Plot your Course

to

Adventure

How to Be a Successful Cruiser

by

Roger Olson

authorHOUSE

1663 Liberty Drive, Suite 200
Bloomington, Indiana 47403
(800) 839-8640
www.authorhouse.com

© 2004 Roger Olson
All Rights Reserved.

No part of this book may be reproduced, stored in a retrieval system, or transmitted by any means without the written permission of the author.

First published by AuthorHouse 09/29/04

ISBN: 1-4184-0577-9 (e)
ISBN: 1-4184-0576-0 (sc)

Printed in the United States of America
Bloomington, Indiana

This book is printed on acid-free paper.

Edited by Roz Gordon
Cover & Typographical Design by Manuel de Lizarriturri
Illustrations & Front Cover Photograph by Roger Olson
Back Cover Photograph by Manuel de Lizarriturri

Acknowledgements

The ideas presented in this book are compiled from years of personal sailing experience and from the interactions I have had with other cruisers. When we cruise, we read books and connect with cruisers from all over the world. We visit their boats and get ideas that worked for them. We engage in conversations and hear their stories. The information we obtain from these exchanges may stimulate new ideas that may apply to our own or other boats. So in all honesty, I must admit that only some of the ideas presented here are originally mine, but most of them come from other cruisers or from modifications of their ideas. This book would never have been written if it were not for the assistance and knowledge provided by Elizabeth Pearce, a single-handed sailor whom I highly admire and respect.

Last, but certainly not least, I would also like to thank Roz Gordon and Manuel de Lizarriturri for their invaluable contributions: the creation of an Index and a Glossary. If this book is at all successful, it will be to a great extent because of their diligent work. Their editorial talents and design skills have transformed my long and oftentimes cumbersome original manuscript into a book that I sincerely hope will earn its rightful place in the limited—and precious—shelf space of your cruising yacht's library.

Dedication

I would like to dedicate this book to anyone who has a dream to break away from the norm and do something different. To go cruising on your own boat is only one way to leave behind the drudgery and monotony of the landlubber's everyday existence.

I admire all those who have the courage to simply turn their backs on the social forces and conventions that seem to keep us with one foot nailed to the ground, walking in circles.

This book is dedicated to all those free-thinking, free-living individuals who dare to consider plotting a course to their own adventure.

Table of Contents

Table of Illustrations

INTRODUCTION

My body is pressed back against the seat as the jet approaches speed for flight. The whole plane is shaking, and the engine is screaming too loud to think or talk. I am looking forward to this flight and for the time it gives me to reflect on my past years. At the other end of this journey is a new life, one I left behind many years ago. I am not looking forward to it, but I really have no other choice.

The departure was late, but I feel damn lucky to have gotten this flight. It took days to get my cat, *Pintle*, cleared to leave Singapore. You'd think it would be more difficult to get a cat into a country than to get it out. First, I had to pay a veterinarian to give him a clean bill of health. Then, there was the fee for the permit required to take him out of the country. Next, a special official had to be paid to see to it that my cat was put on the plane. I could have saved some money if I had left *Pintle* at the baggage area overnight instead of carrying him with me to the airport, but I love this cat too much to even consider leaving him in a strange place overnight. We have been together since I found him in Papeete, Tahiti, over 13 years ago. He fit into the palm of my hand then. After all the years and the experiences we have had together, it is impossible for me to leave *Pintle* alone any more than is necessary. This cat will be with me until one of us dies.

As the airplane ascends, we pass through some black clouds and the plane begins to shake as if it is falling apart. Finally, there is clear sky as we pass through the clouds above Singapore on our way back to America.

This phase of my life started a month ago. I was sailing my small 28-foot sailboat, *Xiphias*, to Europe via the Red Sea. Several hundred miles out of Thailand on my way to Sri Lanka, I got a radio message that my father was going in for open-heart surgery, and my mother was ill. My brother would have gone to be with our parents, but he passed away tragically just over a year ago. He was my only sibling. Now, I am the only one left to help my aging parents, both in their 80's. I heard that Sri Lanka is not a good place to leave a boat; so, I turned around and headed back to Singapore.

It took me nearly two weeks to get back to the States. My father had already had his operation and was doing all right. My mother was better, but was having difficulty looking after my dad. Neither of them had adjusted back to normal after my brother's death. They took it very hard. My father went into severe depression; he has hardly spoken at all since my brother's death. I could see that, at least for a while, my cruising days were coming to an end.

I considered shipping *Xiphias* back to the States, but found that the cost was far above my budget. Reluctantly, I sold her.

The jet has leveled off, and the flight attendant just passed with drinks. I have my seat reclined back to its maximum and a double scotch on ice on the fold-down table in front of me. I close my eyes and try to contemplate how it all began.

It has been over 13 years since I departed to go cruising on my small sailboat. So much has happened during that time. I was happy cruising and feel it was one of the best decisions of my life. When did I make this decision? What ever influenced me to leave the security of home, job, and friends?

My life seemed to be exactly like everyone else's, our goals the same: to be married, to have a reasonable job, a house and children, to accumulate as many essentials and non-essentials as possible, to have vacations to look forward to and dreams for the future.

I was 30 years old and a teacher in Southern California. I had been married for 5 years to the most beautiful young woman in the world. She was 5' 5", 120 pounds, a svelte, perfect body, and natural blond hair to her shoulder. She was bright and witty. She had a sensual, feminine voice and sang like an angel. When she smiled, it made my knees tremble, and my heart would skip a beat. I thought we were happy.

I felt we were exactly like our neighbors. Apparently, my wife wanted something different, so she found someone else who could provide her with more of whatever it was I lacked.

After my divorce, I spent my free time with friends who appeared to have perfect marriages. I studied them to see what they did or had that was different, to understand why my marriage had failed. Some had much more money, but to many of them, it was never enough. They worked so hard to accumulate more and more, sometimes losing sleep worrying about the future. Some had homes that were never big enough even though they had more bedrooms than occupants. Others thought their homes were in the wrong neighborhood. Some had more cars than family members to drive them. Most lived and planned for their weekends and vacations.

It seemed no one was really happy with their reality: they wanted to be richer, better looking, smarter, healthier, more adventurous. Perhaps it is the striving for more that makes them happy. But for some, like myself, there is a vague feeling that there is something missing.

After a few months of adjusting to the reality of being single, I felt as if I had been released or unzipped from a bag full of social restraints and values. I didn't have to answer to anyone, and this newly found freedom opened itself to many roads I had never before considered.

I do not want to sound anti-marriage. Sometimes I envied my friends and their friends for the happiness they seemed to have. Simply, I realized that I was alone without any responsibility. Since I wasn't ready to step back into a relationship or attempt to achieve something I didn't need, I began looking for something different to occupy my time and interests.

Now as I look back, I wish I had stayed married or at least re-married. I could have still gone cruising, but with a wife and even a family, instead of alone. To live a life as I have can be—and has been—lonely. However, it is better than the rut I was in before.

The only way it could have been better would be to have had a loving partner who shared the same dream.

I always loved the water and especially admired the ocean with its never-ending mood swings. As a youth, I had enjoyed water sports, spending much of my teens skin diving and SCUBA diving. Now with this newfound freedom, I returned to my love of the sea. I would drive down to the coast just to watch the sunsets and sunrises over the ocean.

Many of my weekends were spent looking for a spot where the waves would break against the rocks sending wind-driven spray high into the air. I enjoyed feeling the earth shudder from the crushing blow of the waves and to taste and smell the salt air. I would find a place high enough above the water to see the far distant horizon and to dream.

Usually, I was with a girlfriend, a bottle of fine wine, and a cracked crab. Sitting on the rocks with the seat of our pants wet from the dampness, we would snuggle close, arms wrapped around each other and talk about visiting distant lands, islands, and exotic places together.

Soon, I discovered it was a one-sided dream. My girlfriend would listen and agree with the idea, until I mentioned doing it on a sailboat. I don't know why a sailboat came into my mind, but it seemed to be the logical way to do it for someone without any money. As soon as that magic word was uttered, I felt a sudden distance and hesitation in our conversation. I wasn't concerned at the time, because I felt that it would be easy to convert her to accept my dream; that is, if I were really serious about it myself. Unbeknownst to me, she also intended to change my course. Her dreams included a small ranch with a few horses. She tactfully began humoring me and explaining why I would never sail across an ocean. There were times I thought she was right. I had little money, no experience, nothing for my future, and I needed a newer car.

I decided to begin slowly and bought my first boat, a Chinese Junk. I chose it because it had character and, more importantly, fit my budget. Then I progressed to other boats as my finances and experience improved. These were the years of learning and building confidence.

My free time was spent reading books about sailing and making short sailing trips to Southern California's outer islands. I progressed to making trips up the coast to San Francisco and back. For years, I spent my summers sailing in the Sea of Cortez, Baja California, Mexico. The more experience I gained, the more I realized how little I knew. No matter how confident I was, I kept running into new and different situations and made many stupid mistakes. Finally, I concluded that I would never know it all, but I had enough confidence to commit to an offshore cruise... alone.

I wasn't always alone; I managed to find female crew now and then. However, I found that it is difficult for a woman to give up everything she has, including job security, to take off into the unknown with an unknown.

During my travels, I experienced many wonderful places, adventures, and friends I would keep for life. I also encountered life-threatening situations including storms, hurricanes, a loss of life, a flash flood, dragging anchors, and more. But I continued to cruise.

When asked why I continued after so many bad experiences, I answer by saying that the good times are so good that they offset the bad ones.

Pintle made it home safely and lived another 5 years in the comfort of a warm, loving—and motionless—home. I found my parents were doing much better and just wanted the security of knowing I was close if they needed me.

I soon realized that I needed a job. Fortunately, I had saved some money while working overseas and from the sale of *Xiphias*. I went to work for, and ended up buying out, the company that had built my boat. After five years of working closely with an incredible crew of master boat builders, I thoroughly learned about the construction of quality ocean-going sailboats from the ground up. During this time, I built a boat exactly like *Xiphias*; this time, with all the bells and whistles. *Nereus* will be my last boat.

Soon after my new boat was completed, my father passed away but my mother was in excellent health. At her request, I returned to cruising. I sold the company and took off down the coast of Mexico. I intended to return home for a visit every few months and when I was needed. I kept daily contact with my mother via on-board email.

Unfortunately, she had a stroke during my first visit home. As I write this, my boat sets on the hard in La Paz, Mexico, waiting for my return. I am now a full-time caregiver to my 88-year-old mother.

The purpose of this book is to express the reality of cruising—both good and bad. I can only hope that the reader will read between the lines and understand that the 25 years I have been sailing and cruising have been the most rewarding years of my life.

The information in this book was gained from 12 years and over 25,000 nautical miles of coastal cruising. Additional experience was gained from another 13 years of offshore cruising—about 50,000 nautical miles. During these 13 years, there were many yacht deliveries and great experiences while working ashore in foreign countries. Finally, and most importantly, is the experience gained from the 9 years I worked as the owner of a reputable boat building company.

This book is written to provide information. Its intent is to answer as many questions as possible that relate to cruising. There are many illustrations to help clarify written details and to assist the reader in better visualizing the situations and the techniques suggested. My own experiences will augment what I am attempting to explain.

There are also some true stories that are unrelated to the technical information. They are included because they are interesting and happened as a result of going cruising. These events are recounted from the best of my memory, my ship's log, and assistance from those who shared these experiences.

I feel compelled to disguise the true identity of some, while others remain the actual parties... as myself. Being single, I often had female crew or partners who discovered that the lifestyle—or I—was not to their liking. They have continued on a different path and may not want others to know about this part of their life.

Sailing and cruising is a complicated sport or lifestyle, and there will always be differences of opinion. This book is written based on my own experience. The reader should draw his or her own conclusions.

I will attempt to explain the cruising yacht design, different techniques and methods of anchoring, some basic storm strategy, how to prepare for the cruise, and some simple ideas to make life aboard easier; in other words, how to make the cruise successful. It is not the purpose of this book to explain how to sail a boat or even how it works. It is presumed that the person considering going cruising will already have a basic understanding of sailing. However, if that is not the case, I suggest reading basic sailing books and taking sailing lessons before, during, or after reading this book.

It is difficult to write an opinion without sounding too opinionated. When I feel the situation could have alternative responses, I have tried to give both pros and cons, so the reader can arrive at his or her own conclusion. This is difficult, however. In some situations, if it worked for me, I cannot help but feel it will work for others.

I want to make sure that it is clearly understood that no matter what I write, safety for personnel comes first. There may be words used that might be interpreted differently, but that is not the intention. I ask that you keep this in mind as you progress through this book: *safety first*.

If you are considering taking a boat offshore and crossing oceans, I would like to suggest that you take some quiet time to seriously evaluate this idea. Most importantly, if you have a partner, be certain he or she is involved in the decision, or you may find yourself sailing alone. All too often, the desire to go cruising is only one person's dream, and the partner goes along because it is expected. One really unhappy person aboard a small boat can take away all the enjoyment of the adventure for everyone.

The reasons not go cruising usually increase the older you get, so there will always be a rational reason not to attempt to live your dream. It takes a truly devoted person to overcome or ignore the objections to the cruising lifestyle. Just remember: the time is not too far away when you may say, "Now, it is too late".

There are some that are more adventurous than others. There are those who have no desire for adventure at all. Then, there are those who live vicariously through others' adventures. This book is for those who are considering sailing on their own sailboat to the far corners of the world, or for those who just want to sail along the coast to experience something new and different.

A cruise can take you to new countries with different cultures and customs. Perhaps you will discover uninhabited islands where you can sit on a beach totally nude without fear of being caught. Or maybe, you will find a populated island where you are invited to join in a local ceremony that is rarely seen by outsiders, where there will be new foods with different smells and tastes. There will be crystal clear, warm, tropical waters to swim and dive, unlike any ever before seen or experienced. You will have the flexibility to leave for a new location whenever you want.

The reasons to go cruising will vary by individual. Some may wish to escape the social pressures, financial burdens, and the violence so prevalent in our society today. For others, it may be as simple as having the desire to experience something different from the norm. Maybe it's the challenge and feeling of accomplishment. For the romantic, it may be the whisper of the ocean rushing along the hull of a well-founded vessel as it is propelled by the wind, under clear skies or a star lit night, on its way to a strange place that is only a spot on the chart. Others are looking for the freedom to move with the seasons to different countries. And for some, it is simply because it is an inexpensive way to live.

Regardless of your reasons, this book will help make your dream come true.

Chapter One

BEFORE YOU GO CRUISING

It is the purpose of this chapter to help answer some basic questions a person might have who is considering spending a few years cruising on their own small boat. Items that will be covered are: where to go cruising, when to leave, and how to afford it.

Cruising the oceans and seas of the world can fulfill dreams and desires for those that do their research, are properly prepared, and are on a sound vessel. The lifestyle permits movement when and where you want; there are few if any time schedules. The boat can be securely anchored or moored to tour inland to see sights not available from the boat. One of the pleasures I enjoyed was simply laying back and reading a good—or even a bad—book. If the cruiser is in the tropics, the warm, clear water is inviting day or night. The scenery and sea life to be experienced will remain in your memory for a lifetime. New friends are made from many parts of the world, and they all have the same interest and desire to cruise. Even if for a short time, it is worth trying this adventure.

Cruising can be an inexpensive way to travel, depending on the needs, habits, and the number of family members aboard, Many cruisers leave for only a year or two, and discover it is so affordable that they continue for much longer. Some even settle and retire in a foreign country where their savings will go much further.

Depending on the cruising area, the average couple can live comfortably for as little as $10,000 a year. This will depend on how much time is spent in the more expensive countries and towns and on their budget. The more time spent in outer islands, living like the locals, the less expensive it is to cruise. Also, if you have certain skills and are in the right place when that skill is needed, it is possible to earn money along the way.

I remember a book I read by Sterling Hayden entitled, **Wanderer**. In just a few sentences, Sterling summed up everything that I would like to express to you now. I used to have this quote taped to the mirror to help keep me focused on my dream.

"To be truly challenging, a voyage, like a life, must rest on a firm foundation of financial unrest. Otherwise, you are doomed to a routine traverse, the kind known to yachtsmen who play with their boats at sea... 'Cruising' it is called. Voyaging belongs to seamen, and to the wanderers of the world who cannot, or will not, fit in. If you are contemplating a voyage and you have the means, abandon the venture until your fortunes change. Only then will you know what the sea is all about.

'I've always wanted to sail to the South Seas, but I can't afford it.' What these men can't afford is not to go. They are enmeshed in the cancerous discipline of 'security'. And in the worship of security we fling our lives beneath the wheels of routine - and before we know it our lives are gone.

What does a man need - really need? A few pounds of food each day, heat and shelter, six feet to lie down in - and some form of working activity that will yield a sense of accomplishment. That's all - in the material sense, and we know it. But we are brainwashed by our economic system until we end up in a tomb beneath a pyramid of time payments, mortgages, preposterous gadgetry, playthings that divert our attention for the sheer idiocy of the charade.

The years thunder by, the dreams of youth grow dim where they lie caked in dust on the shelves of patience. Before we know it, the tomb is sealed.

Where, then, lies the answer? In choice. Which shall it be: bankruptcy of purse or bankruptcy of life?"

Sterling Hayden

This quote makes me want to do away with the term "cruising", but the reality is that we all start our departure as a cruiser. For those just beginning to enter this adventure, I will continue to use the term cruiser. As we become more acquainted with the lifestyle, hopefully, many will become wanderers.

Where to go cruising?

In the United States, we are fortunate to be living in a country surrounded by two oceans with excellent cruising grounds. Most beginning cruisers feel more comfortable by doing some coastal cruising to gain experience and confidence before attempting to cross an ocean. This is probably a good idea until they feel ready.

Ironically, most accidents and damage to vessels happen along the coast. When sailing in the open ocean, there is little to worry about because there are no rocks or reefs to hit. Of course there are other concerns, but a well-built, sound vessel will take care of her crew. An ocean passage can be—and often is—one of the most gratifying experiences for a cruiser. Not only does it take you to a new country with new customs and values, but also there is the unforgettable feeling of accomplishment of crossing an ocean.

Most of those who have cruised extensively would agree that one of the most enjoyable aspects of offshore cruising is to be hundreds of miles from any land, set the windvane, and sail along at 6 knots in a light breeze. You can listen to the water rushing by the hull as the miles pass, all with the power of the wind over the sails. This is the time to watch the beauty of the open ocean and the clear skies. Nighttime brings more stars than can be imagined. The sense of solitude and self-fulfillment is overwhelming. There is a feeling of humbleness and respect, for the thought of the power of the sea is always in the back of the mind. It is at times like this that God feels close.

Planning the voyage is one of the most enjoyable aspects of the cruise, because your mind becomes a playground for your expectations and experiences. Dreams are of sailing upon the seas to foreign places and different cultures.

Careful planning can make the difference between success and failure for your cruise. Be sure to involve the whole family during this planning period, especially when it comes to making decisions. Include even those who will not be going, because they will be living the cruise vicariously.

Try to plan your trip with a minimum of upwind sailing. It is also a good idea to start the voyage in short legs. Even if the plan is to cross an ocean, begin by doing some coastal sailing. Try to keep each leg less than 50 nautical miles, so there is some time left at the end of the day to enjoy an evening meal together in a safe anchorage. This will give the crew time to adjust to the vessel's movement and to get their sea legs.

Most cruisers will depart from their homeport. There are some that will ship their boat to a place closer to their final destination, making the cruising distance shorter and perhaps safer. This would depend on the plans, time limits, and finances of the crew.

The East Coast of the United States offers great coastal cruising and inland waterways, a good way to get started. When the time feels right, if there is a desire, Europe is not all that far via Bermuda and the Azores.

However, most cruisers on the East Coast will sail down to the tropical Bahamas, West Indies, and the islands of the Caribbean Sea. Then they can choose between South America, the Gulf of Mexico, or the Panama Canal, the gateway to the South Pacific.

Those who are in the Gulf of Mexico or Florida will want to do much the same. Again, there are inland waterways and great coastal cruising to gain the experience and confidence.

Then there is Cuba. I have spoken with many cruisers who have nothing but positive comments about their visit. They say the people, including officials, are friendly and courteous. I hear there are fantastic anchorages, excellent food, and warm weather. What more could a cruiser ask for?

For those on the West Coast, there is a minimum of inland waterways. For those already in the northwest, Puget Sound is a must. However, to sail up the coast to get there can be difficult for the beginning cruiser, as the entire trip is to weather. North central California has the Sacramento River Delta, but you have to begin and return via San Francisco Bay, another challenging cruising ground for the beginner.

The sail south down the coast is very rewarding, and the prevailing winds are from the stern. Most will sail to Mexico and spend some time cruising the Sea of Cortez; then, when ready, continue south. Some will sail down to the Panama Canal and cross over into the Atlantic, while others may continue down to South America. At any time, the cruiser can make a right hand turn and enter the tropical South Pacific. The more confident cruiser may want to head directly to Hawaii and enter the South Pacific without the coastal sail south.

Regardless of the place of departure, most cruisers eventually head for the tropical South Pacific. This is a good choice because the Pacific got its name from lack of storms and bad weather. The Pacific is covered with hundreds of islands and atolls that are fairly close together, reducing the number of overnight sails. The islands are all beautiful, and each one has different inhabitants, customs, and values. Most Islanders speak English and are some of the friendliest natives the cruiser will ever encounter. It is rare to lock the boat when going ashore.

Many sailors will first head for the Marquesas, then on to the Tuamotos of French Polynesia. From there, it is not far to Tahiti and all its friendly islands. From Tahiti, the cruiser can follow the "Coconut Milk Run", as it has come to be known. This route takes in the Cook Islands, both Samoas (American and Western), Tonga Islands, Fiji, New Zealand, and Australia. With few exceptions, the passages are short between islands and most cruisers eventually spend some time in New Zealand and Australia.

There are other routes available and equally appealing. From Northern Australia, there are several decisions to make. The cruiser could enter the Indian Ocean, which means a commitment to make a circumnavigation, or they may decide to stay in the Pacific.

From Australia's Queensland coast, it's a week's sail to the islands of New Caledonia. From New Caledonia, it is a much shorter distance to the islands of Vanuatu and Solomon's.

After the Solomon's, the decision has to be made to either head for the Philippines, Hong Kong, Japan, and back to America by sailing across the North Pacific, or to continue to Papua New Guinea, Indonesia, Singapore, Malaysia, and Thailand, where more decisions would have to be made.

From Thailand, it is possible to continue north to the Philippines and follow the route home mentioned above.

If a circumnavigation is intended, the cruiser will have to choose between the Red Sea and South Africa. Whatever the decision, a few weeks or even months in the Chagos Islands will be long remembered.

These are only a few of the possibilities that exist, and they are the most common ones cruisers follow. There are always the less traveled routes that will appeal to those who want to go to the out of the way places other yachts choose to miss. For the more courageous cruiser, there are the colder climates of the Arctic and Antarctic.

Regardless of the destination, some research must be done about weather, currents, and storm probability for the time of year of departure. I strongly suggest a copy of ***World Cruising Routes*** by Jim Cornell for the boat's library. This book does exactly what the title indicates: it gives the best time and course between points all over the world. It will answer most questions.

However, it should not be used as an absolute answer. You still need to buy government copies of ***Sailing Directions*** and ***Pilot Charts*** for your intended cruising area. The ***Sailing Directions*** is primarily written for large ships, so it will give all the details and what to expect entering larger ports but little help to the real out of the way anchorages.

The ***Pilot Charts*** are of large sections of oceans and are available in months of the year. Each chart will give that month's expected wind and current strength and directions. It will also break the large area into grids and give the percentage chance of a gale.

By using the ***Pilot Charts***, a cruiser can select a course with the highest percentage of winds from the desired direction and the lowest percentage of storms. I know of cruisers who followed such courses and made a circumnavigation never experiencing winds in excess of 35 knots.

There are other materials available with up-to-date information on tides, lights, etc. These should be considered but are not nearly as important as the two above because they are only valid for one year and are often out of date by the time they are needed.

Today, there are more and more cruising guides written by cruisers, with additional information on particular areas. Some of these should be aboard. Be aware, however, that many of the anchorages are sketches and not to any scale. I have found many errors in these local cruising guides; they should be used as a reference only and not as absolute.

Do not go out and buy all the charts for your intended cruise routes before departure. Plans have a way of being changed along the way. Other countries have their own charts at a far lower price than American or British Admiralty charts. Charts can also be traded and copied from other cruisers. This works particularly well if the charts are in good condition. Often there are hand written notes on the charts about anchorages and other important information.

When deciding where to go cruising, always remember the route home. If it is a hard beat to windward, then perhaps choose something a little simpler for the first year. It is better to break your plans into short legs, so if something goes wrong or someone wants to go home, it is possible without too much difficulty. It is best to keep the first year simple. As you gain experience and confidence, the destinations can become more challenging.

When to go cruising?

One of the most difficult decisions to make after the cruiser has decided where to go is when to leave. There are many situations that will influence the timing. The time to leave should involve all members of the family, even those remaining at home. Finances, jobs, obligations, season, etc. will all have an influence. The problems increase depending on the number of family members involved. Each problem should be confronted realistically with all persons concerned and in the order of importance.

There really is no age that is too young or too old; it only means that adjustments have to be made, perhaps for all aboard. The skipper must take into consideration the ages of all concerned, including him or herself, when determining the amount of time to be spent away from home. There are many couples in their 70's and older who are living aboard their boats in various parts of the world and have no desire to return to the States to live.

Children adjust to the cruising life better than adults and usually complain less. They easily meet other children from all over the world with common interests and complaints. Many children's education continues through correspondence courses arranged in advance of departure. Those children who have daily schedules set aside for study time normally improve faster than their shore-side peers. All the children I met while cruising, including a 10-year-old on my own boat for a year, were bright, mature, and proud of themselves and their achievements. The number one reason given for their success was that their parents were available 24 hours a day and showed sincere interest in their studies.

After most of the questions are answered and time is allotted to resolve them, it is time to set a departure date. This date should not be a general idea of when it would be best to leave, but the actual day, month and year to depart. The date set can be months or even years away, but it must be a *specific* day. Some will even set the date before they have the cruising boat. Try not to make it too far in the distant future, because the longer it takes, the more reasons not to leave will surface.

Sit down with all involved and discuss the timing. Listen carefully to each person's concerns. If someone feels they are leaving prematurely or leaving something behind, he or she will be unhappy and may make the rest of the crew miserable.

Once you have made the commitment, your life will change and have focus. This will result in cruiser's tunnel vision, which will keep the objective in sight. Every penny you spend, every vacation you take, every sailing trip you make, every lecture you attend, and every book you read, will have a purpose.

After setting the departure date, inform all your friends and relatives so they can prepare themselves. This is important because you will feel honest about your commitment if you tell others. Some interesting aspects of this are the remarks, comments, and advice that will be given by others. They will bring up every possible scenario as a reason why you should not go. Just remember that the cruiser is not like everyone else. If those who are making the negative comments had the courage and skill, they would be going as well.

If you find that a multitude of reasons prevent you from setting the date, then you may be living a fantasy and really don't want to go. You may be an armchair cruiser, living vicariously through others who do succeed. This is a major point to think about. Perhaps it is best to know now and turn your efforts, precious time, and money in other directions.

How can you afford to go cruising?

Now that the location to cruise is confirmed and the date set for a departure, all that needs to be done is to figure out how to afford it.

All debts should be paid so there is no worry about being encumbered by payments while away. If debts cannot be settled before departure, arrange for a responsible person or even your bank to handle payments. This should not be an obstacle or concern when thousands of miles away.

During my first year cruising, I ran into a young couple that bragged about how they had provisioned their boat with electronics and food with a credit card then quickly departed. Months later I ran into them and they informed me that they were heading back to the States because he had to pay back his father-in-law who had paid the bills for them.

Start thinking about your spending habits. Don't buy the new car you wanted or the bigger TV. Instead of buying non-essentials, concentrate on buying what is needed for the boat. Think about what will make the cruise enjoyable for all aboard.

What to do about the family house or home while away? Each family's requirement will be different. Some will rent out their home for the time they are gone. Others will sell and invest the money and cruise on the interest. It may even be necessary to use the proceeds to buy the cruising yacht. The final decision will vary according to each family's situation.

Figure out what expenses will be required and set a budget. This will vary by each person's requirements and finances. The amount of money available to spend is the amount of money that will be spent. I must refer back to Sterling Hayden's quote, *"If you are contemplating a voyage and you have the means, abandon the venture until your fortunes change. Only then will you know what the sea is all about."*

I am sure he is referring to learning to live off the sea and eat the same foods as the local natives. When I learned how to fish and find food from the locals, my life changed. Not only did I save money, but I also learned survival and basic living skills that I never knew.

Think about it: if there were no bills to pay, if you did not have to dress for work, if you did not have to drive to work so that a car was not necessary, what would it cost to live right now?

There are many things to consider when figuring your budget. One is the size of the cruising vessel. The larger, more complex the vessel, the more it will cost to maintain and refit after years of cruising. This is a serious concern if you have a large vessel and a small budget.

The major cost for the cruiser will be diesel fuel, which can be more expensive overseas than at home. Since there really aren't any time schedules, why not sail more and motor less?

Cooking fuel is inexpensive because most other countries use the same kind of fuel—kerosene and propane—for all their cooking. Propane fittings can be a small problem, but adapters are available and easy to make on location.

There is an old saying that cruisers are drinkers with a sailing problem. Drinking spirits can be a major expense if quantities are required. In most places in the world, the cost of drinking alcohol is much higher than in the States. On the other hand, some countries are much cheaper for their local brands of alcohol: local wine, beer, and rum are often better than imported brands.

Personally, I enjoy a dark red wine like a Cabernet Sauvignon, Merlot, Pinot or Shiraz. I was amazed at the low cost of good quality wines in Australia.

Beer will vary in different countries. Those countries that brew their own can be quite inexpensive and much better than we have in the States. Of course, this depends on your taste.

Another cost concern is both boat and medical insurance. Again, this will vary by individual needs and finances. Many cruisers do not carry either, because the cost can be prohibitive. In some cases, a couple can cruise for one full year for the cost of one year's insurance.

If the cruising vessel is well built and sound, the chances of major damage are less likely. The same applies to medical insurance. Healthy young sailors will require less medical expenses than unhealthy or older sailors. If a tourist-type medical insurance is carried, consider that this type of insurance is aimed toward the tourist on land. If a sailor requires major medical care, he must be evacuated back to the States. This requires that the boat be left securely moored or anchored in a foreign country. The country may require a huge deposit to leave the boat unattended.

This happened to me unexpectedly. It was a serious problem that could have ended up a disaster. I would like to share the experience.

While I was in the Solomon Islands, I received word that my brother was on his deathbed. I wanted to be with him and my parents. I found a secure anchorage, put out three anchors, and convinced an Australian couple to stay aboard while I was away. This was good for them because my boat was bigger than theirs. When it came time to depart, the immigration officials insisted I leave a cash bond in the amount of one-third the cost of the vessel.

When I entered the country, I had placed a high value on my yacht. I thought that if it were worth more, it would open more doors.

I valued it in excess of $100,000. So the official was insisting that I could not leave the country until I paid a $33,000 bond.

I went to his superiors who would not flex an inch. I ended up discussing my problem with the number one man. Finally, I got permission to leave only because I convinced him that I had someone staying on my boat while I was away.

I understand their concern. There are those who leave their yachts to go back to the home country. While they are away, a squall or storm causes the yacht to drag into other boats or to end up on the rocks. The yacht has to be dragged off the rocks or away from other boats at government expense. Some may blame the authorities for damage to their boat. This could result in litigation and could end up being the government's responsibility.

The government policy about leaving boats should be understood when entering a country and before you place a value on your vessel. You never know: emergencies can occur aboard or at home, requiring a quick departure. It may even require taking the boat out of the country.

Medical costs are another concern. Many cruisers continue to pay their insurance in the States while they are away. I can't say this is good or bad; it depends on the individual.

Most countries outside the United States have socialized medicine, so the cost for a medical problem is far less than at home.

I was on an island called Langkawi in Malaysia. I rented a motorcycle to tour inland and was hit by a car. My right foot was pinned under the motorcycle as it slid along the pavement for yards. The accident took all the skin off the right side of my foot.

I was taken to a local doctor who informed me that I needed a skin graft and should go to the hospital. I was taken to the hospital, where they confirmed the diagnosis. I refused the skin graft because I did not want to have to deal with a wound on my foot and one on my butt too. I was treated every week and the cost per visit was $3 USD. The total cost was less than $50 USD. The foot healed in time, and I contribute it to good initial medical care.

There are many countries where similar socialized medical costs apply. At worst, it would cost what the government pays its doctors; this would still be much less than back home in the States.

Another way to save money is to forego processed American or other imported foods and eat local fare. Part of the reason for cruising is to try new things. Food in other countries is different: usually fresh, nutritious, and without an abundance of preservatives. It can be fun learning how to cook these new vegetables and roots. For the carnivores, beef, pork, and chicken are cheap and fresh. You may even see them butcher the animal right in front of you.

Clothing can be a big saving if the cruise is in the tropics. A simple colorfully patterned piece of lightweight cloth, which is wrapped around the body, is all that is required. Most locals don't even wear anything under this wrap. A pair of thongs or flip-flops on the feet and a hat completes the daily wardrobe. For the more formal events, carry lightweight clothing aboard from home. You will be surprised how little use it will get.

One of the major costs is boat maintenance and repairs. A cruiser should be able to maintain his or her vessel without hiring outside help. If there are a lot of gadgets and electronics aboard, do not depend on them; consider them a convenience. Especially in the tropics, the humid environment will corrode or destroy electronic connections quickly.

Depending on the age and use of the cruising vessel, a major refit will be required every seven years or so. This may involve new standing rigging, new sails, engine overhaul, and even a major bottom job for osmosis. Depending on the size of the vessel, this can be a big expense.

The budget will vary by family size and individual needs. More importantly, the budget will be how much is available.

If the budget is set too low, it may become necessary to find work along the way. There are many ways to earn money while cruising. The easiest is to deliver yachts from one location to another. I found the best place to find deliveries was where sailboat races terminate. These racing vessels have to be returned to their home. There are always some positions open. It may be as the skipper, who earns the most money, or it may be as crew, navigator, or even cook. Sometimes the owner will want to go along, but this is not too common.

The cost for deliveries varies depending on the position available, number of crewmembers, distance, time, etc. Some deliveries are paid by the mile, while others are paid by the time it takes to deliver the vessel. Another cost consideration is the time allotted for the delivery: can the vessel stop along the way and enjoy the delivery, or is it necessary to get the boat to its destination as soon as possible? What is the expected weather? It will cost more to take a boat upwind and less for downwind. Often, after delivering a lightweight, fast racer, you appreciate the soundness of your own heavy displacement cruising yacht.

For sailors who are handy and can build, repair, or fix things on boats, there may be more work than they want. There are many sailors from all corners of the world who are excellent sailors but couldn't properly repair a broken drawer. Unfortunately, fellow cruisers don't want to pay a lot, so set a minimum price before work begins.

The most common demands are in the areas of electronic and refrigeration repairs. Because of the array of equipment and electronics available today, it is tempting for the cruiser to take it all. There are generators, inverters, solar panels, and regulators to run TVs, videos, refrigeration, freezers, microwaves, and air conditioners. The list of electronics for navigation is endless, and they all eventually break down.

Engine repair is another skill in demand. Most cruisers know how to service their engines, but many cannot make repairs.

Varnishing and painting boats can make money. It may be as simple as helping someone sand and paint the anti-fouling on the bottom of a boat at the local yard. For those who are really talented at varnishing, there is lots of work. The best way to get varnish jobs is to keep your own boat in excellent display condition. Many people think that anyone can do a varnish job, but it is not that simple. A proper varnish job takes skill, knowledge, and time, and it is expensive to have it done properly.

All of the above is aimed at making money from local sailors and fellow cruisers. There are excellent opportunities ashore as well. Even in developed countries, jobs are available to the computer literate for instruction, operation, programming, and repairs. There are also jobs available in the trades such as carpentry, painting, welding, electronics, plumbing, etc.

The best money making opportunities are in developing countries where they are learning technology that the developed countries have already mastered. They offer the cruiser the opportunity to live in their country and show them how to coordinate, construct, operate, design, and configure whatever it is they require.

In order for local business personnel to import the talent they require, it would cost them airfares, housing, and salaries equal to what would be earned in their home country. So when a cruising yachtie arrives with the needed skill and knowledge and has his home with him, it is a welcome windfall for both parties.

Some of the trades and professions that are in demand in many developing countries are: all fields relating to computer use and programming and all medical skills such as doctors (some countries require a local license, but apparently doctors from developed countries are more highly trained so it may not be a problem), dentists, nurses, dental hygienists, physical therapists, etc.

The easiest way to find employment is to be in the right place at the right time. Sail to places where there is work related to your skills. If there is a lot of construction, there are jobs available in all related trades. If you are a tradesman, look for places where there has been a recent disaster, like a hurricane or an earthquake.

Engineers and geologists will find that the mining industry pays very well and is scattered all over the Pacific. I was fortunate to get a job in a copper mine on Bougainville Island, Papua New Guinea. I started by working for a local contractor until a position in the mine opened. I applied for the job and got it. Fortunately, my superior was a sailor and was building his own yacht on site. When his contract ended, he returned to Australia and I was given his managerial position. I was paid far more than I would have ever dreamed.

Finding work in a foreign country can be difficult and illegal. I want to make sure it is clear that I do not encourage breaking the law in any country. However, there is a way to work around the problem of finding work while on a tourist visa.

Spend time where the local businessmen frequent, like the local yacht clubs and pubs. When you make acquaintances, they often presume you are rich—how else could you afford to sail around like you do? Be certain it is clear that you are not rich, that you work your way as you go. The question will arise about your skills or what it is that you do to earn money. It is critical that you have some idea of what is in demand and that your skill will be needed. Try to keep the definition of your skill as broad as possible to keep more doors open. Often the locals will know someone who needs to hire a person with your skills and will make the introductions.

Remember that you are not permitted to look for or be paid to work. Do not discuss earning money. Ask if you can volunteer to work for free for a few days or weeks just to help. If you prove you have the ability, you will be offered a job. Be careful not to accept any money for the time worked. If your future employer is insistent, you can ask to have it applied to future paychecks or toward travel expenses.

It is the employer's responsibility to get you the working visa. It may require that you get the visa outside the country. It may also require a post-dated letter from the employer asking for you to come to work for him. Each country is different. I encourage you to abide by their laws.

Even if you are financially secure, there is no better way to get to know the local people and their customs than to volunteer your time to help in some way. You may even want to take the opportunity to move off the boat for a while and live ashore while you make some changes or additions to your boat.

This only touches the surface on how to finance your cruise. The opportunities are endless. Each person will have to figure out his or her own budget, and try to live within it. If it is necessary to find work, the particular skill to sell will vary by situation, availability, and demand. I do not encourage trying to sell a skill that you really don't have. This will only make the situation worse and perhaps make enemies, especially if it costs the employer some out of pocket money to correct the errors you made.

Chapter Two

GAIN EXPERIENCE BEFORE DEPARTING

The amount of sailing experience required before going cruising may depend on the amount of courage you have. I met several cruisers who had little or no sailing experience at all before they departed.

One such family was from France. I met them while sailing through the Marquesas. They explained to me that they were about to get a divorce because the husband was working too many hours with his landscape business. To preserve their marriage, they decided to sell the business and their home and move to Australia where they had relatives.

They got more money than expected from the sale of the business and their home, so they decided it would be an adventure to sail to Australia on their own boat. Their only experience consisted of no more than a few day sails on a friend's boat. At a broker's advice, they bought their cruising yacht. Fortunately, the broker gave them good advice and sold them a heavy, well-built, very forgiving yacht.

They moved aboard and spent less than one month learning to sail before they departed. They loaded the boat with a pile of sailing, cruising, and navigation books to study underway. This was before the electronic navigation devices of today. They told me that they sailed in open ocean by dead reckoning for a week before they learned celestial navigation. When I met them, they were happy, confident, and excellent cruisers. The important factor is that they had a sound vessel that could look after them when they made mistakes.

I do not encourage this method and use it only to illustrate that the amount of experience required will vary according to those involved and the level of their desire to cruise. Needless to say, more experience results in more confidence and reduces the chance of an accident.

I feel my own personal sailing experience was just above average before I left. I began sailing on a 30-foot Chinese Junk. After a few years I sold her and moved to a smaller but more versatile 20-foot trailer-sailer. For years, I trailered this little boat down to the Sea of Cortez during the summer months. I progressed to a 40-footer so I could live aboard. It was full of dry rot, so it took me more than a year of work before I could sail her. I sailed it from Southern California to San Francisco and back four times. Finally I bought my 28-foot Bristol Channel Cutter; this was the boat that I cruised on for 13 years.

I would like to share a few true stories about these boats that will more clearly illustrate how I started sailing and worked my way to gaining the experience and confidence to leave.

I had long hair, bellbottom trousers, and wore a headband when I bought my first sailboat, a 30-foot Chinese Junk. It was the early 70's. I did not have a clue how to sail, so I spent much of my time making her look authentic. I cast her name in solid bronze using English letters in a Chinese style. I called her *Peace O' Junk*. Her Chinese Junk mainsail was yellow with a huge red peace sign sewn in the center.

I learned to sail by trial and error. I read all the books I could find and spent hours in the library researching Chinese Junks. Slowly, I was gaining confidence sailing in and out of the Long Beach Harbor in California. I finally made my maiden voyage to Catalina Island on a windless, foggy, winter day. The distance was a little over 20 miles to the Isthmus Harbor. On board with me was Joan, my girlfriend at the time, and my best friend, Jerry.

We sailed the total distance by compass only because I did not have any other navigational devices aboard. I didn't even have the time or the knowledge to swing the compass before we left. Luckily, it was accurate.

I remember the sail to Catalina Island as if it were yesterday. We got a late start. Two hours outside of the Long Beach Harbor breakwater, the wind died and fog encompassed us.

Before we left, I knew the bottom of the junk was badly fouled and would slow our progress down considerably. I did not realize that we were only making 2 to 3 knots using the 20 horsepower outboard. We had been motoring for hours and hours; I had no idea where we were when night set in. It became darker than I had ever experienced. I looked down, it was black; I looked up and it was the same blackness. It was like being in a black void. The only light was from our prop wash and the flashlight we used to see the compass. That's right, no compass light. I was near panic.

In the darkness, I turned to Jerry and said, "I don't want to risk running into the island in this pea soup. I think we should turn around and go back, but I don't have a clue how far we have to go. I think we must be about half way; what do you think?"

Jerry's nautical skills exceeded mine and he appeared much calmer. In his calm voice he suggested, "We should continue to follow the compass heading and watch for any change in the darkness that might indicate land mass or other boats. There is also the possibility that the fog may lift."

More hours passed. Our flashlight was slowly getting dimmer and dimmer and the sea was dead calm. Suddenly, Joan let out a scream; my heart jumped as we hit something. Closer inspection revealed that we were bumping into mooring buoys. Somehow, we had managed to sail right past Bird Rock. This large rock (or small island) is located in the center of the entrance to the Isthmus Harbor. Somehow, we never saw it.

I continued to sail the *Peace O' Junk*, but mostly inside the harbor. She always had a slow leak, so I installed an electric bilge pump with an automatic float switch. This relieved me of the worry of her sinking while I was away during the week. My problem was that I did not want to cut a hole through the hull for the discharge until I was certain of the location; I just hung the hose in the engine well, wedged against the outboard.

On a Thanksgiving Day, I had put my back out badly. I got a call from the marina that my boat had sunk at the dock. In great pain, I drove to Long Beach to discover that only her cabin top was above water. There was a Long Beach fireboat tied behind her. A diver in the water was yelling that the engine well had to be closed off. He passed up the 20-hp outboard, grabbed some canvas, nails and a hammer and disappeared below the surface. The next thing I knew, there was a loud roar as a cannon size stream of water began shooting off the fireboat; slowly, my Chinese Junk began to rise.

I will never forget how efficiently the firemen worked and how nice they were about the entire episode. They explained that I must have placed the bilge pump discharge hose into the engine well deep enough to reach the water. When the bilge pump turned on, it filled the hose. When it stopped, it siphoned the ocean back inside. It must have pumped it out and siphoned it in over and over until the battery died.

Even after many hours of trying to rehabilitate it, the outboard never ran again. I found a huge German-built, single cylinder diesel engine. It was about three feet tall and weighed hundreds of pounds, but the price was right, and I wanted diesel. The only place it would fit was way forward. I considered a long shaft, but to install it was too complicated. I decided to use a hydraulic pump, lines, controls and motor to drive the prop.

I fabricated a female cylindrical insert that was fastened inside the engine well. This insert accepted a male, 15" diameter cylindrical tube that I could slide up and down the engine well. At the bottom of the cylinder, I fastened the hydraulic motor with prop attached. To this motor, I ran hydraulic lines inside the cylinder to the controls in the cockpit. It worked perfectly. When under sail, I could raise the cylinder enough to reduce the drag from the hydraulic motor and prop. When motoring, the cylinder was set into stops to make it go straight, or it could be rotated up to 90° to make it easy to get in and out of tight places. The only problem with this design was that the single cylinder engine was too big. People would tell me that I was the first boat they had ever seen that made a 360° wake when motoring.

I sold the Chinese Junk and bought a 20-foot Balboa trailer-sailer. The person I bought the boat from was a friend of the boat's designer, Lyle Hess. At the time, I was not aware that Lyle had designed *Seraffyn*, the little 24-foot cutter that Lin and Larry Pardey had sailed around the world without an engine.

Karl, a fellow teacher, bought a Balboa 20 before I bought mine. Taking his boat day sailing convinced me that I wanted a Balboa too. It was this little Balboa that really got me sailing and increased my interest in cruising. I could put this little 20-foot sailboat on a trailer and take her anywhere.

During spring vacation a few years after buying my Balboa, Karl and I decided to take his 20-footer out from the Channel Islands Harbor in Oxnard, California, to Santa Cruz Island, about 20 miles off the coast. It was to be a shakedown sail before we took one of our Balboas to the Sea of Cortez in Baja California, Mexico.

It was a perfect day, but as we were ready to cast off, a harbor patrolman drove up, stuck his head out the car window and said, "If you guys are heading out to the island, you're nuts. There are gale warnings for this afternoon, and I wouldn't be surprised if you get winds in excess of 40 knots inside the channel."

Karl had little sailing experience and mine wasn't much better. All I had done was to sail the *Peace O' Junk* to Catalina Island a few times, but even this was more than Karl.

The events of that day play out again on an inner screen. I see Karl, tall and lanky with short blond hair. Even though he and I are of similar build, he towers over me by inches.

"So, what do you think?" I asked.

Karl's tone revealed a slight irritation—or maybe it was over confidence—when he said, "Hell, man, we're out here this weekend for a shakedown; we'll get winds over 40 in Mexico. Let's go for it."

His enthusiasm annoyed me and my stomach started to get that nervous twitch which happens just before I do something that involves some risk. Trying to hide my apprehension, I said, "If we're going to go, let's hightail it for Smuggler's Cove on the southern end of Santa Cruz Island. There, we can anchor and sit it out if it gets too rough."

As an answer, Karl yanked the starter rope to the 2-hp Seagull outboard engine, and we headed for the breakwater leading to the Santa Barbara Channel. The swell ran about three feet high out of the north; the wind was light: six to ten knots out of the northeast. Unfortunately, that's the direction to Smuggler's Cove, so we would have to tack back and forth to get there.

I hoisted the mainsail, raised the large genoa headsail, then returned to the cockpit to help Karl pull the sheets to adjust the sails. We pulled the mainsail almost to the centerline of the boat. Next, we snugged the genoa along the port so that the wind was coming from our starboard. Soon the wind had us heeled over to a 15° angle, and we stowed the engine in the lazarette compartment.

It was obvious that we couldn't point directly towards Smuggler's Cove, so we steered for the southern tip of Anacapa Island, about ten miles downwind of our destination. The light winds were ideal for the boat; we coasted along effortlessly at five knots. If we had to tack back and forth at this speed, it would take us at least 8 hours to get there. Hopefully, the winds would shift a little later in the day.

After about four hours, the winds freshened and dark clouds began floating overhead, hiding the sun. Soon, we passed Anacapa on our right and continued windward on a starboard tack out to sea.

Karl relieved me at the helm. I was convinced that the gale force winds would never develop. I went below, rummaged in our ice chest, and grabbed Karl and me a beer. He popped the lid, put both legs out straight, and attempted to lean back.

"This is the life," he said with a smile. I joined him in this smugness and said, "Right, the only thing that would make it better would be two naked dancing girls."

As we talked and joked about the gale force winds that never developed, the winds freshened and the genoa sail forced us over to such an angle that the lee side was under water most of the time.

I gulped a slug from my second beer. "Let's put on a smaller sail, and then we'd better turn around on the other tack."

"What smaller sail?" Karl said, "There's just this big genoa." He sipped his beer and turned to look at the building seas without a thought about what he had just said.

I also stared at the white caps and said, "We can let the sail out so only the end of it will carry some wind while the rest flogs; I think they call that a Fisherman's reef. Can you at least shorten the mainsail?"

With an assured voice, he answered, "Sure, no problem; I have a roller reefing boom on the mainsail just like yours."

"No Karl, I don't have a roller reefing boom; I have slab reefing. I think the previous owner did it. Mine is different than yours," I tried to explain.

We tacked around so the wind was now coming from our port and plowed our way back towards Anacapa Island. Even though the sheets were let out considerably, the genoa carried too much wind. We were heeled so far over that our rail was constantly under water.

As we neared the island, I realized that we had made little if any progress upwind toward our destination. We were back to almost where we had passed the end of Anacapa. Again, we brought the boat around onto the opposite tack and returned seaward.

I realized that we were carrying far too much sail and there might be a current against us. We had to reduce our angle of heel by reducing sail area. Facing forward, I turned to Karl at the helm and asked, "How do you reef your main? We've got to reduce sail area."

Confidently, Karl responded, "We bring the boat up into the wind and let the halyard that raises the sail loose a bit so the sail will come down. Then pull the boom aft out of its square spring catch and start rotating the boom until you have taken down as much as you want. When finished, release the boom and it will spring back into place, then raise the sail taut again." It sounded easy enough, but when the sea is this rough, things are not as easy as they seem.

"Do you have a safety harness?" I asked, afraid I already knew the answer.

"Never got around to buying one, just never needed it," Karl responded.

Scooting on my butt, I worked my way to the mast. I released the halyard holding the mainsail up the mast and waited for Karl to bring the boat upwind. As soon as the mainsail was luffing, I released some tension on the halyard and pulled down about five feet of sail.

Next thing I knew, the genoa was backwinded, and we were being forced over onto the other tack. The boat heeled so far over that I had difficulty holding on. We were dead in the water, heeled over at about a 70° angle. Karl released the sheet to the genoa and let it fly across to the other side, then pulled in on the other sheet. We were now on the other tack, and the wind was howling across the deck at 90°. I was still trying to hold on to the main halyard and boom as we screamed along at over 6 knots.

Karl managed to bring us up into the wind again, but this time he did not point quite so high into the wind. I scooted aft a little to get a better grip on the boom. Then I pulled the boom aft, felt it snap out of its socket, and began rolling up the loose bottom of the mainsail. After I had pulled down and rolled up about half the sail area, I let it spring back into its socket. I worked my way back to the mast and raised the mainsail back up taut.

It didn't take long; I could see that we were losing the shape of our mainsail and the airfoil that drives the boat into the wind. The leach was being pulled forward by the strong wind. If there were a grommet at the end of the sail where the reef meets the boom, I could have tied a rope around the boom to prevent it. There was another problem: the mainsail shape is like a right triangle; as the foot of the sail was being rolled around the boom, the longer leach permitted the aft end of the boom to drop considerably lower. Now it could more easily hit us in the head.

On this seaward tack with the mainsail reefed, we tried to point high up into the wind, but just minutes later, the entire mainsail unrolled. We tried to reef it again, but the same thing happened. Apparently, the force of the wind on the sail was stronger than the force of the spring holding the boom in its square socket. Again, grommets in the sail would solve much of this problem, but there weren't any. I was glad that I have slab reefing on my Balboa and not this spring roller boom idea for reducing sail area.

We struggled to make some windward ground. The leeward rail was under water all the time; the winds steadily increasing. We buttoned up our jackets and took turns at the helm. Karl's smile was gone and no one was talking anymore.

He focused on steering, while I hung over the windward side. I was holding on to the wire shrouds that support the mast in an attempt to have my weight help reduce our angle of heel. A wave hit the side of the boat with a mighty crash, and water covered everything. My pants and old navy Pea coat were so soaked that I must have been 40 pounds heavier. My every movement became an effort.

Karl's voice quivered when he said, "I think we should tack now."

"Not yet," I responded, trying to sound more confident than I really felt. "We need to make our anchorage in one tack, and it's going to get dark soon, so keep going."

Nothing would reduce our heel. We had far too much sail up. We decided to drop the mainsail to reduce sail area. It took most of my strength to get it down, tie it to the boom, tie the boom to the cabin handrail, and manage to stay aboard. Now we were not heeled over so far, but we couldn't begin to point high enough into the wind to make it to Smuggler's Cove. We would be lucky if we could even make it back to Anacapa Island.

We were both afraid to move out of the cockpit because a wave might wash us overboard. The seas were about 5 feet high, and it was a fight just to steer the boat. This went on for hours; the sun hid behind black clouds massed on the horizon. I calculated that we had made only two miles to windward on this tack, and it would be getting dark soon.

I turned to Karl and said, "We won't reach our anchorage tonight, not at this rate. Do you think your outboard will push us into this wind and sea?"

Karl was fighting the tiller, trying to steer us as high into the wind as possible, but with the full genoa, we couldn't make any gain to windward. Karl said, "What do we have to lose? You drop the sail, I'll grab the engine."

I crawled forward to the mast and dropped the genoa into the water. Karl reached for the engine, only to find the compartment full of water. Still, he fastened the Seagull onto the transom bracket, where, amazingly, it started on the first pull.

I managed to get the genoa aboard and lashed it to the lifelines. The sound of the engine was reassuring. Surely we'd be able to find some protection behind Anacapa Island.

I went below to study the charts. "Head as high as you can for Anacapa," I yelled from inside the cabin while rummaging for the charts.

"This damn engine won't point us upwind. We're going…"

His words were lost as a wave swamped us, leaving the cockpit full of water. Karl just managed to stay on board. Water rushed down through the companionway into the boat. The engine quit and wouldn't start.

"Where the hell are your charts?" I could feel my fear rising.

Defensively, he answered, "I didn't bring them because I knew we'd be in sight of land at all times."

I heaved an exasperated sigh, then said, "We'll have to go inside the channel for smoother water; you raise the sails." While Karl raised the mainsail and genoa, I took the helm.

With the wind and seas now at 80° to the side of the boat, we catapulted forward. As we headed back for the southern tip of Anacapa, I was aware that I was freezing. I also realized that we were losing all our windward ground, but hoped we would find quieter seas inside the channel, maybe even a place to anchor.

The sky to the east was dark. Silhouetted against the remnants of light from the setting sun, the island appeared deep purple. On the unstable black surface of the seas, we could barely distinguish the top of the waves from the dark sky. The boat rose, rolled, dropped, shifted, and yawed, making the movement almost unbearable.

As we approached the island, we tried to stay close to the southern end for protection. I could hear the seas roar ahead and my mouth dried. We were entering a dark, forbidden world, and I knew we were in trouble. Suddenly, a mountainous wave loomed above us, the top breaking. Before I could think, the rumbling wave was towering over us.

"Hold on!" I shouted, as I grabbed for the lifeline behind my back. The water smashed over us with unbelievable force. My mind was spinning. We were under water. Then, the next thing I knew, the boat was lying sideways on the water. We hadn't sunk, but the starboard side was submerged. The sails appeared fluorescent laying flat against the inky surface of the water.

My feet pushed against the opposite edge of the cockpit; my elbows were wrapped around the lifeline. I stood and peered down into the foam, waiting for the boat to right herself. Where was Karl?

As if in answer, I heard, "Man overboard!" I thought, "How nautical of Karl at a time like this."

It was so dark that I could only see the frothing water, then noticed two white-knuckled hands clinging on to the mainsail sheets where they connect to the boom. No head was to be seen. He struggled from under the mainsail and yelled something unintelligible.

Then another wave defeated us, pushing us along the surface like a piece of driftwood. Tons of water flowed over the boat, but thank God, we didn't go further over or under. I think that the flat surface of the sails on the water prevented it.

The wave left us still on our side. "Karl!" I screamed, for he was gone. I feared that the last wave pushed the boat over him and that he might drown. "Karl!"

I was beginning to think that we were going to die. There was no way we could get help. "We'll sink and I'll drown just like Karl, but I don't want to die, not like this, I..."

"Get me the hell out of here!" Not so nautical this time, came the sweet sound of Karl's voice from somewhere behind the stern. Then I saw him, only an arm's length away, but at this angle, he couldn't get aboard.

I shouted, "Hold on to the stern rail!" With my right hand, I reached down and released the jib sheet and the main sheet. Almost immediately, the boat righted itself. There must have been suction created from the sails being flat on the water that prevented the boat from righting. I tugged Karl onto the deck. He lay on his stomach, stretched out across the cockpit catching his breath.

We were way too close to the sheer cliffs of Anacapa Island, and I knew that I must get away before we hit the rocks. I figured that the next wave might capsize us again. The wind was nearly on our bow; the boom was swinging from side to side at great speed. I crawled forward and dropped the mainsail. The genoa was flogging violently in the wind.

Karl pulled on the genoa sheet. Immediately, wind filled the sail and we took off like a shot downwind, back to the open sea.

Karl controlled the tiller and genoa sheet. I gathered the mainsail together the best I could and roughly fastened a line around the sail and boom. This would hold the whole mess together until we decided what we were going to do next.

As soon as we rounded Anacapa, we were heading back out to sea where we were before, except we were further downwind. If we kept on our present course, our next landfall would be Australia!

This had all happened too quickly; we needed time to think. We dropped the genoa to stop our progress. Below, I found an old canvas 18-inch sea anchor, which I hoped would bring the bow up to the wind and prevent our drifting further downwind. I tied it to the end of a 3/8-inch anchor line and threw it off the bow. I let out about 100 feet of line and secured it to the bow cleat. Suddenly there was a jerk, but the bow didn't point up to the wind to stop our turbulent rolling and drifting. We were still beam to the seas and were being tossed around like a cork. Apparently, the sea anchor was too small or the rope too short. At least we didn't seem to be moving away from the island as fast.

Karl appeared dazed, perhaps in shock. I hurried below, grabbed a saucepan, and began bailing out the water inside. I grabbed two life jackets and passed one out to Karl and put the other one on myself. When I returned to the cockpit, nothing was said; we both stared at our black surroundings. Anacapa Island could be seen as a black silhouette against the dark sky. We were frightened, wet, and cold. If we had a radio, we could have called for help, but we didn't. I took our foghorn, which operated on compressed air canisters, and repeated the SOS sequence several times: three short blasts, followed by three long blasts, ending with three short blasts (...---...), but who could hear us?

We could clearly see the white light atop the cliffs on the uninhabited island. I turned to Karl and asked, "Is the lighthouse on the island manned?"

Karl shrugged and said, "Anything's worth a try," and he disappeared below. He came topside with a handful of flares. They were the kind used in automobiles, the kind you light and lay on the road.

He took one, broke off the end, and scratched it to the flare. After it ignited, he stood on the cabin top. Clutching the mast with his left arm, he waved the flare back and forth with the other.

"Damn it!" he yelled, as fiery liquid flowed down his arm, singeing his hair and burning holes into the fiberglass deck and mainsail. He flung the flare into the ocean and shouted, "Drowning's preferable to burning."

"Not funny Karl," I yelled at him.

In the silence that united us, I heard Karl's teeth chattering as he tried to say, "Isss therrree annyyyy way weeee cannn reaccch Anacapaaa and tie to the kelp?"

"Hell no," I responded in irritated fear. "We can't get to Anacapa; it is now too windward of us and the seas are too big."

We stared at the black tip of the island in silence; then Karl said, "Our only chance is to head back through the channel between the islands and the mainland. We'll lash ourselves to the boat so we don't get washed overboard and just use the genoa."

As I tried to visualize being beam to those huge, steep seas, I chattered, "We'll be broadside to the wind and seas like we were before and we'll get knocked down." My mind began to feel it happening as I continued, "We may be knocked over but the boat should come back up each time if we don't have the main up."

We really didn't have any other choice without charts. We had no idea what was downwind of us; it might have been open ocean.

I looked at Karl and said, "If we tie ourselves to the lifelines with slip knots, we can easily release ourselves in case we go completely over or sink." I was more scared than I have ever been in my life. "Karl must feel the same," I thought.

With Karl at the helm, I inched forward to bring in the sea anchor. Fighting the violent roll of the boat, it seemed to take forever just to bring in a few feet. Sitting on top of the genoa on deck was slippery; it seemed to want to slide overboard with me on it. I pulled and pulled on the anchor, but there was too much resistance. I was too cold and weak to continue. I decided, "Screw it, I'll buy Karl a new sea anchor and line." With that in mind, I cut the anchor loose with my pocketknife that, thankfully, I had sharpened just before our departure.

The wind, seas, and the incredible rolling made crawling back to the mast nearly impossible; I just held on for a while. For the first time, I thought about seasickness and immediately dispelled the notion, fearing it might come sooner if I thought about it.

Each time I moved, the damn genoa slid out from under me. Every roll of the boat caused more sail to go into the water until the entire genoa was tugged from under me. I laid arms outstretched, hands locked on to the lifeline, my feet dangling into the sea. Except where it was connected on to the headstay, the genoa was completely in the water.

I waited until the boat rolled, lifting me, making it easier to reach the mast. Grasping the mast with one arm, I raised the genoa halyard as much as possible by hand. It was enough for the sail to catch air and we started moving. I returned to the cockpit to tie myself to the lifeline beside Karl.

With the genoa full, sailing on a broad reach, we sailed in silence, deep in our own thoughts. "How did I ever get myself into this? I just wanted to enjoy sailing." I felt as if God was punishing me for something, but couldn't figure out what it was that I had done. My mind relived a few arguments and lies I had told my parents in my younger years. There were some girls in college I had made love to; I didn't really love them but I think I said I did. I hadn't ever done anyone any harm. Basically, I've tried to live by the Golden Rule; I loved people in general and revered life.

"Yeah, I'm being punished for chasing after women, but I always treat them with respect. I am a gentleman, even when I don't want to be. Hell, I'm single. I believe in equality for women; even voted in favor of doing away with bras while in college. But, hey, maybe I'm not being punished, but tested. Do I have stamina for survival? Am I good enough to ride upon Mother Ocean's surface? Perhaps I entered Her too early, and she's expressing her dissatisfaction. If I get back alive, I will never set foot on another sailboat, ever."

As we approached the end of the island, near where we were previously knocked down, I heard the roar of the breaking seas inside the channel. Fear of drowning interrupted my thoughts. Over my shoulder, the dark sky disappeared as a darker surface rose overhead. It began to turn white on top and started to roar down upon us. I screamed, "Turn into it! Hold on!"

Karl shoved the tiller hard to starboard. The boat rounded up into the wind as the mountain of water broke over us. Yet we stayed upright and—most importantly—aboard. The wave, passing as quickly as it came, left the cockpit full. As soon as the genoa caught air, Karl put us back on course.

Each time a wave approached, the sky vanished. We lost some of the wind in the troughs because the seas were so high, but we maintained steerage. As the wave passed, we were carried to the next crest where the wind filled the sail and thrust us forward towards land.

About 3:00 a.m., we saw the lights of Channel Island Harbor. Exhausted and relieved, we sailed into the harbor, where a patrol boat greeted us. "You guys just come out of that stuff? You're crazy to be out there in that little boat. You all right? It's been blowing over 40 in the channel. We lost two boats and the 82-foot Coast Guard cutter was damaged." One of the men flung us a line and began towing us to the protection of the harbor.

All Karl and I could do was shake our heads and smile. Maybe we had passed the test after all.

That summer, we did take my Balboa 20 to Baja California, Mexico. In fact, we did it during the summer vacation for the next three years. My last trip was with Jerry, who had sailed with me on my Chinese Junk. He was still in the Navy and had taken an extended leave to make this trip with me. We sailed from San Diego all the way down the Pacific side around the tip of Cabo San Lucas then up to the town of San Felipe at the northern most end of the Sea of Cortez. There, a trailer was waiting to take us home.

The trip was basically uneventful except for one incident that I remember only too well. It will illustrate how anything can happen.

We were sailing in the midriff island group. We had sailed through a narrow passage to a great anchorage on one of the little islands. Jerry is slim and tall. He towers over me by about 4 inches and weighs about 200 pounds, 40 pounds more than I. He has dark hair that was thinning prematurely, and it bothered him. Since we were in a kind of no man's land in mid July, there was no one to see him but me, so he had nothing to worry about except sunburn.

Except for a pod of Finback Whales that swam right next to our boat for half an hour, we had not seen another living thing for almost a week. It was even a little frightening to be so alone.

During this particular day's sail, we had encountered tidal currents in excess of 9 knots, which created whirlpools that were big enough to threaten our 20-foot boat. The north end of the Sea of Cortez has 18-foot tides, so when it floods or ebbs, the currents can be dangerous, especially near the islands where the Venturi Effect increases the speed of the current.

It was nearing sunset when we set the anchor at this uninhabited island. Jerry thought we should climb to the top of the hill and take a picture of the sunset. We rowed our dinghy across the smooth waters to the shore. It was a rocky hill, and after quite a struggle, we neared the top. From our bird's eye view, it was impressive. The only living things within sight were a few stalks of organ pipe cactus and some sea birds. We could see the sea's currents were running strong with whirlpools scattered about.

We accidentally set some loose rocks tumbling down the hill, starting a small landslide. Suddenly, there were creatures flying all over the place. They must have been under the rocks to get away from the heat and light of the hot summer day.

"Vampire bats!" Jerry joked.

I ignored him. The sun had just set and it was too dark to determine if they were bats or small birds, but they were flying just over our heads. We crouched down until they finally settled back under the rocks.

By the time we got back to the boat, it was dark. It had been a long day and we were exhausted, so we had a quick dinner and decided to hit the rack. We took our cushions outside to sleep in the cockpit because it was hellishly hot and the sky was full of stars. I was just dozing off when I heard loud deep breathing on my side of the boat. I flicked on the flashlight that I keep at my side at night, but it was too late. I caught a glimpse of the top of a black head going under water some distance from the boat. My first thought was of a whale, but that wasn't likely considering the narrow shallow entrance.

About ten minutes later, I heard it again, but louder and closer. It even woke Jerry. This time the flashlight beam caught the rough top of its head as it went under. Perhaps I wouldn't have been so concerned except that this spot was primitive and unusual. Anything could live here, and who the hell would know what it was. I had just finished reading that there was evidence that a giant squid may live in the deep waters of the Sea of Cortez. History has documented them big enough to sink large vessels.

"How big was this head?" Jerry asked. "Did you see a hole or a spout of water come from it?"

"No," I responded. "It looked rough like it may have barnacles on it, but no blow hole."

We sat in silence waiting for it to surface again, but nothing happened. We figured that it must have left, so we decided to try to get some sleep.

I was just beginning to doze when there was a loud hammering on the underside of the boat, as if we were bouncing on the rocks. Something was breathing very loudly right beside me. I jumped to the other side, landing on top of Jerry.

"What the hell is it?" he yelled.

Bang! Bang! It continued hitting the underside of the boat; I figured the thing was trying to put a hole in our hull. The breathing intensified. We couldn't move. I expected to see a claw or tentacle come over the side, but nothing happened.

Finally, I gathered up enough courage to lean over with my flashlight. There it was! An immense reptile hand reaching up for me! I ducked back, then stole another look. No, it was an enormous sea turtle banging his shell against our hull and poking his head up almost to the topsides of the boat.

Needless to say, we had a restless night's sleep.

Over the years, the obsession to go cruising grew. After the Chinese Junk, it was the 20-footer. Now, I was more committed to sailing over the horizon and needed a larger boat. Joan, my girlfriend, insisted I buy a much bigger boat if she was going to be doing any sailing with me.

We found a used 40 footer which had been finished by its original owner. She was named *Mrs. M.* The only way I could afford a boat of this size was to live aboard. Joan was insistent that this was a boat she could sail on and big enough to store some of her clothes. So, with a bit of reluctance, I bought her. Soon after I made the commitment, I changed her name to the *Marionette.*

I soon discovered that *Marionette,* big and comfortable as she was, drained all my finances. As a high school teacher, I wasn't wealthy. Marina fees were high, and the *Marionette* demanded continual maintenance plus the monthly boat loan payments. It would be seven years before she would be paid for, and we could leave. By then, she'd need new rigging and sails, and it would be time to repeat nearly everything I had just finished.

I had owned the *Marionette* for about six months. I was driving to work one morning, thinking about the problems I was having with this boat. It seemed to be my nemesis. Joan was insistent that this is what I should name the boat, *Nemesis.* My mind was more on my boat than my driving. I signaled out of the fast lane, then grinned. That could be my metaphor—get out of the fast lane permanently. But, it couldn't be on the *Marionette.*

To handle her required two full-time crew. If the weather turned bad, the person on watch would have to wake the other crewmember to help make sail changes or reefs. When the winds freshened at night, the larger the boat, the more likely that it would be the first boat to drag at anchor. This was especially true with the *Marionette,* which had a huge cabin with lots of windage. When the anchor is dragging towards the rocks, to get a large boat underway in a hurry requires more than one extra hand. So, I felt I shouldn't go cruising with less than 3 persons aboard, and finding good crew wasn't easy.

Most of my sailing friends had different working schedules than mine. My hippie-type, non-working friends were, well, unreliable. After being caught in 100-knot winds while anchored behind Santa Barbara Island, off the California coast, my single teacher friends had had their fill. Wives of my married teacher friends usually wouldn't let their husbands go for longer than a day sail. Some wives just didn't like sailing at all.

Sailing with women in general had proven to be disappointing. I do feel that it was largely my fault. The type of women that I was attracted to were bright, beautiful ladies who wore hose, high heels, and had long fine hair. Unfortunately, those types weren't keen on their long hair blowing in a breeze over 10 knots, and they were more interested in suntans than in learning the effects of the sail slot while sailing to windward.

As I exited the freeway, I thought of Joan, my first and last relationship since my divorce 7 years ago. Soon after I bought the *Marionette,* I moved aboard. It took Joan another few months to take the plunge and move aboard with me. She was so unsure this was really what she wanted to do, that she continued to pay rent on her apartment, just in case. It was just before the start of the rainy season.

After the first rain, we discovered a leak in the teak deck over the hanging locker holding Joan's expensive clothes. The next morning, she left for work in a wet dress spotted with brown water stains. There was little communication for the start of this day.

The following night, a new leak brought a continuous stream of water, slightly smaller than the size an infant boy could produce. It was directly over the center of our queen-size bed in the aft stateroom.

At 3:00 in the morning, without speaking, we rigged, tied, shaped and wedged aluminum foil and various items under the leak with duct tape, and re-directed it into a metal bucket beside the bed. I tried to ignore the shambles we'd created while locating all the paraphernalia needed to accomplish the job. Cranky and irritable, we crawled back into bed. I reached for Joan only to find that the leak had soaked the center of the mattress. The stiff way Joan held her body told me she really didn't feel like getting close anyway.

The small stream of water flowed constantly into the bucket with the sound of a fire hose. Thirty to forty-five minutes later, I sat up, put my feet on the cold, soggy, shag carpet, picked up the overflowing bucket, and whispered, "Shit!"

"You said it," Joan answered from the far side of the bed. Spreading moisture forced us to the respective edges, and eventually into the salon where we slept on opposite settees.

At 6:30 a.m., the alarm rang. It was still raining. With a clenched jaw and complete silence except for an occasional grunt, Joan quickly dressed and departed for work without breakfast, coffee, or a good-bye.

She and I returned home that evening at about the same time. She smiled and asked about my day. "Ah, things are back to normal," I thought. It wasn't until we got aboard that we both suddenly stopped dead when we saw the completely soaked aft stateroom. Most of our luxurious shag carpeting lay under water.

"The mattress shouldn't be too wet," I pointed out as we stared at the piece of plastic I'd used to cover it with that morning before I left for work. But the plastic had prevented the mattress from drying. "I'll just move it into the salon near the heater where it will dry quicker. After it dries, we can sleep on the floor."

Silence.

I removed my shoes, waded to the bed, and yanked. The mattress didn't budge. It was as if it were fastened down. Again I tugged; it was so waterlogged that I couldn't budge it. Like a huge funnel, the plastic had directed all the water from the deck leak to a small hole in its center.

"A drink?" I suggested.

Dispirited, we turned into the salon. I poured glasses of Chardonnay, but we couldn't sit on the settees—they were now wet too. The shag carpet squished beneath our feet as we moved to the raised galley, the one dry spot on the boat. Here, Joan looked me straight in the eye with the expression that said 'do not say a word' and said in a low, slow voice, like I did not understand English, "I'm gathering up my sodden, ruined clothes and stuffing them into one of the plastic garbage bags. Then I'm getting into my car and driving back to Newport Beach, where I still have a warm, dry apartment waiting for me. Join me if you like. I truly don't give a damn."

I didn't join her.

I saw Joan at work occasionally, and she remained cordial. We went out in the evenings once in awhile, but for certain, she would never set foot on the boat again.

I had to resolve the leaking deck problem. As I went through the process of elimination, I discovered that the whole superstructure and deck was full of dry rot. Over the years, water had found its way under the fiberglass at the large sliding windows in the main salon and rotted the wood beneath. The rot spread everywhere; the damage was extensive, and to repair it was far more than I could handle. I was broke, still owed 7 years of payments on the boat, and I was living aboard... alone.

At the advice of a friend, I called a Maritime Attorney. He agreed to see me for a free consultation. He informed me that I had a good case against the surveyor who, only 6 months earlier, had given her a clean bill of health. But I could not sue for an unknown amount; the repairs would have to be completed first.

I contacted a local boatyard for a quote on the repairs. They gave me an estimate of $15,000. At the lawyer's advice, I contacted the surveyor in San Diego, where I had bought the boat, and threatened him with a lawsuit. He agreed to meet me and the guy from the boatyard to check the damage himself. He admitted negligence and gave some sort of excuse. He said he did not have any money, but would give me $4,000 cash if I signed a release. Otherwise, I would have to see him in court.

Since I did not have any money of my own to pay for the repairs, I had no choice but to accept. I sold my car and got an old clunker. I sold all my expensive camera gear and anything else that was a non-essential. Including the $4,000 from the surveyor, I then had about $8,000 cash.

I found an ad in a local marine chandlery for a shipwright looking for work. He drove up in a new white Cadillac—that should have waved a red flag. After surveying the damage, he said he could make the repairs for about $5,000 if I did all the clean up and painting after repairs were finished. We made up a hand-written contract. He wanted $3,000 now and an additional $1,000 a month for two months.

I moved off the boat. With my tail between my legs, I moved in with Joan. She constantly reminded me of why I was there. My life was miserable. There was nowhere for me to go, and the little money I had was for boat repairs. I really think she enjoyed having the upper hand, and I felt my balls were slowly being squeezed to the size of grapes.

Everyday after teaching, I drove down to Long Beach to check on the progress. The entire upper structure had been removed, but the deck remained intact. After two weeks, the shipwright said he needed the rest of the money to buy all the materials because there was going to be a major increase in material costs. He signed the contract that it was paid in full, but the work was not complete. I never saw him again.

Now I had a boat without a cabin, $3,000 left, and I was living with someone who was making my life hell and enjoying it. I bought some tarps, covered the boat, then moved back aboard. This was better than being squeezed to a lifeless form.

I found a Swedish shipwright who talked like he knew what he was doing. We agreed that I would pay him $6 an hour, and I could work with him to reduce the cost. It was summer, and I had almost three months off to work on the boat.

This guy was great. He knew exactly what he was doing. I worked alongside him as his apprentice. That summer, I learned more about boat building and repairs than most people learn in a lifetime. By the end of the summer, we were finished, and the *Marionette* looked like a brand new boat.

§

It was now apparent that I'd probably be sailing solo, and I needed a craft I could handle alone. So, I put the *Marionette* up for sale. I hung a large sign on the headstay that read, "For Sale, Price Negotiable".

On an early Saturday morning while I sat in the cockpit drinking coffee and fantasizing about a new, smaller boat, a chubby little bald-headed man walked out on the finger pier. Without asking permission, he stepped on board.

"I'm Robert T. Whitfield, and I'm here to buy your boat," he said in an authoritative voice.

My coffee mug clinked on the cockpit table. "Sure," I almost laughed. "Cash or check?"

He tugged a checkbook from his rear pocket. "For a retainer, I'll give you $3,000." From his shirt pocket, he pulled a pen. "How do you spell your name?"

"R-o-g-e-r O-l-s-o-n," I stuttered.

As he wrote, I said, "Hey, you're going to give me $3,000 without even knowing my asking price or how she sails?"

"I'm not concerned about price." Ripping the check from the book, he laid it on the table. "We can discuss it during our sail later this morning. I'm meeting some business associates at 10:00; I'll bring them with me. Have plenty of food and some good Scotch on board. See you at 11:00."

As quickly as Whitfield had appeared, he left. Stunned, I picked up the check. Then, as reality sunk in, I made a quick run to the store, grabbing up bread, cold meat, chips, nuts, and a quart of Johnny Walker Black Label.

By 11:00, I had the sail covers off, the sails ready to be raised, and the engine warm. Fifteen minutes later, Whitfield arrived dressed in a white T-shirt and white shorts that accentuated his large belly and made his legs look exceptionally thin. He wore no shoes.

Even though he stood 5 feet away, I could smell alcohol on his breath as he said, "My associates couldn't make it. Let's go."

Soon I had the *Marionette* sailing hard to windward, moving beautifully as if she were showing off. I felt proud of her performance. In rapid succession, Whitfield ate two sandwiches and downed three glasses of straight Scotch.

"The *Marionette* is great in a blow," I said. "In a storm, she heaves-to comfortably with the main fully reefed and the storm jib backed."

Through a full mouth, he mumbled, "I don't care about that; I just anchor."

"But what if you're out at sea and the water's too deep?" I asked.

As if he had done it a hundred times, he said, "I just drop the anchor into deep water, and when I get into shallow water, it will grab on to something."

I knew Mr. Whitfield was full of crap, and that I shouldn't care as long as he bought the boat. I've always had a big mouth, so I couldn't leave his statement unchallenged. "You need some storm strategy," I insisted. "Your method would work in moderate conditions in shallow water, but sometimes it gets awfully rough, and you have to go to sea to get away from land or a lee shore."

He smiled and drained the glass. "I'm not going to sail her. She'll serve as my office on Lido Island. I own a real estate business and intend to sell yachts as well as land and houses."

The thought that my boat wouldn't be used at sea hurt. I really shouldn't care; I needed the money. I quoted him the price.

Whitfield didn't blink. "I'll have cash Monday. I'm buying other boats, too. Could you get me more Scotch, please?"

As I went below for the bottle, his voice trailed me down the companionway, "I'm also buying the *Queen Mary*."

With my foot poised on the ladder, I reconsidered. Maybe I better not take the quart topside. I poured a little liquor in his glass, then hid the bottle.

"What are you going to do with her?" I asked when I handed him his drink.

"Gambling ship." He gulped the Scotch. "Outside the country limits, naturally. I'll fly guests out on a helicopter."

"Humor him," I thought, as I brought the *Marionette* about and steered back toward the marina.

I asked, "How do you plan to get her seaworthy again? I am sure she isn't able to motor out of Long Beach Harbor even if her motor works."

He continued to ramble on about engineering experts, how well he knew the President, and how rich he was. It never stopped.

As I inched the *Marionette* back into her slip, he offered to help me tie her up. I was afraid he was too drunk and might fall in the water, so I insisted he remain aboard.

Trying to sound a bit desperate, I said, "Mr. Whitfield, I really need some cash now. If you'll give me a hundred dollars as a retainer, I'll write a receipt and return your check." I figured this would more than cover my cost for the food and booze.

Without hesitation, he agreed, "Sure. I have cash in my hotel room; I'll go get it for you."

Rapidly slipping on my thongs, I suggested, "I'll go with you so you don't have to come back."

"First, we have to find my car," Whitfield announced as we proceeded along the dock. "I don't remember where I parked it, and the hotel keys are in the glove box."

Although quite drunk, he walked straight and his description of a white Cadillac convertible, parked near Harpoon Henry's restaurant, was but a bit slurred.

We rounded a corner. There sat a vintage 1959 convertible, half on the sidewalk and half in the street. Its hood was wired down and stood agape by 6 inches. There was no trunk lid, a cracked windshield without wipers, a missing interior instrument panel cover, and upholstery that had experienced the butts of thousands. How had this car managed to stay on the road? There was a ticket shoved into an opening where the wiper should have been.

Whitfield was delighted, "Oh, here it is." As he rummaged through the glove box, minus a door, I felt despair. "Maybe he's an eccentric," I assured myself. As long as there was a chance this man would make my dream possible, I'd stick with him.

When he couldn't find hotel or car keys, I accompanied him the short distance to the Dana Point Hotel. Here the elderly female clerk behind the desk addressed him by name. I felt hopeful, but she quickly added, "The police were here asking for you, but I told them they couldn't search your room without a warrant. What's…"

"Damn." He beat his fists against the counter top. "They do this to me whenever I'm handling a big business deal. Well, just give me the spare set of keys."

She shook her head. "Remember you lost your first set of keys this morning, and I gave you the spare set then. All I have left is this last set, and I am not permitted to release them."

Whitfield leaned his big belly against the edge of the counter and bent far over so his nose nearly touched the clerk's forehead. In a voice of quiet authority, one that again raised my hopes, he said, "I have come to your hotel on business, big business. I have a client with me. I don't care about your keys. I'll buy this damn place and put you out in the street if you don't let me into my room instantly."

Obviously impressed, she handed over a key. Whitfield punched the elevator button, and we rode to the second floor. His room commanded a great view of the marina and, once more, I was unsure of him. He fumbled for his checkbook.

"No check. Cash," I said, as he began to write.

As if awakening from a dream, he said, "Well, why didn't you say so? My cash's hidden in the car."

Hope fled. I wanted to get away and eagerly left with him to go back to his car. When the elevator door opened on the lobby level, he blanched at the policemen talking to the clerk. They were facing the counter and could not see us. Whitfield gripped my arm, jerked me to one side, and hurried me out a rear door, whispering something about finding his secretary by the pool.

He started on some wild story about a metal plate in his head as a result of some war. He told me to feel it, but I didn't. He continued on about becoming deranged when he spotted a man in uniform, any uniform. I interrupted him and yelled, "Hey, Whitfield, or whatever your name is, you're so full of bullshit you can't see for the brown in your eyes. You haven't any money, and if your check bounces, I'm going to prosecute."

With considerable dignity, he drew himself up. "I can't blame you for what you must think. In your shoes I'd feel the same way. Take my check to the bank on Monday. I'll be back next weekend with the rest of the money; you can apologize then."

Continuing to hold himself erect and mustering as much dignity as any man can with half a quart of Scotch in his belly, he strolled back toward the hotel. Once more, weak hope nudged. Could he be legit? But suddenly, just before the door, he turned into the shadows and was gone from sight.

His check bounced, but I saved it as a souvenir of the day I met the guy who was going to buy the *Queen Mary*. The check reminded me of what I'd go through to sell a boat and buy another.

Amazingly, a few weeks later, a genuine buyer accepted my asking price. I paid off my loan and began looking for my cruising yacht.

§

There is some specific knowledge that a cruiser should acquire before departure. The list is long, but fortunately, most of the items are common sense. Following are a few of the most important and often overlooked experiences or techniques one should have before leaving on a cruise.

There will come a time when the engine will not start. Sailors today have much bigger boats with bigger engines to power them. Unfortunately, many cruisers could not sail their boat to or from the dock, raise or set an anchor under sail, or get underway in a hurry without the engine.

There are many examples of boats or even lives being lost because cruisers relied too much on the engine. In many cases, the sail covers were still on the sails and could not be deployed in time, even if the cruisers knew how to sail to safety.

There are many reasons why the engine may quit unexpectedly, causing the cruiser to depend on his or her sailing skills. The radical rolling and pounding of a boat in rough weather will stir up sediment in the fuel tank and plug the filters, thus killing the engine. If the fuel tank is not full, the radical rolling may cause air to be sucked into the fuel line, which can also affect the engine. The fuel line may break or come loose at the most inappropriate time. Or, a line or netting can get caught in the prop, causing the engine to die.

§

Being able to sail when the engine died and having emergency tools and parts readily available saved me from some serious trouble. I had recently crossed the Torres Straits between Papua New Guinea and Northern Australia on my way to Darwin, Australia. There was a narrow pass between the mainland and an island which had to be navigated with the tidal current. Fortunately, there is a protected anchorage just before this pass where a sailor can wait for the tide to change. I spent the night in this anchorage planning to catch the changing tide before sunrise.

This particular morning, there was little—if any—wind. I started the engine and raised all sails including my light wind drifter. I raised anchor and began motoring to the narrow passage that protected the anchorage. The water was as smooth as a mirror. There wasn't even a whisper of a breeze, so the drifter hung loose in the centerline of the boat as I motored forward.

Using my spotlight, I could see the narrow pass ahead. I turned on my echo sounder that read to 60 feet. I was only yards away from the pass when the engine alarm sounded. It was overheated. It was too late to turn around; I was already in the pass. I dashed below, tore off the engine cover, and immediately saw that the fan belt, which drives the cooling pump, was gone. As I dashed topside, the depth sounder alarm sounded at 10 feet, and then the engine died.

I suspected that I was too far to starboard, so I turned to port, and the depth sounder went to 6 feet. My boat will hit bottom at about four and a half feet, so I didn't have much time. I pushed the tiller to port, and slowly the boat turned to starboard. The depth sounder went back to 10 feet. Unfortunately, the tide had turned and began to flood, causing a slight current that pushed me back to port.

I figured I would hit the rocks at any moment. Since there was no swell or waves, I was not too concerned about major damage, but I did not want to get stuck on any rocks. I grabbed my boat pole in preparation to fend off, when suddenly, there was the slightest of breeze that lifted the drifter and gave me just enough way to move slowly to starboard.

I grabbed my tiller autopilot and set a straight course. Then, I dashed down and changed my belt in record time. Fortunately, I always kept a spare belt and the necessary size open-end wrenches within arm's reach in case of just such an emergency. It is frightening to think about what could have happened if a large swell was running and the drifter hadn't caught a little air.

§

The more skill the cruiser has to sail the boat in tight quarters, in calms, or in adverse weather, the greater the chance of someday saving the boat and perhaps even lives. An easy way to get some experience without the possibility of damage to your own boat or others is to set out markers as obstacles and to practice sailing around them. As confidence is gained, place the obstacles closer together until you discover your boat's limitations. Heavier boats will maintain headway when tacking through the wind, while lighter boats may stall. Depending on the keel design, some boats will not turn as rapidly or as tightly as others. Change the positions of the markers, so you can practice in various wind directions.

Another important consideration is that there should be at least two people aboard who are capable of sailing the boat alone. This may sound unnecessary, but the time may come when the boat has to be single-handed.

If a person is on watch, he or she should be able to handle most situations alone, without waking other crewmembers. This includes reefing and changing sails.

The boat may have to be sailed single-handed if others get sick or injured. A common problem is unexpected seasickness when the weather turns rough. A problem many men encounter is a painful back that may even prevent standing upright.

There may be an emergency, and one or more of the crew may have to return home leaving one person on board. The boat my have to be moved to a more protected anchorage or even out of the country. There are many places in the world where crew is not easy to find, so the ability to sail the vessel alone may be necessary.

There should be enough experience, so the skipper and crew know how the boat will respond in as many different conditions as possible. A bad time to learn that your boat won't heave-to is during a gale at sea.

While in familiar waters and near protected waters, take the boat out when others are coming in for protection. Experiment with different heavy weather strategies to see how your boat responds. If something goes wrong, you can always motor back to protected waters.

I don't feel that a person planning to leave on a cruise can have too much experience. Nonetheless, sailing and cruising is a continuous learning experience. You will never know it all. It is up to you to decide when and where to draw the line and begin your cruise.

Chapter Three

THE CRUISING YACHT

One of the most important considerations when deciding to go cruising is the vessel that you choose. Not every boat is capable of accomplishing the challenge of crossing the seas of the world.

In this chapter, my intention is to address the aspects of a boat that are an integral part of the ship's construction; these are features that cannot be changed. I will leave things that can be altered, added, and deleted, for another chapter.

I will attempt to summarize my views about those yacht features that would help make a better offshore cruiser. There is no attempt to compare these vessels to offshore racers. Only those designs that I feel are practical for offshore cruising will be mentioned. I am neither a Naval Architect nor a design engineer. The formulas mentioned should be considered guidelines, not absolutes.

My opinions are based on 25 years of my own cruising and boat building experience. The wealth of material I researched for years before buying my own boat, as well as recent books and articles, are included. The comments and opinions of fellow cruisers who sail and cruise on many different yacht sizes, rigs, and designs are considered.

Delivering a variety of yachts has also given me great insight into good and bad designs. I feel that my 9 years of owning a reputable boat building company gave me an intimate knowledge of the structure and features required to make a vessel truly worthy of being called a blue water cruiser. Material is also included that was gleaned from my many conversations with Lyle Hess, a renowned boat designer and friend.

Selecting the vessel in which to live and cruise for an unlimited amount of time is one of the most difficult decisions a prospective cruiser will have to make. This vessel must meet certain criteria before the cruiser will be satisfied with it as his or her floating home.

Bear in mind that there is no perfect yacht; they all involve a compromise. To gain something, something else must be sacrificed. It may only be the additional cost of an item or, more often, an important detail. It will be up to the readers to decide which features are critical to them. This is why there are so many models available: each buyer places more emphasis on a particular aspect over others. When it comes to boats, there will always be a difference of opinion.

Most buyers will visit boat shows to see what type, make, and size boats are available. They are also good places to get new ideas. It is interesting to listen to salesmen who have little—if any—real cruising experience. Many of them make comments that are completely unfounded, and may embarrass themselves and the company they represent.

The same applies to many marine surveyors. Many are excellent and highly qualified, but there are too many who really do not know a properly designed or soundly built vessel. So, when the search for the vessel begins, listen to all the 'experts', including this author, with a skeptical ear. The buyer has to draw from all the information that is gathered and then select the yacht according to his or her particular needs and budget.

It is the purpose of this chapter to reveal as much information as I can, both good and bad, about a sailing vessel's design and construction. I will leave the final deduction to the reader. It is possible that I might miss an item or two. The number of pros and cons can extend into minute details that have little need to be considered in this book.

There is one concern that should take precedence over all others: *the safety for vessel and crew*. The vessel should be stoutly built and able to take the punishment from the pounding of the seas over many years of use. Many prospective cruisers may be highly qualified as sailors, but may lack the knowledge of the proper design and construction methods that make a cruising vessel safe. A lot of money can be spent on a yacht that may not have the necessary qualities to go offshore.

The prospective buyer should begin compiling as much information as possible. All sailors have opinions based on their experience or the experiences they have heard from others. Sometimes this information is distilled from stories they heard over their 10th beer at the local saloon, so use caution when listening to fellow sailors. The more experience a sailor has, the more one should listen to what he or she has to say.

It is surprising how many sailors will voice an opinion about the sailing characteristics of a boat they have never sailed on. I had heard many negative stories about a particular boat model. Yet when I sailed on one or alongside one, I discovered my original conception was in total error. It had been based on the unsubstantiated opinion of others. When someone volunteers such information, be sure to ask what he or she is using to base his or her comments. Try to draw out as much information from this person's source, so you can feel confident that what is being said is factual. Then listen to what they have to say, but file it under "needing further research".

Read all the books available on boat design and construction. When the model and type of boat is narrowed down to a few, ask many surveyors what their opinion is about the boats under consideration. Again, listen and file under "needing further research".

I feel it is important to contact as many boatyards as possible to get their opinions. Boatyard workers have firsthand knowledge about certain aspects of some boat models. It is only when a boat has to be repaired that some of the true construction methods are revealed. During my travels, I saw many boats of a particular manufacturer that had severe osmosis. These boats were being repaired all over the world. Boatyard interviews may reveal such a problem.

If the boat under consideration is still in production, visit the factory to see, firsthand, how the boat is put together. Some boat builders will hide flaws, knowing that they will never be seen unless the vessel is damaged. These companies are an embarrassment to the industry. Be extremely cautious if the builder will not permit you to visit the factory or a particular part of the facility.

The cruising vessel should be able to sail well. This does not only relate to speed but to all aspects of sailing. Of course, the boat should be able to get you to your destination quickly; no one wants to spend years sailing and never exceed 5 knots. The speed of a vessel is directly related to her weight, design, and the skipper's sailing skill. If the boat is a slug, then she is too heavy and/or poorly designed. Either of these factors could also affect the safety of an ocean passage.

I feel safety should take precedence over speed. This would not only involve the vessel's soundness, but her ability to heave-to in severe weather. She should have some weight and directional stability to sail in heavy winds. She should have the ability to sail to windward, so she could sail off a lee shore in a blow. In case of a knockdown, she should right herself quickly and without hesitation.

The size of vessel

There is a misconception that larger is better. Perhaps this is the case in other matters, but it does not apply to cruising boats. There are boats over 60 feet long that are not nearly as seaworthy as some boats that are 20 feet long. Seaworthiness is based on design and structural integrity, not size.

Most cruisers consider that the average size boat for two people should be about 34 feet. This is not an absolute; it could be longer or shorter. I would consider a boat over 40 feet for two to be pushing the limits. The safe size boat for two will depend on its rig configuration, balance, displacement, hull design, skill and even age of the crew. So when the term 'larger' is used, it will be based on the number of crew required to sail the boat. The number aboard will increase proportionally to the length.

The larger yacht does require more crew. When I was delivering yachts, a basic criterion many delivery skippers used for determining the number of crew required was the size of the mainsail. When it came time to reduce sail area by either changing sails or reefing, how many crewmembers would be required? It was felt that in severe weather, about 300 square feet of mainsail was all one person could handle. Since the mainsail is the primary driving sail going to weather, it became a measuring stick because all other sails would be proportionate in size and difficulty in handling.

This is not taking into consideration electric reefing winches and additional devices that make working the sails easier. All too often, these devices, especially electrical ones, fail just when they are needed the most. At the very least, they are not 100% dependable. Try to remember that when things go wrong or break, it is usually when they are stressed to their limits. There may be no sign of a problem until the time comes when you need to rely on them.

Larger vessels have many advantages. As a home underway, they have more living accommodations. There are more places to move around and space for "private time", those moments needed to be away from others. Each person or couple may have their own private stateroom, perhaps with head and shower.

The bigger the boat, the more general comforts and gadgets it can have. There may be forced heating and air conditioning, hot running water, showers and baths, microwaves, freezers, and generators to provide power to every electrical device imaginable. The list goes on and on. The additional storage space will allow the cruiser to carry several dinghies, bicycles or even motor scooters, kayaks, SCUBA gear with compressors, etc.

If the larger vessel is properly designed and constructed, she will be more seaworthy and will have a more comfortable motion at sea. This can be a major factor for families. The smaller the boat and the lighter the boat, the more radical will be her motion. Severe motion will have a tendency to irritate and could cause mutiny. However, most sailors become accustomed to this movement, while others can't—or won't—adjust.

The longer the waterline on a boat, the faster she is expected to sail and motor. Because she will carry more sail area and have a bigger engine, she will have more driving force going to windward or plowing through rough seas.

While I was cruising, I noticed that most cruising boats under fifty feet averaged 100 nautical miles for a 24-hour run. Many boats of various sizes will leave port on the same day and reach their destination a week later at about the same time. Of course, there are going to be exceptions to this, but it is more common than uncommon.

The larger boat has all these advantages, but not without some compromise. Larger vessels have deeper drafts, restricting movement into shallower waters and increasing the chances of going aground. If she does go aground, her additional weight and surface area will make it more difficult to get her off and floating again. This can be more or less of a problem based on the keel's configuration.

Because of the longer length, there are many places the larger vessel cannot go due to its inability to maneuver in small areas. This problem is compounded when there is wind or strong currents. I found one of the major advantages of the smaller vessel was her ability to go up shallow, narrow rivers or bays to find perfectly smooth waters with beautiful surroundings.

A vessel with more weight and additional windage requires much heavier ground tackle. Depending on the size and draft of the vessel, it may have to anchor further out in deeper water. Thus, it will be more exposed to stronger winds and seas. This could cause the vessel to drag sooner than the smaller vessels, and depending on crew aboard, make it more difficult to get underway in a hurry.

The larger vessel will cost much more to maintain. The amount of money spent on one mainsail for a 50-foot yacht may be as much as the whole set of sails on a smaller one. The average 40-foot yacht will require 4 to 5 gallons of anti-fouling paint per coat while a 34-foot yacht may require less than 2 gallons per coat. The cost will go up proportionally by yacht size for repairs, replacement parts, and even regular maintenance. All of this may be of little concern if the owner can afford these additional expenses.

The larger yacht has more amenities that have to be maintained, serviced, and may require repair. Most electrical devices are short-lived in warm, humid, tropical climates.

The larger vessel will pay much more for harbor fees. Many countries have a set fee for a minimum length, usually about 30 feet. This size is considered the maximum length for a pleasure craft. When the vessel exceeds this length, it is approaching commercial size and will be charged more for each additional foot. Another interesting factor is that the locals will see the larger vessels as "rich folks" and will expect more money for any work or service provided.

In summary, I feel the smaller boat is best for a limited number of crewmembers on a low budget. If money is not a problem, then the larger vessel is going to provide more comfort and perhaps safety. Keep in mind, however, that as we get older, simple tasks become more difficult. This can lead to laziness or reluctance to reef early or put out more anchor scope. As older sailors, we like more comfort and usually have more money, so the tendency is to buy bigger, more comfortable boats that may be more difficult to handle.

The type of sailing rig

There are many kinds of sailing rigs. By rigs, I am referring to the number of masts and the general sailing configuration of a boat. It has nothing to do with the hull shape or design. The most common types of sailing rigs are the Sloop, Cutter, Ketch, Yawl and Schooner. Other rigs like the Chinese Junk, Lateen and Clipper will not be covered, because I do not consider these designs applicable for family cruising.

Also not included in this chapter are racing boats, which use a special material for their sails that is expensive and does not last long. Many racing hulls are made of lightweight materials and light construction that may not be strong enough for the offshore cruising yacht. These hulls are designed for speed, but may not survive a collision or severe storm.

Then there are the multihulls. Because of their lack of a keel, their shallow draft, and lightweight construction, their performance will be different than the monohulls. When comparing the effects of the performance of different rigs, there will be a basic difference because of the hull types. Multihulls will be covered in more detail later in this chapter.

The information provided in this section will be based on the sailing performance of the various rigs using normal cruising sails made from normal sailing materials on the standard monohull design.

Before I can begin to discuss the different sailing rigs, I need to explain a few sailing terms, so that the explanations are clearly understood. There are three terms I want to review briefly: the sail's "center of effort", the hull's "center of lateral resistance", and the "slot effect".

The center of effort for the sails and the center of lateral resistance on the hull and keel work together to balance a boat. These affect her ability to sail to windward and are responsible for lee helm and weather helm.

To obtain a sail's center of effort, as shown in Figure 1, draw three lines bisecting the angles at the head, clew, and tack. Where these three lines intersect is that sail's center of effort. A boat's center of effort is the point where the wind forces are centered on all the sails at one time. It is the average point of effort of all the working sails. This point may vary as different size sails are dropped or set. So for our purpose, we will work on the standard working sails of the designer's sail plan.

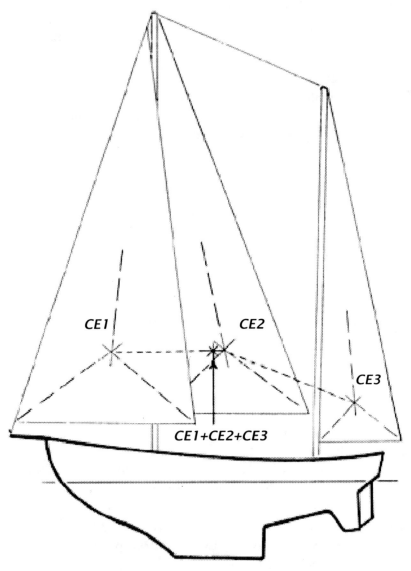

Figure 1. A boat's center of effort

A hull's center of lateral resistance, shown in Figure 2, is a point where a hull will pivot if it were to slide through the water sideways. Imagine this point as a line of resistance that will not move easily, but will move when the hull is pushed against it.

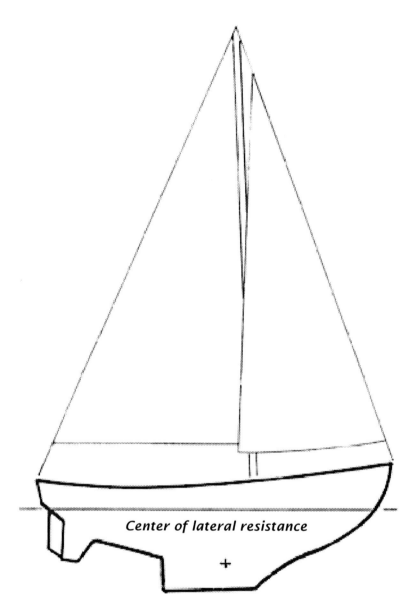

Center of lateral resistance

+

Figure 2. A boat's center of lateral resistance

If the center of lateral resistance is properly located, the hull will slide sideways without pivoting around this point. If the point on the hull is too far forward, the stern will be forced away from this point, and the bow will point toward the source of pressure. If the point is too far aft the opposite will happen. The sail's center of effort may change. However, because the center of lateral resistance of the hull and keel is built into the design, it will never change.

A sailboat's balance is the ability of the boat to sail a straight course with minimum use of the rudder. It is normally applied when sailing to weather. When off the wind, it is more difficult to make a boat sail perfectly balanced. It can be done, but it takes more diligent effort and skill.

In general, to have a boat perfectly balanced, the boat's center of effort will be in the same vertical axis over the hull's center of lateral resistance. An exception to this rule is when a boat is heeled over so far, that the center of effort moves outside the boat, if viewed from above. However, I don't think it necessary to go into so much detail for the purpose of this discussion.

If a boat were to sail out of balance, then the boat will have a tendency to sail into the wind or off the wind in relation to the centerline course.

If the boat's center of effort is forward of its center of lateral resistance, the boat will sail to leeward, or away from the direction of the wind. This condition is called a "lee helm", as shown in Figure 3.

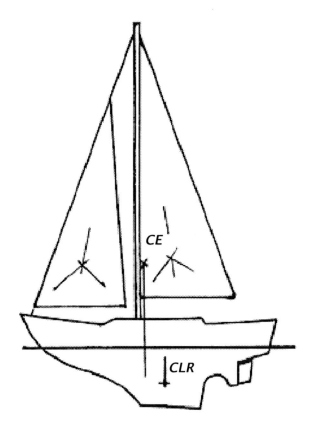

Figure 3. A boat with lee helm

If the boat's center of effort is aft of its center of lateral resistance, the boat will have a tendency to sail up into the wind. The boat is said to have a "weather helm", as shown in Figure 4.

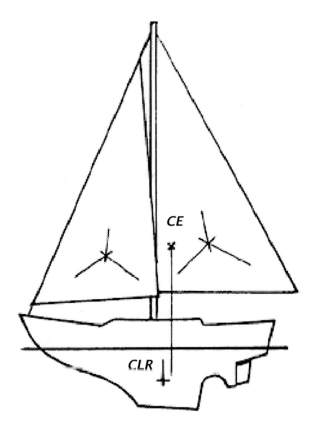

Figure 4. A boat with weather helm

If a boat has a weather helm and sails up into the wind, it will eventually reach a point where the wind has no drive over the sails. The sails will luff and cause the boat to lose all its forward momentum. The boat will then be "in irons", as shown in Figure 5.

Figure 5. A boat in irons

On the other hand, if the boat has a lee helm and sails off the wind, the boat will continue to sail around until the sails are suddenly forced across to the other side, or "gybe" (jibe) across. This is a very dangerous situation if it is not controlled. In an uncontrolled gybe, the boom and sails fly across the boat with tremendous force. The boom may hit someone in the head. If the boom is not on a boom vang, it may lift, hitting and breaking the backstay. Thus, an unexpected gyb" is an uncontrolled, flying gybe, and needs to be avoided at all costs. For this reason, all sailboats are designed with a small amount of weather helm for safety.

Before I can explain the "slot effect", there must be a basic understanding of what makes a sailboat sail upwind. The mainsail is sewn into the shape of an airplane wing. In an airplane, it is the shape or airfoil of the wing that permits the plane to fly. As the wind hits the leading edge of the wing, part of it is deflected over the wing, and another part of it is deflected under the wing. Because of the airfoil shape of the top of the wing, the wind that passes over it is deflected considerably above it; this leaves an area of less dense air (less pressure) directly on top of the wing, causing lift. The wind that passes under the wing has a slight force that pushes up on the bottom. This little push under the wing and the area on top of the wing with less pressure causes the wing to lift upward. As it does, so the void or less dense air continues to lift with it, and so the wing goes up and up.

If the wing were set on a vertical axis, it would be the same effect, except that the wing would not lift, but rather would be pulled forward. For a wing to lift, it must have air speed passing over it. This speed of air is created by the plane's engine. Thus, theoretically, an airplane cannot just lift straight up off the ground; it has to be moving forward and will rise at an angle to the wind. Likewise, a vertical wing will not pull directly into the wind, but must be pulled at an angle. This is why a sailboat cannot sail directly upwind, but must sail at an angle. This angle to the wind narrows as the boat points higher into the wind. This is the result of good shape of the sails as well as the boat's balance.

An airplane gets its wind speed from the engine. A sailboat gets its wind speed from the prevailing wind strength and the boat's speed into the wind. Creating a Venturi effect between the headsails and the airfoil side of the mainsail can increase the speed of the wind on a sailboat. If the boat is sailing to windward at an angle, the wind will pass over the bow into the headsail, which directs it back over the main. As the area between the leach of the headsail and the mainsail narrows, the wind speed increases, thus giving more lift to the mainsail, pulling it forward. This Venturi effect is called the slot, shown in Figure 6.

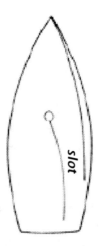

Figure 6. The slot effect

Sailing rigs

The sloop

The sloop is the most common rig on sailboats (see Figure 7). It has one mast with only one headstay. If the headstay goes all the way to the top of the mast, it is a "masthead sloop". If it only goes partway up the mast, it is considered a "fractional rig sloop". The sloop normally carries only the mainsail and a single sail on the headstay.

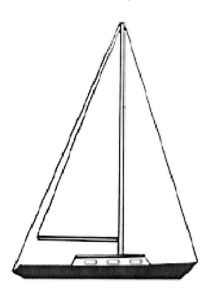

Figure 7. The sloop rig

Because this rig can carry only two sails, it is easily balanced. That is, getting the sails' center of effort nearly over the hull's center of lateral resistance is much easier. Thus, a sloop has a tendency to point a little higher into the wind, giving it a better windward performance than other rigs.

The sloop rig requires a smaller sail inventory than the other rigs with two masts. Because there is only one mast and one headstay, the cost of standing rigging is also reduced. And because there is less standing rigging, there is less windage aloft. This may be an important factor in strong winds.

Since the sloop only has one headstay attached to the stem or bow of the boat, it is safer to change sails from the security of the deck, rather than going out on a bowsprit normally found on other rigs. However, because there is only one headstay, varying wind strength will require more frequent sail changes. More importantly, if the sloop's only headstay were to break, the sloop would lose its mast.

Often, roller furling is used on the headstay, making it easier to reduce sail area. However, this makes it difficult or even impossible to set a storm jib in severe weather. There are storm sails designed that wrap around the roller furling headsail, but since I have no experience using them, I cannot comment on their effectiveness.

Since the sloop only carries two sails, they must be of considerable size or square footage to drive a large boat. This results in a much larger mainsail, making it more difficult to handle for limited crew. For this reason, it is rare to see a larger cruising boat that is sloop rigged. Of course, racing sloops would be the exception.

The cutter

The cutter is similar to the sloop in that they both have only one mast (see Figure 8). Unlike the sloop, the cutter has two stays forward supporting the mast, each carrying a sail. The forward most stay is called the headstay, which is usually attached from the end of a bowsprit to the masthead. The second, or inner stay, is called the staysail stay or inner stay. It is attached to or near the stem like a sloop, but it only goes up about 75% of the mast, similar to a fractional rig on the sloop.

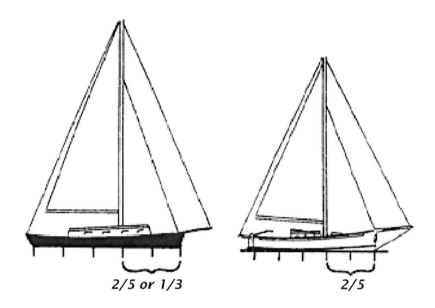

2/5 or 1/3   2/5

Figure 8. The cutter rig

During my research, I discovered that there are several definitions of a cutter. One defines a cutter as a sloop with two headstays instead of one. If we use the double headstays as a definition of a cutter, then a sloop could be converted to a cutter by adding an inner stay. This is not correct because if a sail were set on both the headstay and inner stay, it would change the position of the sloop's center of effort, thereby changing the boat's balance.

A cutter uses the sail area of the inner sail, or staysail, as part of the total sail area to figure the boat's center of effort. It is more accurate to say that the mast on a cutter is stepped aft of the stem where the inner or staysail stay is located, 1/3 to 2/5 of the waterline length. The headstay is moved forward until the sail's center of effort is properly located above the hull's center of lateral resistance. It would be difficult to make a cutter out of a sloop, unless the mast was moved aft and a bowsprit added.

Now that we know the difference between the sloop and the cutter, we can compare the two. Because the cutter has the headstay considerably further forward than the sloop, it moves the boat's center of effort forward. This will increase the "J" measurement or surface area between the mast and the headstay, forcing more air through the slot, which may increase windward performance. This will depend on the vessel's rig configuration and the design of the sails.

Because the cutter can carry two headsails, they can be smaller and still maintain the necessary balance. The smaller sails make sail handling easier, and they can stay up longer before they have to be changed. However, it may mean that changing the headsail requires going out on a bowsprit, also known as a "widow maker". Installing a roller reefing headsail or using a downhaul often overcomes much of this problem.

The inner sail or staysail is small enough that it can be left up and still maintain the boat's balance when other sails have to be reefed. If a storm jib is set on the inner stay, and a storm trysail is set on the main, this also makes for a good balance, especially when it becomes necessary to heave-to.

Of course, the cutter does require the extra inner stay. The load on this stay must be counterbalanced or supported aft by either running backstays or intermediate stays. This is an additional cost and creates windage aloft.

Most cutters require a bowsprit to achieve balance. There is the added cost and maintenance of the bowsprit and the extra rigging to support it.

When sailing a cutter in light conditions with a light wind genoa or drifter on the headstay, it is more difficult to tack these larger headsails across the slot between the headstay and inner stay. This can be overcome by installing a large pelican hook on the base of the inner stay so that the base and stay can be easily removed and set against the mast. This opens the entire area between the headstay and the mast, but it also means more expense.

The yawl

Depending on the sail configuration forward, the yawl is just a sloop or cutter with a small mizzenmast stepped aft of the rudderpost, as shown in Figure 9. The yawl's center of effort does not take into account the jigger sail on the aft mizzenmast, because it is so small. Thus, most of the advantages and disadvantages are the same as the sloop or cutter.

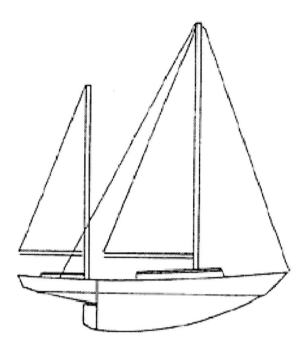

Figure 9. The yawl rig

The main advantage of this design is that the aft jigger sail can help improve the boat's balance if she has a tendency to go to windward or leeward. Also, it can act like a weather vane at anchor or while hove-to. It will help bring the bow up closer to the wind.

Depending on the strength and design of the mizzenmast, it can carry a mizzen staysail or spinnaker between the main mast and the mizzenmast. This is not too common, because the mizzenmast is too small to carry much of a sail between the two. But, there are some that will use it when sailing off the wind.

The major disadvantage of this rig is the difficulty to properly install the mizzenmast. Since it must be installed aft of the rudderpost, it will often require the installation of a boomkin and added rigging to support it. There will be additional costs to maintain, repair, and replace the extra mast, rigging, and sails.

Usually, the boom on the mizzenmast overhangs beyond the stern of the vessel, making sail handling difficult and dangerous. It also makes it difficult to install a windvane.

The ketch

The ketch (see Figure 10) has two masts and can have either one headstay like the sloop, or two like the cutter. The aft or mizzenmast is larger than the one on a yawl, and it is located forward of the rudderpost, making it much easier to install and work the sails.

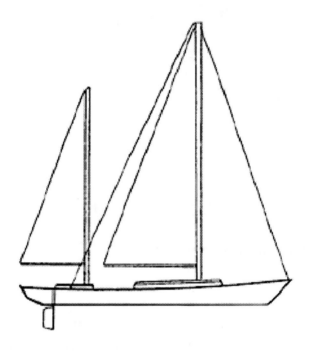

Figure 10. The ketch rig

Unlike the yawl the ketch uses the mizzen's sail area when determining the boat's center of effort. This means that in order to have the boat properly balanced, all the working sails must be set, working together. When sails are changed or dropped, the boat's center of effort must be taken into consideration to maintain the boat's balance.

The primary forward driving force of the sails is from the foresails and the main. Because there is no slot effect over the mizzen, this sail has little forward driving force and, in some cases, may even cause more drag. Many ketches drop the mizzen when sailing to windward.

This will move the center of effort forward, causing lee helm and preventing the boat from pointing as high into the wind as the previous rigs discussed. There are exceptions to this, but they are rare. Some ketches will sail very well with the headsail and mizzen only. This will still maintain a balanced helm.

The ketch will sail great when sailing just off the wind where the mizzen will give the boat some drive. They are known to fly on beam to broad reaches. However, there is a point where the mizzen will blanket the mainsail, and one of the two sails must be dropped.

Comparing a sloop, cutter, and yawl to the ketch, all carrying the same amount of sail area, the ketch's sails will be more in number, but smaller in size. The smaller size sails require less sail changes and make sail handling easier. However, the smaller size working sails will not give as much drive in light airs, so the sail inventory will have to include light wind sails. Because the ketch has smaller sails to achieve the required amount of sail area, it makes an excellent rig for larger vessels.

Like the yawl, the mizzen mast can have a small sail set which will aid in pointing the boat upwind at anchor or while hove-to. Depending on the ketch's design, some will heave-to with the mizzen sail only and the helm tied to leeward. Since the ketch's mizzen mast is set on deck and not stayed to a boomkin, it is stayed stronger and is taller than the yawl's, making it better for flying a sail, like a mizzen staysail, between the two masts.

The ketch will have additional costs for the extra mast, sails, and rigging. It will also add to the weight and windage aloft.

The schooner

The schooner (see Figure 11) replaced the old Square Riggers because they, like the Square Riggers, could make remarkable speeds off the wind, but the schooner could also sail closer to the wind.

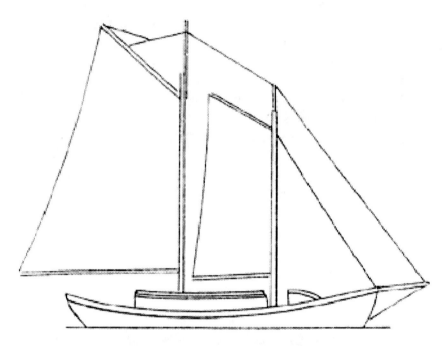

Figure 11. The schooner rig

The schooner has two or more masts of equal height, or the aft mast is taller than the forward mast. This is a beautiful boat to look at under sail. She has old traditional lines that warm the heart. Today, its primary use is for charters, and it is not practical for the small cruising family. However, for those who get emotional over the lovely lines of the schooner, why not take it cruising?

Because the aft mast or main mast is usually the taller of the two, it carries a huge sail. Often, this sail is gaff rigged, which requires the top of the sail to be attached to a small boom called the gaff. The gaff is raised in order to haul up the mainsail. This requires a lot of blocks and lines and creates additional weight and windage aloft.

If the mainsail is gaff rigged, she cannot be tacked without the gaff hitting the backstay; this means running backstays are required. To tack the sail requires preparation and should not happen accidentally.

To keep the sail's center of effort nearly above the hull's center of lateral resistance is more difficult due to the large main. The next sail forward on the foremast is called the foresail. The foresail is often on a boom, but on some schooners, it has a free flying foot. The headsails are similar to the cutter rig. Usually, a long bowsprit is required to move the center of effort forward.

Because the schooner carries two or more masts and large sails, this rig is restricted to bigger vessels. Because of the sizeable sails and a large variety of sails, the schooner performs well in light winds and has a reputation of sailing at respectable speeds when the wind is abaft the beam.

Since both masts are heavily built and stayed, they can carry a lot of sail area and a variety of light wind sails between the two masts. However, because these larger, stronger masts are normally heavily stayed, there is considerable windage and weight aloft.

The schooner does not have a reputation for sailing close to the wind. I suspect this is because of the difficulty creating a slot effect over the large main that is set further aft. However, she will sail well on all other points. When the wind is abaft the beam, the large main will blanket the other sails. However, this is not a problem, because the size of the main alone allows it to drive the boat.

Fortunately, the schooner rig is on larger boats, which can carry the large sail inventory required for all the different weather conditions. A schooner also requires a considerable number of crewmembers to handle all these sails.

Hull shapes and sterns

The shape of the hull as it passes through the water will affect many aspects of the yacht's performance and stability. In this section, I want to compare a few hull shapes from a cross-section perspective. The shape, location, and weight of the keel will be covered in another section in this chapter. Here, I will briefly discuss the multihull, hard and soft-chined hulls, round and wine glass shaped hulls, the champagne glass hull, as well as transom sterns vs. canoe sterns.

Multihulls

There are two designs of multihulls: the catamaran and the trimaran, as shown in Figure 12.

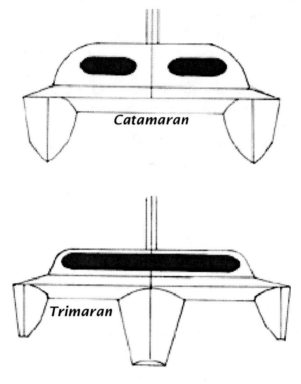

Figure 12. Multihulls

The trimaran has three hulls. The center hull is the primary area for living, while the other two hulls are much smaller and act as floats to keep the boat relatively horizontal to the water's surface. Often, the trimaran is nearly as wide as it is long.

The trimaran is made for speed. However, sailing at speed requires stoutly designed rudders with an almost perfect foil to eliminate vibrations. It is built light, so it will plane at higher speeds. For this reason, it has a shallow draft. In order to maintain steerage at speed, when the hull begins to plane, a daggerboard or equivalent is required. This shallow draft will permit the boat to go into shallow waters; it can even be beached for cleaning.

Because of the wide beam, the trimaran won't heel, so it has a more level surface underway. Unfortunately, because of its width, it is sometimes difficult to find slips or a place to keep her at a marina. This wide beam also provides for more storage space. On the other hand, as the weight increases, the advantages of the trimaran decrease. Hence, even though there is extensive storage space, it can only carry light items.

The monohull will heel when there is a strong gust of wind, thus reducing the stress loads on the sails, mast, and rigging. The trimaran will not. Therefore, the mast must have heavier rigging to take the stress. The wide beam, though, makes stepping the mast stronger and may not require spreaders. This will reduce the weight and windage aloft.

Because the boat is light and wide, it has initial stability, but unlike the keeled mono-hull, it does not have ultimate stability. It can flip over in certain conditions. Since there is no ballast, it is difficult to bring it back upright. However, they will not sink. Some trimarans actually have trap doors on the bottom for escape in case they capsize. A capsized trimaran is difficult—if not impossible—to be turned back upright.

Because the trimaran has a shallow draft, the boat will not heave-to in severe weather. Instead, it must be sailed or set to a parachute anchor. If the boat has to be sailed in foul weather, it must be diligently steered to maintain control so she will not yaw or broach, causing it to flip over.

The stresses on the struts between the main hull and floats are substantial, and some actually break from fatigue. This is not common, but the engineering and materials used must be considered carefully.

I am reluctant to comment on the trimaran's windward sailing ability. If a trimaran is under consideration, take her for a sail and see how she points, then draw your own conclusion about that particular boat.

The catamaran has two twin hulls. There are more cruising catamarans on the market today than ever before. These boats have most of the same advantages as the trimaran, with less possible problems. They have two hulls of equal size and depth. The area between the hulls is the living quarters, which can be quite substantial. The catamaran has a deeper hull than the trimaran, so it has better tracking ability and is not so sensitive on the helm. For this reason, they are not as fast as the cruising trimaran.

Now I am going to have to eat my words when I think about "*Enza*", the New Zealand catamaran that made world record speeds. My commentary regarding the speed of the catamaran is aimed at the average, family-size cruising boat, not one made for record-breaking speeds.

Catamarans will not heave-to in rough weather, unless they have a deep daggerboard in both hulls. They do not have ultimate stability, so they can flip over in certain situations. Like the trimarans, however, they will not sink. And like the trimarans, capsized catamarans are difficult—if not impossible—to be turned back upright.

Monohull shapes

The monohull can have different shapes when looked at in cross section.

Hard and soft chined hulls

Chined hulls are shown in Figure 13. The hard-chined hulls have flat surfaces with sharp angles where the flats meet. This is common on hulls made with plywood, steel, and aluminum. Their only advantage is that they are cheaper and faster to build.

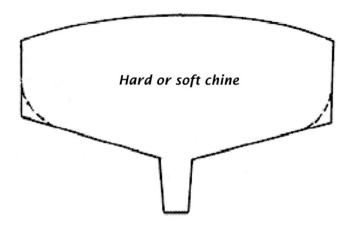

Hard or soft chine

Figure 13. Chined hull

Depending on the hull design and keel design, the hard-chined hull may sail as well as other mono hulls. The only real problem is that they may pound hard in rough conditions because of the flat surfaces.

The soft-chined hull is similar to the hard-chined, except its corners are more rounded, reducing the amount of flat surface. The advantages and disadvantages are the same as the hard-chined hull, but with less pounding.

The round and wine glass shaped hulls

Round and wine glass shaped hulls are shown in Figures 14 and 15. These hulls can be round like a portion of a circle, semi-round, or shaped like a long stemmed wine glass. The point is that there isn't a flat surface on the hull.

The round hull has less wetted surface, thus less resistance when moving through the water. Because of the round shape of the hull, it is restricted to a narrow beam, and there is no stability or resistance to heeling. The stability must come from the keel shape, depth, and weight of the ballast. This narrow beam also restricts living and storage space.

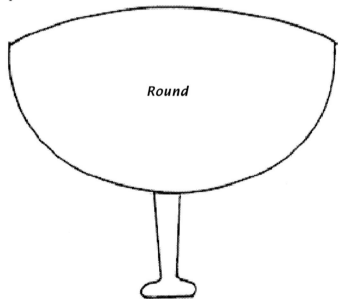

Figure 14. Round hull

The round hull is most common on racing boats, because it is normally faster than other shapes. Today, racing boats have a shallow, rounded hull to reduce resistance and a deep, narrow, fin keel for stability.

Wine glass

Figure 15. Wine glass shaped hull

These boats will have greater ballast to displacement ratio. It is not uncommon to see the ballast as 50% of the boat's total displacement.

The champagne glass shaped hull

The champagne glass shaped hull is shown in Figure 16. This is the most common hull shape for cruising boats, because it has more "form stability". The hull design has a flatter surface under the hull, requiring more pressure to force the boat to heel. It is easy to visualize if you compare the stability of a flat bottom canoe to that of one with a round bottom.

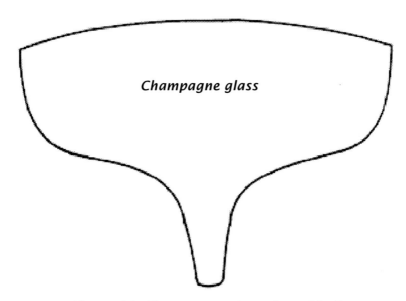

Champagne glass

Figure 16. Champagne glass shaped hull

Because of its form stability, it has a wide beam. Since the additional beam and flatness of the underside of the hull resists heel, the keel and ballast can be shallower and lighter than narrow beam, round hulls.

These boats have lower ballast to displacement ratio. The ballast is normally about one third of the boat's total displacement.

The wider beamed vessel will have more living and storage space than the round shaped hull with a narrow beam. However, the wider beam will have more wetted surface, so it will not sail as fast as the rounder hulls with fin keels.

Stern shapes: transom sterns vs. canoe sterns

The canoe stern is shaped like a canoe's end. The term double-ender is also used, referring to a boat whose stern is similar to its bow. Although there can be some differences in design, for the general purpose of comparison, the canoe stern and the double-ended stern will be considered the same.

The transom stern has a flat butt or a flat stern, as if it were cut off across the back. The transom stern will provide more efficient lift of the waterline. On a canoe stern, the waterline curves back under the aft overhang meeting in the center; this reduces buoyancy at the stern. On the transom stern, the waterline continues back to the transom in a more direct line, never meeting in the center; this provides more buoyancy at the stern. The buoyancy of the transom stern helps prevent the stern from squatting or dropping when sailing at or near hull speed, as shown in Figure 17.

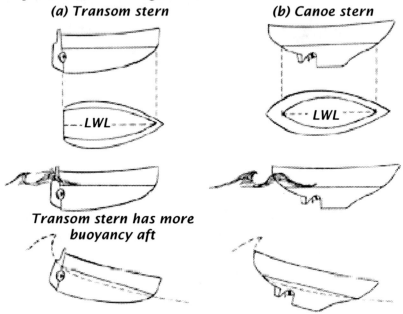

(a) Transom stern

(b) Canoe stern

LWL

LWL

Transom stern has more buoyancy aft

Figure 17. Transom sterns vs. canoe sterns

The transom stern provides more living and storage space on deck. Most transom designs have a large lazarette for storage. Because the transom stern is flatter than the other sterns, short waves coming from the stern will hit it, making an annoying slapping sound. The canoe stern, being more pointed, will break these waves, resulting in less slapping. These waves are not big enough to cause any danger to either design; it is more a matter of the degree of annoyance caused by the noise.

As the stern waves get taller and break, the transom stern will be more vulnerable to the forces. It will be pushed forward and could cause a broach. Because of the stronger design of a canoe stern, it will break the force.

When stern waves begin to rise to a point where they are towering over the boat's stern and may break aboard, the transom stern will have more buoyancy and lift and move forward. With less buoyancy, the canoe stern will bury deeper into the wave before its buoyancy will lift and push it forward. If the wave poops both designs, the canoe stern will take on more water.

There are differences of opinion on the effects of the two designs in rough seas. I would advise the readers to draw their own conclusions.

Basic formulas for expected performance and stability

These formulas are included only as a rough reference, to help the reader get an idea of what could be expected. Keep in mind that the formulas do not always consider a number of factors. Here is a partial list: What if the depth of the ballast below the water surface was considered? Would a hull designed with maximum beam forward or aft make a difference in its performance? How would the general shape of the entry and the total hull affect a boat's performance? Would a flat bottom boat be more stable than a "V" bottom? Would a taller mast with the same sail area change the boat's performance or stability?

With that said, hopefully these formulas will serve as guidelines, not as absolutes. Use them as additional pieces of data when selecting your cruising boat.

Beam to length ratio

Beam to Length Ratio = Beam ÷ LOD
Beam in feet divided by length on deck in feet, equals about 0.350.

If the number were greater than 0.350, the boat would be so beamy that it might sail like a barge. A smaller number would not have as much beam, so it would be considered less stable, or more tender. Basically, a flat bottom, wide beam boat will have more resistance to heel than a narrow beamed, round hull.

Displacement: heavy, medium and light

Medium Displacement $= (0.8 * LWL + 4)^3$

(0.8 X length of waterline in feet + 4) cubed = a medium displacement boat.

If the boat exceeds this number by 10%, it is considered a heavy displacement vessel; if it is 10% less than this number, it is considered a light displacement boat. Remember that these numbers are generalized, and the conclusions that follow could vary depending on factors mentioned previously.

The weight of a vessel is measured by its displacement (the weight of the volume of water the boat displaces). When a vessel is put into water, it will displace a certain amount of this liquid. This can be compared to filling a glass to the brim, then dropping in an egg. The water that overflows is the displacement of the egg. If this water could be weighed, it would weigh exactly the same amount as the egg.

A boat that is heavier will have a different performance and motion than a lighter one. The heavy displacement hull only has a few advantages, but they are important ones. Because of her weight, she will plow through the seas rather than plane over them. Thus, it will have a more comfortable sea motion. Additional weight for supplies and gear will have little effect on the performance. The location of additional weight is not as critical as it is on lighter boats.

On the other hand, the heavy displacement boat may not sail well to weather. In fact, it may not sail well at all, unless the wind is near gale force. Of course, this will vary depending on the amount of sail area carried and the shape of the hull and keel.

Heavy displacement boats are more difficult to stop quickly, but will maintain momentum during a tack or while maneuvering in tight quarters. The heavier the boat, the heavier the ground tackle; hence, the heavier the equipment needed to lift the ground tackle.

Light displacement boats will sail faster than the heavier boats. They may sail over the water rather than through it. Because they weigh less, they perform better in light airs, but may be difficult to handle in rough seas. Often, a light boat will be stopped dead by a steep wave on the bow, whereas the heavier boat will plow right through it.

Most light displacement boats require continuous steering, because they are sensitive to a sudden, quick motion. The light boats are very sensitive to additional weight, because it makes the boat set deeper in the water, affecting its performance.

One of the major disadvantages of the lighter hull is that it is more difficult to heave-to in rough weather. Because of its lightness, it is more susceptible to be pushed around by the seas.

So it appears that a middle displacement boat would have a little of both the advantages and disadvantages of the two.

Sail area to displacement ratio

Sail Area to Displacement Ratio= $\sqrt[3]{(\text{Sail area} \div \text{Displacement})^2}$

Sail area in square feet divided by the displacement in cubic feet (displacement in pounds divided by 64) to the 2/3 power (square the answer, then take the cube root) equals between 12 to 15.

A boat is considered to perform better or worse depending on the amount of working sails she carries to push or pull the weight she displaces. This formula should be used only as a rough guide. The final number should be between 12 and 15. A lower number would indicate too small of a sail area to move the heavy boat. The higher numbers would be just the opposite.

Ballast to displacement ratio

Ballast to Displacement Ratio = Ballast weight ÷ Displacement Weight

Ballast weight in pounds, divided by displacement weight in pounds equals the ratio between the two.

The ballast of a monohull is what keeps the boat upright when there is wind pressure on the sails trying to push it over. The more force on the sails causing the boat to heel, the more the gravity pull is on the weight of the ballast.

Since the total weight of a boat (or its displacement) includes the ballast, it is important to know what percentage of the total weight is below the surface, helping to keep the boat upright. If the percentage of ballast weight is too much, the yacht is considered stiff and will not heel as readily. This may sound good initially, but the major disadvantage is that the boat will not heel with the gusts, thus spilling some of the wind force. Instead, the force is placed directly on the sails and standing rigging. This is what causes sails to rip and masts to collapse.

On the other hand, the boat with a low ballast to displacement ratio will be too tender, or will have too much movement and could be knocked down more easily. So, you want a boat that does not have too high nor too low of a displacement to ballast ratio.

A ballast to displacement ratio of 40% to 50% would be considered a high ratio, resulting in a stiff boat. This would be expected on a narrow, round hull, which does not have any 'form stability'. It could be that the boat has a tall mast and needs the additional weight ratio to keep her from heeling too far. Regardless, these higher ratio boats need stronger masts and standing rigging, as well as heavier constructed sails.

If the ratio is below 30%, the boat is considered to have a low ratio. It would need a wide, flat beam to provide some 'form stability' and a smaller sail area. This ratio would be more common on racing boats, where the crew will hike out to windward to help reduce heel with their weight. These boats would be considered extremely tender. All this could be negated if the hulls were really beamy or the ballast was quite deep.

It appears that the ratio between 30% and 40% would be most common on a cruiser. Again, the 'form stability', height of the mast, working sail area, and depth of the ballast would have positive or negative effects on this ratio.

Capsize screen or positive stability

Capsize Screen = Beam $\div \sqrt[3]{\text{Displacement}}$

Beam in feet and tenths of a foot, divided by the cube root of the displacement in cubic feet (displacement in pounds divided by 64) equals 2 or less.

If the answer were above 2, the boat would be considered too susceptible to capsize. As the number gets smaller, the chances of capsizing are reduced. This formula was developed for racing boats. It can be applied to cruising vessels, but like other formulas, it should not be used as an absolute.

Hull speed

Hull Speed = $1.35 * \sqrt[2]{LWL}$

1.35 times the square root of the waterline length, equals maximum efficiency hull speed.

This is a formula used to determine the hull's expected speed. It is based on displacement boats that will not plane over the water. It is not the maximum speed a boat can reach. It is the maximum efficient speed of a hull. A boat can exceed these numbers, but the additional speed would cause more drag, resulting in the hull dropping deeper into the water.

In the classic days of the Clipper Ships and Square Riggers, the boats used to sail so fast that the hull would actually sail herself under the water. The force on the sails would push the bow down. The excessive speed of the hull increased the friction, causing the hull to drop deeper in the water.

Keel shapes and ballast types

The shape of the keel and how it is connected to the hull determine the profile shape of the hull, an important aspect of a yacht's performance and stability. I will attempt to compare various common designs that I feel are practical for the cruising vessel: the full or long keel, the swept-back keel, the cut-away or 3/4 keel, and the fin keel. I will summarize the difference between these designs. If after reading the following, more detailed information is required, I highly recommend C.A. Marchai's book **Seaworthiness, The Forgotten Factor**.

The full or long keel

Hundreds of years ago, the classic, traditional boats had a full, long keel that was nearly parallel to the waterline, as shown in Figure 18.

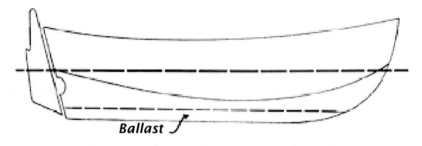

Ballast

Figure 18. Full or long keel

This was great for directional stability, permitting the vessel to hold its course with the minimum of steerage or effort. The downside of this design is that it is difficult to maneuver in tight quarters or point high into the wind. The reason is that there is too much surface area under the water forward, which causes resistance when turning or attempting to point upwind. Because the long, full keel covered a considerable surface area, it made the vessel a heavy displacement boat, with all the advantages and disadvantages of this design.

Any keel design that is long and nearly parallel to the waterline is much more stable and safer when standing on the hard, because the boat's keel is solidly supported fore and aft. Whenever boats topple over, they are usually fin-keeled boats or boats with minimum stable surface area where they set on the hard. When the wind is strong, it causes vibrations in the rigging that pass through the hull, slightly loosening the supports, causing the boat to pivot on its narrow base. Since the fuller keel is supported more along the length of the boat, it will not pivot, even if it does vibrate.

Keels that are long, or proportionally so, will set to the directions of the current in light winds, while narrow keels will set more with the wind. Fuller, long keeled boats are heavier, and therefore require more speed to tack in light airs. However, because of their weight, these boats have momentum that will help carry them through the tack.

Depending on the hull design and placement of weight, the longer keels can hobbyhorse. This normally occurs on designs where the ballast is almost the whole length of the keel. As the ballast is set more toward the center, the hobbyhorse effect is reduced. Sometimes, a full-keeled boat will carry heavy ground tackle right on the bow and additional anchors and chain in the extreme stern. This will increase the boat's probability of hobbyhorsing.

On many designs, the full keel will have a deep bilge aft of the ballast. This can make it difficult to clean or to pick up something dropped. However, the deep bilge will carry a lot of water without splashing out onto the cabin sole.

The swept-back keel

In order to improve a full-keeled boat's windward ability, there have been variations to this design. One that manages to maintain most of the advantages and reduce some of the disadvantages is the swept-back keel, shown in Figure 19.

This design removes much of the surface area forward. The keel begins at the stem's waterline. It then makes a slow, curved, sweep down and back until it levels nears the stern. This design, being a flowing curve with a narrow entry, permits the water to flow aft with minimum disturbance. This will improve the vessel's performance.

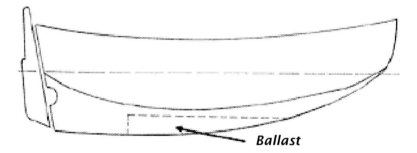

Ballast

Figure 19. Swept-back keel

Where the keel terminates will vary. One design carries the keel all the way back to where it meets a line down from the transom. This design requires an externally hung rudder.

Another design will have the keel terminate further forward, leaving more buoyancy aft of the keel. This design requires the rudder to be on a rudderpost, which goes through the hull. The only differences between these two designs are the rudder location and the total length of the keel.

The swept-back keel maintains directional stability, which makes steering less sensitive. This design works better for windvanes than hulls with a narrower keel design.

Because of its size, the swept-back keel will have more wetted surface, which will reduce its ability to sail at higher speeds. The additional surface area will result in a medium to high displacement hull with its expected effects.

One of the major, unexpected advantages of this design is that it is much more forgiving if it runs aground or hits something.

§

I remember sailing at over 6 knots one night off the coast of Papua New Guinea. I hit a huge tree that I never saw until I was stopped dead in its grasp. The swept-back keel design did not stop abruptly like other designs would have, but carried my boat up, on to the tree with little damage. After my sails were dropped, I slid backward off the tree and managed to power in reverse away from it.

I experienced another advantage of a swept-back keel when I was racing my boat between Malaysia and Thailand, down the Malacca Straits. I noticed that several faster, narrow fin-keeled boats were stopped dead in the water. My initial thought was they had gone aground. Then I noticed some people in the water. I presumed someone had fallen overboard. Just then, I heard a small bump against my hull. I looked over the side and noticed that I was sailing over fishing nets on floats. The fin-keeled boats were caught in the nets, while my swept-back keel slid right over them.

The three quarter or cut-away keel

This design, like the swept-back keel, has similar advantages and disadvantages as the full, long keel. The cut-away or three-quarter keel removes surface area forward, as seen in Figure 20. This design begins at the stem's waterline. The keel sweeps aft, similar to the swept-back design. At about one forth of the way back, it makes a rather abrupt turn downward to the bottom of the keel where it levels off more parallel to the waterline. Some call this turn in the keel a 'dogleg' shape. The abruptness of this 'dogleg' turn varies by boat.

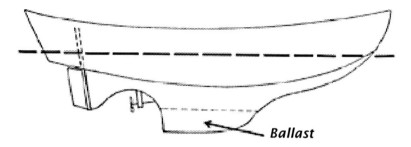

Figure 20. Three quarter or cut-away keel

The advantage to this design is that it removes surface or wetted area forward, which improves windward and steering performance while maintaining directional stability.

One of the disadvantages to this design is that the keel is rather wide where it makes the dogleg turn downward. This width, even if rounded, disturbs the flow of water aft of this point. It also causes more resistance through the water. It would be like the resistance of a 4" or larger diameter pole moving nearly vertically through the water.

The dogleg shape of the leading edge of the keel also provides a more abrupt stop when going aground or hitting something. However, whether the keel is a swept-back or a cut-away design, both are more forgiving than the fin keel when the boat goes aground.

§

I remember when I was sailing through the South Pacific, I kept arriving at major ports just after a boat had been pulled off the reef. It was always the same boat. All the fellow yachties gave him the nickname of "Eddie the Reef Hopper".

I finally met Eddie in New Caledonia, where he had also gone on to the reef. I had pulled out my boat to clean and paint her bottom. I was set right next to Eddie. He was in the process of installing a 2" X 8" piece of timber to the bottom of his keel. It wasn't until I questioned the purpose of the unusual addition that I realized I was talking to "Eddie the Reef Hopper". He explained that going aground on the reefs was beginning to wear on the bottom of his keel.

The boat was a 32-footer with the cut-away design where the bottom of the keel was nearly parallel to the waterline. The ballast was internal, set inside the fiberglass hull. On close inspection, I saw that a considerable amount of gel-coat was missing, but that there was no sign of any serious damage that would threaten the boat's integrity. Neither had she ever lain over on her side. This was after at least five major groundings on coral.

After meeting Eddie, I found that he was a professional and very intelligent. When I asked him to explain how all the groundings took place, his answer was that he did not realize the water was so shallow.

Eddie and I built up a friendship and began sailing in tandem. My boat was faster and pointed higher than his, so we would wander apart, especially at night. I always arrived at the anchorage considerably before Eddie. We kept radio contact so I could talk him in to the anchorage if he had a problem.

There was a particular time, in the Solomon Islands, when we had to power through a narrow passage to reach the anchorage on the other side of the island. I was securely anchored and had radio contact with Eddie. I informed him that the water was shallow after he rounded a certain point, and that he should stay in the deeper blue water. I sat on my boat and watched him round the point and then head directly into the shallow water. I stood up to yell, but it was too late. Bang! True to form, "Eddie the Reef Hopper" was up on the reef again, his boat at a 30° angle.

I raised my anchor and motored over to where he was aground. I anchored in deeper water, then took my dinghy over to talk to Eddie about a plan to kedge him off the reef. When I boarded his boat, I asked him why he didn't stay in the dark blue water and avoid the shallow green water. He looked at me, dumbfounded. Until that moment, he never realized that he was colorblind—he could not distinguish blue from green.

Fortunately, the tide was flooding. After waiting a few hours, we got him off easily. With this new discovery about his color blindness, Eddie decided to stop cruising. He managed to make it back to Australia, where he shipped his boat back to the States.

The fin keel

The fin keel is nearly vertical, as shown in Figure 21. It is deeper, thinner, and much narrower than the other designs. They are usually deeper to get the same righting moment as the longer keels. Because the keel is thin and narrow, it has less wetted surface. The ballast is deeper and sometimes at the very bottom of the keel, making the boat light and stiff. The reduction in wetted surface and weight permits the boat to sail much faster than the previously discussed designs. The fin keel also permits the boat to turn quickly or sharply for faster tacks.

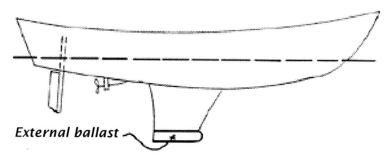

External ballast

Figure 21. Fin keel

This keel is rarely formed as part of the hull; instead, it is bolted on using keel bolts. This external fastening of the keel could be a problem if it hits something or goes aground, especially at hull speed.

The deep, narrow keel provides little directional stability. Therefore, the boat must be steered all the time and it will have difficulty staying hove-to. I will discuss this further in the storm chapter of this book.

The deep, nearly vertical keel catches ropes, nets, seaweed, and more. I have seen several incidents where a fin-keeled boat was passing close to anchored boats and its keel caught the rope anchor rode of these boats, causing havoc.

These keels are usually on narrow beam boats. The narrow design makes it less stable and more difficult to stand safely on the hard. It is nearly impossible for a fin-keeled boat to career (lay over on her side) to clean when the tide ebbs.

These designs do not have much of a bilge, so when water enters the boat, there is little space to trap it. When sailing gets a little rough, the bilge water sloshes up and over the cabin sole.

Fin-keeled boats are faster, point higher, and are lighter than the other keel designs. Thus, the fin-keeled boats are mostly used for racing. Some manufacturers market the fin-keeled boat as a cruiser/racer. I feel there is always the danger of hitting something hard or of going aground at a speed that could tear the fin keel off the boat or at least do major damage. It is the opinion of this author that the fin-keeled boats should remain as fast racing boats while the full, longer keeled vessels should be for cruising.

Internal vs. external ballast

This is a controversial issue, and I am not sure I will resolve the question here. However, I will state my feelings on the matter, and the reader can draw his or her own conclusion.

The internal ballast is also referred to as encapsulated ballast. The hull mold is made with the shape of the keel as part of the design. This provides a cavity to accept the lead ballast, so the ballast material never makes contact with water.

This design has many advantages, but it depends on the type of ballast material used. If the ballast consists only of loose lead shot, a small hole in the hull would permit the shot to trickle out. This system was used in much older and owner finished boats. A solid casting of lead ballast is much preferable. If the ballast is steel and salt water makes contact with it, the steel will rust and swell, causing problems with the hull shell.

Encapsulating the ballast makes it a solid unit that cannot move, shift, or ever make contact with water. The process is accomplished by pouring liquid resins under the ballast until the level of resin rises above the top surface. It is then covered with multiple layers of fiberglass. This assures that the ballast will remain securely in place, in case of an unfortunate rollover. An internal, encapsulated ballast, constructed in this fashion, will last the life of the boat and has the added advantage of making an extremely strong base on which to step the mast or the mast support.

The area of the hull where the internal ballast is encapsulated, must be thick to take the stress and weight. The additional thickness will prevent the hull from being badly damaged in case of a hard grounding. Even if the boat does hit something hard, it would be difficult to penetrate the bottom of the keel to reach the ballast; if it did, the encapsulated ballast would not be affected.

The internal ballast rarely extends to the underside of the cabin sole, leaving room to set water tanks. This is an ideal location for this additional weight: the center of the boat and as low as possible.

The internal, encapsulated ballast rarely extends the full length of the keel, leaving a deep bilge in the stern. This provides space for a water or fuel tank. However, since it is a bilge, which is often wet, the tank must be constructed of a non-corrosive material.

The cost of a boat with internal ballast may be higher. The hull mold must include the shape of the keel to accept the internal ballast. This requires more material and labor, making the hull more expensive to build.

The internal ballast is limited to designs of full-keeled boats such as the swept-back or cut-away. A deep narrow fin keel is difficult to mold into the hull and thus achieve the necessary strength required to take the forces of the leverage and weight of this design.

The external ballast is cast separately from the hull in lead, steel, or iron. It is then bolted through the underside of the hull. This has two major advantages. First, it permits the keel to be deep and narrow, reducing wetted surface. Second, the hull can be constructed of any material and the ballast added later, making it less expensive to produce.

Some will argue that there is another advantage: the external ballast, being lead or steel, will absorb the impact of going aground so the hull will not be damaged. This is partly true. Certainly, the external ballast will be dented, but not seriously. As long as the boat stays upright, the ballast will take all the damage.

Grounding of a fiberglass boat with internal ballast would lose some gel coat. If it is properly built, however, the hull will be thick enough to take the punishment. If the ballast is encapsulated, the entire bottom, under the ballast, could wear away which would only expose the ballast.

Most of the serious damage done to a boat that goes aground is not to the keel, but to the side of the hull. What causes a boat to be lost when it goes aground is that it lies on its side. The hull, being much thinner at the turn of the bilge, will abrade away from the movement and pounding.

Regardless of the type of ballast, whether internal or external, boats that go aground on a hard bottom and remain standing, mostly upright, can be kedged off before any serious damage occurs. The key is to get the boat off before the side of the hull is grinding on the bottom.

A concern with external lead ballast is the softness of the lead. Over time, the extreme weight and working of the keel will compress the lead between the top surface of the ballast and the bottom of the keel bolts. If this happens, the keel bolts will extend slightly, causing the nuts to become loose. If the ballast becomes loose, it will permit water to enter, causing weeping around the keel bolts.

When I was building boats, I subscribed to a magazine for boat builders named **The Professional Boatbuilder**. There was an article in one issue that had a title something like, *"Those darn keel bolt nuts keep coming loose"*. The basis of the article was that the keel bolts are bent at the bottom where they are embedded in the lead ballast during casting. The extreme weight of the ballast and the momentum loads will cause the lead, where the keel bolts are located, to compress. The force of a boat going hard ground will make the situation worse. This may loosen the keel bolts or elongate them. This is a problem that will always exist with external lead ballast and only reveals itself after years of use or a severe grounding.

Eventually, the ballast may separate from the hull just enough to permit water to ingress between the ballast and the underside of the hull, causing weeping through the keel bolts. Tightening the keel bolt nuts may solve the problem temporarily Placing a gasket or caulking under the nuts may prevent water from seeping into the hull, but this does not prevent water from entering between the ballast and the hull, which could create a much more serious problem. So, keel bolt nuts must be accessible to check and tighten. That being the case, water tanks should never be set on top of the bolts.

§

An example of a problem that can occur when water enters between the keel and hull happened to a fellow boat after we completed the Darwin-Ambon race from Northern Australia to Ambon, Indonesia. At the completion of the race, one of the faster fin-keeled boats hit a reef. There was a considerable amount of water weeping through the keel bolts. I was asked to check it out and assist in delivering it back to Darwin for repairs, if necessary.

At close inspection, it was apparent that the stainless steel keel bolts had been weeping salt water for quite some time; the recent grounding only made it worse. We attempted to set the weight of the boat on its keel by tying it to some pilings, then waiting for the tide to ebb. While the boat was resting on the bottom, we tightened the keel bolt nuts as hard as possible.

When the tide came back in, we still took on water. Consequently, during the next low tide, we put a three-foot cheater pipe on the end of the socket wrench and put some leverage to it. This broke off one of the one-inch stainless steel keel bolts.

A one-inch bolt is only as strong as its minor diameter. This is the diameter of the solid part of the bolt below the bottom of the thread grooves. For a one-inch bolt, the minor diameter was reduced to about three-quarters of an inch, as shown in Figure 22.

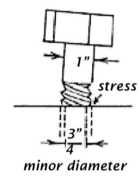

minor diameter

Figure 22. Fatigue break

Upon further inspection, we discovered severe corrosion on the broken bolt at the point where it entered the ballast. This was caused by either oxygen starvation or crevice corrosion, a common problem with stainless steel submersed in salt water for long periods of time. The stainless steel at this point had been eaten away another 1/8-inch around its circumference, reducing the core diameter to about half an inch (see Figure 23). The boat had to be taken back to Australia to get a new ballast installed.

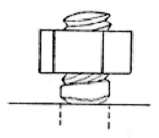

Figure 23. Electrolysis

Stainless steel should not be considered as a material for constant submersion in salt water. It is susceptible to oxygen starvation corrosion, crevice corrosion, and electrolysis. Electrolysis occurs when a less noble metal sacrifices its electrons to a more noble metal. This will be discussed in more detail later in this chapter. Also, stainless steel is more subject to fatigue failure than many other metals. If you are considering a boat with external ballast, this author strongly advises the use of silicone bronze or monel for keel bolts, not stainless steel.

The external ballast, unlike the internal ballast, can act as an excellent dissipation ground plane for single side band radios or as a lightning ground. This will be discussed in more detail in another chapter.

A big advantage of the external ballast is that it can have more weight at the very bottom of the keel. This is seen in keels that taper from the top down to where it is widest at the bottom. One extreme design is the Australian Wing Keel.

The wing keel became popular after the Americans lost the America's Cup to Australia. It is an external ballast design with a wing foil at the bottom. This wide wing is shaped like an inverted "T" with a foil on the bottom that grabs the water as it heels. There are different names given to this design, but basically, they all work on the same principle of getting the weight lower and resisting heel. The more radical the design of the wing keel, the more it belongs on racing boats. As the design moderates and is not so wide, it becomes more applicable to the cruiser.

Since this design has more weight at the bottom of the keel, it does not have to be so deep. There are some builders, however, who provide a wing design that is shallower, but which results in the rudder being deeper than the keel. You can imagine the consequences of a severe grounding with such a design: the rudder could be severely damaged.

If a wing keel design goes aground in sand or mud, it acts as an anchor. I know of several boats that have been lost just because the wing keel buried itself into the bottom; no matter how hard or from which direction it was pulled, it failed to let go.

The hull construction

As mentioned earlier, the size of a boat has little to do with its seaworthiness. The most important elements are design and structural integrity. Unfortunately, to build a boat that is strong enough to cross an ocean costs much more money than to build a coastal cruiser.

The boat building company I owned built ocean going cruisers. To show our boats to the public, I participated in local boat shows. I was often asked why our boats cost so much more than a considerably larger boat. I would hear comments like "a boat should cost about a thousand dollars a foot, but your boats are over five thousand dollars a foot". My response was, "I will build you a boat twice as long as the other boat you mentioned, for one-tenth the cost they are asking, as long as there is no consideration about the materials I use and how I use them."

I further attempted to explain that a better measure of value would be to compare the cost per pound of a boat. For an offshore vessel, weight is usually proportional to its strength.

However, this is not an absolute. Today, racing boats are being built out of lightweight Kevlar and other expensive, stronger, lighter materials. This technology is slowly being carried over to the offshore cruiser, but they certainly are not less expensive.

I would like to explain some of the factors that distinguish boats that are well built from those that are not so well built. Take this information to the next boat show, and see what you can deduce for yourself.

Today, I see modern boat designs emphasizing the living comforts, while sacrificing structural strength. The boat builders are cutting back on hull thickness, explaining that they are getting the same structural strength by using new, lighter materials. If this were the case, the new materials should increase the strength of the hull. The reality is that they are cutting financial corners.

As a boat builder, I was aware of many ways to cut costs of construction and labor. With little exception, these new materials, techniques, and devices sacrificed some of the existing strength that we felt was imperative. What I am trying to say is that it is very easy to hide things while building a boat.

One simple example is the use of pieces of Styrofoam stuffed into the insulation cavity of the icebox. This would never be detected unless the icebox was torn out for some reason. There are many aspects of boat construction where the builders can—and do—cheat. Buyers beware.

Hull material

Imagine the power of a three-foot breaking wave at the beach. Now, take that same wave and have it hit the side of a cruising vessel every 30 seconds for 5 years. Perhaps this sounds extreme to some, but the reality is that this would be about the average punishment a cruising boat may encounter after 10 or 15 years of use.

Boats are built from many different materials. The ones that are most common for cruising boats are steel, aluminum, wood, ferro cement, and fiberglass. I will attempt to briefly discuss these materials, placing the emphasis on the most common one: fiberglass.

The steel hull

Steel is probably the strongest of the materials to be used in boat construction. It is easy to repair by welding and is resistant to fire. Many cruisers claim they do not carry insurance because their boat is built of steel.

When I used to race my fiberglass boat in Papua New Guinea, one of my major competitors was a well-designed steel boat. Every time I would have the right-of-way and would yell out, "*Starboard!*" the steel hull boat would respond, "*Steel!*" It was an effective way to gain the right-of-way.

Most boats that are made of steel do so for strength. This may result in a hull too heavy to perform well. However, I have encountered both those that are heavy slugs and those that sail astonishingly well.

Even with the remarkable strength of this material, it has some limitations. Since it is built out of sheets of steel welded together, it has to be built one at a time—a one-off. It is costly to build because of the extensive labor.

Steel hulled boats are often hard-chined, because the thicker steel plates are difficult to form. If thinner sheets of steel are used, the steel plates can be formed to achieve a soft-chined boat; however, this may sacrifice hull strength. Also, the hull made from thinner steel sheet will eventually dimple between the steel ribs; this is not a structural problem, only a cosmetic one.

Steel, being more difficult to shape, does not lend itself to hydrodynamic hull design. Often, steel-hulled boats do not sail too well. I hesitate making the preceding comment, because I have seen some great hull designs out of Holland that sail every bit as well as fiberglass boats. However, these are the exception.

Steel hulls have a major maintenance problem because of rust. I have seen very few steel boats that do not have a constant weeping of rust somewhere on the boat. To prevent this, many boats have expensive epoxy paint jobs over expensive base coats. Even then, they chip, or water may work its way under a fitting, causing the rust.

§

Two of my closest friends, who I met while in the Marquesas, were a couple on a boat called *Vela*. He was from Denmark and she from South Africa. They had been cruising for years and were getting really frustrated maintaining their steel hull. Finally, they found a paint that almost perfectly matched the rust color on their boat. The whole boat was painted this color, radically cutting back on the routine touch-up.

§

One of the more serious concerns with steel construction is over-grinding welds. Since the boat is built out of sheets welded together, the welds are usually ground down to make a smooth surface, hiding the weld. The weld, if properly done, may be stronger than the material being welded. However, it is susceptible to human error, especially where there is a hard chine. The tendency is to grind as much of the weld away as possible to round the edge. This can create a weak point that will crack under stress or fatigue. It is impossible to detect this possible problem in advance without using expensive specialized testing equipment.

There is an additional problem with steel from electrolysis. This will be discussed in more detail in the following section.

The aluminum hull

Hulls made from aluminum are relatively new. Like the steel hull, it is built as a one-off, so it is expensive and takes a long time to build. It is strong, easy to repair, and fireproof. It is constructed using sheets welded together; therefore, it may be hard or soft-chined, depending on the thickness and ductility of the aluminum. Because it is much lighter than steel, the aluminum hull is often used on offshore racing boats.

Aluminum is not as strong as steel but is more ductile. Because of this ductility, the aluminum is easier to form, so a better-shaped hull may be achieved. The ductility may make the sheets dimple between the ribs and stringers; however, it will take more pounding before fatigue breaks down the aluminum.

§

The following story will illustrate the ductility of aluminum. I was on one of my approaches to Australia, when I encountered the remains of Cyclone Tia off the Queensland coast. Because the seas were too big, the officials would not give permission to enter Morten Bay to check in at Brisbane. After waiting a couple of days, hove-to off Morten Island, permission was given to enter at Maloolaba, further north. The wind was blowing over 60 knots from the starboard quarter. With storm jib and storm trysail set, I flew toward the breakwater entrance. I knew there was only one shot; it was all terra firma ahead if I missed the entrance. With the huge seas running, strong wind blowing, and the rain horizontal, it would be impossible to turn around and sail back out to sea.

I was about to abort before I got to the point of no return, when I suddenly saw an orange and gray powerboat come out of what seemed to be the entrance. He was plowing through the seas right towards me. Then suddenly, he turned and headed back. I figured he decided it was too rough.

This fortunate maneuver led me directly to the entrance side of the breakwater; it appeared to have huge breaking waves across it. The powerboat made it in, but not without its prop coming out of the water as he came off a huge breaker, almost causing him to broach. He narrowly missed hitting the lee breakwater wall. I was petrified, but totally committed. It was after sunset and almost totally dark. The visibility was poor because of the heavy rain.

I had no control over my speed so could not time my entrance between waves. I hugged the windward breakwater, trying not to come too close to the lee side if I were picked up by a wave. As I entered, I was only feet from the rocks. A wave picked me up and catapulted me forward. I threw the helm hard over to starboard.

As the wave passed, I was inside the breakwater. Because of my speed and with the helm hard over, I shot toward the inside of the windward breakwater rocks. I narrowly missed them. I still think I should have hit the bottom. The rocks were so close, I could have stepped off the boat onto them.

When I got inside the harbor, I tied between two pilings and waited out the rest of the storm. The next morning, there were officials in uniform waving from a pier. When I went ashore, I discovered that the orange and gray boat was the Pilot boat. Its skipper had asked the authorities if he could go out and lead us in to safety. This was my first exposure to Australian hospitality.

After clearing into Australia, the skipper of the Pilot boat asked me if I would like to go with him to Nusa Heads to look at some boats that were driven onto the rocks from the storm. When we arrived, I saw two boats setting on the rocks. The steel hull fishing vessel was holed and flooded. The aluminum sailing boat was sitting near the steel boat, but it was not holed. When we checked it out, we discovered that the aluminum had taken the shape of the rocks as it pounded, but did not fracture like the steel hull. This was a great example of the ductility of aluminum.

§

The same problem of over-grinding the welds applies to aluminum as it does to steel. Using a welding rod with a dissimilar metal can also adversely affect the weld.

The major concern with aluminum is its susceptibility to severe corrosion. When I returned to the States, a friend and I found work repairing teak decks on an aluminum boat. There were places where the teak rose in huge bumps and had even separated from the other teak strips. When we removed the damaged teak, we found a white acid-like paste between the aluminum and the teak.

We discovered that the heat had distorted the aluminum deck during welding. This resulted in high and low spots. The deck was then smoothed, using epoxy-type putty. The epoxy filled the low spots to the level of the higher ones. This left places where the teak made direct contact with the aluminum deck. Apparently, the teak was not properly bedded during installation. Water got trapped between the two, and the resulting corrosion ate through the aluminum deck in many places.

Aluminum is very low on the Galvanic Action Table. What this means is that, in time, it can be totally dissolved by electrolysis. All metals are made of molecules with different electrical charges. The more noble the metal, the less the chance it will lose its electrons to other metals. This brings us to the principle of the anode and cathode. The nobler the metal makes it a stronger cathode. The less noble the metal makes it an anode. This means that the anode electrons will move from the anode to the cathode. This is the process used during electro-plating. This is why boats use zinc as the anode on shafts and other external metal parts. It will sacrifice itself to the more noble metals, thus protecting the metals nearest it.

Below is a list of the metals in order of their galvanic scale, with mercury being the most noble or the strongest cathode. All the metals below it would be an anode to it, but a cathode to the others, as it goes down the scale.

The galvanic scale

Mercury
Monel
Silicone Bronze
Copper
Phosphor Bronze
Manganese Bronze
Lead
Stainless Steel
Cast Iron
Wrought Iron
Mild Steel
Aluminum
Cadmium
Zinc and Galvanized Metals
Magnesium

It is important to have a basic understanding of this electrolysis action, so that two radically dissimilar metals are not put together, especially below the hull.

The wooden hull

Wooden hulls have been around for hundreds of years. The wooden hull, like the steel and aluminum hulls, is made as a one-off.

The wooden hull requires a keel backbone with ribs and stringers over which the hull is laid. There are different ways of laying up the hull. The lapstrake-planked hull is where each plank overlaps the edge of the other. The planks are usually wide and have a pleasing appearance. Advocates of this method claim that the overlap at the edge makes a stronger hull.

On a carvel-planked hull, each plank butts against the other. To ensure watertightness, there is usually cotton, followed by caulking, pounded between each plank. An advantage of this method is that it results in a smooth hull; however, it does require re-caulking periodically.

Diagonal planking uses thin wide planks laid at an angle over the hull frame. Additional layers are applied and glued over previous layers at an angle, until the desired thickness is achieved. It results in a formed plywood hull, where the grain of each layer runs at a different angle to the previous, creating a smooth, strong, watertight hull. The hull is normally light, because the wood used must be soft and light to absorb the glues. Most all diagonal planked hulls are covered with epoxy saturated cloth. Some call this system the 'West System' because West Epoxies and materials are used.

The most recent wooden hull building method is strip planking. Narrow strips of wood are applied over the frame; then, they are butted, screwed, and glued together. The advantage of this method is that the narrow strips are easy to form over the frame, making more complex designs possible. It results in a smooth hull finish. Like the diagonal hull, it is usually, but not always, covered with epoxy saturated cloth.

On all the methods mentioned, the ballast must be external or bolted on after the hull is completed. Although there may be some exceptions to this, I have never encountered them.

The wooden hull, if properly built and maintained, is strong and could last many lifetimes. Unfortunately, often they are not properly maintained and problems occur. There is a multitude of ways in which water may enter the wood: the epoxy coating may delaminate, or a collision or grounding may loosen the seal between the planks, permitting water to seep into the wood.

Both dry rot and wet rot are probably the biggest enemies of wooden boats. There is a fungus spoor that grows in wood fiber when it remains wet from fresh water, without circulation of air. Like a cancer, it can spread rapidly or slowly. It is difficult to detect until there are apparent signs of very soft wood. By the time the rot is discovered, it may have spread through the core of the wood, making it difficult to treat.

Often, the signs of rot are superficial, and only the superficial damage is treated or cut away. However, the spoors may have already penetrated deeply into the wood, making it impossible to detect. In time, the rot spreads.

There are no absolute guarantees that a wooden boat does not have some rot. Even a good marine surveyor can miss dry rot spoors that have not reached the surface. The best way to search for rot is to check places where fresh water might stand, and there is little air circulation. If the hull is not protected, it may occur at the waterline where fresh water sits on top of salt water. Tapping the susceptible area may reveal a softer sound than the surrounding area. When dry rot is severe, it has a strong fungus odor of dampness.

There was a recent discovery that some metals will react to wood, creating a type of electrolysis around the metal that softens the surrounding wood fibers. This would be a major concern around hull fasteners. If the wood around a screw were to soften where the plank meets the stem post, the plank could break loose; therefore, depending on the material used, the fasteners should be checked periodically.

Another major concern for wooden boat owners is the teredo worm. These little worms live in salt water and eat most all wood, except teak. They eat their way deep into the core of the wood, leaving small tunnels that can affect the hull's structural strength.

Wooden hulls require a substantial structural frame on which to lay the planking. This skeletal form of ribs usually has ceiling strips over them on the inside for cosmetic reasons. The frame and ceiling strips reduce living space inside the boat by many inches.

Wood and fiberglass hulls, unlike steel, aluminum, and the concrete hulls, can burn. A major advantage of a wooden hull, however, is that it can be easily repaired almost anywhere in the world.

The ferro cement hull

Ferro cement hulls are not as popular as they used to be. Because the hull was relatively easy to build by the layman, many were built in back yards. It consists of a basic frame that is thrown away when the hull is complete. Outside this frame, reinforcing steel and a screen hold the cement together. A special concrete is used to form the hull. The result is a relatively strong, medium-weight hull that is inexpensive to build. Because of the method of making the hull shape and the material used, the ballast could be encapsulated inside the hull.

The concrete is easy to repair, but the strength of the repair is questionable. Many repairs are not done with the diligence required. The concrete has to be chipped away around the damaged area, until only solid concrete remains. If the reinforcing steel is damaged, it has to be exposed to good steel and screen; then, new reinforcing metals need to be applied.

Another problem with repairs is that the concrete continues to cure over time. The older hull may not have the same expansion and contraction as the new concrete used for the repairs.

One of the major problems with the concrete hull is that it will pulverize if damaged by a severe grounding.

§

I first experienced this while I was working at a copper mine on Bougainville Island in Papua New Guinea. A storm broke the mooring lines to a ferro cement boat; the boat ended up on the rocks and was quickly holed. I assisted the owner to re-float her.

When the tide was at its lowest, we went aboard and noticed the hole was about 8 inches in diameter. It took us over 24 hours to arrange to get the materials necessary to make the temporary repairs. The next day, we arrived at low tide. When we entered the boat, we discovered that the hole was now 2 feet in diameter, and the concrete around it was pulverized. We were surprised because the harbor was well protected, and there weren't any waves to cause abrasion. The additional damage was caused simply by the rise and fall of the tide.

Fortunately, we brought extra material. The temporary repair was made by using concrete nails to fasten one-quarter inch plywood over the hull-damaged area. Then, we applied underwater epoxy putty over the hole on the inside. It took many gallons of this expensive putty, because it washed away before it would settle and cure. The repair held long enough to get the hull pumped dry and towed to a location where a crane could lift her out for more a permanent repair.

§

There is also the problem of fastening bulkheads and furniture to the interior of the cement hull. I have seen many of these boats where some of the furniture was mostly floating inside the hull. It was in place, but provided no additional strength to the hull.

The major concern with the concrete hull is its structural integrity; a great deal depends on the skill and diligence of the builder. Buying a used ferro cement boat could and should be a concern. Although these hulls have been around for over 20 years, their life expectancy is still unknown.

The fiberglass hull

Fiberglass is the most common hull material used today. A female mold is used, so many hulls can be 'pulled' from the same mold. This process lends itself to mass production.

If the material is properly applied to a reasonable thickness, the fiberglass hull can be structurally strong. The hulls are flexible, so they can absorb the punishments of the seas for many years. We still do not know the life expectancy of these hulls, but they have already been around for over 50 years.

Since a mold is used to make the hull, any design can be achieved. This is a racing boat designer's dream. For this reason, most fiberglass boats have a pleasing appearance. Some look classical, while others look like they are going fast while at anchor. The flexibility of design makes it possible to have internal, encapsulated ballast or external ballast. Since the hull is from a mold, there is little need for ribs and stringers taking up living space. If an interior liner is used, however, it has the opposite effect and will take up much of the interior space.

As long as it is properly prepared and applied, fiberglass bonded to fiberglass makes an excellent adhesion. Because of this excellent bonding, bulkheads and interior furniture can be fastened to the hull and remain there for the life of the boat. There should be no attempt to bond polyester resins to epoxy resins; they do not bond. However, epoxy will bond to polyester resins.

Some fiberglass hulls have developed a problem called osmosis, the ingress of moisture into the fiberglass material, which causes blistering. There are many reasons this can occur and will be discussed in more detail later in this chapter.

If the hull is not properly constructed, or if it is too thin for its intended purpose, it can be damaged easily by going aground or by hitting something hard like another boat. The thinner the hull, the more it will flex. This can cause fiberglass fatigue where there are hard, inflexible points, like bulkheads and stringers. This is commonly seen on small powerboats that pound on the waves. Cracks develop in the fiberglass where the floor's reinforcing beams make contact with the hull.

Repairs to fiberglass can be difficult, unless there is access to the proper materials and equipment. Because of this, major repairs are more difficult in some out of the way places.

Today, many boat builders use a molded fiberglass liner for the interior. This is a great way to cut construction costs. If a liner is used, it should be bonded to the hull in as many places as possible to provide the needed strength. These liners, though, may create a problem where they do not have access under or behind them.

I could cite many examples of boats that have had hull problems that could not be accessed from inside without cutting away a great deal of the interior. I have friends who deliver boats that insist on carrying battery driven saws, a fireman's-type axe, and crowbars for emergencies.

If there is minimum access behind the liner, it is very difficult to clean. Fungus, mould, insects, and rodents can find their way under liners and be difficult to remove.

The liner restricts any possibility of changing the interior layout. This means that every boat produced will have the same interior design. This is not necessarily a bad thing, if the interior design is satisfactory to its owner. Most of these interior designs are carefully thought out with personal comfort and maximum living space as the primary concerns. Most owners are happy with the interior layouts.

Some fiberglass boats with fiberglass liners have the water tanks molded into the liner. This may create a problem if it is difficult to access for cleaning. Some fiberglass water tanks never lose the taste of fiberglass. There are ways to resolve this problem, but good access is required.

As mentioned previously, fiberglass hulls will burn. Not only will they burn, but it is also difficult to stop the fire.

Fiberglass hull construction

As I mentioned previously, most fiberglass hulls are made in a female mold. The most common exceptions to this are fiberglass hulls made by the home builder. The female mold can be in one solid piece or in two or more parts. The more complex the hull shape, like with tumble home, the more pieces to the mold; this enables the 'piece' to be removed. This is important when it comes to an in-turning flange on which to set the deck.

If the mold is one piece, the hull shape cannot have any tumble home (any part of it turning inward), or the 'piece' cannot be removed from the mold. It can, however, have an out-turning flange. If it has an out-turning flange, it must be narrow; otherwise, it might tear itself off when along side the dock or another boat. The narrow out-turning flange will take a deck, but there is little surface area for bonding; hence, it will likely separate in rough conditions. Since the out-turning flange is narrow, it has little strength to hold the hull shape when it is removed from the mold. This is not a problem as long as the hull is properly supported symmetrically before the deck is installed. The out-turning flange is used on smaller, inexpensive, coastal boats, and not offshore cruisers.

If the mold is in two or more pieces, it can have an in-turning flange of any width. To remove the 'piece,' the mold must be separated in half, lengthwise. The in-turning flange, if wide enough, makes an excellent surface on which to set the deck. The wide, in-turning flange will maintain the hull's shape before the deck is set in place. This wider surface will accept lots of bonding material and more fasteners.

Since the mold is in two halves, it is easier to make a cavity to accept an internal ballast. This is not done on narrow fin keels, but on longer, wider keels.

To lay up a hull using a two-part mold, the two halves of the mold are separated and laid flat. A special wax called a mold release is applied over both halves of the mold and polished. If there will be a different color for the boot top, it is masked off before applying the hull color gel coat. Then, the gel coat color is mixed with catalyst, and a thin coat is sprayed over the entire mold. When this first coat is nearly cured, another coat is applied.

Before the hull gel coat completely cures, the masking tape is removed for the boot top; this is then gel coated the required color. When the gel coat cures, some boat builders will apply a darker gel coat over the lighter colors so that no light can be seen though the hull; it also makes it easier to see air bubbles during lamination.

A mistake made by some builders is applying too much gel coat at one time. The outer coating, which is exposed to the air, cures more rapidly by evaporating the solvents on the surface. This traps solvent in the uncured gel coat between the cured outer surface and the previous coat against the inside of the mold. The inner gel coat cures chemically, but the solvents remain entrapped. Eventually, when moisture mixes with this solvent, gel coat osmosis may occur. This type of osmosis is not a danger to the structure of the hull, because it only affects the gel coat, not the lamination.

A thin coating of fiberglass matt and roving is applied over the final gel coat coating. Then, the two mold halves are clamped together for the rest of the structural lay-up.

At this point the methods of laminations vary by builder. Some use special materials and special resins. Resin has little structural strength by itself: it is too brittle. To achieve the proper strength, the resin must be applied to a reinforced clothlike material. The most common material is fiberglass, but there are others that are lighter, stronger, and much more expensive, like Kevlar.

The most common kinds of reinforcing materials are: (a) fiberglass matt, a loose fiber material used to absorb the resins, (b) fiberglass roving, a strongly woven material for strength, and (c) fiberglass cloth for a strong, smoother finish. The matt should be used with the roving or cloth because it has more absorption. One layer of matt and a layer of roving or cloth are considered as a single lamination.

When the 'piece' cures, it is removed from the two-part mold, leaving a seam line down the center where the two halves were gel coated before assembly. Many people misinterpret this as a seam where the hull was made in two halves and then bonded together. This was done on some boats in the past, but because of the increased chance of failure along this seam, it has mostly been discontinued. If a builder is still using this method, I am certain that they have developed a construction technique that makes it structurally strong. I am aware of some reputable builders in Europe who still make the hull in two halves and join them together after they are removed from the mold.

A critical factor in hull lamination is removing air bubbles, known to cause osmosis in the laminate. Depending on the severity of the bubbles, this type of osmosis can affect the structural integrity of the hull.

There are several ways to cause air bubbles and several ways to eliminate them. Shooting the fiberglass matt on the hull mold using a 'chopper gun' often creates air bubbles. Since the fibers are loose and mixed with resin as it is shot onto the mold, bubbles may get trapped and cannot be easily removed. If an additional layer of roving or cloth is applied over the chopped matt, the bubbles can be removed by squeegee or by vacuum bagging.

What is important is that all the fibers of the matt are applied evenly throughout the mold. For this reason, most builders use sheets of matt instead of the chopper gun. Also important is that the combination of matt and roving must be thoroughly saturated after the bubbles have been removed. Excessive passes with the squeegee can remove too much resin, as well as the air bubbles.

To get a complete bond between coats, each subsequent lamination layer should be applied before the previous coat has completely cured. If this is not possible, a rough sanding is required before the next application.

Another critical factor in achieving a strong hull is the removal of excess resins. As mentioned earlier, resin alone has little structural strength. Imagine liquid resin spread over a 4' X 8' sheet of plywood covered with waxed paper. After the resin cures, it would be impossible to remove the hard resin from the plywood without it shattering into many pieces.

If a layer of resin saturated matt and roving were applied to the waxed paper plywood and cured, it would be much stronger. However, if the excess resins were not removed, the surface would be irregular, resulting in weak spots. If it were removed and rolled around a barrel, it would break at the weakest point and cause pieces of excess resins to shatter.

If the same application was used, but all the excess resins and bubbles were removed using a squeegee, the sheet would easily bend over the barrel without breaking. This same procedure should apply to hull construction.

The American Bureau of Shipbuilding specifies that a pleasure boat fiberglass hull must have a minimum breaking strength of 6,000 pounds per square inch. This would apply to coastal boats and should be at least three times that strength for an offshore vessel.

The same strength can be achieved with less laminations by using new, expensive materials such as epoxy resins, vinylester resins, and Kevlar sheets. The boat building company I used to own built their standard 28-foot hulls with a breaking strength of 24,000 pounds per square inch. Recently, a customer wanted a much stronger hull to take to the Antarctic. By using Kevlar and vinylester resins, a hull was laid up to the same thickness or number of laminations that resulted in a breaking strength of between 90,000 to 100,000 pound per square inch. However, the cost was more than double that of a fiberglass, polyester resin hull.

All boat builders use hole saws to cut holes through the hull to install through-hull fittings. A prospective buyer should be able to look at the plugs extracted from the hull saws to see how many laminations were used and whether all the laminations were of equal thickness. Take into consideration that different parts of a hull will require a stronger, thicker lay-up. I would expect the bottom of the keel area to be about twice as thick as the hull at the sheer. There should be more lay-ups forward and also where the chainplates are located. Ask the builder about these concerns.

The hull to deck join should be as strong as possible, so it will not separate when working in a heavy seaway. There are many different methods to achieve this join. Regardless of the method used, the key factors are a large matching surface between the hull and deck, a strong bonding material between the join, and many strong fasteners through-bolted to hold the join together.

I have seen some embarrassing construction by some builders on the hull to deck join. I remember going to a boat show and asking the salesperson what he used to bond the deck to the hull. He responded that they used a polysulfide caulking and sheet metal screws as fasteners. When I questioned him about why they used something that did not have excellent bonding, his answer was so that the deck could be removed to repair it if it leaked.

Conversely, there are builders who will use a substantial contact surface between the deck and hull, then fiberglass over it. This is excellent, but only as good as the amount of matt and cloth used, and whether it is done on both the inside and outside of the join. To use only resin will not work; it is too brittle.

Even if the deck and hull are properly bonded together, there is no guarantee that they will never separate. The fiberglass hull works or flexes with the seas. There may be severe yawing or twisting of the hull, placing tremendous sheer forces on this join. The only way to properly prevent this action is with the installation of bulkheads bonded to the hull and the underside of the deck. The more bulkheads there are, the less the twisting effect and the stronger the boat, as shown in Figure 24.

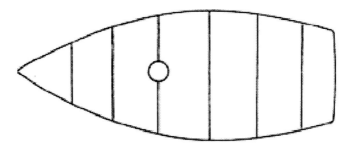

The more bulkheads, the stronger the boat

Figure 24. More bulkheads

The fewer the bulkheads, the more interior living space a boat has, but the hull is not nearly as strong, as shown in Figure 25.

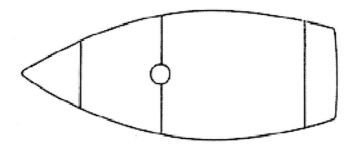

Few bulkheads mean less strength; hull may twist

Figure 25. Fewer bulkheads

This is a bit of a sore spot for me. I go to boat shows and go aboard boats that have few—if any—bulkheads, but the living space is enormous. Where is the line drawn on these designs? I realize that living space and comfort are important considerations, but the structural integrity of the vessel should not be sacrificed.

The most important bulkhead on a boat is at or near the mast. This is for several reasons. This area is the major point of flex and twist. It is also where the standing rigging is pulling down on the mast, which pulls inward on the hull. Without a properly installed bulkhead, the deck will pump or rise as the stresses are pulled toward the center. There are builders who say that they have engineered structural beams across the deck so it cannot pump; however, how would this prevent twist unless there are more bulkheads?

Basically, the more bulkheads a boat has, the stronger the boat. To have its maximum structural effect, a bulkhead should be bonded with multiple layers of fiberglass to the underside of the deck and cabin, as well as to the hull.

After the bulkheads are installed, their structural strength will depend on the bulkhead material, the width of the bonding material, and the method of installation. A proper bulkhead is constructed of any strong material that will not break down under the stress that prevents the twisting or yawing of the boat. Most builders use marine grade plywood, because it absorbs fiberglass resins for bonding.

Some builders call the attachment of the bulkhead to the hull and deck, tabbing. I define tabbing as using narrow strips of fiberglass of about 2 to 3 inches wide to connect the bulkhead. I consider bonding stronger, because the strips of material used should be about 10 to 12 inches wide.

This bonding or tabbing is the process of permanently fastening the bulkhead to the hull, using resin-soaked fiberglass matt and cloth. If the builder uses 2-inch tabbing, one inch is on the hull and one inch is on the bulkhead. This narrow tabbing may break away from the hull or bulkhead when the boat is under its greatest stress, or over years of normal sailing. The wider this bonding, the stronger the bulkhead attachment, because the stress loads are spread over a wider area. Proper bonding should always be applied to both sides of the bulkhead. I have seen boats that only use small pieces of tabbing spaced every few inches around the bulkhead.

This bonding of a bulkhead to the hull and deck is hidden on the completed boat. However, there are things to look for, in order to determine how much material was used. The best place to look is inside the lockers. If this does not reveal the bonding, look under the cabin sole.

A builder that uses teak or mahogany plywood as the bulkhead material must hide the bonding material with wood trim. The width of the wood trim will reveal the maximum width used for the bonding. If a vinyl headliner is used, check the width of the trim. More than likely, the builder didn't use wooden trim at all, because there wasn't any tabbing used under the cabin top. This is revealed if the vinyl top uses a vinyl rope for the trim.

Better builders will apply a veneer of some material over the bulkhead to conceal the bonding, so a narrower trim can be used. This may make it difficult to see the size of the bonding.

Since this bulkhead can create a hard spot where it makes contact with the hull, as shown in Figure 26 (a), there should be something between the two to absorb some of the impact from waves, or when hitting against a pier. Some builders just leave a space between the bulkhead and hull, while others use foam or rubber, as shown in Figure 26 (b).

Methods of attaching bulkheads to hulls

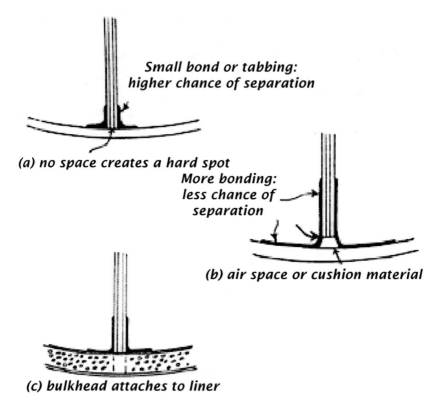

**Small bond or tabbing:
higher chance of separation**

(a) no space creates a hard spot

**More bonding:
less chance of
separation**

(b) air space or cushion material

(c) bulkhead attaches to liner

Figure 26. Bonding of bulkheads

A bulkhead that is installed against the inside of a liner seems to defeat much of its purpose of preventing the yawing stresses; the stress is now transmitted to the liner. How stoutly the liner is installed will determine how effective the bulkhead is. See Figure 26 (c).

Try asking the builder the size of the tabbing or bonding used; inquire if it is also used under the deck and cabin. If he uses wide bonding, find out how he conceals it. Even more importantly, if the company is still building boats, visit the factory.

The same bonding principle applies to all the internal furniture and the cabin sole. Wherever something is bonded to the hull, it is strengthened at this point. On much larger boats, where there is considerable space between pieces of the interior furniture, longitudinal stringers are bonded to the hull to give it additional strength. If the furniture is bonded to the hull, it should be bonded on both sides if possible. Unfortunately, it is costly to build this way; hence, most builders use fiberglass liners.

Liners that are properly designed and installed are fine. The problem is that it may be difficult to access the space behind the liner to do adequate bonding to the hull. If the bonding is done properly, it will add to the structurally strength of the hull. Therefore, if you are considering buying a boat with a fiberglass liner, look in the back of the lockers, in the bilge, and anyplace you can access to see how the liner is attached to the hull.

Some builders use a core, such as balsa or rigid foam, in the hull. This will make a hull much lighter and, perhaps, stiffer. If a fiberglass straw was filled with balsa or foam, it is apparent how much stronger it would be. If the same straw were filled with solid fiberglass, it would be even stronger, but much heavier.

Let's imagine that we have a fiberglass lamination of 1/8" thickness applied to a surface covered with wax paper. While the lamination is still wet, we apply double that thickness—1/4"—of a lightweight core material. This is followed by a final 1/8" of fiberglass lamination. The end result would be a fiberglass core 1/2" thick. To lift this sheet and try to bend or twist it would be difficult because of its stiffness and thickness.

Now, let's make a sheet of solid fiberglass laminations to the same half-inch thickness. Both sheets would be equally rigid, but the core sheet would be much lighter. Lay the two between two sawhorses, and hit each with a sledgehammer. You can imagine the results: the cored sheet would break, while the solid fiberglass sheet would only have superficial damage.

If we were to make a solid fiberglass sheet only as thick as the two 1/8" laminations, it would not be as strong. The cored material provides stiffness with far less weight, but is susceptible to impact damage.

The major problem with cored hulls is the severity of osmosis. We know that polyester resins will absorb moisture. The thin laminations or skin coats on the outside of a cored hull will more readily permit this to happen. If the core material will hold or absorb this moisture, it can create severe osmosis problems. In some cores, the lamination can actually separate from the core. Using resins and core materials that are more resistant to moisture absorption can reduce much of this problem.

The best test of a cored hull is time. This is when it is a good idea to visit boatyards and go on the Internet to find out as much as possible about the boat you are considering.

The rudder

The rudder is as important to a boat as the steering wheel is to a car. Without the rudder, it is difficult to steer the boat. The rudder design, shape, attachment, and construction are all important factors to consider. Many owners give little thought or concern to the rudder, until a problem arises.

The location of the rudder determines the turning arc of the boat. A rudder set considerably forward of the stern will turn the boat much sharper than the rudder set aft of the stern. However, the further aft the rudder is set, the less steering is required. This is an advantage when going on long straight sails, but a disadvantage when racing around the marks.

A rudder's construction and design are important. Most are constructed from fiberglass with a foam core. Others are made of laminated wood or various types of metal. The materials used for the rudder have the same advantages and disadvantages as the material used for the hull.

I have seen rudders in which the fiberglass shell had separated from the core after being left out of the water and exposed to the sun for long periods of time. The most important factors to consider are the rudder's design, and how it is attached to the hull.

The spade rudder

The spade rudder is most commonly used on racing boats with fin keels, because it has minimum resistance and wetted surface. These rudders hang by themselves, as shown in Figure 27. They are set considerably aft of the keel, and thus are exposed to damage.

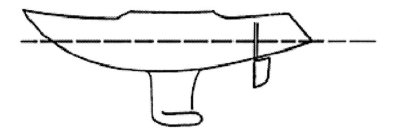

Figure 27. The spade rudder

The spade rudder is only supported where the rudderpost passes through the hull. It is not supported at the bottom of the rudder, like other designs. This requires a strong, heavy rudderpost. Depending on the rudderpost material, it is possible to get electrolysis on the shaft, which can affect the seal where it passes through the hull.

The rudderpost, being exposed and unsupported, is susceptible to damage if it hits something, or something hits it. If the post is bent, it can push the top aft end of the rudder against the hull, so it cannot move. Or, it may break the seal where it passes through the hull.

On most designs, if the spade rudder is damaged, it cannot be removed from the boat while it is in the water. If the boat is set on the hard, the rudder's bottom is near the ground; therefore, to remove the rudderpost requires either digging a deep hole, or lifting the boat.

The spade rudder will catch nets and anchor ropes, but so will the fin keel. If an obstacle passes the keel, it will probably also pass the rudder. The biggest concern is a log that may hit the keel, then pivot around and hit the rudder.

I know of cases where the rudderpost retainer and seal were not properly tightened, and the rudder fell completely out of the boat. Depending on the installation design, this could permit water to enter the boat. However, most designs have the rudderpost inside a pipe that extends above the waterline.

The skeg rudder

The skeg rudder is similar to the spade rudder, except that it is supported at the bottom, as shown in Figure 28. The rudder is also on a rudderpost; consequently, it would have similar problems to the spade rudderpost.

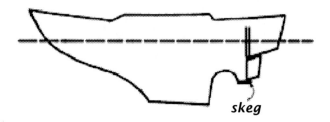

skeg

Figure 28. The skeg rudder

The aft end of the keel or a separate skeg supports the bottom of the rudder. For the purpose of comparing rudders, the rudder attached to the aft end of the keel has, basically, the same advantages and disadvantages as the skeg rudder. Therefore, although the rudder that is attached to the aft end of the keel is not literally a skeg rudder, the term will be used for both, but the differences should be apparent.

If the bottom of the rudderpost is attached to the aft end of the keel, it would be considered strongly supported and better protected. If the bottom of the skeg rudderpost is attached to a separate skeg, the rudder is only as strong as the attachment of the skeg to the hull. If the skeg is part of the hull mold, it is probably more than strong enough to support the rudder. However, if the skeg is added to the hull later, the method of attachment is critical. If the boat goes aground or hits something, the skeg must take the punishment in order to protect the rudder. Depending on the rudder attachment, both the keel and the skeg will deflect ropes, netting, and logs.

The external rudder

The externally hung rudder does not have a rudderpost, so it does not go though the hull; instead, it is attached to the transom or stern of the boat with pintles and gudgeons, as shown in Figure 29. Thus, the external rudder has none of the disadvantages of a rudder with a rudderpost.

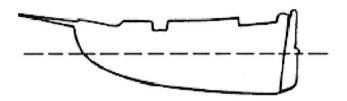

Figure 29. The external rudder

The external hung rudder is attached to the stern of the boat with male pintles on the rudder that fit into matching female gudgeons on the boat's stern. The materials used to construct these are susceptible to electrolysis below the waterline. Stainless steel is not a good choice, unless it has an anode attached and is inspected often. By checking the galvanic scale, you will note that silicone bronze would be the best choice for these fittings.

Because the rudder is hung off the stern, it can be removed while in the water; this is one of its major advantages. This, of course, depends on its design.

The stern hung rudder is usually much larger than the spade or skeg rudder; therefore, there is a higher steering load on the helm, especially when making sternway. If this load is too heavy, it may damage the pintles and gudgeons. Since the rudder is accessible, rudder stops can be easily installed to prevent the rudder from going hard over.

If the boat has a fin keel or a keel that does not extend to the stern of the boat, the external rudder will hang unsupported and unprotected at the bottom. This would result in the same problems as with the spade rudder: it could be damaged, or catch ropes and nets.

On the more full-length keels, the external rudder is also attached at the bottom of the keel. This bottom gudgeon is set a few inches above the bottom of the keel to protect it during a grounding. With this method of attachment, the keel will protect the rudder from damage caused by logs, ropes, or nets.

The boat with an external rudder will have a much wider turning radius than a spade or skeg rudder, where the rudderpost is closer to the center of the boat.

Since the rudder is set directly behind the prop, there may be vibration from the prop wash. An aperture or notch is often cut into the leading edge of the rudder, so that the prop wash has more clearance. This all will affect the performance and efficiency of the rudder, both under sail and under power.

The external rudder is easy to access for inspection and repair. Because of its design, it can be reproduced in plywood or any laminated wood in an emergency.

An often overlooked advantage to the external hung rudder is the simplicity of attaching a trim tab to the rudder's trailing edge. This trim tab can be connected to a windvane or to an inexpensive tiller-type autopilot to steer the boat on passages with minimum current draw.

Steering methods: tiller vs. wheel

The tiller

Steering with a tiller is more common on smaller boats. The rudder's load to the helmsman is direct; this would be overwhelming on larger boats. The only load reduction between the rudder and the tiller is the length of the tiller. Depending on the size of the rudder and the length of the tiller, steering for long periods can be a chore in rough conditions. Most offshore cruisers that have tiller steering have a windvane and/or an autopilot to steer the boat and relieve the helmsman.

Since the rudder's load leads directly to the helmsman, there is a more sensitive feel of the helm, allowing the helmsman to detect the smallest weather helm or lee helm. Because of this direct load, the rudder will respond immediately to the helmsman; this is great in close quarters, but arduous if steering a straight course for a long distance.

Depending on the length of the tiller, it can swing from one side of the cockpit to the other, making sitting anywhere in this arc difficult. However, in my opinion, the best thing about tiller steering is that the tiller can be removed when it is not needed. At anchor, the entire cockpit is free for entertaining or sleeping outside. If a reliable trim tab-type windvane or autopilot is used, the tiller can be removed while underway as well. However, after it is removed, it can be lost overboard if not properly stored.

The tiller is normally made of laminated wood for strength; the rare possibility exists that it could break. However, if it did break, it could be easily replaced with something aboard, like an oar. A new one can be built out of material available most anywhere in the world.

There are different ways in which the tiller is attached to the rudder. There is a tremendous load at this point; whatever the method used, it must be strongly constructed and routinely maintained.

Wheel steering

Wheel steering, unlike tiller steering, will absorb much of the rudder's pressure to the helmsman. Wheel steering is more commonly used on rudders that have a rudderpost, because it is easy to attach a quadrant, which is like a pulley that is one quarter of a circle.

The wheel's shaft or axis is connected to a pulley inside the pedestal. Some type of linkage is used between the wheel pulley and a series of pulleys below deck that lead to the rudder's quadrant. The most common linkage used is chain and cable. Both of these must be properly tensioned so there is no play in the wheel; this requires a turnbuckle or equivalent somewhere in the system. The chain uses shackles for attachments, while the cable uses Nicro Press-type fittings or cable clamps. The pulleys and the quadrant are attached to their respective shafts using setscrews, pins, or keys, such as square keys or Woodruff keys. The problem is that there are many movable parts and connections that can slip or fail at the worst time—when there is a heavy load during a storm.

A stronger, more reliable direct linkage between the wheel and quadrant is the worm gear, or the rack-and-pinion. Both of these use threads or gears to transfer the movement between the wheel and rudder. There is nothing that will stretch, slip, or require adjusting like cable and chain. There are far fewer connections. The only problem that I am aware of is that the pins or keys holding the gears to the shaft may shear in rough conditions. Routine inspection and necessary replacement will help prevent this from occurring.

The hydraulic steering method has the lightest load on the helmsman. There is little—if any—feedback from the rudder to the wheel. A hydraulic pump and motor absorb the rudder's load; this makes steering a boat like driving a car with power steering. There are variations to this design, but basically it consists of a hydraulic pump at the wheel that pumps hydraulic fluid through high-pressure hoses to a hydraulic arm that is attached to the rudder's quadrant or rudder arm.

One disadvantage of hydraulic steering is that there will always be some liquid slipping past the pump, so it is difficult to keep a mark on the wheel to show when the rudder is dead center. The other problem is that most of the hydraulic system's load force is in one direction. There is little feedback from the rudder to the helmsman, making it almost impossible to detect a weather helm or lee helm. It also makes it impossible to attach a windvane to the rudder.

Depending on the wheel steering mechanism used, the load and response time is considerably less than with tiller steering.

All the wheel steering designs have the possibility of breaking down at a time when it is under the heaviest load, like in a storm. To repair the system in rough conditions is difficult. Therefore, the rudderpost must have a fitting to accept an emergency tiller.

In my opinion, the biggest disadvantage of wheel steering is that it requires a pedestal, which cannot be removed. It is like having a tree stump in the cockpit for the life of the boat. This may not be a problem on larger vessels, but could be a continuous irritation on smaller ones.

Deck design and construction

The deck design

A properly designed deck can provide safety and comfort. Many sailors like large cockpits with lots of room for entertaining. This is fine on larger boats, but it uses up much of the living space below on smaller ones. I feel that the cockpit seats should be at least long enough to permit sleeping outside comfortably.

On the other hand, the cockpit well should be as small as possible, so it will not jeopardize the safety of the boat when filled with water if pooped. One cubic foot of water weighs about 64 pounds. A cockpit well that is 5 feet long by 3 feet wide and 2 feet deep has a total volume of 30 cubic feet. If pooped, it would weigh 1920 pounds. This is a lot of weight in the stern of a boat when running in a storm.

It is also important that the companionway opening to the inside of the boat does not extend down into the cockpit well. Any water entering the cockpit well will end up inside the boat. Depending on the size of the boat, this requires the companionway entry to be on deck, with a low sill. This makes the opening smaller and perhaps a little more difficult to use. This design varies considerably among boats. What is important is to keep the water out of the interior of the boat.

On most boat designs, the cockpits are at the stern of the boat. This is not necessarily bad, but it does expose the helmsman to stern breaking waves. The further forward the cockpit, the safer and dryer it is. Unfortunately, moving the cockpit forward puts it above valuable living space.

Another popular design is the mid cockpit. This cockpit is set near the center of the boat, above the deck level, so it takes up less vital living space below. This higher cockpit provides better visibility. However, if the cockpit is set too high, it may add too much windage and could be unsafe in severe weather.

Mid cockpits are used on larger boats. The cockpit, being above deck level, requires a larger cabin. Usually, the larger the cabin is, the larger the windows or ports are. This is not always the case, but it is more common than uncommon.

If these windows or ports break, they would permit a lot of water to enter the interior of the boat. On my own 28-foot boat, I had 7-inch diameter portlights. I was on a beam reach. There was a moderate sea, but nothing to be concerned about. I had a portlight open on the windward side for ventilation. A single freak wave broke against the side. Instantly, there must have been over 50 gallons of water inside the boat. It soaked all of the cushions, and the cabin sole had about 6 inches of water over the top. This much water came inside from just one wave and one 7-inch portlight.

To prevent larger windows from breaking, most boats have safety covers when the weather gets rough. The problem is that the wave that does the damage is usually not expected, and all too often, the storm boards are put in place too late.

During my travels, I have seen many examples of the odd unexpected freak wave completely smashing these larger windows. In one instance, a sizeable boat with a substantial cabin had the entire cabin removed in a gale between Australia and New Caledonia. Upon inspection, the construction of the cabin to the deck was inferior. The boat was built for harbor or coastal sailing; unfortunately, it was not marketed that way.

The deck should have plenty of wide walking space around the cabin so that moving forward, even while dragging a sail bag, can be done safely. The larger the deck space forward, the easier it is to handle sails. It also provides space to set the dinghy as low as possible.

Personally, I like to have some bulwarks around the outer edge of the deck. This solid wall, regardless of its height, will prevent feet from slipping over the side and provides a place to stoutly fasten lifeline stanchions.

The deck construction

All fiberglass decks have a core. The core makes the deck rigid, with less weight. The core material is usually balsa, rigid foam, or marine plywood.

Foam core is light, but provides little compression strength. In other words, wherever there is compression like a through bolt or a deck-stepped mast, the core material will eventually compress. This may permit water to enter the core and cause the core to separate from the laminate.

To prevent this from happening, most builders add a piece of marine plywood or solid fiberglass at these locations. Plywood has excellent resistance to compression, but it can absorb moisture and rot. Solid fiberglass would be even better than plywood to fill the areas of compression. This compression piece should be added wherever there will be a bolt passing through the deck; however, it is difficult to know the location of all the through bolts. The builder knows the location of deck cleats and winches, so that is not the problem. After the boat is complete, careful consideration should be given to the location of any additional through bolts for things like dinghy chocks, anchor windlass, fairleads, etc. Some builders will tell you that it is not a problem as long as a backup plate is used to distribute the compression. This is true, although it depends on the core material, the load, and the size of the backup plate.

I have seen boats' deck cleats torn completely through the deck, with their back-up plates still bolted to them. One boat had the anchor windlass torn out, leaving a gaping hole in the foredeck.

Balsa core is the same as the foam core, except that it has a slightly higher resistance to compression and is somewhat heavier. Like the foam core, marine plywood, or solid fiberglass, balsa is used at high compression locations. Since balsa is soft, it will absorb moisture more quickly than other core materials. This could result in rot, causing major problems if it spreads though the core. To prevent this, some balsa cores are made from small squares on a cloth backing, which will permit resins between the separate squares. If it is properly saturated, the rot could be localized.

The marine plywood core has more weight than the other cores, but has excellent compression resistance. However, if fresh water gets into the plywood core, it could rot; this would be difficult to detect and repair.

Since marine plywood core is so resistant to compression, through bolts can be added anywhere, as long as they are properly bedded. Some builders will use an epoxy sealant in the drilled holes before the bolt is installed. This seals the end grain in case water does get in through the bedding.

Regardless of the core material, proper bedding of hardware is essential. Since the bedding will also compress in time, the nuts should be accessible so they can be tightened periodically.

The deck should have added strength or thickness where the higher loads are expected, including where the mast is stepped or where it passes though the deck or cabin, at the location of the cleats, and at the anchor windlass. This added thickness to the deck core is impossible to detect after the boat is finished, because the headliner hides it. Again, visit the factory where the boat is built.

If you are buying a used boat with a cored deck, two concerns are delamination from the core or rot in the core. You can usually detect delamination by tapping the deck with the handle of a screwdriver and listening for hollow sounds. Rot, on the other hand, cannot be detected until the damage is severe. A way to detect problems early is to remove questionable through bolts for visual inspection and then to poke at the core. However, this is not always possible prior to buying a boat; few owners or dealers would permit it.

The non-skid materials and designs used on molded fiberglass decks are practically useless. In order for the deck to be removed from the mold, the non-skid must be relatively smooth. This almost negates its purpose. These molded fiberglass decks were the main reason special shoes were invented to help gain traction.

Some boats have teak decks, which are skid resistant and beautiful to behold. However, they require a great deal of maintenance. Older teak decks were screwed to the underdeck using hundreds of screws. The teak had to be properly bedded during the fastening process to prevent water from entering any screw holes. The teak had to be a minimum of 5/8" thick, so it could have teak plugs over the screw heads and still have enough teak under the screw to pull it down onto the bedding and underdeck.

As time passes, the softer teak fibers wear away; this results in a rougher gray deck that is less pleasing to the eye. Eventually, it gets sanded smooth. How many sandings will the deck take until the teak plugs are gone, and the screws are exposed? This depends on the original thickness of the teak. Eventually, the time will come when some of the screws will have to be removed, re-countersunk, and replaced. How much teak is under the screw to keep it strongly pulled down on the underdeck?

The teak deck requires caulking between the slats. This is more difficult than it appears. Teak is a waxy wood that prevents rot and worms, but it also prevents good adhesion of most caulking materials. Most good caulking requires a special primer on the teak before application. No matter how good the caulking, the time will come when it has to be removed and re-caulked. This is a long and nasty job.

Today, many teak decks are pre-made on a thin sheet of plywood. This pre-formed deck is epoxy glued to the underdeck or existing deck. This requires fewer screws, less maintenance, and reduces the chances of water entering the underdeck.

If maintenance of a teak deck does not discourage having it on a boat, consider its weight and color. Teak is a heavy wood that adds substantial weight above the waterline. Because teak is dark, it is hot under bare feet. Even when it turns gray, it is still hot in the tropics.

Another excellent non-skid material is ground walnuts or silica sand applied with a paint or epoxy coating. This does not have as pleasing an appearance as teak or the molded non-skid, but it is effective.

Personally, I like the non-skid product called Treadmaster. It is a corklike material that is purchased in sheets and can be epoxy glued to any deck. It has remarkable non-skid capabilities and is far stronger than I ever imagined. The disadvantages of this material are that it is almost too non-skid, and that it is uncomfortable to sit on without clothes. Also, like teak decks, it gets hot in direct sunlight.

The mast and rigging

Deck-stepped vs. keel-stepped masts

There are two ways a mast is installed on a boat. One is where the mast goes through the deck or cabin and sets on the keel. This is a keel-stepped mast. The other is a mast that is set on the deck or cabin top, with additional support beneath provided by a compression post, a bulkhead, or a crossbeam.

The keel-stepped mast

The keel-stepped mast is much better supported than a mast set on top of a deck or cabin top. The base of the mast is set on the keel, which will not compress or move, and it is supported where it goes through the deck or cabin top. If all the rigging were removed, the mast would still stand.

Since the mast is set on the keel, it must have something solid that will not compress or rot, between the mast base and the keel. This will prevent bilge water from settling on the mast base.

I have been to boat shows where the salesperson who is selling a boat with a deck-stepped mast tells me that if the keel-stepped mast loses its rigging, it will take out the cabin or deck when it falls over. This is absolutely absurd, unless the deck and cabin top are made paper-thin or of a material so weak that it would not even support human weight. Most masts are hollow. Being hollow, they will break at the point where they go through the deck or cabin; the only exception would be a solid mast of any material.

The keel-stepped mast is like a tree growing out of the center of the boat. It will always be there; hence, the boat's interior has to be built around it. To remove the mast, it must be lifted up the distance it is buried to the keel. This can be difficult if there isn't a crane available. It is not something that can be done in one's backyard.

Where the mast passes through the deck, a raised mast collar is installed. The mast must be properly aligned inside this collar, so it is not resting against a hard spot. After the mast is properly adjusted in place, it must be sealed to keep out water. On wooden masts, wooden wedges are used to center the mast in the collar; then, a waterproof mast boot is slipped over the collar to keep out water. The mast boot it sealed around the mast and the collar with sealant and hose clamps.

On aluminum masts, the wooden wedges may create too much of a localized hard spot. For this reason, I like thick rubber strips that are driven in between the mast and collar, around its circumference, until the mast is centered. After the mast is centered in the collar and supported by the rubber, a sealant is spread over the entire surface. Plenty of sealant must be applied to the mast sail slot. Over all this, the same mast boot is installed, sealed, and clamped.

The deck-stepped mast

The deck-stepped mast is necessary on boats with tabernacles. Tabernacles are used for raising and lowering the mast when trailering or going under bridges. Deck-stepped masts have the advantage that they can be removed from the boat without affecting the deck or cabin's watertightness.

Since the mast does not go through the boat into the interior, it opens more alternatives for the interior design: the tree growing out of the keel is gone.

The mast set on deck creates tremendous compression loads on the deck, its core, and the support between the deck and keel. Some boats have a compression post below the deck where the mast is stepped; this is like having a smaller mast in the same location. Other builders will put a bulkhead at this location for strength. Others will only reinforce the underside of the deck with a crossbeam. Regardless of the method used to take the compression of the deck-stepped mast, it has to be carefully engineered to take the compression loads from years of use.

Another concern is where the mast sets on the deck. I have seen boats where the deck has become saucer shaped from years of compression. This may permit water to enter where the mast step is bolted to the deck.

There is a well-known, older boat model that has the compression post set on top of a piece of steel shaped like an inverted U. This sets on the ballast, and its purpose is to keep the base of the mast out of the bilge water. The fiberglass liner covers this steel support. In time, the steel support rusted out and the mast collapsed it, breaking the mast. A huge hole had to be cut through the liner to access the steel support for replacement.

Mast material

Masts are made of wood, aluminum, or a modern fiberglass material like carbon fiber or Kevlar.

Wood

The wooden mast is more common on older wooden boats. It can be a solid wood mast, which is much heavier and perhaps stronger than a hollow mast. The hollow mast is usually made of laminated spruce or a vertical grain Douglas fir. Spruce is lighter and more common, but is becoming less available. A properly built wooden mast, made with a good long grain wood, will be as strong as—if not stronger than—an aluminum mast. From my own experience handling both wood and aluminum masts, I think the properly constructed wooden mast is stronger.

The wooden mast makes fastening hardware an easy job, as long as it is properly bedded. If a screw strips in the wood, a dowel can be glued in place to make it like new. The major problem with the wood mast is maintenance: to prevent water entering the fittings causing rot.

Aluminum

The aluminum mast is the most common mast used on boats today. It is strong and flexible like the wooden mast. Depending on the finish, it may require minimum maintenance. Some masts are anodized, which will prolong the time before corrosion becomes a problem. Most aluminum masts are painted with a linear polyurethane paint; properly prepared and applied, it will last many years before re-painting is necessary. The mast, however, will eventually corrode and require repainting.

Because the aluminum mast is a metal, it provides some natural reflection to radar. Aluminum is low on the galvanic scale, so it is susceptible to electrolysis. Any dissimilar metals must be properly bedded, including the fasteners and rigging. This is important because the fasteners are a different metal—like stainless steel—which causes electrolysis. This could eventually cause the fastener to fail, resulting in a serious problem.

If a fastener is stripped in the mast, it may be difficult to remove or replace. It cannot be plugged and re-drilled like the wooden mast; normally, a larger screw is required, or welding over the hole is necessary.

Aluminum is a great conductor of electricity, so a lightning strike may lead directly to an external ballast for dissipation. However, this will permit the lightning to enter the inside of the boat. If there is internal ballast, the mast can have lightning protection led outside of the boat. This will be discussed in more detail in another chapter.

Carbon fiber

Carbon fiber is a new material used for masts and is gaining popularity on cruising boats. Carbon fiber masts are exceptionally light and flexible, but very expensive to build. Like the aluminum mast, it may be a little more difficult to fasten hardware. If a screw strips, it is difficult to repair or replace. I think the only major disadvantage to this mast is the cost.

Standing rigging

It is not my objective to get into discussing metallurgical terms, metals, and alloys. However, I feel it is necessary to mention some basic differences in the most common materials used on boats, so that a boat owner can have a better idea of the best way to meet his or her particular needs.

Standing rigging wire, connections, and plates are made of either an alloy of stainless steel or an alloy of bronze. It is important that any boat owner should know the difference between brass and bronze.

They are both alloys of copper, with copper being the largest percentage of the alloy.

Brass is copper mixed with zinc. If you refer back to the galvanic scale, you will see that zinc is a strong anode; that is, it will sacrifice its electrons to any other more noble metal. Thus, brass should not be on a boat unless it is inside, protected from the elements.

Bronze is a mixture of copper and tin; it is much more resistant to corrosion or electrolysis. The more copper it has, the redder it becomes and is called red bronze. If silicone is added, it becomes silicone bronze. Adding manganese makes it manganese bronze, etc. Each alloy has its own advantage.

For standing rigging hardware, such as chainplates, I prefer to use silicone bronze for its resistance to fatigue and corrosion, as well as for its strength. When exposed to salt air or water, it protects itself by turning brown and will eventually get a green patina look. This is about as far as it will corrode. Some people do not like this appearance. Personally, I feel it has the classical nautical look that only bronze can produce.

Bronze is not used for standing rigging wire because it will stretch too much and does not have the required strength. It is most commonly used on boat hardware and fittings for the standing rigging, such as chainplates and turnbuckles.

Stainless steel is the most common metal used on standing rigging and related hardware. The problem is that stainless steel, unlike bronze, will fatigue and corrode more readily. Stainless can develop cracks at stress load points, like where chainplates go through the deck or where they are bent, as shown in Figure 30. These cracks will hold salt water, and corrosion will occur deeper into the crack, increasing the problem. This is called crevice corrosion.

Unfortunately, these little cracks cannot be seen by the naked eye and must be tested using special dyes and a strong magnifying glass. If the cracks are just below the surface or on the inside of a bend, the problem may never be detected, until it is too late.

Stainless steel is basically a mixture of iron and chromium. All stainless steel will rust to some degree if exposed to salt water in warm climates. The amount of iron determines how badly it will rust. Nickel is added to this alloy to make it more resistant to corrosion and to give it additional strength. This is referred to as a 300 series of stainless steel.

A variety of this alloy, which has less carbon, is 304 stainless steel. This is stronger and more resistant to corrosion. It is used mostly where higher strengths are required, like chainplates, tangs, and fittings for the standing rigging.

If molybdenum is added to this alloy, it becomes 316 stainless steel, which is yet more resistant to corrosion, but not as strong as the 304 stainless steel. The 316 stainless steel is used mostly on the standing rigging wire. Again, let me emphasize that 304 is stronger than 316, but also more corrosive. It can leave rust stains on the sails.

There are more and more variations to these alloys, improving their use. Most have brand names that are too numerous to mention.

Stainless steel standing rigging is wire or rod. The rod is stronger, so a smaller diameter can be used; this is important, especially on racing boats. The trouble with rod rigging is that there is a crevice corrosion problem at thread grooves. The rod must be threaded. It is where these threads are hidden inside the turnbuckle that the corrosion or fatigue occurs. It is almost impossible to detect, until it fails. However, there are some exceptions to this where threads are not used.

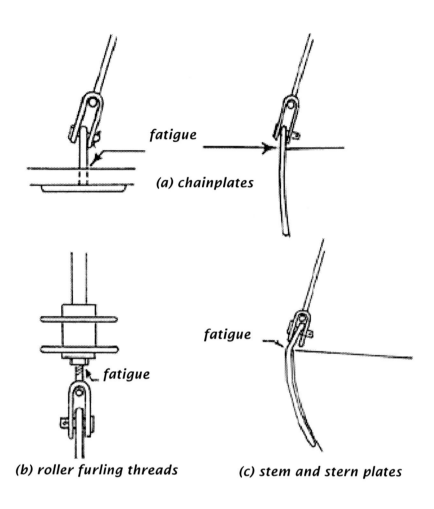

fatigue

(a) chainplates

fatigue

(b) roller furling threads

fatigue

(c) stem and stern plates

Figure 30. Stress fatigue points

Stainless steel wire comes in two common forms: 1 X 19 wire (see Figure 31) and 7 X 19 wire (see Figure 32). This refers to the number of stainless steel strands used to make the wire clusters.

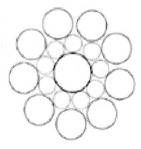

Figure 31. 1 X 19 wire

The 1 X 19 wire has a single core wire surrounded by 18 wires all twisted together as one single cluster. This is strong and stiff and most commonly used as standing rigging.

Figure 32. 7 X 19 wire

The 7 X 19 wire has 7 cluster strands made up of 19 wires each, all twisted together. This wire is flexible and not as strong as the 1 X 19 wire. The more flexible, softer wire is used as running rigging, such as wire halyards. This softer wire makes it possible to splice it to rope.

If the softer 7 X 19 wire is used for standing rigging, terminals and fittings can be fastened to the wire by wrapping the wire around a thimble, then connecting back to itself. The methods used for this connection are hand splicing, Nicro Press-type fittings, or cable clamps.

Splicing is an excellent method, but requires someone very knowledgeable in the process to do it successfully. Splicing without any wires exposed that could rip sails and skin is very difficult. This method is a great way to make the connection stronger, but it requires many hours of skilled splicing.

Another way to connect the softer wire is by using Nicro Press-type fittings. The wire is also wrapped abound a thimble; however, it is clamped to itself using a special sleeve that is compressed around the wire using a special tool. It is much easier to make this connection using this method rather than hand splicing, but it is not as strong.

There are two major advantages to the methods mentioned above: one is the lower cost, and the other is the fact that the owner can install it.

Another factor not usually considered is that the wire normally begins to fatigue at the extreme bottom of the thimble. Small, outside strands begin to break loose from the others. This is the first sign that the wire needs to be replaced. See Figure 33 (b).

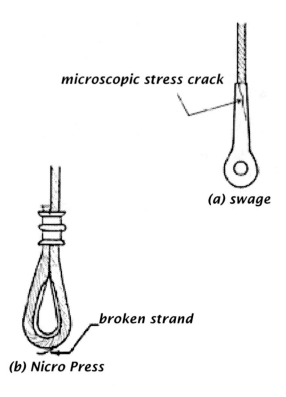

microscopic stress crack

(a) swage

broken strand

(b) Nicro Press

Figure 33. Stress points in rigging wire fittings

Swage terminals are normally used on the more rigid 1 X 19 wire. They are made of 304 stainless steel for strength or 316 for less corrosion. They are the most commonly used terminals on sailboats today. This terminal is formed with a hollow tube the same size as the 1 X 19 wire. The wire is pressed into the tube. The tube is then compressed around the wire using tremendous pressure created by a special hydraulic press. This is an extremely strong bond. If the proper terminal, wire, and pressure are used, the bond will never separate.

Depending on the boat's use, these swage terminals on the standing rigging should last many years. The problem comes from stress fatigue where the wire enters the terminal tube. These cracks cannot be detected by the naked eye. See Figure 33 (a).

When I entered Papua New Guinea, I got a job working in a copper mine on Bougainville Island. I took the opportunity to remove my mast and repaint it. While the mast was out of the boat, I had my standing rigging tested by the company's riggers. When it came back, almost every single swage fitting had hairline cracks.

I was really surprised, because I had only been cruising for four years, and the boat was only 6 years old. I closely inspected my rigging hardware and terminals every time I left on a passage that would take me to sea for more than two days. Unfortunately, these cracks are difficult to see.

The swageless terminal is more expensive than any of the above. They are identified by their brand names like Norseman, Sta-Lok, and others. The terminal has a split cone, which is slipped over the core of the 1 X 19 wire. The outside wires are bent over the back end of the cone. Then, it is pressed inside the threaded terminal base. A water-resistant sealant is added before a tapered cap is threaded down over the cone, pressing it against the formed inside of the terminal.

The end result is a very strong terminal fitting that will not have stress fatigue cracks from the hydraulic press, like in the normal swage fittings. These terminals can be installed by the owner and are simple to do, as long as directions are carefully followed.

Stainless steel threaded to itself may result in the metal bonding to itself. This is called galling of metal. You may have experienced this phenomenon. Have you ever attempted to remove a stainless steel nut from a stainless steel thread, found that it started to unthread, then froze, and that it could not be tightened or loosened? This is galling. For this reason, the turnbuckles should not be made of stainless steel, if the rigging threaded terminal is stainless. Most stainless steel rigging uses chrome plated bronze turnbuckles.

The standing rigging is attached to the boat's hull with chainplates, bow plates, and stern fittings. The rigging is attached to the mast using split tangs or plates, which should be insulated from the aluminum, if it is an aluminum mast. The wire between the mast plate and hull plates must have free movement in all directions to prevent stress on the fittings. This is accomplished by using toggles. This is an important point. Every boat should be closely inspected to see that there are no restrictions in the free movement in all directions, or stress fatigue will result.

Conclusion

I would like to conclude this chapter with a short story of how I found the boat that perfectly fit my own personal needs.

I decided that I needed to get rid of the *Marionette*, the 40-foot Anacapa sloop, and find a smaller boat that I could more easily handle alone or with one other person. I called Lyle Hess, who had designed the little Balboa 20 I enjoyed so much, as well as many other boats, including the famous *Seraffyn* and *Taleisin* of Lin and Larry Pardey. Lyle asked me to come over one morning to discuss my needs.

What a mind-awakening experience it was! I never realized how little I knew about boats. He took the time to explain many of the more important factors that make a safe offshore cruiser. He even mentioned some brand names I should look at. One was the Bristol Channel Cutter that he had designed in fiberglass. When he said it was 28 feet long, I concluded it was too small for me.

I began looking at some of the brands Lyle had mentioned. I also looked at many wooden boats. They all left me unemotional, cold, and discouraged. Most looked alike. Out of frustration, I decided to take a look at the 28-foot Bristol Channel Cutter Lyle had suggested.

The Sam L. Morse factory was in Costa Mesa, California, not far from where I was living aboard the *Marionette*. As I drove into the yard where the cutter was being built, I saw a bare hull sitting in the parking lot. "My God, what nice lines," I thought, as I parked my used Pinto wagon.

I walked up the stairs where Sam had his office. Sam was sitting behind his desk. He was nearly bald. I walked up to him and extended my hand. "Roger Olson," I said, "I'd like as much information as possible on the cutter."

He took a brochure from the top desk drawer and handed it to me. I skimmed the facts: 28 feet on deck, 37 feet overall with her bowsprit, 10-foot beam, a hull with a swept-back keel. The waterline was a respectable 26' 3", her draft 4' 10", 14,000-pound displacement, encapsulated internal ballast of 4,600 pounds of cast lead. She carried nearly 700 square feet of working sail, aluminum mast, stainless steel rigging, and a 13 horsepower Volvo diesel.

"Come on," Sam interrupted my reading, "you can see one under construction."

I followed him into the yard. As we entered a huge tin building, he said, "We get the hull and deck strength in the many layers of matt and roving which are hand laid and hand squeegeed between each layer."

We neared the boat hull where workers were wearing masks. "You can have any desired thickness by adding more layers," he continued. "This keel will be over one inch thick on the bottom of the keel and 5/8-inch to 3/4-inch at the turn of the bilge, leaving nearly a 1/2-inch at the top of the hull."

"Let's go take a look at another boat we're building," Sam said, "she's nearly finished."

I inhaled deeply as Sam continued to talk, "Most of the cutters are sold unfinished or as boat kits. Helps keep costs down and enables owners to finish them personally."

He nodded ahead, "This one, however, was ordered by an Australian doctor who wanted his boat completely finished and equipped."

A guy in paint-spattered jeans was painting the name *Kikorangi* across the transom. As I neared, I stopped dead in my tracks. She was beautiful. From the end of the boomkin to the tip of the six-foot bowsprit, her lines flowed in a smooth curve. In awe, I stepped closer, looking at all the teak. She had teak everywhere: on the decks, taffrail, cockpit coaming, bulwarks, walestrake, hatches, and skylight. Not only was all the exterior wood teak, but also the entire cabin interior was trimmed in teak. The workmanship was the best quality I had ever seen.

The solid bronze portlights gleamed. The full keel swept back gradually in a slow continuous curve to the transom-hung rudder. "Damn," I said, "she sure looks salty. She belongs on the sea. How does she sail?" I asked.

Sam shrugged. "I honestly don't know. Believe me, I'm as anxious as you to find out, because everyone asks the same question. Considering her 26-foot 3-inch waterline and large sail area, nearing 700 square feet, I'd predict she should be quite fast. That long bowsprit with jib and staysail should permit her to point pretty high and…"

Entranced with the cutter, I, quite simply, was in love. Minutes slipped by before I tried to ask casually, "How much you figure this *Kikorangi* will cost when completed?"

Sam stared at the boat, lifted his hands to rest on his hips and cleared his throat. "Our boats are not mass produced, you know. There are no assembly lines. We build to customer order exclusively, so we take great care. We use the best materials and the highest standard of construction."

Sam spoke slowly, but never losing his flow, he continued, "They're not cheap, because it costs more to build this way, by hand. As custom builders, we must use shipwrights to construct these boats. It's not like a production boat built with a fiberglass liner that 'snaps' together by a worker off the street. It takes one full year to build a completed boat." For a second he paused and then added, "These cutters aren't for everyone."

He'd talked around price, so I pushed. "Okay, how much for *Kikorangi*, with sails and all? Give me a sail-away number."

He did, and my knees shook. Hell, I could buy a brand new 35-foot production boat for that price, and this one was only 28 feet. I couldn't look away from her; she was the most beautiful boat I had ever seen. Here was my dream cruising boat, but—damn it—one I couldn't afford. Discouraged, I forced myself to thank Sam, assured him he'd hear from me, and climbed into my car.

A naked woman could have walked in front of me at that moment, and I wouldn't have noticed. My total concentration was on that boat. I wanted one and, by God, I would have one.

As I drove back down the freeway, my mind swam with pictures of the cutter and how well she was built, while on a deeper level, I kept hearing Sam's voice quoting the price. "I must have it," I thought, "that's that". Of course, I felt the same way the first time I saw Bo Derek. Like a mantra, I repeated, "I have to have her!" (A Bristol Channel Cutter, that is).

I felt I could afford to buy a hull and deck and finish the rest myself. I put the *Marionette* on the market, keeping the price low enough to sell, but steep enough to get me out of debt. I hung a hand-printed sign on the bow and waited for the line to form.

I went on a crash saving program, placing a large portion of my monthly paycheck into the bank, so I could draw upon it later. I learned to do without, to stay home nights, to eat out and drink less, and to spend money only on bare necessities. On weekends, I did odd jobs for other boat owners. I sold more personal items and excess gear off the *Marionette*. Then I started selling the metal sculptures that I had been making over the years, but had previously refused to sell. I made gold and silver jewelry from lost wax casting as well. I never claimed the title of an artist, but I seemed to be good at it, and it brought in extra cash.

Finally, the *Marionette* sold. Immediately, I went to see Sam and ordered a partially completed boat. I christened her *Xiphias*. My life has never been the same.

Chapter Four

ANCHORS AND ANCHORING

To write a book that uses technical terms and techniques is difficult. No matter what I write or how I write this and other chapters, there will be those who will feel I used the wrong technique, method, comment, or term. I need to remind the reader that the methods and opinions in this book are those of the author, based on my own experience. It is my purpose to relate what I learned so that future cruisers will not have to learn by bad experiences or by trial and error.

It becomes increasingly difficult when it comes to using nautical terms. Other countries use different words that have the same meaning as ours. Or, they may be the same word, but spelled differently. Some of these terms have become part of my nautical vocabulary. I will attempt to use American terms throughout, but I am certain that I will occasionally make a mistake.

In this chapter, I will use the words rope and line interchangeably. I realize that rope becomes line when it comes aboard a boat. However, when it is no longer on a boat, it returns to rope. It remains rope if it is on a spool or in a coil, even if aboard the boat. Depending on where you are from, the anchor rode may be called anchor rope or anchor line. When an anchor is deployed, its rode may be called anchor rope, not anchor line, until it is back on deck. It is interesting, though, that the ropes that tie the boat to the dock are always called dock lines, not dock ropes.

Having said that, if you feel that I use the wrong term, just try to understand my purpose.

Before I get into the technical information in this very important chapter, I would like to write about an experience I had during my first year cruising. It will illustrate what can happen unexpectedly, even when you are certain you anchored perfectly. As you read the following, try to imagine that you are in a similar situation and see what could go wrong and what you would have done differently. You may find that there was little that could have been done; it was just an unfortunate situation.

§

I had just returned to the harbor at Papeete, Tahiti, from one of my many trips to nearby Moorea Island. My intention was to anchor between an American 32-foot yacht named *Mintaka*, which was downwind, and another small boat from Australia, named *Eshepe*, which was upwind.

Because there are so many cruising boats in Papeete harbor, they all anchor using the Mediterranean method: the stern is tied ashore, and one or two anchors are set off the bow. The boats set relatively close together, so it is necessary to use two stern lines, one from each quarter, and two anchors set apart to prevent the boat from moving sideways.

As I approached, I yelled to see if there was anyone aboard the two boats. It was apparent there wasn't anyone aboard *Eshepe*, so I had no idea where her anchor was set. I saw an elderly gentleman aboard *Mintaka*, so I yelled over and asked, "Where is your anchor set?"

The elderly man yelled back, "We have a single anchor on a chain and rope rode set directly off our bow, out about 200 feet. We don't have a clue what *Eshepe* has out; they were already here when we arrived."

I considered the space between the two boats was small enough to justify two anchors set about 30° apart. The prevailing wind was light from the starboard beam of the boats already anchored. This would push me away from *Eshepe*, but onto *Mintaka*, and would make anchoring more difficult.

To make sure I had enough room to anchor and that there weren't any unexpected shallows or currents, I backed into the space where I expected to set.

Feeling confident that there was room and no obstacles, I motored out in front of *Eshepe*. When I was about 200 feet in front of her and slightly to her port, I dropped my 45-pound CQR off the bow in about 40 feet of water.

Slowly, I backed the boat up until I had about 225 feet of 5/16" chain paid out. As I motored in reverse, the wind kept pushing me toward *Mintaka*; I had to keep giving it a burst in forward to get me back in position. Fortunately, the bottom was soft mud, so the chain rode moved freely as I maneuvered.

Finally, when I was in position, I put the engine in neutral. The moment I stopped backing, the weight of the chain catapulted me forward. I motored back until I got into a position where I was anchored on the weight of the chain. Now, with the wind from my starboard beam, I was blown into *Mintaka*.

The owners of *Mintaka* were on deck watching my every move. They saw my problem and set fenders along their starboard side. The elderly man calmly said, "Toss me a line; you can rest against us while you take your stern lines ashore."

It all went well. With fenders between *Xiphias* and *Mintaka*, I coiled 300 feet of my stern anchor rope into the bottom of the cockpit footwell so it would run free off the top. I piled what I expected would be needed to reach shore into the dinghy. I rowed ashore and found bollards set in concrete all along the waterfront. Using a bowline, I tied a loop and slipped it over a bollard that was considerably upwind of my stern. I had to cross over the port stern line from *Eshepe*.

I returned to *Xiphias* and pulled in the slack until I was no longer resting against *Mintaka* and was centered between the two boats. I secured the line to my starboard stern cleat. As I pulled my stern line taut, my bow began falling off towards *Mintaka*. I ran forward and winched in enough chain so that I was now secure fore and aft with the wind against my starboard beam.

I returned to the cockpit and turned over the coil of rope so I could get to the other end. Leaving the excess rope in the bottom of the cockpit, I repeated the same procedure. I piled what I needed into the dinghy, rowed it ashore, and tied a loop around a bollard set to my port. It also crossed over *Mintaka's* stern line.

I returned to *Xiphias* and secured the line to the port stern cleat. Leaving the excess rope coiled in the bottom of the cockpit, I went forward and winched in some more chain until I was setting securely in the center between *Eshepe* and *Mintaka*.

I put my 25-pound Danforth anchor into the dinghy, followed by 50 feet of chain and several hundred feet of 5/8"nylon line. The bitter end of the line remained tethered to *Xiphias* as I rowed out the second anchor. Since this anchor was mostly line, I decided to use all 300 feet of line and the 50 feet of chain. I rowed out in front of *Mintaka* until I was out considerably further than their anchor and dropped mine.

I returned to *Xiphias*, pulled in all the slack, and tied it off to the port bow cleat. I continued to bring in more chain from the first anchor and line from the second until I felt *Xiphias* would not move much in any direction.

I sat there for a few moments to review what I had done. I looked around at the other boats. They all seemed to be about the same except that the boat upwind of "*Eshepe*" was quite close to her.

The owners of *Mintaka* hailed me over for a drink. I was ready. In their sixties, Charles and Nita were a very fit couple indeed. They were from Montana, where they had finished a partially completed boat. They sailed it to the Washington coast via the inland waterways.

As Charles explained all the details, I thought, "He's a typical cowboy-type, minus the hat." He had a full head of thick dark hair with some gray streaks. He was tall with broad shoulders; he had the rugged outdoor look, and his drawl produced images of chewing tobacco and wearing six shooters.

Nita was petite, svelte, and had a full head of gray hair cut just above her shoulders. She wore a continuous grin that made her look mischievous. They were two of the most pleasant cruisers I had yet to meet. They invited me to stay for dinner.

The next day, I met Roger on *Eshepe*. He was Australian, taking his time cruising the Pacific. He informed me that he had only one anchor set, and it was out about 150 feet. We both felt confident that my anchor would not interfere with his.

A few days later, on a very windy, warm, late afternoon, Charles and I sat on our respective bows drinking sundowner cocktails. We were both watching the huge waves coming through the main pass into Papeete. Charles yelled over to me and said, "Have you noticed the barometer has dropped considerably?"

"Yeah," I responded, "this wind may be the beginning of a storm heading our way."

Charles pointed toward the entrance through the pass, "Ya know those waves comin' through the pass must be at least 30 feet high."

Over the wind, I shouted, "Sure glad I'm not out there. I doubt any yacht could make it through the pass in these conditions."

"Good Christ," Charles yelled back, "the Moorea boat is going to try it."

Horrified, we both stared. The 90-foot steel motor vessel that transported cargo and passengers to and from Moorea was attempting to enter the pass.

As we watched in silence, we lost sight of it in the trough. Suddenly, it came high onto the crest. It was apparent that the waves were much higher than 30 feet, but how much higher was hard to judge. As it came off the crest, it suddenly broached. It didn't roll over, but instead, in the wink of an eye, was turned end for end. Thank God, it was still upright, going in the opposite direction, back out to sea.

I called over to Charles, "Now that was close. He's real lucky he didn't capsize."

"Look," Charles responded, "that idiot's going to try it again."

Sure enough, as we watched, the vessel returned to the pass. I couldn't help but wonder why he was so determined to enter in these conditions. There are other passes that lead into the lagoon that are far better protected. In fact, the local fishing boats returning to Papeete had all chosen an alternate entrance.

As the 90-footer approached the pass, it was lost in the trough once more, then rode high on the crest of a wave. This last wave caught it.

"Oh, God, he's going over," Charles screamed.

The bow pointed down the monstrous wave that dwarfed the vessel. The stern pointed high into the air. The bow buried itself into the water. I was sure she going to pitchpole, stern over bow! The crest of the wave lifted the stern, and the whole boat rolled on its side; then, it turned upside down. The waves continued to carry it into the pass. We could see only its bottom.

I jumped below to summon help on channel 16 of my VHF radio. Since I didn't know enough French to even say "Help!" I repeated, "May Day, May Day, Moorea tourist vessel overturned in the pass!"

No one answered. I kept on, but still no response. I decided to leave it to the French and hurried topside to see one of the fishing boats en route to give aid. I heard someone else try the radio and heard the corresponding silence that greeted the transmission. Soon a large tug moved out, but it was too late. The Moorea ferry was on the reef. I felt frustrated and powerless. All I could do was watch as other fishing boats rescued survivors. Later I learned that one person died in this mishap.

After things settled a bit, but still unnerved by the tragedy, I said to Charles, "Seems this storm's gradually shifting. Do you think it will be bringing those waves in our direction?" We looked to where the waves were being directed further down the beach.

"Naw," Charles said, "the reef extends a long way out the other side. It'll break up any major waves that enter the harbor."

As I studied the situation further, I thought, "I'm not sure he's right," but I decided not to worry.

It began to rain, so I went below to make dinner. As the night progressed, the anchorage grew rougher. Waves four to six feet high smashed onto rocks close behind my stern.

At 2300, in order to get away from the breakers, I let out a little on the stern lines and pulled in a bit on both bow anchors. Charles was doing the same thing. He yelled, "It's going to be a long night."

I looked up and down the row of yachts; all were violently pitching at various intervals; all had lights on. No one was asleep.

I went below to get out of the cold rain. Suddenly, I heard a loud crash. I darted back on deck to see that *Vengila*, the boat next to *Eshepe*, was broadside on the rocks.

I turned on the VHF and heard them calling for help. Topside, I stood helpless as the ketch banged her steel sides against the rocks, her mast leaning into the trees.

Xiphias was pitching so frantically that I had to hold on to keep from being knocked off my feet.

Immediately it seemed, the harbor tug arrived and threw a line to *Vengila*. A hawser followed and was secured to her bow. With a thrust of the throttle, the tug churned up the bottom and freed the ketch. As the tug towed the yacht to the main pier, I began to wonder if I had enough anchor rode out. I had brought a lot in making adjustments.

As I started to go below, Charles shouted, "Roger, you're going!"

In seconds, I was against *Mintaka*. My starboard anchor wasn't holding. It must have been tripped by *Vengila's* anchor or by the tug's prop wash.

Charles was desperately trying to fit fenders between our two boats. The wind and surge made holding me off impossible. My port side was banging against *Mintaka*. Out of synch, we pitched and rolled causing loud scrapes and the tearing of wood.

I ran to my anchor windlass and began pumping the handle to bring the chain up taut. "Please hold you big 45-pound CQR," I prayed, "please grab hold." *Xiphias* bucked wildly. Her bow aimed high and then almost dipped under water. Harder, I pumped harder. "Bang!" Something broke in the windlass, and chain began to run out. I grabbed what I could and threw it around the bitts, which held the chain fast.

I had set the clutch on the gypsy too tight, which didn't allow slippage against the sudden load from the steep waves.

Poor Charles was still struggling to fend me off, but it looked as if our boats would make slivers of each other.

Before the windlass broke, I had brought in at least 20 feet of chain, which included my snubber line with a chain hook at its end. As a rule, I put a length of rope between the last 20 feet of chain and the bow, then let the chain between bow and end of the snubber slacken. That way the snubber rope absorbed the stretch, preventing unexpected jerks that could break the chain. This worked well while anchored, but served no purpose when bringing it aboard.

I had to get the anchor to re-set. Leaning over the bow, I attached the chain hook that was tied to the end of my snubber line to the chain. I led the snubber line to the halyard winch on the mast and began cranking. Finally, the anchor took hold. Slowly, *Xiphias* pulled away from *Mintaka*. Fortunately, there was a lull in the wind which made it all easier. I continued to crank on the halyard winch to make sure the anchor had reset, but it didn't—it continued to drag.

While the remaining length of chain and anchor were heavy enough to pull me clear of *Mintaka*, my other anchor, set out to port to prevent movement to starboard, was ineffectual.

"I must get out now before the wind resumes," I thought. I started the engine and was going to put it in gear to move forward when I realized that *Xiphias* had moved much further aft and the stern lines were under the boat. If I put the engine in gear, the prop might catch the lines.

I would have to cast off my stern lines first. I'd retrieve them tomorrow. I had used one continuous 300-foot length of line from shore back aboard the boat, around the inside of my backstay, and back to shore on the other side. "Shit! I have to cut it," I thought. I seized my rigging knife, then noticed two people watching me from shore. Cupping my hands, I shouted, "Please undo those two ropes tied to those two posts."

In the darkness, I didn't know if they were French or native Tahitians. If they didn't understand, I'd cut. As I watched, each ran to a line. In a few moments, my stern was free.

Fortunately, the wind was still light as I piled the line into the cockpit. I still couldn't go anywhere until I raised my starboard anchor.

From out of nowhere, a young couple appeared in a dinghy. "Need a hand?" the guy asked, and without waiting for a response, tossed me his dinghy's painter line.

As soon as they boarded, the wind returned to push us back against *Mintaka* and back toward the rocks. The man and I fought to get the chain aboard.

I yelled to the woman, "Put the engine in forward to take up our backward movement." She shoved the engine into gear. This stopped our movement aft, but we still banged against *Mintaka*.

Furiously, the man and I got chain and anchor aboard. I yelled back to the woman, "Okay, motor forward, slowly, until we are past *Mintaka*. Try to steer to starboard." We began making slow headway, but the wind forced us hard against *Mintaka*.

My new friend was smart enough to pull in on the slack port anchor line as we moved forward so it would not get caught in our prop. I dashed aft and took the tiller from the woman and gave it more throttle in an attempt to move away from *Mintaka*.

In the meantime, Charles was exerting all his strength to keep the boats apart. Just as *Xiphias's* stern passed *Mintaka's* bow, the wind pushed us to port. Suddenly, the engine died. In a strangely calm voice Charles said, "You've caught my anchor line in your prop."

The stranger on the bow had my second port anchor line taut. This anchor was now holding and kept the bow from being blown completely back onto *Mintaka*.

Grabbing my underwater flashlight and facemask, I leaped over the side. In the dark, dirty water, I saw nothing. *Xiphias* rose above me one second, then banged down on top of me the next. I shone my light in the direction of the prop and tugged myself down along *Mintaka's* anchor line. There, I could just see the prop. It had only two wraps. I worked to release it, but it was far too tight. I tried to spin the prop, but there was too much pull on the anchor rope.

Xiphias arched high above me, at least six feet. To keep from being lifted too fast, I let go of the anchor line. I swam backwards, but not fast enough. *Xiphias* beat down on my shoulder, pushing me under the surface. I touched bottom just as I opened my mouth. Muddy water filled my mouth and throat. I shot to the surface and coughed, retched, and for a few seconds, couldn't breathe. This wasn't going to be easy, but I must succeed or *Mintaka's* anchor line will be cut and break.

I grabbed *Mintaka's* anchor line and yelled up to Charles, "Can you try to give me a little slack?"

"Hell," he answered, "if I give you slack, I'll be on the rocks." I heard a quiver in his voice as he said, "Waves are breaking at my stern now."

I yelled back, "If you wait until I dive, then let out a few feet, I can have it released in a second; there are only two wraps. Then, you can bring it back taut without losing any stern way."

Charles, still calm as if discussing fishing techniques, answered, "When you're ready."

I waited for a momentary lull in the wind, inhaled deeply, stuck the flashlight in my mouth, and submerged. I pulled myself down to the prop. Damn, *Xiphias* rose again. I would have to stay with her. As she yanked me up, my mask ripped off my face, but at that instant, I felt slack line in my hand. Seeing absolutely nothing, I gave a quick twist.

It was free! I held on to *Mintaka's* anchor line as *Xiphias* continued to rise. I must get out before she descends. I was too late. She whammed hard on my head and shoulders pushing me down fast. Again, I felt the bottom. Everything went black.

Dimly, I realized I was grasping something and someone was speaking. I couldn't move.

"Are you all right?"

Stunned, I peered up through the blur of salt-water eyes. As if disembodied, I saw my arm stretched upward; someone had hold of it and was tugging. That someone, this stranger, was leaning over the taffrail and kept repeating, "You all right?"

Thankful to be alive, I answered, "Think so." With his aid, I climbed aboard *Xiphias*. By now, we had moved parallel to the wind, 90° to the boats, and swinging free on her remaining port anchor. We were safely away from the other boats and the surf.

Charles called out from his bow to see if I was okay. I didn't want to yell. There was too much noise with the wind blowing and the sound of the waves crashing on the rocks; I gave him a thumbs up and a wave.

As my senses returned, I assured the stranger and his wife that I was fine, only a bit lightheaded.

"Well, if you really are okay, we have to go look after our own boat." And the couple jumped into their dinghy and started off.

I held on to the shrouds as *Xiphias* rolled with the swell. "I can't begin to thank you. I'll see you when this mess is over. Which boat is yours?"

From out of the darkness came the answer, "*Vela*."

Aware that if the wind changed course again, I would collide with other yachts, I went through the arduous task of raising the Danforth anchor. I motored to the center of the bay, away from everything, and dropped it. If I had to move, I would, but now I needed rest. To hell with the harbor rules. I poured myself a stiff drink and collapsed in my berth.

At sunup, a man on a tugboat shouting in French awakened me. I needed no interpreter to get his meaning. I signaled that I would return to my original spot.

In calm waters and non-existent wind, I set my anchors again, but this time I used all the rode I had available. I ran separate stern lines around the bollards back to the boat, so I could cast off from the boat if necessary. By this time, Charles appeared on deck to say, "Come over for breakfast."

We discussed the problems that occurred. I originally let out 225 feet of chain, but about 50 feet of that was piled on the bottom. This prevented me from swinging into *Mintaka*. I brought in more to take up the slack after securing my stern lines. When the waves were forcing *Xiphias* back towards the rocks, I let out more stern line and pulled in more anchor chain to move me away from the rocks. I suspect I only had about 100 feet of chain set in 40 feet of water. No wonder I dragged. However, the problems could have been the results of the tug pulling *Vengila* off the rocks.

The damage to both our boats was repairable. It took me a week to repair *Mintaka's* wooden rub rail. That week was the beginning of a long-term friendship that lasts till this day.

§

I consider this the most important chapter in this book. More boats are lost as a result of poor anchoring techniques than for any other reason. Unfortunately, most sailors think it is simply a matter of setting an anchor, backing down so it doesn't drag, and that's it.

Most areas of the States do not experience violent, unexpected squalls that can hit without notice in the middle of the night. If the correct anchor and rode is used, if it is set correctly, and if the appropriate scope is deployed, the chances are the anchor will not drag. However, it might. No one knows for sure what the anchor has grabbed unless someone dives on it.

I remember having a conversation with a sailor who had little cruising experience, but had all the answers. The comment was made, "an anchor will never drag if it is set properly and has enough scope." I thought about this and remembered the number of times I was sure I had anchored correctly, but still dragged. I do not believe there is any way to set an anchor and be absolutely certain it will not drag. There are too many factors that could cause it to drag. Anchor the best you can; then, if there is a change in the wind direction or current, check to make sure it is still set. Even diving on it is not an absolute guarantee that it won't drag. All we can do is anchor as well as we can, and keep a skeptical eye open to the possibility that it may drag.

If you cannot afford insurance for your boat, spend at least one year's premium on good anchors and anchoring equipment. *This is not the place to cut corners.*

This chapter is broken down into different sections. Basically, it is in two parts: the anchoring hardware and equipment, and anchoring suggestions and techniques.

A common error many sailors or beginning cruisers make is choosing the wrong anchor for the situation and conditions. New anchor designs continue to show up on the market. There is no way I can cover them all. Therefore, I have listed the most common designs, which may include different brands with radically different qualities.

Anchor types and their use

When you read the material about a particular anchor and its holding ability, the information is normally provided by the manufacturer's own tests. These tests are generally done in the most ideal conditions and on the bottom that best suits the design. If you can find an independent study comparing various anchors in various bottoms and conditions, it will have more credibility.

When you think of an anchor, most sailors only look at its holding ability. In normal anchoring situations, that's all that may be required. However, in tropical anchorages, an unexpected squall may bring strong winds and waves from a different direction. This may create pulling forces on the anchor from another angle. Depending on the bottom, some anchors will pivot with the pull, while others will not. Some will even break away from the bottom and will drag until they reset. For this reason, some anchors are better in different bottoms and directions of pull.

I will attempt to discuss the advantages and disadvantages of the most common designs. This will not cover all the makes or manufacturers of a particular design, so there may be some considerations that are not mentioned.

Navy-type

This is the most common of anchor designs, shown in Figure 34. When people think "anchor", it is this design that generally comes to mind. The reason is that it is the type used on large vessels and readily seen hanging off the bow of Navy ships. These anchors are similar to the fluke design discussed later. The major difference is that the flukes are rounded on the Navy-type; it has less holding ability, but it is much stronger and heavier.

Big ships use this anchor for its weight and strength, not for its holding ability. If the anchor begins to drag, the ship motors into the wind or raises the anchor. This is not so easy for the pleasure craft that does not have someone on watch 24 hours a day.

Figure 34. Navy-type anchor

These Navy-type anchors have all the disadvantages of the fluke-type anchor mentioned below and few—if any—of the advantages. What I like about this anchor is its strength and weight. These anchors are readily available and normally inexpensive. However, they do not belong on a pleasure craft because they just do not hold well enough.

Fisherman, luke and yachtsman-type

There are other names and designs for this type of anchor, but they are similar in principle. The crown is shaped into an arc with pointed, flattened flukes or palms at both ends, as shown in Figure 35. At the inside center of the crown is the shank. The shank may be welded, forged, or cast to the crown. At the upper end of the shank, opposite from the crown, is the stock. The stock passes through the shank at 90° to the crown. The stock forces the crown to turn, so one of its flukes must grab the bottom.

Figure 35. Fisherman, luke and yachtsman-type anchor

Most designs have removable stocks, so they store flat. They can be assembled rapidly, but not so quickly that they can be relied upon in an emergency.

The flukes at the ends of the crown have a small surface area, so its holding ability in soft sand and mud is limited. However, because of its design, it will grab on to rock and coral with less chance of being fouled than other anchors.

Some cruisers carry this type anchor as a storm anchor, because these anchors are large, heavy, and easily stored in the bilge.

Personally, I do not like this anchor for several reasons. For its weight and size, it has poor holding ability in the most common bottoms. This design is prone to being fouled by its own chain or the chain from another boat's anchor. The stock, being 90° to the crown, forces the crown's fluke into the bottom. This will always leave the other half of the crown and the other fluke sticking above the bottom's surface. If the boat swings 360°, its own chain will wrap around the exposed crown. If the wind picks up, the chain may be pulled like a knot around the crown. The wide fluke may prevent the chain from slipping off the tip of the crown, so it may never reset.

Danforth, performance, fluke-type

This anchor comes in many different makes and designs. Basically, it is like the Navy-type, but with flat, wider flukes, as shown in Figure 36. The flukes are welded to both ends of a rod. The shank pivots up and down about 32° in both directions around the center of this rod. Thus, when the anchor lies flat on the bottom, the flukes want to pivot downward. When there is pull on the anchor, the flukes' points begin to dig into the bottom. Depending on the bottom, the flukes may pull the anchor deep indeed. These designs set quickly if the bottom is soft.

Figure 36. Danforth, performance or fluke-type anchor

Since this is a relatively flat design, the anchor will often set below the bottom's surface, making it impossible to be tripped or fouled by its own chain or the chain from another boat. However, if the bottom is hard rock or coral, it may not set as deeply and could be fouled by its own chain.

This design is one of the best holding anchors in soft mud or sand in a straight-line pull. I do not feel it should be used in rock, coral, grass, clay, or a hard-packed sand bottom.

After the anchor is properly set, changes in wind or current will be swinging the boat, so the pull on the anchor is from a different direction. If it is soft mud or sand, the anchor will pivot with the pull. However, if it is rock, coral, grass, clay or packed sand, it may not pivot and will break itself out from its hold. If the bottom is soft mud or sand, it will quickly reset. This is not a problem as long as there is room for the boat to drift back until it sets.

The problem occurs if the anchor breaks loose and catches a piece of rock, coral, clump of clay or grass between the shank and the flukes. This would hold the flukes in that position. As the anchor breaks out and turns upside down, the flukes will not pivot down to reset.

The fluke-type anchor may not penetrate grass, hard clay, or packed sand to set deep enough to hold in a blow. This is a concern. It may hold while backing down with some power, but if it does not continue to bury as the pull increases, the anchor may pop out of the bottom when the wind or tide shifts.

This brings up another point. As mentioned earlier, when the boat swings with the wind or change of tide, the anchor will not pivot with the boat, unless it is a soft bottom. The cheaper anchors with mild steel shanks will bend, while those that are dropforged or tempered will not. You will pay considerably more for the better anchor. If this type anchor is going to be the primary anchor, used by itself, the better anchor will be well worth the extra money. However, if the boat is permitted to swing, I do not recommend this type of anchor as the primary anchor, regardless of its cost or the type of bottom.

I do not feel good about this design in aluminum. The lightweight aluminum will not be as strong as forged or tempered steel, so the shaft would bend more readily if the pull were from a different direction. The advantage of the aluminum anchor is its lightness, making it easy to handle and deploy. Also, some can be disassembled for ease of storage. It is the weight of the anchor's flukes that will force the tips down into the bottom. I feel the fluke-type anchor should be built out of as strong a material as possible and have some weight to it.

I like the fluke-type anchor, but I have had my share of problems with it. I would like to share a short story about the first time I learned about one of the disadvantages of its design.

§

It was during my first months cruising aboard *Xiphias*. I was in the Marquesas Islands and wanted to go ashore to buy some carvings and painted Tapa. The wind was light, blowing on shore. I set a single 25-pound Danforth off the bow, then let the boat pivot around facing into the wind. I was not concerned because I knew the Danforth had excellent holding power in sand on a straight-line pull.

While ashore, the wind shifted, and I saw my boat slowly being blown away from the island out to sea. I jumped into my dinghy and rowed toward my dragging boat at a speed someone could have water skied behind.

As soon as I reached *Xiphias*, I started the engine. The anchor hung down, touching nothing in the deeper water. I brought it aboard and found a baseball size piece of coral caught between one fluke and the shank, so it would not move up or down. Apparently, when the wind shifted and the boat swung 180°, the anchor broke loose with this piece of coral caught in the flukes. It never would have reset.

I have seen many similar situations on other boats. It has happened to me, too, on more than this one occasion.

Bruce or claw-type

The Bruce or claw-type anchors are solid, with nothing that pivots, as shown in Figure 37. Most are cast, providing substantial strength. It is shaped like a claw so it grabs the bottom. The design allows the anchor to set quickly in sand or mud bottoms. Like the fluke anchor, when it is set, there is little above the bottom surface to catch its own or another boat's anchor chain.

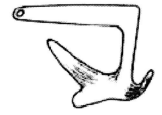

Figure 37. Bruce or claw-type anchor

This anchor, like the fluke-type anchor, is best in sand and mud and should not be used in coral, rock or grass. This does not mean it won't set or hold in these bottoms; it simply implies that there could be problems.

If the boat swings, the same problems that exist for the fluke-type anchors apply to the claw-type anchors as well: the claw-type will swing with the boat if the bottom is soft, but may break out if the bottom is hard, rock or coral. If something gets trapped in the claw, it may never reset.

The anchor may set in grass, but it depends on the thickness of the grass. In order for this anchor to hold, it must get below the grass surface. If it grabs a large clump in its claw, it will not properly set. The grass may hold the anchor in mild conditions, but if it is just the grass holding it, the anchor could break loose with the clump of grass in its grasp and never reset.

The same applies to a clay bottom. The anchor may set well, but as the boat swings, the anchor may not swing because of its strong grasp to the clay bottom. When the pull is near 180°, the anchor may break loose with a clump of clay held firmly by the claws and never reset.

I do not feel the claw-type anchor should be used in rock or coral. The main reason is that the claw shape can grab a rock or piece of coral like a clump of grass or clay and never properly set or reset.

Because of its shape, this type of anchor is more difficult to store than other anchors. However, its design and hardy construction make it relatively expensive.

I like the claw's quick and strong holding ability, but like the fluke anchor, I feel it belongs in a straight-line pull and should not be used in a situation where the boat will swing. If the bottom were soft, this would be less of a concern.

I have seen several situations where this problem of grabbing something in its claw caused the boat to drag. One was in French Polynesia, shortly after the storm mentioned previously had passed.

§

I was anchored behind the reef on Moorea Island in French Polynesia, with two anchors deployed off the bow. The reason for two anchors was that the bottom was shallow soft sand over hard coral, so one anchor wouldn't bury deep enough to hold well in severe conditions.

One day, a trimaran anchored some distance from me. I saw them deploy an anchor and back the boat down until it was set. Then, they all went ashore. After a few hours, the wind picked up. I watched the trimaran slowly move backwards. I wasn't sure if it was dragging or if it was just the chain stretching out. Soon, it was apparent—it was dragging.

Steve on *Blown Away* and I both rowed over to see what we could do. There was no one aboard, no other anchor on deck, no key in the ignition, and the boat was locked tight. It was apparent that we did not have time to get an anchor off our own boats. The trimaran was moving quickly towards the beach. Fortunately, it was mostly sand.

The boat hit harder than expected. We didn't know quite what to do because the owners were not aboard. If we brought in the anchor, they might think we did something to cause it to drag. Also, we had no idea if the boat was damaged.

We went to Steve's boat, which was much larger and had a bigger engine than mine. We raised his anchor and motored over near the trimaran. We were considering towing it back out to deeper water, but if the boat was holed, it would make matters even worse.

Fortunately, the owners returned before we did anything. We anchored near them and went ashore to assist. As soon as they went aboard and unlocked the companionway, they discovered the thin plywood center hull had been pierced by a piece of coral. She was slowly taking on water. We were lucky we hadn't towed her off to deeper water.

I dove down to check their anchor. It was a large Bruce and it had a piece of coral that fit perfectly into its claws. Apparently, the coral had been attached to the bottom. The anchor grabbed it and held while they backed down. When the winds increased, the coral must have broken loose, and the anchor would not reset with the piece of coral in its grasp.

I have heard many similar stories from fellow cruisers. Even though it has this limitation, some still swear by their claw-type anchors for their quick and strong holding ability.

CQR, plow-type

This anchor looks like and works like a plow, as shown in Figure 38. There are two types: one in which the head of the anchor or fluke pivots sideways, and one which is solid and will not pivot, such as the Delta-type shown in Figure 39.

Figure 38. CQR or plow-type anchor

The plow-type anchor is not the best holding anchor. Because this anchor is shaped like a plow, it holds like a plow. It will slowly drag in a soft bottom if there is a substantial pulling load.

This design is what I consider to be an all-bottom anchor. Because of its plow shape, it will bury beneath grass and will not grab and hold coral or rock to prevent it from resetting. However, this anchor does not have a good reputation for setting in a hard-packed sand bottom. Because the tip is large, without a sharp point, it may skip over the hard bottom and may never penetrate its surface. If it does take hold, it won't hold well unless it can bury deep.

The CQR or plow-type anchors have additional weight added to the point on the head of the fluke, which improves its ability to set quicker. The CQR or the plow with the head that pivots will set a little quicker than the plow with the solid head. Both types have equal holding ability after they are set.

Figure 39. Delta or plow-type anchor

There are many manufacturers of these anchors, and care should be given to check the material used on the shank. The ones that are high tensile or dropforged will not bend. Those that are cut out of mild steel plate will bend. If the shank is ever bent, it will have difficulty setting on the curved side.

There are rare situations when this type anchor will land on its head, upside down. If the bottom is smooth, it may drag indefinitely without flipping over onto its side.

I prefer the CQR plow as a primary anchor for several reasons. It is the design that has the least possibility of fouling on its own chain. It will set in any bottom even though it may take longer to set. It will not break out of the bottom when the boat swings and there is pull from a different direction.

In all my years of cruising, there were only two incidents when my CQR seriously fouled. One was between Papua New Guinea and Australia, which I will discuss later in this chapter. The other was in Malaysia, when I was anchored up a river where the current took precedence over the wind.

§

I dropped my CQR on all chain and backed the boat down until I was confident it was set. The bottom was soft mud, so if I backed down too hard, it would just plow the bottom. With the weight and pull on the anchor, it took time to set deep enough to hold properly.

I stayed there for several days without a problem. One night, there was a squall that came through with gusts exceeding 40 knots. It looked like I was slowly dragging. I figured the plow was plowing in the soft mud, so I let out more chain. I continued to drag, and it seemed a bit faster. I started the engine and put it in gear to take the load off the anchor. In about 20 minutes, the squall passed, and I went back to bed.

The next morning, I decided to check to see if my anchor was holding. I started the engine and put it in reverse until I felt all the slack in the chain was gone and it was taut. I gave it more throttle; sure enough, I was moving backwards.

I decided to raise the anchor and reset it somewhere else. As I was bringing it up off the bottom, I noticed it was unusually heavy. When it broke the surface, I could see a piece of concrete wedged in the curve of the fluke. It was the type of concrete used as tire stops in parking lots. The CQR had grabbed it in the center. It was wedged in tight. No matter how hard I tried to kick it loose, it would not release its grip.

I set another anchor to hold me while I attempted to remove this chunk of concrete. I got into my dinghy and began hammering on it with a hammer and cold chisel. It took half an hour to finally get it free.

I consider this situation rare. However, it does illustrate how any anchor, no matter the design, can get fouled.

Grapnel-type

This anchor has a series of curved flukes on the end of a shank, as shown in Figure 40. Some have just curved rods that hook something hard, while others have cast steel flukes shaped like a pointed spoon. Those with spoon-like flukes are cast steel and have better holding ability in a soft bottom than the ones with curved rods. Even the spoon-shaped flukes on the grapnel are too small, with minimum surface area, to provide adequate holding for a large boat in a soft bottom.

Figure 40. Grapnel-type anchor

The grapnel anchor usually is available with flukes that fold, which makes them easy and safe to store. However, they are not strong enough to really hold a boat under a load.

Because it folds and is light, I like this anchor for the dinghy. Since the dinghy is light, the grapnel will hold it without danger of breaking off one of the flukes.

Basically, the grapnel just hooks on to something on the bottom. Even if it grabs on to rock or coral, it may break loose if the boat swings. This anchor is normally used when anchoring temporarily, like when fishing or doing temporary repairs.

I think every boat should have a grapnel aboard. The time may come when it is needed to snag a chain or rope rode that was cast off in a hurry or by accident.

Anchor size

The size of an anchor should be based on the displacement and windage of a boat, not on its length. If there are waves slamming against the hull, it is the displacement or weight of the boat that will be pulling against the anchor. If there is wind with the waves, add the force of the wind against the exposed surface. Therefore, choosing the correct size anchor to use will depend on the conditions and the weight and configuration of the vessel.

Every boat should carry at least three anchors for general use. If the boat is large enough, a storm anchor may also be stored below decks.

The primary anchor is carried on the bow ready to deploy instantly. It should be the strongest of the three anchors. It should permit the boat to swing freely 360° or more without worry of fouling its own chain or that of another boat. This anchor should pivot as the boat swings.

The secondary anchor can be any good holding anchor, because it is usually used in conjunction with the primary anchor, normally in a bow and stern situation. For this reason, the primary consideration is holding ability. However, if the secondary anchor is to be used off the bow without a stern anchor, careful consideration must be placed on its ability not to be fouled by its own chain or drag when the boat swings.

The tertiary anchor, like the secondary anchor, is normally used in a straight-line pull, so holding ability is the primary concern. Personally, I prefer the tertiary anchor to be the same design as the primary anchor, but smaller. The reason for this is that it can substitute for the primary anchor if necessary.

It is apparent that I feel there are really only three anchors to be considered for the mother boat. I will list the size I recommend as the primary anchor for the approximate displacement weight of the boat. If the anchor will be a secondary or tertiary anchor, its size could be slightly reduced.

Since there are different makes for each type anchor and sizes will vary, use the following table only as a rough guide. If you have to choose a different size, always consider the larger.

Displacement	plow-type	fluke-type	claw-type
8,000 #	25 #	15 to 20 #	15 #
15,000 #	35 #	20 to 30 #	20+ #
20,000 #	45+ #	30 to 40 #	30+ #
35,000 #	65+ #	40 to 50 #	40+ #
45,000 #	95+ #	60 + #	60+ #

Table I. Displacement and anchor weight

I consider it most important that a second anchor be on deck and ready to deploy in an emergency. There are many reasons for this. For example, if the owners are not aboard, someone else can set the anchor.

On *Xiphias*, I carried a Danforth fluke-type anchor against the port bulwarks. I stored a 2" X 6" X 8' long board between the bulwark stanchions, forward, inside the shrouds. This provided a pocket to hold the anchor and 75 feet of chain. When it was necessary to tie alongside a dock with pilings, I could use this board as a fender board.

The anchor was set on its side with the shank facing forward and the stock up. I installed a stainless steel ring around the aft lower shroud that slipped over the anchor's stock, holding the anchor tightly against the shroud. I also installed rubber chair leg guards to both ends of the stock to protect the deck.

Most of the 75 feet of chain was stored in this pocket next to the bulwarks. The chain ran over the lifeline, around and under the whisker stay, to the deck pipe. Just inside the deck pipe, the chain was attached to the rope. This kept the rope out of the sun when not being used.

Where the chain left the bulwark pocket, a small line held the chain to the base of a lifeline stanchion to keep it from moving. The line around the chain was tied with a slipknot for quick release. Where the chain passed over the lifeline, there was another piece of small line that held it in place with another slipknot.

To deploy the anchor, I had to release the slipknot holding the chain at the base of the lifeline stanchion and the one on top of the lifeline holding the chain. Then I had to lift the stainless steel ring off the anchor stock. At that point, it was simply a matter of tossing the anchor overboard and paying out rode. It took about 20 seconds.

This system saved my boat, and possibly my life, in a flash flood in New Zealand. I would like to relive the experience with you, so you can see the importance of such a set-up.

§

It was pouring rain. It began about four hours earlier. There was thunder and lightning, which frightened my cat *Pintle*. He ran to hide behind some sail bags in the forepeak. The rain was heavier than I had ever experienced. It was so dense that I couldn't see through it until there was a lightning strike. I wasn't worried, because I was securely tied between two pilings up the Keri Keri River in New Zealand. I remember thinking how glad I was that I wasn't at sea.

I coaxed *Pintle* from his hiding place with a tasty treat. I lay down and held him for a while to comfort him, or more honestly, to comfort both of us. His warm, soft body was snuggled between my body and my left arm. His head pushed into my chin. I could hear and feel his calming purr. We both were totally relaxed.

I had spent the day installing a new interior on *Mintaka*. They were tied a few pilings upriver from me. We had an early start and worked until well after dark. When I had finished for the day, they gave me a few gin and tonics. I returned to *Xiphias* to prepare a quick dinner. The drinks plus dinner made me drowsy, so I was ready to go to sleep with *Pintle* snuggled against me.

The pelting rain, intense thunder, and lightning was keeping me awake, so I grabbed the book I had started several days ago. Suddenly, I had an inspiration. I had begun taping a message to my girlfriend on the cassette recorder the previous night. This would be an excellent time to continue taping so she could hear the rain and thunder in the background. It would make it more realistic.

I spoke into the microphone telling her about progress on *Mintaka's* interior, about Charles and Nita's kindness, about *Pintle*, and the unusually heavy rainstorm.

My words flowed easily, freely. Suddenly, I was abruptly interrupted as *Xiphias* jerked first to port, then to starboard. It happened again and again, each time more rapidly and violently.

I shrugged on my foul weather jacket and noted it was just past 2300. I realized that this deluge hadn't abated in over eight hours. I went on deck to see what was causing the sudden jerking motions.

The once docile river was flowing swiftly, so swiftly that *Xiphias* was steering herself back and forth into the raging current. I secured the tiller amidships, so the rudder wouldn't zigzag us back and forth. I let out more stern line, so she would more easily point directly into the strong current. I turned to go below and saw a light on *Mintaka's* deck. Charles was three pile moorings upstream from me. A small boat was ahead of me, with his stern line tied to the same piling as my bow line. There was a vacant mooring or set of pilings ahead of him. *Mintaka's* stern line was tied to the front piling of the vacant mooring. Off Charles's bow, there was no piling, so he'd set two anchors.

I cupped my hands and yelled, "Everything all right?"

"Anchor's dragging a little, but think I'm okay," came Charles's reply.

There was a bolt of lightning. I could see what appeared to be an unmanned boat drifting broadside down river towards *Mintaka*.

I yelled, "Charles... a boat... coming..."

There was nothing Charles could do. The boat bashed hard into *Mintaka*. Through the sound of the storm, I could hear wood crunching. The unmanned boat headed towards me. My dinghy was tied alongside, and it would be crushed or torn away. I released the clip holding it to the lifeline, ran it back to the stern, and re-clipped it.

Incredibly, without touching, the boat passed and vanished into the darkness. I pulled my hard dinghy, *Fillet of the Xiphias*, on deck and lashed it to the inside of the shrouds on the port side. This gave me free movement on the foredeck, just in case I had to cast off.

With the next lightning flash, I saw *Mintaka* broadside to the current and moving downstream. No, she was swinging around on the piling where her stern was tied. She did 180°. She now set in the vacant mooring with her stern pointing up stream.

"Charles," I yelled, "what can I do?"

"Both my anchors didn't hold, but my stern line's holding fast to the pile," Charles replied.

Mintaka, a Dreadnaught 32, has a large outboard rudder like the one on *Xiphias*. That rudder was now taking the full force of the current, which put severe pressure and strain on the rudder and its fittings.

"Can you bind your rudder amidships?" I yelled out.

"No," he answered, "you have my tiller." Right. We had stored it on my boat to make room for all the wood to redo his interior. There was no way I could get it to him.

Xiphias continued to whip back and forth on her pile mooring. I let out a little more slack on the stern line, hoping to reduce the sudden jerks.

Through the rain I heard Charles, "Another boat's coming down on us."

The rain was so dense I couldn't see anything. Every few seconds, the sky was lit by lightning, making it possible to see. I caught a glimpse of not only the large boat, but also several smaller ones tearing down river with it.

We were moored on the inside of a hairpin turn of the river, probably the worst location to be rammed by floating objects in a current out of control.

Wham! A 44-foot sailboat slammed hard against *Xiphias*, grinding and tearing. Then, like a ghost monster, it was gone in the darkness.

Charles's voice was faint as I strained to listen, "Current's much too strong against my stern. I managed to get a line around the piling off my bow. I'll release my stern line. We'll swing down alongside the boat in front of you. Then, I'll try to let out enough line to drift back close enough to you so you can hand me my tiller."

As I tried to interpret Charles's words, a lightning flash revealed that *Chucklyn*, a Canadian yacht, was being swept broadside down the middle of the river; surely she was moving at well over ten knots.

I could see Carl and Lynn on deck. I called out, "You all right?"

"We've lost all anchors," he answered. "Our steering is jammed, and a line's snagged around our prop."

In the drenching rain, I stood motionless, feeling helpless as I watched *Chucklyn* head for imminent disaster.

As soon as *Chucklyn* passed in the darkness, I watched as Charles released his stern line and rapidly swung around, banging hard against the boat in front of me. Even with his fenders alongside, it sounded like it was a hard hit.

His bow now faced upstream. He attempted to adjust the fenders between the two boats. He slowly let out on the bow line. I grabbed his tiller and climbed out on to my bowsprit. I stared down at the roaring current. This was not the time to drop the tiller or fall overboard.

The river had risen considerably. I had wrapped my mooring lines around the piles and had led them back to the boat, so I could cast off from on deck if necessary. When I first did this, the line was horizontal, even with deck level. Now it was under water at a 40° angle. The river had risen considerably. There was at least eight feet of pile post still above water, so I wasn't too worried about the river rising above it.

As I sat out on the bowsprit waiting for Charles to reach for his tiller, I saw other boats, trees, and debris swirl past me at incredible speed. Suddenly, I noticed the pile in front of me was no longer eight feet above water level. In only seconds, four feet had vanished.

"Charles, the water's rising," I yelled.

Terrified, I watched my bow line become nearly perpendicular. I jumped back on deck, tossed Charles's tiller aside, untied the bow line and started letting it out, so *Xiphias* would lift with the rising water.

Seconds later, the piling was so far below the surface, I couldn't see a trace of it. I was certain that I, too, would soon be carried away. "That piling won't hold me," I thought.

I was worried. If I continued to let out the bow line, *Xiphias* would fall back over the stern piling and could be holed. I tied it off and dashed back to cast off the stern line, so *Xiphias* would swing freely in the current. "Shit!" I had wrapped it in some stupid way around the cleat when I last let some out. I couldn't see the problem. I tried to feel how to undo it. As I struggled with the knot, I heard Charles yell, "I'm going!"

My mind said, "That means we all are going." *Mintaka* and the other boat tethered together by the common piling shot past me. The stern line from the other boat must have broken where it had been tied to *Xiphias's* bow piling.

Suddenly, my bow began to swing behind them. My first thought was that *Xiphias* would go over my stern pile, and it might put a hole in the hull.

As *Xiphias's* bow quickly swung around, I managed to get my stern line free and cast it off. As I did this, my keel slammed into the submerged stern piling, turning me 180°. *Mintaka* and the other boat were gone in the darkness.

A lightning strike showed that we were all being catapulted at high speed towards a large powerboat still on its mooring. I threw the rudder over, knowing it was futile. Because we were moving with the current, the rudder would have no effect. We were flying towards that boat like an arrow.

In an instant, *Xiphias's* bowsprit buried deep into its side. The impact threw me to the deck. The sound of wood splintering filled the air. Momentarily, we were frozen. Suddenly, the current grabbed *Xiphias's* stern and bore us around, so we were moving backwards.

The boat I'd just impaled was moored at the bottom of the hairpin bend. Had I not hit it, I would have gone directly into the rocks behind. I still might go into the rocks, for there was no way *Xiphias* could be swept around such a sharp bend without hitting something.

In an instant's flash, just ahead of me, I made out *Kimimoana*, Keith and Angela's 50-foot ketch. It set hard against the mountainside at a 30° angle with its stern mostly submerged. This is where the hairpin curve ended. It was open river after this point.

Before I realized what was happening, I passed over her submerged stern, and I was in the trees. Thick limbs flew by at a terrific speed. A branch hit me in the head and knocked me into the cockpit. I remained there, crouched low, as *Xiphias* went over the side of this hill. Next, my dodger was ripped off. "Damn!" I had seen *Pintle* under the dodger only a minute ago. I screamed, "*Pintle*! Oh God, have I lost him?"

As fast as it had begun, everything was quiet. I staggered below for my spotlight. I made a quick survey for *Pintle* and looked for water. Neither was found.

I thought I had stopped. With my spotlight, I surveyed ahead. Through the heavy rain, I saw *Mintaka* not far from me.

"Charles, is it over?" I yelled at the top of my lungs.

"Not yet. We're in the middle of the river. The worst is yet to come. I need my tiller! I have no control," Charles yelled back.

I shone my light into the trees along shore; they were only a blur. Suddenly, I realized I was being propelled down the straight part of the Keri Keri River at a tremendous speed.

It all happened so quickly, I hadn't had time to even start my engine. I started it, hoping I could motor over to reach *Mintaka*. It had no effect, for the river current was too powerful. There was lots of debris in the water; I was afraid I might catch a log in the prop, so I put it in neutral. I was left to the raging current of the river.

I watched helplessly as the darkness concealed Charles's whereabouts.

I stiffened, for I heard rapids. My first thought was that I'd been cast into a river with a fall. The sound of roaring water grew deafening. When I aimed the spotlight ahead, I saw nothing but white rapids.

At the same instant, my keel scraped against rocks. Suddenly, we stopped. *Xiphias* heeled over so far she was lying on her starboard side, the mast nearly horizontal. My feet were on the side of the cockpit coamings. I was standing nearly vertical, holding on to the lifeline above my head with all my strength. Water poured over *Xiphias* as it would a sunken stone. It was like being inside a waterfall.

"Thud! Thud!" *Xiphias* started pounding hard against the rocks. "She is finished," I thought, but I held on for my life.

She began to move sideways, dragging her keel along the bottom. Finally, we came upright in the middle of the white, roaring rapids. I had no idea where I was, but it made no difference. I had no control. I was at the mercy of the river.

When I had hit bottom, the spotlight had gone into the river. I grabbed the electric wire to the light and yanked it aboard. I was surprised to find it was still on. I shone it into the blackness at... a roof of a house... a car that hadn't sunk yet... a 30-foot powerboat tumbling over and over, all flowing with the fast moving current down river. In that moment, I realized I'd just passed where the Waipapa River merged with the Keri Keri River.

Ahead, the river widened and then spilled into the Bay of Islands. Oyster beds lay in the shallow water at the river's mouth, so if I were going to drop anchor anywhere, it would have to be there.

I was being carried broadside by the river's current.

I untied my 45-pound CQR anchor, which was in its bow roller. It was ready to deploy. I released the clutch to the gypsy so chain could run free. Just then, a lightning strike revealed a steel marker, just breaking the surface, directly ahead. Unable to avoid it, at about 15 knots, I hit the marker broadside in the center of my hull. *Xiphias* heeled, then pivoted, with sounds of gouging and scraping all along the hull as we were torn by this steel railroad rail used for these river markers.

When the next lightning flashed, I saw open bay just ahead. I figured the current would not be as strong in the wider bay. *Xiphias* was moving so fast, I knew I had little time to get an anchor out before I would be in the shallow rock oyster beds in the center of the channel.

I heaved the anchor over the side. The chain ran out so rapidly that it created a high-pitched sound like a chain saw. In only seconds, 300 feet of chain would be at its end. Immediately, I began tightening the brake clutch to the gypsy on my windlass. Now the sound came slightly lower, but chain was still going out in a blur.

Using the winch handle I use for the halyard winches, I pounded on the brake until the chain produced a jackhammer sound and finally stopped. At this point, the bowsprit and bow went under water, the stern rose several feet higher than normal; the current was washing over the foredeck.

Slowly, the bow came up, but the bowsprit's end remained just at the surface of the raging water. Using the spotlight, I saw that I was holding fast. As long as nothing collided with me, I would be all right. "I've made it! Thank you God," I shouted.

I inspected the chain—275 feet had gone out in only seconds. Another 25 feet and I would have lost it all. I readied my second anchor, a 25-pound Danforth, just in case I started dragging back towards the rocks. Checking behind me with the spotlight, I picked out wrecked boats on the rocks, but because of the thick rain, I couldn't tell how many.

Ahead of me, the spotlight revealed unmanned boats still riding the river's current into the bay.

I moved the beam a few degrees and moaned, "Oh God, please not now!" A full-grown tree was charging straight at me at a high speed. Rocks weren't far behind my stern. It was impossible for my anchor to hold *Xiphias* and that tree in this current. "It's not over yet!" The tree struck the chain first, then drove the chain into the stem of the boat, wedging itself between the bow and the bottom.

The tree, and *Xiphias* with the anchor and chain, began going slowly backwards. As the tree tried to pull the anchor chain under *Xiphias*, the bow again went down, raising the stern.

I threw the other anchor over the tree; it was followed by the chain and then, the rope. I threw a few wraps of the rope around the bitts. Rope continued to fly overboard, but now I had some control. After I thought that at least 100 feet of anchor rope had passed over the tree, I began pulling tighter and tighter on the anchor rope around the post until I felt it grab and then slow us to a stop.

Using the spotlight, I surveyed my surroundings to determine if I was still dragging backwards. It appeared I was stationary. The shallowness of the water here saved me; the tree was resting on the bottom.

Now, I had to prevent debris from accumulating on the tree, or I'd be delivered into the rocks for certain. Yet, before I did anything else, I had to find out if *Pintle* had been washed overboard.

I went below. "*Pintle!*" I called. Unless hungry, he was never one to come running at my call, but now I heard a faint, "Meow."

I found him wedged between two sail bags. Soaking, with ears flattened, tail hanging to his feet, he was a wonderful sight. I caressed his sodden body, kissed his head, and put him back where he felt more secure.

When I returned to the bow, I discovered a large amount of debris had already piled itself into the tree branches. "The only way you can get rid of that stuff," I told myself, "is to go out on the tree, use the boat pole, and push away the bigger pieces."

I tied a line around my chest and climbed out on to the tree. The rope just got tangled in the branches, so I cast it back on deck.

Thank God, the current had subsided considerably because the river was much wider at its mouth. I poled away what I could reach and prayed that no more trees, boats, houses, or cars would rush down on me.

For the remainder of the night, I paced back and forth on the tree that held me in bondage.

Near morning, the rain tapered to erratic sprinkles. As dawn approached, I saw a large blue sailboat next to me that appeared to be anchored. Later, I learned that it had been moored with chain and shackle to a steel railroad rail. The boat, tethered to its steel mooring rail, was washed away by the flood. The rail acted like an anchor and stopped the boat just short of the oyster beds.

When I looked behind me, I saw the top of a car and several boats half-submerged. Far to my left up river, I saw *Mintaka* resting against a French boat aground in shallow water. Further up river, *Chucklyn* sat nearly upright about 30 feet above the river's water. I wondered how they would ever get her down to the river again.

Within minutes, a powerboat pulled up and tried, unsuccessfully, to tow the tree that had me in its grasp. I told them to go help others; I could take care of it myself.

I deployed my dinghy, grabbed the oars and my extendable boat pole. I checked the depth—it was no more than 7 feet. The strength of the current had reduced to a flow that I could swim against, if necessary.

I decided to remain anchored on my second anchor, which I had thrown over the tree. I would cast off the remaining chain on my primary CQR and pull the chain from under the tree on the other side.

I jumped back aboard and pulled the few feet of remaining chain on deck. I tied a buoy to the end and cast it overboard. Then, I flung myself back into the dinghy.

Cautiously, I rowed around the tree and began dragging the boat pole along the bottom until I hooked my anchor chain. I pulled the chain up to the dinghy and pulled myself along until I was near the CQR.

No matter how hard I tried, I could not get it to break its hold on the bottom. I jumped into the water. I could almost reach it without diving under, but not quite. It took a few dives to get it to break loose; it was really dug in deep.

Back aboard the dinghy, I lifted the anchor aboard, then began pulling on the chain. As the chain came aboard, I was being pulled back to the tree. I continued to pull until I saw the buoy on the other end of the chain begin to move. I jumped back into the water, swam around, and untied the buoy from the chain.

I pulled the remaining chain from under the tree, then returned the CQR and all the chain back aboard *Xiphias*. I let out some more line on my secondary anchor and motored around the tree to retrieve it. Then, I went to check on my friends.

We were told it was the second flash flood in the history of the Keri Keri River. Wouldn't you know, I had to be there.

Anchor rodes and strengths

There are really only two types of anchor rodes: one is chain, the other is chain combined with rope. Some actually use wire cable, but this is impractical on the small cruising vessel.

It is important to remember that for an anchor to properly hold the boat, the pull must be as horizontal as possible. The more weight on the rode, the more likely the anchor will not break loose. For this reason, chain should always be used in conjunction with rope. The only exception to this would be using a heavy sentinel that would hold the rope rode on the bottom.

Nylon rope

The advantage of nylon rope is that it is light, simple to handle, and stores easily aboard the boat. Nylon rope has far more stretch than dacron rope and is less expensive. Nylon rope will stretch about one quarter of its length before it will break. This makes it an excellent anchor rode that will absorb the shock of a wave crashing against a hull.

Nylon will lose much of its strength after long periods of exposure to direct sunlight. There are no signs of the deterioration; it just gets weaker. This is not a problem if a particular area of anchor rope is not exposed for long periods of time. The concern is when the same spot is left exposed 24 hours a day.

Many will advise to use three-strand nylon over braided-nylon rope. I am not sure I agree or disagree; there are advantages and disadvantages to both.

Braided rope is stronger and less likely to abrade where it passes through or over the anchor chock and roller. Yet even though it is stronger, it will not stretch as much as the three-strand nylon.

Braided rope is a little more difficult to backsplice around a thimble. It can be done, but it requires some skill and a special tool for each size rope. On the other hand, three-strand nylon is easy to backsplice around a thimble, even by the inexperienced; it is also considerably cheaper than braided rope.

What I don't like about the three-strand is that it will kink if it is forced to twist with, or against, the lay of the rope. I am sure every sailor has seen this twisted kink in nylon rope. If this happens under a strain, it will greatly reduce its strength at this point. The kink can be removed by stretching and twisting the rope in the correct direction; however, this will always be a weak point of the rope.

Nylon rope is heavy enough to sink to the bottom. This makes it easy to snag on rock or coral. Since the rope is soft, it will chafe through rapidly. The major disadvantage to any rope rode, including nylon, is the ease of chafing.

§

I remember when Jerry, my closest friend, and I were sailing my little Balboa 20-footer down the Baja coast. We had anchored behind a windy bluff named Punta Colnett. I had set my Danforth anchor on a combination of chain and nylon rope. We tried to get in close to the cliffs to get away from the winds blowing over the bluff and the swell coming around the point.

We were exhausted and went straight to bed as soon as the anchor was set. During the night, I kept hearing sounds like gunshots from under the boat. I couldn't figure it out, so I just went back to sleep. I was really tired.

Early the next morning, we awoke to find the winds had died. We were setting broadside—only feet from the breakers.

I started my little 5-hp outboard and began bringing in the anchor. After I brought up about 15 feet, I found that the 1/2" nylon anchor line had several kinks. It had completely worn through two of the three stands and over half of the third. We were being held by about 1/8" of nylon line.

During the night, we must have swung around several times with the shifting wind, eddies, and current. The nylon rope had caught around the swing keel. Whenever there was a load on the rope, it chafed through, causing the gun shot sounds under the boat. We were lucky indeed.

Polypropylene rope

Because this rope is so inexpensive, you will see it on local fishing boats in most foreign countries. Polypropylene rope is a synthetic rope that is not as strong as nylon. It will break down in sunlight much quicker than nylon. Polypropylene rope is slippery and stiffer than nylon. Care must be taken when splicing or tying knots, so they do not slip.

The major advantage to this rope, other than its cost, is that it floats. This makes an excellent line to tie ashore if the bottom is rock or coral, or anywhere a floating rope would be better than a rope that sinks to the bottom.

This rope is available in many colors, which can have its advantages. I like to use yellow for tying ashore because it is easier to see at night. I also use various colors to mark my anchor chain. This will be discussed later.

One thing I don't like about polypropylene is that small stiff strands will break away from the larger strands, and the ends are sharp. When the rope gets to this stage, it will be hard to handle and should be replaced.

It should be obvious why this type of rope should not be used as the primary anchor rode. As long as care is taken to inspect and replace it often, polypropylene rope is okay to use on other anchors or to tie ashore.

Chain

Chain is the most common rode used on cruising boats. It is strong, heavy, and will not chafe like rope. There are many different kinds of chain, so care must be taken to buy the right chain for anchoring.

Chain is available in low carbon steel, high tensile steel, and stainless steel. The low carbon chain links are always used in the longer links called Proof Coil. It is also used on the shorter links called BBB.

High-test chain, which is made from high carbon steel, is about double the strength of low carbon steel chain. Because of its additional strength, many cruisers will use a much smaller diameter link for less weight aboard, and it requires less storage space.

However, I feel this is a mistake for two reasons. Since it is the weight of chain on the bottom that provides horizontal pull for good holding, the same length of the smaller, lighter chain will not achieve the same results. If the additional strength is a concern, use the HT chain but of the same size link as would be used if it were low carbon.

The other concern is finding a shackle with the same strength as the chain. This may not be even possible, because the larger shackle pin may not fit through the link. Like the old saying, a chain is only as strong as its weakest link—and it may be the shackle.

Regardless of whether the chain is made of low or high carbon steel, it will rust quickly in salt water, unless it has a protective coating. Steel chain is available with zinc electroplate, cadmium electroplate, or hot-dipped galvanized. The zinc and cadmium plate is thin and will rust away quickly, so it must not be used under water and really does not belong on a boat in a salt-air environment.

Hot-dipped galvanized chain is produced by dipping the chain through an acid bath to make it absolutely clean. Then, it is passed through a bath of melted zinc. The zinc evenly coats each link. The chain must then be hung, and all the excess zinc shaken off the chain.

Galvanized chain will last a surprisingly long time in a salt-water environment. When the zinc begins to wear off, the chain can be re-galvanized. *Be sure you select a company that has the ability to hang and shake the chain.* The problem occurs if the chain is piled before the zinc has had a chance to harden: it ends up being one solid pile of galvanized chain.

Stainless steel chain is relatively new as a chain anchor rode. It is stronger than low carbon steel chain, but not as strong as high-test. The major advantage to this chain is that it is more resistant to rust.

The major disadvantage is that it is more than double the cost of low carbon chain.

Personally, I am not convinced that stainless steel is good for anchor chain. I know that stainless steel will fatigue quicker and easier than low carbon or high-test steel. There are no warning signs that this is happening until it breaks. Also, stainless steel is susceptible to oxygen starvation corrosion and crevice corrosion. I am not sure this applies to chain links, but it is something I wonder about.

Another concern I have about stainless steel is the method used to weld the link together. I have seen stainless steel links where each link is welded slightly differently, which indicates the possibility of error. I am not sure if it is produced the same way as high or low carbon links.

Personally, I think stainless steel chain needs to be around a little longer for me to feel comfortable using it. When the wind and seas are threatening, I do not want to have to worry about something that might break or give way at just the wrong time.

If stainless steel is a serious consideration, I suggest you gather as much information about the chain as possible. How is it tested? How is each link welded? How many links are tested?

Chain comes in two types of links. The most common is Proof Coil. Its link is longer than the other—or BBB—chain link. Proof Coil chain tests every 20th link to make sure it meets the required standards. This chain is most commonly used in general industry, because it is strong and inexpensive. The link is made of low carbon steel or stainless steel. The longer link will not fit the gypsy on most windlasses. I have never seen this longer link in high-test, but this does not mean it does not exist. For the reasons stated above, this chain is rarely seen on cruising boats.

BBB link is shorter than Proof Coil. It can be made of low carbon, high-test, or stainless steel. If BBB chain is made of low carbon steel, it will have the same strength as Proof Coil, but *each link* is tested, rather than every 20th link. Because the link is shorter, there is less chance that it will deform under a load. The shorter link fits the gypsy on most anchor windlasses. Thus, the BBB link is most commonly seen on cruising boats.

It is important that one continuous length of chain is used for each anchor. All too often, the minimum length of chain is purchased.

Later, the buyer realizes that more is needed. Where two chains are connected becomes the 'weakest link'.

If it is essential that two chains be connected together, the strongest method is to use a Mid-Link Connector, shown in Figure 41. This is a solid dropforged double clevis with a clevis pin on each end. It is as strong as chain, but it is longer and wider than a standard link. The length would be similar to welding two links together. Because of this additional length and width, it will not go around a gypsy properly and may slip at this point. Also, it may not make the turn to drop down into the chainpipe. In addition, these connectors are hard to find in hot-dipped galvanized coating.

Figure 41. Mid-link connector

An alternative, which is not as strong as a mid-link connector, is a Split Chain Connector, shown in Figure 42. This is an actual link, which is dropforged and heat-treated in two halves. The halves are like cutting a link in half lengthwise, so it appears that there are two links. This connector has rivets molded into its shape; when they properly match, the rivet of the male half fits the hole of the female half. The rivets are then peened over to lock the two halves together. This connector is still not as strong as the original chain link, but they are the same size. They come in both BBB and Proof Coil lengths. The shorter link is a little more difficult to find, but if you can find it, it will fit the gypsy on the windlass.

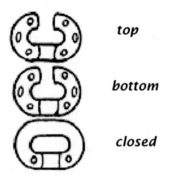

top

bottom

closed

Figure 42. Split chain connector

There are other connectors available. None of these are really acceptable, because they just are not strong enough. If you find one that you like, make sure it will be as strong as the chain being connected.

If I had to connect two lengths of chain together, I would use the proper size shackles and a high-test solid swivel. The swivel would provide at least equal strength, with the weakest point being the shackles. The additional swivel would help prevent the chain from twisting and getting kinks. Of course, the downside is that it would not pass around the gypsy and may not pass down into the chainpipe.

Quality chain links are hot fused together. That is, after the link is bent around the previous link, the place where the ends meet is heated to a point where it nearly melts; then, it is forced together under high pressure. The result is a slightly raised area where the link was fused together. The better chain has its trademark stamped on the link at this point—cheaper chains do not.

Be skeptical of chain links that appear to be welded together. All too often, the weld does not penetrate to the center of the link material, leaving a weak spot in the weld. *Always be sure to cut a link on the opposite side of the weld, to see if it bends on the side with the weld.*

§

While I was working in a boatyard in Singapore, I needed to put *Xiphias* on a mooring. The bottom was soft, deep mud silt, so anchors did not hold well. The available moorings were plastic barrels filled with concrete. Only the weight of the mooring held the boat, so when the wind picked up, they would drag along the bottom. This was not acceptable for me; I wanted my own mooring.

I made one out of molded concrete with a 1" eyebolt cast in the center. The only thing that I needed was some chain and a mooring rope. I went to a local hardware store in Changi Village, near where my mooring would set. They only had Proof Coil chain, so I selected 75 feet of half-inch hot-dipped galvanized chain. I watched as the Chinese owner took the bolt cutters and began to cut the chain on the weld. I told him that it was more difficult to cut on the weld; he should cut on the opposite side. But, he was adamant.

This worried me, so I insisted he cut it opposite the weld. As soon as he cut through the side of the link, opposite the weld, the link broke into two pieces. On inspection, I could see that the chain link was only surface welded. There was no penetration at all. He insisted that it was only that one link that was welded like this. I took the bolt cutters and began cutting one link at a time. Each one broke in half. After ten links were cut, he shrugged his shoulders and said, "Chinese chain."

I had great difficulty finding quality chain. I finally found some in a marine store an hour's bus ride away. There was no way I could carry the chain back on a bus, so I had to hire a taxi.

§

Chain can be used in conjunction with a rope rode, as long as there is no rock or coral on the bottom. It can be attached to the rope by using a thimble, or by splicing the rope to the chain. If the chain and rope must pass over a windlass's gypsy, a thimble may not work. Also, because the thimble size required to fit the rope is large, it may not fit down the chainpipe.

For these reasons, some will splice the rope onto the chain. There are two ways to do this. One way is to splice the rope through many links of chain and seize the ends. The other is to backsplice the rope through the last link. If the rope is considerably larger than the inside of the link, it may not pass through; therefore, a shackle must be used.

Both of these splicing methods are susceptible to chafe and are not as strong as using a thimble. If the rope is spliced, it should be inspected regularly.

Consideration should be made to match the strength of the chain to the strength of the rope and shackle. Remember, it is the weight of the chain that is important. Do not reduce the size unless there is no other choice.

Approximate breaking strengths of nylon rope, chain and shackles.

The following chart compares the strength of the same size nylon rope, chain, and shackles. Since different manufacturers have different strengths, these figures are averages. When buying chain, rope, and shackles, check to see that the particular brand you buy has compatible strengths.

It is a good idea to select at least one size larger nylon rope, because it will lose some of its strength when exposed to sunlight, and it chafes.

If you look at the following chart, you can see that a good combination for 5/16" BBB low carbon chain would be 5/8" nylon and a 3/4" shackle. However, it is impossible for a shackle of this size to fit the chain, so the largest, strongest shackle must be selected. It will still be the weakest link.

Diameter	3 Strand Nylon	BBB Low Carbon	BBB High Test	Shackle
1/4 "	1,800 #	2,600 #	6,500 #	1,200 #
5/16 "	2,600 #	7,500 #	11,500 #	1,500 #
3/8 "	4,000 #	10,500 #	15,000 #	2,500 #
1/2 "	7,500 #	12,500 #	22,000 #	4,000 #
5/8 "	12,000 #	14,500 #	33,000 #	6,500 #
3/4 "	15,000 #	20,500 #	46,000 #	9,500 #
7/8 "	19,000 #	24,000 #	———	14,000 #
1 "	24,500 #	31,000 #	———	18,500 #

Table II. Approximate breaking strengths of nylon rope, chain and shackles

It can be seen by this chart that if high-test chain is used, it will require a shackle considerably larger to match its strength. The larger shackle will not fit the chain link. This seems to defeat the purpose of the high-test chain if it is being used just for its additional strength.

Since chain is heavy and sets on the bottom, the boat will have a tendency to swing on just the chain until the wind or current strengthens. This is not a problem as long as other boats in the area are not on a rope rode with a wider swing. Also, the chain lying on the bottom can drag along the bottom's surface and possibly trip its own anchor, or it might wrap itself around a large rock or coral head.

§

I lost my 45-pound CQR in such a situation. I was sailing from Papua New Guinea to Thursday Island in Northern Australia; this passage is called the Torres Straits. It is about 200 nautical miles long, shallow, and littered with coral reefs and small islands. This is that point of water where the Pacific Ocean meets the Arafura Sea of the Indian Ocean. The currents are quite strong, and often the wind will blow against the current, causing dangerously steep seas. Because of the many reefs and atolls, it is dangerous to navigate at night; I had to anchor two nights to make this crossing.

The first night was in the lee of a coral atoll. I anchored in 15 feet with a coral bottom. I would have preferred sand, but there was none available. The night was spent with the chain wrapped around coral, causing the boat to come up tight with each wave. I broke one snubber line that night.

The next night, I found some sand in the lee of another atoll. It was also about 15 feet deep, and the current was running strong. I set out plenty of scope, so I wouldn't drag into the reef behind my stern.

During the night, I could hear the chain grinding against coral. I knew I would swing with the change of the tidal current, so I was quite certain my chain was fouled. There was nothing I could do about it at night; I just kept letting out more chain as it came up taut.

When morning came, I could not raise the last 50 feet of chain and the anchor. It was badly fouled. I had to wait until slack tide to safely maneuver in the strong tidal current. There was only about 20 minutes between tidal currents, and they were always strong. When it was spring tide, the current ran at 5 to 6 knots. This day, it was at the top of the spring tide.

Just before slack tide, I began motoring around the coral heads to free my chain. I got most of it up, except for the last 25 feet. I grabbed my facemask and fins and dove into the warm water. Fortunately, I was near the chain. Since the current was so strong, it jerked my body perpendicular to the chain and tore the mask right off my face. There was no way I would be able to do anything until a totally slack tide. A few minutes later, the current was nearly still, so I pulled myself down the chain. It was shallow and easy to do just holding my breath.

When I reached the bottom, I saw the problem. It was mostly sand, except for two large coral heads about three to four feet high. One had grown partly over the other. My anchor had originally been set a few feet up current of these coral heads. The chain must have lain right over the top where the two coral heads met. When I backed down to set the anchor, the chain pulled between the two chunks of coral, and the anchor pulled under their base.

I peered under the coral and could see that the sand was shallow over a hard coral bottom, so the anchor never did really set. Instead, it had dragged under the coral until it snagged the coral's base. It was too far under the coral to reach, and there was no room for me to get to it.

Luckily, the polypropylene line I use as a pick-up line, attached to the head of the anchor, was accessible. No matter how hard I pulled, it would not pull the anchor back out. I figured that *Xiphias* was holding the anchor against the coral, and I was trying to pull her and the anchor.

I climbed back aboard and quickly deployed my dinghy. I set my second anchor and some chain into the dinghy, then rowed it out beyond the coral heads. When I returned to the boat, I took up the slack until I was anchored on the new anchor.

I released some slack on the primary chain, so I could pull the anchor out backwards. I slipped on my SCUBA tank and jumped in the water. I pulled and pulled on that line, but the anchor would not budge. The current was quickly returning. I managed to get aboard just in time; the current would have been much too strong to swim against.

With no other choice, I took the bolt cutters and cut the chain. Then, I pulled in my second anchor and headed for Thursday Island.

§

Another disadvantage of chain is its weight. The chain should not be stored above the waterline. The additional weight could affect the righting moment. Nor should it be stored too far forward. It is this additional weight forward that can cause a boat to hobbyhorse. Likewise, there should not be too much weight aft, which can have similar effects.

The best place to store this weight is as far aft toward the center of the boat as possible, and deep in the bilge. This is impossible on boats with "V" berths, unless they want the chainpipe in the middle of the bed.

The chain should be stored so it can pile without difficulty. This is not a problem on larger boats, but as the boat gets smaller, there is less depth to accept the chain. The chain locker should be deep enough that the weight of the chain will continue to pull the rest of the chain into the locker. The distance between the bottom of the chainpipe and the bilge should permit the chain to pile without difficulty. If this area will not take all the chain, it may be necessary to pull some of it back to another compartment. This can be both good and bad.

If the chain can be pulled further aft, it moves the weight aft during passages. This may improve the boat's performance and reduce hobbyhorsing. However, if the area where the chain piles is not large enough or deep enough to accept all of the chain before the anchor breaks bottom, you will have to run down and pull some chain back or tip the pile over. Meantime the anchor, now on almost zero scope, may break loose. This is much less of a problem if there is a crewmember aboard to pull the chain back.

Chain does not stretch or give. It is the weight of the catenary of the chain that takes the shock. In deeper water, the weight of the chain must lift off the bottom as the boat moves aft. The deeper the water, the more chain has to be lifted. In shallow waters or in severe conditions, the catenary may not exist, and it may be a straight-line pull between the anchor and the boat. If there is a sudden shock or load from a wave, it may break the anchor out of its hold, or even break the chain or a shackle. For this reason, an all chain rode should always be attached to the boat with a snubber line to absorb this sudden load. This will be more thoroughly discussed later in this chapter.

Chain left on deck during a passage can cause considerable damage if it is not securely fastened. Often, this is only discovered when the conditions are too dangerous to go forward to secure it.

Chain will hold mud or clay in its links. If this mud gets into the bilge, it will begin to smell. It is best to have a washdown pump on deck or some other means to remove this stinky mud before it gets inside the boat.

Each time the boat swings, it will cause a twist in the chain. If the twist is near the anchor, a swivel between the chain and anchor will prevent the development of kinks. Most commonly, the twist is near the boat and goes aboard before it can untwist itself. Over time, the twist will get worse and eventually develop kinks in the chain. These kinks can cause weakness and prevent it from passing through the gypsy. I have had kinks so bad that the chain could not be deployed because a kink would not pass through the narrow chainpipe. I could not anchor until I went below to remove some of the kinks.

If you are cruising and anchoring often, the chain should be laid out on the ground and untwisted by hand once a year. Another way to remove the twist is to let the chain hang straight down in deep water for a while. *Make sure you have a rope tethered to the bitter end and a strong windlass to bring it all back aboard.*

The anchor windlass

Because anchor chain is heavy, it requires an anchor windlass to bring it aboard. It can be done by hand until the time comes to raise the chain and the anchor together. If the water is 50 feet deep, the weight of the combined chain and anchor may be too heavy to lift without some mechanical assistance.

Most anchor windlasses provide a mechanical advantage. The advantage will vary by type, model, and manufacturer. If the anchor and chain has to come up directly with no advantage, it would have a 1 to 1 ratio. The only advantage would be in the length of the handle used to work the windlass. If the windlass has a 5 to 1 ratio, then the lifting power is 5 times greater than the 1 to 1 ratio. Most windlasses will have a much higher lifting ratio, so the load is reduced considerably. However, as the ratio increases, it also reduces the speed the chain comes aboard. This is something many cruisers do not consider until it becomes an issue. There will be more on this later.

It is critical that the windlass be properly located on deck. The windlass gypsy must have a straight line pull from the anchor roller to the gypsy, or the links may not engage properly. The windlass should be located over a deep part of the bilge, so all the chain will fall and pile without requiring someone to pull it back. Because of the chain's weight, this pile should be as far aft as possible.

This may be difficult on some boats, so an angled chainpipe may be required. The angle of this pipe must not exceed the ability of the chain to pull itself down by its own weight. The chain must drop vertically from the end of the angled chainpipe to pile in the chain locker.

This may cause a problem when it is time to deploy the chain. There is a heavy load and abrasion where the chain passes over this angled edge. This will restrict the chain from running out freely and will quickly wear though at this point. If the angle of the chainpipe is considerable, it should have a roller at this edge or at least be rounded.

All chainpipes should have a slight angle, so the chain will always rest against the backside. If the pipe is vertical, the chain will swing and thump the sides of the pipe, driving all onboard crazy.

There is a considerable load where the windlass is through-bolted through the deck. This must be substantially reinforced with backup plates. This is such a common problem that there are always stories circulating about a windlass that was torn off the boat, taking a section of the deck with it.

An anchor windlass must be built stoutly, with strong fasteners and parts. When I departed to go cruising, the windlass I had aboard was part steel, part stainless steel, and had an aluminum body. It was nicely painted white on the outside, but the inside had no protection. Over the years of cruising in a salt-water environment, the body nearly disintegrated. The steel parts had to be replaced because of severe rust. The stainless steel axis rusted, making it almost impossible to remove the locking nuts. If any part of the windlass will attract a magnet, it has too much carbon steel that will eventually rust. The windlass should be easily disassembled so it can be serviced, inspected, and repaired if necessary.

Most windlasses come with a capstan for rope rode and a gypsy for chain. Because of its weight, chain will fall through the chainpipe into the chain locker. Rope will not. If a combination of rope and chain is used, the rope will have to be shoved or pulled into the locker until chain is reached. Often, this requires that the rope be left on deck, then pushed or pulled down into the locker.

This does not apply to all windlasses. Some claim that the rope will fall and pile on its own. I have yet to see this actually work, but as the chainpipe increases in diameter and as the chainlocker gets deeper, the chances increase that it will fall on its own. If the primary anchor is a combination of chain and rope, then this is something to check before spending a lot of money on a windlass.

The chain must fit the gypsy perfectly to prevent it from slipping when there is a load. When buying a windlass, it is a good idea to take a short length of your anchor chain to check the match.

Every gypsy must have a chain stripper to remove the chain from the gypsy. I have seen some that are poorly designed and constructed.

I have seen strippers that permitted the chain to pass the trip lever, binding everything up so badly that the windlass had to be disassembled to clear the jam.

There are two designs of anchor windlasses. In one type of windlass, the axis is horizontal, and in the other, the axis is vertical. Both designs are available in manual or auxiliary power.

Horizontal axis windlass

The most common manual windlass has a horizontal axis. It is readily available and relatively inexpensive. It has a central body, which houses the axis and gears. On one end of the axis is a capstan for rope, and on the other end, a gypsy for chain. If it is a manual windlass, a vertical handle is inserted into the top of the windlass. As the handle is pumped back and forth, the axis turns, bringing in the anchor rode.

The pull can be single or double action. If it is single action, the axis only rotates when the handle is brought back to its original position. If it is double action, the axis rotates as the handle is pulled and pushed. The chain will come up much faster if the windlass is double action. Because this windlass uses a handle placed vertically on the top, it permits the operator to stand while bringing in the chain.

The capstan is part of the axis and will rotate at the same speed. Unlike the gypsy, it does not have a clutch. To bring in line, it is wrapped around the capstan several times, then pulled tight so it grabs the capstan as it rotates. If the pull is slackened, the capstan continues to turn while the rope slips.

The gypsy must have a clutch or some method of adjusting the friction. To deploy chain, the clutch on the gypsy is released, so it rotates freely. When bringing the chain aboard, the clutch is tightened, so the gypsy rotates with the axis. *It is of utmost importance that the clutch not be tightened too tight; it must slip when a wave hits.* If the gypsy won't slip, something has to give. It may strip the threads on the clutch, as it happened to me in Papeete. It may break the axis where it passes into the body, or it might break the chain or a shackle.

I feel the horizontal axis windlass has some limitations. As mentioned previously, the body must be non-corrosive inside as well as outside. To keep water out of the interior of the windlass, the axis must be properly sealed where it passes through the body. This is difficult to maintain because the load is always against one side of the seal. It must be inspected and replaced as necessary.

The threads on the clutch must be strong. This is where most horizontal axis windlasses fail. If the clutch is set up too tight, the load is applied directly to the gypsy, creating excessive torque on the clutch and its threads. This is why it should never be tightened too much.

Chain passes over the top of the gypsy and drops at 90° into the chainpipe. This permits about 2 or 3 links to actually set into the recesses for the links. The smaller the diameter on the gypsy, the less links it will support, as shown in Figure 43.

This is important, because the design of the horizontal windlass has the axis considerably high off the deck. If there is a load on the chain, it will become taut. When there is no load, it will form a catenary down. This pumping of the chain can pull the few links being held off the gypsy. The larger the diameter of the gypsy, the more links make contact, reducing this problem.

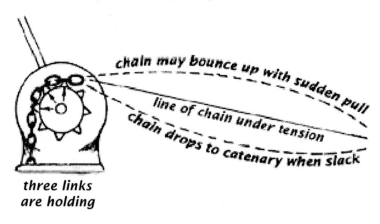

three links
are holding

Figure 43. Horizontal axis windlass

As mentioned previously, it is critical that the horizontal windlass be mounted so the chain leads on a straight line from the bow roller to the gypsy. If it does not, the chain will come off when it is under a load. This leaves little choice about its mounting location, which may not be over a deep part of the bilge. Depending on the distance between the bow rollers on the bow, it may be impossible to have the secondary rope rode lead directly to the capstan, and the chain lead to the gypsy.

Another problem occurs when the rode is a combination of rope and chain. Since the capstan is on the opposite side of the gypsy, it may be difficult for the rope and chain to fall into a common chainpipe. Often, the rope must be piled on deck until it reaches the chain; then, the rope must be pushed or pulled down the chainpipe, followed by the chain.

An additional concern exists if the wind is blowing and there is a load on the rope anchor rode when it reaches the chain. It is difficult to transfer from the capstan to the gypsy without releasing the line from the capstan.

The horizontal axis windlass always has a reduction in its lifting ratio to increase the mechanical advantage. This will give the windlass the power to break the anchor loose from the bottom. The better and more expensive ones are two-speed, which means the advantage can be changed. The greater the lifting advantage, the slower the chain is raised. This is not a problem until the anchor breaks bottom. If the anchor is deep, it may take a considerable amount of time to raise it to the surface. Meantime, the boat is moving.

§

This was a problem for a fellow cruiser and I while in the Bank Islands. It was getting late, and we needed to find an anchorage before dark. We found a well-protected cove, but the bottom was 60 feet deep and all huge coral heads. The only other choice was to continue through the night; we didn't want to do this because there were many reefs. Also, there were more local islands and anchorages that we wanted to visit before we continued to the Solomon Islands.

I was more naïve then. I figured I needed a minimum ratio of 3 to 1 in this deep water. Needless to say, all my excess chain just got wrapped around coral. The more I let out, the more got fouled. Even when the tide was at it lowest, the excess chain wrapped around coral. During the night, I got up about ten times to let out more chain. By morning, I had let out nearly my entire 300 feet. It was all wrapped around coral.

Wearing my facemask and fins, I dove into the water. It was crystal clear, and I could easily see where the chain was wrapped around the coral. I went back aboard and slowly managed to get my chain up a little at a time. Finally, my anchor hung straight down between two coral heads—there was no way I was going anywhere.

I swam over to the other boat. By floating on the surface, I could direct them which way to maneuver to release their chain. After it was all up except the anchor, I returned to my boat. Slowly, I pulled on my chain, but the anchor was fouled. I let some chain out, then pulled it back. I continued doing this until my anchor was free.

My windlass permitted me to pull the chain aboard quickly. It was a vertical windlass that worked like a sheet winch. In one direction, I had a reduction. In the other direction, I could raise the anchor as quickly as I could turn the handle. When I was free, I motored over to the other boat and rafted alongside.

Their anchor was badly fouled. I explained to the skipper that my SCUBA tank was empty. I could reach the bottom holding my breath, but I could not linger. There was a light breeze blowing, causing a load on the chain. I asked him to wait until I reached the bottom, then let out some chain for a few seconds, bringing it back up as quickly as he could. I figured that I would be able to free his anchor when the chain was slack.

I pulled myself down the chain until I reached the bottom. I saw that the anchor was fouled under a coral head. As soon as the chain became slack, I pulled it loose. I surfaced and watched the anchor come up inches at a time until it fouled again. This happened over and over. Because it had a high reduction ratio, the damn horizontal windlass would only bring in a few inches of chain with each pump of the lever. I had to dive down repeatedly to free the anchor until it cleared the top of the coral heads.

§

Vertical axis windlass

The vertical axis windlass has a wide base, with the gypsy just above the base. If there is a capstan, it is above the gypsy, as shown in

Figure 44. The vertical axis windlass is the most common design for electrical windlasses. However, some manual ones are also available.

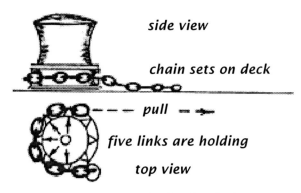

side view

chain sets on deck

pull

five links are holding

top view

Figure 44. Vertical axis windlass

The manual windlass is operated like a sheet winch, with a winch handle that rotates the capstan or gypsy. To use the manual vertical windlass, the operator must bend over or be on his or her knees. This can get old very quickly.

The gypsy, being at deck level, prevents the chain from forming a catenary or pumping up and down. Instead, the chain slides on the deck. Obviously, this can be a problem if there isn't some kind of protection on the deck to prevent abrasion.

Unlike the horizontal windlass where the chain must have a straight line to the gypsy, the chain on a vertical axis can lead to the gypsy from a slight angle. This is because the gypsy lies flat or parallel to the deck, and the chain goes horizontally around the gypsy. This makes it possible to vary the mounting location.

Since the gypsy is near deck level, the chain leads directly down the chainpipe. This design permits a shield or cover to fit over the chainpipe to reduce water entering it from forward. However, if there is a lot of water, it will enter the chainpipe from the backside.

There are some manual vertical axis windlasses available, but they don't have two speeds or the ratio variations I would like. Most have ratios of 5 to 1. This is only moderately strong enough for breaking the anchor out, and it brings the chain up too slowly.

The major advantage of the vertical axis windlass is that the chain wraps around the gypsy 180°. There are twice the number of links held in the recesses of the gypsy, so there is no way the chain can slip.

I think I had the perfect manual vertical windlass on *Xiphias*. I bought it from a chap named Jim Bates in New Zealand. He designed, cast, and assembled this vertical windlass in his home. It was all solid bronze with a 3" diameter axis. It used stainless steel pin bearings on the gypsy, which was at deck level. Just above the gypsy was the clutch, which had three large handles to grab for adjusting the friction. They were so strong that they could be hit with the winch handle or a hammer if necessary. The clutch was threaded to the 3" axis with acme threads. This made it strong and easy to adjust up or down. The bottom of the clutch had a male bevel or taper that perfectly matched the female bevel on the top of the gypsy; therefore, as the clutch was tightened down on the gypsy, they eventually locked together as one. The capstan was above the clutch, which rotated with the axis and independently of the gypsy. When the clutch was tightened against the gypsy, the whole unit moved as one.

The winch was two-speed and worked like a sheet winch. When the winch handle rotated counterclockwise, the pull had a ratio of 10 to 1 for heavy lifting. When rotated clockwise, the ratio was 1 to 1, so the chain and anchor could be raised as quickly as the handle could be rotated.

I used this windlass for years without a single problem. It was strong, and I could raise the anchor off the bottom faster than most electric windlasses. Unfortunately, Jim Bates sold the drawings and patterns to someone who never produced another windlass. To my knowledge, such a windlass is not available anywhere today. If there were, I would gladly purchase it over an electric windlass.

Power vs. manual windlasses

I think everyone would prefer to have a powered windlass, as long as it was reliable and had an efficient manual backup. Unfortunately, most are not that reliable and few, if any, have an efficient manual override that can be put into effect immediately. Most manual overrides are a 1 to 1 ratio, which is of little use when it is time to break out the anchor.

The most reliable and powerful windlass is driven by hydraulics. Because this requires the engine to be run and uses heavy, bulky pumps, motors, lines, and fittings, they are not practical on small pleasure cruising boats. They are more common on commercial vessels that leave the engine running almost all the time.

The powered windlass that is available for sailboats is electrical, and it is expensive. The better the quality, the more it costs. For this reason, many cruisers choose a manual windlass.

Electrical windlasses are strong and make raising the anchor and chain a simple process of pressing on a foot switch. Normally, there are two switches: one to raise and the other to lower the anchor. The foot switches are on deck near the windlass, so it is easy to see what is happening with the anchor. Some also have remote controls or switches in the cockpit, so the anchor can be raised from the helm.

The electrical windlass is rated by its load-lifting capacity, current draw, and the number of feet of chain it raises per minute. Care must be taken to get the correct electrical windlass for the size and weight of the chain and anchor.

The windlass must have a heavy load-lifting capacity to easily lift the chain and anchor, even when under a load. If there is too much weight or load and the gypsy is set up too tight, the breaker switch will trip. This will stop the chain from being raised until the circuit breaker is reset or the manual override is engaged. This usually happens just when there is a load trying to break the anchor from a firm grip on the bottom. If the breaker does trip, there is no scope, and a small passing wave may break the anchor's hold. Now, the boat is moving with the wind or current, with the chain and anchor skipping along the bottom until the windlass is back in operation.

To prevent this problem from happening, select a windlass that has more load-lifting capacity than you expect to need. Also, always adjust the clutch so it will slip when under a heavy load.

Another concern is the amount of electrical current it draws. The higher the load-lifting capacity, the more amps required. The average size windlass will draw about 60 amps when under a load. If the current is being drawn from a single 90-amp battery, it will quickly kill it. For this reason, most cruisers start the engine before engaging an electrical windlass. As long as the engine is charging the battery, the number of amps it draws shouldn't be important. The time may come when the engine will not start, or the batteries are dead, and the anchor must be raised; then, a manual backup is essential.

An additional worry is the number of feet it will raise in one minute. I feel the minimum rating should be 60 feet per minute. This number is based on a minimum load in shallow water. If the water is deep, the weight of the chain and anchor will be more, and the lifting speed will be considerably reduced. As I mentioned previously, I feel it is important to get the anchor up off the bottom and on deck as quickly as possible.

I have mixed feelings about the use of a down switch to deploy the chain. I feel the gypsy should be able to be completely released, so the chain will run freely even if the windlass is not engaged. This is for obvious safety reasons. After the anchor is set, the down switch can be used to let out more chain if needed.

I particularly like to have an up and down switch in the cockpit, or to have a remote that can be used from the helm. Sometimes, only one person is available to do the anchoring. This makes it easy to raise or deploy the anchor from the helm. When raising the anchor, be sure to permit the clutch to slip, so when the anchor reaches its chock, it will not be torn off the bow.

Anything electrical on a boat will eventually fail. I know how pessimistic and absolute this sounds, but it is more common that it will fail sooner or later, than never fail at all. For this reason, a good, quick, manual backup is necessary. Unfortunately, I have yet to see one that really works well, or that can be quickly engaged in an emergency. However, any backup is better than no backup.

It is better to prevent an electrical failure than have to deal with it. The best way to prevent failure is to have a good sealed motor with waterproof switches and connectors. The most common failure is at the crimped connections. Personally, I do not like to rely on any crimped connection. Past experience convinces me to crimp and solder.

Marking anchor rodes

Anchor rodes must have markings, so the amount of scope deployed can be properly determined. There are many ideas and methods for doing this, and they all work. What is important is to find a method that will last a long time, can be seen at night, and will be difficult to miss.

It is not necessary to mark the rode every ten feet. I use every 25 feet; after all, it is easy to guess if it is about half way between a 25-foot mark and the next mark. If there is any doubt how much has been let out, continue deploying rode until you do know. *It is better to err with too much rode than with too little rode.* I mark the chain at 10 feet above the anchor. This tells me that the anchor is nearing the surface.

Most boats will carry 300 feet of anchor chain aboard. Most anchoring situations require about half that, or about 150 feet. Most small cruising boats anchor in water 30 feet deep or less. If a 5 to 1 scope were to be used, the length of chain would be 150 feet. This results in the first half of the chain losing its galvanizing before the other half, which sits in the bilge. Eventually the chain will be switched end for end; therefore, *mark the chain from both ends to the middle, so when it is switched around, the same markings exist.*

Marking the chain ten feet from both ends will indicate when you are near the bitter end, or near the anchor. If a bright color is used, it will be easier to see. I like to use red at the ends, so when I see red again anywhere along the rode, I know it cannot be the ends.

Rather than discuss the various methods available and explain their pros and cons, I would like to describe what worked for me for many years.

I bought three 10-foot lengths of three-strand polypropylene rope in three contrasting colors. The size or diameter of the rope depends on the size of the chain. I used three-strand because I could unravel the strands into three separate 10-foot lengths. First, I cut the 10-foot length into four 30" lengths. Then, I separated each length into three strands, which would yield 12 lengths, each 30" long, of each color. This is more than enough to do one chain rode marked every 25 feet, or even two chain rodes, if they are marked at 50 feet.

I selected colors of polypropylene rope that could be seen in the dark. This eliminates black or dark blue. The most common colors are white, red, and yellow. I also like orange and light blue. Try to find colors that contrast. If the yellow is too close to white, don't use it. The same applies to the orange being too close to the red. The difference in contrast will vary by manufacturer.

After the pieces are cut, I weave the 30" length loosely between each link where I want the mark. The end result is about 18" of exposed marking. The ends are seized to the link with monel wire. The wire is wrapped around the link and rope several times, then pulled tight, twisted, and cut. The twisted cut is rotated to the inside of the link, so it doesn't snag something.

It is important to weave the rope tight enough, so it moves as part of the chain and will not have a loose loop that could snag something when it turns or bends. The size or diameter of the polypropylene strand must not be so big that it prevents the chain from passing through the gypsy. Too thick a strand is a common mistake. The rope will compress as it passes through the gypsy, but if it is too thick, it won't compress enough.

On *Xiphias*, I used 300 feet of 5/16" BBB chain. Depending on the tightness of the lay of the rope, I used either 3/8" or 1/2" three strand polypropylene rope. After the strands were separated, they were small enough not to interfere with the gypsy and still be easily seen.

I found it necessary to re-seize some of the ends occasionally, because the rope would slip out of the wire. I found that I would have to replace the markings about once a year, depending on the bottom. Coral is hard on the polypropylene rope, and the sun will make it fade. I know of some cruisers who employ the same method, but utilize colored webbing instead the polypropylene rope.

The following is only an example of what I used. Notice that the markings are the same at both ends until they meet at the common center.

25-foot markings

I tried to use a new color at each 50-foot marking, then add a white after it at the next 25-foot mark.

10 ft.	Red (both ends)
25 ft.	White
50 ft.	Yellow (New Color)
75 ft.	Yellow-White (10" apart)
100 ft.	Red (New Color)
125 ft.	Red-White (10" apart)
150 ft.	Red-Yellow (10" apart - half chain mark)
175 ft.	Red-White (10" apart)
200 ft.	Red
225 ft.	Yellow-White (10" apart)
250 ft.	Yellow
275 ft.	White
290 ft.	Red (both ends)

50-foot markings

I tried to use a new color at each 50-foot marking, except for the ends.

10 ft.	Red
25 ft.	White
50 ft.	Yellow
100 ft.	Red
150 ft.	Red-Yellow (half chain mark)
200 ft.	Red
250 ft.	Yellow
275 ft.	White
290 ft.	Red

I am sure that there are even better choices of colors and marking strategies. This is provided as an idea. See what you can come up with for your own needs. Try to make it so it is easily seen, even at night, and not so small of a marking that it can be missed with the blink of an eye. It must last a long time before it has to be remarked. Lastly, it should be a color code that is easily remembered.

Suggestions for anchoring

This section consists of a series of suggestions that might make anchoring a little safer. These suggestions are not necessarily techniques, which I tried to save for the next section. These are ideas that I feel are important, but they may not apply to everyone, or to every situation. There are too many variables involved in anchoring to make these comments anything other than suggestions. The purpose is to stimulate thinking about the particular subject and how the idea might apply and be altered to fit a particular situation.

In this and following sections, anchoring in coral will be addressed. I want to make it clear that I do not encourage this, because the anchor could destroy some of this living coral. However, for the sake of safety for the boat and crew, sometimes it may be necessary. I feel it is better to know how to do it, than to ignore it because it shouldn't be done. Live coral is colorful. *If you must anchor in coral, try to anchor in white or dead coral.*

Avoid letting the chain sit in water in the chain locker.

Most boats carry more chain aboard than will ever be used at one time. It is there, just in case, for safety reasons. Normally, about half the chain is used for anchoring, while the remainder sits in the bilge. If it sits in salt water, it will eventually rust away. If possible, put a grate under the chain to keep it out of the water. Also, give the chain locker a fresh water wash now and then to remove the salt.

The chain locker should be watertight.

No matter how hard you try, chain will bring stinky sludge into the chain locker. If it drains into the boat's bilge, this stinky stuff will smell up the boat. Seal the chain locker so it is watertight; then, install a manual or electrical bilge pump to remove the water. This also makes it easier to clean or rinse with fresh water.

Terminate the bitter end of the chain with a safety line.

Before the chain is installed in the boat, tie a piece of line to the last link and the other end of the line to an eyebolt, or some strong structural member in the boat's chain locker. The line should be strong enough to hold the weight of the chain under a load, but small enough to be cut through quickly. I use one-quarter inch, three strand nylon on my 5/16" chain. The line should be long enough to permit the chain to reach the deck, with enough extra so that it can be cut or untied if necessary.

Stern anchor line shouldn't pass through a deck pipe into the locker.

The time may come when the bow anchor will drag, and the stern anchor will have to be thrown overboard in a hurry. If the stern anchor line is led through any opening like a deck pipe or hawsehole, every foot of remaining line will have to pass through this hole before the boat can get underway. *If the line passes through a hawsehole to a cleat, always pass the line back through the hawsehole so it can be released to run free.*

On my own boat, I keep my stern anchor line and chain in a bag in the lazarette. The stern anchor is tied to its chock on the boomkin or on deck. When I want to deploy the stern anchor, I have to attach the chain to the anchor swivel with a split pin or Cotter pin.

I deploy the anchor by hand and lead it out by hand until I get the scope I want. I pass a loop of anchor line through the hawsehole, around the cleat, and back out the hawsehole. Now, I have some control.

After the anchor is set, I secure the line to the cleat as normal, but the remainder of the anchor line is fed back out the hawsehole, then to the bag. I tie the stern anchor bag to the outside of the stern rail or pushpit with a slipknot.

If something happens and I must get underway in a hurry, all I have to do is cast the rope off the cleat, pull the slipknot, and it's gone.

A float could be put inside the bag so it floats while the line sinks, but I advise against it. When the stern anchor is suddenly released, the boat is usually making sternway. A float could get caught in the prop.

§

I would like to share an incident that happened to me when I was anchored in Lumut, Malaysia. I am certain these ideas prevented my boat from being severely damaged.

I was anchored up a river in front of a quaint, casual, local yacht club. Boats would normally set with the bow facing against the river's current. If the wind was fresh and the current light, the boats would swing broadside to the current, or sometimes, they would begin swinging 360°. Therefore, most boats anchored using a bow and stern anchor in order to remain pointing into the current. I followed my fellow cruisers' lead.

One night, a severe squall hit, with 40-knot winds gusting to 60, and horizontal rain. It came from the same direction as the river's current. I peered out my portlight to check if I was dragging. I could see the boats on either side were stationary, so I was sure I was okay. Suddenly, horns began to blow. Spotlights hit my boat. The horns warn all boats that someone is dragging. The spotlight is shone on to the boat with the problem. The spotlights were on me.

Stark naked, I jumped on deck. I looked around and confirmed that I was not dragging. Then, the spotlights moved off me, perhaps because I was naked, to a barge full of gravel heading right for me. It was apparent that the barge had broken loose from its mooring up river. It was nearly over my bow anchor already.

I started the engine, cast off the stern line at the cleat, and threw the anchor bag overboard. Then, I ran forward and released the snubber line from the bitts. I released the clutch on the gypsy so chain ran free. *Xiphias* began moving backward with the wind and current at about the same speed that the barge was coming down on me.

I ran aft and shoved the engine in reverse, then ran forward and grabbed the diving knife I store on the mast. Chain ran out quickly. With no one at the helm, my stern began to move to port. As soon as the rope that was tied to the last link reached the deck, I cut it. I ran back to the helm and reversed out of the path of the barge. It missed me by only a few feet. This all took less than one minute.

Keep a float near both bow and stern anchors while anchored.

If it becomes necessary to cast off the anchors, a float will assist in finding them later. *However, only use the float if there is no chance it will get caught in the prop.* It is better to use a grapnel to try to recover the anchor chain later, than to have a float catch in the prop.

Use hand signals while anchoring.

It is fun to watch an inexperienced sailor anchor. Usually, the man is forward, facing forward, yelling out instructions. The boat in front of him hears every word clearly. The person at the helm, who is meant to hear the instructions, can't hear a thing over the sound of the engine directly beneath the helm. Perhaps the man on the bow realizes that there is no response to his orders, so he turns around and yells, "turn to port" while he points to starboard. We have all seen this happen, and it's probably happened to everyone in his or her early years of sailing.

Hand signals look professional, and they work. There is no need to take a radio or megaphone forward. There are only a few hand signals required: forward, reverse, neutral, port, starboard, stop, fast, slow, anchor's down, anchor's set, anchor's up and anchor's dragging. Make up your own signals; it can be fun and unusual. As you know, everyone will be watching; it'll provide a good opportunity for you to put on a little show.

I have a dear friend who uses the following signals:

Forward: the right arm shoots forward like a jab.

Reverse: the right elbow is shoved back.

Neutral: using both hands over the head, making a big circle with the thumbs and forefingers.

Port and **starboard**: the arm and finger points in the appropriate direction.

Stop: baseball's 'safe' signal.

Fast: the military double time with the fist pumping up and down.

Slow: the palm is flat, extended out at shoulder height and moved back and forth slowly.

Anchor's down: both hands slap the butt.

Anchor is set: the fist is raised and dropped suddenly like in the 'yes' sign.

Anchor's up: both hands go up like football's 'touchdown' signal.

Swivels should always be used.

When a boat is anchored on a single anchor, it will often swing 360°. Over the years, this will cause a twist in the rode. This twist can cause kinks, which can affect its strength. These kinks can jam in the chainpipe when deploying the anchor and can be difficult to clear in a hurry. Adding a swivel where the chain meets the anchor can reduce this twisting. If it has a rope at the end of the chain, an additional swivel can be added to further reduce the twisting.

A washdown pump will help keep the chain clean.

A washdown pump should have enough pressure and a nozzle that will direct a strong, straight stream of water onto the chain. This will help clean mud and slime from the chain before it enters the interior of the boat. It also comes in handy for water fights.

Anchor cleats or bitts should be heavy duty.

Not only should these cleats or bitts be strong, but they must also be through-bolted with backup plates. This is not a place to have any doubts. If you think it might not be strong enough, change it or strengthen it. When you are away from the boat, you are relying on this fitting to hold her in any condition or situation.

Never leave the boat anchored with the chain on the gypsy.

If there is a sudden surge, the total load is on the gypsy and windlass. If the clutch is left to slip, it may continue to slip until all the chain is gone. If it is set up too tightly, it may strip the threads on the axis of the gypsy. Depending on the windlass and how it is installed, it could be ripped off the deck. Always secure the chain with a chain stopper or to a cleat before it goes to the gypsy.

Use a snubber line if anchoring with all chain.

The snubber line should be three-strand nylon with a breaking strength less than that of the chain. The objective is to let the snubber take the shock. If it breaks, the chain is still attached to the boat.

I prefer using a rolling hitch to attach the snubber to the chain. I tried a chain hook and found it difficult to keep it from falling off the chain during deployment. *However, a chain hook should be aboard to bring in the chain, in case the windlass breaks down.*

Set the anchor as normal. After the anchor is set and the proper scope is deployed, attach the snubber. Then, let out more chain with the snubber attached. I like to back the boat down so the chain is taut and the knot to the snubber is just above the surface. I secure the snubber to the boat and then let out more chain to create a catenary. This hanging chain loop increases the weight that must be lifted before the snubber comes up taut.

I like to have my snubber line about 50 feet long, so I can let more out if I am concerned about needing a little more scope. It is easier to let more out than to bring the chain in, untie the rolling hitch, let more chain out, and retie the snubber line. However, sometimes it may be necessary to do so. The longer the line, the more it will stretch, reducing the jerking motion of the boat.

Use caution when terminating snubber lines at the bobstay fitting.

Sometimes this is called the anchor tang, which is located on the stem, at the waterline. The reason I do not like this is that it makes it difficult to cast off in a hurry. In order to release the snubber, the chain must be brought aboard to access where the snubber is attached to the chain. In an emergency, there may not be time for this. If you feel the line must lead to this point, use a block so the line can be cast off from on deck. However, if you can reach this tang easily to cut the line if necessary, then it would be less of a problem.

Leading a snubber line on a bowsprit.

Using all chain rode and a snubber is always more difficult on a boat with a bowsprit. If the rode is deployed at the bow rollers on the stem, the snubber and chain will rub against the bobstay as the boat tacks back and forth. To prevent this, I use a heavy-duty swivel block attached to the underside of the Cranse Iron, which is on the end of the bowsprit, as shown in Figure 45.

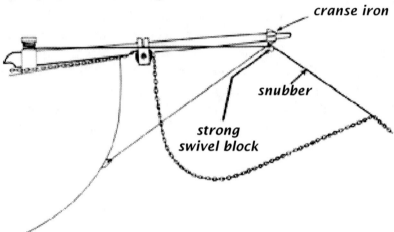

cranse iron

snubber

strong swivel block

Figure 45. Leading a snubber line on a bowsprit

To store the snubber line when not in use, one end is lead from the deck, passed through the block, and back to the deck. To deploy the snubber, one end is released and tied to the chain. The other end controls the length. When the chain is brought aboard, the snubber remains fed through the block with both ends on deck, tied to a cleat.

I have been asked if I am at all concerned about the load it puts on the end of the bowsprit. My response is that the bottom end of the bowsprit is supported by the bobstay. The top is supported by the headstay and backstay, which are putting the mast in compression. The whisker stays take any lateral loads. I have never had any indication that this could be a problem.

Secure snubber and anchor lines to cleats so they can be easily removed.

It is common practice to lock the line to a cleat or bitts with a final half hitch or clove hitch. If this is practiced, be certain the knot is not taking the load, or it will be difficult to remove. Wrap several passes around the base of the cleat before locking the line. I like a Tugman's hitch on bitts, which can be easily released. I rarely lock my line to the cleats anymore. Too many times, I have had the strain pull on the knot, making it impossible to untie. Now, I wrap the line around the base of the cleat several times, then do the normal figure eight. If I feel confident the load is on the wraps, then I might use a locking hitch.

Avoid securing snubber or anchor lines using a spliced or a tied loop.

This can be disastrous if the loop is passed under the cleat and back over it. If there is a load on the line, it is much more difficult to release than wraps of rope. *Loops belong on dock lines only, not when anchoring.*

When using a snubber or a rope rode, freshen the nip at the first sign of wear.

Chafe normally occurs in the nip where the line passes through a block, a chock, or a hawsehole. If you are going to be anchored for a while, use an anti-chafing sleeve over the line. If it is for a short time, check it regularly.

Be cautious using chain stoppers.

When bringing in chain while the boat is under a load, the chain stopper will not permit the chain to give when a wave shoves the boat aft. The chain may come up taut, and the chain or a shackle may break. It is better to leave it directly on the gypsy with the clutch not too tight so it will slip under a sudden load. The chain stopper can be used under normal conditions without a problem.

Always have a second anchor ready to deploy.

If there is an emergency and the primary anchor drags or the rode breaks, *a second anchor should be ready in an instant.* If it is hidden in a locker or if it has to be assembled, its purpose is defeated.

Attach a lifting line to the head of the anchor.

During a passage, I like to bring the anchors on deck so I can securely tie them to a chock or the shrouds. I don't want an anchor coming loose and hitting the hull when the weather turns rough.

To bring the anchor aboard, I attach a yellow polypropylene line to the head. It is short enough so there is no way it could reach the prop, yet long enough that it will float to the surface before the anchor. On the end, I splice a large loop so it can be easily grabbed with a boat hook.

Anchor chain rollers should be strong, with high cheeks and a chain guard.

This means they should have a method of locking the two sides together, so the rode cannot slip over the top.

This problem is all too common. Many anchor rollers are built and designed to take the load directly off the front of the roller. When the boat swings, the load is transferred to the cheeks or sides of the roller. The rope or chain might slip over the cheek, resulting in damage to the boat's caprail. If the chain is under a load, it can make it impossible to put the chain back into the rollers.

There should be a chain guard, such as a pin or arm, that fits over the top between the sides of the roller, locking the cheeks together. This will prevent the rope or chain from coming out of the roller. When the load is from the side, it will also help prevent the cheek from bending.

Display an anchor light when anchored.

Most boats have an anchor light on the masthead. Others may use a light hanging from the headstay or backstay. I know that many like to use kerosene anchor lamps.

Most sailors display these lights in a place where they are easy to reach. All too often, the dodger or windvane obscures the light. This light has to be seen by other boaters from a distance. In many foreign countries, powerboats will roar through an anchorage at night and may not see the light until it is too late to maneuver and avoid a collision.

Personally, I like to know that my anchor light is seen at night. I am not a great fan of the anchor light on the masthead, because it is difficult to see when approaching close to the boat. Also, if the masthead light is not bright enough, it will blend in with the stars.

My first choice is an 18-inch fluorescent 12V DC trouble light that has been waterproofed. I first saw these on the local fishing boats in Malaysia. The fluorescent light has a bluish color that makes it stand out against other lights in the anchorage. Because it is fluorescent, it draws little current. Its length definitely distinguishes it from any stars.

Avoid entering an unfamiliar anchorage at night.

When tired from a long passage or after a storm, we fantasize about a calm anchorage for the night. This might lead us to take unnecessary chances. In developing countries, the lights on the chart may not be lit, or they may not even exist anymore. Sometimes there might be a recent, uncharted, artificial reef, or a wreck that blocks the expected passage into the anchorage. If you are determined to enter a strange anchorage at night in rough weather, it could end in disaster. Each situation must be considered carefully. Nonetheless, I feel *it is best to heave-to and wait until daylight.*

When you enter an anchorage, decide if you intend to stay the night, regardless of the weather.

Survey the situation before setting the anchor. If the anchorage is exposed to the open sea from any direction, a severe squall could bring huge waves in the night, making it dangerous to stay. Set one anchor so it is easy to get underway in a hurry.

If you intend to spend the night, regardless of what the weather will bring, then set two anchors off the bow and one off the stern to prevent the boat from swinging. Only do this if you are exhausted and certain you want to spend the night. If a squall hits, it will be comforting to know the boat is secure.

This is a general rule to consider at each anchorage; it may not always be applicable. If there are other boats in the anchorage that are anchored differently than the way you prefer, *you have to follow their lead.*

Avoid taking a strange mooring.

It is impossible to know how safe a strange mooring is, unless you personally dive on it, or have firsthand knowledge or assurance that it is safe for your size boat.

I have attempted to use many moorings during my travels. I could move at least half of them under power. Some, I even broke. If the owner of the mooring is available, ask if you can test the mooring before paying. If he agrees, make sure there is a little slack in the mooring line to the boat. Then give the boat full throttle until the mooring line jerks the boat to a stop. This is still not a guarantee that the mooring will not drag or break in severe conditions. *Don't make the mistake of setting an anchor as well.* The rode will get wrapped around the mooring, making it difficult to retrieve. However, this would not apply if it were a stern anchor to prevent the boat from swinging.

Before anchoring, make certain the rode will deploy freely.

When I anchor on chain, I always bring about twenty feet on deck to make sure the chain runs free from the chain locker. Sometimes, the top of a pile of chain will tip over and trap the chain underneath, restricting it from being deployed. This will normally be discovered as soon as the first 20 feet are brought on deck.

The same applies to a rope rode. It is easy to get kinks or knots in rope. Sometimes, it will snag something inside the locker. If time permits, lay most of it on deck, so it will deploy from the top.

Make a pass where you intend to anchor.

Survey the area to see if there are any surprises that could interfere with anchoring. Check to see if the boat might swing into other boats or obstacles. It is good to know if there is a cross current, or if the wind shifts where the boat will set.

Boats that are already anchored have privilege over boats that anchor later.

It is usually the inexperienced sailor who does not respect this rule. It does not matter if a boat is in the middle of the anchorage with bow and stern anchors already set. *Any boat that comes in later must avoid the boat already at anchor.* If there is a problem because the anchorage is getting crowded, offer to assist the privileged boat to shift or change its anchoring method, but do not insist. Usually, by the time it becomes this crowded, there is nowhere else to go that would provide the same protection.

If possible, know the bottom before dropping the anchor.

This is not easy, because this information is not always correct on charts. I found that using a fish finder depth sounder increases the possibility of determining the bottom. It will show coral heads and large rocks, even wrecks. Different colors will indicate a soft or hard bottom.

For years, I sailed with an echo sounder that read to 60 feet and then would make another revolution starting at zero. It was impossible to tell if the bottom was 20 feet deep or 80 feet. Today, depth sounders are digital, eliminating the problem.

§

When I was working in Papua New Guinea, I ordered a fish finder that read to 2,000 feet. It lost much of its reliable clarity over 1,200 feet, but that was still deep enough to use for navigation if necessary. It came in handy at night or in fog to see when I passed over different depth contour lines. The problem was determining where I was on this line.

I loved this depth sounder, because it had different colors to indicate the type of bottom. It was always 100% correct; any error was with the operator. I found that I just did not take the time to interpret its reading clearly before dropping the anchor.

I forgot to properly read my fish finder when I set my CQR in 30 feet of water on the lee side of Panang Island, Malaysia. After a couple of days enjoying this lovely island, it was time to raise the anchor. I had great difficulty getting it to the surface. I figured I must have snagged a mooring chain or something heavy like a small wreck. I turned on my fish finder and there, clearly outlined, was a bunch of tires attached to my anchor. I managed to get it to the surface and discovered my CQR had penetrated one of the tires that was chained to hundreds more. It took hours to cut the wire-reinforced tire off the end of the anchor.

Presume the boat upwind will drag down on you.

Obviously, there is no way this can be predicted. However, if you consider that it could happen, it might influence your anchoring location.

I try to avoid anchoring anywhere near charter boats. All too often, the people who charter these boats are not experienced, and rarely anchor properly. Okay, I can hear the thoughts of some of you now. Of course there are exceptions to this, but how am I to know if the guy at the helm in his Speedos is an experienced cruising sailor?

Locate the anchors of other boats before setting your anchor.

This is not always possible because sometimes there is no one aboard the other boat when you are ready to anchor. Even if there is someone aboard, he or she may not be certain where his or her own anchor is set. The objective is to leave no stone unturned. The more knowledge you gather before dropping the anchor, the less chance you will have of bumping in the night or fouling someone else's anchor.

The boat anchored on chain and rope will swing wider than the boat anchored on all chain.

Always try to determine the type of rode the surrounding boats are using, so collisions in the night can be avoided. This especially applies during light wind conditions. If the boat's rode is all chain, the boat may be swinging on the weight of its own chain. It may swing in a small arc until the wind picks up, stretching out the chain.

The boat with chain and rope will have a much wider swing in light conditions. The more knowledge you have, the better your chances of avoiding problems.

Full-keeled boats may set with the current; powerboats and fin-keeled boats may set with the wind.

It is apparent that this will depend on the strength of the wind and current. At least take this into consideration when selecting the spot to set the anchor. Often you will see two boats setting feet apart, pointing 90° to each other. This is probably the reason.

Keep the decks clear of obstacles.

Everyone will eventually have an anchor drag, or have some other boat drag down on them in the darkness of night. Running around on deck can be a problem, if the deck is cluttered with SCUBA tanks, dive gear, fishing poles, etc.

§

While I was in Thailand, a squall hit in the middle of the night. A local charter boat began dragging. In the rush to get the boat under control, a crewmember shoved his foot deep into the tip of a spear gun that was left on deck.

If you are laying beam to the wind, you are probably dragging.

If you find you are setting beam to the wind, immediately check to see how other boats are setting. Also, take bearings to see if you are dragging. It might be that the boat is setting with the current instead of the wind, but never ignore this situation.

Have a plan in advance on how to depart in a hurry at night.

My example of the barge drifting down on me should illustrate the importance of having a plan in mind to get underway in a hurry. Each crewmember should clearly understand his or her particular

responsibility if the boat must get underway in the middle of the
night.

Try to avoid using the dinghy when setting and raising anchors.

If the dinghy is used to set the anchor, more than likely, it will
also be required to raise the anchor. No matter how many anchors
need to be set, they should be set by the mother boat whenever
possible, so that they can be retrieved the same way.

There are always exceptions to this suggestion: it might be close
quarters; it might be the current or wind strength and direction; it
might be setting the anchor in shallow water or ashore. Or perhaps
your boat is already anchored, and another anchor needs to be set.
And the list goes on. In all of these situations, the use of the dinghy
may be required.

If the dinghy must be used, be sure to put the anchor, chain, and all the rode you expect to use in the dinghy.

It is impossible to row, towing several hundreds of feet of rope
behind the dinghy. Even if there is a motor on the dinghy, it is still
easier to pay the rode out from the dinghy than to tow the rode.
Needless to say, if the rode is all chain, it may be impossible to use
the dinghy.

I feel too many cruisers rely too much on their dinghy's outboard
to set and raise their anchors. I am not trying to talk anyone out of
outboard engines; they are an essential part of the cruising boat. I just
want to state that all too often the outboard will not start. Perhaps the
motor is onboard the mother boat, and the waves are short and steep,
making it nearly impossible to mount it on the dinghy's transom. The
outboard could be out of gas when it is needed the most. If the dinghy
can be rowed into the wind, it will be a bonus when the engine fails.

There may be times when the weather and seas are so severe that
it is not safe—or even possible—to use the dinghy to set another
anchor. If necessary, tie the anchor and chain to a float, or to a few
fenders tied together, and swim it out.

I learned about this method from Lin and Larry Pardey. Fortunately, I have never had to put it to the test; however, I do know how many fenders I need to float my anchor and chain, just in case.

Anchoring using the engine

This section covers the basics for setting anchors in various circumstances using the engine. The suggestions provided are not absolutes. Because every anchoring situation is different, each requires a special strategy. I will discuss as many as possible. My purpose is to relate ideas and techniques that can be carried over to other situations.

I wish I could take credit for all of these suggestions, but I can't. These techniques were gained over many years from personal experience, watching others, and reading books on anchoring. Some of the ideas mentioned are from books written by Lin and Larry Pardey, and they all seem to work.

Scope

When determining the length of scope to use, always figure the height from the transducer to the bow roller as part of the depth. *Don't forget to add high tide as well.*

When anchoring with all chain, the general rule is a 5 to 1 ratio: 5 feet of chain for every foot of depth.

If a combination of chain and rope is used, a ratio of 7 to 1 is considered appropriate. This will depend on how much chain is used and its size.

These ratios are only estimates; there are many variables that should also be considered. If the rode is all chain and the water is deeper than 40 feet, this ratio can be reduced because of the additional weight of the chain. If the bottom is hard, grass, or shallow sand over coral, the anchor will not set properly; then, the ratio should be increased. If unsettled weather is expected, increase the ratio. Regardless of the reason, *it is always better to err by increasing the ratio, rather than by reducing it.*

Trip lines and anchor buoys

I know that many authors recommend using a buoy on the anchor. When anchoring in rock or coral, the anchor will often foul, and it is presumed that a buoy will make it easy to retrieve. Unfortunately, this is not the case. More often than not, the anchor buoy causes more problems than it solves. The major advantage to the anchor buoy is to indicate the location of the anchor.

With few exceptions, I find the anchor buoy line will twist around the chain as it sinks to the bottom. If it does twist around the chain, it will be of little help if the anchor is fouled. Also, the line may be too short for the buoy to reach the surface.

I tried to throw the buoy way out before I released the anchor and chain, but it still wrapped around the chain on the way down. It did this more often than not. I tried to hold on to the float line, using it to let the anchor sink to the bottom. This worked, but it was a hassle. One person could do it, if the water was shallow. Deeper water made the chain and anchor too heavy to control by hand, so it required someone on the float line and another at the windlass. If the boat was moving, it made the process even more difficult.

If an anchor buoy is to be used, the line should not sink. This means is should be polypropylene line, not nylon, unless the nylon line has floats attached.

§

When I first began cruising, I often fouled my anchor or wrapped chain around a coral head. I decided to tie a strong nylon line and buoy to the head of the anchor, so I could easily free it. The result was that this so-called trip line always got fouled on the coral. Many times, the anchor and chain was near the surface, but the fouled trip line held it fast. I had to dive to free or cut the line.

I finally got rid of the nylon line and used polypropylene, which floats. It worked better, but it still fouled too often.

The anchor buoy line must be slightly longer than the depth of the water at high tide. When the tide drops, there will be excess line floating on the surface. A passing boat might catch this line in its prop or rudder, tripping the anchor.

The buoy line might catch the boat's prop or rudder when the boat swings with the changing tidal currents or winds. It may not be your own boat; it may be someone else's. If the engine is started, it will make the situation worse, as shown in Figure 46.

Even if all goes well and there is no excess line floating on the surface, the buoy will be an annoyance when it bangs against the hull in the middle of the night. This problem, however, can be eliminated if the boat is anchored bow and stern.

Some sailors will advise leading the trip line back to the boat. This may be okay if the boat will not swing and the line will not float on the surface. Just keep in mind, when a line is attached to the head of the anchor, and if it catches something, the anchor will trip.

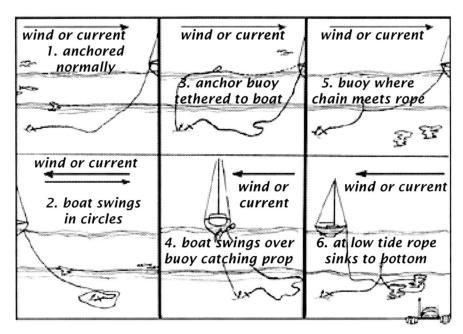

Figure 46. Anchoring problems with trip lines

I discovered two methods that work to help prevent the line from snagging the prop or rudder. One is to tie the line to the bottom of a Dan buoy, as shown in Figure 47.

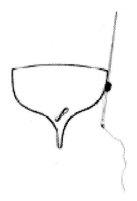

Figure 47. Using a Dan buoy as anchor float

The bottom of the pole sets deep enough that the line will not snag the boat. A weight can be added about 5 to 10 feet below the bottom of the pole to ensure the excess line does not float on the surface. The problem occurs when a passing boat tries to pick up the Dan Buoy.

Another method that I learned from a dear friend, Elizabeth Pearce, is to use a fender as the float. Attach a small swivel block to the bottom of the fender. The trip line is passed though the block and a lead weight attached to the end of the line, as shown in Figure 48.

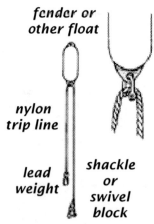

Figure 48. Using a fender as anchor float

The result is a float that will rise and fall vertically with the change of tides and cannot foul on the prop or rudder, as shown in Figure 49.

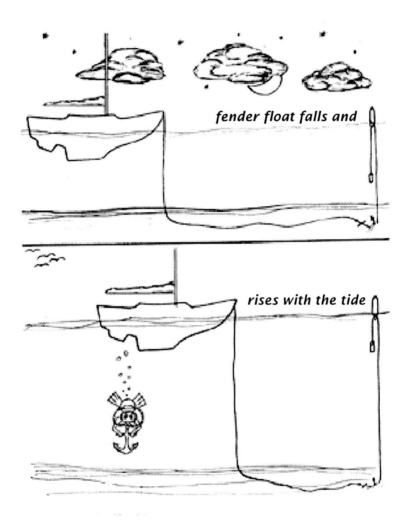

fender float falls and

rises with the tide

Figure 49. Trip line with fender float that does not foul on prop or rudder

Setting the primary anchor under power

Prepare the anchor and rode. Make certain the anchor is ready to deploy. I like to hang it over the bow just above the water. I always have ample amounts of chain piled on deck, so it will lead off the top.

Check to see how other boats are anchored, and ask where they expect their anchors are located. Then make a pass where you intend to anchor, and check the depth and swinging room. Determine as accurately as possible where the anchor will be dropped.

When you are in the position you expect to set, stop the boat momentarily to determine if the boat will drift with the wind or the current. Motor back out to where there is more room to maneuver, and gather your thoughts. Discuss your intentions with crewmembers, and clearly assign duties.

Motor back to the area where the anchor will be set. Slowly, approach upwind or up current, whichever is stronger. As the drop area nears, reduce speed so you have control and can quickly stop the forward momentum.

Put the engine in reverse just before reaching the location. The boat should continue to drift slowly past the drop area before it begins to make sternway. While slowly moving in reverse, drop the anchor when you pass over the spot where it will set.

Many beginning sailors make the mistake of stopping the boat, then dropping the anchor and the chain in a pile. This increases the chances of the anchor being fouled by its own chain.

Continue in reverse, letting out rode. Keep the rode under control, do not let it just run free. If the boat has a tendency to move sideways while backing, put it in neutral and wait until it is back in line with the anchor, or motor forward to get back into position.

When the appropriate amount of scope has been deployed, let out another 20 to 50 feet. Then, signal the helmsman to put the engine in neutral.

If using a chain rode, slowly snug the gypsy until it stops running out. If using a line rode, take one wrap around the capstan, bitts, or cleat, and slowly control the boat to a stop.

When there is no load, secure the rode to something permanent like the bitts or a cleat. Then, signal the helmsman to reverse slowly.

As the rode slowly becomes taut, put your hand or foot on top of the rode to feel if the anchor is dragging. If it is dragging, you will be able to feel it skip along the bottom. This is more readily felt with chain than with rope. If it does drag, let out more scope.

When the anchor feels set, let the engine continue to run slowly in reverse until the scope is taut. Hold it at this slow speed for a minute, then slowly increase rpm.

Continue to feel the rode to see if the anchor is dragging, and have the helmsman *slowly* increase rpm. If too much rpm is used too quickly, it will break the anchor out before it is properly set.

After you are certain the anchor is set, put the engine in neutral. If all chain is being used, the boat will catapult forward from the weight of the chain.

If excessive amount of scope was deployed to set the anchor, the excess can now be brought back aboard. However, you might want to consider leaving the extra scope.

Tie the snubber line to the chain with a rolling hitch, and let the chain back out. Put the engine in reverse until the snubber line and anchor rode are equally taut, and the knot is just above the water. Secure the snubber line.

Let out another 10 feet of anchor chain so the load is entirely on the snubber. Then, secure the chain to the chain stopper, cleat, or bitts, *but not to the gypsy*. When the snubber is taut, there should be a loop of chain hanging between the bow and the knot.

Take a depth reading, and sight your position. Record the depth and bearing, so they are not forgotten. If at any time, the boat swings to 90° or more from the direction the anchor was set, start the engine, and back down to make sure the anchor is still secure.

If possible, always dive on the anchor to visually check that it is properly set. However, I don't advise this in areas where salt-water crocodiles are common, like Northern Australia.

§

I was anchored in Darwin harbor and wanted to change my prop from a three-blade to a two-blade before the Darwin-Ambon race. As soon as I got out of the water, an official boat from the yacht club came by and began to chew me out. Apparently, salt-water crocodiles frequent the area to eat the garbage from the boats. They really like human meat.

Anchoring bow and stern anchor under power

Only anchor bow and stern when it is necessary. It may be because the other boats in the anchorage are already bow and stern. Or, you may want the bow to point into the wind, waves, or current. There could be danger close by if the boat were permitted to swing. Perhaps you want to spend the night with two anchors off the bow and a stern anchor to keep the boat from swinging. I am sure there are many other reasons.

Regardless of the reason, always try to use the same scope on the stern rode as the bow, if there is any chance the wind will shift from that direction, as shown in Figure 50. Otherwise, use a little more scope where the strongest wind is expected.

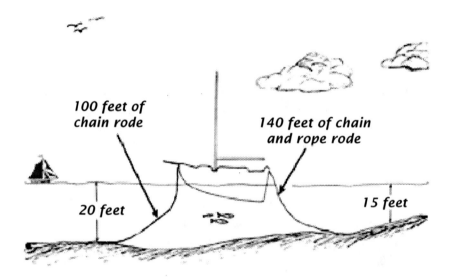

100 feet of chain rode

140 feet of chain and rope rode

20 feet

15 feet

Figure 50. Anchoring bow and stern under power

Ready the stern anchor with the rode on deck, so it will deploy off the top of the pile and will not snag something during deployment.

Set the bow anchor as mentioned above. After it is set, motor in reverse until at least double the required scope is deployed off the bow. If the boat has a tendency to pull to port or starboard, put the engine in neutral until it sets with the wind or current. If this does not work, move the rudder to steer where you want the boat, then give the engine short bursts in forward until back in position.

When the bow rode is out with double the required scope and taut, drop the stern anchor.

With or without using the engine, slowly pull in on the bow anchor rode until the stern anchor sets. If there is help aboard, it is easier if a crewmember controls the stern line, keeping pressure on it while the bow rode is brought aboard. This will help set the stern anchor while adjusting the boat between the two. Make sure the stern crewperson understands that you are pulling the boat forward, so he or she uses minimum tension.

When the boat is positioned between the two anchors, the engine can be used to properly set the stern anchor. Make certain the stern line is free to cast off quickly if necessary.

If strong winds, waves, or current are expected from the bow, use a little extra scope on this anchor. Use anti-chafing at the areas of concern, if strong winds are expected and the rode passes through a chock or hawsehole.

Dive on the anchors whenever it's possible and safe to do so.

Anchoring on a steep drop-off

Sometimes, there is a steep drop-off a narrow shelf of shallow water, making it difficult to swing on one anchor. This is most commonly seen in the tropics, where the coral suddenly drops off to great depths. The shelf is usually deep enough for a boat to anchor, but without swinging room. If the boat swings out over deeper water, the anchor would be pulling downhill; this is dangerous because the anchor could easily break free.

Set the bow anchor over the side of the shelf, so it will be pulling uphill, as shown in Figure 51. This requires much less scope. Then set the stern anchor following the same steps previously mentioned.

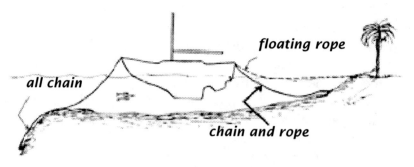

floating rope

all chain

chain and rope

Figure 51. Anchoring on a steep drop-off

If there is not enough room to set a stern anchor, or if the holding is poor, use the dinghy to take a line ashore to a rock or tree. *It is important that the stern line be passed around the tree and led back to the boat, so it can be cast off from the boat, if necessary.*

Pass the stern line as high as possible up the tree to keep it from setting on sharp coral or rocks. If this is not possible, then you should use a line that floats, so it does not chafe on the bottom. If the bottom is sand or mud, this is of little concern.

If there is any possibility that there will be other boats in the area, *be sure to mark the stern line by tying floats or fenders to the line to warn others.*

Anchoring parallel to a steep drop-off

This method should not be used unless absolutely necessary. It is shown in Figure 52. This technique has some limitations and dangers. Carefully consider each step and potential problems that may occur before using it.

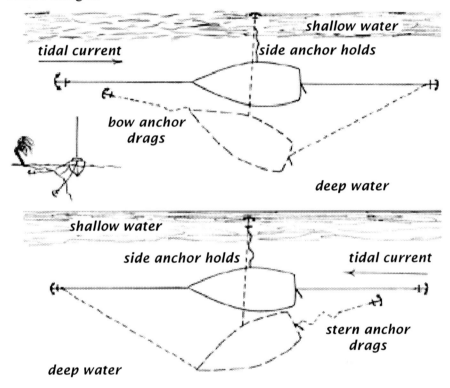

Figure 52. Anchoring parallel to a steep drop-off

I used this method when I anchored in a large protected bay on the southern tip of the Celebes in Indonesia. There was a fishing village soon after we entered the bay. All the local fishing boats were on bow and stern moorings, which were no more than chain permanently wrapped around pieces of coral. The water was either too shallow to anchor, or it dropped steeply to great depths. The shelf was not deep enough to allow me to anchor using the previous method. The only possibility was to anchor bow and stern, parallel to the shore. The current ran in opposite directions when the tide changed. It ran at about two knots, parallel to the shore. If either anchor gave way, we would be aground in the coral.

We motored into the current, parallel to the shore, in about 20 feet of water. We were about 30 feet from the shallow water with a coral bottom.

I set the anchor off the bow and slowly let the current carry me back, so I was at least double the scope I intended to use. Then I set my stern anchor and centered myself between the two.

I dove on both anchors. There wasn't any sand, just dead white coral.

Since the coral was not very big, there was danger that either anchor could break the small bump of coral that held it. I tied the helm over, so the current forced the bow to point away from the shore. If the bow anchor gave way, the boat would swing out to deeper water and around 180°. Then the stern anchor would be holding the boat. The chances were high that the stern anchor might not hold with the pull 180° from the way it was set. There was also the possibility that the boat could swing into the shallow water.

I took another anchor ashore and set it in the shallow water. The other end I secured at my midship cleat. Now, if the bow anchor failed, the boat would swing out to deeper water until the midship anchor held her fast. This would give me time to get underway or re-anchor.

Now, the problem was when the tidal current changed and was coming from the stern. If the stern anchor failed, I would have the same problem. However, with the rudder still in its same position, the stern would be pushed into the deeper water. The same midship anchor would keep me from doing 180°.

The only remaining danger was if the wind changed and came from the beam, pushing us towards the shallow water. There was little I could do about that. The drop-off was nearly vertical, so setting an anchor on the deep side would not solve the problem. All I could do was to bring both rodes up taut to restrict as much movement as possible.

Fortunately, the wind never shifted from this direction. We spent several days anchored in this fashion and had a great time. We were the only cruising boat that had ever visited this bay and village. That's what cruising is all about.

Anchoring on a coral head

This method, shown in Figure 53, is not common. I have used it several times when anchoring inside the lagoon of a coral atoll. Generally, tropical atolls do not have much sand. The sand that is available is usually shallow over hard coral, so the anchor may not set properly. *This is not a procedure I would recommend, except when there is no other choice.*

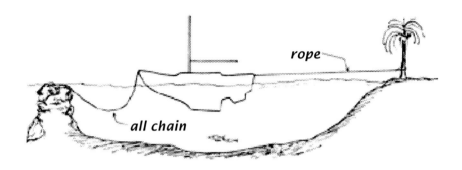

Figure 53. Anchoring on a coral head

§

The first time I used this method was at Ahe, a coral atoll in the Tuamotus, between the Marquesas and Tahiti. There was a narrow pass where the current ran strong with the tides. This is common if the lagoon within the atoll is totally protected by a surrounding reef. When the tide changed, all the water had to run through the pass, instead of over the reef. The only safe way to negotiate the pass was at slack tide or just as the tide turned. It was possible to go with the tide, but sometimes it flowed very fast. There may have also been coral heads in the pass that nearly reached the surface; if the current were running strong, it would be difficult to avoid hitting one.

The anchorage was in front of a village across the lagoon. The lagoon was filled with coral heads that just reached the surface, making it dangerous to navigate at night.

When it was time to depart, we learned that slack tide was at first light. We did not want to try to reach the pass in the darkness before sun-up. So that afternoon, we sailed to just inside the pass, looking for somewhere to anchor. We couldn't find a place that would not put us on a lee shore and exposed to the strong Tradewinds that often blew across the lagoon.

We found a large coral head where the water between it and shore was deep enough to accept *Xiphias*. There was a tree on the beach directly behind the coral head.

While in the safety of the deep lagoon, I took my CQR out to the tip of the bowsprit and tied it there with a slipknot. The chain led back through the bow roller and piled on deck, so it would lead off the top.

While my girlfriend motored in a slow circle, I took the dinghy and a long length of polypropylene ashore to tie to the tree. I rowed the line out to deeper water, and my girlfriend motored over to me. I climbed aboard with the dinghy alongside.

I put a single wrap around a stern cleat so that it would slip and still maintain control. I continued to pay the stern line out, as my girlfriend slowly approached the protected side of the coral head. It was a vertical drop-off, so we could motor right up to its edge. I secured the stern line and left the engine idling in forward. My girlfriend stayed at the helm, while I ran out to the bowsprit and dropped my anchor on top of the coral head, right at the edge.

I returned to the helm, put the engine in neutral, and began pulling back on the stern line. The weight of the chain off the bow kept the stern line taut.

When I felt we were safely away from the coral head, I rowed the dinghy out to check that the anchor was grabbing a big chunk of coral. It wasn't.

I returned to the boat and took another line from the bow to the coral and tied it to a strong chunk. Then my girlfriend pulled in the slack and secured it to a cleat. When she felt the boat was securely tethered with the new line, she let out some on the primary anchor chain, releasing the load. This gave me the slack I needed to move the anchor to a better location. I set it behind a large piece of coral that was even closer to the edge, which would make it easier to raise from the bowsprit in the morning.

I left this temporary line from the bow to the coral, just in case the anchor did give way. I knew I would not be able to retrieve it in the morning, because it was tied too far over the coral: the price we pay for a little extra security.

Next, I took another polypropylene line from the boat, wrapped it around the tree on the beach, and back to the boat. Then, I released the first line I had tied to the tree. This now permitted me to release the new stern line from the boat.

The next morning, we started the engine and motored over the bow anchor to lift it aboard, while keeping tension on the stern line. As soon as the anchor was aboard, we pulled the stern line aboard. We were on our way through the pass at slack tide.

I am sure you can imagine all the things that might have gone wrong. There was always the possibility that the stern line could have chafed through on a piece of coral. The chunk of coral holding the anchor could have broken off the coral head. In the morning, there might have been wind blowing against our beam, making it dangerous to release either bow or stern line.

There are other things that could have gone wrong, but I felt the anchor was secure. The stern line was passed around the tree as high as I could reach to keep it above the coral to prevent chafe. If I had to do it over again, I think I would use a sacrificial piece of chain looped around a chunk of coral. I would have then passed a line through this chain loop, so I did not have to get so close to the coral head. Of course, this would have required using the dinghy and more time.

This method can be used on boats without a bowsprit, but it requires the use of the dinghy to remove the anchor, unless there is a chain loop left on the coral.

Anchoring in deep water with coral bottom

This is about the only anchoring situation where a 1 to 1 scope would be used, based on high tide. See Figure 54. I gave an example of this type of anchoring earlier in the chapter, when I discussed the importance of the speed in which the anchor windlass can lift the anchor off the bottom.

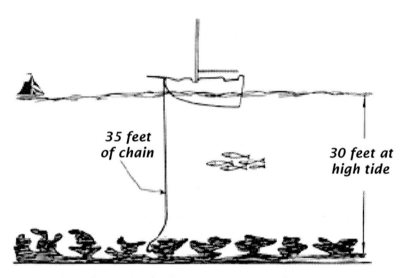

35 feet of chain

30 feet at high tide

Figure 54. Anchoring in deep water with coral bottom

If at all possible, never anchor in coral, particularly when the water is deep. However, sometimes there is little choice. If it is necessary to anchor this way, be aware that it will be a restless night. The boat will come up hard on the chain with each wave. The sound of the anchor in the coral will travel up the chain and be heard throughout the boat. At least, the boat will not go anywhere, and as long as the anchorage is protected, it will be a safe night.

Setting two anchors in tandem

There are times when it may be necessary to set two anchors on the same rode, as shown in Figure 55. I use this method when there is only a foot or so of sand over a hard coral bottom. One anchor will not bury deep enough to hold, but using two increases the holding ability.

Anchor A: fluke or claw type
Anchor B: plow type
Anchor C: fluke or claw type

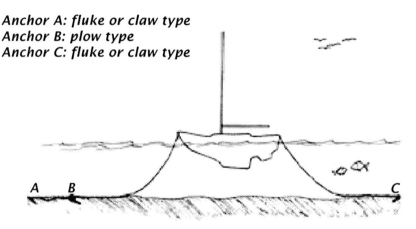

Figure 55. Setting two anchors in tandem

Another reason to use this method is that there may be boats on either side of your boat already anchored with two anchors set apart. To do the same would certainly cross someone else's anchor.

If this method is used, it is advisable, not mandatory, to use a stern anchor. The reason is that the boat will swing on the anchor closest to the boat, which will take most of the load. If this anchor is not properly set, it may turn over and never reset. Also, there is the possibility that the chain can foul on the first anchor as the boat swings in circles.

To set two anchors in tandem, select the area where the boat will set, as mentioned previously. Then, prepare all anchors. I prefer using a fluke or claw-type anchor on the end of the chain. These anchors are best on a straight-line pull and hold well. After the first anchor, I like to set a CQR plow-type because it will plow, transferring the load to the first anchor. Also, the plow-type anchor will allow for some swinging and still remain set.

Set the fluke or claw-type anchor first. It should have about 50 feet of chain followed by a rope rode. After it is properly set, bring in the rode until the thimble, where the chain and rope are connected, is reached. Take off the shackle to remove the rope and thimble.

Shackle the end of the chain to the head of the CQR, and seize the pin as normal. Depending on the depth of the water, bring up more chain so there will be enough slack to set the second anchor.

Drop the CQR on all chain, and back down until it is set. If there isn't enough slack in the first anchor chain, the second anchor will not set.

After both anchors are set in tandem off the bow, continue in reverse in order to set the stern anchor as described previously.

Setting two anchors at 30° to 60° apart

I feel more comfortable having at least two anchors set if I am tired and really need some sleep, or if I intend to leave the boat to go ashore for a few days. I also set two anchors off the bow if I expect severe weather.

When the wind or tide changes, the boat may swing 360° or more, twisting the two rodes. For this reason, a stern anchor should also be used so that the boat doesn't swing, as shown in Figure 56.

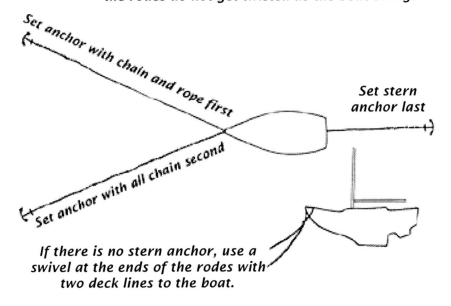

Best to use a stern anchor when using this method, so the rodes do not get twisted as the boat swings.

Set anchor with chain and rope first

Set stern anchor last

Set anchor with all chain second

If there is no stern anchor, use a swivel at the ends of the rodes with two deck lines to the boat.

Figure 56. Setting two anchors 30° to 60° apart

If there is a reason that a stern anchor should not be used, then the two bow anchors should terminate at a swivel below the surface. Also, try to set the bow anchors far enough apart so that they don't foul on each other's chains when the boat swings. This will also prevent the chain from dragging along the bottom and snagging a rock or piece of coral.

However, if the boat will swing, I prefer not setting the anchors 30° to 60° apart, but 180° apart. This will be covered in the next topic.

If the wind is blowing, set the first anchor more to windward; this will make it easier to set the second anchor. *Always set the anchor that has the chain and rope rode first.* Set it as described previously. If the anchor with all chain is set first, it is much more difficult to raise it and pay it out when trying to set the second anchor.

After you are confident that the first anchor is properly set, bring the rode back aboard until the chain is reached. Then motor sharply away from this anchor, being careful not to go the wrong way and cross over it. Pay out rode as you approach the location to set the second anchor. When you are over the spot where you want the anchor set, drop it and set it as normal, while paying out the rode to the first anchor. Then, adjust both rodes so the scope on the rope rode is about a 7 to 1 ratio, and the scope on the all chain rode is about a 5 to 1 ratio. This takes some advanced planning.

If a stern anchor is to be used, set it as normal, letting out double the scope on both bow anchor rodes before dropping the anchor.

Perhaps the boat will swing, and there is no need for a stern anchor. In that case, a swivel must be used where the two rodes meet. This is done by paying out both rodes until the end of the chain rode is reached. Attach a heavy-duty swivel to the last link. Then tie two heavy lines to the top of the swivel. Pass one of these lines to the other side of the bow so there is a line on each side of the bow attached to the top of the swivel.

Using this bow line, pull the swivel around to the other side of the boat, and bring it aboard. Attach another large shackle to the bottom of the swivel. Through this shackle, pass the end of the rope rode, and pull up any slack; then, tie a bowline. Remember that the rope rode needs more scope than the all chain rode. If there is a lot of excess rope, coil it and tie it together, then cast it overboard.

If everything was done correctly, the chain and rope rodes should be attached to the bottom of the swivel, and there should be two lines tied to the top of the swivel that lead to opposite sides of the bow.

Let the weight of chain sink the swivel down below the keel, and secure both lines on deck. The two lines on top of the swivel prevent it from rotating with the bottom half, forcing it to swivel.

Setting two anchors opposite each other

In this situation, the anchors are set 180° apart, as shown in Figure 57. I like to use this method if I want to leave the boat for a day or two, and there is limited swinging room.

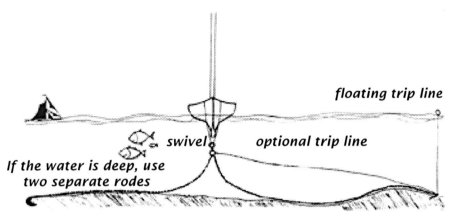

floating trip line

swivel

optional trip line

If the water is deep, use
two separate rodes

If the water is shallow, use one continuous 300 ft. length of chain

Figure 57. Setting two anchors opposite each other

It can be done two ways. In the first method, a single 300 feet of chain is used for both anchors, with the boat tethered to the middle of the chain. In the second method, it can be done similarly to the procedure stated previously, using two separate anchor rodes meeting at the boat.

If the water is shallow and has good holding, the boat can be anchored on one 300-foot length of chain. This is done by setting the primary anchor rode as normal. After it is set, continue to reverse until the 150-foot mark, or half its length, is reached. At this point, attach a large swivel.

If the swivel has a pin that fits through a link, it may not be strong enough. If the swivel is high tensile, it will fit and be strong. Presuming there isn't a high tensile swivel available, use a shackle that will fit over the chain. Keep this large shackle in place by using smaller shackles through the links on both sides of this large shackle. Attach the swivel to this large shackle.

Tie two deck lines to the top of the swivel. One line should be about double the depth of the water and be buoyed. Toss this line and buoy overboard. The other line should be at least 150 feet long, so it will reach the end of the chain. It should remain aboard. Of course, you could use the buoyed line and motor back to this line after the second anchor is set.

Continue to reverse, paying out chain and this longer line. It is best if they are paid out from opposite sides of the boat, so that the rope does not tangle with the chain. When the bitter end of the chain reaches the deck, attach the other anchor appropriately. A swivel will not be necessary. At this time, I suggest attaching a trip line to this anchor to make retrieval easier.

When the anchor is ready, continue to reverse until all the chain is taut; then, deploy this second anchor. Using the trip line, let it down slowly. The boat will still have the rope aboard that is attached at the middle of the chain. Using this line, pull the boat back to the center of the chain while paying out the trip line.

If possible, lift the center of the chain to the surface to grab the other line that was buoyed. If the chain is too heavy to lift to the surface, motor over to grab the buoy, being careful not to catch the other lines in the prop.

Bring both lines aboard, one on each side of the boat, to keep the top of the swivel from rotating. Now back down, setting the second anchor. This should provide enough slack in the chain to be able to raise it to the surface. Attach the second anchor trip line to the bottom of the swivel. If the chain and swivel still cannot be raised to the surface to attach the trip line, it may be necessary to dive and tie it to the bottom of the swivel.

If this is out of the question, then the trip line should be an anchor buoy; it will have to be shortened to just reach the surface at high tide. This can be done when it is set, or later, using the dinghy.

When it comes time to raise the anchors, the trip line will make it much easier. If a trip line is not used, it may require diving on one of the anchors in order to bring it aboard.

For maximum holding ability, or when the water is deeper, use two rodes. This is done as mentioned earlier. When the bitter end of the rode of the first anchor is reached, it can be buoyed and dropped overboard, or an additional line can be attached. This line must be long enough to set the second anchor.

Set the second anchor as explained previously. It is not necessary to buoy this anchor, because it will be retrieved as normal. If the end of the first anchor rode was buoyed, motor back, paying out the second anchor rode until the buoy is reached. If there was a long line tied to the end of the first anchor rode, pull the boat back to the end.

Bring both ends of the rodes aboard and attach them to the bottom of a large swivel. Attach the two deck lines to the top of the swivel, and bring them aboard on opposite sides of the bow. Let the swivel sink below the keel.

Raise the anchors as normal, one at a time.

The anchor mooring

This idea for the anchor mooring came from Lin and Larry Pardey, and is shown in Figure 58. When I had to leave the boat for an undetermined amount of time, I found it worked perfectly. I prefer this method to a questionable mooring. The only problem would be if the anchor mooring were set in a busy anchorage. Other boats could hook the rodes and trip the anchors. Buoys set at each anchor with the word "*anchor*" clearly marked on them may help. Unfortunately, there is always someone who will raise the buoy to see what is at the other end.

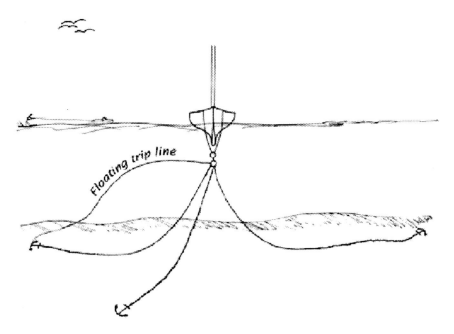

Figure 58. The anchor mooring

The boat will be left for a considerable amount of time and will have to survive any weather. Consequently, make sure the anchors are set as far out as possible, using all their rode. Try to set the anchors as close to 120° apart as possible, as shown in Figure 58.

Figure 59. Pre-assembled swivel with shackles

When setting the anchor mooring, plan on having some time on your hands. I suggest you have a swivel with appropriate shackles already made up, ready to use, as shown in Figure 59.

Set the first anchor as normal. After all the rode is deployed, attach the bitter end to the bottom of a heavy-duty swivel. Tie a line with a float to the top of the swivel, and let the rode settle to the bottom so the float is accessible. I like to use the Dan Buoy for this because it is easy to grab from the deck of the boat.

Try to judge the direction and distance to set the second anchor. It is set like the first anchor, then the boat is brought back to the float that is tied to the bitter end of the first anchor rode. Using the float, raise the swivel to the surface, and attach the second anchor rode to the bottom of the swivel's shackle. Let the swivel settle to the bottom with the buoy. Then set the third anchor like the other two.

After all three rodes are attached to the bottom of the swivel, a killet can be attached to it to keep it all well below the keel or on the bottom. This additional weight will help keep all three rodes on a more horizontal pull, as shown in Figure 60.

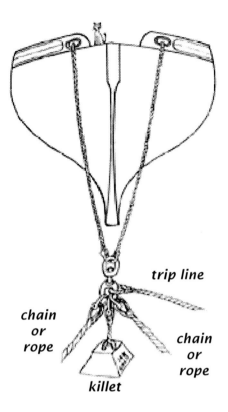

trip line

chain
or
rope

chain
or
rope

killet

Figure 60. Using a killet to keep swivel under keel

If the boat will be left on this mooring without moving on and off, then lead two lines from the top of the swivel to both sides of the bow.

If the boat will be moving on and off the mooring, the mooring line should have a float to keep it off the bottom when not tethered to the boat. Refer to the section on setting a mooring later in this chapter.

Setting anchors under sail

Every cruiser should be able to set the anchors under sail. The time may come when the engine does not work, and there is no other choice. *The keys to anchoring under sail are preparation and control of speed*. It is important to know how far the boat will coast, and how it will maneuver after all sails lose their drive. This only comes from experience.

The best way to accomplish this is to practice where there aren't any other boats or obstructions. I used fenders as markers and placed them where I expected other boats would set. If I bumped into the fender, I just wiped out someone's boat.

Setting the primary anchor upwind, under sail

First, sail past the location to determine where you want to set the anchor. If there is room, put the boat in irons to determine if the boat will drift with the wind or current. Presuming the boat will set with the wind, sail out to more open water. When there are no obstacles, prepare the anchor so it will drop quickly, and the chain will run freely.

If the approach is from a distance, the main and headsail can be used. As you get closer, furl or drop the headsail, and sail only on the main. If the winds are fresh, put in a reef or two to have better control of the speed. *The objective is to just make headway, not speed.*

Make the approach slowly, sailing at an angle to the wind with just the mainsail, as shown in Figure 61. (Some boats will not sail to windward well on the main alone. If that is the case, a foresail may have to be deployed.) It is important that the boat gradually be brought upwind to reduce speed as it gets closer to where the anchor will be dropped. Just before you are over the location to drop the anchor, bring the boat upwind so the mainsail luffs, and the boat stalls.

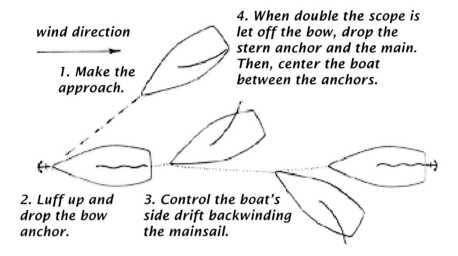

wind direction

1. Make the approach.

4. When double the scope is let off the bow, drop the stern anchor and the main. Then, center the boat between the anchors.

2. Luff up and drop the bow anchor.

3. Control the boat's side drift backwinding the mainsail.

Figure 61. Setting the primary anchor upwind under sail

Now, it is important to *make sure the main sheets are let out,* so they are totally free. The boat will eventually fall off to one side or the other. If the main is in too tight, it will start driving forward again. The mainsail sheets cannot be too loose either.

Slowly, drop the anchor when the boat stalls, so the chain does not pile on top of the anchor. Leave just enough resistance on the gypsy, so the chain won't fall from its own weight. This is not as important if there is a crewmember at the windlass to control the run-out.

As the boat begins to drift backward, the bow will have a tendency to fall off to port or starboard. It is important that there be some resistance on the chain to help keep the bow into the wind.

The side drift can be controlled by backwinding the mainsail by hand. Regardless of the direction the bow falls off, push the main into the wind, and hold it there until the boat is back in position. If the bow falls off to port, push the main out to starboard, and vice versa. If the boat does not respond, there is not enough resistance on the bow rode. It may be necessary to tighten the gypsy a little.

The rudder can be used to get the boat back into position, but more than likely, there is not going to be enough sternway for it to have any effect. I usually secure it amidships.

Continue backing the main to keep the boat in position, while paying out chain. When the appropriate amount of scope is deployed, secure the boat as normal. If it is a chain rode, connect the snubber.

After everything is secure, backwind the main on both sides of the boat to help set the anchor. Then, drop the main.

Setting bow and stern anchors upwind

If a stern anchor is to be set, follow the same procedure described above, but continue to pay out rode until it is about double the scope needed, as shown in Figure 61. Drop the stern anchor, drop the main, and pull the boat forward, while setting the stern anchor. Secure both rodes and the boat as normal.

Setting one anchor downwind

If the current is running 90° to the wind, it may be difficult to set the anchor by sailing into the wind as described above. In this situation, the boat must have speed to maintain control, so the anchor can be dropped in the selected location.

Using this method, care must be taken if the wind is blowing on shore. If the anchor does not grab or set, there must be room to sail off shore. For this reason, this technique should not be attempted unless the skipper is relatively sure of the bottom, so the anchor will set quickly and have good holding.

As normal, sail through the anchorage to determine the location to set the anchor. Then, sail out to clear waters to make the necessary preparations. Unlike the methods mentioned above, there should be little—if any—resistance to the rode as it is being deployed. *It is advisable to have all the rode on deck, so it runs freely and the end can be clearly seen before it is reached.*

Determine the required scope, and pile the rode on deck. If there will be a crewmember on deck, the end of the rode should be led around a cleat or bitts one turn, so it can be controlled to stop the boat more slowly. If single handing, the end of the rode will have to be terminated to a strong cleat or bitts, and the boat will have to be slowed to a near stop before the rode comes up taut. *Do not leave the chain on the gypsy.*

In order to sail slowly, yet maintain control, reduce the sail area. If the main is to be used, put in the necessary reefs. If roller furling will be used, roll in as much as needed. Determine if the boat will be sailing on a port or starboard tack. The anchor will be deployed from the windward side of the boat, or the opposite side as the sail, as shown in Figure 62.

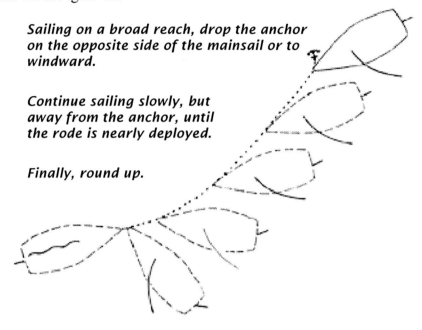

Sailing on a broad reach, drop the anchor on the opposite side of the mainsail or to windward.

Continue sailing slowly, but away from the anchor, until the rode is nearly deployed.

Finally, round up.

Figure 62. Setting one anchor downwind under sail

As you can see from Figure 62, the boat is on a broad reach, on a starboard tack. When the boat passes where you want it to set, drop the anchor off the windward side. *Make certain there is a rode guard or retainer on top of the bow roller cheeks, to prevent the rode from slipping out as it is being deployed.*

Slowly, sail in a slow curve, away from the anchor, so the rode does not pass under the boat. Eventually, the boat will be on a dead run. If there is a crewmember on the bow, he or she should inform the helmsman of the amount of rode still to be deployed. When there is about 20 to 40 feet of rode left, throw the helm hard over, so the boat will round up just as the rode comes up taut.

It is important that the anchor not be deployed from the lee side of the boat, or the same side as the main. This would require the mainsail to gybe when the rode comes to the end. The boat will have to pass over the rode, which could cause a rope rode to catch on a fin keel or a spade rudder.

Depending on the length of the boat, the rode, and the number of crew aboard, this method can be varied by deploying the anchor off the stern. The anchor and most all of the rode are brought back to the cockpit. *Be sure it leads outside of all shrouds, lifelines, and sheets.*

The rode at the bow is tethered as mentioned above. The anchor is deployed off the stern, so the boat can sail a straight line. When the rode is nearly gone, the boat is turned sharply upwind, so it is almost stalled as the rode comes up taut.

This method works well using the headsail instead of the mainsail.

Setting bow and stern anchors downwind using roller furling headsail

This method works best if the boat has roller furling, because the speed can be better controlled. In Figure 63, both a bow and stern anchor will be set. As mentioned above, I do not like to set bow and stern anchors with the mainsail, because of the possibility of an accidental gybe.

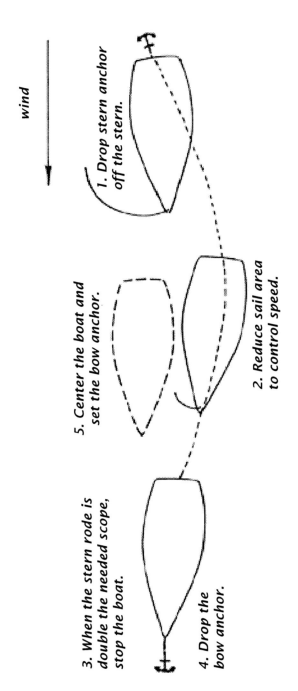

wind

1. Drop stern anchor off the stern.

2. Reduce sail area to control speed.

5. Center the boat and set the bow anchor.

3. When the stern rode is double the needed scope, stop the boat.

4. Drop the bow anchor.

Figure 63. Setting bow and stern anchors downwind using roller furling headsail

As normal, make the pass through the anchorage to determine the anchor location. Return to clear water to prepare.

Roll up enough headsail so that the boat is moving slowly downwind. Drop the stern anchor, and begin paying out rode. Continue to sail downwind, reducing speed by furling in headsail area, until double the scope is deployed; then, roll up the sail to stop its drive.

If this is done properly, the boat will be nearly stopped when the rode comes up taut. Now, drop the bow anchor and pull back on the stern rode until the boat is in position between the two. The bow anchor has to be set by the tension exerted on the stern anchor.

I like this method because there is less chance of the main causing drive. If the boat has to get back under sail, the roller jib can be deployed instantly.

If you want to anchor on only one anchor and you want the boat to point into the wind, set the stern anchor as described above. After the anchor is set, move the rode from the stern to the bow. Or, the anchor rode can remain tethered to the bow and deployed off the stern, as mentioned in the previous section.

Retrieving anchors under sail

If there is only one anchor set off the bow, it is better to bring the anchor up sailing to windward. *Before raising the anchor, take plenty of time to evaluate and locate dangers and obstacles.* Select the tack that has the most room for leeward drift, because the boat will have to fall off before enough speed is gathered to have steering control.

Raise the main with any necessary reefs. Leave the mainsheet free, so the main will not start driving the boat before the anchor is up. Bring in the anchor rode with the windlass or by hand, until the anchor is ready to break loose from the bottom.

The boat will now begin to tack back and forth into the wind. Raise the anchor just as the boat is beginning to come onto the tack you intend to sail.

This is easiest if there is a person on the bow and one at the helm. However, I have done this many times alone. To do it single-handed, tie the helm amidships with a quick release knot. I have a small eye pad with small cam cleats on both sides of the tiller to make it easy to adjust and release. Pull in the main sheets, so the main will provide some drive when the boat falls off to about 60°.

Raise the anchor when the boat is on the proper tack. Continue to bring it up as the boat begins to fall off and start sailing. If necessary, run back to the cockpit and make adjustments to the main or helm. However, this should not be necessary if it was properly planned. The boat should continue to sail on a close to beam reach as the anchor is brought aboard.

Continue to sail on this tack while securing the anchor. If there is danger near, then take over the helm and sail to safety first.

If the boat is anchored bow and stern, the wind direction will determine which anchor will be raised first. If the boat is facing into the wind, as shown in Figure 64, fall back while deploying more rode off the bow, until the stern anchor can be brought aboard. Then, follow the procedures described above for picking up an anchor to windward.

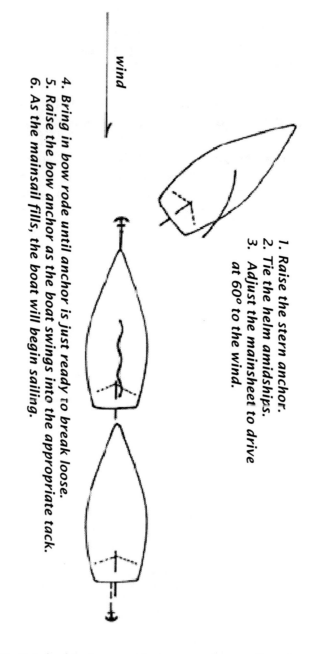

1. Raise the stern anchor.
2. Tie the helm amidships.
3. Adjust the mainsheet to drive at 60° to the wind.

4. Bring in bow rode until anchor is just ready to break loose.
5. Raise the bow anchor as the boat swings into the appropriate tack.
6. As the mainsail fills, the boat will begin sailing.

wind

Figure 64. Retrieving bow and stern anchors when boat is facing upwind

If the wind is from the stern, as shown in Figure 65, let out stern line while pulling in on the bow rode, until the bow anchor can be raised. Then move the stern line around to the bow. If there is enough line, it can remain tied to the stern cleat while the excess is brought around to the bow, outside the shrouds. If the line is too short, tie another line to the stern line and around to the bow.

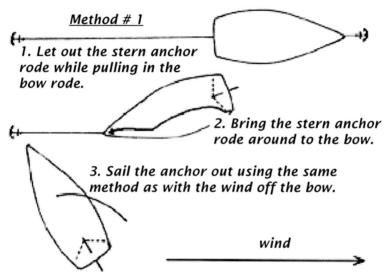

Method # 1

1. Let out the stern anchor rode while pulling in the bow rode.

2. Bring the stern anchor rode around to the bow.

3. Sail the anchor out using the same method as with the wind off the bow.

wind

Figure 65. Retrieving bow and stern anchors with wind off the stern and sailing upwind

Cast off the stern line from the cleat. After the boat swings into the wind, begin to bring in the stern anchor as normal, then sail out as mentioned previously.

If there is a reason the boat cannot be sailed to windward, then it can be sailed out downwind. If the wind is light, the bow anchor can be raised first while the stern anchor remains tethered to the stern. The stern rode will have to be brought aboard from the stern by hand until it is ready to break its hold. Then, raise or unroll the headsail, and sail downwind to safety before raising the mainsail, as shown in Figure 66.

If the wind or current is too strong to pull the stern of the boat back over the stern anchor, move the stern rode to the bow, as mentioned previously. Break out the anchor as normal, and let the boat fall back onto a tack. As soon as the wind is on one side of the boat, raise the headsail and sail to the safety of clear waters; then, raise the main.

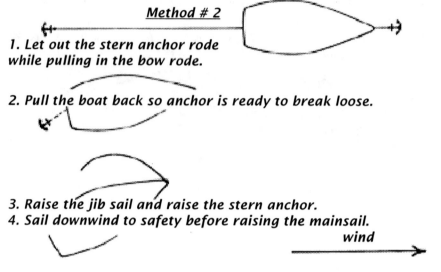

Method # 2

1. Let out the stern anchor rode while pulling in the bow rode.

2. Pull the boat back so anchor is ready to break loose.

3. Raise the jib sail and raise the stern anchor.
4. Sail downwind to safety before raising the mainsail.

wind

Figure 66. Retrieving bow and stern anchors with wind off the stern and sailing downwind

Different anchoring situations

Sailing at anchor

If the wind is fresh and there is only one anchor set off the bow, the boat may sail back and forth through the eye of the wind. This can make things uncomfortable aboard. The boat can be stabilized in two ways. One method is to add more windage as far aft as possible, causing the boat to weathercock, or point more into the wind. This can be accomplished by raising a reefed mizzen sail, if there is one. If the boat only has one mast, a riding sail can be raised up the backstay. This sail is usually a small sail, like a storm jib, and it is sheeted to the mast or boom. This sail must be set up flat, so it doesn't snap across with the wind.

The other way to stabilize the boat is to force it to set to one side of the wind. You can easily accomplish this by adding a line to the anchor rode or chain with a rolling hitch, then leading it back to a mid-ship or stern cleat. The bow anchor rode is paid out while adjusting the line tied to the side, until the boat sets comfortably at an angle, as shown in Figure 67.

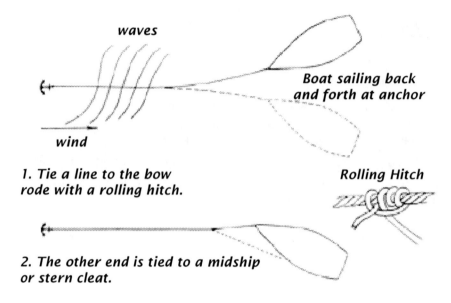

waves

wind

Boat sailing back and forth at anchor

1. Tie a line to the bow rode with a rolling hitch.

Rolling Hitch

2. The other end is tied to a midship or stern cleat.

3. Adjust this line so the wind or waves come from one side.

Figure 67. How to prevent the boat from sailing back and forth at anchor

Anchoring against a wall

At the beginning of this chapter, I related a story about anchoring in this manner, when I was in Papeete, Tahiti. This is sometimes called the Mediterranean method, probably because it is commonly used in the Mediterranean. Basically, two anchors are set off the bow, and stern lines are tied ashore. The stern lines are used to adjust the boat close to the wall, so the crew can go ashore. See Figure 68. When the stern lines are released, the weight of the bow rode pulls the boat safely away from the wall.

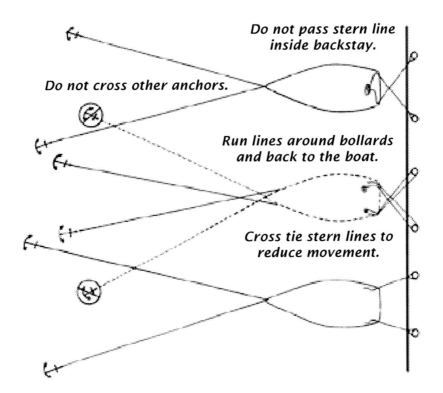

Do not pass stern line inside backstay.

Do not cross other anchors.

Run lines around bollards and back to the boat.

Cross tie stern lines to reduce movement.

Figure 68. Anchoring against a wall — Mediterranean method

If possible, it is important not to set your bow anchors over someone else's. This is difficult because there may not be anyone aboard, they may not speak your language, or they may not know where their anchor is set. It would be great if an anchor buoy had been set, but most people don't use one for the same dangers mentioned previously.

It is difficult and dangerous to set these anchors under sail; consequently, the engine should be used. If the weather is calm, it can all be done from the mother boat, without using the dinghy. If there is a wind blowing or a cross current, then the dinghy must be used.

Set fenders on both sides of the boat, just in case the boat drifts to one side or the other.

First, back into the place where you intend to set to see if there is a crosswind or current. If there is, use the method discussed in the next section.

Presuming there is no wind or current, motor out far enough to allow time to prepare all anchors and lines. In this situation, it is better to have more scope than normal; it also helps if the anchor is pulling uphill. *Set the anchor with the rope rode first.* Back down and make sure it is properly set. (If the chain rode is set first, it is difficult to control the boat with the weight of the chain on the bottom, while setting the second anchor.)

If the anchors cannot be set as far apart as you would like, consider running the anchor rode from opposite sides of the bow. This will increase the angle. However, if the bow rollers are close together, or if the rodes will chafe on something or each other, don't bother. Two anchors in tandem will work, but there must be room to allow the bow to move sideways.

Motor forward to set the second anchor on chain. *Be sure to bring the rope rode aboard as you motor forward.* Set the second anchor and reverse back, letting out both rodes.

As mentioned previously, if the boat has a tendency to reverse to one side or the other, set the rudder in the direction to get back in-line, then give the engine short busts in forward.

Continue to reverse until the boat is close to the wall. Keep the engine in reverse until a line can be set to a bollard ashore. If the bollard is close, it may be possible to throw a line over it. Perhaps there is someone ashore who can take the line and wrap it around the bollard. It may require sending a crewmember ashore.

If the bollards are set close together, cross the stern lines to get the maximum angle, in order to keep the stern from shifting. *It is important that separate lines are used, and that they are passed around the bollards, then back to the boat, so that they can be cast off from the boat.*

Anchoring against a wall in a cross wind

If there is a cross wind, or a cross current, the dinghy must be used, as shown in Figure 69.

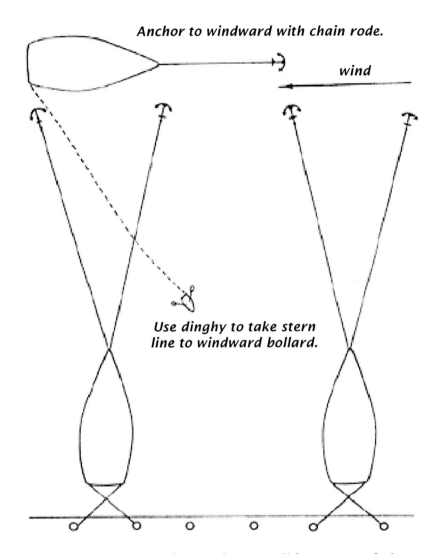

Anchor to windward with chain rode.

wind

Use dinghy to take stern line to windward bollard.

Figure 69. Anchoring against a wall in a cross wind

In this situation, set the primary anchor on the chain rode first. Set it to windward or up current as normal. Then, attach a long line to the same side of the boat at the stern. Put this line in the dinghy and take it ashore. Probably, it will not be long enough to go around the bollard and back to the boat; additional lines can be tied together, or it can be done after the boat is in place.

Pull the stern to the wall while adjusting the bow rode. Since the wind or current is from one direction, the single anchor and stern line will hold the boat in position, while the second anchor is rowed out and set. Then, pass new stern lines around the bollard as discussed above.

Anchoring up a river

If possible, select a location just inside of a turn in the river, as shown in Figure 70. This will deflect much of the strength of the current, and will provide more protection from debris.

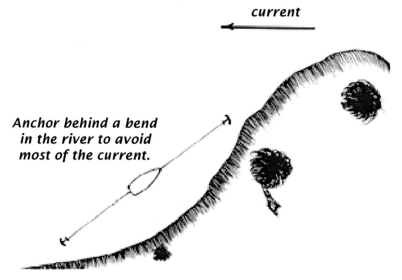

current

Anchor behind a bend in the river to avoid most of the current.

Figure 70. Anchoring up a river

The boat will usually set with the current. This makes it easy to set one anchor and let the boat drift back with the current. There should be swinging room, in case the winds increase and take precedence over the current. If swinging will be a problem, then set a stern anchor as normal.

Tying between pilings

The most common mooring in foreign countries is to tie between two pilings. This is not difficult, as long and there isn't a crosswind or current.

Some pile moorings will have lines permanently attached to the piling. These can be used, as long as they are strong and not too old or chafed. If there is any doubt, use your own lines.

The procedure is similar to setting an anchor. First, determine which is stronger, the current or the wind. In the following procedure, presume the current is stronger and there is little, if any, wind.

The bow pile mooring is approached up current, as shown in Figure 71. When the piling can be reached, pass a line around the piling or grab the line already on the piling. Depending on the boat's bow, it may be necessary to bring one side of the bow alongside the piling to do this. As the boat drifts back, pay out line until the boat is close enough to the stern piling to throw a line around it or to grab the line that remains on the piling. *Again, let me emphasize the importance of being able to cast off from the boat.*

1. Sail up current or windward to pass line around bow piling.

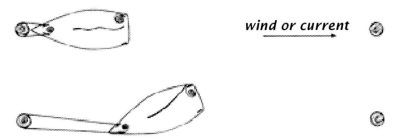

wind or current

2. Drift back, controlling side drift backwinding the mainsail.

3. Pass stern line around stern piling and back to the boat.

4. Center the boat between bow and stern pilings.

Figure 71. Tying between pilings under sail

If the mooring is to be done under sail, care must be taken to control the speed approaching the bow piling. After the line is passed around it, the boat can be controlled by backwinding the mainsail to keep it in-line with the stern piling.

If there is a crosswind, tie to the bow piling as mentioned above; then, use the dinghy to take a line to the stern piling.

§

An embarrassing situation happened to me when I was in Mooloolaba, Queensland, Australia. I was moored up a river between two pile moorings, directly in front of the Mooloolaba Yacht Club. There were two sets of pile moorings parallel to each other, so there were two lines of boats parallel to the shore. (Years later, these have been replaced by a marina with docks and slips.)

The pilings had their own lines that were hung on a huge hook, making them easy to grab. For weeks, I approached the pile mooring up current, which was often against the wind, making it necessary to use the engine.

One day, I decided to try to pick up the mooring line sailing downwind. As long as I had some headsail deployed, I sailed slightly faster than the current, which ran against it. By using the roller furling jib topsail, I could control my speed to nearly a standstill.

Slowly sailing against the current, I approached the first piling that would hold my stern at about a 20° angle and as close as possible. When close enough, I grabbed the line and threw the helm hard over, so that I was aiming directly into the current, and the wind was nearly dead astern. I continued to pay out line until my bowsprit was nearly touching the other piling, downwind but up current. I left the sail up, so the current wouldn't push me back. I found I could control the position of my bow with the rudder.

When I had the bow just where I wanted it, I walked out on the bowsprit and reached the bow mooring line. Then, I rolled up the sail and positioned myself between the two pilings.

After mooring like this successfully several times, I decided to tie a loop in the line that was attached to the stern piling. With this loop around my stern cleat, the line was just long enough to bring my bowsprit inches from the other piling when it became taut.

On weekends, when the yacht club was full of members with guests, I would single-handedly pick up my pile mooring lines under sail. I would just pass the first piling, grab the line, and throw it around the stern cleat. The boat slowly sailed up current as I calmly walked forward. I would be standing on the end of the bowsprit, ready to grab the other line, when the stern line came up taut. Then, I would go ashore to get all kinds of compliments and, often, free beer.

One day, the wind was a little stronger than normal. I missed my first line, and *Xiphias* continued sailing downwind, hitting the other piling. This shoved me into the center between the two sets of moorings. I did not have time to roll up my sail because I was running from side to side fending off the other boats.

Fortunately, no damage was done to any of the boats. I cut my finger badly and my ego was deflated. I got a real ribbing from my Aussie friends ashore. They have a name for people like me, but I don't think I will use it here.

Dragging anchors

After anchoring, always take compass bearings on anything nearby. Record these bearings on a piece of paper for a quick referral if necessary. If a squall hits, visually assess if the boat is dragging. If there is any doubt, take a compass bearing to confirm if you are dragging or not.

Usually, the first sign of a dragging anchor is that the boat will turn sideways to the wind. If the boat is dragging, the first thing to do is get out of any danger. If there is only one anchor set off the bow, the boat can motor over the anchor, then reverse to drag the anchor along the bottom until out of danger, as shown in Figure 72. Then, the anchor can be safely raised.

***Motor away from danger. It is difficult to steer the
boat dragging the anchor while motoring forward.***

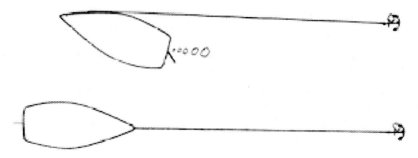

Tow the dragging anchor in reverse until clear of danger.

Figure 72. Dragging anchors

Do not attempt to motor forward pulling a dragging anchor along
the bottom with its rode off the bow. The bow will just be pulled
down, and the rode may even catch in the prop. If the boat is reversed,
the boat can pull the anchor with more control.

If the anchor is dragging and there is plenty of room behind the
boat, more scope can be deployed. Personally, I do not like paying out
more rode. The additional weight of chain may stop the boat from
dragging, but this does not necessarily reset the anchor. You could be
misled to a feeling of false security.

If room permits, a second anchor can be deployed. Be careful not
to set the second anchor on top of the rode of the dragging anchor.

If the boat is anchored bow and stern, the stern anchor should be
brought aboard, if time permits. If not, throw the rode overboard.
*Care must always be taken not to catch the stern rode or buoy in the
prop.*

The primary objective is to get the boat out of danger. If there is
no danger, then you have plenty of time to raise all anchors and reset.

Fouled anchors

Given enough time, everyone will eventually foul an anchor. It may be on coral, rocks, mooring chains, sunken trees, artificial reefs, or a wreck. Depending on where you are cruising, most likely it will foul on coral. If you suspect the chain or anchor is fouled, avoid applying too much lifting load. This may make the foul even worse.

If all the chain is up except the anchor, it is only the anchor that is fouled. If there is more chain than depth, then the chain is fouled. It serves no purpose to try to remove the anchor until all the chain is free.

The moment you feel the chain is fouled, *stop pulling on it*. If it is calm and no apparent current running, attempt to free the chain by hand. The windlass takes too much time. First, let out about 10 feet, then bring it back aboard. This should be repeated several times and from different angles. When the chain is brought back aboard, the boat will be pulled in the direction where it is fouled. While the boat is still coasting and the chain comes up hard, immediately let out another 5 feet to see if it will clear some of the chain.

If the chain is still fouled, or if there is some wind or current, then the engine will have to be used. With someone at the helm, release the 10 feet of chain; slowly motor in one direction to see if it comes free. If it gets tighter, then go in the other direction. Continue to release 10 feet of chain and bring it back aboard; it may not work on the first or second attempt, so keep trying this in different directions. If the chain is still fouled, it is time to grab the facemask. If you can see the problem, let the helmsman know which direction to motor.

After the chain is cleared, the anchor may also be fouled. Without releasing any more than about 5 to 10 feet of chain, power in different directions to see if it will release. Be careful not to let out too much chain or it may foul again.

If the anchor is still fouled, a loop of chain can be dropped down the chain to the anchor, then pulled from different directions. *Again, don't foul this loop of chain.*

If the water is clear, use a facemask to see where the anchor is fouled. It will be easier than just experimenting to determine how to get it free.

Moorings

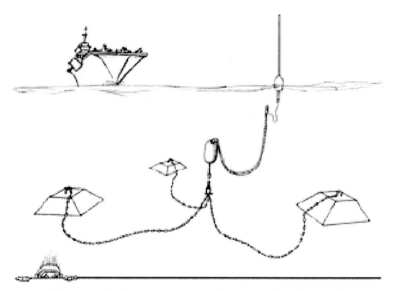

Figure 73. Concrete moorings chained together

There are two types of moorings: temporary and permanent. If the mooring is to be used as a temporary safe place to keep the boat, use the anchor mooring discussed previously in this chapter. If the mooring is to be permanent, try the following methods.

Many moorings in foreign countries are no more than plastic barrels filled with concrete and chained together. These only provide weight and have little—if any—design to prevent them from moving. Most boats could move one of these moorings under their own power.

Some moorings are made of huge chunks of metal chained together. This is better than barrels filled with concrete. The problem occurs when there are dissimilar metals, causing electrolysis to attack the less noble metal. If the shackle happens to be the less noble metal, there would be a problem in a short time.

§

While I was in Papua New Guinea, I worked for a copper mine on Bougainville Island. Most of the employees were from Australia; they had their private boats moored in front of a small yacht club that they made themselves. The shallow water was limited, so many of the moorings were set in water over 100 feet deep.

The copper mine was a large open pit mine that had millions of dollars in equipment, parts, accessories, and everything imaginable. Most of the moorings were made from useless engine blocks or obsolete mining equipment chained together. This created a huge underwater battery. Shackles had to be replaced every few months. Even the moorings set in concrete had their shackles affected by electrolysis. Nearly every time a severe squall passed, someone's boat washed up on the beach. There was no way to solve the problem without removing all this metal.

§

It is much simpler to make a single large mooring than several smaller ones chained together. The difficulty is getting this single, large, heavy mooring out to deep water. This will require a substantially large boat, barge, or float.

In most cases, though, the mooring has to be set by the boat it will hold. Needless to say, a large single mooring will not work in this situation. However, a smaller mooring that can be moved by the boat can also be moved in a strong wind. Consequently, several smaller moorings chained together may have to be used.

I like to make the mooring out of concrete; it is cheap and it reduces the problems arising from electrolysis. Concrete loses much of its weight in water, due to air bubbles trapped in the concrete. For this reason, the mooring must be designed to increase its holding ability. The common mushroom mooring relies on its design, instead of its weight.

Xiphias weighed about 17,000 pounds. For a mooring, I used two concrete blocks. Each was about 3' X 3' square and between 1' to 2' thick. The sides were tapered about 30° from the bottom to the top. The bottom was concave. When this type of mooring is set, the tapered sides will eventually gather sand or mud around the bottom edges, adding to its holding ability, and the concave bottom will create suction after it settles.

I made a single plywood form with tapered sides. I nailed 2" X 4"s on the outside for reinforcement. To make the bottom concave, I formed a mound of sand and covered it with plastic. I placed the plywood form over this mound.

I used a single 3-foot piece of 3/4" concrete reinforcing steel rod to form a loop that would hold the mooring chain. The center was bent, shaped like a large 'U'. Six inches of the ends were bent outward to a 100° angle, to form the 'feet'. The distance between the bottom 'feet' and the top inside of the 'U' was about 10 inches.

Inside the form, I placed pieces of reinforcing steel rod and wire mesh, all wired together. I wired the steel loop to this reinforcing steel in the center of the mooring, with the 'U' shape inverted. The bottom of the loop extended three inches above the top surface of the mooring form.

By hand, using a shovel, I mixed the appropriate amount of concrete, lime, sand, and gravel. I poured about 6 inches in the bottom of the form, then added large rocks, bricks, even steel pieces, and more concrete until it was filled to the top. I made two moorings in this fashion.

I attached some oversize chain to the top of the moorings, to keep the rope from chafing on the bottom and to add some weight. The length of the chain was enough to reach the surface, plus at least another 10 feet, so that the moorings could be chained together.

I tied a sacrificial float to a rock and placed it where I wanted to set the moorings. The distance between the moorings had to be about the depth of the water, so that the two chains could be attached together. Before setting the moorings, I attached a rope and float to the ends of the chains, so I could bring the chain to the surface later.

To get the moorings down to the water, I used steel pipes as skids. By wedging a pipe under the mooring as a lever, the mooring end could be raised, so that the pipes could be slid underneath. Using this same pipe, the mooring could be pried down to the water, as deep as possible. It had to be deep enough so I could get my boat over it at low tide. I had to wait until spring tides to have the lift I needed.

As the tide was beginning to turn, I motored over the mooring and brought the chain up snug to the deck. I used some old rope to tie the chain to the base of the mast. I intended to cut the rope to release the mooring. The nylon rope began to stretch before I cut it through; it broke like a gunshot and flew out at the speed of light. I felt lucky I wasn't injured. If I had to do it over again, I think I would have used a quick-release lever instead.

On my first attempt, I tied the mooring at the bow. When the tide came in, the bow went down and the stern rose. The stern was so high out of the water that I was afraid the prop would not grab. I waited until the next day and tied the mooring to the stern; this worked better.

After both moorings were set, the chains were connected with a large shackle and a large swivel. Instead of using seizing wire to secure the pins, I peened the excess thread over so it was impossible to undo; it would have to be cut off.

To the top of the swivel, I attached the mooring rope, which was already backspliced to a large thimble. Over this rope, I slid a fishing net float, the kind with a hole in the middle. The purpose was to keep the mooring rope from reaching the bottom. At the other end of the mooring rope was the pick-up float. This float was another fishing net float with a bamboo pole weighted on the bottom.

The advantage of this setup was that both moorings would have to drag together before the boat would begin to drag. The chains between the moorings were long enough so that the connection could be brought to the surface for inspection.

Another easy mooring to make is by using tires with concrete inside. Be sure the eye that will take the chain is part of the reinforcing steel in the tire. The tire is set on a flat or a hump and filled with concrete. In order to drag, the tire must tip on its side. I am not saying use only one tire, but many tires set apart and all chained together.

There are many other ways to make moorings. Try to avoid just one mooring unless there is a large vessel available to set it.

Anchoring in preparation for a storm

If a storm is expected, it is important that the boat be safely and strongly secured. Avoid tying alongside jetties or wharves; the wave action will make slivers of the boat. Also, avoid a mooring, unless you feel confident it is strong enough to handle the storm. Try not to anchor where there are rocks directly behind the boat. The more room to drag or swing you have, the better off you will be.

Try to find an area to anchor that is protected from the wind and seas. Anchor behind reefs and jetties only if they are high enough to take the higher tides that come with the storm. Some tides will rise as much as 20 feet. Mangroves have strong, deep roots, which makes them good for protection and for tying a line.

Depending on the protection and the severity of the storm, it may be necessary to go to sea. *I would only consider this if it is a gale or less—not a storm with a name.* Life is more important than the boat. I have sat through hurricanes, and I assure you that there was nothing, **nothing** that would have made me go to sea.

Select the area to anchor carefully. The biggest problem is not how you anchor, but how others upwind of you anchor. You can have all the anchors out to set through the strongest of hurricanes, but if a boat comes down on you, it would make little difference. Their anchor will foul on yours. They will either trip your anchors, or your anchors will hold theirs. If your anchor or chain holds their anchor, it may position their boat so it is banging against yours. *Therefore, the most important factor is to select a location where other boats will not drag down on you.*

This may be more difficult than it sounds. You may have all your anchors properly set, with the boat secure, when someone anchors in front of you. There is nothing you can do about this. I suggest you try to help them set all their anchors properly, so they don't drag.

It is important to know from which direction to expect the wind and waves. Set the anchors off the bow, facing the direction of danger.

If the eye is expected to pass over or near, the wind and waves could come from any direction. In that case, set all anchors as mentioned previously in anchor moorings.

One of the safest places to anchor is up a river, where large waves cannot reach the boat. The problem with rivers during a cyclone is that they will flood, causing strong currents and debris.

Select a place on the inside, behind a curve or bend in the river. As the current strengthens, the point of land will deflect most of the current to the other side of the river, as shown in Figure 74.

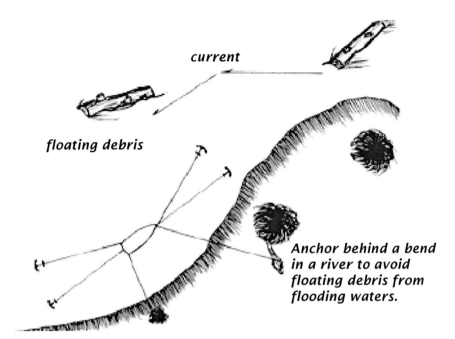

current

floating debris

Anchor behind a bend in a river to avoid floating debris from flooding waters.

Figure 74. Anchoring up a river in preparation for a storm

The boat must anchor so it faces the current; this may not be the same direction as the expected winds. Set as many anchors as you can off the bow and stern. Then, tie to trees, mangroves, or anything that will survive the storm and support the boat.

After everything is properly set, place lots of anti-chafing material where the lines pass though fairleads, hawseholes, and chocks. Leather is the best to prevent chafe, but there may not be enough aboard for all the lines. Use hoses, rags, plastic bags, or anything that will help.

It is important to remove as much windage as possible. Remove the roller furling headsail and all the sails you can. If your boat has a dodger that can be removed, take it off as well. The same applies to any additional fuel cans, water jugs, dinghy, and anything that can be put below decks. Anything that must remain on deck must be securely lashed so it does not come loose.

If the storm is a severe one and you do not feel 100% safe with the location, move off the boat and find protection ashore. If you intend to stay aboard, have the engine running so it can be put into gear to reduce the force against the anchors. It is not advisable to be out in the cockpit doing this, so devise a method to increase or hold the rpm's at the desired speed from inside the boat. This is normally done at the engine throttle linkage.

If it is possible to put the boat on the hard, be sure that it will be safer than if you leave it in the water. I have seen hundreds of boats severely damaged because of one boat falling, causing the domino effect.

The surface where the boat will set should be flat and solid, like concrete or pavement. Avoid dirt or sand, because they will shift and erode with the heavy rains; however, if there is no other choice, put large surface plates under the boat supports, so they don't sink. Then, tie the supports together with chain, so they will not shift. Boats fall over because of the vibration created by high winds in the rigging. This causes the supports to shift.

Let's hope that none of these storm preparation methods will ever be needed or put to the test.

Chapter Five

STORM STRATEGY

Because this book is about cruising, I feel it is necessary to include material on storm strategy. However, I am somewhat reluctant to write this chapter, because I certainly do not consider myself an expert on the subject. I have encountered some nasty weather, even the edge of major cyclones, but nothing compared to those who have written entire books on the subject.

Not only do I lack the necessary experience to tell the reader how to handle a major storm, but also I feel like I am "beating a dead horse". There are so many other excellent books written on the subject by qualified authors. Consequently, what I can offer may be redundant. Nevertheless, I have had many years and many nautical miles of experience, and I feel confident that I can contribute some insights that will be useful to a prospective cruiser.

I intend to include information from my own experiences, as well as material that I have gathered from others on the subject. I strongly advise the reader to do as much research as possible and to compare what other authors and I have to say. When all sources agree on a particular method or idea, then it should have a star next to it. Where authors disagree, the readers should draw their own conclusions, based on their own boat and their own experience.

Let's face it: there isn't an author who can comprehensively cover all aspects of any single subject about sailing. There I go again, making an absolute statement. Well, there may be such an author, but I feel that in sailing—especially storm strategy—there are too many variables that could influence a particular technique. No two boats are alike, and they all handle differently in heavy weather. Some will not even heave-to, while others do so almost automatically. The severity of the weather, the variation in the state of the seas, the expected duration of the storm, and the condition of the boat and its crew can all have an influence on the strategy used. These are only a few of the many variables that can affect the choice and outcome of a particular method or strategy.

The only way an author could validly comment on how a boat will handle storm conditions is to be on that particular design and to experience the storm firsthand. Since that is impossible, most authors will generalize about specific techniques and apply them to all boats. While I do not necessarily agree with this, I intend to write about what happened to me: the conditions I encountered, what I did wrong, and what I did right. This may not apply to every vessel afloat, but it is more information for you, the reader, to put into your memory files.

Before we can discuss strategy, we must decide what a severe storm is. It is amazing how yachts, only a few miles apart, report radically different conditions. This is not to say that they don't experience different conditions; it is quite possible that they do. There may have been a slight variation in the depth of the water between the boats. If the contour of the bottom between the vessels is steeper, the sea conditions will change. Of course, there is the current strength and direction, the size and frequency of freak or rogue waves, and how the wind conditions vary. All of these things can differ in relatively short distances. However, it may also be due to the interpretation of the conditions by the people on board. The more experienced sailor will have a tendency to play down the storm, while the less experienced one will see the waves and winds as much more severe and threatening.

The boat's size, its design, and weight will vary considerably, resulting in a different interpretation of the storm. Of course, the strategy used will also affect the sailor's impression of the conditions. If the strategy used worked without a problem, the severity of the storm will probably be played down. However, if it failed or did not work as expected, the harsh conditions of the storm may be blamed.

Consequently, a storm to some may be 30 knots of wind with 10-foot seas, while to others, a storm is a storm only if it is a storm with a name. So, what is a storm? Briefly, let's discuss the Beaufort Scale, which is most commonly referred to by licensed captains and professional weather personnel to measure the wind and sea conditions.

The Beaufort Scale was developed by Rear-Admiral Sir Francis Beaufort of the Royal British Navy. He was born in 1774 in Ireland and devised the scale in the early eighteen hundreds as a force scale. The scale did not have wind speed, but instead was based on the force of the wind against the seas and sails of the Man-of-War ships of that era. It wasn't until many years later that wind speed was added.

The following is condensed from the original. I have added my own response to the conditions in the column labeled Possible Action.

The Beaufort Scale

Scale	Wind Speed in Knots	Wind Description	Sea Conditions	Possible Action
0	0	Calm	Calm, mirror-like seas	Motoring or swimming
1	1 to 3	Light airs	Ripples in patches, 4" wavelets	Sailing slowly or motoring
2	4 to 6	Light breeze	Ripples all over, 6" to 1' wavelets, not breaking	Great sailing
3	7 to 10	Gentle breeze	Large wavelets; crests start breaking. Scattered whitecaps	Great sailing
4	11 to 16	Moderate breeze	1'6" to 4' waves, some are breaking	Great sailing or 1st reef
5	17 to 21	Fresh breeze	Some white caps, 4' to 8' waves, half are breaking	1st or 2nd reef
6	22 to 27	Strong breeze	White caps overall, 8' to 13' waves, most are breaking.	2nd or 3rd reef
7	28 to 33	Near gale – Small Craft Advisory	Waves have white foam in streaks. 13' to 19' waves, most are breaking.	3rd reef or heave-to
8	34 to 40	Gale warning	Streaks of foam off the crests, 18' to 28' waves of greater length.	Small boats go to protected harbors; if at sea, run or heave-to
9	41 to 47	Whole gale	White water, seas begin to roll. Spray affects visibility. 23' to 32' waves.	Run or heave-to
10	48 to 55	Storm warning	29' to 41' waves with overhanging crests, sea white with spray	Run, lie ahull or use parachute anchor
11	56 to 63	Violent storm	Dangerously high waves.	Run, lie ahull or use parachute anchor
12	63+	Hurricane or cyclone	Vertical mountains, air filled with foam, dangerous situation.	Parachute anchor and prayers.

Note: The Beaufort Scale does not take into consideration the possible actions mentioned above.

The vessel

When it comes to surviving a true storm with minimum damage, it really depends on the vessel. As I mentioned above, no two vessels respond the same to a particular storm strategy. I know this firsthand because I have delivered many yachts and was amazed at the variations in the way they handled rough weather.

To prevent repetition, I suggest you refer to the comments I made in Chapter 3, The Cruising Yacht. However, there are certain aspects that are worth repeating, so the reader can more fully understand their importance.

The heavier boat with a long keel will handle heavy seas better than the light fin-keeled boat. The long keel will hold it in a hove-to position, creating a slick behind the keel as it drifts to leeward. This slick will smooth the breaking waves, protecting the vessel. Also, the vessel will set better to a parachute anchor. The heavier boat will be more forgiving and will not be whipped around as much as the lighter boats. Refer to Figure 18 on page 88, Figure 19 on page 89, Figure 20 on page 91, and Figure 21 on page 93, for keel configurations.

Perhaps even more important than the boat's keel and weight is its construction. Try to imagine your boat lying broadside to a 5-foot wave breaking against her side repeatedly for hours, or even days.

Remember that it is not necessarily the length of a boat that makes it safe; however, there is no question that comparing two boats of similar design and construction, the larger one would be safer. The problem occurs in the construction of the boat. I have seen small sound vessels come out of a storm without any problems, while poorly built larger boats suffered extensive damage. One of the most important factors to consider is the number of bulkheads installed and their method of installation. Refer to Figures 24 and 25 on page 115, and Figure 26 on page 118, for bulkhead installations.

Under storm conditions, there are excessive stresses placed on the hull, deck, and all the rigging. The better the boat is constructed, the better it will handle these stresses.

Many owners don't think too much about the standing rigging prior to a storm, and unfortunately, this is where most failures or problems occur. Refer to Figure 30 on page 137, and Figures 31 and 32 on page 138, for problems with standing rigging.

The waves threaten the vessel's hull. The wind and radical whipping of the boat, as she jerks from one side to the other, threaten the rigging.

Another concern is windage aloft. The more windage, caused by the surface area exposed, and the more weight aloft will increase the stress and radical movement of the vessel. A multi-mast vessel will have much more weight and surface area exposed to the forces of the wind than a single mast vessel. Those who leave roller-furling sails attached will also have more wind force.

I often hear sailors explain why they went to much larger standing and running rigging. I have no objection to stronger rigging, but how much stronger? Consider a single stay that is a 1/4" in diameter and 50 feet long. It will carry more than the necessary loads in storm conditions for this particular boat. Now, let's increase that diameter to 5/16". This means for every foot of length, there will be at least an extra 1/16" of windage and weight; therefore, for a 50-foot wire, it would be about 8 square inches of surface area and several pounds. Now, multiply this against all the standing rigging, and there may be nearly 100 additional square inches and an equivalent amount of additional weight.

This also applies to running rigging. Sure, it's great to have nice fat lines that are easy to grasp, but the larger the line, the more windage and weight exposed aloft.

A wind speed of 60 knots will have about 12 pounds of force per square foot of surface above the waterline. Winds of 100 knots will have about 34 pounds per square foot of pressure. Consequently, a mast that is 45 feet tall with its rigging will expose about 75 square feet of surface area. This does not take into account antennas, radars, radar reflectors, the hull, cabin, or other surface area above the waterline. I am talking about just mast and rigging. If the wind is blowing 60 knots, it will be providing nearly 1000 pounds of pressure above the waterline. Much of this is compounded as the mast gets higher. Imagine the forces as the exposed surface increases. Now, put this additional weight and surface area on a boat that is rocking in heavy seas. You can imagine the results.

All I am trying to say is that there must be a happy medium. Think about your boat and its rigging. Do you really want to increase the size, or do you just want to replace it with the same size? I have heard that a boat should be able to be lifted by any two shrouds. Check with a rigger to find out the expected strength of wire and lines that your boat needs; then, use your own judgment. The results will definitely have an effect on your boat's performance in a storm.

There are many other things to consider about the vessel for storm conditions. Because there are too many to cover in detail, I will talk about some that I consider more important.

This must include tall, strong lifelines. I see too many boats, with too few lifeline stanchions, spaced too far apart. It is the stanchions spaced at close intervals that are going to support the lifeline and prevent it from sagging or giving when a 200-pound man is thrown against it.

I wonder why so many boats go to sea with stanchions that are short, weak, and poorly installed, when someone's life may depend on them. For a lifeline stanchion to work properly, it must be strong enough to take the weight of a heavy person being thrown against it with considerable force. Have you ever gone to a boat show and pulled on or leaned against a lifeline stanchion and been told to stop, because you might bend it?

Most lifeline stanchions are made of stainless steel tube. They should be double walled, so that they do not bend. Most importantly, they should be stoutly installed. That means: through-bolted through the deck and through the bulwarks, if you have them.

Since I am writing about lifelines, I want to bring up the question: should you have single or double lifelines? Most would jump up and vote for the double lifelines, because a person can be washed under a single lifeline. This is true and is a serious consideration. However, most people fall overboard over the top lifeline. If there are double lifelines, the tethered person who fell overboard over the top lifeline must return the same way. This can be difficult to impossible if the person is stunned and unable to help him or herself. It may be impossible if the vessel has a high freeboard.

§

I have some close friends who I buddy boated with for years that had a tragic accident between Madagascar and the African coast. There was a bad storm. Somehow, in the middle of the night, the husband fell overboard. He was wearing his harness and was tethered to the mast. The boat was heeled over, being steered by the windvane.

Fortunately, he fell over on the lower side, the lee side of the boat. His wife ran forward to help, but he was stunned and could not assist himself. He was being dragged along at the sheer. If there wasn't a second lifeline, she could have rolled him aboard; instead, she had to get him over the top lifeline. Because he was limp, she was afraid that if she let go of him, he would slip out of his harness. She held on to him as long as she could, then concluded that she had to let go of him to release the windvane, so the boat would round up into the wind. It only took seconds, which was too much time. He slipped from his harness. She never found him.

§

Another safety feature in yacht design are wide working decks so a person can move safely along the boat. I like decks wide enough that I can drag a sail bag along it, without having it snag on rigging, or having to heft it onto my shoulder. Along with this, there should be strongly installed handrails to grab as a person moves along the boat.

The size and type of portlights or windows on your boat need to be considered in a heavy weather situation. If your boat has large windows, they must have storm boards that can be quickly and easily installed. All too often, they are put into place too late, when the weather has already turned bad.

I would be reluctant to have the plastic portlights or windows that are common on many production boats today. I do not think that plastic can survive the forces of a knockdown or waves breaking against them. If there were some way that you could take a fire hose and hit these windows or portlights with its full force, it might give you an indication of their strength.

Other design elements that I personally do not like are clubs and gaffs on boats. I could state several situations where people have been hit hard by these swinging clubs in a storm.

§

I remember when I was in the Marquesas; a boat from South Africa arrived and told me this story.

On board were the skipper, his wife, their daughter, and their daughter's boyfriend, who was taken along as working crew. During a storm in the middle of the night, the skipper went forward to drop the staysail onto its club. He did not wear his harness. His wife, at the helm, yelled at him to wear his harness. The commotion woke the crewman who ran out on deck and went forward to assist the skipper. He, too, neglected to put on his harness.

As they were securing the sail to the club, a wave hit and broke over the boat. They both wrapped their arms around the club with its furled sail. Their combined weight and the pressure of the wave caused the end of the club to break away from the line holding it in place. The club swung outboard with the crewman still holding on to its end. When the boom came to an abrupt stop, the crewman slipped off the end, into the water.

The boat was sailing at good speed; in only seconds, the crewman was out of sight. The skipper ran back to the cockpit and immediately threw a life ring overboard. They did not have a Dan Buoy with a light. When the crewman surfaced, the boat was almost out of sight. He saw the life ring and swam to it.

As he held on to the ring for his life, he saw the boat come about and drop all sails. As they motored back, he realized that they would be too far downwind to hear his shouts or to see him. He watched as the wind continued to push them further away.

He evaluated the situation and decided to leave the security of the life ring and begin swimming. Fortunately, he was a strong swimmer, and he lived to tell this story.

§

The ability to sail off a lee shore in heavy weather is a very important skill. Frequently, when a storm hits, we head for the protection of land. Unfortunately, many times the skipper is unable to find the proper entrance, or decides it is not safe to continue towards land. Then, it becomes necessary to get away from the land which is downwind of his or her position. Too many sailors rely on their engines at this time, and all too often, the engine dies from sucking air or sludge during the violent motion of the boat. It may be necessary to sail back out to safety.

I remember when I entered Australia. I was hove-to off Morten Island, on the Queensland coast, waiting for the authorities to give me permission to enter Morten Bay. Cyclone Tia was coming down the coast, and I had winds in excess of 40 knots blowing me onto a lee shore. The authorities informed me that I could not enter because the seas were too big in the shallow bay. I would have to wait.

I felt safe hove-to, but I was being slowly blown onto a lee shore. I needed more sea room to spend the night. I was considerably low on fuel and was worried about not having enough to get back. There was also the possibility of sucking air into the fuel line.

With my storm trysail set and my storm jib back winded, I released the helm and released the windward sheet to the storm jib. It shot across and I was underway. The wind and heavy seas would not let me point any more than about 80° to the wind. My leeward slide made up the other 10°, so the best I could do was to parallel the coast. I decided to unroll only a handkerchief-size bit of headsail. Cautiously, with great concentration, I let out about three feet of the roller-furling jib. I shot forward, making a comfortable 60° off the wind and about 4 knots into the head seas. Had I not been able to get off the lee shore, I could have been in serious trouble.

Preparing the boat before departure

One of the most important things to consider in sailing and making any passage is preparation for the expected—and the unexpected. This includes having the items aboard that may be needed. I would like to mention a few things that I consider important to remember.

The boat should have proper storm sails that can be easily accessed and set. Because these sails are rarely used, they end up under all the other sailbags and other items that must first be moved. Since they have not been used in a long time, the hanks may be frozen, making it impossible to attach them to the stay. A storm is a bad time to discover the problem.

I feel that, depending on its size, the mainsail should have at least three reef points. The sail should be strongly reinforced at each reef point. It should be easily reefed, without threatening the safety of the person doing the reefing. This would lead one to conclude that reef lines should lead to the cockpit. I would agree, if it can be done properly. I have seen and delivered boats where reef lines leading to the cockpit did not work unless the boat was brought up into the wind. This can be a dangerous maneuver.

When the boat is brought around into the wind to reduce the pressure on the sail, the boat may be too near the eye of the wind. A sudden wind change while the boat is in the trough—or an unexpected wave—may push the boat suddenly onto the opposite tack. This would backwind the headsail, which could cause a knockdown or broach.

I like to be able to reef the mainsail without changing my point of sail. This is not always easy, unless the sails are cut for this purpose. I like lazy jacks that support the weight of the boom and the sail when the halyard is released. However, if the sail has a roach with battens, the sail's roach will get hung up on these lazy jacks when trying to raise the sails. For this reason, I like to have my headsail without a headboard or battens and with a negative roach. This reduces the chance of it getting hung up on the lazy jacks. It may still be necessary to loosen the leeward lazy jack, if the boat is sailing well off the wind.

The boom can be set in any position. The sails can be dropped or reefed down into the lazy jacks until the reef is set. Then, the sail can be raised from its existing position. This will be further discussed in detail later in this chapter.

When things get really bad, I also like to have a storm trysail aboard. Normally, the third reef on the mainsail has about the same surface area as the storm trysail. So, why even have a trysail if you have a third reef? A third reef in the mainsail will still retain some of its windward driving shape. This can be important to sail off a lee shore. However, if the sail is ripped at the third reef point, the mainsail becomes totally useless.

The storm trysail is built flat and made of heavier material than the mainsail. It should have at least 4 rows of stitching, so the force of the wind will not rip out one of the panels. The storm trysail, though built strongly, has little shape for windward driving force. I like to use the triple reefed mainsail when the weather has slowly reached a point where the boat sails more comfortably with the third reef, if further deterioration of the weather is not expected and when the winds are steady.

If there are strong gusts or if the weather may get worse, I like to set the storm trysail. That way, I do not have to worry about doing it later, when the weather may make it dangerous to do so. This is not always an easy decision to make in advance, because you may not know what to expect. *When in doubt, always prepare for the worst.*

The storm trysail should be easily set or deployed. I really dislike the storm trysail that uses the same track as the mainsail, where each slide must be forced into the track. However, if the design works well, and it is easy to make the change, it should be all right. I like to have a separate track that is devoted just to the storm trysail, next to the mainsail track. I also like to have the storm trysail permanently attached to this track, so it is easy to raise as soon as the main is dropped.

It is important that the storm trysail is setup with the sheets and pennant attached to the sail. Before the sail is raised, the sheets should lead back to the proper blocks and cleats. There should also be pre-marked points on the sheets where it is to be cleated. This is to prevent violent flogging when the sail is raised.

The storm jib is usually less complicated but more difficult to set in rough conditions. The first consideration is where to set the storm jib to maintain sail balance. This is usually the inner stay on a cutter-rigged boat and the headstay on a sloop.

If the storm jib will be set on the staysail stay on a cutter, the headsail should be removed to reduce windage. This may sound simple, but it can be very difficult if the headsail is roller furling. If the wind is blowing, the sail can be blown all over the place as it leaves the roller furling extrusion. Therefore, depending on the wind and sea conditions, it may be better to just leave it rolled up on the headstay. If this is done, *be sure that it is rolled up as tightly as possible and that the sheets are pulled tight so there is a curve to the headstay.* This will help prevent the headstay and sail from vibrating too much in strong winds. It is this vibration that causes sails to unfurl and fittings to fatigue quickly.

If the storm jib is to be set on a sloop, the headsail will have to be dropped and the storm jib attached. Again, this can be a problem if the headsail is roller furling, and the wind is already blowing too strongly to make it safe to drop. There is a saddle-type device available that goes over roller furling for just such a situation, but I have never used one, so I can't comment on its reliability in storm conditions.

If the boat is a sloop and an inner stay is added just for this purpose, it may be used, as long as it is strongly attached through the deck to a bulkhead and to the mast with proper backstays or intermediate stays to support it. Also, it must not radically affect the balance of the boat. I am reluctant to advise this. All too often, this inner stay is not properly attached at both ends, and the boat is radically out of balance. However, more than likely, a storm jib set on this inner stay will give the boat a little more weather helm; this may make it easier to heave-to.

On smaller boats with limited space for extra sails, a reef in the existing headsail may be required. If this is done, careful consideration must be paid to the strength of the winds and the sea conditions. In heavy weather, green water comes aboard. If a wave slams into a reefed jib, it may rip it to shreds.

If the existing sail is to be reefed, *be sure the reef points are at a radical angle to the horizontal, so water that catches in the excess sail at the foot can flow out easily.* On *Xiphias*, I had a reefed staysail. It was a real pain to reef when the weather was rough. After I finally got it reefed and raised it again, I found lots of green water gathered in the rolled up sail material at the foot. Then, when the sail began to flog, it forced the water out, carrying with it the original clew. The clew then began to flog violently, causing more problems; sometimes, the reef stops would untie.

Another consideration before departure is whether to carry a life raft. I feel that it is a safe practice to carry a life raft adequate for all aboard, just in case. On my own boat, however, I have chosen not to.

For those who refuse to leave their vessel and whose motto is, "I'll go down with my boat," there are the flotation bags. These suitcase-size bags are fastened to the underside of the deck at specific locations in the boat's interior. When the appropriate number have been properly installed in the correct locations, they will keep the vessel afloat when inflated. The problem is that these bags are quite large, and many are required to make the boat, filled with water, buoyant. This is not an option to consider on many boats.

As mentioned earlier, during storm conditions there are extreme stresses on all parts of the boat; this includes hoses and through-hull fittings. It is a good idea to have wooden plugs loosely tethered to each through-hull fitting, just in case they are needed.

Especially during heavy weather, there is no such thing as having too many bilge pumps. Too often, a bilge pump clogs-up, preventing it from pumping properly; therefore, have as many as can fit aboard. Also, they should be as large as reasonably possible. I like to have at least one electric bilge pump that can be set to operate automatically when the water reaches a certain level. Usually, the sound of the electric bilge pump going off automatically is the first sign of a problem. The others can be manual pumps.

On my own boat, I have a diverter valve at the salt-water intake, so I can flush the engine with fresh water. I keep a stainless steel strainer on the pick up end of the hose. In an emergency, this can be used as an additional pump. Plenty of buckets are good to have aboard. It is amazing how fast a boat can be bailed out, if all on board are frightened and have a bucket in their hand.

Jacklines and safety harnesses are other pieces of necessary equipment. Place strong safety harness jack line fasteners at the extreme ends of the boat and on both sides. When the jack line is attached to these strong fasteners, it makes uninterrupted movement possible to any location on the boat. Personally, I do not like to get myself in a situation where I have to disconnect my harness tether to move about the boat's exterior.

Another problem that often occurs from the violent motion of a boat is that the boom will come loose from its hold and begin swinging about. Make sure the method of fastening it is strong and reliable. I am a great lover of boom gallows where the boom can be lashed snugly, slightly to port or starboard.

I feel every boat should carry some basic emergency hull repair supplies. This would include thin sheets of marine plywood that would form to the curvature of the hull. Be sure to also store some concrete nails, wooden wedges, and some underwater epoxy. On smaller boats, it may be possible to use bin lids and other items already on the boat. The key is to have an idea what you can use before it is necessary to use it.

There are commercial collision mats and umbrella-type devices available. I don't have any personal experience with these, so I will not make any comments. If you are considering any of these items, study the design, construction, and ease of use for the possible locations that may need repair. All too often, the damaged area is behind a locker or somewhere that is difficult to access with something that is too long or too large.

Another safety precaution is to be sure that bin lids and locker tops have some method to secure them. You don't want them to open in case of a severe knockdown or roll over. During my first cyclone at sea, I had a knockdown that emptied the lockers on the high side of the boat and threw items everywhere. I was finding cans in the strangest places for months.

If you will be cruising in colder climates, it is a good idea to have heavy wet suits or survival suits aboard for each crewmember.

I think it is unnecessary to mention the need for an EPIRB and updated flares. The problem is that the flares do not have a long shelf life; they should be replaced when they go out of date. The EPIRB is only as good as the distance to someone who can provide assistance. The ones with the built-in location finder are excellent, although expensive.

The SSB and ham radios can be useful when there is an emergency. No license is required in an emergency. However, you would probably want to use it at other times as well, so it is a good idea to get the license.

§

I remember when I was in Vanuatu, there was a Mayday call. An American sailor said his wife had fallen overboard during the night. They were about half way between Hawaii and Vanuatu. The problem was that neither Hawaii nor Vanuatu would acknowledge that the boat was within their waters. It took two days before the search began. The bottom line is: *when you are out there, you are on your own.* Don't expect any help.

§

As I mentioned earlier, because of the violent motion in a storm, fuel tanks can suck air into the lines if they are close to empty. This will depend on the tank's design and mounting location. I like to have a sump built into the bottom of my tank. This sump has a drain cock to remove water and sediment. This provides a pocket where there will always be some fuel, which reduces the chances of sucking air. However, because it is a sump, it can accumulate sediment; this could clog the lines and filter if not regularly drained.

Other items that each boat should carry are a hacksaw, bolt cutter and cable cutter. In case the mast were to fail, the rigging could be cut, if necessary. If this did happen, I like to leave the cotter pins or split pins to the standing rigging clevis pins spread slightly, like a "Y", so I can rapidly pull them out with a pair of pliers. Of course, they have to be in a location where they cannot catch on sheets, sails, or skin. Outboard chainplates make this a little easier.

There should be some method to slow the boat down in rough weather. Anything that will slow a boat is called a drogue. This would apply to sea anchors, tires, and large diameter ropes—anything that could be trailed off the stern to slow the boat's speed. Of course, I would question the wisdom of running off the wind in a storm. It is mentioned because it just might be the best solution, used for a short period of time, to reach a safe harbor.

When things get to the point where heaving-to is no longer a safe strategy, I believe in a parachute anchor. The size of the parachute anchor will vary by the size and weight of the boat. The ones recommended by the various manufacturers are adequate, but many are based solely on the size of the boat. I think the weight or displacement of the boat is probably more important than its length. The amount of windage a boat has is another consideration. I think between a sloop and a ketch of equal length and displacement, the ketch would require a larger parachute because of windage.

The following was taken from Para-Tech Engineering. I provide it only as a reference. I suggest the various manufacturers be contacted directly for their professional opinion regarding the size needed for your particular boat.

Parachute anchor size vs. boat length

Boat length	Parachute anchor size
20 ft.	6 ft.
25 ft.	9 ft.
35 ft.	12 ft.
40 ft.	15 ft.
45 to 50 ft.	18 ft.
50 to 90 ft.	24 ft.
90 to 110 ft.	32 ft.

There is some controversy and some agreement about the size, the material, and how to properly prepare and deploy the parachute anchor. Although I don't consider myself enough of an authority to give advice on this subject, I would like to relate what I did, the results I had, and what I would have done differently. Because an entire book could be written about this, and I am devoting only a small chapter to it, I strongly suggest that you read material provided by the parachute anchor's manufacturer, as well as other books on the subject.

If you are confident that you have everything aboard that may be required during a storm, the time to actually prepare for the storm is before you leave port. It is of utmost importance that all crewmembers aboard know how to reef the sails almost instinctually. This also applies to the method used to heave-to. When the weather gets rough, it is difficult to think clearly because of fear, fatigue, and even seasickness. The only way to gain this knowledge and confidence is from experience, and the only way to gain experience is through practice.

Before departing, check that everything is working properly, and check out anything that could possibly create a problem. We all think about a wave causing the boat to roll 360° and pray it never happens. More than likely it won't happen, but a severe knockdown is possible. It is a good idea to think about—and prepare for—the worst. Consequently, let's consider the necessary preparations in case of a rollover.

This means that all tanks on the boat must be strongly secured so they do not shift or break loose, flying around the cabin. This also applies to bin lids, locker tops, and even any removable lids in the cabin sole.

Check that the batteries are secure and will not break loose. These are heavy and full of acid. A battery is not an item to have flying loose inside the boat.

I have heard of gimbaled stoves coming out of their bracket during a knockdown. Make sure there is some way to keep it in place. If necessary, it can still be removed.

I see too many boats that have their books and dishes restrained with bungee cords. Bungee cords will never hold something that heavy in place in a knockdown.

Go around the boat inside and outside, looking for anything that could come loose or open. You certainly don't want knives flying around the boat.

On the outside, it is possible that anything on deck will be torn off and washed overboard. This would apply to extra fuel, water tanks, and the dodger. The dinghy may also go; again, this would depend how you secured it to the boat.

It is during storm conditions that things we rely on fail. One such concern is the fasteners and fittings on roller furling stays. These have almost constant movement and take severe stress when the sails are flogging. It is important to make certain that the bearings and bushings are working properly. Check for any sign of fatigue cracks in the stainless steel fasteners and hardware used to attach the unit to the boat. Remember that anything that is threaded is only as strong as the minor diameter of the threads, or the diameter distance between the bottom of the threads. If this fastener is hollow inside, it is more likely to fail. Refer to Figure 22 on page 97.

Inspect all the standing rigging regularly. This means checking for any hairline cracks or any sign of possible failure in all the hardware that supports the mast and sails. This is not easy because most cracks are not visible to the naked eye. There are products used in welding that are available which will make it easier to detect small cracks.

The standing rigging continues to stretch, especially in the first few years of continuous use. If it is an older boat that has not been used extensively, the rigging may still stretch.

The greatest chance of failure on chainplates is where the pull or stress is not in a direct line with the pull or force it is intended to support. Refer to Figure 30 on page 140.

Check that the mast is properly tuned. A mast that is adjusted too tight is just as dangerous as one that is adjusted too loose. Because it should be done regularly, especially on newer boats, it is a good idea to know how to do this yourself.

Check for anything that could foul sails, sheets, lines, and halyards. When reefing, always try to keep the slack out of the other reef lines. The same applies to the halyards, guys, lifts, and anything that could catch on something that would require the necessity of a crewmember moving into more exposed areas to unfoul.

It is important that propane, gasoline, and anything combustible be securely fastened. Check all the fittings and hoses to be sure that they could not cause a problem or leak if there were a knockdown.

Service all the through-hull valves so they do not fail when they are needed. This applies especially to the cockpit drains.

Make sure all the storm sails have the head, tack, and clew properly marked. If the configuration requires separate port and starboard sheets, be sure they are also properly marked. Review and practice the procedure for setting these sails, so it requires little thinking.

I like to keep a sharp dive knife and flashlight within an arm's reach from the cockpit. On passages, I also fasten a dive knife to the base of the mast. Needless to say, these knives must be held securely, so they don't come out of their scabbard accidentally.

I always have various short lengths of rope and line loosely tied to the dodger supports and on my pin rails. If something needs to be secured in a hurry, you don't want to be searching in cockpit lockers for rope or line.

As mentioned earlier, be sure jacklines are strongly attached to the boat and are strong enough for their intended purpose. Lin and Larry Pardey tie a line from the boom gallows to the upper shroud at chest height. I really like this for two reasons. First, it gives more security while moving between the cockpit and the mast. Second, I like to fasten my harness tether to this line, so it does not drag along the deck keeping those below awake.

Clean the bilges to reduce the chances of sludge or other debris fouling the bilge pumps. One common problem that occurs when water enters the boat is that paper, rags, and towels end up in the bilge, fouling the bilge pump intake.

While you're at it, why not service the bilge pumps? Take them out, clean them, and make sure the valves are all clear and working properly. If not, replace the part now, before it is really needed.

Although I know I am repeating myself, I cannot emphasize enough how important it is that all aboard know instinctually what to do during a storm. This means reefing, sail changes, storm sail deployment, method for heaving-to, setting the parachute anchor or drogues, and any possible emergency situation that can be imagined. This would include sending distress messages, activating the EPIRB, deploying the life raft and its supplies, and abandoning ship.

Avoid the storm

It is far better to avoid a storm than it is to have to deal with it. I know of cruisers who have followed the safest course, during the safest months, and have made circumnavigations never encountering winds more than 35 knots. Unfortunately, this is not always the case. However, your chances of running into a storm can be radically reduced, by knowing where most storms occur and when the storm season starts.

This requires updated **Pilot Charts** aboard, covering the area you expect to cruise. The Defense Mapping Agency provides **Pilot Charts**. Their purpose is to help mariners select the fastest and safest route to a destination. They are compiled using many years of reports from ships and past weather information for a particular area.

The **Pilot Chart** provides lots of information that the cruiser can use to plan the cruise. Study the **Pilot Chart** for the months you intend to make the passage. If that month has too many gales or too much wind, plan your departure when the conditions are better.

The information is not an absolute; it does not necessarily mean that you will encounter the same situation indicated in the chart. It is simply an average of the reports they have received.

Each monthly chart will provide the following information for each 5° square:

Prevailing winds and calms in the wind rose

Average wave height
Typical barometric pressures
Percentage of gales
Average current direction and strength
Tracks of previous hurricanes and cyclones
Air and water temperature
Recommended routes

Avoiding the storm

The entire map is covered with wind roses. Most sailors are familiar with this rose and know how to interpret it. However, if this is new to you, let me explain the basics. See Figure 75.

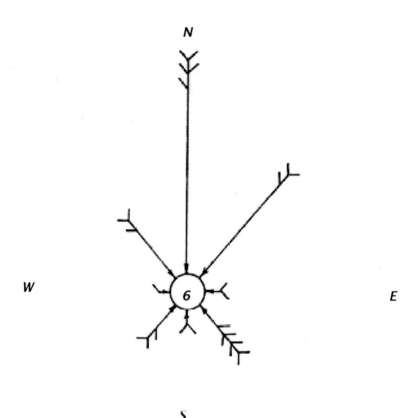

6% calms, indicated by the number inside the circle.
Predominant winds are from the North at force 5.
Strongest winds are from the Southeast at force 7.
Minimum winds are from the West at force 1.

Figure 75. The Wind Rose

There is a circle in the center with a number that shows the percentage of calms for that particular 5° square.

An arrow pointing toward the center of the circle indicates the percentage of wind from that direction. The direction the wind blows is the direction the arrow goes toward the circle of calms.

The arrow's length indicates the percentage of wind from that direction for that particular month in that 5° grid. If the percentage of wind from one direction exceeds 30%, it will have a number indicating this percentage.

The arrow has short angled feathers at the outward end. Each hash mark at an angle indicates one force on the Beaufort Scale mentioned previously.

Sometimes there is a blue line going through the wind rose that indicates the direction and strength of the current in that area. There is a number on this line to record the expected current strength.

The track of previous hurricanes and cyclones are shown in a rectangle in another section of the chart.

Another important bit of information available on the *Pilot Chart* is the Percentage of Gales in a particular 5° square. This is also located at the bottom of the chart. See Figure 76.

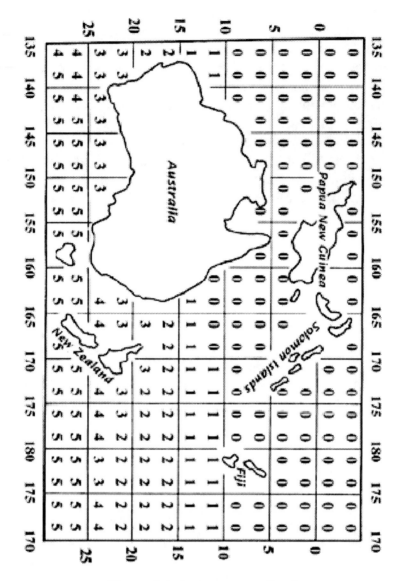

Figure 76. Percentage of gales

Each number in the center indicates the number of gales reported in that grid during the month of the chart. The one I used in the illustration is not an actual chart, but an example of the information provided in the Percentage of Gale Chart. The major difference is that the number may be inside the circle of a windrose. Do not get this confused with the standard windrose on the rest of the ***Pilot Chart***, where the numbers represent the *percentage of calms* in that 5° area. It would be wise to plan your route where there are all zeros, and there are no numbers anywhere around it.

After you have decided which would be the best month to leave and the safest route, be sure to get a weather report before you depart. Fortunately, tropical storms take time to build before they are considered dangerous. A tropical storm begins as a low pressure; then in a few days, it may progress to a tropical depression. After another few days, it may become a tropical storm. A name is given at this time, because the odds are that it will increase into a cyclone. It will take another few days to become a cyclone. The winds and seas increase as the low becomes a storm. Consequently, if there are no lows indicated along your route, you can expect about 5 days before anything could develop that would be a serious threat.

While I am at it, let's clarify that a hurricane is the same as a cyclone and a typhoon. The term hurricane is commonly used in the Americas, while the rest of the world uses the term cyclone or typhoon.

Most sailors have heard the saying, *"Never leave on a Friday"*. This originated in the early days of the British Royal Navy. Too many ships were being lost on Fridays, so many sailors refused to sail on that day of the week. As a result, the British government had to eliminate this superstition. So, they laid the keel to a new ship on a Friday. They christened her the *HMS Friday*. She was launched on a Friday and left on her maiden voyage on a Friday. She was never seen again.

I do not know if this is a fact, but I have read this account and heard the story many times. Now, I admit that I have left on a Friday and nothing has happened. However, I do make it a point to never leave on an overnight passage on a Friday.

One thing I personally encourage and practice myself is to listen to your gut feeling. There have been many times when I felt something was wrong, and that I should not leave on the scheduled day. Or, I may be sailing and just feel that something is not right. This has happened to me many times. I will suddenly get this feeling; I'll go on deck, and in the distance is a ship heading right towards me, or there are rocks or shallow water in sight. Perhaps my personal sensitive sensors subconsciously pick up sound that my consciousness does not. I realize there is no proof that this really works; however, I still listen to my gut feeling before going to sea. If I feel something is not right, I wait until I feel better about leaving. There have been many times when I was glad that I did; there have been other times when nothing has happened. Some people believe in this more than others, but I think it is worthy of being mentioned.

Basic weather information

No sailor should ever go to sea without some basic weather knowledge. The more information gathered and understood, the better. If you have access to weather fax, you should know how to interpret the symbols and deduce what type of weather might be expected.

As we all know, weather prediction is difficult even for the professional. However, I would like to mention a few items that should be considered. I strongly advise taking a comprehensive nautical weather course. At the minimum, I suggest you carry along some books on the subject that can be used as a reference.

This is not a chapter on weather lore. It is not close to being a comprehensive study. Hopefully, the general comments and ideas provided here will encourage further thinking on the subject and the desire to search for more information. I want to discuss some simple weather reading ideas that may be of assistance to the cruiser.

Before I begin, I want to make sure that everyone knows that *major weather patterns rotate in an opposite direction in the Southern Hemisphere*. Most weather books emphasize the Northern Hemisphere; therefore, if you do not understand the difference, you could find yourself in trouble. In the Northern Hemisphere, low-pressure depressions rotate counterclockwise. High-pressure systems or anti-cyclones rotate clockwise. In the Southern Hemisphere, low-pressure depressions rotate clockwise, and the high-pressure systems rotate counterclockwise. Some may feel that this is elementary, but I mention it just in case; it is important if you intend to cross the equator.

Using this information, if you are in the Northern Hemisphere, put your back to the wind, and the low-pressure system will be slightly to your left. In the Southern Hemisphere, it will be to your right.

Another item that may be common knowledge to some, but is worthy of mentioning, is that the hurricane or cyclone seasons are also during the *opposite* months in the Southern Hemisphere. In the Northern Hemisphere, our storm season is from June through November, while in the Southern Hemisphere, it is from November through May.

Wind will flow from a high-pressure system to a low-pressure system. Since the equator is a constant low-pressure, the wind in either hemisphere will flow in that direction. Because the earth rotates from west to east, it pulls the wind in an easterly direction. This becomes more predominant closer to the equator. This is why the tradewinds in the Northern Hemisphere flow from the northeast. In the Southern Hemisphere, the tradewinds flow from the southeast.

You have heard the saying, *"Red sky at night, sailor's delight. Red sky in the morning, sailors take warning"*. This saying is based on the fact that the earth rotates from west to east, so the earth is rotating in the direction of the rising sun; therefore, *"sailor take warning"* means that the earth is heading toward the storm. If it is in the west, or between us and the setting sun, *"sailor's delight"* means that the storm is behind us.

In the Northern Hemisphere, if a low-pressure system and a high-pressure system are near each other, the wind will flow from the high-pressure system, in a slightly clockwise direction, toward the low-pressure system, until the isobars merge. Here, the low-pressure system takes precedence over the wind, and it will begin to change to a more counterclockwise direction. In the Southern Hemisphere, it will move from a high-pressure system, in a slightly counterclockwise direction, towards the low-pressure system. Then, the low-pressure system takes precedence, and the winds will move in a clockwise direction.

A high-pressure system has warmer air than a low-pressure system. As the moist warm air enters a low-pressure system, it rises and condenses until precipitation occurs, and a storm develops. The greater the difference in the pressure between the two systems determines the severity of the storm. This is why it is important to understand and keep record of the barometric pressure.

In America, we use inches to measure this pressure. The rest of the world and all government reports are in metric millibars. I found that I really prefer the metric millibar system to the inch system. Inches are more difficult to interpret than millibars. Also, millibars are in smaller increments than inches and parts of an inch. *I strongly advise that you have a barometer that reads in millibars and get in the habit of using only millibars.*

The average daily pressure is about 1013 millibars or about 30 inches. This pressure will vary during the day. This change is called the semi-diurnal change; it is normal, and it will not have any effect on the weather. It will rise a few millibars in the afternoon and drop a few in the early morning hours. This is easy to determine by watching your barometer regularly. This should not be applied to the major change in pressure.

The actual barometer reading is not as important as the rate it drops or rises. If you are in a high-pressure system, the barometer will read in the lower to middle 1000 millibars or in the lower 30-inch range. While in a low-pressure system, it will be in the 900 millibars or in the 28-inch range. If the drop between the high-pressure system and the low-pressure system is rapid, there is the likelihood that the storm will be more severe.

The barometer should be read and recorded about every three hours, if a sudden drop is noticed. The following was taken from Alan Watts's book, ***Instant Weather Forecasting***.

Fall in pressure	Fall in millibars in 3 hours
Slow Fall	Less than 3
Moderate Fall	Between 3 and 6
Rapid Fall	Between 6 and 8
Major Fall	Between 8 and 10

Based on a reading taken every 3 hours

However, this is not an absolute. As the following story illustrates, a sudden drop in barometric pressure doesn't always mean a storm is brewing.

§

I was sailing in the Vanuatu Islands. I had just been to Tana Island to visit a live volcano. On the way back to Port Villa, the capital, I noticed that the weather was unsettled, and my barometer was dropping rapidly. I could almost watch the needle move. It dropped about 10 millibars in three hours and continued to fall. I figured I was in for the ultimate cyclone.

The weather was not severe, and the winds were variable, but fairly strong. By the time I arrived in Port Villa two days later, the barometer was back to normal. Later, I discovered that I had encountered a compression of isobars.

§

Isobars are lines of barometric pressure separated by a certain number of millibars of pressure. This varies by the type of chart. In the British Isles, each isobar is separated by 1 millibar; in the North Atlantic, it varies by 4 millibars; on large-scale charts, it is 8 millibars.

The distance between the isobars will affect the strength of the wind. As isobars get closer together, the pressure gradient increases. Most synoptic weather charts, ASXX charts and FSXX charts, have a scale that shows the wind strength between isobars. This is the Geostrophic Wind, which is not affected by surface friction.

Here is a hypothetical example: let's say there is a gradient change of 4 millibars between two isobar lines. The distance between the two isobars is about 200 nautical miles. According to the scale on the chart, there would be about 20 knots of wind expected. If the distance between isobars was 50 nautical miles, then about 50 knots of wind might be expected. This is only an example for the purpose of clarification. See Figure 77.

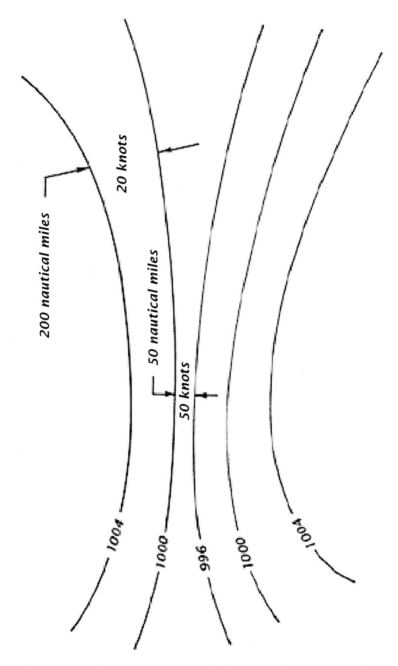

Figure 77. Distance between isobars and wind speed

Unfortunately, there is no standard rule that will apply to all charts. The reason is that different charts have different scales and the millibar distance between isobars varies by the type of chart. Therefore, you need to check each chart for this graph, which measures wind strength based on distance between isobar lines.

Studying the upper and lower cloud formations is another important way to determine the expected weather. This is too extensive to try to cover in a single chapter. There are excellent books available that have photos of the cloud formations and what they may indicate. Again, let me recommend Alan Watts's books *Instant Weather Forecasting* and *Instant Wind Forecasting*. I like to carry these books aboard for quick and easy reference.

There are different types of winds: surface winds, geostrophic winds, lower winds, and upper winds that carry the clouds and may indicate a change in the wind direction. In the tropics, the surface winds blow just above the ocean's surface. These are our sailing winds. Lower winds carry the normal clouds, like cumulus, stratocumulus, and others we see daily. These flow in the same direction as the wind between the isobars. Upper winds are influenced by the freezing temperatures aloft and are, apparently, very high up. These winds will often flow in an entirely different direction than the lower or surface winds.

The isobars will be roughly parallel to the center of the high or low-pressure system. They will begin to change shape as they get further away from the center.

The surface winds do not necessarily flow parallel to the isobars like lower winds, but will flow at about 10° to them, predominantly blowing from the high-pressure system to the low-pressure system. If you are in the Northern Hemisphere, to find out the lower wind direction, stand with your back to the surface wind, then rotate clockwise about 10°; your back is now facing the lower wind. If you are in the Southern Hemisphere, turn counterclockwise 10° and your back will be facing the lower wind. The surface wind is strongly influenced by landmasses, so be sure this is done at sea.

While you are standing with your back to the lower wind, look up at the clouds in the upper wind. If they are flowing parallel in either direction to the flow of the lower wind, there will probably be no change in the winds and weather. However, if the upper wind is blowing at 90° to the lower wind, there may be a change.

It is difficult to tell how long it will take for the change to happen. It could be only hours or a full day. It would depend on the type of clouds in the upper winds. I suggest you buy a good book on the subject. I got this information from Alan Watts's **Weather Forecasting: Ashore and Afloat**, one of my favorite books.

Preparation for the storm's arrival

Let's assume we discover that the barometer is dropping too rapidly. The clouds indicate a worsening of the weather, and a weather fax shows a deep depression on our path that will be impossible to avoid. Now is the time to make preparations for the worst.

Check to see that everything on deck—as well as below—is properly secured, and that there is no possibility of anything coming loose. The dinghy is always a problem. If it is an inflatable, perhaps it should be rolled up and stored below.

It may also be better to store the anchors below or in a locker. If not, make sure they are secure, and there is no possibility of them coming loose. A flogging anchor is something you don't want in a storm. While you're at it, consider plugging the chainpipe with rags or clay to prevent water from entering below.

Install the inner stay if you are on a sloop. Remember to check that it will not change the boat's balance too much.

If the weather permits, remove the roller furling headsail, or at least, have it rolled up tightly and pulled aft to make it bow. This will reduce the oscillating or vibrating in strong winds.

Consider removing cowl vents and installing deck covers. This will depend on the severity of the storm expected and the temperature inside the boat. In the tropics, this could make it miserable inside. Careful judgment must be used on this one.

The jacklines for safety harnesses should already be in place. Make sure every person who may have to go on deck has a safety harness. It may be necessary to wear them around the clock.

Activate your lightning protection if it is not automatically built into the boat. Also, disconnect any electronics that will not be of use.

Consider closing the head and using a bucket. I know this is a difficult one, because trying to dump a bucket in rough seas could be worse than a plugged head. At least make sure the head is securely fastened, so if someone is sitting on it and the boat makes a sudden lurch, it will not break loose. This may sound silly, but it happened to me on one of my deliveries.

Have leather or other anti-chafe material readily available, in case the parachute anchor will be needed. Have the parachute anchor prepared and ready to deploy easily.

Charge the engine batteries. Replace any replaceable batteries that might be old, and have more new ones available. Make sure everyone knows where they are located if needed in a hurry.

As mentioned previously, have a plan and assign duties so everyone knows what to expect and how to respond to the situation. This point has to be handled carefully. You do not want to instill fear, but to show confidence in your own knowledge and skills.

Assign watch duties. In rough weather, the watches should be short. The time and length of the watch can be changed if necessary, but everyone likes to have an idea when they can get some rest. This brings up another important point. Have everyone get as much rest as possible; this is easier said than done.

Consider issuing seasick pills to everyone aboard, even the ones who are not prone to seasickness. The radical movement of a boat in a storm, combined with fear, can make the most able seamen ill.

Make up quick and easy food beforehand. It will be nearly impossible to cook during the storm. It will be dangerous to do so without getting burnt. Only provide food that is easy to eat and digest. Sandwiches are excellent, as are crackers and sweets. By now you know what the crew likes and dislikes. Don't serve anything that could aggravate someone else's stomach.

Make it a point to keep frequent and accurate records of your position, speed, course, and expected destination.

I know there are many more items that I have not mentioned. I would advise you to have your own checklist for your boat and its crew.

Strategies for handling the storm

Before I begin to discuss the best strategy to apply in a particular situation, we should discuss the basic strategies available. These will vary by boat design and sail configuration, weather and sea conditions, as well as the experience of the crew.

Reefing sails

One of the first strategies in rough weather is to reduce sail area easily and properly. Most sailors already know all about reefing and probably already do so efficiently. I merely want to review the basic systems available and how they work.

Roller reefing headsails

One of the first things you will do is to reduce sail area, while still retaining steerage control. One of the most common methods to reef the headsail is using roller reefing or roller furling sails. The reason I mention roller reefing separately from roller furling is that roller reefing will hold its shape as it is rolled up and can be used for reefing. Roller furling sails are just what the term implies, the sail can be stored on the headstay. It can be totally unrolled to sail or totally rolled up on the headstay to store. This sail does not hold the necessary shape and should not be used for reefing except in light to mild conditions.

The problem is that manufacturers do not separate the two in their marketing packages. The reason for this is not necessarily the mechanical unit itself, but the sail that fits the unit.

There are several factors that can influence effective reefing of this sail. One of the most important is the size of the roller furling system in relation to the size of sail. Unfortunately, many sales people try to sell a cruiser too small a system. I don't know why they do this; you would think it would be just the opposite.

One of the major considerations is the size of the center axis of the drum, or the diameter of the drum, that rolls up the reefing line. The larger the diameter, the less effort needed to roll up the sails. When the wind begins to flog the sails, things begin to happen rapidly. Knots suddenly develop in sheets. Sheets wrap around cleats, winches, etc. The best way to roll up a sail is to have some load on it, so it is not flogging too violently. If the drum is big enough, this can be accomplished more easily.

Another concern is the shape and cut of the sail. The more hollow sewn into the sail, the less shape it will have as it is rolled up. Foam luffs do help solve this problem. Over time, however, the foam becomes more flattened, reducing this positive effect.

Personally, I think that the most important factor is the angle of the sheet lead to the headstay. I am not a sailmaker, so I don't feel that I have the expertise to go into all the reasons why this is important. What I do have is experience, and I'd like to relate what I have found.

The angle of the sheet lead to the headstay should be as close to a 90° angle as possible, with nearly the same amount of sail area above and below the sheet lead line. To me, this just seems logical. When the sail is rolled up on the furling system, the sail will roll up more evenly on the top and bottom of the sail, thus holding its shape better.

Also, the sheet lead to the sheet block will not change as the sail is reduced. Thus, the block remains in the same position at all times. See Figure 78 (a).

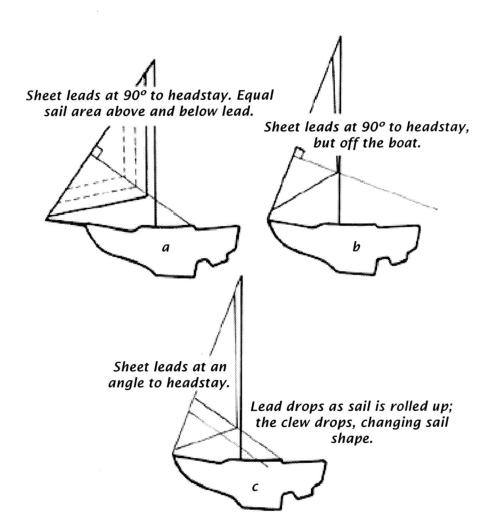

Figure 78. Jib sheet lead to headstay

Of course, the problem is getting the airfoil shape needed when the lead is at 90°, and there is equal sail area above and below this sheet lead. There must be a compromise to be able to achieve both.

Unfortunately, this is impossible on many or even most boats. The angle of the headstay is such that to have the sheet lead as near to 90° as possible, with fairly equal sail area above and below this line, would mean that the sheet will lead off the stern of the boat, as shown in Figure 78 (b).

The closer the angle between the mast and the headstay is to a right angle improves the situation. This is most commonly seen on low aspect ratio masts (boats with shorter masts) and boats with bowsprits.

Most boats have tall masts with the headstay closer to the mast, hence, with a smaller angle. Thus, for the sheet lead to stay aboard, it must lead to the headstay at an angle. This lead to the headstay is critical so that the sail's leach can be pulled down, and the foot pulled aft at about equal pressure, giving the sail the needed shape to provide drive. As the sail is furled or reefed around the headstay, the lead must change where it meets the deck. This requires a track and car so the block can be moved to maintain this critical angle, as shown in Figure 78 (c).

Check your own boat. See how far up the headstay you have to go to get the 90° angle and still lead to the boat. Even if there is more sail area above than below this line, it may be better than what you have. I suggest you discuss this with your sailmaker and express your concerns. He or she is the professional and could better advise you on your particular boat than I.

Another concern when reefing existing sails is the weight or thickness of the sail. For a headsail to provide the necessary shape and drive in light winds, the weight of the sail should be much less than if the winds were considerably stronger. So, either the sail must be changed for various conditions, or an average weight is used for normal conditions. This sail is too heavy for light conditions and too light for heavy winds. So, when the sail is rolled up, the remaining sail that is providing drive must survive the existing conditions. If this sail is ripped, then the sail is useless until it can be repaired. Also, it may be difficult to effectively furl a torn sail. For this reason, reefing headsails in anything but moderate conditions is not advised.

Slab reefing headsails

This is the traditional way to reef headsails. There are several ways this can be done. One is by the traditional slab reefing method, and the other is with a removable panel that Larry and Lin Pardey like so well.

It is possible to slab reef the headsail, as long as you feel it can be done safely. I strongly discourage this on a bowsprit. However, if the boat has a bowsprit, it probably has a staysail or inner stay to take the storm sail. Therefore, the headsail can be removed early, or it can be pulled down with a downhaul and lashed to the bowsprit, whisker stays, or lifelines.

To reef a headsail or staysail, the sail usually has a downhaul that makes dropping it quicker and more efficient. It also helps keep the sail on deck, so the wind doesn't raise it when not holding it down.

The sail is dropped to access the reef, which is at the bottom of the sail. This requires that the tack and clew be moved to this higher reef position. The tack normally has a longer pennant, so the sail is higher off the deck and will not catch as much green water.

The clew becomes more of a problem. To move the sheet lead higher, it must be easily transferred. If a knot is used on port and starboard sheets, the knot will often come loose before there is a load on it. I have had this happen several times. The other alternative is to have a quick release snap shackle or equivalent on the sheet. This is a heavy, hard piece of hardware. You don't want to take any chances of being hit in the head when it flogs—and it will flog. I have not yet found a solution to this problem; I still use a snap shackle and try to be very careful.

After the reef tack is in place and the sheets are now connected to the reef clew, the foot of the sail below this reef point must be rolled up. This requires removing any hanks connected to the stay. Then the clew must be folded towards the center of the sail, and the foot rolled up to the reef point. There should be sail stops at the reef points to secure this roll. There should also be a line that can be tied to the folded clew to prevent it from being forced out of the roll when the sail flogs.

Next, the sail is raised and sheets adjusted. The sail will flog radically until the lee sheet is set.

The reef line should be at quite an angle to the deck. If the reef line is horizontal or anywhere near horizontal, water will gather in the roll and balloon between the reef stops. This water has to go somewhere, usually out the clew end of the roll, carrying with it the clew. Sometimes, the water will force the reef stops to release, making the ballooned foot worse.

This problem is easily resolved by having the angle of the reef line at 20° or more to the horizontal, so the clew is considerably higher than the tack. Water will run out the tack side of the roll. To accomplish this, the problem arises on the lead of the sheets to the block. With this higher clew, the sheet may not lead where it provides the best shape for the sail. Again, I advise you check this and discuss it with your sailmaker.

The removable panel is much easier to reef. The sail is dropped, and sheet and tack are moved to the new reef position as above. Then, the bottom foot is unzipped and removed entirely.

The only problems I can see with this system are chafe at the zipper and zipper failure. As any offshore sailor knows, salt is the biggest enemy to all zippers. The zipper can have a cover sewn over it, but it still should be checked and serviced often.

If you are considering this panel method of reefing, talk to your sailmaker and get his or her advice and suggestions.

Roller reefing mainsails

This is still a bit controversial for me. The old method, where the boom was rotated and the sail was rolled around it as it came down, was never a good solution for reefing the mainsail, as you may recall from the story of the shakedown cruise on a Balboa 20 that I related in Chapter 2. Because the leach of the sail is so much longer than the luff, the end of the boom drops, causing all kinds of problems. If it drops low enough, it increases the chances of hitting someone in the head. If the boat was on a run with following seas, the boom would dip into the water. The boom could break where the boom vang was attached, or somewhere else.

The other problem with this design is that the pressure on the sail causes the leach, where it is wrapped around the boom, to move forward, changing the sail's shape. This can be resolved by having an outhaul grommet installed and reinforced. There is still the problem of getting a line through this grommet and strongly attaching it to the boom. This requires that the boom be inboard long enough to accomplish it. It also means that the person who is doing this job has to stand near the boat's edge.

If your boat has this method of reefing the mainsail, I strongly advise you to forget it and change to slab reefing. This will be discussed shortly.

Another method of roller reefing the mainsail is rolling the foot of the sail inside the boom. What I like about this method is that the end of the boom, where the leach rolls around the axis, is wider than the forward end. Thus, the boom does not drop, and the sail maintains its shape as it is reduced. The shorter it is or the more it is reefed down, the flatter it becomes; this is good in strong winds.

What I am concerned about, however, is the reliability of this roller system inside the boom. It may be difficult to access if the sail is already partially rolled up. This will depend on the manufacturer, construction, and design.

Another concern with in-boom roller reefing is that it requires a considerably larger, thus heavier, boom. This may be a problem depending on the size of the boat and the boom. It is just something to consider before buying one.

I have often seen roller reefing on the luff of the mainsail. It may be rolled up inside the mast, or on a vertical stay or extrusion just aft of the mast. I have looked closely at these, but have not really used one, so I am reluctant to comment. However, I have sailed alongside boats with them and found that they all seem to work well in light to moderate conditions. The real question is how it will work when it is needed the most: in a storm. Here I can only speculate.

First, let's look at the idea of roller furling or reefing mainsail. The sail is inserted into an extrusion or hanked to a stay that goes up the mast. The mainsail, to have the airfoil needed to sail to windward, must have a hollow sewn into the sail. As the luff is rolled up, it takes this hollow or airfoil and moves it forward, thus reducing the airfoil shape quickly.

Then there is the problem of the sheet lead. As mentioned previously, the ideal lead for roller reefing is at or near 90° to the luff, with nearly equal sail area above and below this sheet line. This is about the only way a perfectly even roll can be achieved. On a vertical mast, it is totally impossible to achieve, but there are different extremes.

On a boat with a boom, the foot of the sail must be loose footed and not lead into the boom. The luff and foot are nearly at a right angle. This means that the sheet pull on the clew must be down and aft to flatten the leach. As the sail's luff is rolled up, the lead must move forward to maintain the same sail shape. So the sheet lead must go to a floating block on the boom. As the sail is rolled up on its luff, the clew moves forward. There is nowhere else to have this lead except at the top of the boom.

The wishbone boom looks and works similarly to a sailboard's boom. There is a curved rod on both sides of the sail. The clew leads to the point where the two sides meet. This can provide an excellent lead for the clew and a good angle to the luff. Each system would have to be looked at closely to feel confident that this type of wishbone boom is properly designed, constructed, and attached to the mast.

The roller furling or reefing mainsail that leads to a horizontal boom would not be able to achieve as good of a sheet lead as the wishbone boom. Again, each system would have to be evaluated and used before any conclusions could be made.

Personally, I cannot see how roller reefing the luff of the mainsail could efficiently maintain the airfoil required to provide the necessary lift. I think it would be a good method of furling, but question its effectiveness for reefing. I know there are many that will disagree with my comments. As I mentioned earlier, I do not have personal experience with this method and will leave the door open to the possibility that I am wrong.

Slab reefing the mainsail at the mast

I am from the old school and believe in the old fashioned system of slab reefing the mainsail. There are no moving parts to fail, no drums to jam, no swivels to freeze, no fittings to come loose or break, and the list goes on. This is the method for reefing the mainsail that I will discuss at length.

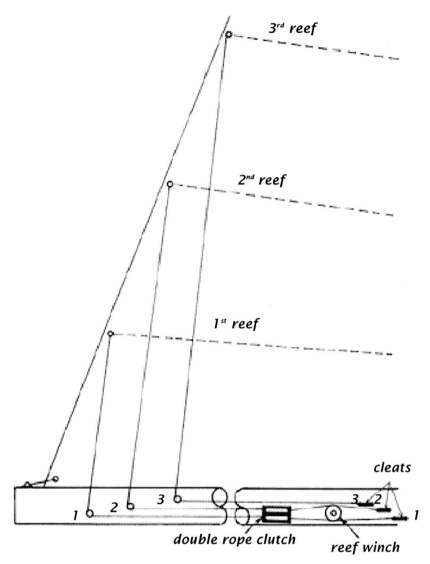

Figure 79. Slab reefing for three reef points

The mainsail has reinforced reef points sewn into the sail from the luff to the leach. Each reef point should raise the boom's end a little higher to prevent it dipping when the boat rolls while on a run. The idea is to drop the sail by the amount of area between the reef points.

The reefing can be done at the mast or from the cockpit. During most of my sailing, I did the reefing at the mast. Now that I am older,

I have the lines led to the cockpit. I would like to explain both methods.

Let's start with the more traditional way of reefing the mainsail at the mast. If I were to reef the sail from the mast, my boom must be equipped with some basic hardware. Let's say there are three reef points in the sail. On the starboard side of the boom, there should be a strong turning block set aft of the outhaul reef grommet or the last reinforced grommet at the leach of the sail for each reef.

The block's position is based on the location of this grommet when the sail is down on the boom. This outhaul grommet is pulled aft until the sail is taut along the reef line. The turning block should be installed several inches aft of this position. The objective is to pull the reef clew down and aft. As the number of reefs increases, the bottom of the sail piles, so the turning block should get progressively further aft with each reef point.

Assuming there are three reef points, the first or aft most block should be mounted just below the centerline of the boom, so it does not bind or interfere with the other two reef points after it is set taut. The second reef turning block should be located forward of this first block and near the centerline of the boom. The third reef turning block would be further forward and just above the centerline of the boom. The objective is to keep them close to the centerline of the boom, but not interfering with one another.

There are three ways the outhaul line can be led through the outhaul grommet. One is to strongly install an eyestrap to the boom on the opposite side of the turning block. The outhaul reef line is tied to this eyestrap. The reef line leads up and through the outhaul grommet, down to the turning block, and forward.

The second method is to tie the end of the outhaul reef line to the boom, or under the boom to the end of the turning block. The line then leads under the boom and up the port side, through the outhaul reef, down to the turning block, and then forward. Both of these methods give a slight advantage to the force to pull the leach of the sail down.

The last method is to tie the end of the outhaul reef line directly to the outhaul grommet, down to the turning block, and then forward. This does not provide any advantage to help pull the sail's leach down.

Regardless of the method used, these outhaul reef lines go through fairleads, which prevents the slack in the line from dropping below the boom and catching on something while tacking.

The first two outhaul reef lines lead to a double rope clutch. The third reef line leads over the top of the rope clutch.

In Figure 79, a double rope clutch is mounted considerably aft of the gooseneck on the boom. The distance aft is determined so it can be safely reached if the boom is set far out on a run. *You don't want to be leaning over lifelines to access this rope clutch.* It should be mounted slightly below the centerline. This location will vary depending on the size of the boom.

Forward of this rope clutch and closer to the mast is a reef winch. The size and ratio will depend on the size of the boat. The distance aft must provide clear access to operate it while at the safety of the mast, not too close to the rope clutch, and still with plenty of room forward to mount cleats. The top of the winch should be almost inline with the lead from the top opening in the rope clutch.

Forward of the winch are the three cleats to terminate the outhaul reef lines. The first reef cleat is below the centerline and forward of the others. The second reef cleat is near or on the centerline and further aft. The third reef cleat is above the centerline and furthest aft.

There must also be a downhaul for the luff of the sail at each reef point. Most masts will have a horn on both sides of the gooseneck, so the luff reef grommet can be hooked over this horn. This may work for the first reef, but is much more difficult as the sail gathers with each reef. Some sailmakers sew in a floating ring on strong webbing so additional reefs can more easily be set around this horn.

I hate this horn idea. Unfailingly, after I hook the grommet or ring around the horn, it drops out before I can raise the sail. I have also found that the length of the pennant or webbing for the second and third reef is too long or too short. The reef point should be as close to the boom as possible. If there is a large amount of sail gathered, it may be difficult to pull or compress the sail to get the ring over the horn. If it is easy to do, then it is probably too long.

I like to remove this horn and use a single luff downhaul that leads to a cleat mounted below the boom on the mast, as shown in Figure 80.

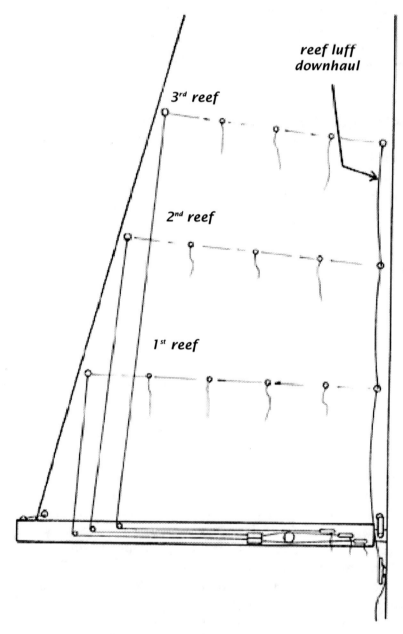

reef luff
downhaul

3ʳᵈ reef

2ⁿᵈ reef

1ˢᵗ reef

Figure 80. Reef luff downhaul

One line is used for all three downhaul reef points. It begins at the third reef grommet. I use a bowline to attach the end of the reef line. Then it leads down to the second reef, so there is minimum slack in the line when the sail is up taut. At the second reef grommet, the same line is tied with a bowline. The line continues down to the first reef grommet and is also tied with a bowline at this point. The rest of the line continues down to the cleat mounted on the mast under the boom. The length of line between each reef point determines the distance the cleat is installed below the boom. There has to be enough line to wrap around the cleat.

The sails can be reefed without turning into the wind, if there is a method to support the boom and the loose foot of the sail when the halyard is released. This can be accomplished by using lazy jacks. The boom can be let out until it luffs, or as far as possible to reduce the wind's pressure. The lazy jacks will support everything. This will be discussed in more detail later in chapter 6.

To put a reef in the mainsail is simple, except that there must be someone at the mast to do the reefing. The following procedure goes from the first reef to the second and the third reef.

1. Keep the boat on its course either by windvane, autopilot, or hand steering.
2. Let the boom out until the sail has minimum pressure. If on a dead run or broad reach this is not possible because there is no way to reduce the wind's pressure. It will simply require a little more strength to pull down the luff of the sail.
3. Release the halyard to a predetermined or marked position on the line. (This must be marked in advance while in port). The sail may not drop because there is still wind pressure in the sail. The boom will not drop because of the lazy jacks supporting it.
4. Now, pull down on the luff downhaul line until the first reef grommet is down as near as possible to the boom; cleat this line to the cleat on the mast, under the boom.
5. Raise the halyard until the luff is taut. *Each subsequent reef is done the same way.*
6. *The first reef* leach outhaul line leads through the bottom of the double rope clutch then to the top of the winch.

Crank in the outhaul until the outhaul grommet is to the top of the boom. Lock the rope clutch and release the line from the winch. Run this line under the winch directly to the lower, forward cleat on the boom. Gather up extra outhaul lines to the other two reef points, and wrap them around the spare unused cleats. At this time, the second outhaul reef line should be wrapped around the winch, ready to use if necessary.

7. *The second reef* outhaul line leads through the top of the double rope clutch then to the top of the winch. Crank in the outhaul until the outhaul grommet is to the top of the boom. Lock the rope clutch and release the line from the winch. Lead this line over the top of the winch to the center cleat on the boom. Gather up the excess outhaul reef line to the third reef. Wrap it around the winch in preparation for a third reef if necessary.

8. *The third reef* outhaul line leads over the double rope clutch to the winch. The third reef outhaul is cranked down on top of the gathered sail foot already reefed. Leave this reef line on the winch and lead it to the top cleat where it will remain until it is time to shake out the reef.

Slab reefing the mainsail from the cockpit

It is safer to reef the mainsail from the cockpit, but it takes some additional blocks and hardware to do it efficiently. There is a system called single point reefing, where one single line is lead through both the leach outhaul grommet and the luff downhaul grommet, then to the cockpit. The reef line begins at an eyestrap on the aft port side of the boom, or under and around the boom, then up through the outhaul grommet. It then goes down to the outhaul reefing turning block, then forward to another turning block at the forward end of the boom, up to and through the downhaul luff grommet, and down and back to the cockpit.

There are three major problems with this method. First, there is far too much friction where the reef lines pass through both grommets. Second, there is too much line involved. The excess line for the other reefs gets caught on things and ends up being a heap of reef line in the cockpit, if all three reefs are set. Finally, it takes far too long to put in a reef. This requires using a winch to get the advantage to pull the sail down evenly. It takes forever to winch in so much line. Thus, I strongly discourage using this method.

The only way I could ever get this system to work efficiently was to bring the boat almost dead into the wind to reduce almost all of the wind's pressure on the sail. Then, I could pull most of the reef in quickly by hand and use the winch for the last few feet. *I do not like to bring the boat around into the wind under any reefing circumstances, because a change in wind direction might cause the boat to tack when you don't mean to, with the inherent danger of broaching.*

I like to use a separate reef line for the outhaul and a separate line for the downhaul for each reef point.

The layout will vary by boat design and its obstructions as the reef lines leads back to the cockpit, as shown in Figure 81.

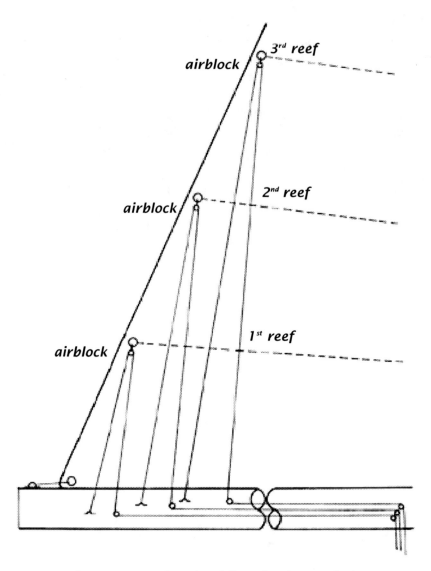

3rd reef

airblock

2nd reef

airblock

1st reef

airblock

Figure 81. Reef outhaul lines lead to cockpit

The reefing rope clutch and winch on the boom are moved back to the cockpit area. If an existing sheet winch can be used, there will be no need for a reefing winch at all.

I use a strong airblock of the appropriate size at each outhaul grommet to reduce friction. I do this by finding a strong, closed eyestrap where the eye will pass through the grommet, and the mounting screw holes lay over the stainless steel part of the grommet.

I pass this eye through from the starboard side of the grommet, so the eye is on the port side of the sail. See Figure 82.

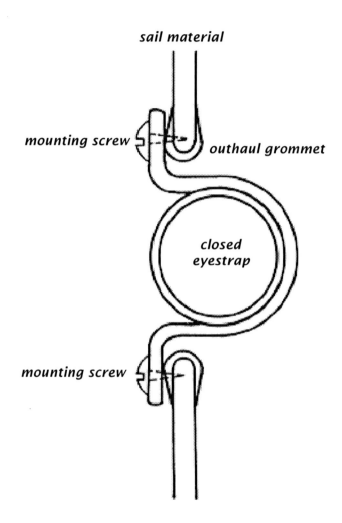

Figure 82. Closed eyestrap through sail grommet to take airblock

I mount the swivel airblock to this eye. The pull is on the other side of the grommet, and it is impossible for the eyestrap to pull through if it is screwed to the grommet.

The side of the sail where the eyestrap is installed is not as important as being sure that the leach outhaul reef lines do not interfere with the luff downhaul reef lines. If it is on the same side of the sail, there may be six lines all leading back to the cockpit.

On my own smaller boat, I like to have the downhaul luff reef lines on the same side of the sail as the halyard, the starboard side. This means I have to run the leach outhaul line on the port side; there is not enough room to do otherwise.

Another strong eyestrap must be installed on the boom some distance aft of the turning block at each leach outhaul reef point. This will help prevent the reef line from twisting. It will twist initially because of the twist in the new rope. After a few uses, however, it will stop twisting.

The outhaul reef line begins at this aft eyestrap on the boom. It leads up to the outhaul reefing airblock, then down to the turning block. From here, it leads through fairleads to another block at the forward end of the boom, leading the lines down to the cabin top or deck. The type of block used will vary by each boat's design and sail configuration. It is important that this block does not create any friction, making it harder to pull the sail down.

From the boom, the line leads to another set of blocks that lead back to the cockpit. *It is important that this block be as near to the vertical axis of the boom's gooseneck as possible, so it does not change the tension as the boom swings out on a run.*

From here, the lines lead to the cabin top or deck, then through more blocks to the cockpit. This is probably the most difficult part of the whole set up because there may be limited space to lead these lines without obstruction and friction.

It may be easier to use deck organizers to lead these lines aft. The deck organizer has multiple blocks already mounted in a single frame. The objective is to reduce line friction by using these blocks.

The leach downhaul reef lines are a little simpler. The reef lines are tied to the reef grommet, then led down and back to the cockpit, similarly to the leach outhaul reef line. If room permits, it can be done on the same side of the boat as the outhaul reef lines; if not, it must be on the opposite side.

Normally, all these reef lines lead to the aft end of the cabin or coach roof. This depends on the boat. These lines may lead through or around dodgers, depending on the design of the vessel.

The lines must pass through at least one fairlead before going to the reefing hardware. This is to ensure as frictionless a lead as possible. From this last fairlead, the lines will go to the double rope clutch, like it was on the boom, then to the reefing winch or other sheet winch that might be used for this purpose.

To reef from the cockpit, the main halyard must also lead to a rope clutch on the same side as the luff downhaul line. This is normally the starboard side. There will have to be at least one double rope clutch for the outhaul reef line and perhaps a triple rope clutch for the halyard. You may want to use a separate clutch for the halyard.

On my own boat, I leave the existing winch and rope clutch on the boom just in case something goes wrong with the cockpit hardware. I use my staysail winch to reef the lines at the cockpit. This requires another single rope clutch to hold the staysail sheet while the winch is being used for reefing.

This method of reefing is the same as reefing at the mast, except that it is done from the cockpit. The procedure is as follows:

1. The boat remains on course.
2. The halyard is released to a predetermined mark.
3. The luff downhaul is winched down to the boom, and the rope clutch locked.
4. The luff downhaul line is released from the winch.
5. Using the same winch, raise the sail with the halyard. After the halyard is taut, lock the rope clutch and remove the halyard from the winch. Wrap the next reef line in case it will be needed.
6. Bring in any slack in the other reef lines.
7. The leach outhaul reef line is winched in, until the grommet is near the top of boom. Lock the rope clutch and remove the line from the winch. Prepare for the next reef.
8. Take in any slack in the other reef lines.

A major problem with this method is getting battens hung up in the lazy jacks, when the sail is raised after winching in the reef. This is not easily resolved. If the head of the sail does not have a headboard, it reduces the problem quite a bit. The problem is also lessened if the sail has a negative roach, so no battens are used.

The lazy jacks can be set more forward than normal to reduce the chances of being hung up. Personally, I like to make the leeward side of the lazy jacks really slack before I reef, or even consider reefing. The windward lazy jack still supports the boom, and the lee lazy jack will still support the foot of the sail. The extra sail area at the foot always falls to leeward, which further pushes the leeward lazy jacks away from the head of the sail. You will have to work something out on your own boat.

Lazy jacks are not the only solution to support the boom and foot of the sail. I mention it for illustration because it is my favorite method, and the one I know the best. You may want to consider other methods available. I know some use the Scotsman system: a monofilament line is used, passing through grommets near the center of the sail in line from the middle of the boom to a spot on the topping lift. This line (or lines) is parallel to the mast.

Personally, I have never used this system and wonder how well it would support the boom and sail weight. How much would it increase the friction while trying to reef off the wind? I have talked to those who have used this system, and who are happy with it. I have not been able to locate anyone who has used it in heavy weather, or while sailing off the wind.

The reefing methods mentioned are not necessarily suitable for all boats. They have worked well for me for many years. I realize that there may have to be modifications to the systems mentioned for your particular boat. The objective is to get the sails reefed as quickly and safely as possible.

Setting a drogue

A drogue is anything set in the water that will reduce the boat speed and help maintain steerage or control. This strategy is normally used to reduce the risk of a broach or other problem and is not used as a technique for survival.

Perhaps this is a good time to mention that I am not a strong advocate of using a drogue at all. I feel that it exposes the stern of the boat and the helmsman to the seas. A breaking wave over the stern could carry the helmsman hard against the wheel or the cabin, breaking bones or even worse. Also, boats can broach while running off the wind in heavy seas. A drogue will reduce the chance, but it will not entirely prevent it.

Some sailors believe that running with the storm will create a slick, preventing a wave from breaking aboard. This may be the case if the boat is being sailed dead downwind; however, this is not practical unless the boat is flying a storm spinnaker that will fill dead downwind. Most boats will sail slightly off the wind to keep the sails full on one side of the boat. This will not leave the slick directly behind the boat, but to one side. I have tried to sail downwind in rough conditions and have been pooped more than once. One wave nearly washed a lady crewmember overboard. She was fortunate to grab on to the lifeline as the rest of her body went overboard. When this happened, I was not sailing dead downwind, but at a slight angle to prevent a gybe.

This doesn't mean not to carry a drogue. There may be a time when you need to get to a safe harbor, the boat is moving too fast, and more control is needed. A drogue will help maintain control and perhaps prevent a broach.

There are commercial drogues on the market. Some are a single drogue, shaped like a coned bucket, while others may be a series of small cones on a long line. There are many different designs available, and they will all have some effectiveness. Actually, anything can be used as a drogue, as long as it creates drag to slow the vessel and help maintain control.

Some examples of a drogue would be long lengths of rope, strong buckets, tires, sail bags full of rags, or anything to create mass. The list is limitless. But, you should decide in advance what will be used, and be certain that it is easily accessed.

Drogues are deployed over the stern to slow the boat's forward speed. There are some that have suggested using a drogue off the bow; this is wrong in technique or perhaps in interpretation. Again, the drogue's purpose is to permit the boat to continue on a course, but to slow its progression while increasing steerage control. Boats do not progress on course in reverse.

For our purpose, the drogue will be deployed off the stern. When preparing your drogue, remember that eventually it has to be brought back aboard. Consequenly, if you tie a tire to the end of a rope and throw it over the stern, it may work well as a drogue, but may be difficult to bring back aboard. For this reason, some cone-shaped drogue anchors or buckets have trip lines at the end, so they can be pulled back aboard by reversing them.

Perhaps this is good time to mention that I do not like a trip line of any kind on drogues or parachute anchors. I have never been able to successfully deploy and set it without it twisting around the main rope or line that carries the load.

There are two kinds of drogues that I prefer. The first is a thick old rope about 300 feet long or longer. It is set out in a loop from both sides of the stern. To retrieve it, just release one end. If the rope alone does not create enough drag, items like tires or buckets can be slid down one end to the bottom of the loop. Of course, these items will be lost when you release one end to bring the rope back aboard.

If there is not a long enough rope aboard to make an efficient loop, a drogue may have to be tied to the end of a shorter rope. For this, I like to use a sacrificial, inexpensive, old tire.

On *Xiphias*, I had three old mini car tires that cost me nothing. I made a strong nylon bag to hold each one. The top of the bag had Velcro to keep it sealed. The bag had two-inch webbing sewn all the way around it, leaving a longer loop at the top. When I put the tire in the bag, I could use it as a fender. If I needed it as a drogue, I took the tire out of the bag and tied it to the rope.

Heave-to under sail

To heave-to under sail is to stop, or at least radically reduce, the vessel's progression. This is done by using the sails. There are those who say that any method of stopping this progress is still heaving-to. That may be the case, but for my purpose in this chapter, the sails are required in order to heave-to.

To heave-to requires that the boat's sails be properly balanced, and that the boat has the appropriate keel and hull design for it to hold the position after it is hove-to. As mentioned previously, the light displacement, fin-keeled boat may not hold the position and will sail onto the other tack.

The strategy to heave-to is normally used after the sails have been reduced considerably, or after the last reef is set. This is not necessary, but generally what occurs. It is not a strategy normally used from full sail to heave-to. However, some sailors will heave-to when having lunch or doing some boat repairs.

The reefed mainsail or storm trysail remains set. It is the sail that determines the angle the boat will set to the wind and seas. The reefed headsail or storm jib is backwinded or sheeted to windward, so the bow is forced off or downwind. As the vessel's bow begins to fall away from the wind, the mainsail or trysail begins to fill and provide drive, moving the boat slowly forward.

If the rudder were set to sail downwind or off the wind, the boat would continue to sail away from the wind until it gybed, which could be disastrous. Therefore, you don't want the rudder to be set in this position. If the rudder is left amidships, the vessel will find a balance where the mainsail will provide drive, and the jib will eventually find an equal balance. Thus, the boat will continue sailing slowly on a rather straight line.

For the boat to heave-to properly, the rudder must be set to turn the boat back into the wind, as if attempting to go onto the other tack. When the boat begins to gather a little forward speed from the drive on the mainsail, the rudder turns the boat upwind, so the mainsail loses it drive, and the foresail forces the bow back downwind. You can see how important the angle of the mainsail is to properly heave-to. If the mainsail is set up too tight or close to the wind, the vessel may gather speed and tack before wind begins to spill from the main, stopping its drive. If the mainsail is set too far off the wind, it may be setting beam-to the wind and seas, which could be dangerous. Each boat is different, so you will have to find what works for your boat.

Let's go through the procedure, shown in Figure 83.

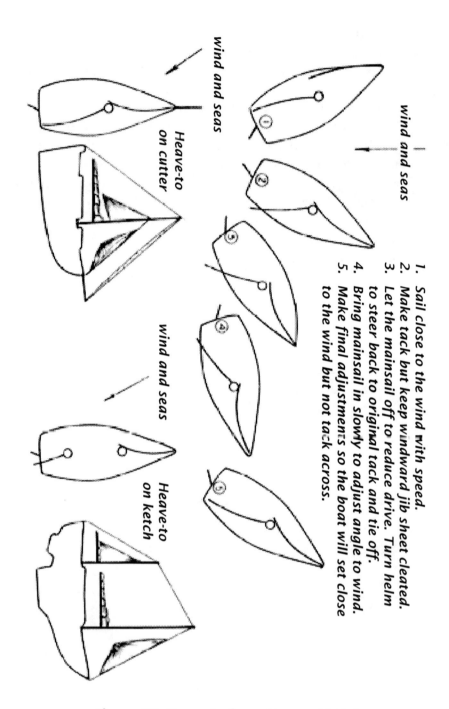

1. Sail close to the wind with speed.
2. Make tack but keep windward jib sheet cleated.
3. Let the mainsail off to reduce drive. Turn helm to steer back to original tack and tie off.
4. Bring mainsail in slowly to adjust angle to wind.
5. Make final adjustments so the boat will set close to the wind but not tack across.

wind and seas

Heave-to on cutter

wind and seas

Heave-to on ketch

Figure 83. Heave-to for cutter and ketch

Assume that we are sailing on a close reach, so the wind and seas are just forward of the beam. Actually, the point of sail is not really important. We have already reduced our sail area to maximum reef, or we have set storm sails. The boat must be fairly well balanced with the sails set.

1. Bring the vessel close to the wind, but not so dangerously close that the boat could go onto the other tack or lose its drive. Speed is important to tack through the wind.
2. As the boat gathers speed, keep an eye on the waves. Try to choose a smaller wave. Just after the wave passes under the boat, throw the helm over onto the other tack, but do not release the windward jib or storm sail sheet.
3. As the boat falls off, let the main out a little to reduce heel and to reduce the possibility of it driving the boat back through the eye of the wind.
4. Slowly, turn the helm so the boat wants to sail back on its original tack or upwind.
5. Adjust the mainsail to get the angle to the wind you feel best suits your boat.
6. Tie the helm in this position. Be sure to tie it so you can quickly release it.

If you feel it would be dangerous to tack the boat to backwind the jib storm sail, then the headsail can be winched across. This is not easy if the winds are strong.

On ketches, the mainsail is normally completely dropped, and the mizzen sail provides the drive. See Figure 83. Again, each boat reacts differently; this is why practice is very important.

Some boats can heave-to with just the mainsail or trysail. The same principle is used; however, there is no need for the headsail to force the bow down. It is critical that the boat not be set too close to the wind using this method. I have also heard of ketches doing the same thing with only the mizzen sail set.

Setting a parachute anchor

If the boat is hove-to and you feel that the conditions are worsening, or you feel that being hove-to is no longer safe, you may have to set a parachute anchor off the bow. Because it almost stops the boat, I don't think anyone would advise setting it off the stern—you wouldn't want breaking waves over the stern of the boat.

The parachute anchor is often referred to as a para-anchor. There are several commercial ones available, and they are excellent. A military cargo chute can also be used; it is referred to as a Bourd, a term that is derived from the Bureau of Ordnance. In the past, these were readily available in Army Surplus stores, but I have not seen one in many years.

The most critical aspect of the parachute anchor is getting the right size for the boat. I think the boat's displacement and windage is more important than the actual length.

To find out what size would best suit your boat, you can refer back to the chart provided earlier in this chapter, which was taken from Para-Tech Engineering. However, I feel it would be better to contact one of the reputable manufacturers directly to get their professional advice.

For a parachute anchor to work properly, it should nearly stop the boat completely. Lin and Larry Pardey strongly encourage some leeward drift to provide a slick that will confuse the breaking waves. I am in general agreement with this; however, if the drift is too fast, it can also damage the rudder and its fastenings. For this reason, the difference of only one foot in diameter could make the difference between too much drift and not enough drift. Understandably, this will also vary by the severity of the conditions. Since the size is critical to work effectively, it is best that it be proven on your particular boat. In Victor Shane's book, *DDDB* (Drag Device Data Base) there are many letters from users of the parachute anchor, relating the size that worked for them as well as the details of the storm. I strongly advise this as essential reading material.

Some suggest deploying the para-anchor while standing at the bow. This would have to depend on the size of the boat, the conditions at the time, and the ability to do it safely. Because I am getting older, I guess I feel more secure doing it from the cockpit. Also, on my small 28-foot boat, it can be too dangerous to do so from the bow.

Before the parachute anchor can be deployed, it must be properly rigged or prepared. If a commercial unit was purchased, most of the work is already done; all that would be required is the nylon rope rode and a float. If you are considering using a Bourd, you will have to set it up yourself.

The parachute itself is called the canopy. The canopy has many small nylon lines attached, at equal distance apart, around the entire outside circumference. These lines are called suspension lines. The suspension lines terminate together at one end of a strong swivel. The other end of the swivel is attached to the nylon rode.

When the parachute is soaked, it is no longer buoyant; therefore, a float on a line should be attached at the apex or outside center of the canopy's dome. The length of this line should be at least the diameter of the parachute, but preferably three times as long. This float must be buoyant enough to support the weight of the soaked parachute anchor, thimbles, shackles, and the swivel; an appropriately sized fender works perfectly.

The first time I tried to practice using a parachute anchor, I attached a trip line from the crown that led back to the boat. Every time I tried to deploy the parachute, it began to spin slowly and twisted the trip line around the main rode. I finally cut the trip line off and deployed it without a trip line or a float.

It set perfectly and held the boat even with the engine hard in reverse. When I put the engine in neutral and began to pull the parachute aboard, it sunk. By the time I was directly over it, it was about 100 feet straight down under the boat. Using my anchor windlass, it took all day to get the thing back aboard. I learned the hard way that a float is absolutely necessary.

At the other end, anti-chafe gear is also essential, because there is a heavy load on the nylon line, which will create friction and chafe wherever it passes though a chock, hawsehole, or any other lead. It is also a good idea to have some extra line so the nip or point of chafe can be changed.

The only time that I set to a parachute anchor was when cyclone Tia was approaching down the Coral Sea, off the Australian coast. I knew it was coming, so I had plenty of time to prepare and set it properly—at least I thought it was set properly.

On *Xiphias*, I led the line though a special rounded stainless steel fairlead under the cranse iron at the end of the bowsprit. This prevented the line from ever going under the bobstay.

The 10-foot Bourd parachute anchor held *Xiphias* with minimum sternway. I did have the helm tied amidships to minimize any possible damage to the rudder.

Even though it held firmly, *Xiphias* tacked to radical extremes from one side to the other. When she was in the trough, she set at a slightly different angle to the wind than when she was on the crest. So when she reached the crest, the wind hit the side, driving her hard over. She would sail under bare poles on this tack. When she entered the next trough, the pull on the rode brought the bow through the wind onto the other tack. At the crest, the same thing happened again, but on the other side. So it went for nearly two days. If I had it to do over again, I would follow the Pardey's suggestion of setting it slightly off to one side of the bow.

How far to one side to set it will depend on the boat, its configuration, and location of chocks, fairleads, hawseholes, and cleats. The line must lead so it cannot come out of the chock and do some serious damage to the vessel's sheer or caprail. Where the line passes out of the boat should have a minimum of friction.

Most boats do not have bowsprits, whisker stays, and bobstays to worry about, so the location of bow deployment will depend on what is available along the side.

Since the parachute anchor and the rode will be leading off to one side of the boat, *it is important that the line remain on the same side of the boat.* If the boat tacks across, the line will have to pass under or around the bow, causing it to quickly chafe through. To avoid this, using another line to hold the rode away from the bow is recommended. I believe this method was the original idea of Lin and Larry Pardey, who wrote many cruising books; their ***Storm Tactics Handbook*** is excellent.

Their objective is to have the boat lie to a parachute anchor at a 50° angle, so the boat slowly drifts downwind, creating a slick that would help break the waves before they reach the boat. To accomplish this, they used a snatch block on the main parachute anchor rode. The snatch block is attached to another line, which is led back to a sheet winch near the stern of the boat. The angle of the boat can be adjusted by adjusting this line. I do not want to tread on their information or repeat what they have already written, so I strongly advise their book be part of any cruiser's library.

During my first real storm, I realized that I was not able to deploy the parachute anchor after the wind and seas had grown to the point of making it dangerous to do so. I know I should not have waited so long, but the circumstances led me to believe it would never get as bad as it did. The story is included at the end of this chapter.

Thereafter, *I always prepared my parachute anchor while in port.* I set it up so I could deploy it at anytime from the cockpit. I understand now that my method was not something new and is still being used by others today.

First, let's assume that the parachute anchor will not be led directly straight off the bow, like I did, but will lie slightly to one side of the boat. To achieve this, on one side of the bow, there must be a hawsehole or closed fairlead through or over the boat's sheer for the main parachute anchor rode. If there is no place to lead it off one side, then it may be necessary to install one.

The best way to set up the parachute anchor in advance is to set it up completely in mild conditions. This includes the float, lines, swivel, anti-chafing, and the bridle or method to be used to keep the parachute anchor to one side of the boat.

The side bridle must lead from the main rode aft to a winch, in order to make the necessary adjustments to the angle of the boat to the wind and seas. Lin and Larry Pardey suggest using a snatch block where it attaches to the main rode to prevent chafe. I have tried this and found it difficult to accomplish after the parachute is set; it must be done in advance. You may want to consider attaching this side bridle line to the main rode with a rolling hitch; however, you will not be able to change its position if you do so. Personally, I prefer the rolling hitch, but I may have to eat my words when, or if, I actually have to use it in a real storm.

After the parachute anchor is deployed and all adjustments are made to the angle of the boat to the wind and seas, bring it back aboard, leaving the line in the chocks and attached to the cleats.

Disconnect the parachute anchor from the nylon rode, leaving the swivel and float on the parachute anchor. Let it dry, and then fold it according to the manufacturer's instructions. If you do not have the instructions, fold it accordion style, so it will deploy without fouling on its own lines. Stuff the whole thing into its bag, leaving the end of the swivel exposed.

Bring all the remaining rope, including the line that will be used as part of the adjusting bridle and the snatch block if it is used, over the lifelines, outside all rigging, into the cockpit. The only line not in the cockpit is that which leads forward through the chock to the cleat and the little extra left for adjustment.

Beginning at the bow, using some light line that will easily break, tie the line to the top of the lifeline every 10 to 12 inches, until you reach the point where the line passes over the lifeline to the cockpit. I suggest using a standard cotton sewing thread or even electrical tape. The objective is to have it break away from the lifeline when it is pulled away by the parachute anchor.

Using a little stronger piece of line, securely tie the rope to the top of the lifeline where it leads into the cockpit. This will help prevent the rope from coming lose accidentally.

Lead all the main parachute anchor line into the footwell, or where it will remain until it is needed. Coil it carefully, beginning at a point just after the place where the rope comes over the lifeline, until the end with the thimble is on top. Now, use short pieces of line or stops to hold the coil together. Each stop should be tied with a slipknot, making it easy to release.

In a separate bag in one of the cockpit lockers, have the parachute anchor, float, suspension lines, and the shackle to the swivel, all assembled and within easy access.

To deploy the parachute anchor from the cockpit:

1. Leaving the parachute anchor in its bag, attach the exposed swivel shackle to the rope's thimble and secure the pin as normal.

2. Release all the stops to the nylon rope coil so it can run free.

3. Remember, the parachute anchor must be deployed on the side it has already been set. If hove-to, release the helm so you can steer by hand and begin sailing slowly off the wind, leaving the storm jib backwinded. If not hove-to, then just sail slowly with whatever sails are needed, even bare poles.

4. Slide the bag off the parachute anchor and throw the float over the windward side of the boat. Begin to pay out the float line until the parachute anchor can be thrown

overboard. Throwing it over the windward side will prevent any possibility of the line passing under the boat, catching the prop or rudder.

5. Continue to pay out line until the parachute anchor begins to fill and provides some resistance.
6. Let the line run free, being careful not to get your foot or something snagged by the line as it goes overboard.
7. The moment the line begins to reach the end of the coil, turn the boat around into the wind.
8. The boat will continue downwind as the line is torn off the stops on the lifeline, until the boat is setting to the parachute anchor off the windward side of the bow.

I only did this once, but it worked without a problem. Also, I had my side bridle tied to the main rode with a rolling hitch. I have not done this using the snatch block, so cannot comment on it.

Lying ahull

This is what I consider the last resort. If everything else fails, let the boat take care of you. Unfortunately, to lie ahull, the boat will set with her beam to the wind and waves. It is only a matter of time until a wave will knock her down or even roll her over. If it doesn't, the movement would be so radical that it might seem better to abandon the boat and accept the consequences. Keep in mind that the storm is a temporary thing and will end soon. *If you do consider abandoning the boat, remember that all too often the crew is never seen again, but the vessel is found sound and still floating.* The only thing that can really be done is to have everything as secure as possible in preparation for a roll-over or a severe knockdown.

I don't even want to discuss abandoning the vessel in a storm. If the storm is so severe that it is sinking the boat, there is little chance that a life raft would survive the same storm. Of course, this does not take into account hitting something that caused the vessel to sink. All I am trying to say is this: do not leave the safety and security of a floating vessel for a small rubber life raft—not until you *have* to do so. Remember the old saying that goes something like, *"you should step up from the boat to get into the life raft."*

When the storm arrives

The severity of the storm will determine which of the above strategies should be used. Most importantly, if it is a major storm, like a hurricane or cyclone and it has a name, you need to find shelter, if possible. There is no need to threaten life; a boat can be replaced.

This is not as straightforward as it may seem. *You do not want to head towards land with the possibility of the storm blowing you onto a lee shore.* Before you make the decision to head for shelter, you should be certain where the storm is located and the direction it is moving. You should have a good idea of the strength and the direction of the winds to be expected. If you feel confident that you know all this and can still make it to a safe harbor in time, then that is what you should do.

If you cannot find shelter in time, then the boat must be maneuvered as far away from the storm—and from a lee shore—as possible. Find out where the dangerous semi-circle (where the winds are the strongest and the waves the steepest) will be, and avoid it. Figure out what it will take to get the boat as far away from this semi-circle as possible and into the semi-circle of least danger. These quadrants are different between the Northern and Southern Hemispheres.

The time to progress to another storm strategy will depend on the storm severity, the way the boat is handling the conditions at the time, and the boat itself. However, keep in mind that *you should always make the change when you first consider doing it.* All too often, we wait too long, thinking it won't get any worse. Sometimes, we really don't want to make the change because it is a lot of work, and it's wet and cold. *Believe me, if it does get worse, it will be much harder, colder, and wetter later.* In some storms, the time may come when you refuse to move about the boat and will stay below, regardless of what happens on deck. If you do end up using the next strategy and it turns out that it wasn't necessary, so what? Look at the experience gained from just going through the motions.

Before the storm actually arrives, you will have a day or two to try to reach shelter. If you can't reach shelter, get as far away from the storm as possible, or at least, get into the safer semi-circle. During the early stages of the storm, it is unlikely that you would be sailing to windward, but instead would be sailing on a beam to broad reach.

It is common for the winds to increase at night. Therefore, if you are using a whisker pole or spinnaker pole, be sure to drop it before there is any danger of it dipping in the water while moving at speed. I discourage using any kind of downwind pole in storm or rough conditions. There is the danger of the boat rolling to an extreme that could dip the pole and break it. Shorter poles, set higher, are less of a problem.

The same applies to the main boom. This will depend on the boat, length of the boom, and how high it is off the water. The reef points should not be parallel to the boom, but at a slight angle going up from the luff to the leach. As the mainsail is reefed, the boom's end should lift with each reef.

When on a run, the boom is set out over the water as far as possible. A boom vang must be used to keep it from rising with the variations in wind and to keep the shape of the mainsail. Often, the boom vang is also the preventer, used to hold the boom out over the water. If the boom is long, or if there is any possibility the boom's end could dip in to the water while sailing at speed, it could break the boom where the boom vang is attached.

On my own boat, I have a long boom which sticks out far enough that it could—and does—dip into the water. I used a boom vang on an elastic strop to hold the boom down. As I put in each reef, it raises the boom end considerably. However, on a run in mild to moderate conditions, before I put in a couple of reefs, it will dip into the water. To prevent the possibility of the boom breaking where the boom vang is attached, I run a preventer line from the tip or end of the boom, forward to the bow chock, then back to a cam cleat in the cockpit. If I want to gibe the mainsail, I can disconnect or control the preventer from the cockpit. This line is always stored under the boom. A snap shackle is used on the boom's end or the bail. The line is led forward to the gooseneck where I have a cleat attached to the underside of the boom. I do the same with the boom vang. It is also stored under the boom at all times. After the boom vang is set, I can easily reach the preventer near the gooseneck, lead it outside the shrouds forward, and back to the cockpit. I learned to do this after trying to pull in the boom by hand and leaning out over the lifeline to attach the preventer line. After a few close calls, I decided to install the preventer permanently.

As you attempt to get away from the storm, you will probably be sailing with the maximum sail area that the boat can handle safely in order to put as much distance between you and the storm. *It is important to know when it is time to begin reefing.* This is a difficult question to answer, because each boat is different. Some need to reef at 10 to 15 knots, while others don't begin until 15 to 20 knots. Get to know your boat. *It is always better to reef early, before it gets too rough or sails are damaged.*

It is also important to know when it is time to heave-to. *I strongly advise heaving-to, rather than trying to run with the storm.* I think most authors and offshore sailors will agree that to run in a severe storm is not a safe technique. Running with the storm or wind is okay, until the seas become too steep and the boat's speed is too fast to handle the steep seas safely. You will have to make this decision earlier rather than later.

I know I talked about using drogues while running as a strategy. I only mentioned it because there may be a situation where there is no other alternative. As long as there is a choice, *I would strongly discourage using a drogue.*

When sailing off the wind, you may encounter considerably higher and steeper waves than normal. These are created if there is a current running against the storm, or if there is a variation in the depth of the water. Therefore, if you are running for shelter and the waves are already high and steep, they will get much worse as the boat nears land.

Always be prepared for the occasional larger wave. I read somewhere that every seventh wave was larger than the others. I have counted the waves and could not notice any difference by their numbers. However, there certainly are waves that are considerably bigger than the rest. These are called rogue waves or freak waves. The average rogue wave at sea is normally about twice the size as the normal waves; however, in different parts of the world, they are as much as three times bigger.

Another controversial subject is turning on a strobe light in storm conditions; it would depend on where you are and if there are ships in the area. Personally, I do not like any lights on at night, unless I am in waters where I know there are other boats. I can see better at night without lights, and I am relying on someone being on deck on watch at all times. If there are ships in the area, or any possibility that there will not be someone on watch at all times, then I turn on the running lights. If I am hove-to or set to a parachute anchor, I will turn on the strobe light because I cannot maneuver and want to be seen. This is not legal, so I do not encourage it. Just consider it my admission of guilt.

If you are sailing off the wind, *it is important that reefs can be set without turning the boat around anywhere near the eye of the wind.* This is just too dangerous; the boat could be accidentally forced onto the other tack, backwinding the jib. This could cause a knockdown or a broach.

If you are sailing a cutter-rigged boat off the wind and the conditions are not too severe yet, consider sheeting the staysail hard down the centerline of the boat. This will help reduce the boat's rolling motion.

Assuming I am sailing off the wind and the winds and seas are slowly getting worse, the following is the sequential procedure I would use. This may not apply to all boats, but the procedure would be similar.

1. While sailing off the wind, try putting the first two reefs in the mainsail before you begin to reef the jib or headsails. This will help keep the boat steering downwind. If the main is carrying too much sail area, it will have a tendency to rotate the boat on its 'center of lateral resistance', whereas the pressure on the foresail will be like pulling the boat along, making steering easier.

2. On a ketch, if the mizzen sail is set on a run, it will have even more of a tendency to make the boat round up. Reefing the mainsail or mizzen sail will depend on the ketch's sail balance and design.

3. The next step would be to reduce sail area forward. If roller-furling headsails are used, roll up a substantial amount of sail area, leaving considerably more sail area exposed than the reefed mainsail (or mizzen sail on a ketch).

4. As the conditions worsen and there are already a couple of reefs in the mainsail, the next step would be to drop the mainsail and set the storm trysail. If there isn't a storm trysail, put in the last reef on the mainsail.

5. This decision is more difficult on a ketch. If the main is dropped and a trysail set on the mizzen, the boat will have more of a tendency to round up. If it is on the mainsail and the mizzen is dropped, then the boat cannot heave-to without dropping the main trysail and moving it to the mizzen. You will have to check your own boat and see what works the best. It may be better to set it on the mizzen and sheet it hard amidships to help prevent roll and to reduce the tendency to round up.

6. If the weather continues to deteriorate and it is safe to do so, drop and remove the roller-furling jib, and set the storm jib. If this is not possible, roll up the entire sail tightly, and set the storm jib on the inner stay; if she is cutter rigged, set a reefed staysail. If you have a storm jib that goes around the rolled up jib, and you are happy with it, then use it now.

7. Now we are sailing with storm jib or reefed staysail and a storm trysail or reefed mainsail. If conditions worsen, it is time to stop sailing and heave-to.

8. Time your turn when the waves are not too high, and a wave has just passed under the boat. Make the move quickly. The storm jib should automatically back wind when the boat passes through the eye of the wind. Most boats will set well like this in conditions from force 7 to force 9. *Always try to heave-to on the same side that you will set the storm anchor.* It will really simplify the process later.

9. If it seems that the winds and seas are overpowering the boat, drop the storm jib and heave-to on the reefed main or storm trysail. If on a ketch, it would probably be the reefed mizzen or trysail set on the mizzenmast.

10. If conditions worsen or the boat feels overwhelmed, set the parachute anchor as mentioned previously, and drop all

sails. A ketch may be able to still fly the storm trysail, but it would depend on the boat and conditions.

These are not absolutes and could vary according to the storm conditions and the way the boat is handling the storm. The more practice and experience gained will make this all much easier. This is provided as a guideline only.

The one piece of advice that I wish to emphasize is this: *do whatever is necessary sooner rather than later*. Hopefully, the following story of my personal encounter with my first storm will illustrate this point. You can draw your own conclusions as to what I did right and what I did wrong, but most importantly, to what I didn't do in time.

§

I was in Tahiti, in the South Pacific, and it was the cyclone season. I had a girlfriend who had a few days vacation and wanted to join me in American Samoa. Normally, I would never make a passage during the cyclone season; I would stay in local waters where I knew the protected areas.

I intended to make this passage alone. I sailed over to Moorea to spend the night. There, I met a guy named Jim who was looking for a crew position. He agreed to sail with me as far as American Samoa.

We had an enjoyable and uneventful sail to Souverou Island in the Cook group of islands. The passage convinced me that Jim was valuable crew who I could rely on to carry his load. We stayed in Souverou for a few days to catch up on our rest.

The only weather forecast we could get was available via WWVH every hour.

I had been recording our barometer reading three times a day and noticed there was a slow but definite drop; we decided we should get to American Samoa before anything developed. Early the next morning, we departed for Pago Pago, American Samoa.

I remember that trip as if it were yesterday. It went something like this:

On our second day out, I noticed the barometer continued to move downward. The winds had shifted from the southeast to east by northeast. There was a large swell running, and it was getting cloudy.

I felt a little seasick. I didn't want to shoot any sights because doing that always made me feel worse. Yet, I had no choice. I had to take a sight to be sure where we were in case the weather closed in on us. In order to shoot sights, I needed to coordinate my watch with GMT, Universal Time, or WWVH out of Hawaii. This ensured that I had the correct time, to the second, when I set the sun on the horizon. I turned on WWVH to get the time. When I turned the radio on, they were giving weather warnings for the South Pacific. "Warning! Warning! Hurricane Clouda at Naana Dagy South, one seven zero west moving southeast at terty knots."

I turned to Jim, "What the hell did he say?"

"I couldn't understand a word of it. What's the story with that woman talking in Japanese over the warning?" Jim asked.

We had noticed this in the past; often, there was a Japanese woman speaking over the English weather report. It had never been as bad as it was this day.

I said, "I suspect we are in that zone where both Japanese and English reports overlap."

"Why not wait another hour and listen again," Jim said.

"Yeah, I'll even record it," I responded.

Sixty minutes later, when the report was repeated, I taped the message and played it back. It sounded like gibberish with both languages going at once. This time I was quite certain I got the word "*Claudia*", instead of "Clouda."

Over and over, we played the tape. I wrote down each word and we ended up with something close to this: "Warning! Warning! Hurricane *Claudia* located at 9° South; 170° West, moving slowly southeast at 30 knots."

"But that can't be!" I yelled, "It must mean it's moving more like three knots."

I checked our last fix and figured we were about 13°, 40 minutes South; 166°, 30 minutes West. We might have been directly in the hurricane's path, but we still weren't sure where it was, or which way it was going.

"I say we go northeast. I think we'll have a better chance of it missing us than if we sailed in any other direction," I said.

Jim was sitting at the helm. The windvane was steering the boat. He grinned and said, "You're the captain." Then, he immediately altered course.

For a day and a half, we sailed northeast, listening hourly to the weather. With each broadcast, there was this Japanese woman's voice over the English. It was impossible to tell what was being said.

I finally resorted to the ham radio, sending out a CQ for any South Pacific station. A New Zealander responded to my general call. He phoned the weather station at Wellington and reported the cyclone's location as 19°, 20 minutes South; 171°, 30 minutes West, moving south at 10 knots.

What a relief; it was south of us, moving south.

Jim and I both shot sights and compared our results. Then, we changed course back towards American Samoa. We'd lost over 100 nautical miles from our original course. Now the winds were steady out of the southeast making our sail easy.

Over the next two days, the barometer continued to drop. The swells were getting quite large, but spaced far apart. There was a constant cloud cover that seemed to be thickening. Winds were still southeast, but now a steady 20 knots with higher gusts. We still were not concerned, because even if it were a new storm developing, we would be in Pago Pago before it got severe.

Within hours, the wind had increased to 25 knots and gusting higher. Jim was sitting at the helm, but not steering. The windvane was doing an excellent job without our help. I was below studying the chart. We had already put in two reefs in the mainsail and had rolled up the jib's roller furling headsail. All we had up forward was the staysail set on the inner stay.

I stuck my head out to the cockpit and yelled to Jim, "The barometer is still dropping, and the conditions are getting worse fast; I think we should heave-to now before it gets worse."

"Sure," Jim responded, "just tell me what you want me to do."

Together, we dropped the mainsail and set the storm trysail. Then, we dropped the staysail, put a reef in, and raised it again. We were ready to heave-to.

Fortunately, the seas were not yet dangerously high. I expected this was just a small local storm or squall that would pass in an hour or two.

We were sailing on a starboard tack on a broad reach. I took the helm and disconnected the windvane to hand steer.

I turned to Jim and said, "I'll bring the boat more up into the wind so we can get some speed to tack through the eye of the wind. I'll handle the trysail sheet. I want you to pull in on the port staysail sheet so it continues to draw as I get closer to the wind. When I yell, 'coming about,' be ready to pull the port staysail sheet taut. Don't let it go; we are not tacking!"

Conditions were ideal. The seas were not too high, and the boat was screaming along with the storm sails set.

The tack went perfectly. The boat heeled over about 40° until I let out on the trysail. After we were setting at about 60° off the wind, I pushed the tiller to starboard so the boat wanted to sail around to port. She held the angle perfectly.

After all this was done, we settled down to a quick canned stew dinner. It was too rough to do any real cooking.

By 2000, the winds had picked up to 35 knots, gusting to over 40 knots. All I had to measure the wind strength was one of those little handheld wind meters that have a little Styrofoam ball floating inside a plastic tube with a scale alongside the tube.

We were about 150 to 200 miles from Pago Pago, American Samoa, when I raised an AM radio station out of Pago Pago. An English voice said, "Warning! Warning! Cyclone *Claudia* heading for Samoa Islands. Cyclone *Claudia* is currently located at 12°, 20 minutes South; 170°, 10 minutes West, heading southeast at 12 knots."

Astounded, Jim stared at me and said, "Holy shit! There must have been two cyclones. The one we heard about the first time and the one the New Zealander mentioned. I bet the first one, '*Claudia*', has always been there, just taking its damn time." Now I knew why the conditions had worsened.

In the gusts, *Xiphias* held her own, heeling far over. Jim and I waited below for something to go wrong. I realize that was a pessimistic attitude, but it seemed if something was going to happen, it would do so at night, during a storm.

According to a later update, the center would now go south of Samoa, with winds predicted at 75 knots in Pago Pago. We'd be sitting it out right in its path.

I turned to Jim and asked, "The seas are getting huge and breaking. Do you think we should run with the storm?"

Jim jumped back at me, "Hell, you're the sailor; I'm just around for the fun. You tell me what you want me to do, and I'll do it."

Feeling insecure in making the decision, I decided to discuss the situation with Jim. "If we run with the storm, we may cause a slick which may prevent the seas from breaking aboard. This is all theory... I have never done it. We'll have to be careful that we don't broach on a steep wave; this also means we will have to be outside steering the boat every second."

Jim turned his head toward me and raised one of his hairy eyebrows, but said nothing.

I continued, "If the slick doesn't prevent the waves from breaking aboard, we will be exposed to the possibility of being pooped and carried overboard, thrown against the back of the cabin, or carried to the end of our harness, which could break the harness or a few ribs."

I guess I did not paint a very good picture of what to expect, because Jim came back immediately, "Why can't we just stay like we are, hove-to, so we don't have to sail or be outside?"

"We can," I responded, "but if we are not going to sail downwind, we need to drop the reefed staysail. We have too much sail area up to remain hove-to. Do you want to do it?"

Jim was short with his response, "No."

I had no choice but to do it myself. After all, it was my responsibility, not his.

I turned on the deck lights so I could see. I slid the companion slide open and removed the top weatherboard. I reached out and clipped my harness on to the pad eye next to the companionway. Then, I carefully went out into the cockpit.

I sat there for awhile, looking around at the seas, the boat, the mast, and the reefed staysail that was hardly reefed anymore. The clew that was originally folded and stuffed into the foot of the sail before it was rolled up, was now flogging about wildly.

I let a little out on the storm trysail sheet because I did not want to take a chance of the boat sailing around after I dropped the backwinded, reefed staysail. After letting a little out, we were setting at about 75° off the wind. This was a little too much. I figured I would be able to drop the backwinded, reefed staysail quickly, which would bring the boat up a little.

Carefully, I unclipped my harness and clipped it on to the port jackline. Slowly, I crawled forward. Just as I was reaching the mast, my harness came up taut. The wind had picked up the harness tether and wrapped it around the cowl vent. I worked my way back and freed the line.

I noticed Jim's head sticking up above the companion slide. He looked like the old drawing of 'Kilroy was here'. I could only see his fingers on the companion slide and his eyes peering over the top. Everything else blended into the darkness. He was watching my every move. It made me feel less alone, knowing he was there if something went really wrong.

When I got to the mast, I released the staysail halyard, but the sail did not come down. I knew there was too much load on it. I yelled at Jim to let off on the windward port staysail sheet that held the sail backwinded.

Suddenly, the sail was violently flogging on the starboard side and still was not coming down. The flogging port sheet was hitting me in the head like a club. It really hurt.

I store my hard dinghy, upside down, over the scuttle hatch on the foredeck, so it was between the flogging staysail and me. To get to the starboard side, I dove over the dinghy, dragging my belly over the top. I made it, but my harness tether was hung up on the port halyard winch. I could not quite reach the staysail stay. "Damn, I hate this fucking harness," I yelled at the top of my voice. Then, I unclipped my tether at the harness.

I wedged myself between the lifeline and the dinghy. By now, the reefed staysail was halfway down. I pulled it almost all the way down, but it would not drop the last four feet. The halyard was hung up on something, and the sail would not drop.

Now, angry instead of frightened, I stood up and released the snap shackle pin. The sail dropped to my feet, and the halyard sailed off into the wind. "Shit, shit, shit," I yelled.

I managed to get the sail all gathered together. I noticed that the sheets were slack to make it a little easier. Apparently, Jim had taken any tension off the sheets as soon as the sail hit the deck.

I always keep various lengths of rope on my pin rails between the forward and aft lower shrouds. I reached back and grabbed anything I could. I took these lines and wrapped them around the sail and around the bulwarks.

As I was doing this, a wave broke over the bow. Green water went over and under the dinghy and soaked me. I felt that the dinghy had taken the force of the wave and protected me from being washed overboard. Suddenly, I wished I had not disconnected from my harness tether.

I finished lashing the sail to the bulwarks and began slowly working my way back to the mast. When I got there, I clipped my harness back to the tether. I grabbed the staysail halyard at the mast and tried to pull it up to the block so it would not flog in the wind. It was too late; it had wrapped itself tightly around the shroud. Because it was above the deck lights, I couldn't see where it was or how badly it was wrapped. All I knew was that the halyard was not moving, so I secured it to a cleat.

Carefully, I scooted on my butt back to the cockpit. We were now hove-to with just the trysail set. I checked our position to the wind and brought it in a little. We now set about 60° off the wind. I felt good with this and went below.

Jim met me with a towel and a shot of straight brandy. Actually, it was an excellent Cognac that I saved for special occasions. Jim felt this was just such an occasion. He was right.

After I changed clothes, I sat down and waited.

Jim asked, "Well, what happens now?"

I began to rattle off what came into my head, "If it doesn't get any worse, we will be fine. If it gets worse, I really don't know what we will do. I don't know what's going to happen; we may even be rolled over. Hell, Jim, I haven't ever been in a storm this bad before. I don't know."

Jim turned to me, with a serious look on his face said, "Didn't you tell me you had a parachute anchor or sea anchor you could use in real bad weather? Where is it?"

I almost laughed when I said, "Jim, it's in the lazarette. It has to be fastened to the anchor rope forward and set off the bow. Do you want to do it? I'm certainly not going back out there."

There was no response.

I continued, "Hell Jim, had I known we were in the path if a cyclone, I would have set it a long time ago, but I had no idea that cyclone *'Claudia'* existed."

By 2300, we had winds in excess of 60 knots. I know this because my wind meter only reads to 66 knots and the Styrofoam ball was stuck against the top.

It seemed that every other wave hit us so hard that I thought we were under water. We heeled over to 75°, then came back up.

As the night went on, the winds howled. Looking out the portlight, all I could see was white water in the night. When the boat came out of the trough, the winds hit the sail hard and we went over, way over, but still not a complete knockdown.

I thought about the storm trysail and if it would blow out. It didn't matter if it did or not; I was not going outside.

We were either in a trough with no winds, or on the crest in howling winds, so I stuck my head out of the companionway and held up my wind meter. It was still pegged at its maximum reading of 66 knots. The seas had become mountains. For a moment, I was chilled with the total reality of how small, how vulnerable I was.

Back inside the cabin, I studied Jim. He was so worried that he lay back with legs propped to either side of his bunk reading *Tai Pan*. I tried to affect calmness as I sat in the opposite settee, consuming coffee with a touch of cheap brandy and biting my fingernails.

Then a wave lifted us, throwing *Xiphias* on to her side. I flew across the boat and landed on top of Jim. Never taking his eyes from the book, he said, "If you don't mind, this bunk's only big enough for one."

I shoved my way back to my feet, "Oh, I just came over to reassure you. I could tell you were worried."

He smiled and kept on reading as I cleaned up coffee spilled all over everything and picked up all the cans that had flown out of the unlocked lockers.

It seemed like only moments later when another one hit. This one resulted in a complete knockdown. I was thrown back against Jim, and more cans came out of their locker. My bedding and pillow followed. Everything that had at one time been on the port side of the boat was now on the starboard side. We stayed over for what seemed like an eternity; then, we came back upright. The bottle of cheap brandy broke when it hit the bronze knobs of the portlight. It was about a 100° knockdown.

I was concerned about the mast and trysail, so I slid back the companion hatch just enough to stick out my head. Everything looked okay; the trysail was shedding water like a waterfall so it must have been under water. The cockpit footwell had some water in it, but not nearly as much as I had expected. I closed the hatch and went below.

Neither Jim nor I felt like joking anymore. This was serious, and it was time to worry about what to do next. There really wasn't anything to do until daylight. We just had to sit it out.

By sunrise, the gusts had diminished some, and by 0630, the winds registered about 40 knots, but the seas were still huge. I hooked on my harness and went outside to inspect any damage. The storm trysail was still intact. Everything seemed normal, except we had lost our diesel jerry jugs.

The staysail halyard was tightly wrapped around the upper and intermediate shrouds. The snap shackle at the end was flying in the wind. I figured I could reach it with a boat pole. We decided to wait until the conditions improved a little more.

By 0900, the winds were about 20 knots, gusting to 30. The seas were still huge, but not breaking anymore. I untied the boat pole I keep lashed to the aft lower shroud and managed to reach the staysail halyard snap shackle. I pulled it down the shroud until I could grab it. It was not difficult to release the wraps after I had the end in my hand.

I walked it back up forward and clipped it to the reefed staysail that was still tied to the bulwarks. I returned to the mast and took up the slack on the halyard, then went back to the cockpit.

An hour later, it seemed the conditions had further improved. The barometer was rising. Encouraged, we raised the reefed staysail and got back on course for Pago Pago, American Samoa.

Suddenly, we were on our side again. Fortunately, I had seen it coming and yelled, "Hold on!"

I held tightly to the port lifeline. My feet were at the top edge of the cockpit well, and I was standing nearly vertical and parallel to the deck. The boat came up as quickly as it had gone over, and I found myself lying prone in the cockpit.

I heard Jim cursing below. He was in the process of making coffee when we had our knockdown. The coffee can had flown across the boat leaving grounds everywhere, even stuck to the overhead; most of it ended up in the handrail.

"I say we wait just a little longer," Jim said. We backwinded the reefed staysail and hove-to again. We took our time and ate cold cereal without milk for breakfast.

By 1100, we could sail. Throughout the day, we gradually shook out reefs and adjusted to the lessening winds and clearing skies. We turned the AM radio on as we got closer to Pago Pago. For some reason, the radio made us feel excited that American civilization lay ahead.

Approximately 70 miles from Pago Pago, we heard a voice interrupt the program. "Gale warning for American Samoa. It will hit Pago Pago at midnight tonight."

In unison, Jim and I both screamed, "Shit!"

For your own notes

_____
_____
_____
_____
_____
_____
_____
_____
_____
_____
_____
_____
_____
_____
_____
_____
_____
_____
_____
_____
_____
_____
_____
_____
_____
_____
_____
_____
_____
_____
_____
_____

Chapter Six

HOW TO MAKE THE CRUISE A SUCCESS

There are some things that will make the time away from home more fun, comfortable, enjoyable, and simply more successful. The list of ways to accomplish this is limitless. In this section, I will discuss some of the better ideas that I have found and used. These may not apply to all cruising boats or cruisers; however, think about the intention of the suggestion, and see if you can modify it to suit you own needs.

Most cruisers spend about 10% to 15% of their time at sea and the remainder at anchor. So, the boat should be most comfortable at anchor. This does not mean there should be huge king size beds and a Jacuzzi aboard. Sure, it would be nice, but most boats do not have the space for such luxuries. Therefore, there must be a compromise. Consider how comfortable it is aboard your boat while at the slip, on a mooring, or on short overnight sails. You may want to make some changes before you head offshore.

The ideas and suggestions that follow may seem trivial or common sense to some sailors. I admit that I almost did not mention some of them for that reason. I also realize that there are beginners who will be reading this who are not as knowledgeable as others. Please bear with me if you feel some of this is general sailing knowledge; someone else may gain from it.

Psychological and physical concerns

Self-confidence

Knowing as much as you can about what to expect and gaining personal confidence are two of the most important factors that will help to make your cruise successful. Try to soak in as much information as possible. Start by reading sailing and cruising books and watch cruising videos. If they are available in your area, attend navigation and cruising classes.

When your friends and people at the marina hear you are going cruising, they will all volunteer their advice. Everyone has an opinion and suggestions (including this author). Listen to all and everything, but keep a skeptical open mind. There are many marina experts who do not have the experience, but are more than ready to give their advice. Sometimes, if the advice is incorrect or misleading, it can get you into trouble.

Know your vessel

After the yacht has been purchased and is approaching a cruise-ready state, it is a good idea to live aboard before departing. This will be your new home for an undetermined amount of time, and familiarity with your boat is essential. Making local trips is a good way to get to know her. How much time should you spend living aboard before leaving? The longer, the better. This should apply to everyone who will be aboard during the cruise.

Slow down

If you really want to escape the pace you are now living, don't try to carry it with you by setting time schedules and rules. The only rules should be the ones that apply to safety. Initially, when you depart, you will find it difficult to relax, because of the worry and uncertainty of what will happen tomorrow. Try to look forward to these surprises. After all, you could be driving to and from work and living where each day is indistinguishable from the next. Learn to relax and to take everything in stride. Try to ease yourself into this new lifestyle. The sooner you adjust to 'slowing down', the sooner you will begin to enjoy yourself.

One of the biggest mistakes most beginning cruisers make is setting time limits in anchorages and for passages, so they can be at a particular destination on a prearranged date to meet someone. This can quickly ruin a cruise.

During my years cruising, I encountered two cyclones at sea. On both occasions, I was sailing during the cyclone season to meet a girlfriend on prearranged dates. If you are going to meet friends or family members on a certain date, be at the location ahead of schedule. If possible, be there before the arrangements are made. Try to avoid meeting someone during the cyclone season. If this is impossible, make certain the location to meet is well protected, in case a cyclone does develop. If possible, be there before the season begins.

It is better to see a few places thoroughly, than to pass by many without really learning anything about the people and their customs. A common mistake is to try to go around the world in three years. This will only permit time to stop at major cities where visas are stamped in and out. By setting these time limits, you force yourself back into the schedule you are trying to leave behind. If time limits must be set, adjust the itinerary to spend plenty of time in the places you enjoy the most.

It is best to sit out the cyclone season in a place you really enjoy. Spend the months touring inland and learn as much as you can about the culture. Set the departure date at the end of the cyclone season. This will allow more cruising time before it is necessary to search for a safe location to sit out the next cyclone season.

Admittedly, there will be occasions when you have to sail just when you are beginning to enjoy the place. You may have to leave because of visa expirations, or the approach of the cyclone season where there is no safe place to stay. Let these be the reasons to move on, not because "we don't have enough time". If you are enjoying a place and its people, give yourself a chance to share your culture with them and allow time to absorb their values and customs.

Acquire navigation skills

All aboard should know how to navigate as well as sail the boat. A little celestial navigation is a great help in building self-confidence and may be necessary if a lightning strike wipes out all electronics aboard. One of the greatest thrills of cruising is making that first landfall after a week or two at sea. It is even more gratifying if it is done using celestial navigation.

This does not mean that there should not be a GPS aboard. On the contrary, one or more GPS units aboard will make everyone feel better, knowing where they are at all times, regardless of weather conditions. To know a minimum of celestial navigation will just add another dimension to navigation and an appreciation of the method. It can be fun to teach all aboard how to take a simple noon sight and explain that this is how oceans were crossed hundreds of years ago.

Keep detailed instructions in clear steps on how to do celestial navigation; it is quickly forgotten if not used. If for some reason it becomes necessary, or if someone aboard wants to play with the sextant, the simple recipe method works well.

Remove tension

It is critical to remove any tension aboard. This applies to interaction between skipper, crew, and family members. Most tension is a result of fear. The more experience gained, the more comfortable everyone will be aboard. If the captain exudes sincere confidence, the others will also feel more relaxed and secure. On the other hand, if the skipper shows fear, all aboard will be frightened. Confidence is gained from experience. Take as many short and long sails as possible. Each time you go for a sail, try to imagine a situation that could occur and plan on a response. Ask all aboard how they think the situation should be handled. This will create a lot of thought and imagination. Listen to everyone; then, act out each of the suggestions until everyone agrees on which technique works the best. This will help reduce many surprises and instill confidence.

The more all aboard know about sailing and boat handling, the more help they will be when and if something goes wrong. There is always the possibility that something could happen to the skipper. The others aboard should feel confident that they are able to safely reach land and help. As confidence builds, fear and tension decrease.

Tension can be further reduced if everyone feels the boat is under control at all times. Reduce sail area at night, so a random squall will not cause a knockdown, throwing all aboard into panic. It is fun to drive a boat in the daytime and watch the miles pass under the hull, but at night, slow it down and make it more comfortable. It might be interesting to let everyone aboard vote on the amount of sail area to carry at night and try it. If the skipper feels the voted sail area is still too much, it can be reduced later. If the captain feels it is too little, he or she can explain why. However, be aware of the consequences of having too much sail area. An unexpected squall can make a crew want to mutiny.

If the weather deteriorates, don't fight it or worry about it. Show confidence and safety, heave-to early, and get some rest. Rest is one of the most important factors in safety at sea for all aboard. The mind does not work as clearly when you are fatigued: that is when the most serious mistakes are made.

Night watch

When sailing at night, there should always be someone on watch. This is sometimes easier said than done. Again, fatigue must be avoided. If there is still some tension aboard from fear, take a little time to calm everyone down at night. If you are out of the shipping lanes and have not seen a ship for days, turn on all the deck lights and crawl into bed for a cuddle for an hour. Try not to go to sleep, but talk about happy things and experiences. Tell jokes and generally try to give assurance that everything is going to go just right. Be sure to stick your head out once in awhile, listen to the sounds of the boat, and pay attention to your instincts. This technique becomes more important as the weather worsens. Remind yourself that there is no rush, the destination will still be there, even if you arrive a few days later than expected.

While I was cruising, I met an older single-handed sailor I highly respected. His name was Sid, and he was sailing a boat named *Doreen Beatrice*. She was named after his late wife. They were planning on making the cruise together, but she suddenly became ill and passed away before they could leave. He decided to continue on his own to keep her dream alive. To my knowledge, he never did take on crew. I asked him why and he said, "This was Doreen's and my dream, not someone else's. She sails with me." He was always overdue entering ports where we, his cruising friends, waited and worried. I learned that he heaved-to all night long, every night. He commented that he was always rested and enjoyed the day's sail much more.

It is difficult to advise on the actual hours of standing watch, because there are many variables to consider. Some sleep deeper and go to sleep more quickly than others. People who can do this get much more rest than those who can't, so some may fatigue quicker than others. Rougher weather conditions require shorter watches. This is because the sea conditions can change rapidly, causing one person to spend the whole watch working their tail off, while the next watch has nothing at all to do. When the weather is rough, all aboard will get less sleep, or useful deep sleep. Often, the rougher weather will require two people to handle the sails. If the weather is rough and there is enough crew aboard, have two people on watch for longer periods. If shorthanded, have a single person on watch for less time.

Watch standing is really a personal matter. Each skipper will have to determine the length of the watch, depending on the condition of the crew and the weather. When I had crew aboard, we normally stood three-hour watches when the weather was calm to moderate. If the weather was rough, we stood one or two-hour watches. It is nice to have extra crew aboard during a passage, so when your watch is finished, you have more hours to get needed rest.

Keep everyone busy

Try to have all personnel aboard participate in something. Designate duties according to age and ability. The more useful a person feels, the more they will have the sense of contributing to the success of the cruise. No matter how trivial the chore, make it into something important.

I found that having crew do navigation is a great way to keep them occupied. Not only do they learn navigation, but they can also see where they are on the chart and figure their time of arrival.

Issue simple chores like sewing anti-chafe to anchor lines, practicing tying knots, making ornamental knots or mats, polishing brass, making fishing lures, and the list goes on. If the job shows some actual results, the person will feel more useful.

The cruising life never gets boring; there is always something new to learn. This never changes, no matter how many miles under the keel. Every place, every situation brings with it a new experience.

The boat

As mentioned in a previous chapter, there are certain characteristics about a boat's design and construction that will affect her speed, movement, and comfort level at sea. These are items that are part of the boat's design and cannot be changed without radical construction efforts. This would include the boat's sailing rig, keel, hull design and general layout, especially if it has a fiberglass liner. If you find you do not like some of these characteristics, you will need to consider buying a different boat, or you will have to learn to live with it.

I feel I should remind the reader that *all boats are a compromise*. The perfect vessel has yet to be produced and never will be. There are some things that we all learn to live with. If you think about it, I'm sure you will see that even in our everyday lives, there are many compromises.

Exterior

Removable tillers and steering wheels

One of the most important concerns for making a cruise enjoyable is the ease of steering the boat. The type of steering on the boat may not be changeable. It is often too complicated to change a boat from wheel steering to tiller steering and vice versa. What is important is that steering can be done with relative ease. Larger boats will normally have wheel steering, which requires less effort, while smaller boats have tiller steering.

Regardless of the type of steering, it is nice to be able to remove the wheel or tiller while at anchor. It makes it much more comfortable for moving around the boat and perhaps even sleeping outside. *Be sure to have a safe place to store the wheel or tiller after it is removed, so it does not accidentally go overboard. Equally important is the ability to reinstall it in a hurry.*

It is much easier to remove, store, and quickly reinstall the tiller than the wheel. The wheel has a key or pin in the hub to prevent it from rotating on the drive axis. Normally, the wheel is held on to the axis by a nut. If a pin is used, try replacing it with a quick release pin that has a friction stop. If a key is used, try using a good adhesive to hold the key in place on the axis or in the wheel hub. The retainer nut can be a wing nut to make it easier to remove and replace. Most cruisers who remove their wheel at anchor often reinstall it when they go to bed at night in case it is needed in a hurry.

If the wheel is attached to the axis with a taper fit, it will be more difficult to remove easily and may have to remain on the pedestal. Tillers, on the other hand, are attached directly to the rudder or the rudderpost using various methods. It should not be too difficult to figure a way to make it easy to remove and replace the tiller quickly.

Cockpit footwell cover

In the tropics, I like to sleep outside. If the wheel or tiller can be removed and a filler used to cover the footwell, the whole cockpit becomes a single surface for sleeping. To fill or cover the top of the footwell will require some thinking for each boat.

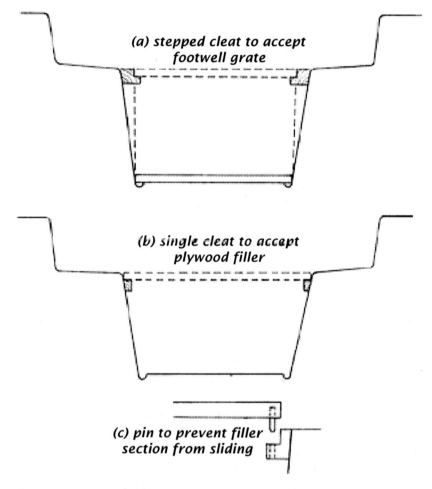

(a) stepped cleat to accept footwell grate

(b) single cleat to accept plywood filler

(c) pin to prevent filler section from sliding

Figure 84. Cockpit footwell covers

On my own boat, I have a grating in the bottom of the footwell that is in two halves. Depending on how much space I need, I can use only one half or both halves. The two halves fit on to cleats fastened to the top inside edge of the footwell.

The cleat may have to be quite wide if there is a substantial taper or draft to the sides of the footwell. See Figure 84 (a).

If a grating is out of the question or undesirable, a cover can be made using single or multiple pieces of plywood, as shown in Figure 84 (b). Because a plywood cover does not have to live in the bottom of the footwell, it can be made to snugly fit the top, thus reducing the width of the cleat. The plywood pieces can be stored in the lazarette or under the deck in one of the cockpit lockers.

If the cover will be in two or more pieces and only part is needed or wanted, there must be a method to prevent them from sliding along the cleat when the boat heels. If the footwell has a recessed drain around the edge, a pin can be installed in the bottom side of the cover piece that matches a hole in the cleat. See Figure 84 (c).

Fenderboards

The boat will often have to set against unprotected pilings. Because the pilings are round and the boat moves with the swell, it is difficult to keep fenders in place. A fenderboard set between two or more fenders will help protect the boat's side, as shown in Figure 85 (a).

Fenderboards are difficult to store. I used a fenderboard set on its edge and lashed to the inside of the bulwarks on both sides of the boat, as shown in Figure 85 (b). It does slightly interfere with the free movement on deck; however, its advantages far outweigh this disadvantage.

I found I could store my secondary anchor and 75 feet of anchor chain in the space between the bulwarks and the fenderboard. If your boat does not have bulwarks, this may not be possible.

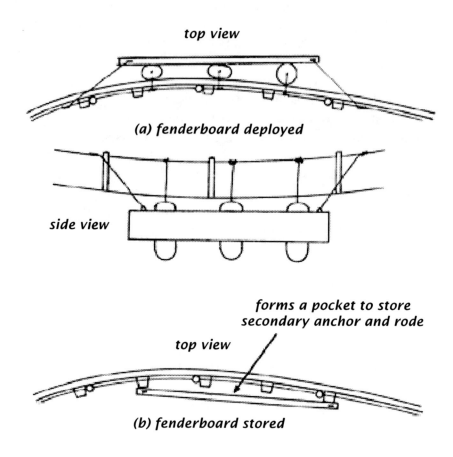

top view

(a) fenderboard deployed

side view

*forms a pocket to store
secondary anchor and rode*

top view

(b) fenderboard stored

Figure 85. Fenderboards

Rubrails

A situation may occur when there is not enough time to remove and set the fenderboard. For this reason, I suggest a metal rubrail along both sides of the boat. Most boats already have rubrails. It is important that they extend far enough outboard to protect the boat's sides when it is rolling.

Watertightness

Another consideration of utmost importance is to make sure that the vessel is watertight. The whole trip can be ruined if clothes, bedding, and electronics get wet. Unfortunately, it is almost impossible to simulate the conditions that cause a boat to leak. When the boat is at sea, it is working, causing stress on hull to deck joins and hardware. During these conditions, it is very difficult to find the source of the leak; all too often, it is feet away from where the water or dampness is seen or felt.

It is much easier to locate and repair a leak in port. Since the working conditions at sea cannot be simulated at the dock, all that can be done is to use a fire hose, which has some pressure. If this is not possible, a good garden hose is better than no test at all.

Spray the whole boat from different directions and angles for a long period of time. If you have an idea where the leak is located, direct the force of the water at and around that location for some time. It often takes a while for the water to weep through the leak and reach a place where it can be seen.

Non-skid decks

Most fiberglass boats have the non-skid pattern molded into the deck. Because these patterns are made in a female mold, they must be slightly rounded to be able to remove the deck from the mold. These non-skids are only good when the deck is dry.

There are other non-skid materials available. I like Treadmaster the best. It is available in different colors and patterns. It really does provide a non-skid surface. In fact, if you sit on it wearing your birthday suit while the boat is rolling, you will find your skin is quickly removed.

If you are considering Treadmaster, be sure it is properly installed. I like to leave a space between each sheet for water drainage. I also suggest that the fiberglass deck be thoroughly ground to remove any smooth surface. The Treadmaster is usually applied using epoxy glue. There are other glues available that may work just as well. It is important that it be weighted down during installation. If this is not possible because of the contour of the deck, at least add weights to the edges.

A good non-skid deck can also be applied using paint and a non-skid material like silica sand or ground walnut shells. There are other materials available, like ground tennis balls; however, I don't have any personal experience with them. I have seen one boat with it. It looked all right, and it felt like a good non-skid surface, although I don't know how long it would be expected to last in the tropics and salt-water environment.

Boom gallows

I realize that many—or perhaps most—boats could not use boom gallows because their booms are too short. If your boat has a long boom, you might want to consider installing boom gallows.

The boom gallows are normally installed at the aft end of the boat to support the end of the boom. Without the boom gallows, the boom is supported by a topping lift and a stop or line to the backstay to keep it from swinging. I hate this because the boom will still swing a few inches; these few inches can hit someone in the head. If the boom is raised above head level, it still makes noise as it swings from stop to stop. When the weather gets rough, this stop may even break.

I like to drop my boom into the middle or either side of the boom gallows. If the weather is rough, I can even lash the boom around the boom gallows to ensure that it will not come loose even in a knockdown or worse.

I have an awning stored on the aft end of my dodger that extends back to the underside of the boom gallows for sun and weather protection over the helm. It has an additional piece that can be rolled down to connect to the stern weather curtains, which provides shade and protection from the stern. By adding removable panels to the sides of this awning, you can completely enclose the cockpit. This will be discussed later in more detail.

I store my fishing reel and fishing pole bracket on the boom gallows uprights. I know of others who store their outboards, barbecues, life ring and more on these uprights.

I especially like the advantage of being able to tie a horizontal line from the upper shrouds to the corner knees of the boom gallows. This line is just about chest high and acts as an additional lifeline and jack line that keeps the harness clip from dragging along the deck at night.

The boom gallows uprights provide a strong place to fasten the lifelines. I find this much stronger than having them fastened to a sternrail, or a pushpit as the British call it.

Another unexpected advantage to the boom gallows is that I can stand behind the gallows and rest my arms over the crown and steer with my feet. This provides much better vision when in a crowded area; it is also comfortable if I sit on the sternrail. I even installed a swing-up seat on my sternrail just for this purpose.

There are several possible disadvantages that I can find with the boom gallows. The first is if they are installed too far forward and you sit directly beneath them, you can hit your head when you stand. Also, depending on the lines of the boat, it may not be pleasing to eye. There is also a more serious concern: depending on how close the boom gallows are installed to the main sheet lead, the chances of the sheets getting caught behind or in front of the gallows during a gibe may increase. Most of these problems are a result of installation location; these situations can be prevented by proper testing before installation.

Interior

As I mentioned above, the boat should be comfortable both at sea and at anchor. Much of this comfort is based on the interior layout. Often, the interior layout is not something that can be easily changed, especially if the boat has a fiberglass liner. However, there are some changes or additions that can make it more comfortable.

Berths

Probably, the most important part of interior comfort is the sleeping berths' sizes and locations. If they are not comfortable both at sea and at anchor, the chances for sound sleep are not good.

The ideal location for the berth is right in the center of the boat at the waterline. This is where there is minimal movement. Of course, this is almost impossible to do on a small boat. Keep in mind that as the berth moves outboard, fore and aft of this point, the movement increases proportionally.

Many modern boats have the berths in the stern of the boat. I like this as an alternative, but I don't like the waves slapping the hull next to my head when the boat is tied or anchored bow and stern. Most stern berths are located in their own devoted stateroom with a door. This provides privacy and a place to go when one wants some solitude. In some cases, it may even have its own head and shower. The stern berth will have far less movement than the berth at the bow.

Probably the worst place for a berth is on the bow. When the boat is underway, the bow is where the boat gets the most movement. If going to weather, it is impossible to get a good night's sleep. Also, the forward berth is close to the anchor chain. Consequently, when the boat is at anchor, you can hear the anchor chain sliding in the chock or the anchor rope stretching under load.

This is also the location of the chain locker. The berth must be totally away from the anchor chain or rope locker, or there will always be moisture and odor. If the chainpipe is installed near the berth, the sound of the chain banging back and forth within the pipe will drive one crazy when the boat is rolling.

Another problem with the berth in the forepeak is that the wavelets slap against the hull whenever there is a wind. Of course, none of this is of any importance if you are sitting in a marina or in well-protected waters.

The forepeak is normally where sail bags are stored. They may be damp, causing additional problems. Also, it may be possible that they must be moved each time the berth is needed for sleeping.

Another factor to consider with berths is their width and length. At anchor, a wide berth is welcome, so your legs and arms can stretch out and two or more can sleep together. However, the wide berth at sea is miserable to sleep in because as the boat rolls, so does your body. I agree with other sources that the best single berth while underway is about two feet wide and at least 6 inches longer than the person using the berth. This will minimize body movement, and additional cushions or pillows can be wedged along the sides to make it even more comfortable.

Many boats have separate quarter berths and pilot berths for use while underway, with larger double berths forward or aft to use while at anchor. If the boat only has large double berths or the berths are too wide, they can have inserts or removable partitions added to make them into narrower berths to use while underway.

On my own boat, when the weather is a little rough, I put the pilot berth's cushions in the middle of the cabin sole and stuff additional cushions along the sides. This provides a berth in the center of the movement athwartship and fore and aft, which radically reduces the motion. With the additional cushions wedged against the sides, there is nowhere to roll. When there is compatible crew aboard, we alternate using this cabin sole berth when changing watches.

Fitted sheets

Since I am writing about berths, consider making fitted sheets for the cushions. It seems more difficult to make up a berth on a boat than at home. Fitted bottom sheets certainly make it easier. If all the cushions have expensive or new upholstery, a fitted cover would be nice to have while underway. It is much easier to wash sheets than the upholstery.

Leeboards or leecloths

All underway berths need a method to keep the crewmember from falling out of his or her berth when the boat is heeled or rolling at sea. Using a leecloth or a leeboard accomplishes this, as shown in Figure 86.

There are many different designs for leecloths. The most common is usually a piece of canvas or similar material about 4 to 6 feet long and about 2 feet wide with a rope sewn into one edge. The other edge is fastened to the top, outboard edge of the berth, under the cushion. This is where the leecloth lives until it is needed. There may be about four equally spaced lines sewn to the rope edge of the leecloth. Tied to the other end of these lines are rings or hooks that attach to matching connections on the handrail or underside of the deck above the berth. These lines are long enough to reach these matching connections when the leecloth is used. See Figure 86 (a).

**If leecloth hooks overhead, it's difficult to get out.
If leecloth hooks horizontally, it's easier to climb over.**

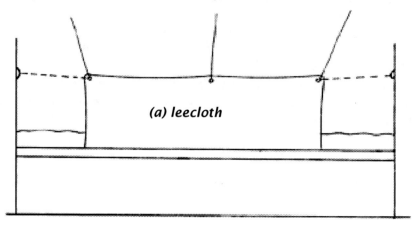

(a) leecloth

**Insert removed to climb into bunk.
Insert placed between leeboard and
cushion when sleeping.**

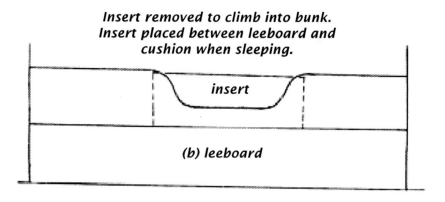

insert

(b) leeboard

Figure 86. Leecloths and leeboards

When at sea, the leecloth with the rope and lines sewn into its edge is pulled out from under the berth cushions and fastened to hooks or to the handrail above the berth. This provides a cloth wall to hold the person in the berth. The only problem with this leecloth design is that it is difficult to get out of the berth, if the boat is heeled far over so the crew's weight is against the leecloth. This weight makes it almost impossible to release the hooks above the berth.

Because the berth with a leecloth may be difficult to get out of in a hurry, I like leeboards. As with leecloths, there are different designs for leeboards. Most leeboards are permanently fastened to the side of the berth. Its height is usually about 8 to 10 inches above the top of the cushion to keep the crew in the berth when the boat heels. Near the center of the leeboard, there is a low cut opening to cushion level, which makes getting in and out easy. However, this opening is normally located where the hip is when sleeping, so it does not restrain that part of the body. See Figure 86 (b).

What I like about this method is that the opening makes it is easy to get in and out of the berth. When it gets rough, a small, thin, removable board can be inserted in this opening to close it off, so the crew cannot fall through. This removable board must be a little longer than the opening, so the ends are supported when there is weight against it.

To install the board, it is slipped down the inside of the opening, between the cushion and the permanent leeboard. To get in or out of the berth, the board is simply slipped up and out of the opening, then replaced after the crewmember is in. It is normally stored under the berth cushions when not needed.

Seacocks below the waterline

Some beginning sailors do not really know the difference between a standard through-hull fitting and a seacock. Many think that a ball valve is a seacock; this is incorrect. A seacock can have any kind of valve: a gate valve, ball valve, or expanding plug valve. The real difference lies in the method used to fasten the valve through the hull. See Figure 87.

Any valve can be connected to a regular through-hull fitting that has its own nut to hold it firmly to the hull. The through-hull is placed through the hull and held in place by a nut over its threads. The valve is then threaded over the exposed threads of this through-hull fitting, as shown in Figure 87 (a) and (b).

The problem with this method is that the strength of the through-hull fitting is limited to the thickness between the hole inside the fitting and the bottom of the thread. Most through-hull fittings begin with a wall of about 1/8-inch thick. After the threads are cut into the wall, the actual strength could be less than half that. If electrolysis or etching occurs, a hole could quickly penetrate this wall.

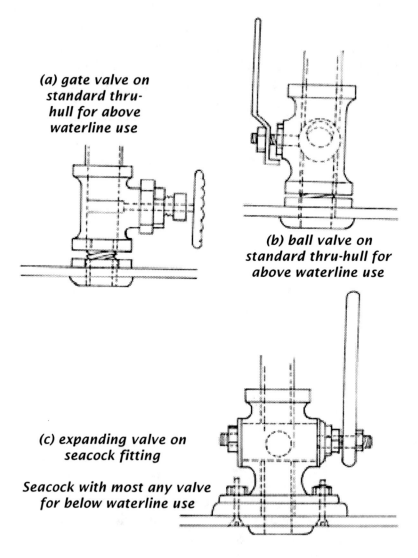

(a) gate valve on standard thru-hull for above waterline use

(b) ball valve on standard thru-hull for above waterline use

(c) expanding valve on seacock fitting

Seacock with most any valve for below waterline use

Figure 87. Seacocks and valves

The seacock is a valve that has a bottom-mounting flange cast as part of the valve, as shown in Figure 87 (c). The inside of this flange is threaded to match a through-hull fitting. This flange is through-bolted through the hull. The through-hull fitting is threaded into the valve from the outside, after the valve has been mounted. This makes the through-hull fitting impossible to break.

Only seacocks should be installed below the waterline. Above the waterline, a standard through-hull and valve can be used.

An interesting note is that if, for example, you are using a one and a half-inch hose, and you order a one and a half-inch seacock, the actual size of the hole in the valve will be one and a quarter-inch. The reason is that the outside of the hose barb that takes the hose must be one and a half-inch, while the inside of the hose barb is one and a quarter-inch or smaller. Take this into consideration when selecting the valves you intend to use.

Propane vs. kerosene

There is no question that propane is far more combustible and dangerous than kerosene. Propane is a gas; it does not catch fire, but it explodes. It is also heavier than air, so if there is a leak inside the boat, it will collect on the bottom of the bilge. For this reason, many boats will not have propane aboard. On the other hand, gasoline fumes are nearly as combustible as propane, and it is safely used on automobiles. The reason autos rarely have fires or an explosion is proper installation of the fuel system. The same safety concerns apply to propane. Have it properly installed, vented, and inspected often for leaks, and there will probably never be a problem for the life of the boat. However, be aware that only one problem is one too many.

Kerosene is much easier to handle and fill than propane. A jerry jug filled with kerosene can be poured into the kerosene reservoir and you're done. With propane, the bottle must be removed and carried to a place that fills propane. The proper adapter must be available for the country being visited, because most do not fit American fittings. Then the filled propane tank must be returned to the boat and installed. The tank cannot be left in the sun or in the heat after filling, because the propane will expand inside the bottle. This may cause the safety valve to release propane.

Both propane and kerosene are readily available in foreign countries, and surprisingly, there is little difference in the cost between the two. The cost difference is in the containers and the fittings needed for propane. This is almost a wash when you consider the cost of the denatured alcohol required to prime the kerosene before it can be lit. Denatured alcohol may only be available in drugstores, and it is very expensive. Shellac thinner is denatured alcohol and costs much less. It is available in most large paint stores.

I know of some cruisers who use propane torches to prime their kerosene burners. These propane bottles have to be carried aboard and in a locker that could leak fumes into the boat's interior. This seems to void the safety of kerosene.

For many years, I cruised with kerosene and refused to have propane aboard for fear of an explosion. However, I carried gallons of denatured alcohol required to prime the kerosene, and gasoline for my two-horse outboard without a second thought. I carried these bottles in lockers in the cockpit.

When I wanted to cook or have a cup of coffee or tea, I had to pump up the container that was mounted below the stove, so it had enough pressure to push the kerosene up to the stove. Then, I poured a little denatured alcohol in the small bowl under the burner and lit it. After the denatured alcohol stopped burning, the burner was hot or primed, so I could light it. But first, I had to turn the burner knob fully in the opposite direction so a little needle would clean the orifice. Then, I could light it. It burned with a nice blue flame, most of the time. If I turned it down low, the burner would lose its heat or prime; then the flame would turn from blue to yellow and leave black soot everywhere. Sometimes, when the flame was turned low, the wind would blow the flame out, but kerosene continued to flow.

Often, right after breakfast, I would have a visitor who came over for a cup of coffee and conversation. If I had just turned the burner off, I had to re-light it. However, if I poured denatured alcohol in the bowl beneath the burner, it would explode when I lit it. The remaining heat in the burner caused the alcohol to turn to a vapor, causing the sudden explosion.

The kerosene burners were always getting clogged and had to be cleaned. The pricking needle had to be replaced occasionally. The burner valve often leaked kerosene, so the seals had to be replaced. I had to carry a lot of spare parts to use kerosene. Not only did this apply to the cooking stove, but to the heater as well.

When I changed to propane, I found that I did not need any spare parts and could light the stove with the turn of a knob and a push of a button. It never burned dirty or left a residue. However, it did not burn as hot as kerosene.

I think most cruisers would prefer using propane rather than kerosene, if it were not for the fear of an explosion. Needless to say, this is a serious concern. If propane is to be used, it is important to make certain there are no leaks in the system. Install a good propane leak detector and have the sensors near and below the stove and heater as well as the bilge. It should be left activated as long as the propane is on and connected to the system's interior.

Most propane installations have a pressure gauge installed after the propane regulator and before the supply hose to show the pressure in the hose. After the solenoid turns the propane off or it is turned off by hand, the pressure gauge should still show pressure. If it drops too rapidly, there is a leak in the system that must be located and fixed. I make it a point to check the gauge an hour after I finished using the stove to see if it still shows the same pressure.

Sinks

I like a large sink that is big enough to set plates flat on the bottom. While underway, I often place several plates in the bottom of the sink in a little soapy water and leave them for a while. All I have to do is rinse them later. The larger sink can also be used to do small loads of laundry. However, there is a compromise: the larger the sink, the more water it takes to partially fill it, so don't get too carried away with its size, unless there is limitless water aboard.

The sink should also be deep enough so water in it does not slosh out while underway. I feel the minimum depth should be eight inches. On many boats, the sinks are installed near the waterline level. *Be careful that you don't install one so deep that seawater sits in the bottom and never drains.*

I like sink drains to go directly to the outside of the boat with a minimum of bends. This makes it a garbage disposal. I can push food particles down the drain, and it provides food for the fish. *Never use this drain to pour oil or anything that is not edible.*

If the boat is big enough to take a double sink, I think that is great. It makes it so easy to wash the dishes and put them in the other sink to drain. *However, make certain the outboard sink will not fill with salt water when the boat is heeled on that side.* The closer the sink and its drain are to amidships, the better the chances are of salt water not coming up through the drain and filling the sink when heeled.

On *Xiphias*, the sink was set too far to port. When I was on a starboard tack, the sink would fill with salt water and slosh into all my galley lockers. I soon learned to close off the through-hull valve when on a starboard tack. This is a real inconvenience if the boat will remain on this tack for some time. Not to mention that I would often tack onto the starboard tack and forget to close the valve beforehand.

Another concern is that stainless steel sinks are designed for the border flange to set on top of the counter. This makes it impossible for any water on the counter to flow back into the sink. This may sound trivial, but it can be a problem. The smaller the sink is, the greater the amount of water that will splash outside the sink and drain into the dry locker behind it.

Sink dam

Even with a large sink, some water will splash outside the sink and run into the lockers behind it. Installing a low teak dam behind the sink to hold the water can prevent this.

Water tanks

It is important to have enough fresh water aboard to make a cruise enjoyable. There should be more than enough water to drink, use for cooking, take showers or baths, and rinse salt water from laundry and dishes. Many cruisers today have watermakers aboard. These are fine. I even encourage having one. However, the tankage volume should not be reduced because you are relying on the watermaker. The watermaker must be looked at as a luxury item and should not be essential to the boat. The reason is logical: they break down and require constant use in absolutely clean salt water.

Personally, I prefer water tanks made of stainless steel because of their longevity, assuming that the proper welding rods were used to make the tanks. I know of many cases where small pinholes developed in the welds as a result of electrolysis of dissimilar metals used in welding the seams. Another advantage to the stainless steel tank is that it makes it easy to install baffles. Baffles are walls within the tank to prevent the water from rushing from end to end. These walls have small holes that permit the water to pass more slowly.

Fiberglass water tanks are popular on modern boats, because they are cheap and are built into the hull or the interior liner. Fiberglass is durable and will not corrode or get electrolysis like stainless steel tanks. Baffles can be easily added before the top is fastened down. The problems are the taste of the water, the chance of osmosis from the inside, and the possibility of cracking from stress over time.

On my own boat, I built a water tank into the deep part of the bilge to get more volume. I coated the interior of the tank with 5 coats of epoxy followed by 5 coats of another brand of epoxy manufactured especially for city water tanks. At the recommendation of the manufacturer, I did not close it up for 6 months, so the solvents would evaporate. When I launched the boat and filled the tank with water, I found it impossible to drink or use for cooking. I could even smell the epoxy solvents as the water came out of the spigot.

I called the manufacturer, and he said I should put a heat gun in the tank for a month or more to evaporate the solvents. After melting my PVC fittings and nearly burning my boat down, I finally got the tank clean of all solvents. Now, there is no taste at all. In fact, this tank is devoted to drinking water only. If I had it to do over, I doubt I would have done the same thing because of the all the time and hassle it took to remove the solvents. Now that I have it, though, I love the extra volume.

Fiberglass tanks should have an epoxy coating on the inside to prevent or at least reduce osmosis. This coating must be completely cured before use. I have heard that waxing the interior of a fiberglass tank will help reduce the fiberglass taste, although I wonder how long the wax will last. I have also heard that blasting the inside with steam helps. The bottom line is, even if we don't taste the solvents, we don't know for sure that we really got rid of them all, or what long-term health hazards might exist.

Any tank that is essential for survival should be accessible for cleaning and removable for inspection and making repairs. Unfortunately, the fiberglass tanks that are built into the liner or the hull's bilge are not removable.

The other alternative tank material is molded polyethylene. This is the same material used for most bottled water you buy at the market. The tanks are made by pouring molten polyethylene into a mold, then rotating the mold so the polyethylene is of equal thickness throughout the tank.

Fittings are installed by friction welding. A hole is cut through the tank where the fitting will be welded. The fitting has a flange that will be welded to the tank's outer surface. This fitting is set into a tool, like a router, and rotated at high rpm. While it is spinning, it is forced down on the tank's surface, over the hole, until the polyethylene material under the fitting begins to melt. The tool is stopped, and the fitting is held in place until the material solidifies. These fittings rarely leak and are permanently part of the tank. This means they cannot be changed later; however, new ones can be installed. The advantage of these tanks is that they are inexpensive, and they do not leave an odor or taste in the water. They are light and available in almost any size and configuration.

The disadvantage to the polyurethane tanks is there may not be a mold available to fit the particular space where it is needed. Another problem is they do not have baffles, so smaller tanks connected together must be used. Because polyurethane is relatively soft, it will wear through in a short time, if it is permitted to move.

Regardless of the tank material, it must be firmly fastened inside the boat, so there is no movement or any possibility of it coming loose. Also, each tank should have inspection plates, so that the tank can be visually inspected and cleaned when necessary. There should be an inspection plate on both sides of the baffles, so the entire tank can be reached.

Water tanks are heavy when filled. There is only one good place for this additional weight: the lowest part of the boat on its centerline. The further the tanks are located away from this point, the more the boat's stability will be affected.

As mentioned earlier, water tanks should be separated with separate fills and feeds. One tank should be devoted to drinking or consumption only. This is the tank the watermaker should feed. I like to have this tank lead directly to its own foot pump and spigot; in this way, it can be totally independent of any water in any other tanks.

The other tank or tanks would be devoted to servicing: to wash dishes, showers, laundry, etc. I like to have a diverter valve between these service tanks and the consumption tank. If I am in a marina or where there is no question about the quality of the water, I can switch from one tank to the others. If the water is questionable, I set the diverter valve to separate the tanks. If there is a real concern about the safety of the water in the service tanks, chlorine can be added; I try to avoid doing this to the consumption tank unless absolutely necessary.

Water filters

When taking water aboard from a questionable source, a filter can be used to filter out sediment, chlorine, and even bacteria. The filters that eliminate bacteria are expensive, don't last long, and are difficult to find. For this reason, most cruisers just use a carbon filter when taking on water.

Consider installing a replaceable carbon filter on the consumption tank inside the boat to remove taste and sediment. Carbon filters are more readily available; however, a reasonable supply should be carried aboard if making a long cruise.

Salt water to sink

No matter how much water you carry, the time will come when you will need to use salt water. While underway, I make it a habit to wash my dishes in salt water and give them a fresh-water rinse. The same applies to doing laundry and taking showers and baths; a salt-water wash and fresh-water rinse will help conserve the fresh water supply.

If you want salt water to the sink, I don't advise a devoted through-hull and seacock for this purpose. It is too difficult to add another through-hull and valve when it really isn't necessary. Put a simple 'T' on the engine intake hose below the waterline that leads to an inline strainer, then to the foot pump before it goes to the spigot at the sink. There are other salt-water sources where the same can be done without adding another through-hull.

Shower ideas

Every boat must have a method for bathing. If the boat has an adequate water supply, a pressure water system can be installed. The pressure water can lead to a hot water system, which makes taking a shower easier and more like being at home. Pressure water systems are great, but they use a lot more water than manual pumps.

There are shower bags that gravity feed the shower water. These bags are not as strong or as durable as I would like. They don't last too long, so several should be carried aboard. If you have a cat, they won't last long at all.

Lin and Larry Pardey like to use a lawn sprayer, partially filled with warm water, to take their shower. I have tried this method and found it works well. The nozzle that came with it, however, produced too fine a mist; it took forever to rinse soap out of my hair. Consequently, I replaced the nozzle with a dishwasher sprayer. This worked perfectly, but I had to repeatedly pump the canister up with air during my shower. If this system will be used, there must be a compromise.

While I was in Australia, I found black polyethylene tanks that were used for storing chemicals. They all have their own tap on the bottom. They were available in many different sizes. I chose a three-gallon tank and connected a plastic hose to the tap on the bottom. On the other end of the hose, I placed a dish sprayer like you would find at home to rinse dishes. I filled the tank about three-quarters full with water and let it sit in the sun all day. By the time I wanted my shower, the water was quite warm. If I arrived back to the boat after dark and the water was cold, I would boil a teakettle of water and add it to the tank. I set this polyethylene tank on deck and let it gravity feed into the shower area. I used this for many years and suspect it may still be aboard *Xiphias*.

Hot water

Since I am writing about showers, I should mention methods for obtaining hot water. The most common method used on smaller boats is the solar heating bladder-type mentioned above, or simply heating the water on the stove.

If the boat has a pressurized water system, there are other alternatives. A common method of getting hot water is to install an insulated tank to store the hot water; the tank is similar to what you would have at home, but smaller. This hot water tank can be heated by heat from the engine or by electricity.

If the engine is used to heat the water, the engine's cooling water passes through the engine and gets hot. Then it passes through stainless tubes inside the hot water tank to heat up the fresh water.

The insulation around the tank keeps the water warm for many hours. This system works really well while motoring, but takes some time if the engine is cold, like when anchored.

The other method to heat the water in these hot water tanks is by electricity. The most common is the 110-volt AC heater. Unfortunately, they are only good at dockside, or if the boat has a generator or an inverter to produce 110-volt AC. Recently, a 12-volt DC unit has come on the market. It is the demand-type, which means it heats the water as it passes through the unit. I hear that these work well, but use a lot of amps. This should not be a problem if the engine is running to keep the batteries charged.

When I owned the boat building company, we usually installed two types of hot water heaters. Initially, we installed the propane demand-type, originally called the Wolter's System. This unit got some bad publicity, stating it produced carbon monoxide, and was taken off the market. Then, we began to install the Isotemp unit, an insulated tank that heated the water by both 110-volt AC and engine heat. We had many excellent reports on its effectiveness, even considering its basic limitation of heating water at anchor when the engine was cold.

On my own boat, I have the old Wolter's demand propane water heater. I really feel they got a bad rap. I used a carbon monoxide detector next to my unit, and it never indicated the presence of carbon monoxide. I installed the unit according to the manufacturer's specifications. It required a flue longer than I could fit on my boat. As an alternative, it could be purchased with an exhaust fan. This is what I did. I must admit that the fan has failed once in the past four years, but this is something I check regularly. As an additional precaution, I never take a hot shower with the place locked up tight. I always leave the hatch open above it.

I have heard others say that you don't want to have a propane water heater inside the boat. If that is true, then there shouldn't be a propane stove or heater either. Propane is safe as long as it is properly installed and tested regularly for leaks.

One of the major problems I have found with showers using hot water is ventilation. Most boats only have a small portlight that is left open. The movement of air is too little to properly ventilate the shower, so moisture from condensation gets into the lockers and other places difficult to access for cleaning. Personally, I really like my shower; it is under the scuttle hatch which I can open when I take a shower. Also, the hatch on my boat will open forward or aft to provide as much ventilation as I need.

Insulation

I feel all boats should be insulated throughout. At the very least, it should be insulated under the cabin top and under the deck. On a hot summer day, feel under the deck that is exposed to direct sunlight; you will be amazed at the amount of heat. Of course, this equally applies to the cold of winter. The more insulation your boat has, the better off you and your crew will be. Some builders will tell you that the core material is the insulation. If the core is not saturated with resin, it may have a positive insulation effect; however, the core should be saturated with resin.

When I owned the boat building company, we used a product made of Ethafoam, a polyethylene foam. Unlike polystyrene, which crumbles and burns, this foam is more like vinyl rubber foam. It can even be bent into a circle without breaking. This makes it easy to conform to the compound curves of a boat. It has the same insulation qualities as other foams. It can be installed with epoxy-type glue or even good quality contact cement. *Be sure to test the contact cement on the foam to make certain the solvents do not dissolve it.*

Ethylene foam is available in various densities. We used denser foam inside the lockers so cans and hard items would not damage the insulation. We used 1/2-inch foam under the cabin top and down the insides of the hull to the waterline. Below the water line and inside the lockers, we used the 1/4-inch denser foam. I think this is the minimum insulation thickness that should be used. Our boats were small, so additional thickness would begin to take up too much space.

Insulating the engine room will reduce engine heat from entering the boat. However, it will also reduce sound, and you want to be able to hear your engine running in order to detect a different sound if something goes wrong. On the other hand, you don't want the engine noise keeping everyone awake while motoring; again, this is a compromise to be considered.

I have mixed emotions about the lead rubber insulation available for this purpose. I have seen this stuff actually melt over time. I am not sure if it breaks down from the diesel fumes or the heat. This does not mean it should not be used, but before you spend the money, check out others who have used this product for a long time; see if they had the same results that I did.

Vinyl headliners

I think the best way to discuss this subject is by relating an experience I had when delivering a boat with a vinyl headliner.

§

The boat's home was in Australia and had spent most of its life in a semi-tropical climate. The moment I boarded the vessel, I could detect a faint odor of mildew. This is common on many boats, especially those that have water sitting constantly in the bilge. After I completed the journey, I wanted to deliver the boat cleaner than when I departed. There were signs of dirt in the vinyl headliner where there was exposed stitching. I tried to undo the zipper along the side, which holds the headliner in place. I found that the zipper would only move about two feet. It was frozen so hard that I could not free it even after using WD-40. When I folded down the exposed liner, I could see and feel a black slimy mould on the inside surface. I cleaned what I could reach, then forced the zipper back to its original position. I deduced that the dirt in the stitching was not just dirt, but mould growing from the inside out. Using diluted bleach, I cleaned the headliner on the outside. I informed the owner of what I had found and suggested he attempt to remove the liner for cleaning.

§

I am not saying that all vinyl headliners will grow mould on the inside. Mould requires moisture to grow. If there is any air space between the underside of the deck and the cabin that is not ventilated, condensation may result, followed by mould. The answer is to prevent condensation from developing; the only way to do that is proper insulation and reduction of air space.

As mentioned in a previous chapter, the size of the beading around the edges of the headliner may indicate the amount of bonding used to install the bulkheads. The bonding must be hidden and something must cover this fiberglass bond. If a wide wooden trim is used to hide the bond, then the width of this trim reveals the width of the bonding. If there isn't any wood trim but only a vinyl bead, it is likely that there is no bonding at all. There is the possibility, however, that the builder may have covered the whole bulkhead with a veneer or other material to hide the bonding before the vinyl headliner was installed.

Accessibility

Every square inch of the hull should be accessible to clean, inspect, and repair if necessary. This is possible on some boats and not on others. On most boats, it is impossible to access behind the icebox because of the insulation between the interior liner and the hull.

I have seen boats that were infested with cockroaches and rats that lived behind an inaccessible liner. They can be killed with poisons, but how do you remove the remains?

Check your boat carefully for possible problems. It may be necessary to cut an opening to get into an inaccessible area. Do this before you leave home, or before you have a problem. This will require some careful consideration, so the cut out does not interfere with free movement and is not an eye sore.

Drawer catches

Many catches and latches on drawers do not hold in rough weather. When I first departed on my cruise, I had a notch cut into the bottom of the drawer so that the drawer dropped down over the cabinet frame to hold the drawer in place, as shown in Figure 88 (a). Before it could be pulled open, the drawer had to be lifted about a quarter inch. My first gale demonstrated that the notch design does not work.

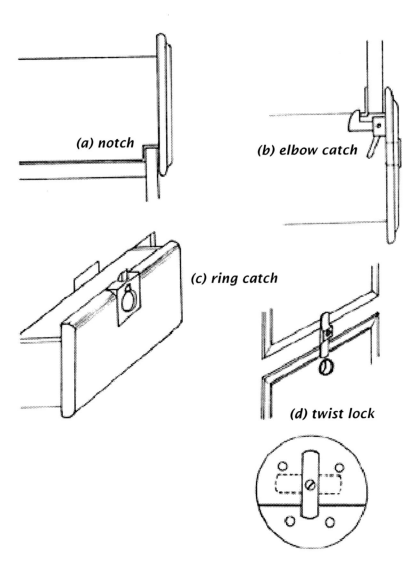

(a) notch

(b) elbow catch

(c) ring catch

(d) twist lock

Figure 88. Drawer catches

I tried installing elbow catches that could be accessed by passing a finger through a hole in the front of the drawer, as shown in Figure 88 (b). When the drawer was closed, the catch held it. To open the drawer, a finger was passed through the hole and the catch released. This system worked well until my next gale. I found that items in the drawer hit this catch, releasing it.

On my new boat, I installed special surface mounted catches that are positive locking when the drawer is closed and can be easily opened by lifting a ring, as shown in Figure 88 (c). It is not possible for something to hit the catch inside, forcing it open. I have not gone through a gale with this new latch, but I feel confident that it will not open accidentally.

If you already have the other type of catches on your boat, consider installing a simple twist-locking bar, shown in Figure 88 (d). The piece is turned to the horizontal position to open the drawer and turned in the vertical position to lock the drawer.

I have seen boats that use quick release pins shoved into a hole through the side of the cabinet, locking the drawer in place. I am sure there are many other ideas available. The important thing is to make sure the drawers do not open accidentally.

Also, all drawers should have stops to prevent them from coming completely out of the cabinet. This can be done easily by using a large washer with a hole drilled in one end. This washer is attached near the top inside back of the drawer with a machine screw, washer and nut that passes through the back of the drawer. When the washer is rotated up, the drawer will not come out. If it is pivoted down, the washer is clear of the cabinet frame and slides out completely. The washer is held in place by the pressure on the machine screw and nut that fastens it to the back of the drawer.

Cabin heater

Most cruisers head for the tropics to get away from the colder climates. If the boat is going to spend the duration of the cruise in the tropics, a heater would only take up valuable space. However, some cruisers will spend some time in colder climates, or in locations where there are seasons. These boats need some way to heat them.

There are several types of heaters available for boats: electrical, wood or coal burning, propane, kerosene, and diesel. The heater that uses electricity is really only good in port and not logical for a cruising boat. Once you leave the American continent, you may never see 110-volts AC again.

Wood or coal burning stoves look nice, feel great, put out lots of heat, but fuel to burn must be carried aboard. For this reason, the wood and coal burning stove is not a good choice for the cruising boat, unless the boat is large enough to have plenty of space for the fuel. In addition, this type of stove burns up oxygen inside the boat; hence, the boat must be properly vented to reduce any chances of carbon monoxide buildup.

Propane heaters are among the most common type used aboard cruising boats. If they are properly installed, they are excellent, although they don't put out as much heat as many other heaters. What I like about it is that the propane heater does not require any priming or kindling. I just light the pilot light with a match and adjust the flame to get the required heat. If it is cold, the pilot light can remain on for the whole day and night.

Diesel and kerosene-burning heaters put out more heat, measured in BTU's, than propane. Diesel and kerosene both require their own devoted tanks. If the tanks are located above the heater, the fuel can be gravity fed to it. If the tank is located below the heater, it will have to be pressurized to force the fuel up to it. This requires the space to access the tank to pump it up to the desired pressure. All this takes up more space.

If the boat will be spending a lot of time in colder climates, I suggest using a diesel or kerosene-burning heater. This can be a bit of a problem if the boat's fuel for the cooking stove is propane, because it means that two or more types of fuel must be carried. If that were the case, then I suggest a diesel-burning heater because diesel is already aboard for the engine.

All heaters require a flue for ventilation. The flue varies in size by the fuel being used. Diesel, wood, and coal burning heaters require the largest size flue. Next is the kerosene, followed by propane, which requires the smallest. This is an important consideration, because the flue pipe takes up lots of room below decks and a considerably large Charlie Noble on deck. The Charlie Noble must be designed and installed high enough so it draws properly, while keeping water out of the boat. If it is set too high, it can catch sheets and other lines on the boat. Look carefully at the size of the flue, the flue's required minimum length to draw correctly, and the size and design of the Charlie Noble before you invest in buying the heater. *You certainly don't want to cut holes in the deck only to discover later that the flue is too high.*

Head and holding tank

There are three primary types of heads available. There is the electrical head that is flushed by pushing or stepping on an electrical button or switch. There are manual heads where the waste is pumped out by hand. Finally, there are the portable heads that are self-contained; these are commonly known as Porta-Potties or Sanipotties.

Electrical heads come with a pump that either sucks out the waste or creates a vacuum to suck it out. Most electrical heads force the waste into a macerator, which grinds it into small particles before discharging overboard or into a holding tank. Some use fresh water and the existing pressure water system on the boat, while others use raw water. These heads are becoming more common on cruising boats because they work exceptionally well most of the time, and it is more like being at home. The only problems I am aware of are the logical ones: the amount of current draw, fresh water use, and electrical failure. It is rare that the electrical head is plugged up by using too much paper; however, there are some limitations to what can be flushed. If the intention is to buy an electrical head, *make certain it has a manual backup*, just in case something goes wrong.

The manual heads work the same as electrical heads except that the waste is removed by using a manually operated pump. In addition, the manual head does not have a macerator as part of the head components. The manual pump is usually located next to the bowl. There is a valve above or near the pump that determines if the head will only discharge, or will also pump in water at the same time waste is removed. These heads have been around for many years and work well.

The problem with the manual head is that the choker valve and flapper valve can become clogged and stop working. In some cases, water may still be pumped in, but the waste does not pump out. This may result in a head full of waste with no way to be removed other than by hand. Since the pump is connected to the bowl, the whole unit may have to be removed to make the necessary repairs. If there is adequate space, the head may be repaired where it is, but first, all the waste will have to be removed. Most boat owners have been through this at least once. If they haven't yet, they will eventually.

Personally, I like the head that has a separate pump away from the bowl. The only one I am aware of is the *LaVac* head from Britain.

The toilet bowl stands alone with no pumps connected to it. Somewhere near, there is a large *Henderson* pump similar to a large bilge pump. This pump has a removable plate to access the interior of the pump to remove whatever is fouling the valves. The pump is above the bowl, so there is no way the waste can run out of the pump during repairs. However, it might be necessary to set a bucket under the pump when opening the screw-on inspection plate, to catch any waste or liquid remaining in the pump.

The *LaVac* head works as a vacuum. There are seals under the lid and the seat. When they are closed, the seals make the inside airtight. The *Henderson* pump is pumped, and the lid and seat seals prevent air from entering. Thus, the pump sucks the waste out, leaving a slight vacuum in the bowl. It is this vacuum that sucks in clean water. As long as the head is pumped, waste goes out and water comes in. It is impossible to overfill this head, because as soon as the vacuum is broken, water stops entering the bowl. If only the waste is to be removed without bringing in water, just leave the lid open. If a little water is needed to remain in the bowl, close the lids and pump it a few times to create a vacuum. Only enough water will come in to break the vacuum. If for some reason, someone continues to pump, it will just start sucking out the excess water as it holds the vacuum. I have used this head extensively for years, use all the toilet paper I want, and the pump has never gotten plugged.

If the bowl of a *LaVac* or any manual head is mounted below the waterline, *there must be an anti-siphon vent installed in both the intake and exhaust hoses to prevent the ocean from siphoning back into the bowl.* This anti-siphon vent is usually located inside the boat, so there is always an odor. This problem can be prevented by installing a hose barb to the top of the anti-siphon vent and running a hose to a 'T' connection to the holding tank vent hose.

Today, in American waters and many other countries, it is required by law to have a waste-holding tank aboard. Unfortunately, it must be large enough to handle the needs of the whole crew for at least a week. It must also be durable, so there is no chance of it breaking or getting a leak.

Most holding tanks are made out of fiberglass or polyethylene, because the waste will attack most metals. Since plastic-type holding tanks are softer than metal, they must be firmly installed so they do not shift and abrade. If they are large, they should have baffles like the water tanks. It is essential that an inspection plate be installed to clean the tank once in awhile.

Odor from the holding tank can be reduced to nothing, if a large vent line is installed. This large vent line prevents the buildup of gases in the tank. I like at least a one-inch vent hose. If the tank is fairly big, two vents should be installed.

The holding tank is rarely used at sea, so diverter valves must be installed; in this way, the head can pump either directly overboard or into the holding tank. This same pump should be able to pump the holding tank overboard. With the *LaVac* head, I use the same *Henderson* pump with two diverter valves. One is mounted before the pump, so it sucks from the head or from the holding tank. The other is mounted after the pump and pushes the waste into the holding tank, or overboard. If not used regularly, these diverter valves have a tendency to clog up with lime deposits. The diverter valve should have a removable cover, so it can be easily serviced.

Then there are the self-contained heads that have none of the above problems. These heads are in two halves. The top is a refillable reservoir that is filled with water. In the center of this reservoir are the head bowl, seat, and lid. The bottom section is another reservoir that takes the waste. There is a hand pump on the top reservoir that pumps the clean water into the bowl. At the bottom of the bowl is a disc valve that permits the waste and water to drop into the bottom reservoir. A chemical is added to the bottom reservoir to break down the solid waste and reduce the smelly gases.

This may seem like the answer, because there are no real moving parts to breakdown, and it is so simple. There are, however, some problems with the self-contained portable heads. Most do not have enough capacity and must be dumped regularly. The bowl may be too shallow to handle the needs of the adult. Although it occurs rarely, sometimes when it is new, the discharge cap may leak; this is easily fixed with a new gasket. The only other problem is that they may get a crack in the bottom reservoir resulting in weeping waste; this, too, happens infrequently.

These self-contained heads are great for weekend sailing and for minimum number of crew. They are really made for temporary use. They are intended to be taken to a land toilet to empty the contents.

They can be used at sea and work well. Unfortunately, many are dumped in the anchorage after dark. I had one on my own boat and managed to live with it for years.

Ventilation

Air movement on a boat is critical to prevent the buildup of mould and keep the boat cool. The best way to get air moving is to have opening hatches, portlights, fans, and vents like cowl vents or solar vents.

The hatches should be able to hinge fore or aft, so they can act as air scoops. To increase the airflow, there are commercial, nylon cloth air-scoops available that fit over the hatches. These work really well, but must be taken down in a blow.

Portlights that open will help bring air in when the wind is from the beam. However, these should not be open while underway, unless the conditions are really mild. The amount of water that can enter through one of these open ports in an instant is unbelievable.

I read somewhere, perhaps in one of the Pardeys' books, the suggestion of using small buckets with a large hole cut out of one side. The bucket is shoved through the portlight opening from the inside, so the hole is facing the wind. The rest of the bucket keeps the rain and spray out. Again, this does not work at sea, because the force of a wave will wash the bucket away from the port. At anchor, it worked really well, but I could not use my mosquito netting at the same time. If the intention is to do some cruising in the tropics, you may want to consider carrying some of these small buckets and fitting mosquito netting over the end.

When conditions get rough or you leave the boat, all hatches and portlights should be closed. Unfortunately, this prevents or reduces ventilation, unless there are cowl vents or solar vents on the boat. I like to have large cowl vents mounted on dorade boxes, which direct air below but keep water from entering the boat. These vents can be rotated into the wind to bring wind into the boat, or away from the wind to suck air out of the boat.

I installed mosquito netting to the bottom of the cowl vents. I used a stainless steel mesh cut to fit the opening on the bottom. I placed this mesh on waxed paper, then I put a bead of 3M 5200 around the bottom of the cowl vent and positioned it on the mesh. I had to let it set up for a few days before the 3M 5200 cured properly.

The air from cowl vents enters the boat, blowing down the vent pipe. By using the appropriate size 45 PVC elbow shoved into this pipe on the inside, the air can be directed where it is needed most, like a berth.

Solar vents also work well, but they do not move much air. If there isn't any wind, they are welcome, regardless of the amount of air they move. If I leave the boat unattended for a long time, I use a cowl vent at the chainpipe forward, facing the expected wind direction, and a solar vent aft, set to remove air from the inside. This ensures air movement throughout the boat.

Not only should the boat be well-ventilated, but the lockers too. This will prevent mould from developing inside them. The simplest way to get a locker ventilated is to have vent holes in the front or sides of each locker. There are attractive louvers or vent covers that can be installed over the holes to hide them.

Chain locker bulkhead

The bulkhead between the chain locker and the rest of the boat should be watertight. The reason for this is that the anchor chain will often bring stinky mud aboard that could end up in the bilge, making the whole boat smell. Since the chain locker is watertight, there will have to be some type of pump installed to remove any water that settles under the chain. This can be an electrical or manual pump. If the chain locker does begin to smell, it is much easier to clean a small area than the whole bilge.

Watertight lockers

Some cruisers feel that the lockers should drain into the boat's bilge. The reason is that the liquid from a broken bottle or leaking can will not contaminate the rest of the supplies in the locker. On the other hand, if the locker is sealed so that liquids are trapped and don't enter the bilge, it makes the removal and cleanup easier. Needless to say, they both have their advantages. Personally, I much prefer to have to clean out a sealed locker, which is a much easier chore, than to have to clean up smelly rotten liquid out of the bilge.

Fiddles

It is amazing how short many fiddles are on boats. Some are just tall enough to tip a glass over if it slides against it. To work properly, fiddles must be at a 90 angle to the surface where they are mounted. I have seen many boats where the fiddles are installed backward: the taper is on the inside, and the flat surface is on the outside. On tables, I prefer no fiddles at all, or at least removable ones. I like to set my forearm on the table to eat, write, or draw. The fiddles make this uncomfortable. At sea, it doesn't matter, because I never sit at the table when the boat is rocking.

I feel that fiddles should be at least 2 inches high on galley counters or working counters, but not on tables. If there is any doubt about installing a fiddle in a particular location, make it removable. This can be accomplished by installing pins to the underside of the fiddle that match holes in the counter or table. I install 1/4-inch brass pins in the bottom of the fiddle that are evenly spaced and match the holes in the countertop. The countertop holes have a copper sleeve so they don't enlarge with use.

The problem is aligning these holes so they match perfectly. One way to do this is to clamp the fiddle where it will be located, then drill up through the surface into the fiddle with a smaller drill than required. This ensures alignment. If that is impossible because it is a countertop with a face, then round the exposed ends of the pins that will go into the fiddle before they are installed. After the pins are glued in place, press the fiddle down on to the surface until it leaves a dimple that marks the spot to drill. Carbon paper may make this easier.

Always start with a smaller drill because this will better align the larger drill. Selecting the final size to drill the hole will vary by the exact size of the brass pin and the matching copper tube. A 1/4-inch hole in the fiddle may be all right for a snug fit for a 1/4-inch brass pin. If the pin is too big for the hole, it will split the wood when driven into the hole. It may be necessary to drill with a 5/64-inch drill. The same principle applies to the copper insert: a 3/8-inch hole may work for a 3/8-inch copper tube, but it may be too tight, so a slightly larger drill may be required.

I like to slightly countersink the inside of the copper tube inserts on the top. Then, I hammer them in flush to the surface. The pins and inserts should be glued in place with a good adhesive like epoxy-type glue or 3M 5200 sealant.

Sails and rigging

Before you begin to make changes to the sails or rigging, be certain you know how to balance the boat correctly. If any changes are to be made, be sure they do not affect this balance. If anything, try to make changes that will improve the boat's balance.

Lazy jacks

When we first learned to sail, we were taught to always bring the boat into the wind to raise, drop, or reef the mainsail. There is no doubt that this procedure makes the chore easier. However, there are times when this can be dangerous. Because this will bring the boat's bow close to the wind, a breaking wave can easily force it onto the other tack, backwinding the jib, which could cause a broach. *Consequently, this procedure of bringing the boat into the wind should only be used in mild to moderate conditions.* There are times, however, when it is convenient and easier if the mainsail can be raised, lowered, or reefed while the boat is on any point of sail. This can be accomplished by making some minor modifications to the mainsail and the addition of lazy jacks, as shown in Figure 89.

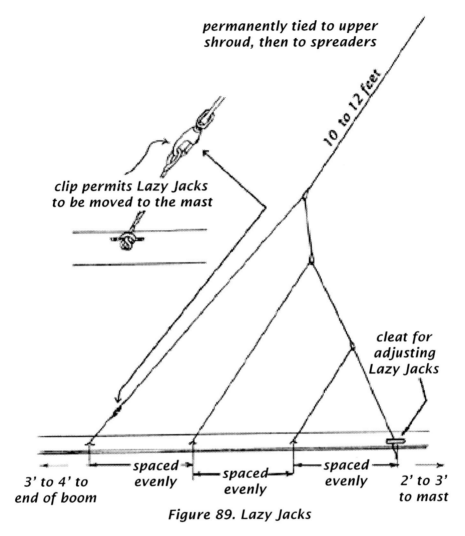

permanently tied to upper
shroud, then to spreaders

10 to 12 feet

clip permits Lazy Jacks
to be moved to the mast

cleat for
adjusting
Lazy Jacks

3' to 4' to
end of boom

spaced
evenly

spaced
evenly

spaced
evenly

2' to 3'
to mast

Figure 89. Lazy Jacks

The objective is to have the boom, in any position, fully supported
with the mainsail completely dropped. Most boats use a topping lift to
support the weight of the boom and mainsail. The topping lift usually
goes from the end of the boom to a block on the aft end of the
masthead and down alongside the mast to a cleat. The problem is that
the topping lift only supports the boom, but not the mainsail.
Personally, I don't like to have the adjusting line running down the
side of the mast. To adjust the topping lift, someone has to go
forward. Also, sometimes this line will slap the mast, driving those
trying to sleep into mutiny frenzy.

As mentioned previously, there are other ways to keep the mainsail on the boom. Most of these restrain the sail, but do not support the weight of the boom and the sail. For this reason, I like lazy jacks. They act as a topping lift, and they hold the mainsail on the boom when dropped. They permit the boom to be set in any position, with the mainsail restrained on the top of the boom.

The only problem I have encountered with lazy jacks is when raising the sails off the wind; if the mainsail has a headboard or battens in the roach, the battens or the headboard can catch under the lazy jacks. This can be resolved by eliminating the battens and sewing a negative roach in the leach of the sail. Also, the headboard can be replaced by making it come to more of a point and using boltrope sewn around it for strength. However, this will reduce some of the sail area and perhaps some windward performance, but I feel the advantages outweigh the disadvantages. If the boat has a bit of a weather helm, this will improve the balance. Of course, the opposite also applies.

Lazy jacks should be made from nylon, so they will stretch. I like three-strand because it is easier to backsplice, and it stretches more than braid. The smaller the size, the more they will stretch. On a 300-square foot sail, I use 1/4-inch line.

To reduce the chance of the head of the sail being caught under the lazy jacks, the top ends can be tied to the intermediate stays or to other shrouds. I use a rolling hitch around the stay, run the line up alongside the stay, and secure the end to the stay or shroud mast tang. This will prevent the lazy jacks from sliding down the shroud. The further outboard they are tied, the less of a chance that the headboard will pass under the lazy jacks. If they are tied too far away from the centerline of the boat, when on a run, their tension may change radically, causing the boom to twist. The distance from the lazy jack top to the centerline will vary by the height of the mast. On my own boat, I like it to be about 12 inches from the stay or shroud to the centerline.

To make the lazy jacks, I prefer using stainless steel thimbles one size smaller than the size of the line. This ensures a snug fit. After the backsplice is complete, I squeeze the ends of the thimble inward to prevent them from catching on sail stitching.

An open cleat at the forward end of the boom retains the excess lazy jack line for making adjustments. The lazy jack line should pass through the opening in the base of the cleat and terminate with a large knot to prevent it from being carried away by the wind.

The stern or aft end of the lazy jack should have about a 12-inch pennant attached to the boom. The loose end of the pennant has an eye spliced at the end. The other end of the lazy jack has a spring clip spliced at the end, so it can be attached or removed from the pennant eye.

The length of the boom or foot of the sail will determine the number of eyestraps needed along the boom to accept the lazy jacks. I think that the aft eyestrap should be at least 4 to 6 feet forward of the sail's clew. The forward cleat should be about 3 feet aft of the gooseneck. These are not critical measurements. Depending on the length of the boom, the distance between these two should be equally spaced. A shorter boom of about 14 feet can get away with one in the center between the two. A longer boom of about 18 feet would need two equally spaced between these two. Longer booms may need more. The eyestraps should be firmly fastened and properly bedded near the top of the boom. This will prevent the tendency to rotate the boom when one lazy jack is slackened. They should be installed at the same location on both sides of the boom.

I suggest that you start with all the lines longer than you think you will need to make the initial proper adjustment. Until the actual lengths are determined, it may be a good idea to just tie the thimbles in place. The lazy jacks are properly adjusted when they totally support the boom and sails when they are down, the same as a topping lift would do. The lines should look the same on both sides when taut.

If the lines are all made to the proper length, the lazy jacks can be moved to the mast to set up an awning. This is accomplished by releasing the aft lazy jack line with the spring clip from the pennant, then walking all the lazy jack lines to the mast. All the lines are pulled alongside the boom, so they are all equal. At the mast, this spring clip should be clipped to the highest thimble that can be reached. Then, the gathered lines are passed around an existing cleat on the mast. If there is not one already in place, one may have to be installed. There must be substantial tension on these lines, so they do not slap the mast in the wind. Not only does this permit an awning to be setup, but the mainsail cover can be installed over the lazy jacks as well.

While sailing, adjustments to the lazy jacks are done at the cleat on the boom where there should be some extra line. When on a run, I like to let the lee lazy jack loose, so the sail does not chafe against it. If there is no wind and I am motoring with the main up, it will slap from side to side with the roll of the boat. I like to adjust the lazy jacks in tight to prevent this violent slapping.

If boom gallows are used, the boom can be pulled down into the gallows as the nylon lazy jack lines stretch. When the main sheet is released, the boom and the mainsail should spring back up above the boom gallows. Then, the boom can be moved into any position, and the sails raised. When raising the sail on a dead run, it may be necessary to pull back on the leach a little until the head and battens pass the lazy jacks.

Mainsail

If lazy jacks are used, the mainsail should not have a headboard; instead, the leach of the sail should have a slight negative roach. If the sail must have a positive roach, then it will have battens. Battens on a cruising boat can cause problems by breaking or chafing through the batten pocket. Get to know your boat. If you feel confident with the battens, then you should use them. Needless to say, the full battened main must have battens, but be aware of the possibility of them breaking.

All working sails should have at least three rows of stitches. I like to have them in three different contrasting colors to the sail. This makes it easier to see torn stitches from the deck. When I discussed this with my sailmaker, he informed me that darker color threads have more UV protection than white threads. Apparently, this is because the UV protection is in the dyes used to color the thread.

Have leather sewn in locations where chafe can occur. This is especially important on the head of the sail and perhaps at all reef outhauls. All reef points should be adequately reinforced to prevent any chance of the sails ripping. If the sails have been used for a while, the chafe points should be apparent. If the sails are being made, discuss the locations where chafe could be expected. Your sailmaker has probably repaired many sails where chafe was serious, so he or she should know.

When the mainsail is dropped, it automatically falls or piles on both sides of the boom. This causes twisting where the sail is attached to the track slide. Therefore, sail slides on the mast should be attached to the sail grommet using webbing or something that will twist easily, instead of a stainless steel shackle. If the connections are made with something hard or sharp, it will chafe or cut into the luff boltrope.

I do not like to have a boltrope sewn into the foot of the sail that slides into a groove on the top of the boom, because this forces me to tie my reef points under the boom. If they are tied under the boom, they will bind the outhaul reef lines. I like these reef lines to be as frictionless as possible. I prefer the sail foot to have slides or slugs, so I can pass my reef lines under the sail, not the boom.

No matter how good of a sailor you are, tell-tales on all the sails will indicate the proper set of the sails. Unfortunately, these tell-tales do not last long, so it may be necessary to install them yourself. If the sails never had tell-tales, you should discuss with your sailmaker the proper locations for your particular sails.

Jib top or headsail

Today, most boats have roller furling headsails. As mentioned in the previous chapter, if they are properly cut, installed, and used as designed, they should provide many years of trouble-free sailing. I would not go to sea without it, especially on a boat with a bowsprit. I know there are those who will disagree with this, but this is my personal opinion. However, if I could not get my sheet lead to the headstay near the 90 angle and the sail area close to being equal above and below the sheet lead, I might have to reconsider the idea.

If the sail is hanked on, it should have a downhaul to make it easier to drop and keep on the deck after it is dropped. I know of some cruisers who lead this downhaul to the cockpit along with the jib halyard, so the sail can be dropped or raised from the cockpit. After the sail is down on deck, I like to have a line tied to the tack, so I can put a spiral wrap around the sail to keep it from coming loose. The length of this line would depend on the length of the sail's foot. It is also advisable to have some additional lines tied to the bulwarks or lifeline stanchions to hold the sail to the boat until it is removed and bagged or raised again.

If the sail has hanks, they must be serviced often. The sliding pin gets corroded, and salt builds up so it will not open or close. Frequent use and lubrication will keep them free and working as intended.

The method of attaching the sheets to the clew has always been a problem. If the sheets will remain rigged while the sails are changed, there has to be a method of attaching and removing the sheets. The easiest way to do this is by using a quick-release device like a snap shackle. These work well, but they are hard and heavy. If the sail is flogging and the shackle hits someone in the head, it could cause a serious injury. This is a real problem when the wind is strong, and the snap shackle is flogging with considerable force.

Some will tie the two sheets to the clew using a bowline. This reduces the danger considerably if the knot hits someone in the head. However, if the bowline is not tied snugly, it may come loose when under a load or on the next tack. There is a lot of stress load on the sheets and bowline, which could make untying the knot quite difficult, especially if the weather is rough. Another thing I don't like about the bowline as a means to attach the sheet to the clew is that the edge of the bowline knot will often catch around a shroud while tacking. The major advantages of this method are that the knot will not release if tied properly, and there is no hard shackle to cause injury or do physical damage.

The jib sheet can be one continuous line with the center of the sheet tied to the clew. This means the sheets must remain on the sail when it is removed. Each sail must have its own devoted sheets that must be run back to the cockpit with each sail change.

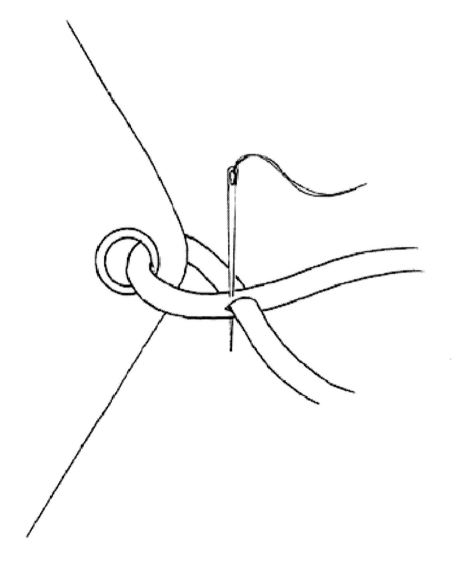

Figure 90. Attaching jib sheet to clew

I like to have the sheets devoted to each sail, but I don't use a knot that can get hung-up on shrouds. First, mark the center of the sheet. It is best if a piece of leather about three inches long is sewn around the sheet at this center point. One end of the sheet is slightly tapered, so it will pass though the center of the rope at the clew. The sheet is passed through the clew to the marked center or leather piece. On the side of the sheet, opposite the tapered end and a few inches from this center mark, a fid is passed through the center of the sheet rope. After the opening in the center of sheet rope is large enough, pass the tapered end through this hole, as shown in Figure 90. The rope is pulled through the hole until it is up loosely against the clew. Using a sail needle and waxed sewing thread, make multiple passes through the sheet at this point. After you feel confident that there are enough passes to prevent it from slipping, wrap more thread around it many times.

Working jibs or headsails should be cut so that the clew is high enough that it cannot catch green water or dip into the water while on a run. This would be less important on light wind sails like drifters and reachers, because they're only meant to be used in mild to moderate seas.

Like on the mainsail, all the headsails should have tell-tales properly located to indicate that the sails are adjusted correctly.

Mast and boom

Sail tracks

Most masts are made of aluminum or wood. The advantages and disadvantages have already been discussed in Chapter 3. The wooden mast must have an external track, while most aluminum masts have internal tracks. Regardless of the type of track, the sails should be able to be raised and lowered with as little friction as possible, especially if the sail is to be raised, lowered, and reefed while on any point of sail. This means the sail slides must move up and down the track as easily as possible, even when under a load.

I have a frictionless sail track extrusion installed in my existing mast track. I really like this, because the slides are longer to prevent binding in the track, and the track is made of a Teflon material that greatly reduces friction. Because I haven't used it long enough to know how it will last in the tropical sun and cruising environment, I can't recommend it yet. If I find it doesn't last, I can remove it and use the existing track.

Mast steps

I like to have steps on my mast, so I can easily and quickly go aloft to look ahead, inspect rigging, or work on the mast. There are different types available. I feel the safest kind is in the shape of a triangle that encloses the foot, so it cannot slip out of the step when the boat rolls. The ones that are more unobtrusive and have less effect on windage are not enclosed. They are made of cast aluminum and fold up against the side of the mast.

The enclosed steps are normally made from stainless steel, but some are made from aluminum. The problem with stainless steel steps is the possibility of electrolysis eating away the aluminum mast. Good bedding or an insulating material between the mast and step can help reduce electrolysis. Most steps are fastened to the mast using stainless steel fasteners, which increases the chances of electrolysis. The aluminum steps have the same problem if they are fastened to the mast with stainless steel fasteners. A good quality bedding compound made for this purpose will considerably improve the insulation quality of the stainless steel fasteners. Using aluminum rivets can eliminate the problem of electrolysis on the mast; however, if the step is stainless steel, the electrolysis may erode the aluminum fastener at the step. Aluminum rivets are not nearly as strong as stainless steel, so a larger size should be used.

Other problems with the enclosed-type steps are that they are not necessarily pleasing to the eye, they create more weight and windage aloft, and the halyards can get caught behind them. There isn't much that can be done about the aesthetics issue without going to the fold-up steps. Using aluminum-enclosed steps can reduce the weight, but these are usually bigger, increasing the windage.

To prevent the halyards from being caught behind the triangular mast steps, a line can be passed through a couple of holes at the outside end of each step and run up to the spreaders, then terminated at the mast head. Another way to prevent the halyards from catching behind the mast steps is to tie a monofilament line from the end of each step horizontally to the upper shroud. The monofilament line will make the line less visible. However, this creates another problem: birds can't see the line either. There is little doubt that some larger sea birds will leave some feathers on the deck.

If the problems with the enclosed steps are a concern for you, you can install the fold-up steps instead. These are made of cast aluminum; they fold up and lock against the side of the mast. The halyards cannot catch on them, they create less windage and weight aloft, and they are more unobtrusive.

However, I must warn you that there are several problems with these fold-up mast steps. There is only a short raised edge at the end of the step to prevent the foot from sliding off when the boat rolls. This would not be a problem normally, but again, only one slip may be one too many. I am concerned about their strength if a 200+ pound man puts all his weight on the end. The manufacturers state that they rarely break, but even one break could be fatal. There is also the problem that stainless steel threaded screws are used to fasten them to the mast. This increases the possibility of electrolysis with the fasteners.

I installed the aluminum fold-up steps on my new boat. One major problem I found with these steps is that the end of the step can be accidentally kicked up as you climb. This puts the step up at an angle, but not locked against the mast. It is difficult to return down the mast and to find a step if it is not in the horizontal position. It takes some effort to get my toe under the base of the step and pull it up so it will fall back horizontally. I often just skip it, making it one very long stretch. Of course, this would depend on their spacing.

Most mast steps are spaced about 3 feet apart on one side of the mast. The other side is spaced the same, but staggered. This makes each step about 1 foot, 6 inches apart. The spreaders can act as a step as long as you stand close to the mast. When I figured the spacing of my steps, I measured down from the lower spreaders, beginning with a step 18 inches below the spreader. Then, I staggered them 3 feet apart from there to where I could step on the boom or a winch. I measured the distance between the upper and lower spreaders and divided this distance by the length between steps, then adjusted as necessary. From the upper spreaders to about 4 feet below the masthead, the steps were equally spaced at the 18-inch intervals. At the uppermost step, I put one on both sides of the mast at the same level, so I could comfortably stand and work on the masthead.

Another consideration with all mast steps is the number and size of the fasteners. There should not be too many holes drilled into the mast in the same area. Keep the holes as far apart as possible, because this could reduce the mast's strength at these locations.

Boom as whisker pole

Depending on the length of the boom, it can be used as a whisker pole to hold one of the headsails out when sailing off the wind. This can be done in two ways. One is to attach a snatch block to the end of the boom and lead the jib sheet through the block and back to additional blocks that lead to the winch. This may not work depending on the sheet lead and the number of blocks required to accomplish it. The only problem using this method is that it is more difficult to control the position of the boom because it is under a compression load.

An alternative is to use the same snatch block at the end of the boom, but lead the sheet forward along the bottom of the boom to a cleat. Now, the mainsheet can control the boom, which will control the headsail fore and aft to suit the conditions. I have used this method many times when running off the wind and have had two headsails set out wing on wing.

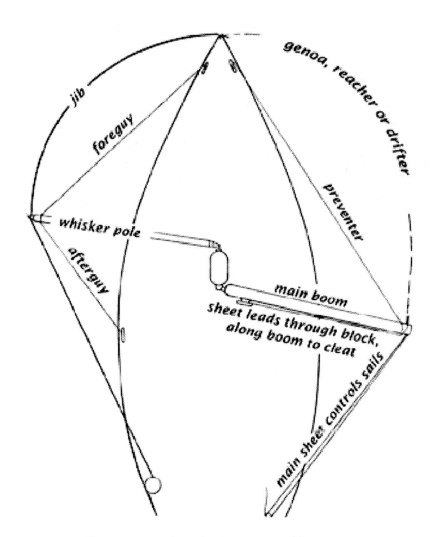

jib

genoa, reacher or drifter

foreguy

preventer

whisker pole

afterguy

main boom

sheet leads through block, along boom to cleat

main sheet controls sails

Figure 91. Using the boom as whisker pole

Using either of these methods, the mainsail can be left up to maintain the boom's height, or the mainsail can be dropped, and the boom height can be controlled by the lazy jacks or topping lift. It may be necessary to use a boom vang and preventer to get the boom in the desired position. I normally drop the mainsail to reduce any chances of a gybe.

Boom vang

As I mentioned previously, I like to keep my boom vang permanently attached to the underside of the boom. This makes it so much easier to store and use. I attach a rubber snubber to the vang bail near the center of the boom, then lead the boom vang forward to a cleat near the gooseneck. The boom vang's snap shackle and excess line is attached to this cleat. After the sail is set in position, I release the forward end of the boom vang that has a snap shackle and lead it to a shackle that I keep permanently attached to the top of the lower aft shroud turnbuckle. I don't like using deck cleats that are designed to have a side pull. The upward pull may break the cleat's seal after extensive use.

I have the cam cleat of the boom vang installed upside down, so I can release the line by pulling it down instead of up. I find it easier to control the line than if the cam cleat were the other way around. The line is led back to the cockpit, so I can control it without going forward. This will vary by the boat and the length of the boom.

Boom preventer

On booms that are short, the boom vang can act as the preventer. On longer booms, using the boom vang as a preventer could possibly dip the end of the boom when running; additionally, the boom vang may cause the boom to break at the boom vang bail. *For this reason, the preventer should be attached to the aft end of the boom.* This creates some problems, because the preventer must lead from the aft end of the boom, outside the shrouds, to a fairlead or hawsehole forward. If the preventer will be controlled from the cockpit, the line must lead back to the cockpit. Before a tack or a gybe, someone would have to walk forward and disconnect the preventer line from its cleat; the preventer would then have to be walked around to the other side and lead outside the shrouds as before.

Another concern is that the end of the boom cannot be reached while on a run. To attach the preventer may require sheeting the boom in close enough to reach it. This is dangerous, because it brings the sail closer to a possible gybe. It is far better if the preventer line is already connected to the end of the boom before the sail is let out on a run.

I have two preventer lines that are tied to the boom bail at the end of the boom. One line is tied on the port side of the mainsheet block and the other to the starboard side. These two lines are slightly shorter than the boom and have a stainless steel ring tied at the other end. These two lines with the rings lead forward under the boom to where they are attached to a hook at the end of a small bungee cord. This keeps the preventer lines snugly under the boom, as shown in Figure 92.

There are two additional preventer lines, one for each side of the boat. There is a snap shackle on one end of these lines. This snap shackle is normally attached to the upper shroud at shoulder level. The preventer line runs from this snap shackle forward, through a hawsehole or fairlead, then back to the cockpit. If the preventer is not to be used, the end at the cockpit is tied to a lifeline stanchion, so it does not interfere with movement along the deck. If the line will be used as a preventer, I move the end of this line to a cam cleat on the cockpit coaming.

To use the preventer, the boom and sail are set out to one side in the running position. The preventer on the same side, under the boom, is removed from the bungee hook and walked to the snap shackle on the upper shroud. The snap shackle is released and attached to this ring. Then, the proper adjustments are made back in the cockpit.

To tack, I bring the boom and sail across while controlling the preventer. When the boom is in position, I release the preventer line in the cockpit. I walk forward to release the other preventer line under the boom and attach it to the snap shackle on the new side.

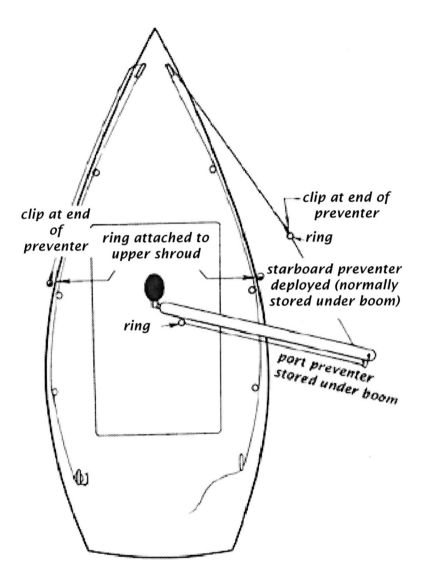

clip at end
of
preventer

ring attached to
upper shroud

clip at end of
preventer

ring

starboard preventer
deployed (normally
stored under boom)

ring

*port preventer
stored under boom*

Figure 92. Boom preventer

Engine and fuel tanks

This section pertains primarily to the diesel engine rather than the gasoline engine. Nowadays, it is unlikely that a cruising boat will have anything other than a diesel engine. However, many of the ideas discussed here will apply to both fuels, so if you do have a gasoline engine, use those items that are relevant for you.

Fresh-water vs. raw-water cooled engines

I prefer the fresh-water cooled engine over the salt-water cooled one, because it reduces the chances of deposits accumulating around the cylinders. A fresh-water cooled engine only has salt water at the condenser or where it cools the fresh water. This is a small chamber and is usually easy to access to clean.

The salt-water cooled engine has salt water circulating through the engine and the cylinder heads. If it is not run hot enough, calcium and salt deposits develop in the engine. As these deposits build up, the cooling effect is reduced. To eliminate the deposits requires removing the cylinder head, and this is a lot of work.

One of the problems with any water-cooled engine is the efficiency of the water pump. Fresh-water pumps use solid or rigid pump blades like in a car. Usually, the only way these fail is when the bearing or seals need replacement. Therefore, they are of little concern. If there is a problem, it will still cool, but not as efficiently.

The problem normally occurs at the raw-water pump. This pump uses a rubber impeller to force the movement of the water. This impeller is sensitive to heat and friction; consequently, if it runs dry, it quickly fails. Like the fresh-water pump, this rarely happens instantly; instead, it reduces the pump's efficiency so that the engine will begin to overheat when run hard.

Another consideration is that the raw-water cooled engine has only one pump to worry about. The fresh-water cooled engine has two. If it overheats, it is normally the salt-water pump impeller. However, if you find it is okay, then the fresh-water pump must be inspected.

Raw-water pressure gauge

In order to record the normal running pressure at cruising rpms, I installed a stainless steel salt-water pressure gauge in the raw-water cooling line after the pump, as shown in Figure 93. If the gauge shows the pressure is not up to its normal reading, it is time to replace the impeller, before the problem becomes more serious.

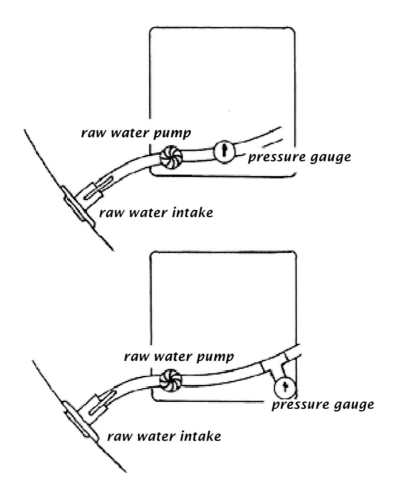

Figure 93. Raw-water pressure gauge

Double fuel filters with diverter valve

Diesel engines have their own fuel filter. Most boats have a primary filter installed to remove water as well as sediment, before the fuel reaches the engine's filter. When this primary filter is dirty or clogged with sediment, it can starve the engine of fuel; therefore, it must be changed. This requires stopping the engine, changing the filter, then bleeding the line of air between the filter and the engine. If air gets past the engine's filter, it goes into the fuel pump and then enters the injector pump and the injectors, which stops the engine. This makes it more difficult to bleed the lines, but it must be done to restart the engine.

Having two primary fuel filters with a couple of diverter valves and a priming pump bulb in the line can prevent most of the above problems, as shown in Figure 94.

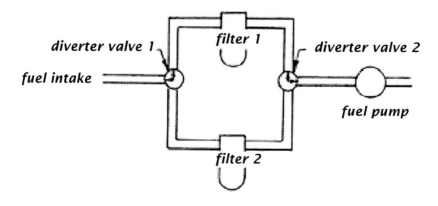

Figure 94. Double primary fuel filters with diverter valves

Hand bulb or fuel pump to prime fuel lines

By installing a priming hand bulb on the fuel line, priming the fuel system can be made much easier. This bulb is like those used on outboard engine fuel tanks, as shown in Figure 95.

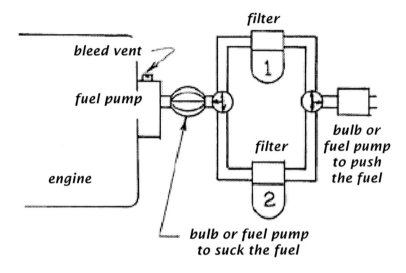

Figure 95. Hand bulb or fuel pump to prime fuel lines

The hand bulb is not Coast Guard approved, so it may be better to use an electric fuel pump with diverter valves. The fuel moves much faster than it does using the engine fuel pump to manually bleed the air out. The bulb or fuel pump can be installed before or after the fuel filters. If a bulb is installed after the fuel filters, the bulb will begin to collapse as the fuel filters get dirty. This could be used as a warning sign instead of the vacuum gauge described below. If the hand bulb is installed before the fuel filters, the air can be bled out at the top of the filters, so it is not necessary to bleed the air at the engine fuel pump. However, this could vary by engine manufacturer. If there is any doubt, it simply requires opening the bleed screw on the engine fuel pump and using the hand bulb or fuel pump to bleed out the air. *The filter not being used cannot be changed and bled while the engine is running.* This can be accomplished by installing additional diverter valves; however, this becomes complicated and does not ensure elimination of trapped air without installing an additional bleed screw.

Vortex-type fuel filter used as primary filter or to polish and bleed fuel lines

Vortex-type filters, shown in Figure 96, do not have elements that must be replaced. Instead, they separate water and sediment by forcing the fuel into a vortex, which forces the water and heavier particles out to settle at the bottom of the filter, where it can then be drained.

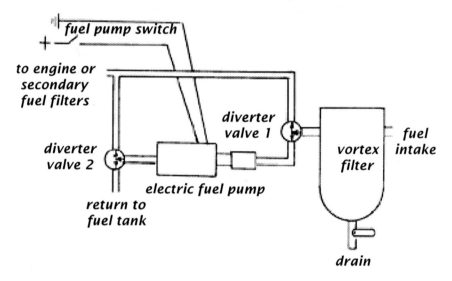

Figure 96. Vortex filter as primary engine filter or to polish and bleed fuel lines

The problem with these filters is that they are designed for higher fuel consumption than most small diesel engines use. However, if the filter is connected to an electric fuel pump, it can be used to polish the fuel and bleed fuel lines. I have one on my boat. Every time I take on new fuel, I run the pump to polish the fuel in the fuel tank. This actually recycles all the fuel through the vortex filter, which keeps the fuel in the tank free from water and sediments.

If the fuel pump and vortex filter are going to be in line with the existing fuel system, two diverter valves are necessary. One diverter valve will direct the fuel from the vortex filter to the engine's secondary filters and engine, or to the electric fuel pump for polishing or bleeding. The other diverter valve is used to direct the fuel from the electric fuel pump back to the fuel tank for polishing, or to the engine fuel lines for bleeding. The system is easy to install and greatly reduces the possibility of fuel problems. I suggest a small or low volume vortex filter as well as a fuel pump that closely matches the filter's rating. This will ensure maximum efficiency of the vortex filter. *Keep in mind that there are electric fuel pumps that are only rated for gasoline and not diesel. Also, some are not Coast Guard approved.*

Fuel vacuum gauge

A vacuum gauge installed in the main fuel line, after the primary filters, will indicate when the fuel filter is dirty. The engine fuel pump sucks the fuel from the secondary filter, if one or more is installed. If the sucking pump has to work harder, it shows on the vacuum gauge. When this happens, the diverter valve between the two filters is switched to the other filter, while the dirty filter is changed.

Start button in engine room

I like to have a start button installed in the engine room, to make bleeding the injectors easier. I release the compression lever and tap the button to turn the engine over, until the air is bled out of each injector. It also comes in handy if the primary start button fails from corrosion.

Engine controls by foot

This seems a bit silly, but the truth is that I often control my engine speed and gears with my toes. This permits me to stand and look ahead without constantly bending down to make the change or adjustment. If the engine control lever is a single lever that controls speed and shifting from forward to reverse, there is a stop or detent at the neutral position to prevent shifting gears without a momentary pause. This detent is a spring stop that requires the fingers to lift the spring before shifting to another gear. To use the toes, this must be removed. The only concern is that the engine is not inadvertently shifted directly from one gear position to another without pausing in the neutral position. This takes some practice.

Dampening coupler

A rubber dampening coupler can be installed between the engine drive flange and the shaft hub. These dampening couplers will reduce vibration and reduce the chance of gear damage if the engine's reduction gear or transmission is forced between gears without a pause. Be sure to consider that this will lengthen the shaft by the thickness of the coupling. In case the coupler fails, it is best not to cut off the shaft. However, I have never heard of one failing.

Kill switch or fuel shut-off

There are rare times when a diesel engine will get hot and continue to run on its own. When this happens, it is almost impossible to stop. One easy and simple way to stop it is to stop the fuel entering the engine. Most engines have a fuel kill switch. It is the most common way to stop an engine. However, if it does not have one, you should consider installing one. If you have to install one, it should be as close to the engine as possible; I suggest between the fuel pump and injector pump. If this kill switch will not stop the engine, then it must be starved of air. A piece of wood over the air intake will work. *Never use a rag; it will be sucked into the air intake. Also, don't use your hand; it can be badly damaged if the engine is fairly big and running at high revolutions.*

Oil drain

Draining the oil on a boat can be a real pain. The drain plug is normally not accessible, so the oil must be pumped out through the dipstick pipe. This makes a real mess and does not remove the dirty oil standing in a lower part of the oil pan.

The next time you remove the engine and can access the drain plug, replace it with an elbow and a special reinforced hose with a valve on the end. Needless to say, this must be done properly, so the oil does not leak through these connections and the hose.

Anti-siphon valve

If the engine is installed below the waterline, an anti-siphon valve must be put in to prevent the ocean from being siphoned back into the engine. There will be a hose connected from the engine's water exhaust to the anti-siphon valve, then back to the engine exhaust. The hose can be installed further down the exhaust line or at the muffler system.

If this valve fails for some reason, water may siphon back into the engine, flooding it with water. This is a serious problem if it is not caught early enough. I have often seen this occur on older boats.

There are two solutions to this problem. The simplest is to check and clean the anti-siphon valve frequently. The other is to eliminate the valve all together. This would entail having an open line to some place above the waterline, where it would be impossible to siphon water back into the engine. This is a simple thing to do. A solid stainless steel tube or quality exhaust hose is connected at the exhaust connection before the anti-siphon valve. This hose or tube then leads overboard far enough above the waterline that it is impossible to siphon water back into the engine. While the engine is running, there will always be some salt water flowing out this outlet.

On my own boat, I drilled and tapped the fitting for the cockpit drain and threaded in a hose barb. I used quality 3/8-inch hot water hose between the engine and the hose barb. The moment I started the engine, I looked into the cockpit drain to see water flowing. This confirmed that the raw-water pump was working properly. The downside to this method is that you would not want to have the cockpit pooped while running the engine. For this reason, some prefer to lead this line over the stern or the top aft side of the boat.

Light in engine room

This seems too obvious to even mention; however, I have delivered boats that did not have a light in the engine room. I had to use a 12-volt DC work light or a flashlight to work on the engine. On my small 28-footer, I have two lights: one so I can clearly see the entire engine and another to see the shaft and exhaust fittings.

Emergency parts and tools readily available

In a previous chapter, I gave an example of how important it is to have emergency parts and tools readily available. The time may come when the cooling pump V-belt breaks, and the engine overheats at a critical moment. It may be essential to fix the problem before there is damage to the engine, or the boat goes on the rocks. If the proper tools and a spare belt are nearby, the job is a lot shorter. On my own boat, I have a small box that has spare V-belts, spare water pump impellers, spare fuel filters, and the necessary open-end wrenches, which are marked for where they are needed. This box is stored in the engine room within an arm's reach.

Spare parts

It is essential that any cruising boat carry as many spare parts as possible. A problem with the engine may occur when you are many miles or days from a large city where parts can be bought or ordered. The following is a list of what I would consider the *minimum* to carry. The quantity of each would vary by the reasonably expected need.

> Primary Fuel Filters
> Engine Fuel Filters
> Oil Filters
> Air Cleaner Filter
> Alternator V-Belt
> Water Pump V-Belt
> Raw-water Pump Impeller
> Thermostat
> Gaskets for all of the above
> Gasket Seal
> At least one Injector
> Copper Compression Washers for Injectors

I should note that the copper washers used on the pressure side of the fuel system should not be reused; they are made of soft copper and intended to compress when properly tightened. However, they can be reused if they are annealed. This is accomplished by getting the copper washer red-hot and dropping it in cold water. This softens the copper material, so it will still compress. *This procedure should not be done too often to the same copper washer.*

Fuel additives

It is common for cruising boats to grow a fungus in their diesel fuel. Water or moisture in the fuel causes the growth of this fungus. This normally happens when contaminated fuel is taken aboard. Water in the fuel tank can also come from condensation caused by leaving the tank low on fuel in warm climates. A drain on the bottom of the fuel tank can help eliminate the problem; however, it has to be drained often.

If there is any doubt about the condition of the fuel, use an additive that will kill this fungus. Do this before it has a chance to grow to the point that the fuel tank has to be removed to clean. This fungus, if picked up by the fuel intake, will quickly clog the fuel filters, stopping the engine. New filters will only provide a temporary reprieve and will soon clog. This will continue until the fungus is removed from the fuel tank. It is far better to prevent it from happening in the first place.

There are fuel conditioners that help keep the injectors clean. When I don't use a diesel fuel conditioner, my transom gets black from the exhaust, and the smell of diesel fumes is strong. When I use a conditioner, I get better fuel consumption, the smell of diesel fumes is negligible, and the transom stays clean. As far as I know, these conditioners can be used regularly. They should not, however, exceed the percentage mixture recommended by the manufacturer. Consequently, if the remaining fuel in the tank already has been treated, only add enough conditioner required for the amount of fuel taken aboard.

Record fuel consumption

It is important to know how much fuel is consumed at various revolutions per minute. This should be recorded and readily available. A situation may arise when you have to motor for a long period of time and don't know if there is sufficient fuel to make it to your destination. If you figure that you are going to cut it close, you can reduce the speed until you feel certain that there will be enough fuel.

You should *never* run too low on fuel, because it can suck air into the fuel line when the boat rolls. A sump in the bottom of the fuel tank will partly, but not entirely, help prevent this.

Run the engine under a load at all times

Most cruisers have a tendency to run the engine in neutral while they charge batteries or cool down the refrigerator. Unfortunately, this will prevent the diesel engine from achieving the proper temperature to thoroughly burn the fuel. If the engine does not reach proper temperature, carbon is developed that can build up in the exhaust system, which will cause the engine to overheat. Not only does running the engine in neutral cause this problem, but running at lower revolutions for long periods of time will have the same results.

Prop puller

Every boat should carry an extra prop and a prop puller to change the prop. When making a long passage under sail, I like to use a two-bladed prop to reduce drag. I use a three-bladed prop when I know I will be doing a lot of motoring. I have had bad luck with prop pullers, because one type is needed for a three-bladed prop and another for a two-bladed prop. They are hard to find in stainless steel, so they rust in the locker.

One way to solve this problem is to drill and tap three holes in the aft end of the hub of the prop so they will take three, 5/16-18 all-thread stainless steel rods, as shown in Figure 97.

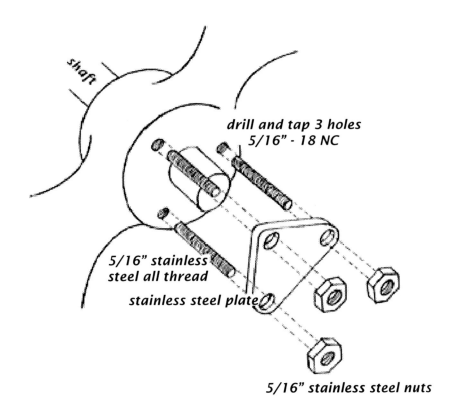

drill and tap 3 holes
5/16" - 18 NC

5/16" stainless steel all thread

stainless steel plate

5/16" stainless steel nuts

Figure 97. Prop puller

It also requires a stainless steel plate that has 3/8-inch holes spaced exactly the same as the holes in the prop hub. When the all-thread rods are threaded into the prop hub, they must be long enough to pass beyond the end of the shaft and still take the stainless steel plate, a nut, and a washer.

To remove the prop, the shaft nut must first be removed. Then the all-thread rods are threaded into the hub. The stainless steel plate is placed over these three all-thread rods, then the washers and nuts are applied. As the nuts are all equally tightened, the plate is pulled against the end of the shaft until the prop breaks its hold. If it doesn't release, it may have to be tapped with a hammer while it is under tension. It helps if the taper on the shaft is greased before the prop is installed. I also use lanolin grease to fill the holes in the prop hub to prevent growth inside the threaded holes. The puller is stored on the other prop aboard.

Bronze prop key

Some sailors use stainless steel square keys on the prop shaft to prevent the brass prop from turning on the shaft. If the prop hits something, the stainless steel key is too strong to shear, so the softer prop keyway or slot that takes the key, will be damaged. It is difficult to repair a damaged keyway inside the prop; a new one would have to be cut.

Using a softer shaft key eliminates this problem. Be sure to carry plenty of extra keys or a long length of key material, so they can be cut off as needed. If possible, try to avoid brass because the zinc in the brass will be affected by electrolysis.

Shaft packing gland

There are many kinds of shaft packing glands on the market today, and I think they all work well. The older type used a packing material compressed between a threaded tube and a matching nut. As the nut was tightened, the packing material compressed around the shaft, preventing water from entering the boat. The problem with this method was that it had to have a little water to keep it from getting hot and damaging the packing material. Consequently, there was always a little water dripping into the bilge. However, it was easy to replace the packing material every few years. Today, there are Teflon packing materials that prevent or radically reduce the amount of water that drips into the boat.

The type of gland that does not let water enter is called a dripless gland. There are many brands available. They all work well, and all have the same advantage: no water enters the boat. They also all have the same disadvantage: they are susceptible to being damaged by sand entering the gland and abrading the watertight surface. This requires the replacement of one part or the whole gland and necessitates removal of the shaft from the engine hub, so the damaged part can be taken out and a new one installed.

Shaft plug

Every boat should have a shaft plug aboard for emergency shaft repairs. This plug must be the same diameter as the shaft, but only about 10 inches long. If you have the old packing gland that uses packing material, it is an easy job. I have done it several times on my own boat in the water.

First, I remove the prop from the shaft. (I have an outboard rudder just behind the prop, so the shaft cannot be removed with the prop on the shaft.) Then, I replace the shaft nut and tie a line snugly around the shaft, so it doesn't drop to the bottom of the ocean.

Inside the boat, I remove the shaft from the engine hub and the key from the keyway. I push the shaft out until the end of the shaft is at the end of the stern gland. Then, I use the shaft plug to push the shaft out of the stern gland. I tighten the stern gland around the shaft plug. This permits me to work on the shaft out of the boat while the boat is still in the water. Unfortunately, most of the dripless glands do not permit the shaft to be removed under water using this method, but it certainly can reduce the amount of water that enters the boat.

Electrical and electronics

Electronics are changing so rapidly in our advancing technological society that whatever I write here will probably be obsolete by the time the book goes to print. Before you run out and buy a piece of electronics, check all models to see which ones are up-to-date and fit your particular needs. Electronics should be one of the last items purchased for a boat, so you get the latest model.

One of the most important ingredients for a successful cruise is to make the boat as comfortable as possible—to have everything you really need aboard. However, when you begin adding electrical items, you must remember that *you cannot rely on them*. If you cannot repair them yourself, cannot find a person who can repair them, or cannot afford to have them repaired, then they will just be taking up space. The usefulness or pleasure they once provided will no longer be there. Their failure should not be essential to the safe functioning of the vessel. They should just be convenience items.

Batteries

I am reluctant to discuss the batteries to use on a boat, because they are so complex and varied that a whole book could be devoted to the subject. It is not my intention to educate the reader on which is better or worse, but to make suggestions based on my own experience.

Batteries on a boat should be deep cycle, which means that the battery can be drained until it is almost dead and take a full charge to get back to maximum capacity. The battery that is not deep cycle, like an automobile battery, will not take a full charge after it is nearly dead. The more times this happens, the less the battery will recharge. *Consequently, only deep cycle batteries should be aboard a boat.*

The types of batteries that are available are flooded or wet batteries, gel-filled batteries, and AGM batteries. The most common battery used is the flooded or wet battery. This battery is filled with acid, which can be accessed to fill when it gets low. Some advantages of this battery are that it will take a higher charge than the others, and there is less chance of damage if the battery is overcharged. If it is discharged and recharged more often, the deep cycle flooded or wet battery also has a longer life.

The disadvantage of the flooded or wet-type is that the acid, which is extremely corrosive, can leak or be spilled out of the battery. They must be installed upright to reduce any chance of spillage. They exude an acidic fume when being charged that can affect any electronics near the battery. They require regular maintenance to ensure that the battery is properly filled.

Gel-filled batteries are not filled with a liquid, but with a gel. This permits the battery to be sealed, so there is no chance of liquid acid spilling or leaking out of the battery. It does not emit an acidic fume when being charged, and it does not have to be maintained. It can be stored on its side with minimum loss of efficiency.

There are some disadvantages of gel-filled batteries. To get the same amp-hours as wet batteries, you need heavier gel-filled batteries. Also, gel-filled batteries are more susceptible to damage if they are not properly charged, and they cannot be serviced if overcharged.

AGM batteries use a dense, absorbent, fiberglass mat between the plates. Like gel batteries, they are sealed, so they cannot leak liquid and require no maintenance. These batteries were designed for the aircraft industry because of their reliability, efficiency, and ability to work in any position except upside-down. They can even be submersed without damage.

There are few disadvantages to the AGM batteries, except that they are expensive and are sensitive to proper charging. They can be damaged if overcharged.

The advantages and disadvantages mentioned are only those that I consider most important. I suggest you do your own research before buying your batteries.

It is important that the batteries you use are all the same type. Because they all have different charging requirements, they should not be mixed. It is also a good idea to replace all the batteries at the same time, rather than one at a time, for the same reason.

On my own boat, I have all AGM batteries, because they take the same charging rate and can be installed in any position. Because of space limitations, I have several mounted on their side.

Crimp connectors vs. soldering

When an electrical item fails, it is usually because of corrosion in one of the connections. This happens far more often in the tropics, where the air is very moist and salty. As long as the boat is on the water, there will be more moisture than on land, and it will eventually have an effect on all electrical items aboard. I soldered all my connections on my cruising boat. I never, in all my years of cruising in the tropics, had any of these electrical connections fail. However, some of the items that were crimped by the manufacturer—or items that I added later by crimping—did fail.

I can almost hear the screams now from those who believe so strongly in crimped connections. I know some say that a crimped connection is as good as a soldered connection—or better. What many do not realize is that for a crimped connection to work as designed, the proper tool must be used with the correct size, matching connector. If you use one of those inexpensive crimping tools that merely makes a dimple in the center of the connector, you can be sure it will fail before the others.

Those who are strong advocates of the crimped connection argue that a soldered connection will break the wire at the end of the rigid soldered section. The rationale is that when the wire moves, it will weaken where the solder prevents movement. It is like taking a wire and bending it back and forth until it breaks. There is some truth to this argument; but let's face it, the wire should not be moving, regardless of the connection used. All wires should be ganged together in clusters or a harness to prevent movement.

I would certainly like to see an unbiased test between the solder connection and the crimped connection done in a tropical environment. Unfortunately, the only information I have ever seen on such comparisons was done by the manufacturers of the connectors and their crimping tool.

Breaker switches vs. fuses

This is another controversial comparison. They both have their advantages and disadvantages. Breaker switches are expensive, especially when you consider the number that may be required. They can corrode or fail internally and must be replaced at considerable cost. They are usually disposable, not serviceable. I have yet to see a breaker switch that can be simply opened to clean the contacts. The major advantage to the breaker switch is that it will automatically break the connection when overloaded and can be reset simply by throwing the switch back to the 'on' position.

Breaker switches must be purchased so they will break the connection just above the expected load of the items they are to protect. If too high an amperage rating is used, the item it is intended to protect may be damaged before the breaker switch breaks the connection. If the amperage rating is too low, the breaker switch will break the connection too early, cutting off power to the unit it is protecting; this can also cause damage. This means that there must be many spares aboard for the different amperage needs. If a breaker switch fails, one of the same amperage should replace it.

On the other hand, the fuse is inexpensive and easy to replace at minimal cost. It does not have a switch to reset; instead, the fuse must be replaced. The major problem I have encountered with fuse boxes is that some have crimped connections, which can fail. Those that are soldered are less of a concern. Unlike breaker switches of the same ratings, fuses of all amperages are available all over the world. Four or five boxes of fuses will take up about the same storage space as one breaker switch.

I feel the only major difference between the two is cost. Personally, I like the breaker switches, although I still have some inline fuses.

E-Meter

Xiphias, the boat I cruised on extensively, did not have an E-Meter. *Nereus*, my new boat, does have one. I don't know how I ever got by without an E-Meter. It monitors the condition of the batteries. Some of the information it provides is the charge of the batteries being monitored, the number of amps being charged or drawn, the number of amps consumed since the batteries had a full charge, and the amount of time left before the batteries will be dead at the present consumption.

It has a series of lights that indicates the charge of the batteries at a glance. As the batteries lose their charge, the number of lights is reduced. When the batteries are low, the color on the few remaining lights changes. I really like this, because I can see the condition of the batteries from almost anywhere inside the boat.

E-Meters are available for a single bank of batteries and two banks of batteries. On my own boat, I have one battery devoted to only starting the engine. I do not have this battery ganged with my house batteries, so its condition is not monitored by the E-Meter.

Mark all wires

A major problem I found on many of the boats that I delivered was the marking or color-coding of the wires. Some boats use many different colored wires, making it impossible to determine which wires are 110-volt AC, which ones 12-volt DC, and which ones are positive, negative, or neutral. The 12-volt DC system on older boats uses red for positive and black for negative. On the 110-volt AC system, black is positive, white is used for negative, and green for neutral. *The problem is that the black 12-volt DC negative wire could get mixed up with the black 110-volt AC positive wire.* For this reason, the black negative wire on the 12-volt DC system has been replaced with yellow.

All wires, regardless of their color, should be marked at the electrical panel and at the item they serve, so the correct wire can be quickly identified. Numbers are normally used to code the wires. There must be a record of this code that is readily accessible, preferably inside the electrical panel.

Access to all wires

Not only is it important to be able to identify each wire, but also each wire should be readily accessible. Wires should not run behind bulkheads, under headliners, or any place where they cannot be inspected or replaced.

One continuous wire should be used from the electrical panel to the item it serves: wires should not be connected because one was too short. There is the possibility that the cover of the connection could chafe, exposing bare wire. Also, if the connection is not properly sealed, moisture can work its way up the wire, under the insulation. If this connection is difficult to access and it fails, it could be almost impossible to locate the problem.

§

I had a similar situation occur with my autopilot on *Xiphias*. My autopilot suddenly stopped working. I tried to find the problem, but could not locate it. I used a volt-ohm meter to check the continuity in order to make sure there were no bad connections, but I found that all the wires had continuity. I connected the autopilot directly to the battery and it worked. I concluded that the problem had to be in the wires that I ran on the boat. As I was following my wires, I remembered connecting two of them together with a crimp connection. I found this connection and discovered that all the wires were broken except one strand. This one strand was enough to indicate continuity, but not enough to carry the required load to operate the autopilot.

Use the proper electrical plugs

One of the major electrical failures on a boat is the plug connection used. Plugs are often chosen so that an item can be installed or removed easily. Unfortunately, many plugs do not have connections that are accessible for cleaning. On *Xiphias*, I had a removable compass in the cockpit. It used a male two-prong plug on the compass and a matching female receptacle mounted in the aft end of the cabin. This plug is marketed as a watertight plug, and it was—for a while.

The male prongs were exposed, making them easy to clean. Each male plug was split down the center, so it could be slightly spread to make a tighter connection. The problem was the matching female receptacle. This receptacle had two small holes to accept the male plug. The inside of these holes corroded and was nearly impossible to clean. Be sure to select a plug that can be cleaned without too much difficulty, because it *will* corrode.

Navigation lights

Most cruising boats have converted to the tri-color light at the masthead. This makes a good light that can be seen for some distance and has a low current draw. The problem is with the steaming lights that are used when motoring. Too many cruising boats have these installed too low on the deck. Even a small wave can hide them. *All steaming and sailing navigation lights on a boat should be mounted high enough to be seen above any wave.* It is against Coast Guard Regulations to have running lights below the boat's sheer line. However, because many older boats had the lights installed forward into the hull, this regulation is not strongly enforced.

I like to have my steaming lights on the sides of the mast, just below the lower spreaders. They are high enough to be seen and far enough away from green water that could affect the connections.

Another problem with steaming lights is the stern light location. Regulations state that there must be a white light that faces forward 180 and a white light that shows aft 180 . This provides a 360 white light. The problem I often encounter is that the stern light is mounted too close to the cockpit, radically reducing night vision. Moving the light further aft and higher can eliminate this problem.

My own boat is under 10 meters long, so it does not fall under the same regulations as the larger boats. A boat under 10 meters long can have the standard port and starboard steaming lights and a single 360 white light. Therefore, when I am motoring, I turn on my port and starboard running lights and my anchor light.

Anchor light

No one likes to leave a light on all night, because it draws too much power. Many cruisers will use kerosene lights or low draw 12-volt DC lights for anchor lights. The problem with these lights is that they cannot be seen until you are close to the boat. Also, many of these anchor lights are low and often hidden by the dodger, boom, or something else on the boat. On the other hand, the masthead light blends in with the stars; unless it is quite bright, it could be missed on a starlit night. Also, the closer you get to the boat, the less likely it is that someone will be looking up to see the anchor light.

Electrical anchor lights draw from 1 to 5 amps. This can draw a considerable amount from the battery in just one evening. One problem is that the anchor light is rarely turned on when it gets dark and off when it gets light. In fact, it can be totally forgotten and left on all day. It is common to go ashore in daylight, knowing you won't return until after dark. So, the anchor light is turned on before leaving and turned off when you get up late the next morning. This can be resolved by installing a small solar switch: a photosensitive switch that closes the circuit when it is dark and opens when it is light. By installing this switch in the anchor light circuit, the anchor light will only be on when it is dark. Turning on the anchor light switch will activate the photosensitive switch.

An anchor light I like is a 12-volt DC fluorescent light. When I was cruising in Malaysia, I noticed the local fishing boats used these lights on deck at night. These lights put out a different color light than the incandescent bulb.

I found a small 12-volt DC work light that was watertight. I used it as my anchor light and noticed that it did not draw as much as my regular anchor light, plus it could be seen from quite a distance. Its distinctive color and shape stood out from all the other boats in the anchorage.

Strobe light

In the previous chapter, I discussed my feelings regarding the use of a strobe light. Here, all I would like to mention is that I think every boat should have one on the masthead, because it can be seen for many miles and can be used as a locator at night in an emergency.

High-output alternators

I really like my high-output alternator and smart regulator. Basically, they generate a lot of amps when the batteries are low and generate less amperage as the batteries take a charge. This happens much quicker than with the standard alternator that comes with the engine. Not only does it put out more amps when it is needed, but it also puts out a little more load on the engine; this helps the engine get up to proper running temperature when at anchor. When installing the high-output alternator, care must be given to increasing the size of the load wires, both positive and negative. Also, it must be more stoutly fastened, because of the additional load required to get the higher output.

Portable generators

I am surprised at how many boats carry auxiliary generators to charge their batteries or service the 110-volt AC needs. Of course, they do serve their purpose by providing the electrical power needed. Unfortunately, most generators use gasoline or petrol, which is highly combustible. Personally, I do not like gasoline on a boat, especially inside the boat. Perhaps the fuel jugs are stored outside, but the generator is stored inside. If there is the smallest leak, it could create a dangerous situation.

My major complaint with permanent and portable generators is the noise they make. I really get irritated when the guy on a boat next to mine starts his noisy generator, then takes off in the dinghy to get away from the noise. There are other ways to charge batteries and even get 110-volt AC power. However, if the owner has brought all their appliances from home, a generator may be needed. Personally, I put noisy generators in the same nuisance category as jet-skis.

Solar panels

Solar panels have been around for quite a while. They are constantly improving by providing more amperage output from a smaller area. There are different types of solar panels. With some types, if there is even the smallest amount of shade covering part of the solar cells, the output is greatly reduced. Other panels are not so seriously affected by a partially shaded area. You would think that everyone would jump at this type. Regrettably, the ones that are not as severely affected by shade do not have as much amperage output in full sun as the other type of the same size or area. Therefore, the location for installation would help determine which type of panel to use.

I feel all solar panels should have a regulator in their circuit. The primary objectives are to stop the panel from overcharging an already fully charged battery and to prevent amps from being drawn from the battery by the solar panel cells.

Unfortunately, for their size, they do not put out enough amps to service a cruising boat's needs. Consequently, many panels must be used. These clutter up the boat or make it look like an alien vessel from outer space.

Another problem with solar panels is the location for installation. They have to be accessible for cleaning. They must be exposed to as much sunlight as possible, and it is best if they can be adjusted to better absorb the sun as it moves across the sky. Also, they shouldn't be located so they interfere with the sails or sheets. For all of these reasons, most boats mount the solar panels behind the cockpit over the transom or stern rail.

On my own boat, I mounted my rigid solar panel between the mast and the upper shroud, as shown in Figure 98.

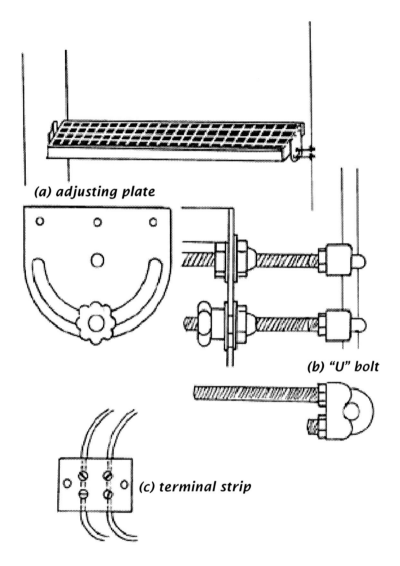

(a) adjusting plate

(b) "U" bolt

(c) terminal strip

Figure 98. Solar panel mount between mast and shroud

There was one panel on each side of the mast, just high enough that I could stand on top of the cabin and clean the panels. I must admit that this was not my original idea. Doug Walling, who had a boat like mine, had installed his in this location.

I communicated with Doug who, at the time, was cruising the South Pacific. He said that they had not created any problems at all after five years of cruising, even in a severe gale. I have had them on my own boat for over four years, and I love them in that location. When in the horizontal position, they are hardly noticeable and create minimum windage. When they are at an angle, they are more obvious, but not objectionable.

I did mount small rounded pieces of teak on the corners, just in case the genoa might rub against them when tacking through the wind. At the middle of each end, I installed a flat aluminum plate that had a center mounting hole and a curved slot below for adjusting the angle, as shown in Figure 98 (a). Because the length of the solar panel was not quite as long as the distance between the mast and upper shroud, I had to fill in the difference. This was accomplished by mounting a flat aluminum cleat against the mast to accept one end of the solar panel. At the shroud, I used 5/16-inch all-thread. I heated and flattened it near the center, then bent it to a perfect 'U' the same size as the shroud wire. I fitted this threaded 'U' rod over the shroud, then slipped on the proper size stainless steel cable wire clamp. After it was clamped in position, one side of the rod was cut off flush with the mounting nut. The other side was left long enough to make up the remaining difference in the length between the solar panel, the mast, and the shroud, as shown in Figure 98 (b).

There are two of these 'U' threaded rods for each side of the solar panel mounting plates. One was on or near the centerline of the panel for the pivot point. The other was located so it fit inside the curved slot on the plate for adjustment. The solar panel was slipped over these threaded rods and held in place with a knob.

I used a terminal strip on the underside of the panel, at the mast, to take the electrical wires, as shown in Figure 98 (c). This made it easy to remove when I left the boat for long periods of time. I soldered the ends of the wire where they fit into the terminal strip to prevent corrosion and improve the connection.

There are only two disadvantages to this mounting location. A shroud or halyard would shade a portion of the panel at times, affecting the amp output. The other problem was that the panels had to be close to the vertical position when raising and dropping sails. However, I found that by leaving the adjusting knobs loose, the panels would swivel up or down on their own when raising or lowering sails.

Wind generators

Wind generators, like solar panels, have greatly improved over the years. They generate lots of power, as long as there is wind. They are much smaller and quieter than they used to be. Wind generator technology is changing rapidly, so be sure to do your research.

Try to select a recent model that has all the bells and whistles. Some have more output than others. Some have feathering blades that self-adjust as the wind increases. Most of them have built-in smart regulators, but be sure to check first. If the wind generator will be mounted on a spreader, select one that is as small as possible to reduce weight and windage. Personally, I don't like the ones mounted on a pedestal on the stern of the boat, because this location may put the blades above the cockpit and could be dangerous if a blade breaks off in high winds.

All wind generators should have some sort of braking system that can be operated from the deck, in case the built-in system to regulate the speed fails. It is also important that the unit is accessible in case it needs to be removed.

I am not a fan of wind generators for two reasons. First, I have seen several break apart in strong winds. On one, the blade hit and damaged another boat many yards away. The other reason I don't like the wind generator is the noise they produce; this even applies to the 'quiet' ones. The larger ones or ones with longer blades cause a vibration that can be felt throughout the boat.

I have a friend who bought one. He intended to mount it on a tall stainless steel pipe behind the transom of the boat. He assembled the unit, then mounted it on the pipe while it was lying on the dock. He raised it to check out how it looked. The prop caught the strong winds that were blowing that day, and it began to spin. No matter which way he rotated or moved it, the prop continued to feather into the wind and spin at high revolutions. He knew he couldn't lay it down on the dock because the blades would be damaged, and he was afraid he couldn't handle the weight and vibration while laying it down. Finally, he sat down and slowly lay on his back bringing the whole unit with him. Eventually, it stopped spinning; then, he tied a rope around the blades so it wouldn't happen again during installation.

Inverters

I think every boat should have a 110-volt AC inverter aboard. It is nice to charge batteries for hand drills and other tools. Many rechargeable tools and appliances available today require 110-volt AC to charge their batteries. I love freshly ground coffee. I have a stovetop, espresso coffee maker aboard, and I like to grind my own coffee beans. I have tried the hand grinders, and they just do not get the fine grind I want. So I use my inverter to grind my coffee beans. I also have a hand mixer that works off the inverter. The inverter permits me to carry more of my shoreside power tools, especially a sander.

Inverters are sold by the number of watts required to run a tool or appliance. The higher the wattage, the heavier or bigger the tool or appliance that can be used. I feel a minimum of 1,000 watts is necessary for average use. Most have higher surge ratings, which means a tool may run at 1,000 watts, but needs 1,200 watts to get it started. The inverter will start the tool but cannot maintain the 1,200 watts; however, it will run at the rated 1,000 watts indefinitely.

They are also available as a combination battery charger and inverter. I think this is okay if the boat will be used in waters where 110-volt AC is available, because that is the power needed to charge the batteries. If there is any question about what you might want, I suggest you buy them separately. If you do buy a combination charger-inverter, make sure that if one fails, the other still continues to operate. This is one of the problems when any electrical item serves more than one function. I prefer to have my charger separate from my inverter.

Remember that the inverter should be used for short periods of time. It should also be considered a convenience, not a necessity.

Battery chargers

I presume all boats will have a battery charger aboard. The type of charger required will depend on the number of batteries to be charged. Some boats carry a huge number of batteries that will require a high output, smart charger. Others may only have one or two batteries and will only need a small capacity one. Even a trickle charger may work.

The larger capacity chargers now come with smart regulators that treat the batteries like a person. It judges the battery's age, capacity, and type and feeds it whenever it shows signs of hunger. The smaller chargers have regulators, but they are not as smart. When the battery is low, it puts out a charge; when it is nearing capacity, it reduces the output.

Remember that the charger will be used while you are dockside. Normally, the boat will be left for some time; consequently, the charger has lots of time to do its job, so a small one will probably be adequate. If you are living aboard and will be using many things on battery power all the time, a larger capacity charger is required. When you leave to go cruising, the only place to charge the batteries with the charger is by using shore power, and it may not be compatible to the 110-volt AC that you have aboard.

Spotlight

A strong or powerful spotlight is *essential* on any cruising boat. It can pick out things in the water or land from a distance. The only downside to a spotlight is that it reflects the light back into the eyes of its user if there is a haze or light fog. This is the same as driving in dense fog with the high beam lights. I like the spotlight that is watertight and has a rubber exterior; if it is dropped, it will do less damage to the light.

Hands-off light

The time may come when you have to go under water at night and need to use both hands. The most common situation is an anchor rope caught in the prop. I like the miner's-type light that fits on the head. These are available as waterproof to 500 feet and provide a bright beam.

An alternative light is one that can be held comfortably between the teeth. I like the StealthLite flashlight that uses four AA size batteries. It has a special xenon lamp that puts out a strong beam, and it is waterproof to 500 feet. I have two aboard: one is an arm's reach from the cockpit and the other in a holder on the side of the cabin, inside.

Red night-lights

The advantage of red night-lights is that they provide enough light to see, but do not damage or interfere with night vision. I am not saying that every light in the boat should have a red light, but those important areas like the chart table, galley, and head should have one. There are many lights available that have both normal white lighting and red lighting in the same fixture.

Autopilots

Every cruising boat must have a method to steer the boat other than a crew person. Sitting at the helm steering for hours is arduous and unnecessary, especially when there are so many kinds and strengths of autopilots available today.

Most autopilots should be used only when motoring. When the weather gets a little rough, many will not handle the loads at the helm for long periods of time. This does not apply to all autopilots; after all, autopilots steer ships. If you are installing an autopilot as the only source of steering the boat and you will not be using a windvane, install one that will take the expected loads, and then some. Remember to carry spare parts, and make sure the connections will not corrode or fail.

VHF radio

It is almost essential that the cruising boat be equipped with a VHF radio. In many countries, you are required to call in on the radio to ask the authorities to come out and clear you into their country. It is also a social radio, like having a phone on a boat, except that anyone around can hear you. Some anchorages have boats that are almost permanently moored and have their own net. Don't overlook this opportunity to talk to fellow cruisers who have been in the locality for a considerable amount of time. They can answer most of your questions and solve many of your problems. Not only do they provide this free service, they enjoy doing it.

The VHF radio is a local radio that works only on line of sight. Most VHF radios will not transmit or receive for more than twenty miles. This will depend on the conditions and obstructions between the two radios. Therefore, the higher the antenna is located, the further it will transmit and receive.

VHF radios are available as portable models or permanently mounted units. The permanent ones use the 12-volt DC house batteries to power the radio. The permanent radios will have more wattage for a stronger signal than the portable VHF radios. The portable radio is handheld. It has lower output wattage than the permanently installed radio, so it cannot transmit nearly as far. Since the handheld portable has its own antenna, it is not high enough to make an efficient transmission anywhere but between short distances.

I prefer to have the VHF radio permanently installed inside the boat, with the antenna on the mast-top. However, I like to carry at least one handheld portable for going ashore or when visiting another boat, so I can keep in touch with someone on my mother boat.

The radio should be mounted inside the boat. This creates a problem because you have to go below to operate it. This is okay if there is crew aboard, but if you are alone, it can be difficult and dangerous. Outside speakers and connectors for the microphone are available. I prefer to have my VHF radio located just inside the companionway, so I can still hear and transmit from outside, with the connections and speaker remaining out of the weather.

A license is required to operate a VHF radio; there is no test, only a small cost to apply. This license will soon become obsolete because of newer, more advanced methods of short distance communications.

Family radio service (FRS) radios

These are small handheld radios, similar to the VHF radios, but they have far less power, so they can only transmit and receive a shorter distance. Like the VHF radios, they also work on line of sight. These are fairly new and are becoming popular on boats, campers, and even around the house.

They have far more channels to select from, because one channel can have 10 coded sub channels. This is nice, because you can select a channel that is rarely used by others, so the conversation might have more privacy. I say 'might' because there is the possibility that someone else may be using the same channel code. In less populated areas, however, this is unlikely to happen.

There is no license required, and compared to the VHF portable radios, they are cheap. The one downside is that they only transmit about two miles in ideal conditions. They are perfect to take ashore to keep in touch with your crew or partner who may be lost in a crowd. It also is great to carry when you visit other boats, so you can have contact with the mother boat. I like to take it hiking; that way, I can keep in touch with others if we get separated.

I feel these are a convenience to have aboard. If you already have a portable VHF radio, it will do about the same thing. Although, unlike the VHF radio, the FRS is small enough to fit into your pocket, and it is much less expensive.

SSB-Ham radio

Many boats have long distance radios aboard, so they can communicate with home, receive weather fax, and send and receive email. These radios are not cheap. They use fairly large antennas and require some knowledge to install properly.

The radio can be purchased as a Single Side Band radio or as a Ham radio. For considerably more money, the radio is available with both, as well as most other frequencies. These are normally referred to as 'all frequency transceivers'.

The question is: do you really need both? In years past, many of the Single Side Band frequencies were restricted to commercial use, like on large ships. This has been relaxed, and the SSB is now available to the cruisers. A license is required to operate the SSB, but unlike the Ham radio, there are no tests to take. There is just a fee, and it can include the license for the VHF radio. The SSB can transmit and receive voice communications for short as well as long distances. It can also receive weather fax and send and receive emails. There is little the SSB cannot do that the Ham radio can do.

The Ham radio uses different frequencies than the SSB. These additional frequencies permit the radio to transmit and receive short to long distance, even on the other side of the earth.

The problem with the Ham radio is that you must take a test to get a license. There are different levels of licenses. As the level of the license increases, so does the number of frequencies available to the licensee. The lower level licenses, Novice and Technician, do not require passing a test to prove your ability to send and receive Morse code. Unfortunately, these licenses are of little use, because the frequencies available are few, and most can only be used with CW or Morse code.

If a Ham radio is to be used aboard, the minimum license you should have is a General class or above. This permits the licensee to use more channels and voice communications. The problem is that you have to learn to send and receive Morse code, but this not as bad as it used to be. The FCC realizes that there are less operators using Ham because of the convenience of the SSB, the cell phone, and global phones. As a result, they lowered the requirement on the code. I think it is only 5 words a minute now; it used to be 12 words a minute. As time passes, I expect the Morse code requirements will continue to be reduced or eliminated. Another disadvantage to the Ham radio is that it cannot be used for any commercial reason.

Both the SSB radio and the Ham radio require sophisticated antennas. This subject is too complex to go into here. If you intend to put in these radios, you should contact a professional who can advise you on the proper antenna installation.

If the cruiser does not intend to send or receive email, receive weather fax, or communicate long distance, there is no need to have these expensive radios aboard. However, for the others, if the budget allows, have both SSB and Ham radios aboard. The reason I suggest the Ham radio as well as the SSB is that the license requirements will be reduced soon, and any frequency can be used in an emergency.

Global satellite phones

Probably the simplest way to communicate is with the cell phone. Nearly everybody has one today, and they work on a boat as long as it is close to shore where it can reach a repeater antenna. However, these are very limited in many foreign countries and when offshore.

The alternative is the cell phone that works with a satellite. The satellite phone permits calls to anywhere in the world from anywhere in the world. Unfortunately, there are not enough satellites for worldwide coverage; however, there probably will be soon.

The only disadvantages to these phones are the cost per minute to make calls and the antenna required on the boat. Since the cost is going down and the antennas are getting smaller, I suggest you wait until the last minute to buy one for your boat.

If I could afford one, I probably would have one aboard. It makes keeping in touch with family, loved ones, friends, and business so much easier.

Depth sounders

Another item that I feel is essential on a boat is a good efficient depth sounder. All depth sounders send out a signal. The depth is measured by the time it takes for the signal to bounce off the bottom and return back to the transducer. The cheaper ones read to about 60 to 100 feet. The older models used a flashing light around a disc with depth markings around the disc. These have become obsolete and have been replaced with the digital readout, which is easy to read day or night. These cheaper sounders may give a false reading in deeper waters, because the signal is not strong enough to bounce off the bottom and make it back to the transducer. This can be misleading and frightening if your depth sounder is reading about 200 feet, then suddenly begins reading 20 feet when in reality the depth is 220 feet. Be sure you know your own depth sounder and how it reads when the depth of the water is deeper than rated.

Most depth sounders are available with two types of transducers. One type sends out a wide signal that can detect shallow water ahead but is limited to shallower depths. The other has a narrow signal that goes to greater depths, but will not indicate shallower water ahead.

The standard transducer should be installed in a vertical position, so the signal it sends will bounce back to the transducer and give an accurate reading. If the transducer is mounted outside the hull, it may require a tapered block to make sure it is vertical. Unfortunately, this also exposes it to damage in a grounding, or if the boat hits a log or other debris. Mounting the transducer outside the hull is bound to affect the boat's speed. If an exterior transducer is to be installed, *do not buy one made of plastic*; it may break much easier than one made of bronze.

If the hull is solid fiberglass, the transducer can be installed inside the hull, so it does not affect the boat's speed and is not susceptible to damage. However, it still must be mounted vertically. The internally mounted transducers lose some efficiency, because the signal must pass through the hull twice: once when it sends the signal and the other when the signal returns. For the transducer to work properly with minimum loss of efficiency, the hull cannot have any air bubbles or voids; this eliminates cored hulls and wooden hulls.

Because the transducer must be mounted vertically, it cannot be mounted directly to the hull if it is at an angle to the horizontal. This requires making a box of some sort that will suspend the transducer vertically. The box is then filled with a solution that will carry the signal with minimum absorption of the signal. Mineral oil works well as a signal conductor. Read the manufacturer's recommendation.

There are transducers available that can be mounted directly to a horizontal area inside of the hull, such as the bottom of the bilge or keel. It can be installed permanently using epoxy adhesive, or temporarily with a silicone adhesive. All air must be removed. In order to achieve this, the transducer must be twisted and forced down to push all the air bubbles out the side. Be sure to check the manufacturer's instructions for the suggested adhesive.

The location of the transducer is critical, so that the signal does not bounce off the keel. This means it should not be mounted too close to the keel or rudder. It is best if it can be mounted slightly forward, so that the depth is indicated before the deepest part of the boat reaches the same location. This is more difficult on full-keeled boats than fin-keeled ones.

I prefer the fish finder-type that reads to as deep as possible. Many will read to 2000 feet. The deeper it reads, the more useful it is for navigation. When sailing in fog, it is nice to know when you cross over depth lines that can be compared to the chart. This will tell you that you are on that line, but not necessarily where you are on the line.

I also like the fish finder's ability to show the contour of the bottom. It will indicate rocks, coral heads, and even wrecks. Some will even indicate the type of bottom: if it is soft or hard.

Some depth sounders are available with a forward-looking transducer. It is great to be able to know what is ahead of you; however, it has one major limitation: the transducer is large and must be mounted outside the hull, forward. This makes it susceptible to damage during a grounding, or if a log or other object is hit.

Knowing the depths is critical, especially when a danger cannot be seen: for example, at night, in dirty water, in direct sunlight, or along the shore after a heavy rain when the water turns brown. Depth sounders are electrical and are susceptible to electrical failure, like any other piece of electronics on board. Previously, I stated that no electrical instrument should be relied on for safety. This is difficult when it comes to the depth sounder. I actually have two. One is the cheaper, shallow, digital-type, while the other is the fish finder. I also carry a marked lead line just in case the other two fail.

Knot-log or speed-log

The speed of the boat is part of general navigation. You have to know your speed over the ground to determine the time of arrival. Today, many cruisers have done away with the knot-log and rely on the speed indicated by the GPS.

Some boats will still want to have an instant accurate source of their speed through the water. This is essential on racing boats, so they can determine if a sail change improved or reduced their speed. The downside to the instant display of speed is that there is a transducer that must pass through the hull to provide the speed. Most are a paddle wheel design, which gets clogged with growth and needs to be cleaned often.

Most transducers are removable from inside the boat, so that they can be cleaned without getting in the water, which will always allow some water to enter the bilge during the change. This is not serious; however, it is always a worry that everything works properly during the change. Another problem that I have found with the speed transducer is that they might leak, just a little.

Most cruisers are not as concerned about their speed through the water as their speed over the ground. The GPS provides an average of the speed over the ground. This eliminates the need for a through-hull transducer, which has to be cleaned often. Most cruisers I know have removed their paddle-wheel transducer and replaced it with the plug.

It might be a good idea to have a knot-log that can be used if the GPS quits working. The Walker log uses a spinner on a line to the speed dial mounted on the stern of the boat. There are others that can be held in the water for a few seconds that will indicate the speed. There is also the traditional method of timing the speed something travels over a known distance. Personally, I find that after a few years of sailing, many sailors can be awfully close to estimating their speed through the water. Try guessing the boat's speed before looking at the knot log or GPS. If you do this often enough at different speeds, your ability to estimate speed through the water will develop quickly.

Radar

I think radar is almost a necessity for a cruising boat. Even a good crewman on watch cannot detect something in the dark or fog. I sailed for the first ten years without radar. During my passage through Indonesia, I encountered local fishing boats anchored in deep water without lights; even bamboo platforms that were permanently mounted to the ocean's bottom were not lit. When I arrived in Singapore, I installed my first radar.

After cruising with radar, I don't think I would like to cruise again without it. Not only does it show the dangers in the dark and in poor visibility, but it will indicate squalls and where the squall is most dense. The better ones can show the contour of the shoreline, making finding the inlet anchorage much easier.

Radars are available based on the distance they can detect a target. Unfortunately, this is a bit misleading. The target has to be something that really has excellent return capabilities, like a land mass. Realistically, the distance should be cut in half; therefore, a radar rated at 16 nautical miles will only begin to give an accurate reading of a target at 8 nautical miles.

Radars are available with monochrome LCD, color TFT, and monochrome CRT screens. The newest screen is the color TFT, which is easy to see in sunlight and has excellent contrast of colors. The other screens still have good visibility, but don't have the same clarity and contrast in sunlight as the TFT.

One of the problems with radar is that it is too easy to depend on, when there should be someone on watch. At night, I found myself paying attention to the radar, instead of looking ahead for lights or other dangers. It was difficult to pull myself away from the radar and keep a diligent visual watch ahead, as well as on the radar.

Some cruisers set the radar's alarm and go to sleep, depending on the alarm to warn them of danger in plenty of time. This is not such a good idea if a ship is on a collision course and moving at or near full speed, or the radar fails to pick up something that does not give a good return. *The radar alarm is good to use while attending to other chores or duties, but should not be the only lookout source.*

Another concern with the radar is determining where to install the antenna radome. Since the radar antenna works on line of sight, the higher it is installed, the better the signal it will provide at a further distance. So if the radar is rated at 34 nautical miles, it serves little purpose to install it 10 feet off the water where it couldn't even reach the distance for which it is rated. The radar antenna radomes are large, heavy, and increase in size and weight proportionally as the range increases. This presents a problem: it should be high enough to work properly, but not high enough to create too much windage and weight aloft.

Most cruisers mount the radar antenna radome on the front of the mast. This works well because it achieves the height and unobstructed view ahead. However, the higher it is mounted, the more the weight and windage affect the boat.

Some cruisers mount the antenna radome on a pedestal or mast aft of the cockpit. The purpose is to keep the weight and windage lower. Sometimes, this actually negates the advantage of mounting it lower, because the pedestal itself adds additional weight and windage, only lower. Another concern with the antenna radome installed aft of the cockpit is that the crew may be exposed to the RF rays.

The radar antenna provides the best signal when it is perfectly horizontal. Consequently, when a sailboat heels over, the signal on the screen will be a little distorted or narrower. To solve this problem, there are gimbaled mounts available that keep the antenna horizontal.

I don't like these gimbaled mounts, because the constant movement can affect the wire where it passes through the mast. Also, in rough weather, the antenna may swing to extremes from one stop to the other. Some mounts are hydraulically dampened to prevent the radar from swinging to a sudden stop. On some gimbaled mounts, when the boat is rolling, the movement of the radar from side to side can be felt through the boat. I feel that the difference of the display on the screen when the boat is heeled is so minor that it does not justify the possible problems that could occur with the gimbaled mount. However, I really have little experience with them, and I have met many cruisers who swear by them.

Personally, I think the minimum range that a radar should have on a small sailboat is 24 miles. It is not that the distance is so important, but that the resolution is better. Also, I prefer my antenna solidly mounted—not too high—on the mast.

The radar comes with many different types of screens that give color and more or less contrast. This is another example of rapidly changing technologies.

Like other electronics, buy the radar just before departure, in order to get the latest model. Select the radar that has the longest range, using the smallest, lightest radome. Even this may not be true, because the best radar may have a slightly larger radome. This will require considerable research before you buy.

GPS

I doubt there is a cruising boat out there that does not carry a GPS to find their position. Most boats carry two or three GPS units, just in case one fails. Except for the few remaining purists, the days of celestial navigation are gone forever.

The GPS is excellent, but does have a few limitations. The GPS is more accurate than most charts. However, the chart may be incorrect; consequently, you may not be where you think you are on the chart. Depending on where you are in the world, the error can be minor or extreme.

While sailing in Mexico, all too often, I found that according to my GPS, I was anchored 500 meters on land. There were other times, though, that I could have navigated a narrow pass with only the GPS. Just be aware that some charts are more accurate than others.

The other downside to the GPS is that we become too dependent on them to find our position. One unexpected lightning strike could wipe out all the GPS aboard, leaving nothing but dead reckoning as the only means of navigating. As I mentioned earlier, do not rely on any electronic device that is essential to the safety of the boat. This is why every skipper should have some basic knowledge of celestial navigation and carry a sextant and almanac aboard.

Chartplotters

Here, I will be brief. Chartplotters are interfaced with the GPS. The charts in the chartplotter are the same as those you would spread across the chart table. Again, the problem is that the GPS is more accurate than the charts. The chartplotter will show your position on a chart on a screen. As long as the chart is accurate, the position of the boat will be accurate. I like the chartplotter as a convenience, but I would never rely on it as my only source of navigation. If you do have a chartplotter, still carry the necessary charts.

Computers

I feel the computer is nice to have aboard, but would not consider it essential. If it is interfaced with the GPS, the computer can be programmed to act as a chartplotter. It can send and receive emails. It can also receive weather faxes. These are all conveniences, but should not be essential on any boat.

I like to have a computer to record maintenance schedules, operating instructions, item location, and more. It is nice to have, but as I've said before, I consider it only as a convenience.

Weather fax

The weather fax can be received by a fax machine devoted to this purpose, or via the Single Side Band radio and a computer. The weather fax is nice to have, if the user can interpret the fax properly. Depending on the budget and size of the boat, a weather fax may be a nice addition to the other convenience electronics aboard. If you already have an SSB radio and a computer aboard, the software for a weather fax is inexpensive and a worthwhile investment.

Use of electronics in the tropics

Electronics are primarily a convenience that provides useful information, but should not provide essential information. Electronics are susceptible to failure from a lightning strike, being dropped or hit, and from corrosion. To reduce the corrosion problem in the tropics, the instrument should be used frequently to keep it warm in order to prevent moisture. This is easier said than done, because of the battery drain. When motoring, you might consider turning on all the electronics to keep them dry.

Safety items and ideas

Lifelines

As I mentioned previously, lifelines should be as tall as aesthetically possible. Their purpose is to keep people aboard. If they are too short, they will trip the person rather than retain them aboard. The general rule is that lifelines should have a minimum height of 24 inches.

To be effective, the stanchions should be as close together as reasonable, so that each stanchion will take the load of the weight of the person thrown against the lifeline. The further apart the stanchions, the more likely the lifeline will stretch and sag under the weight.

The stanchions should be strong enough so they don't bend when put to the test. A single-walled stainless steel tube will not be strong enough. If stainless steel tubing is used, it must be double-walled; that is, there should be another tube inside the outside tube.

There should be some way to prevent chafe to the lifeline where it passes through the stanchion. If a double-walled stainless steel tube stanchion is being used, it should have a small tube welded through the center of the tubing where the lifelines pass through it; there should not be any sharp edges. The welding of a tube through the stanchion will make it retain its strength at that location.

The stanchion should be stoutly mounted to the boat. This means it must be through-bolted wherever it is supported. To weld a plate to the bottom of the stanchion and then bolt it through the deck is not strong enough; the stanchion can break at the weld on the base. The stanchion should be bolted through the deck and supported further up from the base. The higher the support, the stronger the installation. I really like bulwarks for this purpose. Lifelines normally terminate at a ring or loop welded to the stern rail and pulpit. Make sure this is properly welded or fastened; this is the most common location for failure.

As I mentioned before, there are pros and cons to using double lifelines. If a person is tethered and falls overboard over the top lifeline, he or she must be brought back aboard the same way. I have a single lifeline on my boat, but I also have 8-inch bulwarks to help fill the space between the deck and the lifeline.

Remember that the purpose of a lifeline is to prevent someone from falling overboard, regardless of the person's size and weight. Make sure they will serve their purpose. Do not discover that the lifelines are not strong enough or tall enough *after* a person falls overboard.

Steering

If the steering fails on a boat, it can be almost as serious as losing the steering in an automobile, especially if it happens in stormy conditions. The steering may work without any sign of weakness in normal conditions; however, when the weather turns bad, the stresses are much heavier on the whole system. *Routine checks should be made, and everything tightened and adjusted before any passage. This especially applies to wheel steering with a quadrant, which is moved by a wire cable or chain.*

Carry plenty of spare parts and have these and the tools needed to do the repairs close at hand. If the steering fails, you don't want to waste precious time searching for parts and tools.

Jacklines and harness tethers

Jacklines should be strong and extend from the bow to the stern, permitting free movement fore and aft without disconnecting the tether. Jacklines on deck should be made of webbing instead of rope. The rope will roll underfoot, making it possible for the crewmember to fall overboard.

Harness tethers should also be strong and have two clips. One clip should be located at the end of the tether, and the other clip should be much closer to the harness. The one at the end is used when moving along the boat. The clip closer to the harness is for connecting close up to something while doing the necessary job. These clips must be at least as strong as the tether's webbing.

If the boat will permit an additional chest-high rope lifeline to be installed, this will be a real bonus. The harness tether can be clipped to this line, preventing the clip from dragging along the deck and making loud sounds below decks. As a man, I like this chest-high lifeline, because I can lean against it when I drain my bladder—it provides that little extra distance I need to miss the boat.

Deck cleats

The only real concern with deck cleats is that they must be strong enough to take the intended load. All deck cleats should have back-up plates under the deck. If the deck is really solidly constructed, the back-up plate can be a large washer at each bolt. If the deck is foam or balsa cored, a full plate should be used.

I have seen bow cleats torn off the deck when a boat is under tow. This type of stress is similar to being at anchor in a storm. Deck cleats should not tear out or break. Personally, I do not like aluminum cleats for anything but light loads.

Life raft

Although I do not carry a life raft, it does not mean I am against them. I guess I am like the preacher who says, *"Do as I say, not as I do"*. The main reason I do not carry one is that there simply is not enough space on my boat. The life raft, as important as it may be, probably will never be used. They are expensive, and they have to be checked regularly.

My rationalization is that in most cases when I would need a life raft, a hard dinghy would serve the purpose. If I am in a storm that is so severe that my mother boat is sinking, I doubt a life raft or any small dinghy would survive the same storm. If I hit a reef, a rubber life raft may be torn apart; I would prefer a hard dinghy. The major concern would be if I hit something that holed the mother boat while in open waters. If this happened, it would be better to concentrate on stopping water from entering the boat than deploying a life raft. If the boat is going to sink from being holed, chances are that the weather might not be too bad. In that case, I would rather be in a rigid dinghy that could be sailed.

As I see it, chances are that I will never need a life raft. This does not mean I would not like to have one. I probably would have one if I had the room and the money. As an alternative, I made inflatable collars that clip to the sides of my hard dinghy. On a long passage, the collars can be attached, but not inflated until needed. I probably would not feel so cocky if I had a boat of lesser construction. I am putting my insurance in the strength of my vessel. If I am wrong, I am a strong swimmer.

EPIRB

Emergency Position Indicating Radio Beacons transmit a May Day emergency signal using battery power. There are different types of EPIRBs, from the simplest, which only sends out a signal every few seconds, to the very sophisticated, that sends out the GPS position of the EPIRB and identifies the boat. Today, there are satellites that pick up these signals and transmit the distress call to Control Centers.

If there is an emergency on board and you are near land or a ship, the first thing would be to try to use a VHF radio. If the vessel is further offshore, use the SSB or Ham transceiver to make voice contact. If all this fails, then the EPIRB can be activated.

The EPIRB sends out the distress signal every few seconds; the battery will last for about 6 to 8 hours. This is not much time if the boat is in the middle of the ocean. *Before activating the EPIRB, be certain it is a true distress. Never turn it off after is has been activated. Leave it on until the battery dies, then—if possible replace the battery.*

The better EPIRB that transmits the GPS position and identifies the boat would considerably reduce the rescue time. The biggest draw back to these newer EPIRBs is the cost. They are expensive for something that will probably never be needed. It is like the life raft. Do you want to take the gamble?

§

I would like to share a short story about a boat that set off their EPIRB when it was not necessary. The boat was in French Polynesian waters. The skipper and his wife were tired from several days of fighting poor weather conditions and from fear. They were only one full day from their destination when they lost their steering to port. At the time, they did not realize that a bolt had dropped from the pedestal base into the quadrant, restricting its movement on one side. They said they were also low on fresh water. Fatigue clouded their judgment, and they set off the EPIRB. Soon, the French Polynesian Navy sent out a helicopter to make contact. It was night and visibility was poor. The skipper fired his flare gun and hit the bottom of the chopper. The chopper left the scene immediately. Soon a French Navy Frigate arrived and asked them to define their distress conditions. They explained that they had lost their steering and were out of water. The Navy Frigate towed them to the closest city. The Navy discovered that they had not lost their steering, that it could have been repaired at sea, and they still had plenty of fresh water to survive. They had to go to court. The result was that they were required to pay for the entire expense of the rescue or 25% of the value of their vessel, which was determined by the Navy.

Man overboard poles

These are poles that are about 15 feet long with flotation and weighted ballast on the bottom to keep them floating upright. If someone falls overboard, the pole is thrown into the water to better see the person's position. This pole should have a light that is activated when in the water, so it can be seen at night. It should also have a long line attached to the ring buoy or horseshoe buoy.

Normally the line between the pole and the ring buoy is not long enough. The pole is on one bracket and the ring buoy on another. The ring buoy is thrown overboard first, followed by the pole. If the line is too short, the boat will drag the ring buoy until the pole can be released. This may put it quite far away from the victim.

Both the pole and the ring buoy should have quick release brackets and be stored near the cockpit for immediate access. Too many cruisers, including myself, put an extra line on these safety items when the weather gets rough. This only delays the time it takes to deploy. Since I do most of my sailing alone, having one on my boat really serves no purpose.

Lifesling

The purpose of the Lifesling is to make it easier to lift a stunned or unconscious crewmember from the water. Most come with their own quick deploy storage cases. *If there are only two or three persons aboard, one of these Lifeslings is essential.*

Radar reflectors

Another critical item to have aboard is a good radar reflector. Do not rely on the aluminum mast or a steel hull to return the proper signal. Unless the signal hits the mast at just the right angle, the aluminum mast, because of its shape, does not return a good radar signal.

The steel hull will bounce a radar signal back, as long as it is close to the ship sending out the signal. The distance between the two directly affects the efficiency of the return. This is because the radar signal is a straight line or line of sight. If the steel hull sets too low in the water or is below the horizon, it will not return a good signal until the ship is dangerously close.

There are different kinds of radar reflectors available. The more efficient ones are quite large and create a lot of windage aloft. When I was cruising on *Xiphias*, I used one with three interlocking discs. It was permanently mounted on one side of the mast between the lower spreader and the mast, in the water catching position.

One night, while I was sailing across the Gulf of Carpentaria on the northern end of Australia, I got a call on my VHF radio. It was an Australian ship that was charting depths in the Gulf. He informed me that I was not seen on his radar until I was within 8 nautical miles.

This concerned me, because that was not good enough. When I got to Darwin, Australia, I bought two new radar reflectors. The reflector is about 24 inches long and about 3 inches in diameter, filled with aluminum, with flat surfaces at 90° to each other. I mounted one on each upper shroud, port and starboard, under the upper spreaders. I liked these because they were unobtrusive, created less windage, and were easy to install.

While sailing to Indonesia, I contacted a ship on my VHF and explained my new radar reflector. I asked him if he would kindly report on my signal. He continued to give me a continuous report until he was over 16 nautical miles away, then he said he had other things to do.

I know that some people have not given these radar reflectors a good report on their signal return. Before you go out and buy a couple, do your own research and tests.

Most merchant seamen respect the sailor who has the courage to go to sea in a small boat. I have always found them more than happy to assist or help if they can. If you want to check your radar reflector's effectiveness, call a vessel on channel 16 and ask if they could give you a report on your signal and continue to do so until the signal is weak. (Of course, change channels before asking for their assistance.) If there is another yacht in the vicinity, you might ask them what type of radar reflector they are using and have the ship give a report on the return signal of both. If you find you are not providing enough return signal, add more reflectors or change to a better type.

Radar detectors

The value of a radar detector depends on its intended use. The radar only detects ships that have their radar turned on. I had one aboard *Xiphias*. Often, I was below doing something or sitting outside reading when I would see a ship quite close. I couldn't understand why my radar detector did not sound the alarm. I would go below and make fine adjustments to the setting, but it still would not respond. Then much later, the alarm would go off, and sure enough, there would be a ship on the horizon. Each time I saw a ship and the detector did not respond, I tried to contact the ship on VHF radio. Many did not respond, so I suspect that they did not have their radar or VHF radio turned on. Those who did respond to my inquiry always said they did not have the radar turned on. I had always presumed a ship turned the radar on and left it on, but obviously this is not the case. Consequently, if the purpose for the radar detector is to warn of approaching ships while everyone sleeps, it should not be aboard.

If you have a radar aboard, it has a built-in alarm that sounds when it detects a ship or return signal. As mentioned above, if there is no radar aboard, the radar detector will assist in warning of an approaching ship only if it has its radar turned on. *Regardless, the alarm on either or both should not be a substitute for standing watch.*

Know ships' lights

It is important that anyone who will be standing night watches be able to understand the meaning of the color and location of lights on ships. The radar, if there is one aboard, will help to determine the course of a distant vessel. If the radar is not warmed up, batteries are low, or it is out of order, then the lights are the only way to determine the course of the ship.

Not only should the cruiser be aware of the ships' lights, they should also know the rules of the road or the right-of-way, horn signals, and some basic signal flags.

Keep decks clean

I have talked about this before, but it is worth mentioning again. The deck should be clear of obstacles, especially at night. The problem is not the items that remain on deck permanently, but those that are usually stored below decks or in lockers. Items that are not normally stored on deck should be used and then returned to their storage spot. Common items left on deck include: fishing poles, fishing lines, hooks, lures, dive tanks, regulators, spear guns, kites, sail bags, swim fins and mask, wet suits, and the list continues. *There shouldn't be anything on deck to injure or trip a crewmember when his or her concentration is on doing something else.*

Flashlight and knife at arm's reach

The time may come when you need a flashlight or knife immediately. The closer it is, the quicker it can provide the help needed. Many sailors carry knives and flashlights on their body. I did this for about two months, then I decided that they were too uncomfortable and in the way; the discomfort far outweighed any assistance provided. I keep mine mounted on a teakwood box that covers the back of the instruments on the inside, aft face of the cabin.

Gimbaled vs. permanently mounted stove

The concern with both installation methods is being burned or scalded. I was afraid that if I included this discussion in the "General" section of the chapter, someone might skip over it, *and it is too important of a safety issue to overlook.*

Most gimbaled stoves are gimbaled athwartship, because this is the direction of the most violent motion. There may be a few that are also gimbaled fore and aft, but I have never seen one. Therefore, let's presume the stove is gimbaled across the ship, or athwartship. This means that the advantages of the gimbaled stove will not apply to movement fore and aft.

The purpose of the gimbaled stove is to keep the working surface level, so that liquids do not slosh out, and anything being cooked on top of the stove or in the oven does not slide. The stove should be equipped with fiddles and adjustable pot-holders to keep the utensil being used in place when the stove swings to extremes or too violently.

One of the major dangers with the gimbaled stove is adding too much weight on top of the stove, reducing the 'ballast' weight below the pivot point. This usually happens when boiling water for lobsters, crabs, and pasta. One way to reduce this problem can be by adding lead weight to the bottom of the stove.

Another problem with the gimbaled stove is that it can swing to major extremes; therefore, it must have stops to prevent it from swinging too far. I have yet to see a stove that slows down at the extremes; instead, the stove usually swings until it hits its stop, and that is exactly what it does—stop. The point where a gimbaled stove stops will vary by boat.

I suggest you know the stop point, and never use the stove if there is any possibility of it swinging to this extreme. I know of some cruisers who insist on using their stove in almost all conditions and use bungee cords to dampen the movement when it gets near the extremes.

Since the gimbaled stove is permitted to swing, there is a pivot point where the stove is mounted to the cabinet. This must be a stout installation, and the gimbaled bracket must be capable of being locked, so the stove cannot come out accidentally.

Most gimbaled stoves have ovens. On some models, when the oven door is opened, the additional weight of the door, further from the axis, causes the stove to tilt forward. If there is something in the oven or on top of the stove, it could end up in your lap or on your head. Make sure the oven door will slide under the stove, so it does not change the balance. Be aware, however, that the stove will still be a little off balance during the process of opening the door and sliding it under the stove. I think this is how most accidental burns occur.

There should be a stove guard in front of the stove, so the cook is not thrown into it during a more violent roll. I have a three-point cooking harness that is connected to eyes on the ice box bulkhead behind me and to the cabinet on either side of the stove. The eyes that take the clip of the cooking harness are through-bolted. This holds me in place while I cook; however, I cannot move out of the way if there is a spill. I always wear a rubber apron when cooking at sea, although this does not protect my feet.

Basically, the advantages of a permanently mounted stove are that it has none of the disadvantages of the gimbaled one. Since the permanently mounted stove will move with the boat, it must have high fiddles and strong potholders. The pots must be deep and should never be more than half-filled. There is still the danger of having boiling water spill on the cook. I presume it would be difficult to bake bread or cook a casserole in the oven underway.

I prefer the gimbaled stove; however, it must have a lock to keep it held in place permanently when needed. Then, if the weather is rough and I am concerned about using it, I can lock the stove in position and use it like a permanently mounted one. However, if it is really rough, I wouldn't use either stove. I would also add weight to the bottom of the stove to reduce the chances of it becoming top heavy.

Fire extinguishers

Fire extinguishers are available in three basic types. The Class A fire extinguisher is usually filled with water and will only put out ordinary combustible materials like plastic, wood, paper, etc. The Class B fire extinguisher is usually filled with carbon dioxide and will put out flammable liquids like kerosene, diesel, gasoline, paint thinner, etc. The Class C fire extinguisher is filled with a dry powdered chemical and will put out electrical fires.

It is almost impossible to carry all three types. Additionally, there is the chance that the wrong Class may be accidentally used. There are fire extinguishers available where all three Classes are in one extinguisher. I consider this the best type to have aboard a small cruising vessel.

There should be a fire extinguisher in the engine room, galley, and forward. They should be stoutly mounted, but easy to remove.

All fire extinguishers have an expiration date. I like the type that has a gauge to indicate if any of the pressure has escaped, which would make it less useful. The expiration date and pressure should be recorded, and the fire extinguisher replaced or refilled when necessary.

Wooden plug at through-hulls

Older boats had regular through-hulls and marine valves installed under the waterline. There was danger of the through-hull breaking at the base of the threads above the retaining nut. If this happened, there was no way to stop water from flooding the boat. The solution was to carry a tapered wooden plug that could be hammered into the opening.

Today, with seacocks installed below the waterline, the possibility of this happening is greatly reduced. In fact, I think it would be nearly impossible to break a properly installed seacock. The only thing I can think of that would cause a failure would be severe electrolysis below the valve. Therefore, the plug is not as necessary as it once was. This does not mean not to have them; however, if the boat has seacocks, the importance of plugs would be greatly reduced.

Double hose clamps

A regular problem on boats that have been in the water for years is that the hose clamps will rust away, or they will lose their ability to hold. This even happens with all-stainless steel clamps. The stainless steel used in hose clamps is not always a good grade stainless. Even if the hose clamp is stamped with the words 'all stainless steel', check it with a magnet to make sure is does not have too much carbon steel that will cause it to rust.

Also, the threaded screw that does the adjusting is mounted by pinched-over tabs that can loosen and make the clamp fail. *Therefore, it is necessary to have two or more hose clamps on any fitting below the waterline, just in case one fails.*

It is important that hose clamps on new hoses be checked regularly for the first few months. The hose will compress, making the hose clamp less effective. After the few months pass, all the hose clamps should be checked for tightness and inspected for rust at least twice a year.

Hose clamp on shaft

I have a friend who was sailing between the Solomon Islands and Papua New Guinea on a 40-foot fin-keeled spade rudder boat. The prop shaft was offset on a skeg. The wife went below to make coffee and discovered water over the floorboards. There was a rush to find the source of the leak. By the time they decided to check the prop shaft, there was so much water in the boat, the husband had to submerge under water. Sure enough, the shaft was gone. Apparently, it had slipped out of the hub connected to the engine and simply slipped right out of the boat. They did have a tapered wooden plug that was driven into the stern gland.

I like to put two hose clamps on the prop shaft between the hub and the gland. I make sure my two-bladed prop is in the vertical position or inline with the keel before tightening the hose clamps. One hose clamp adjusting screw is on top of the shaft and the other under the shaft. This way, I can see at a glance when my prop is aligned with the keel to reduce drag, then I put the engine in reverse gear to keep it from rotating. The hose clamps also keep the shaft aboard if it should slip out of the hub

No gasoline or propane below decks

It is difficult to find a place to store extra propane tanks and gasoline for outboards. We all know that they should not be stored below decks because of the danger of a leak.

Most boats store the gasoline on deck in jerry jugs. This is okay until the weather gets rough and washes them overboard. Most boats do not have a good strong location to tie jerry jugs.

Propane is a little more difficult, because the tanks and the fittings are metal, which can be quickly damaged if exposed to salt water. These have to be stored in some type of protected locker.

There are several solutions to this problem. One is to build deck boxes that are strongly fastened to the deck. The deck boxes must be out of the way, waterproof, and easy to access. The larger the boat, the easier it is to find a good location. There is little space to spare on smaller boats.

Another alternative is to use an existing cockpit locker. It is essential that the locker be airtight and vented overboard, not into the cockpit. This is where another problem occurs. The vent line cannot have a loop or low spot, which could hold water, preventing proper ventilation. Also, the vent should be as low as possible in the locker; this may make it near or below the waterline. It may be necessary to build a locker within a locker to get the necessary height.

It may not be easy to make this compartment airtight. If the locker is large enough to climb inside, then all openings can be sealed with fiberglass. Use a good seal around the lid and some kind of clamping device to pull the lid down firmly on the seal.

After this is completed, the system must be tested. I use a bicycle pump to pump air into the locker via the vent line, then bend the hose and clamp it with vise grips. After a few minutes, I release the vise grips to see if air is forced out of the vent hose. If it does force air out, it is airtight. If it doesn't, more sealing must be done. This type of seal is only safe if the locker is properly ventilated, and there is no way for water to sit in the hose.

Tape all glass panels

The last thing you need during a storm is broken glass flying around. If you know a storm is on its way, or even if it has already arrived unexpectedly, put strips of duct tape or electrical tape on all large mirrors, windows, or panels.

Know some celestial navigation

It was previously mentioned that any electrical device can and—most likely—will fail eventually. If the GPS fails and the spare does not work, then some minimum celestial navigation will be essential. It is not necessary to have it mastered, but there should be simple instructions aboard that explain how to take and configure a noon sight. This only requires a cheap sextant and an up-to-date almanac.

If you don't have a sextant, at least carry an almanac. If you understand how to use the almanac and understand some basic principles of celestial navigation, you can roughly determine your position by checking the time for sunrise and sunset. If you spend a few minutes reading the almanac, you will discover it is filled with information on how to locate your position.

Comfort

Dodgers

Before I departed to go cruising, I had decided that I would go without a dodger. After all, not all cruising boats have dodgers. I didn't like the way they made the boat look, and they were expensive. Only weeks before our departure, my girlfriend, who was going to make the passage with me, insisted that I install one. On our second day at sea, we were hove-to, cuddling outside under the dodger. We were both too seasick to even think about going below deck. After that, I have bowed to and almost worshiped that dodger. Needless to say, I never did praise my girlfriend enough for insisting that I install one.

Most soft dodgers are made to be collapsible, so they can fold down. Even though this is a possibility, most cruisers never do it. The dodger is so important in bad weather that many sailors would be willing to lose it, rather than to drop it intentionally. This brings up another point: most dodgers are installed to be sacrificial. If they are not, they should be. The time may come when there is a severe knock down, and the dodger is filled with water. This could affect the righting moment of the boat. If the dodger is under water, it will direct the water below decks when the boat eventually rights itself.

Most boats have soft dodgers, which are made out of stainless steel tubing covered with a commonly known acrylic material, which is durable and withstands wet and sun exposure. The major problem I encountered was that after a few years of being exposed to heavy rainwater, this popular boating material allowed water to pass through it and drip. As time passed, it got worse until it had to be replaced. I figure that one will last about three years in the tropics. This problem can be solved by using a different material that will never absorb water and weep moisture. A product I like is Stamoid, which is a reinforced vinyl. It is strong, will not break down in the sunlight, and is 100% waterproof. It may get condensation on the underside, but it will not leak. However, it is expensive.

Since most cruisers will leave the dodgerup permanently, I like a hard dodger. There are different types of hard dodgers. However, they should not get confused with pilothouses. The helm is under a pilothouse, while the dodger only covers the companionway and aft end of the cabin.

Some hard dodgers use a fiberglass crown with exactly the same shape as the canvas-type material. It attaches to the same stainless steel tubing as the canvas-type dodger. Normally, the front face and sides still remain the same canvas-type material. I like these because they will last almost forever and will never leak. Also, if it becomes necessary, they are still sacrificial.

I made my own hard dodger a little differently than the fiberglassed crown-type. I made the crown out of multiple layers of door skins, with a two-inch up-stand all the way around the circumference. When finished, the dodger crown was painted with three coats of primer, followed by five coats of linear polyurethane. The up-stand around the edge provides a good handhold when needed; more importantly, it acts as a rain catcher.

To catch water, I installed a flanged copper tube at the lowest point on both sides. They were roughened with sandpaper, then bedded in place using 3M 5200 sealant. The bottom of the tube extends through the dodger and takes a brass, quick-release hose connection. I have separate hoses with matching connections. These two hoses will reach all my deck water fills.

The top of the hard crown is easy to access to clean, so the water going into the tank is also clean. I even store my awning cockpit cover on the inside of the aft edge of the dodger, so it is always accessible. Also, the hard crown makes it an excellent place to set a portable solar panel.

Eight stainless steel stanchions support the crown. The underside of the crown is strongly reinforced where the fasteners hold the crown to the stanchions. The stanchions are screwed into the top and sides of the cabin. This results in a solid, rigidly mounted crown.

I use three panels made of Sunbrella to surround the dodger; each has a polyvinyl window. The center front window can be unzipped along the sides and bottom to hinge up to the underside of the crown.

This is especially nice to get ventilation in the cockpit when it is warm. If it is really warm, all panels are removable.

I ran wires to the aft center of the hard dodger where I installed a surface light on the underside. This light illuminates the cockpit for eating or entertaining at night.

My hard dodger can be taken off in a few minutes; however, the problem is that there is no place to store it once it is removed. Also, because this type is not commercially available, it must be handmade to fit the boat. If someone has to be hired to build it, it can be expensive.

Wind curtains

Wind curtains normally surround the cockpit to reduce the wind and spray. For personal comfort, these are essential. One of the problems with wind curtains is that, in order for them to be effective, they usually obstruct vision. I know of some boats that actually sew vinyl windows into the curtains. This does not work too well, because if the curtain is effective, the window will be covered with spray.

I like wind curtains to be removable and to have breakaway capabilities. On my own boat, I have the wind curtains attached to the lifeline and stern rail by having it fold over and then fastened with a twist lock. The bottom is attached to the top inside of the bulwarks with button studs and snap buttons. This is where it would breakaway if a wave were to hit. To remove the wind curtains takes less than a minute.

Underway sun awning

Every boat should have some protection from the hot sun while underway. On some boats, it is easy to install an underway sun awning between the dodger and the boom gallows, or on a stainless steel tubing support. On others, it may be a separate fold down awning made similarly to a soft dodger.

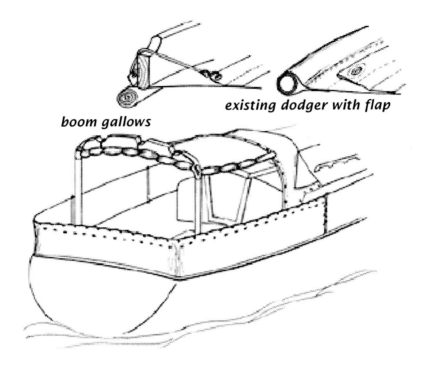

boom gallows

existing dodger with flap

Figure 99. Sun awning for use underway

The problem comes when the main sheet leads down to a traveler in or near the center of the cockpit, because the main sheet must be able to move back and forth from port to starboard. This makes it difficult to keep the cockpit dry, because there must be a split in the awning where the main sheet leads to the boom. I would rather move the sheet lead than attempt to split the awning. The main reason for this is that I like a dry cockpit at all times.

Cockpit cover

One of the most important items that I have on my boat is the total cockpit cover. My cover is made from lightweight Stamoid. It covers the entire cockpit, making it into another room, as shown in Figure 100. The cockpit cover uses the existing underway sun awning and existing wind curtains. The sides and back can be permanently sewn into the sun cover, like in Figure 99, or they can be attached separately. If polyvinyl windows will be installed in the sides and back, it is better if they are removable to prevent damaging the window material.

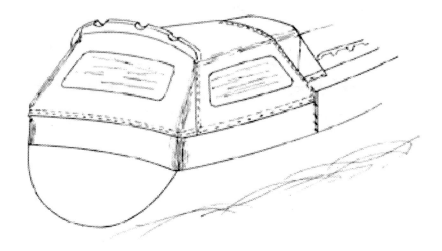

Figure 100. Total cockpit cover

The top of the sides and back panels are attached to the existing sun awning. The bottom is attached to the wind curtains with a small apron hanging over the outside of the top of the lifeline and sternrail. Be sure you have an easy way of getting out of this cockpit cover to move forward. I used Velcro door flaps that I can push open in a hurry.

When the weather is wet or it is rough, I can have the cockpit completely enclosed. If the wind is from one side of the boat, I can lower or cover this windward side and leave the other side open for ventilation.

Awning at anchor

If the cruise will involve a lot of time in warm, wet climates, then a strong lightweight awning that is watertight will be needed when at anchor, as shown in Figure 101.

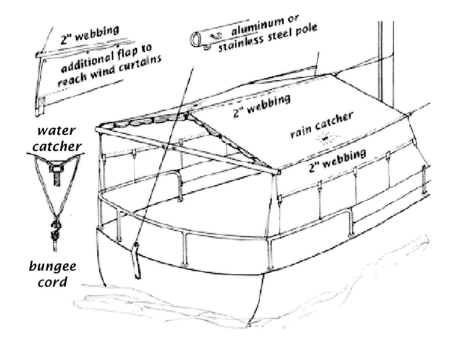

Figure 101. Awning at anchor

Since the tropics have unexpected squalls, it is essential that the awning be strong enough to withstand the blow. When the wind is howling, it is not the time to attempt to remove any awning. If it gets away from you, it could do a lot of damage in a short time. I have had the one in the illustration up in winds in excess of 60 knots. Fortunately, it was only a squall and of short duration.

The awning should be watertight, so water does not drip through the bottom during heavy rains. It should also be able to catch rainwater to fill the tanks.

In the awning illustrated, the sides fold down, and lines are fastened to the top of the lifelines. There is an additional flap inside the existing one to reach the lifeline and wind curtains. The back does the same to provide protection from the stern.

The aft end of the awning should be about 8 inches wider than the pole, which is discussed below. The length is up to you, but it cannot exceed the length to the mast. At the forward end, the awning should also be about 8 inches wider than the beam at this point. These additional 8 inches determine the angle of the gable after it is set. Wider boats will need more and smaller boats less. The angle of the gable should be slight to reduce windage, but enough so that the water runs off without standing.

The awning is made from Stamoid because of its strength and waterproof and sun resistant qualities. The awning has 2-inch nylon webbing sewn inside the full length of the awning at the center and on the sides. No grommets are used, but instead, the webbing is folded back at the ends and sewn to itself, leaving a small loop at both ends of each of the three nylon strips.

The edges all the way around the awning are triple-hemmed and double-stitched. The sides are similarly done, with nylon webbing loops sewn along the bottom, spaced about 2 feet apart. These are used to pull the awning down to the lifelines.

On a single mast vessel, a strong pole is required to keep the awning wide enough to cover the stern. No pole is needed on a ketch, because the awning can be fastened to the mizzenmast standing rigging.

There will be tremendous strain on the pole; therefore, it must be extremely strong, so it does not bend or break. There are many ways to make the pole. A few suggestions would be to use thick-walled aluminum or stainless steel tubing. The problem with this method is that the pole is heavy. Another way is to use two tubes, one inside the other. This is light and makes it possible to telescope for easy storage. The third method is to use aluminum or stainless steel tubing filled with a solid, tight-fitting hard wood rod. On my own boat, I used both of the last two ideas. I found some 2-inch aluminum tubing and another aluminum tube that just fit inside the larger tube. Then I took a piece of teakwood and cut it down so it fit snugly inside the smaller of the two tubes. To protect the sharp ends, I rounded both ends of the wood where it extended beyond the ends of the tubing.

The pole requires two loops or eyes at the center, spaced about 10 inches apart. This allows the pole to be tied to the inside of the backstay. The pole is set against the inside of the backstay, and 1/4-inch line is passed between the loops or eyes and around the outside of the backstay. This permits the pole to slide up and down the backstay.

On the opposite side of these loops, there must be a loop or eye at each end of the pole to take the awning. Again, 1/4-inch nylon line is passed through the nylon webbing loops to the loops at the ends of the pole. I make several passes to pull the awning snugly to the pole. The center of the awning is not connected to the pole. Now, the pole is tied to the inside of the backstay, and the outside ends of the awning are tied to the ends of the pole.

If the awning is pulled taut, the pole will slide up the backstay until it cannot be reached. To prevent this, there are two additional loops or eyes installed on the bottom of both ends of the pole, so it can be pulled down after the awning is set up taut.

If the tubing is thick enough, these loops or eyes can be attached by welding. If welding is not an option, pad eyes, eyestraps, or eyebolts can be used, but they must all be bolted through the tubing.

I keep the awning permanently tethered to the pole. To set the awning, I tie the pole to the inside of the backstay with a line tied between the loops or eyes on the outside of the backstay. This line must not be tied to the backstay, only over it to permit the pole to move up or down for adjusting the height.

Next, I tie the nylon loop sewn in the center of the awning to the backstay. I tie it about 6 inches above the pole, almost as high as I can reach. At the other end of the awning, I run a line from the forward center nylon loop, around the mast, back to the knot where the line is tied to the nylon loop, and back around the mast to get the power needed to pull the awning taut.

After this is done, I take the lines that are tied to the nylon loops on both sides of the awning in the front and run them around the upper shroud and back again to the knot at the nylon loop. This gives me additional pull advantage to make the awning taut.

After the awning is in place, I pull the center of the awning as tight as I can. This will cause the pole to slide up the backstay. To prevent this, I tie more 1/4-inch nylon line from the bottom ends of the pole down to something around the taffrail, like a block or cleat or even the sternrail. I like to run this line down through something and back up and tie it to itself with a rolling hitch, so I can adjust it later. After this is done, the sides can be pulled as tightly as possible until the whole awning is taut.

The last step is to tie the sides down to the lifelines. Again, I like to run the line under the lifeline and back up to where it is tied to itself with a rolling hitch, so I can adjust it.

If the awning was made correctly for your boat and everything is adjusted properly, you have a tight flat surface with a small gable, so water will run off the top.

To catch water, I reinforced a spot near the center of the surface on both sides, but a little closer to the edge. The location will vary by the boat's configuration. I take a piece of nylon webbing about 2 inches wide by about 12 inches long and sew the center 4 inches of the webbing to the underside of the awning at this reinforced point. The remaining 4-inch ends of the webbing that dangle down have a grommet in each end. Next, I cut out the center of the webbing and awning where it is sewn. The hole is just big enough to take a small plastic through-hull fitting. I fasten these through-hull fittings through the reinforced holes with the nut provided. A quick-release garden hose fitting is connected to the exposed threads on the through-hull fittings.

To catch water, a bungee cord is connected to the two grommets and pulled down to hook on to something on deck, like the handrail. This forces a low spot in the awning where the water will flow. By connecting a hose to the fitting, the water can be directed to where it is needed.

To drop the awning, I untie the center at the mast and at the backstay. If the width of the awning is considerably more forward, I install grommets on the forward edge, spaced the same distance apart as the length of the pole. A line is led from the grommets to any stay that will support the awning while being rolled. (These lines do not take any load other than to support the awning while it is being rolled up around the pole.) I then unfasten the side flaps and throw them over the top of the awning. It is a good idea to tie them together, so the wind doesn't blow them off the top while rolling up the awning. Next, the pole is freed from the backstay and the lines untied, so the pole is free, but remains tethered to the awning. The awning is rolled up on the pole from aft going forward. After the awning is rolled up, it will not be any longer than the pole. The weight of the material used and the length of the awning will determine the diameter of the roll.

If length is a consideration, the pole can be telescopic, like a whisker pole, or taken apart. The awning can be folded over and rolled up on the half-length pole.

The key to a successful awning is to use strong materials, lines, and fasteners and to make it taut throughout.

Beanbags

Most cruisers spend the majority of a 24-hour day outside the boat in the cockpit, so cockpit comfort is important. Many boats will use closed cell foam cushions that are moderately comfortable, but they do not support the back or the body when heeled at an angle.

I like beanbags in the cockpit because they form to the shape of my butt and back. I can use them sitting up, leaning back, or even lying down. I can move them to any place on the boat or take them ashore for a potluck. I even use them in the bottom of my dinghy when I go dinghy sailing.

Most beanbags you buy are made of a plastic vinyl material that will not breathe and sticks to the bare skin. A better material is upholstery-type Sunbrella. It is resistant to sun exposure, it breathes, and it is soft. It is not waterproof but water-resistant, however, only for a short time. If it gets really wet, it will take some time to dry.

When I was in Australia, I found a beanbag made out of polypropylene netting. It was filled with Styrofoam beads and was intended for use in swimming pools. I bought a couple and used them for about a year, until the polypropylene began to break down from sun exposure. So, I decided to make my own out of Sunbrella. I made it taller and wider than the standard beanbag, so it would support my head and my body while in the water. The wider bag permitted the Styrofoam beads to float up alongside my body, which stabilized it and provided an armrest. However, the additional width made the beanbag difficult to use on the boat, because the beads would shift, and I ended up sitting directly on the hard cockpit seats. To solve this problem, I opened the seam between two panels. Between these two panels, I sewed in an additional panel made of nylon netting. I sewed a zipper between the two panels, which would hide the netting until I wanted to use it in the water. I also used the same netting on the bottom, so water would drain more easily.

On the boat, the zipper was closed, hiding the netting panel, making it like a normal beanbag, but taller. In the water, the zipper was unzipped, revealing the netting panel. Now the beanbag was wider and would support its user completely in the water. I tried to market these in the States under the trademark name Aqua Lounge, but there didn't seem to be enough interest, so I discontinued making them. If you like beanbags on your boat or in the water, you could make them for personal use. I encourage you to try it.

The only downside to this is that the beanbag is difficult to get completely dry after being in salt water. To dry properly, it really needs a fresh-water rinse. The other problem is that they must be stored in a locker or below decks to keep them from being blown away or from absorbing rainwater. They are also large and take up a lot of room. However, I found that I often would place one beanbag on the cabin sole, making it a comfortable place to read. Personally, I found that the advantages of the Aqua Lounge outweighed the disadvantages.

Windvane

I see more and more boats going to sea without windvanes, but with autopilots instead. I do agree that an autopilot is important on a boat, but I also feel that they draw considerable power and are more likely to break down. The windvane has no electrical connections that will fail. If properly designed and installed, the windvane will steer the boat better than the helmsman.

For the 13 years I was cruising, I used my windvane from the moment I had wind until I lost wind. When the wind died, I used my autopilot while motoring.

I must give credit to Larry Pardey for permitting me to copy the windvane design they used on *Seraffyn*. Larry was kind enough to personally help me take out some of the design problems I had added. I loved this vane so much that I have another one like the Pardeys have on their more recent boat, *Taleisin*.

The Pardey design only works on outboard rudders. It uses a trim tab behind the trailing edge of the rudder. The windvane turns the trim tab in the proper direction to force the rudder to bring the boat back on course. What I really like about this design is that I can use the most inexpensive tiller autopilot to steer the trim tab. It is effortless and draws negligible current. This type of vane is available from Freehand Steering in Newport Beach, California. They are expensive, but when you consider that each one is handmade to fit the boat and it has many handmade parts, the price is reasonable.

There are many different designs of windvanes on the market today that are equally good. I only mention the Pardey design because it is what I use on my own boat, and I know it well. Some other vanes may even work better. I must admit that I have used other vanes and was impressed with how well they work.

If you are considering a windvane for your boat, ask the manufacturer for a list of owners who have the same boat as you so you can call and get their opinion. Also, make sure the vane is easy and safe to use from the cockpit. It should be stoutly built and mounted, and it shouldn't have complicated parts that could not be replaced easily anywhere in the world. It is a real bonus if the autopilot can drive the vane as well.

Non-skid under interior cushions

A problem I continued to encounter while making a passage was that the berth cushion I was sleeping on would slip when the boat was heeled. I finally resolved the problem by gluing Treadmaster strips to the berth top. I hear carpet will also work. I guess it really doesn't matter what you use on your own boat, as long as it prevents the cushion from slipping.

Air-conditioning

Personally, I feel that air conditioning does not belong on a small cruising vessel. On larger vessels that have generators that run 24 hours a day, it is different. To me, the whole idea of cruising is to see different places and interact with the locals. This cannot be done from the comforts of an air-conditioned boat. In time, your body will adjust to warmer climates. The air conditioner will only postpone this adjustment and make going outside in the heat even more uncomfortable.

I have seen a few cruising boats with air conditioners, and those aboard rarely leave their boats for anything but short times and for necessities like checking in or out. They seem to continually complain about the heat.

Refrigeration

For years, I sailed without refrigeration. I clearly remember my first passage from Dana Point, California, to the Marquesas, with my girlfriend. We loaded the icebox with blocks of ice and dry ice. The little room left was for pre-made meals and a few items to make sandwiches. The ice lasted about two weeks. It actually lasted longer than the small amount of food we could fit into the icebox. I was dumping buckets of melted ice water over the side every couple of days. Then I got the idea of using the melted ice water for a rinse after a salt-water shower. I asked my girlfriend if she wanted to go first, but she insisted that she would continue to use the boat's fresh water for her rinse.

When I did my rinse, I noticed there was this odor. It was not revolting, but not pleasant either. Before I was permitted to get close to my girlfriend, I had to take another shower with a fresh-water rinse. She said I smelled of old carrots.

As I continued my cruise for the next few years, I discovered ice was difficult to find. If I found it, it was difficult to get it back to the boat. Let me give you another example: I bought a 60-pound block of ice, then had to take a taxi back to where my boat was anchored. I was alone, so I removed the block from the taxi and set it on the hot road. Then, I paid the driver. Next, I moved the ice down to the dinghy. The additional weight made it nearly impossible to drag the dinghy down the beach to the water, so I set the block of ice on some rocks. I pulled the dinghy down to the water and went back to get my ice which had slipped off the rocks into the sand. Unfazed, I put the ice in the dinghy and rowed it out to *Xiphias*.

Alongside the boat, I attempted to set the block on deck, but the dinghy kept moving away with each try. I decided to do it in one quick motion. The block of ice and I ended up in the water with a capsized dinghy. By the time I got the 60-pound block of ice aboard *Xiphias*, it weighed about 40 pounds. Then, I discovered it would not fit through the opening in the icebox, so I chopped it into pieces. This made it last only about one week, and I had to do it all over again. The next time, it went better, but by the time I got the ice in the icebox, there wasn't any room for food. After a few months of this, I found I really did not need the coolness of the icebox and used it for storage.

When I arrived in Australia, I met a local who installed and worked on refrigeration systems for commercial fishing vessels. He told me that he would explain how to install one, and he would sell me used parts. To make a long story short, I did install an engine-driven refrigeration system and found that it forever changed my life. I would find it very difficult to be without one again.

§

To me, refrigeration provides just that extra little comfort I need. Since I am mostly alone, I find it difficult to make a meal without having a considerable amount of leftovers. I can freeze the extra and have it another day. It also permits me to carry my favorite food. I can stock up on frozen vegetables, fruits, meats, and even ice cream. When I catch a big fish, I do not have to throw any away; I can freeze it.

The question is, what type of refrigeration system to install? Before we can discuss the types, there must be a basic understanding of how the systems work. I am not an expert, so if any of my comments are in error, I apologize. As I understand the working principles of refrigeration, there is a liquid called refrigerant. This refrigerant is put under pressure by a compressor. The refrigerant, in liquid form, is forced through a small orifice, referred to as an evaporator, that absorbs heat. As the liquid is forced through the orifice or evaporator, heat is created, and the liquid turns into a saturated vapor. This process of changing the refrigerant to a saturated vapor draws heat from its surroundings, making the area around the evaporator colder.

The saturated vapor that absorbed the heat is in small tubes that can be surface mounted like you see in older type refrigerator-freezers in homes. These tubes draw heat from the air when the liquid is turned into a saturated vapor. Depending on the quality of insulation, the compressor may have to run almost continuously.

The other method is for the cooling tubes to be encased inside a tank filled with an antifreeze-like liquid. The heat is absorbed from the liquid which will not freeze, but will turn into a frozen slush. This tank is called a eutectic tank or cold plate, and it will hold the cold like a block of ice. The eutectic tank or cold plate will hold the coldness longer, so the compressor does not have to work so often. However, this tank is heavy and takes up valuable space inside the box.

The hot, saturated vapor returns to the compressor via a low-pressure return line. The compressor forces the vapor into a heat exchanger that rejects heat or cools the vapor, which changes the saturated vapor back into a liquid. The heat exchanger that cools the vapor can be air circulating around the tubes of saturated vapor, as seen in home-type refrigerators, or it can be raw-water pumped around the hot tubes. After the vapor turns back to a liquid, the process starts all over again.

There are two types of compressors used in refrigeration systems: the engine-driven compressor, which is similar to an automotive air conditioner compressor, and the electric-driven compressor. The most common is the electric-driven compressor, which is similar to the ones used in home refrigerators. These can run on 120-volts AC, 220-volts AC, or 12-volts DC. The 120-volt AC system is great while in port, but must have another source of power at sea. Thus, many compressors work on a combination of AC and DC power.

Today, the 12-volt systems have become quite efficient. These systems require minimum maintenance. If you are going to spend a lot of time in a marina, you might want to consider a combination 120-volt AC and 12-volt DC system. However, be aware that when you leave the American continent, you may never see 120-volt AC power again.

Electrical compressors are air or raw water-cooled. The location for the air-cooled compressor is critical. You don't want the fan from the compressor and heat exchanger circulating hot air through the inside of the living quarters of the boat, unless you are cruising in cold climates. If it is mounted inside the engine room, the efficiency will drop if a running engine causes hot air to do the cooling. If you select this type of refrigeration system, be sure to review the mounting location with the manufacturer.

The 12-volt DC system draws its amperage from the batteries, so it may require an additional 12-volt charging source like wind generators or solar panels. If these power sources do not provide the required power, then the engine can be started to charge the batteries.

The engine-driven system works like an automobile air conditioning unit, except it is raw-water cooled instead of air-cooled. The compressor is installed somewhere on the engine and is driven by a V-belt from the crankshaft. The engine-driven compressor is equipped with a magnetic clutch that engages and disengages the compressor as required.

The compressor that is driven by the engine is much more efficient than the 12-volt system. It will provide the same amount of cooling in about one tenth of the time, but it does require more items to install, and there are more things that could fail.

The engine-driven compressor requires raw water to change the saturated vapor back to a liquid. The return lines of vapor pass through a chamber which has raw water circulating around it. This requires a pump of some sort to move the raw water. On smaller systems, the engine's pump will serve the purpose, if the heat exchanger is installed between the salt-water source and the engine. On larger units, a separate pump will be required.

The engine-driven system, unlike the electrical-driven system, needs a filter that will absorb moisture. Moisture is the main enemy in any refrigeration system, because it will freeze as it passes through the orifice, preventing free movement of the vapor through the system. Since the engine-driven system requires raw water to turn the gas back to a liquid, it may cause some condensation to enter the system. This is rare, but it does happen.

On my last boat, *Nereus*, I installed a combination 12-volt DC compressor and engine-driven compressor. I love this combination, because when I am motoring, I can bring my refrigerator down to the coldest temperature I set. This extreme cold is held in the eutectic tank or cold plate, so it will take a lot longer before my 12-volt DC system is needed. While in a marina, all I have to worry about is that my battery charger keeps my batteries charged, so that there are enough amps to drive the 12-volt system.

I can monitor the amperage draw of my 12-volt DC refrigeration system using my E-meter. I turn off all electrical items except for the refrigeration system; then I leave the boat for 24 hours. When I return, the number of amps used will show on the E-meter. This gives me a good idea of what the current draw is in one full day. I keep my freezer at about 15 degrees and the refrigerator section at about 40 degrees. For a 24-hour period, it draws an average of 20 amps. Of course, this will vary by the size of the refrigerator, the ambient temperature outside, and the amount and kind of insulation used around the inside of the refrigerator.

I feel any prospective cruiser should at least consider installing some type of refrigeration on their boat. To get maximum efficiency, the box must be properly insulated. Look into vacuum panels. They are expensive, but have great insulating qualities. The refrigeration system you select should be reliable. Recently, when I was cruising in the Sea of Cortez, I found most boats had refrigeration. I found it interesting that one of the more famous brands had far more failures than other brands. Do your research, evaluate your power requirements, and then dig deep into your pockets.

General ideas

Insurance

It is difficult to give advice regarding insurance. I have already stated my feelings on the subject, but I will summarize again just in case it was missed. If money is not a problem, have good medical insurance for everyone aboard. Insure the boat for as much as possible. Unfortunately, the cost of all of this insurance is beyond many cruisers' budgets.

Medical costs in foreign countries are far less than they are in the United States. Don't think that other countries do not have good medical facilities, staff, and physicians. Of course, it depends on the country and the location where you need help within that country. However, the same applies here: the best medical facilities are in or near larger communities.

If you have cruising boater's insurance, it may be difficult to get the proper adjustment on the cost of damage done in some foreign countries. I feel that a cruiser who is cruising near or along the American continent would not have a problem. However, if you are in the Solomon Islands or some other out of the way location, the chances are that it will take a lot of time and red tape to get any claims settled.

Liability is another cause for concern. I would not consider sailing without liability insurance in the States, because litigation is all too common. The same may apply in some foreign countries, but it would be far less likely. Unfortunately, some foreign countries are learning from the United States how to make some easy money.

Glassware or stoneware

Many cruisers feel that it is not a good idea to take along their stoneware or glassware, because it will get broken and will be dangerous to have aboard. There is some truth to this, but being a little careful will eliminate any problems. I used plastic aboard for years and really hated it. Wine or a cognac out of plastic just does not do it for me. However, I can eat off plastic plates until they become scratched from too many cuttings.

While I was in Papua New Guinea, I had a friend make me some stoneware square plates with high sides and cups with wide bottoms. I let her select the glaze and design, and they came out perfectly. Now, 15 years later, this beautiful stoneware is on my new boat, and I still love it.

There is no reason not to have glass on the boat, as long as it is not used when it is rough, and there is a good safe place to keep it stored. While underway, I have a wide plastic bowl that I use for a plate as well as a bowl. I have one plastic cup, but refuse to use it for my coffee or wine.

Nonskid plates and cups

Every plate and cup aboard should have some type of nonskid on the bottom. I use a clear silicone-caulking ring on the bottom of all my stoneware and many other items on the boat. After all these years, it is still firmly fastened to their bottoms. I often illustrate the effectiveness of the silicone bead by placing a plate or cup on the top of the hinged chart table and then raise it to a 45 angle, and the item still does not slide.

If you decide you want to do this to your plates and cups, it is a simple procedure. Place wax paper over a perfectly smooth surface.

Then run a bead of silicone around the outside edge of the bottom of the plate or cup. As soon as this is done, set the item on the wax paper. Do not push down too hard, or you will spread the silicone too thin. Let it set up on the waxed paper overnight or longer. After the silicone has cured, remove the item from the wax paper. Using a sharp knife, cut off the excess around the outside edge of the bead.

Retainers in the oven

Even with a gimbaled stove, it is difficult to bake or to do much cooking in the oven without the items sliding around. I found using cheap, throw-away aluminum pie pans, folded in half, can be slipped in the grill or wedged against the sides to prevent movement. I am sure there are other ideas, but this one works well and can be used over and over.

Garbage

It is difficult to properly dispose of garbage while at sea. As they say, "*You are either part of the problem or part of the solution.*" This is easy to say. However, when you have been at sea for three weeks, the plastic and other non-degradable items that are taking up valuable space could make it dangerous to move about at night.

All foodstuffs or anything edible can be thrown overboard. When it comes to paper and glass, it would depend on how far you are from land and how difficult it would be to carry. If possible, break the glass items or at least fill the bottles with water, so they will sink and not end up on some beach. If the paper goods are waxed or have any kind of plastic coating, treat them like plastic, because they will not sink or break down for many years.

Aluminum cans are another problem. Again, try to carry them to a place where they can be disposed of properly, but this may not be possible. Like the bottles, break them or fill them, so they will sink.

Plastic is probably the most difficult to dispose of. Everything is packaged in plastic today. We carry our shopping in plastic bags. They are everywhere in the world. *Under no circumstances should plastic of any kind be thrown overboard, no matter how far you are at sea, or how much you have.* If it is impossible to carry it, consider burning it at one of the islands or, if possible and safe to do so, on board. I am not encouraging this, but sometimes there is no other option. The local natives have no choice but to burn their garbage, so burning it is an acceptable alternative.

When I was in Singapore, I used my little two-horse outboard on my dinghy to move from my anchored boat to the Changi Yacht Club, some distance away. Almost every time I would catch a plastic bag in the prop. They are everywhere in the harbor. They do not sink and they do not disintegrate. *Please, do not throw these overboard.*

Have you ever anchored in an out of the way place and felt like you were the only ones that have ever been there? I have, many times. All too often, I found beer cans on the bottom.

Barbecue

This is one of those common sense items; everyone carries a barbecue aboard. There is nothing like barbecued fresh fish, and it is a healthy way to cook. Most cruisers do not carry briquettes, because they take up too much room and are not available in many other countries. The alternative is propane. Common propane barbecues use disposable propane canisters. Personally, I don't like these because they are normally stored below decks or in an unventilated locker. On my own boat, I installed a bypass to my existing propane system. There is a shut-off valve, so it will not leak propane into the hose devoted to the barbecue. I ran the hose through the transom, where I installed a stainless steel, male hose connector (the type used on common air hoses). There is a separate hose that has the matching stainless steel female connection. The other end of the hose goes to the barbecue's regulator.

This permits me to use the barbecue from the main propane source, and I can still cook something below at the same time.

Cockroaches

Sooner or later, your boat will get cockroaches aboard. They lay their eggs in cardboard boxes and in places you would not imagine. It is almost impossible to keep them off the boat; however, it is possible to kill them and prevent them from multiplying.

I was in American Samoa when I found my boat infested with cockroaches. I was surprised to see that some even fly, and they are *huge*. When I got up at night and turned on the light, I would often see several cockroaches in the galley or head area. I read somewhere that for every cockroach you see, there are at least ten you don't see.

There was a little café in the harbor where the yachties would meet for breakfast. During one of these occasions, I mentioned my cockroach problem. One of the fellow cruisers suggested I mix about equal amounts of boric acid with sweetened condensed milk, then add flour to make a thick paste. This paste was put on the underside of all the lockers and anywhere I might suspect cockroaches.

I followed these instructions, and in about a month, all the cockroaches were gone. After that, I would see an occasional one and then never see it again. I never had to replace the paste or add more, and as far as I know, it is still working today.

Rats

It is really upsetting to know there are rats aboard. They are excellent swimmers and can easily climb an anchor rope. Usually, they come aboard while the boat is alongside a dock, or while it is on the hard. The best prevention is a cat. There were many occasions when I would hear a rat on deck at night. Evidently, so did *Pintle*. In a matter of seconds, I would hear a splash as the rat escaped the feline hunter.

§

There was one time when I did not have my cat aboard. I was in Lumut, Malaysia, and needed to return to the States for a month. Another cruiser, who also had a cat aboard, agreed to take my cat while I was gone. I set my boat on the hard and locked it up tight, except for two small portlights on either side of the companionway. They had bronze screens, so I left them open for ventilation.

A month later, my flight left California in the middle of the night. I had to fly to Singapore and then on to Kuala Lumpur. After the flight, I rode a bus for eight hours to get to Lumut. Another hour dinghy ride up the river got me to where my boat was on the hard. It was just getting dark. When I arrived, I had had almost no sleep for over 36 hours.

The first thing I noticed was that one of the screens in the stern portlight had a large hole eaten through it. When I entered the boat, I saw two rats take off in different directions. There was pasta, rice, and shredded paper everywhere.

I noticed that they had managed to get into my galley drawer where I kept my eating utensils and had made a nest. They had eaten through the finger pull from the inside in two drawers. The holes were about 4-inches high and 2-inches wide. The whole boat smelled of rat dumpings. It began to rain outside, which made the smell worse.

I cleaned up the mess the best that I could and poured myself a triple scotch. Still dressed, I laid down on my bunk. I fell asleep, but was soon awakened by the sound of rats scurrying around the boat. Angry and tired, I turned on the lights, grabbed my hammer, and went for them. After knocking big dings in my boat and never coming close to a rat, I decided I would have to wait until morning and poured myself another triple scotch.

The next morning, I asked the local owner of the boatyard what I should do. He said that he had rat traps, but seriously doubted that they would work. He explained that rats would not eat if they were frightened or felt threatened.

I set the traps all over the boat inside and out. Two days later, the bait was still there—and so were the rats. I still could not sleep at night from rats scurrying about. I spent a good part of the night sitting in my bed with a flashlight trying to determine where they were hiding out. I discovered they were staying in the chain locker.

The next day, in a daze from lack of sleep and a severe hangover, I grabbed my net dive bag, put on my foul weather boots and leather gloves, and went on the offensive. I held the opened net bag at one end of the lid to the chain locker, then began to open it. In an instant, I had an 8-inch rat in the bag. I immediately stomped on it until guts spilled out if its stomach. I set the dead rat in the cockpit and returned for another.

I killed four adult rats and two young ones. Two more young rats got into my hanging locker and were never found nor heard of again. I expected to smell their dead carcasses in the months that followed, but it never happened. This method of killing rats may seem cruel, but remember, I was nearly out of my mind from lack of sleep, and I was desperate. My next attempt would have been starting a fire inside the boat to chase them out.

§

What I am trying to say is make every effort to keep rats off the boat. Reversed funnels tied to dock lines, as seen in photos on big ships, work well when the boat is tied alongside a dock overnight. At anchor or on a mooring, it is difficult, but I suggest the same reversed funnel. Remember that rats will not take bait if they feel threatened, so find some good traps and leave them alone as if they were welcome. I don't think rat poison is a good idea, because the rat may find an inaccessible place to die.

Preventing weevils in dry goods

No one wants to open a bag of flour or rice and find it full of little moving creatures. This can be prevented by dipping a Q-tip in ether, then wrapping it in foil; be careful not to make it airtight. Instead of foil, some fellow cruisers suggested using an empty 35-mm film canister with holes in it. The objective is to prevent the Q-tip from making direct contact with the flour or rice. This little container is then placed in the same container as the rice or flour and resealed. If you use too much ether, it will affect the smell and taste of the food.

Ether may be difficult to acquire. It has been suggested that bay leaves also work. At this moment, I have bay leaves in my rice and flour on the boat and will know for sure if that method works or not.

Operation manual

It is a good idea to have a detailed manual on how to operate each piece of equipment aboard. This should include operation, maintenance, and elementary repairs. This may be useful if something happens to the skipper, or an urgent situation arises, requiring the captain to return home and someone to remain aboard. There is also the possibility that an emergency would require a delivery captain to sail the boat to a specific destination; this manual will help ensure that everything goes as it should. I would rather have the delivery skipper concentrate on sailing and navigating, rather than trying to figure out how to make something work.

List contents of lockers

When we begin to provision the boat, we have certain locations for canned goods, dry goods, etc. As the months pass, we forget where we put the repair kit for the galley pump or spare parts for the head. Maybe we are cooking a meal and find we have run out of stewed tomatoes. A detailed list of the contents in each locker will make life much easier.

If you have a computer, a database can be used to list each locker and its contents. It can be listed alphabetically. If you want, it can be separated into particular categories. Regardless of your method of listing or categorizing the items, have a hard copy and try to mark it each time you use something. This is the most difficult part of the whole idea. Even if you don't mark off the items used, the list still comes in handy when you need something that has not been used for a long time.

Keep water tanks clean

I hate the taste and smell of dirty water. Even worse is to see little things floating in the bottom of a glass of water that I just drank. Keeping the water tanks clean is important for your health as well as your peace of mind. This means there must be some way to access the inside.

Inspection plates should be installed on the top of all water tanks. If there are baffles in the tank, an inspection plate should be installed on both sides of the baffle. If your water tanks don't have inspection plates, they can be installed later. I found flat deck plates work well. They are available in bronze or polyethylene and come in different sizes. I like the cheaper plastic ones that have a clear, removable cover. If the cover leaks, it may be necessary to use a little dab of cooking oil on the top of the rubber "O" ring before closing.

The best way to clean the tanks is to remove them from the boat; however, in most circumstances, this is difficult. Therefore, they must be cleaned in place. I let the tank get nearly empty, then add a few tablespoons of bleach. Using a clean rag, I shove my arm through the inspection plate and clean it the best I can. For that reason, the inspection plate must be big enough to accept a person's arm and permit it to reach the ends.

After I feel it is clean, I pump this remaining water through the system and let it sit. Then, I pump out the rest of the water and fill it again with about the same amount of clean fresh water. I scrub and pump it out again. I continue to do this until I can't smell the bleach. Then, I add about half a cup of baking soda and fill the tank. The amount of bleach and baking soda will vary depending on the size of the tank, but I don't think it's critical.

Cup holders outside

We have all experienced a drink tipping over when we did not expect it to happen. Many products to hold drinks are available. I particularly like the ones that attach to any upright stanchion with Velcro tape. These are easy to install, adjust, use, and remove. There are others on the market that may be equally good. The point is to have something that will hold drinks while underway.

Cockpit table

Anyone who has sailed in the summer realizes the importance of a cockpit table. It is difficult to give advice on this subject, because all boats are different. The important thing is that the table be sturdy enough so that it does not tip over from the wake of a passing boat or an unstable person. Additionally, it should be easy to install quickly, or it probably won't be used much.

On my own boat, I use my existing table leaf from inside. It is nearly as wide and as long as the cockpit footwell, which makes it about the perfect size. The table leaf is attached to the inside table with take-apart hinges, which makes removing it quick and simple. The underside of the table leaf has a hinged leg attached at each end. In the cockpit, I already have a cleat running around the top inside of the footwell. (This cleat also accommodates the grating from the bottom of the footwell, when I want to raise it and make a flush deck for sleeping outdoors.)

To install the table, I drop down the wide, hinged piece at the aft end of the table. It sits on top of the cleat and screws into the side of the cleat with a threaded knob. The other end also drops down, but the hinged leg goes all the way to the bottom of the footwell. When the table is installed, it is horizontal, rigid, and still provides plenty of leg space.

I can't say that there isn't a better alternative to my design, but this works for me. The point is that every boat is different, and a lot of thought will have to be used to create the cockpit table that works for you.

Net bags

I know that net bags are great on boats, because they permit good air movement around them. The problem that I have encountered is that they must be installed in a rather permanent location, so they cannot swing like a hammock. I used to have potatoes in one of my net bags that turned to mashed potatoes while they were still raw. The bag was installed from the overhead, so it had good air movement around it. In a gale, the bag swung from side to side until every potato was crushed. I even had a bungee cord on the bottom to dampen the swing, but the bungee wasn't strong enough. Another problem is if something goes rotten in these net bags, it will drip out the bottom on to whatever is stored under it.

In some cases, I prefer milk-type plastic crates that have slots for ventilation. These can be stacked and are easy to clean. They are more difficult to install on the overhead, but I have seen it done by hinging one side and putting a clasp on the other.

Instrument slides

There are some instruments that should be clearly seen from the cockpit. Most of the instruments that should be exterior mounted are waterproof, so they can be installed on the aft end of the cabin or on an instrument panel in the cockpit. I like to be able to see my fish finder depth sounder and radar from the cockpit. These are normally weatherproof, but rarely waterproof. Also, they are fairly large and more difficult to install on an instrument panel. For this reason, I like to mount these instruments inside the companionway, so they can be pulled or swung out and be seen from the helm.

There are different kinds of mounts available. There is the swing-out mount that works well. It can be installed on a vertical bulkhead or to the underside of the coach roof to swing out and be seen from the helm. What I don't like about this setup is that because of the wide arc required to swing it in and out, only one instrument can be mounted. Also, if the friction clutch is not tight enough, it can swing back and forth violently. I have never heard of one of these brackets breaking, so I doubt that this would be a concern.

I made a mount so that the instrument could slide in or out without swinging. This permitted more than one instrument to be mounted side by side, as shown in Figure 102. It is simple and anyone can make one, although it does require some welding or silver soldering.

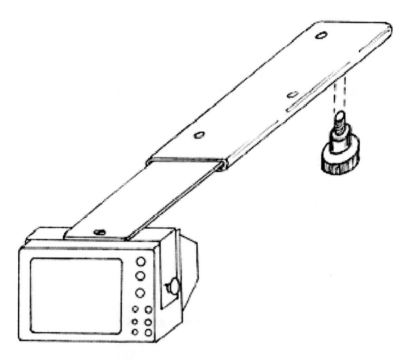

Figure 102. Instrument slide

To determine the length and location where this slide-out bracket would be installed, I measured the length from the side of the companionway, along the underside of the coach roof, to the side of the cabin. On my own boat, it was about 24 inches.

I found a piece of stainless steel plate that was 1/8-inch thick by 3 inches wide and about half the above mentioned length: on my own boat, about 12 inches long. I measured in from both sides half the width or 1-1/2 inches, and drilled a 3/16-inch hole in the center at both ends. Over these two holes, I welded a 1/4-20 stainless steel nut on one side of the plate. I then drilled through these nuts into the plate with a #7 drill. Using a 1/4-20 tap, I threaded through the nuts into the plate, so it was a continuous thread all the way through.

Next, I countersunk the other side of one of the holes on one end. Finally, I polished it with some fine wet and dry paper to make it smooth and to give it a satin finish.

I took the mounting bracket for the instrument to be used and drilled a hole through the center of the mount. Using a round head, stainless steel 1/4-20 screw with washer, I fastened the mount to the stainless steel nut on the plate where the backside of the plate was countersunk. To keep the mount from rotating too easily, I hammered the end of the thread on the screw where it passed through the other side. Then, I ground it down until it was flush. The countersunk recess left enough material to keep the screw from coming out by accident. When finished, the mount could be rotated, but with considerable resistance.

Next, I found a piece of polished 16-gauge stainless steel sheet a little over 4 inches wide by the length I measured from the side of the companionway to the side of the cabin. On my own boat, it was about 24 inches. I set the stainless steel plate with the nuts welded on one side in the center of the longer stainless steel sheet and scribed it along the sides. Along this line, on both sides, I bent it over 180 , leaving enough space to snugly slide the stainless steel plate. The bend on each side ended up being a little less than 1/4-inch wide. I should comment here that stainless steel sheet, like wood, has a grain, and if it is bent along the grain, it will probably break. Consequently, make sure the bend is perpendicular to the grain, or experiment on a piece first.

This stainless steel sheet with the sides bent to 180 had to be mounted to the underside of the coach roof near the companionway. The mounting area of the coach roof had a slight curve, so I had to make a teakwood piece to fit between the stainless steel sheet and the underside of the coach roof. This teakwood back-up piece was nearly as wide as the stainless steel sheet. One side matched the curve of the coach roof, and the other side was perfectly flat.

I drilled mounting holes through the stainless steel sheet and the teak back-up piece. These holes were staggered from side to side, not in a straight line. After drilling the holes, I countersunk both the stainless steel sheet and the flat side of the teakwood. (The stainless steel sheet is not thick enough to accept much of a countersink, so I hammered a tapered rod over the holes to make them concave.)

Using #12 stainless steel sheet metal screws or self-tapping screws, I mounted the teakwood and stainless steel sheet piece to the underside of the coach roof. The stainless steel plate with the instrument mount slides into the bent stainless sheet mounted to the underside of the coach roof. A knob with 1/4-inch thread is screwed into the nut at the other end of the slide. This can be used to hold the slide in any position. It is a good idea to have a hole drilled to accept this threaded knob, when it is extended to its extreme and when it is retracted.

Since the center slide is only about 12 inches long, it will only adjust the instrument in and out about 10 inches. This distance will vary by the amount of space available. The more available length, the further in and out it can be adjusted.

Almanac

As I mentioned earlier, even if you do not carry a sextant, you should carry an Almanac. This government book, published annually, is full of useful information about navigation, time for sunrise, sunset, moonrise, moonset, and a lot more. Knowing the exact time the sun or moon will rise or set can help determine latitude and longitude.

Charts

Charts are available in small-scale and large-scale. The small-scale chart covers a much larger area: the increments of measurement are smaller. The large-scale charts cover a much smaller area: the increments of measurement are larger.

The more small-scale and large-scale charts aboard, the better. The problem is cost. For this reason, many cruisers will buy the necessary small-scale charts to get them to where they want to go and a minimum of large-scale charts, because no one knows for sure exactly where they want to visit. It would be unfortunate to predetermine each location you wished to see before leaving home; you would miss many great places and little known anchorages.

When a cruiser reaches a rather populated city, it is common to make copies of charts from other cruisers. If this is not possible, the local country will have their own charts that are far less expensive than American or British Admiralty charts.

I am not a great lover of American charts, because they come in so many sizes. This makes them difficult to use on a small chart table and to store in a chart locker. British Admiralty charts, on the other hand, are all the same size and just about the right dimensions to fit a small cruising boat's chart table. Unfortunately, they are more expensive than American charts.

I like chart plotters, but would never rely on them as the only source of navigation. If they are interfaced with the GPS, they make navigation easy. They will show where your boat is on the chart at all times. The problem is that the charts are not accurate enough to rely on. You can't presume that you are where the chart shows that you are.

Tide tables

I have mixed feelings about world tide tables. They all require that the tide time be interpolated from a major city. This will often cause some mathematical error. Most countries have their own tide tables. These are easier to interpolate, and in some cases, it is not necessary to do so.

If I were doing a circumnavigation in a short period of time, I would probably carry world tide tables. There are some areas where knowing the exact time that the tide changes is critical: for example, sailing from New York through the battery to Long Island Sound. For the many situations and areas of the world when exact timing is needed, I prefer local tide tables. This does not mean that the world tide tables should not be aboard; I just feel more comfortable with local ones.

Navigation triangles

If you have never used matching triangles for plotting on the chart, you should. They are small, simple to use, and do not require the compass rose to determine a course. To explain how they are used would be too lengthy a discussion for this section. If you do not have any knowledge or experience with these, I would highly recommend doing some research on your own.

Cotton in the tropics

This is another common sense item. However, when I left to go cruising, no one ever mentioned that my polyester clothes were going to make me miserable in the tropics. It did not take long to discover that thin open-weave cotton is the best material for clothing.

I especially love the Thai fishing pants and shirts I found in Thailand. The pants are about as wide as normal pants. There are no belts or belt loops, zippers, or buttons. Folding one side over the other and tucking it in itself holds up the pants. The material is light open-weave cotton and is really comfortable. The shirts are made of a similar material without buttons. They have loose open sleeves and slip over the head like a sweater.

Use a magnet to check fasteners

Many stainless steel fasteners have more carbon steel than other stainless. The more magnetic the stainless, the more readily it will rust. Many fasteners and hardware will appear to be brass or bronze, but are actually steel with an electrical plate coating. A magnet will indicate the difference. I feel there should not be a single piece of hardware or fastener on the boat that will attract a magnet.

Permanently mounted fishing reel

When I was in Australia, I worked for an engineering company that had a lot of metal-working equipment. I decided to make myself a fishing reel that I could mount to any vertical stanchion, shown in Figure 103.

I found a plastic reel that had been discarded by a local welding shop. The reel holds the welding wire used for Mig welding. When the wire is gone, the reel serves no purpose, so it is thrown away. The reel has a 2-inch hole in the center of the axis. First, I machined a delrin or nylon plug that fit snugly into the hole. It was then screwed through the hub into the plug, so it could never slip. After this was done, I drilled a 1-inch hole through its center.

I took a piece of 1/4-inch aluminum angle iron about 2 inches wide and welded a 1-inch solid aluminum rod in the center on one side. The other end of the rod was threaded to take a large nut. I used this larger size angle iron, because I was going to mount it on my boom gallows. If I were going to mount it on a lifeline stanchion, I would have chosen something smaller.

All that was left was to make a handle and a delrin brake. To keep the delrin brake from turning, I had to install a pin in the rod and a matching slot in the delrin brake. After it was finished, I mounted it on the boom gallows with hose clamps.

The fishing line is led up to the top of the boom gallows knee, where it passes through a block which is held to the boom gallows knee with a bungee cord. This acts as a snubber line.

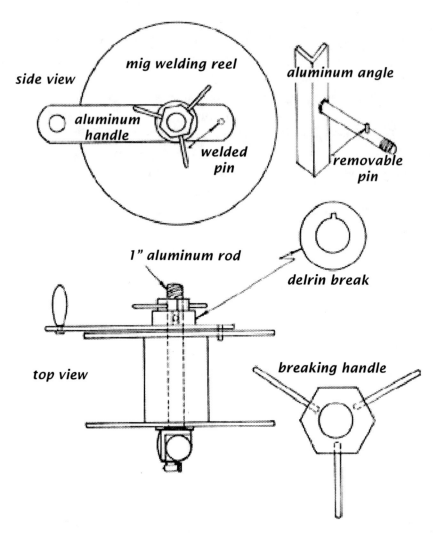

Figure 103. Fishing reel

Lobsters

Most everyone loves to eat lobsters. Unfortunately, they are not very easy to catch. They come out of their hiding places to feed at night, which makes it the best time to catch them. In the United States, it is illegal to spear a lobster; consequently, they have to be taken by hand or with a trap. In many other countries, there are no laws on how to catch them.

I watched some local natives catch lobsters without even getting in the water. They take their dugout canoe, a bright light like a Tilly light attached at the end of a long pole, their hand spear and go hunting for lobster. They only search for the lobster in shallow water, like over a reef or large coral head. The bright light is extended out over the bow about 6 feet. The spear is set in the water below the light, so the deflection can be easily seen. When a lobster is spotted, the spearman on the bow points in the direction to paddle the canoe. When the lobster is under the spear, it is speared and brought aboard.

I am not promoting hunting lobster this way. I only mention it simply to illustrate how locals capture them.

Fishing nets

Fishing nets are not permitted in many countries, so I am not encouraging their use. However, in some countries small personal fishing nets are permitted. A fishing net about 5 feet high and 40 feet long will catch dinner in just a few minutes.

The netting must have weights on the bottom and floats on the top. Corks make great floats. One end of the netting is attached to a pole or oar that is shoved into the bottom in shallow water. The netting is walked out until it is fully extended. Taking this outer end, walk back in a wide arc to the end where the netting is attached to the pole. When the pole is reached, pull the netting ashore to see what is for dinner.

Again, I mention this only as a survival technique. I should also mention that having any fishing netting aboard can create problems in some countries.

Mark cans in bilge

Most cruisers are already aware that the paper coverings on cans can come off and plug the bilge pumps. This not only creates bilge pump problems, but if the label comes off, there is no way of knowing what is in the can. A permanent Magic Marker will last a long time, and it is waterproof. If the cans will be stored where there is any possibility that they may get wet, take the paper labels off and mark the cans.

Lightning protection

I presume that every cruiser is concerned about lightning protection. There are so many theories on the best way to protect your boat, that it is difficult to reach a conclusion. This is not an easy item to address. What I propose here is only a suggestion. I really have no idea if it works; however, I do know that I have never been struck by lightning while using this method.

While I was working for a copper mine on Bougainville Island in Papua New Guinea, one of the fiberglass boats was struck by lightning, and it blew a big hole through the hull. The boat had lightning protection that went through the hull to a dissipation plate. Most of the company's engineers also had fiberglass boats on moorings. A meeting was held to discuss the problem. First, they talked about some characteristics of lightning. Much of what was discussed was far beyond my comprehension; however, I took some notes, which I will attempt to summarize below.

A comment was made about lightning following a pre-charged ionized course. It begins at the grounded surface and works its way up. If there is a way to dissipate these ions, the charge is lost, and the lightning will not strike. However, if the ionized charge goes up without dissipation, it is more likely that the lightning will follow this path. I have heard some sailors say that during a lightning storm, they saw the mast get a green aura around it. They were lucky they were not struck by lightning. The green aura is the ion charge. In the old Man-of-War sailing ships, sailors referred to this phenomenon as St. Elmo's Fire.

The assumption that lightning follows a predetermined charged ionized path was illustrated by the way the company buildings were protected. They installed a lightning rod on the roof with a 14-gauge wire running down to a 5/8-inch by 6-foot long copper-plated rod driven into the ground. As of the date of that meeting, no building had been hit by lightning.

Lightning will not make a right angle or sharp turn. This eliminates the idea of having a wire connected to the base of an aluminum mast at a perpendicular angle or any kind of tight curve.

Another characteristic of lightning is that it will take the path of least resistance, which means it will follow the best conductor that is close to a vertical straight line. Therefore, an aluminum mast is an excellent conductor of electrical current, while stainless steel rigging is a poor conductor. Consequently, the lightning will follow the aluminum mast before it will follow the stainless rigging. A steel hull is an excellent conductor, while a fiberglass hull is a full insulator. For that reason, lightning will pass through the steel hull without any resistance, but will not pass though a fiberglass hull without doing some serious damage.

Lightning requires a means to dissipate its charge when it reaches its ground. If there is no way to dissipate the lightning strike, it explodes on impact. Steel hulls and external ballast provide a large enough surface to dissipate the strike. The real concern is with wood or fiberglass hulls that have encapsulated ballast.

A lightning bolt carries an electrical magnetic charge that can damage any piece of electronics near it. It does not have to hit it directly, only to be close to the item.

There was a lot more discussion, but this is enough to explain what was decided regarding how to protect the fiberglass boats. The primary objective was to keep the boat from being struck at all. This could be done similarly to what was done on the company buildings, by creating a path for the ions to dissipate, eliminating the charged path. A boat with an aluminum mast could have a lightning rod of some sort to dissipate the ions. This rod would be connected to the aluminum mast and would have to reach a ground to complete the cycle.

However, this was not an absolute guarantee that the boat would not be struck by lightning. Therefore, the next objective was to make certain that the lightning strike did not pass through the hull. It was also important to keep a lightning strike outside the boat to protect the electronics and the personnel.

It was concluded that an aluminum wire connected to the mast leading down one of the shrouds or stays to a large dissipation plate set in the water would prevent the lightning strike. If it didn't work, it would at least keep the lightning strike outside the boat. This solution was adequate for the boats on the moorings. There was no discussion about boats underway, so I made my own based on this information. See Figure 104.

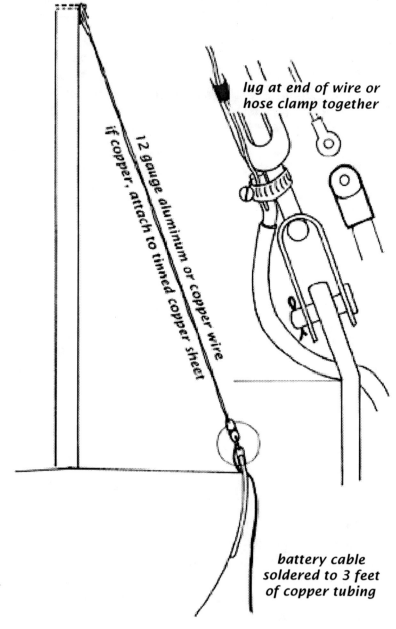

lug at end of wire or hose clamp together

12 gauge aluminum or copper wire if copper, attach to tinned copper sheet

battery cable soldered to 3 feet of copper tubing

Figure 104. Lightning protection

I connected the aluminum wire to the mast between the mast and the lower shroud tang. This wire was taped to the aft lower shroud where it terminated at the bottom of the turnbuckle with a large aluminum lug that would accept a 5/16-inch machine screw.

I found a three-foot piece of 2-inch aluminum tube and connected it to a 2-foot, 0-gauge aluminum wire with a matching lug, the same as the one on the wire on the shroud. I drilled a hole at the top of the aluminum tube, so water would pass through it. When I was concerned about lightning, I connected the wire from the aluminum tube to the wire on the shroud. Then, I dropped the tube in the water. When it filled with water, it nearly doubled the outside surface area for dissipation. I was told that this was probably not a large enough surface area to dissipate a strike, but that it might work.

I have used this method for years, but I changed to all copper instead of aluminum. The aluminum quickly corroded, and the aluminum parts were not readily available elsewhere. At the mast, I took a copper sheet and tinned it on both sides with solder to reduce the chance of electrolysis.

Again, I must say that this is my own idea, and I can't promise that it will work. I include it here only as information to use in determining what type of lightning protection is best for your boat.

Laundry

Most boats are not big enough to have a washing machine, so the laundry is done by hand. I had heard of cruisers who put their dirty laundry in a net bag and dragged it behind the boat for hours before washing. I tried this and found it really did not work any better than letting it soak in a bucket of soapy salt water overnight.

I have seen the small hand-operated machines that, as far as I am concerned, only take up room. The effort to crank the handle to agitate the laundry seems like it would take more energy than doing it by hand.

The best laundry that I have ever had done was by the locals. I would ask for a price ahead of time. Their price would be so reasonable that I could not even consider bargaining with them. In some places, they were so happy that I accepted their first price that they put extra effort into the job. Shirts that I only use for working on the boat, that should have been thrown away, turned out like new.

Having your laundry done by the locals is a win-win situation. Try it and everyone will be happy.

Headphones

For one year, I had my girlfriend and her two children aboard. It was difficult to find any private time together, or to have personal discussions, because little ears were always perked up listening. I already had one stereo installed, so I installed another devoted to the children. I also bought two sets of headphones, so they could listen to their own music or stories without bothering us.

As for my girlfriend and I, our lives changed. We could talk about anything without worry of being overheard. The biggest problem was that the eleven-year-old sang along with the music—off key.

I even put a jack just inside the companionway, so the headphones could be used outside on mild nights while on watch.

Use bucket for head at sea

In the previous chapter, I mentioned that it might be a good idea to use a bucket for a head while underway, or as some would say, "Use a bucket and chuck it". This would depend on the weather conditions, the number of persons, and the compatibility of all aboard. I feel it is especially important to use a bucket instead of trying to go over the side. Too many sailors are lost this way. A simple bucket will greatly reduce the risk.

There are buckets with watertight lids available. A regular toilet seat can be fastened to fit over the bucket if necessary. Of course, the bucket must be strong enough to take the weight of the heaviest person aboard. Also, it must have a substantial handle, strongly fastened, for dumping and cleaning.

Plumber's helper

I found the common plumber's helper (a plunger) comes in handy on a boat. It can be used for what it was designed—to help clear a head. It can also be used as temporary place to hang a towel, tie mosquito netting, or hang a curtain. I found it makes a good agitator for doing the laundry. If there is a through-hull valve that needs to be worked on and you don't want to take the boat out of the water, the plumber's helper can be pushed over the through-hull on the outside of the boat. The pressure of the water will hold it firmly against the hull, as long as it is a flat smooth surface. I have done this several times. First, I cut the handle short, then drill a hole through the end to take a small line. I lead this line aboard, so I can remove the plumber's helper when finished without getting back into the water. I am sure there are many other uses for this item. Use your imagination.

Deck washdown pump

I feel it is almost essential to have a deck washdown system aboard. All too often, the anchor chain brings stinky sludge aboard. It is nice to wash the chain clean as it comes aboard, so it does not stink up the boat when it goes into the bilge.

If you don't already have one installed, consider making a portable one. It is important to use a pump that will provide enough pressure to wash off sticky clay. This pump can be mounted on to a board and a wire led to a 12-volt DC outlet. If the pump is portable, it may be a good idea to have two sets of hoses: one for salt water and one for fresh water.

The salt-water hose can be used to clean the anchor chain and boat if necessary. The fresh-water hose can be used to transfer water from a large container to the boat's water tank. Also, it will come in handy when you need to empty the water tanks for cleaning.

Hiding place

There may come a time when your boat is burgled while you are away, or even worse, while you are aboard. I think it is a good idea to have two hiding places. One would be a little easier to find, and the other almost impossible to find. Keep some valuables in both places, but the most valuable items in the one that is hard to find. If someone comes aboard and forces you to give over your valuables, you can act reluctant and then give in to showing them the place more easily found. *Do not put passports in the hiding place that is harder to find*; the thieves know you have a passport and if they can't find it, they will become suspicious and may make things more difficult for all aboard.

Every boat has places that can be converted to a hiding place. If false floors or partitions are used, make sure it is not apparent that the existing compartment is smaller than it should be. That's a sure indicator that there is a secret compartment. This is something I cannot help you with. Every boat is different. Besides, I certainly am not going to reveal what I did to my own boat.

Leather shoes

If your cruise takes you into the tropics, you will encounter a lot of coral reefs and coral heads. At low tide, the coral is full of good eating items like fish, lobster, and various kinds of shellfish.

When I was on an atoll in the Tuamotu Archipelago in French Polynesia, I was invited to go reef fishing with the locals. They waited until low tide then spread across the reef and began walking. The standing tidal pools had some good size fish stranded until the tide changed. When the locals found such a pool, they herded the fish into shallower water, then killed them with their machetes. If they wanted lobster, they would do it at night. I was amazed at how well this worked.

The major problem was that the coral is really sharp. Without proper protection, feet can be torn to shreds in little time. On this first occasion, I wore tennis shoes and returned to the boat with my shoes in shreds and my feet bleeding badly. The next time, I wore my Topsiders, but they were not high enough and could not be worn in public again. Find some old leather shoes that are devoted to this purpose only. It is fun, the whole family can participate, and it puts fresh fish on the table.

Coconuts

If you have ever tried to open a coconut with the husk on, you know that it is not only difficult, but you can also get injured trying to do so. When I arrived at my first landfall in the Marquesas Islands, I couldn't wait to eat a fresh coconut. That was my symbolic gesture of proving to myself that I was really in the tropics. I had my hearty dive knife with me and began to attack the coconut. I finally got it open, but I sacrificed the blade of my knife in the process.

I learned that the locals use a stout stick with a point on one end. The stick is stuck into the ground with the pointed end up. The coconut is slammed down on to this stick, so the point penetrates the husk. The coconut is twisted downward against the side of the stick. This will tear off the first piece. Then, the sharp point of the stick is shoved between the husk and the shell. The same procedure is repeated until the husk is removed. After you get the hang of it, a coconut can be husked in seconds.

The natives eat the coconut at three stages in its development. Most of us are familiar with the older brown-husked nut. This nut is found lying on the ground under the tree. It has coconut water and hard coconut meat inside. Most natives throw the liquid away and use the meat. The meat is not eaten like a piece of candy as we do. They shred the coconut over a special grater that can be bought for nearly nothing in any local store. The shredded coconut is then put in a clothlike bark found at the bottom of the coconut tree, and the liquid is squeezed out. (Any loose weave cloth can be used.) This liquid is the actual coconut milk. It looks like milk and is used in almost everything they cook. The remaining dry grated coconut meat is often discarded.

The older nut will begin to sprout. A green sprout starts to grow out of one end. If left alone, it will take root and become another coconut tree. If you can find a nut that has just begun to sprout and open it, you will discover a coconut fibrous ball. This ball is sliced; the meat inside is sweet and eaten like candy.

The younger coconut is green and still on the tree. This nut does not have the coconut meat fully developed yet; it is like a silky paste. The water inside is sweet and cool. The husk remains on the nut, and the top is cut off with the machete. Unfortunately, this coconut is only available while still on the tree. When you see the natives climbing the tree, it is this green coconut that they are going after. At this stage, the liquid inside is sterile and can be used as a sterile wash if necessary.

The coconut and the coconut tree is the most important staple in the tropical islands. Each tree belongs to someone—even if it is on a deserted island. Keep this in mind before you begin to cut down a young coconut tree to get to the core to make a palm salad.

Know some basic knots

Knots are designed to serve two purposes: to hold firmly without slipping and to be easily untied after being under a load. Depending on what you are tying, almost any knot may work and will not slip; however, after it is under a load, it may be impossible to untie. For this reason, it is a good idea to know how to properly tie some basic knots. The following are a few of the knots that I consider most important. I encourage you to learn these as well as others.

Bowline

The bowline is the most common knot used to tie a line to anything that you want to be held securely and not slip. It can even be used to connect two lines together, and it can be used to tie a line to a chain. This knot is probably the most used of all the knots.

Rolling hitch

This is the knot I utilize to tie two lines together, or one line midway down another line in order to take a load. I use this knot to tie my snubber line to the chain. It is easy to tie and easy to untie. I also use this knot on my large awning where it is fastened to the lifelines. I can pass the line down, under the lifeline, and back to itself with a rolling hitch. I can then make easy adjustments by sliding the knot up or down the line. If I get an override on my jib sheet, the rolling hitch can be tied to the sheet and taken to another winch to take the load, making it easy to release the override. There are many uses for this essential knot.

Reef knot

This knot is used to tie around something like dropped sails or stops on coils of rope. It is the most common knot used to tie in reef lines. When I use this knot, I like to make it a slip reef knot so it can be released quicker and easier.

Bucket bend

This knot is used for tying a line to the handle on a bucket. There are other knots that can be used, but this one works well for that purpose.

Warm or cold water exposure

Most cruisers do some diving. If the water is cold, they wear a thick wetsuit to keep them warm. In the tropics, the water is not nearly as cold, so a much thinner wetsuit is needed for SCUBA diving and just a bathing suit for skin diving.

Sooner or later, you will encounter tropical parasites when diving. Parasites manage to get into any exposed area, and their bite hurts. I have gone swimming with just a loose bathing suit and had them attack my genitals. I couldn't get out of the water fast enough to get a fresh water rinse. When you intend to dive in waters where there are parasites, wear a full-length nylon suit for protection. You will find it also comes in handy when scrubbing the bottom. These suits are available in ski and diving shops.

Every boat should have a wetsuit for diving in deep tropical waters or water in higher latitudes. The wet suit is one of the best things to wear when the weather gets rough and wet. It keeps the person warm and does not create a stack of wet clothes that have to be rinsed in fresh water and dried before they can be worn again.

Soft bottom paint over hard

For years, I sailed with a hard bottom paint on my hull. Each year I painted another coat over the old. After many years, the buildup was such that it needed to be stripped. This is not an easy process. Stripping the bottom paint can also remove any barrier coat that may be underneath. This problem can be prevented from the very beginning by using the ablative-type paint.

On my own boat, I only used one coat of a hard non-ablative bottom paint and painted it to the top of my boot top. The color I selected was as close as I could get to the actual color of the boot top. I gave the boot top area an extra coat or two. This prevents any growth at the waterline.

After this was dry, I masked off the waterline. This may not be easy, if the coats of hard paint hide the waterline. Perhaps before you begin, you should mark a vertical line along the waterline every 12 inches. This mark should extend above the top of the boot top. Then, measure down from the top of the boot to the waterline, and pencil this measurement above the line. After the hard paint is applied, measure down the distance to where the waterline was, or is, and mark it. Using a long thin batten, connect all these spots to find the waterline. Now mask it.

Some hard bottom paints may require a light sanding before another coat can be applied. Some do not need to be sanded, if the paint is applied within a designated amount of time after the last coat. Select an ablative paint that is close to the same color, but does have some minor contrast. Apply many coats of the ablative over the hard paint. The ablative paint is soft and wears away slowly. Eventually, it will wear away, revealing the hard bottom paint and making it apparent that it is time to add more ablative paint. If the contrast between the hard and soft paint is too extreme, it will be a real eye sore; that's why they should be close to the same color, or at least complementary. Since ablative paint wears away, try to apply extra coats at higher abrasive locations like the waterline, bow entry, prop aperture, and rudder.

The ablative paint must be compatible with the hard paint, or it may not adhere. It is usually safe to use the same brands; they probably use the same solvents. I suggest you call the manufacturer to make certain the two paints are properly matched and to find out if sanding is required.

Hunting vest

This is not my original idea; I read it somewhere and found it an excellent suggestion. Go to a hunting goods store and buy a cheap hunting vest. It is really nice when working on the mast, or when you have to carry many items like cotter pins, screws, nuts, washers, drills, tapes, and small tools.

Flexible fuel tanks or bladders

I am a little reluctant to comment on these, because they may have greatly improved since I had one on my own boat. I used a 15-gallon bladder for kerosene before I converted to propane. I had it solidly fastened in the bilge of the engine room.

I was on the hard in Pago Pago, American Samoa. They use a huge platform that will hold many boats, including commercial fishing vessels, all at the same time. This platform is on a track similar to railroad tracks on a slight incline. As the platform moves up, the vessels are supported with uprights and blocks. It continues up until the entire platform is high and dry.

I had just filled my boat's bladder with kerosene. While we were going back into the water, my automatic bilge pump turned on. My first thought was that I had a leak in the stern gland or a through-hull fitting. That was until one of the locals in the water, who was removing boat supports, began to yell about oil in the water. I realized that it was my boat pumping kerosene into the water. I immediately closed off the switch to the bilge pump and discovered that the bladder full of kerosene had burst and filled the bilge.

As I said, these may have improved by now and will not, or should not, fail. But before you buy one, do some more research. I would never have one again. Just imagine if it had been the head's holding tank.

Mail

I often had difficulty getting mail while cruising. The only way to receive it is through General Delivery. Most countries will only keep General Delivery mail for a limited amount of time. If the words *"Hold for Yacht in Transit"* are part of the address, they will keep it longer. An example of my mailing address would look like this:

Roger Olson, Yacht XIPHIAS
Hold for Yacht in Transit
General Delivery (Poste Restante)
Guadalcanal,
Solomon Islands, South Pacific

I had my Ham radio license then, so had regular radio contact with my parents, brother, and friends. I often knew, in advance, that there would be mail waiting for me.

When I would go to the post office and ask for mail for Roger Olson, care of General Delivery, they would say there wasn't any. In many countries, the last name is actually the given or first name, so they would not call me Roger Olson, but Olson Roger instead. This got me to thinking, so I asked if there was mail under Roger. Sure enough, it was there. After that I found mail under XIPHIAS, Roger, Olson, and even Transit. As a joke, some of my friends included Captain in front of my name or put an esq. at the end. This just made matters worse.

My problem was considerably reduced by using only my yacht's name and not including my name at all. Then, even from behind the counter, I could see if there was mail in the "X" box. The problem is that they ask for verification of identity, so I had to carry my boat papers with me. I also had my boat's name on my passport as my primary address.

What I am suggesting is to "KISS"—Keep It Simple, Sailor. The mail should be addressed to a single word. In following sentences, it can have the person's name or anything else to identify him or her.

When I go cruising again, I will have an address that may look like this:

NEREUS
Hold for Yacht in Transit
C/O Roger Olson
General Delivery (Poste Restante / Lista de Correos)
Etc.

Dinghy

There are two types of dinghies used on boats: the hard dinghy and the inflatable or soft dinghy. There is a lot of controversy on which is best. Those who have inflatables swear that they are the only way to go. On the other hand, the hard dinghy owners feel the same about theirs. This controversy will never be resolved, because they are entirely different and have their own advantages and disadvantages. Each cruiser has to carefully evaluate which one is best for his or her needs. On *Xiphias*, I actually carried both types—and she was only a 28-foot boat.

They both cost about the same for equal length. They are both about the same weight for length, so these two factors are not really a consideration. Both the hard and soft dinghy manufacturers have attempted to make compromises: many inflatable dinghies today have hard fiberglass bottoms, while the hard solid dinghies are available with inflatable collars.

It is my intention to discuss what I consider the pros and cons of both types. The final choice must be made by deciding which type best fits the needs of the skipper and the crew.

The soft inflatable dinghy

The inflatable dinghy is the most common type used on cruising boats today. The reason most owners give for owning an inflatable is that it can be deflated for storage below decks or on deck. In an emergency, it can act as a life raft if necessary. It is stable, so it is good for diving and swimming, and it can carry more passengers than a hard dinghy.

There are several disadvantages to the inflatable dinghy. It can be punctured or ripped more easily than the hard dinghy. It loses its rigidity when it gets cool, making it necessary to inflate at night. If it is inflated at night, there may be too much pressure during the heat of the day. To get the same volume inside the inflatable dinghy, the outside is much larger, thus taking up much more deck space. It will deteriorate in the sun. It won't row well, so it requires an outboard engine. Most cannot be sailed. The inflatable abrades quickly if pulled up on the beach, and it cannot be dragged up on coral. Unless it has wheels, it must be carried. They have a limited life before a new one is needed.

It is rare to see an inflatable dinghy totally inflated while the boat is making even a short passage, because it takes up too much room on deck. Some will deflate it and store it in a locker or below decks. Obviously, this eliminates using it for an emergency life raft.

Depending on the inflatable dinghy's design, a strong wind can get under it and flip it over. I have seen this happen many times when a squall passes.

The hard dinghy

Most hard dinghies are made of fiberglass. Some are made from polyethylene, and some are made of wood. These last two materials would not have the same durability as the fiberglass dinghy. Of course, that is a generalization. It would really depend on the construction of each.

The advocates of the hard dinghy claim that it is always ready to deploy. It is much more difficult to puncture. It rows well, even to weather, so an outboard engine is not required. It can be dragged up the beach, even coral. Most are equipped to sail. It does not break down in sunlight and has a far longer life expectancy.

There are several limitations to the hard dinghy. It is not nearly as stable as an inflatable, making it difficult for swimming or diving. It has limited carrying capacity, so it restricts the number of people and goods it can transport. It cannot be deflated to store away, and it does not work well for an emergency life raft.

§

I would like to share a short story about what happened to one inflatable dinghy while we were in the Marquesas.

My girlfriend and I had just returned to Autona, on Hiva Oa, after spending several days in a little bay named Hana Menu. There was a family living there, Ozane, his wife Maria, and his brother Nick. They had been great hosts for nearly a week. While we were there, we wanted to do some diving, but Ozane and his brother Nick advised against it because the water was too dirty.

When we returned to Autona, we ran into a couple we had met previously, Warner and Inga, on a German yacht named *Caira*. I told them about our anchorage at Hana Menu and the great time that we had with Ozane and his wife Maria. When I mentioned Hana Menu, Warner's features clouded. He began to tell his story.

Warner said, "I will never dive there again. In fact, I may never dive again at all."

"Why?" I asked

Under the shade of a large tree, Warner began, "Inga and I had invited Ozane and Maria to have dinner aboard *Caira*. The sun had set, but it wasn't completely dark. We were through eating, and

Ozane wanted to get back while there was a trace of light. I put them into my inflatable dinghy, and we rowed away from the boat. Suddenly, a shark came out of the water and tore a piece out of the dinghy's right back chamber. My dinghy has three separate chambers, so we stayed afloat. The shark returned for another bite. I grabbed an oar and so did Ozane. We beat him off, but he swam to the other side of the dinghy and tried again. Repeatedly, we beat the shark on the head. Perhaps we stunned him, for there was a break in his attacks, and we paddled back to *Caira*. As soon as I lifted what was left of the dinghy aboard, the shark disappeared. Maria and Ozane slept on board that night. Early the next morning, I rowed them ashore in my hard dinghy."

§

This illustrates the vulnerability of the inflatable dinghy. I realize that occurrences like this one are rare. However, over my years of cruising, I have heard similar stories.

I know of two incidents in which the outboard engines were stolen from inflatable dinghies while they were padlocked to the transom. The thieves simply cut the transom away from the dinghy.

It is probably apparent that I prefer the hard dinghy. It is easy to row, and I enjoy rowing for exercise. I also love to take it sailing just for relaxation. What I don't like is that it is difficult to use for swimming and diving. I had some inflatable collars made. They clip to the sides when I want to swim or dive off the dinghy. The inflatable collars will provide some stability, and they allow the hard dinghy to be used as an emergency life raft if the collars are permanently fastened to the sides of the dinghy. Many cruisers with hard dinghies use boat fenders lashed to the sides for stability.

If you are considering a hard dinghy, find one that has a stem entry to make it drier to use. My first dinghy had a pram bow, or a flat tapered entry. This was okay in mild situations, but when there was a chop, I found that the spray and waves hitting the pram brought lots of water into the boat.

Try to find a dinghy that has a large load-carrying capacity. This usually means a higher freeboard. Look at the method by which the flotation is installed. Be careful of air chambers that have regular deck pipe openings. If these leak—and they will sooner or later—the dinghy could sink. I like flotation that is permanently fiberglassed inside the boat.

If you intend to sail the hard dinghy, it is nice if the seats can be removed or their positions changed. This makes it more comfortable to sail. On my own boat, the seats are removable, and I put my beanbags in the bottom. This keeps me low in the boat and almost too comfortable. I have fallen asleep several times and was awakened when I went aground or hit another boat.

I do not like centerboards on dinghies. The main reason is that it is almost impossible to seal when towing behind the boat, or when the boat is loaded to capacity. It also interferes with my beanbag. I prefer a leeboard that is deep enough to leave on one side and that will swing up when approaching shallow water. The same applies to the rudder; it should also swing up for shallow water, but still steer the boat.

Dinghy wheels

Both inflatable and hard dinghies are heavy and awkward to carry up the beach. If you are anchored where there are extremely high and low tides, the dinghy may have to be carried or dragged a considerable distance. Installing wheels on the transom of the dinghy can reduce this problem.

I installed a wheel at the aft end of the keel between two stainless steel plates. This worked well on concrete, but just sunk deeper into sand. So, I designed the wheels shown in Figure 105. These really worked well for me for many years and are still working today. However, since that time, some excellent ones have become available at any good marine store. I include this illustration only for the cost-conscious sailor, or for those who like to do it themselves.

First, I had to find the wheels. They had to be wide enough so they wouldn't sink in sand and strong enough to roll over rocks and coral. I found the answer with the wheels on kid's toys, like tricycles. They have a nice tread, are durable, and cheap. There are better wheels on the market, but they were not available to me when I made my dinghy wheels.

The major problem with these toy wheels is that they are hollow and may have a hole in them because they are injection molded. Make sure the hole through the wheel for the axle is sealed to the inside of the wheel, not hollow. If the only hole in the wheel is the one used to inject the material into the mold, it must be sealed. I find that 3M 5200 works well for this. You can even fill the wheels with expanding foam first to reduce the chances of water entering.

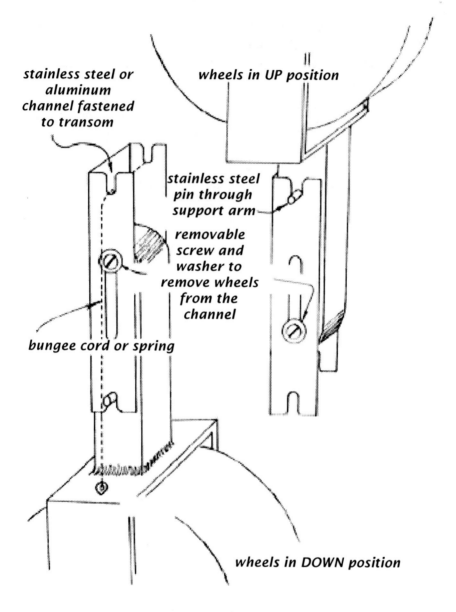

stainless steel or aluminum channel fastened to transom

wheels in UP position

stainless steel pin through support arm

removable screw and washer to remove wheels from the channel

bungee cord or spring

wheels in DOWN position

Figure 105. Dinghy wheels

To fabricate the wheel brace, I found a piece of 1-inch square aluminum tubing. The biggest problem I had was to find a 1/4-inch thick by 3-inch wide flat aluminum plate to make the wheel bracket. I managed to get it bent into a 'U' shape, then had the 1-inch square tubing welded to the top center of the bracket. Next, I found some aluminum channel the right size for the square tube to just fit inside the channel.

The rest was simply a matter of drilling holes and cutting the center slot. If the wheels were not buoyant enough to keep the wheels up in the slot, I used a bungee cord to hold them up. The illustration pretty much explains the way it works.

Dinghy painters

Many boats tow their dinghies behind the mother boat. I really discourage this, except for short distances. Often, the dinghy will capsize, resulting in some damage to the dinghy and the mother boat. When a dinghy is upside down, the entry that is designed to keep the bow above water will now force it below the surface, creating tremendous resistance.

The inflatable dinghy is more susceptible to being flipped, because it has a flat bottom. Air can get under the dinghy and actually lift it just long enough to make it flip upside down. Because of their hull shape, the inflatable with the hard 'V' bottom and the hard dinghy have less chance of lifting and flipping.

If the dinghy must be towed, it should be either tied to or directly behind the transom, or on a long painter, so the pull is mostly horizontal or even down. A small weight in the center of a long painter will cause more drag, but it will keep the bow of the dinghy down. *However, don't forget this weighted line and inadvertently back the boat, catching the dinghy's painter in the prop.*

It is amazing how many sailors forget this until it is too late, but they never make the same mistake again. I have seen inflatable dinghies pulled into the prop and chopped into pieces. I like my dinghy painter made from polypropylene because it floats, thus reducing the chances of the painter being caught in the prop. The downside is that it must be replaced twice as often as nylon or dacron line, because it breaks down more quickly in direct sunlight.

Another problem that occasionally occurs is that the clip at the end of the painter fails. I used to employ a simple spring clip that I could just press over the lifeline, and it would stay there, or so I thought. As it aged, the spring clip did not always spring closed. The jerking motion of the dinghy, created by the wake of a passing powerboat, caused my dinghy painter to come loose more than once. You would think I would have learned from the first time, but I thought that it was my fault for not lubricating the spring. After cleaning and lubricating the clip, it greatly improved; however, occasionally it refused to spring closed, and I would fail to notice. I finally replaced it with a snap shackle that had to be locked by hand. This eliminated the problem.

Another way to tow a dinghy for short distances is to tie it alongside the mother boat. This will greatly reduce any flipping problems, but it may be hard on the sides of the mother boat and dinghy. This method should only be considered for a short duration and in calm conditions.

The dinghy while at anchor

When anchored, most beginning cruisers and sailors leave the dinghy tethered to the transom, trailing behind the boat some distance away. This works well in most conditions, but the time will come when the dinghy moves in front the mother boat, or the mother boat sets with the current while the dinghy sets with the wind. The result will be the dinghy banging against the boat in the middle of the night, as shown in Figure 106.

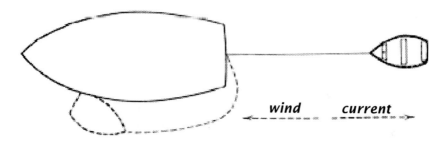

wind   *current*

Figure 106. Dinghy behind transom

Another problem with this method is that if the painter is long, a local powerboat or inebriated sailor may motor between the dinghy and the mother boat, catching the painter in its prop. There are other ways to store the dinghy for the night.

One method I tried is to extend the whisker pole out off the beam and tether the dinghy to the end of the pole, as shown in Figure 107.

If a harness is used, the dinghy can have some water poured inside, to help reduce the roll of the boat. There must be two lines to the dinghy: one is to bring the dinghy out to the end of the pole, the other is to bring the dinghy back to the boat.

I used this method a lot but found there were a few times that I regretted it. The problem with this method is that it takes some time to release the dinghy and get underway in a hurry. Also, it can be a problem if the anchorage is crowded, or there are other boats anchored close. At night, the pole may not be seen and could be hit by a passing vessel.

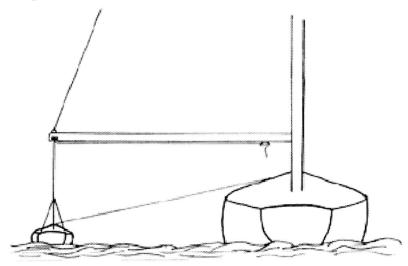

Figure 107. Dinghy on whisker pole

I like to tie my hard dinghy alongside the mother boat when I am at anchor, as shown in Figure 108. For most cruisers, this is probably the most commonly used method. The painter runs forward, and a stern line is run aft to keep the dinghy in place. A couple of fenders between the dinghy and the mother boat prevent the dinghy's side from banging the mother boat at night. The bow and stern lines should be adjusted so that they are quite loose, or the fenders will be screeching against the hull all night. The only downside to this method is that if the dinghy rolls too violently, the fenders will fall inside it.

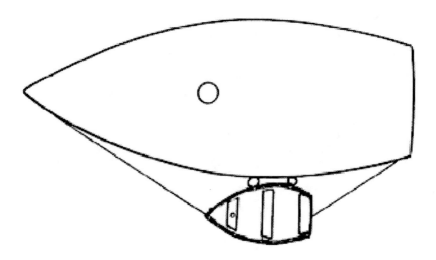

Figure 108. Dinghy alongside mother boat

Another method to store the dinghy at night while at anchor is to raise it with a halyard and rest it against the side of the boat, as shown in Figure 109.

This method is similar to the one mentioned above, except the dinghy is lifted out of the water. The dinghy is tied fore and aft and rests against fenders between the dinghy and the mother boat. To use this method requires that the dinghy have a lifting bridle supported at three or four locations. This bridle is attached to a halyard and lifted free of the water. I often use this method if the anchorage is rough, because if the dinghy is just tied alongside, it could roll under the fenders on the mother boat.

An alternative to this method is to just lift the dinghy so its top rests against the side of the boat. This can be done with the bow up and the stern down. It can also be set alongside the boat sideways, but this requires a two-point bridle.

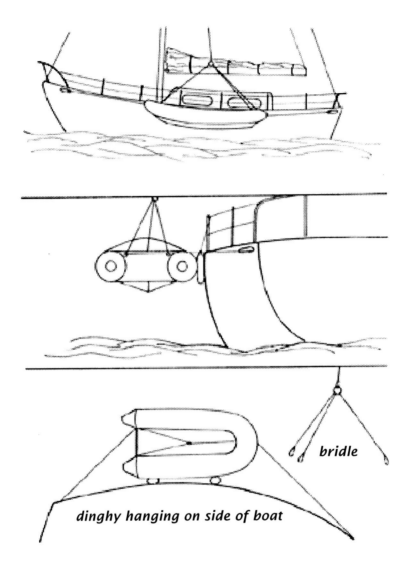

bridle

dinghy hanging on side of boat

Figure 109. Dinghy on the side of mother boat

If the mother boat will be anchored for some time and it has a stern anchor or stern line ashore, the dinghy can be tied to this stern line. This requires a little more work than the other methods mentioned above. This is why I said this technique should only be used if the mother boat will remain anchored for a while. There are several ways to accomplish this. I will mention a couple of my favorites, shown in Figure 110.

One method uses a pulley or block to pull the dinghy to and away from the mother boat, shown in Figure 110 (a). This method requires that a small block be seized to the stern anchor line. The dinghy's painter is led from the bow of the dinghy to the stern of the mother boat. Another line is led from the stern of the mother boat, back through the pulley block, then up to the stern of the dinghy. To bring the dinghy to the mother boat, the stern line that leads through the block is loosened while the bow is pulled to the boat. The opposite procedure is used to leave the dinghy for the night.

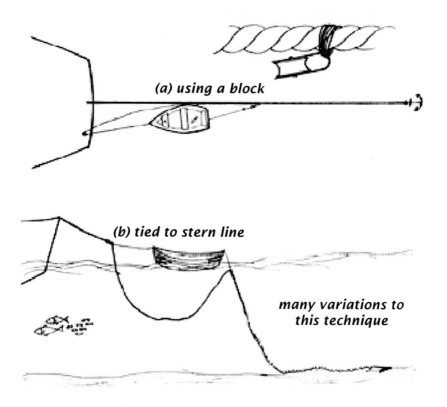

(a) using a block

(b) tied to stern line

many variations to this technique

Figure 110. Dinghy tied to stern line

Another method is to tether the dinghy to the stern line, as shown in Figure 110 (b). There must be some slack in the stern anchor line. This is normally accomplished by the weight of the chain sitting on the bottom. The objective is to tie the stern of the dinghy to the stern anchor line by pulling enough anchor line aboard, then releasing it after the dinghy's stern line is tied to the anchor line.

To do this, first tie the painter to the mother boat. Pull in some of the stern anchor line aboard the boat, and tie it off. Then tie the dinghy's stern line to the stern anchor line with a rolling hitch. When the stern anchor line is released, the weight of the chain will pull the anchor line and the dinghy aft, away from the transom. The dinghy's painter is normally tied to the other side of the transom, so it doesn't take the load of the stern anchor line.

To board the dinghy, the opposite procedure is used. Pull the stern anchor line aboard until the dinghy's stern line can be untied, and then release the stern anchor line. The dinghy is still tethered with its painter to the stern of the mother boat for boarding.

Raising and lowering the dinghy

As can be seen from Figure 111, raising and lowering a dinghy is easy if the boat is large enough to have the mechanical gear to do so.

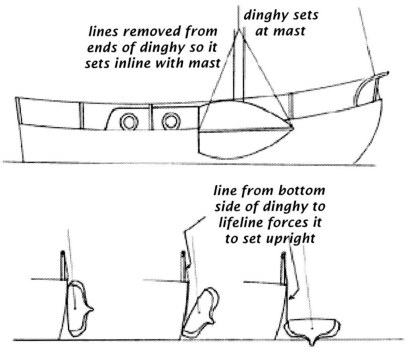

Figure 111. Raising and lowering the dinghy

The problem is with smaller boats and limited crew. The more help aboard to assist while doing this makes the chore that much easier. The problem I always encounter is that I usually must do it by myself.

I store my dinghy on the foredeck, upside down, over the scuttle hatch, as shown in Figure 112.

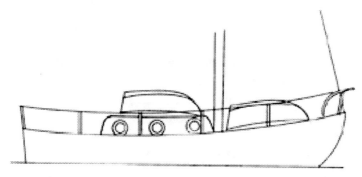

Figure 112. Storing dinghy on deck

I know that many will disagree with this method, because they say it interferes with working the sails forward. I have not found it to be a hindrance at all. In fact, I like to wedge the sail and myself between the lifelines and the dinghy when I am changing or reefing the sail.

The method I use can be applied to setting the dinghy fore or aft of the mast, upside down or right side up, with only minor alterations. To achieve this, the lifting bridle must be attached to the pivot point of the dinghy fore and aft, so when it is raised, it is easily to be turned horizontally, upside down or right side up. If the lifting bridle is attached inside the dinghy, it will set right side up. If it is attached to the outside of the dinghy, it will set upside down.

To set the dinghy upside down, there must be a lifting eye at the pivot point on the outside of the bow and on the outside the transom. In most cases, the existing painter's towing eye and painter can be used as the lifting bridle. There must be an eye installed at the pivot point on the outside of the transom to take the other end of the painter.

If the dinghy will set right side up, there must be an eye or cleat at the pivot point on the inside of the bow and inside the transom. This will require a separate lifting bridle. This lifting line should be about three to four times as long as the dinghy, with a method of attaching it to the bow and stern lifting eyes. In the center of this line, there should be a closed welded stainless steel ring. The position of the ring should be located so the centerline of the dinghy is horizontal when lifted.

As mentioned, if the dinghy will be setting upside down, the dinghy's painter can be used. The ring can be installed in the correct position by slipping the ring over the painter line or bridle to the marked location, then passing the end of the line through itself, pulling it tight, and then seizing it. This ring can remain on the painter or bridle.

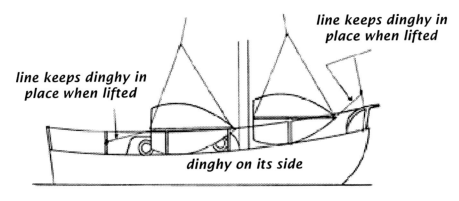

line keeps dinghy in place when lifted

line keeps dinghy in place when lifted

dinghy on its side

Figure 113. Lifting the dinghy

First, let's get the dinghy from the mother boat into the water. Grab one side of the dinghy and lift it until it is setting on its side, leaning against the lifeline and lower forward shroud, as shown in Figure 113. If the mother boat is rolling, I have a small line I clip to the transom eye and to the lower shroud or to the lifeline to keep the dinghy from falling over. My windlass is under the dinghy. If I am anchoring, I have to go through this same procedure, but I also whip the painter around the lifeline as well, to ensure the dinghy will not fall over.

If the dinghy is raised off the deck, the dinghy will fall back to the side of the mast, inside the shrouds. To prevent this, if the dinghy is forward of the mast, I attach a pre-made line to the towing eye of the dinghy and to the staysail stay. This will hold the dinghy in its same position as it is lifted off the deck. If the dinghy is aft of the mast, a line must be led from the dinghy's transom to any place aft, to keep it from moving forward when lifted off the deck.

To lift the dinghy off the deck, if the dinghy is forward of the mast, I use the staysail halyard. If it is aft of the mast, I use the main halyard. I connect the halyard to the center ring on the painter or lifting bridle and take up all the slack.

Then, I put the halyard on the winch and crank the dinghy up until the dinghy is off the deck. The dinghy will have a tendency to roll over either upside down or right side up, depending on which bridle is being used. This is easy to control with your foot or the other hand. If the dinghy is fairly large and heavy, it may be better to use a separate line to keep it on its side. A line can be tied snugly from the upper side of the dinghy to the lifting bridle.

When the dinghy's lower side is only a few inches below passing over the top of the lifeline, cleat off the halyard. If the dinghy is forward of the mast, push the dinghy forward. It will rise as it goes forward until its bottom side passes over the lifeline. Then, let it fall back on the outside of the lifeline until the line between the stem fitting of the dinghy and the inner stay is taut, as shown in Figure 114. If the dinghy is aft of the mast, push the dinghy aft until it passes over the lifeline and falls back on the outside until the stern line is taut. This bow or stern line can now be released to let the dinghy fall back alongside the outside of the shrouds.

dinghy lifted over lifeline

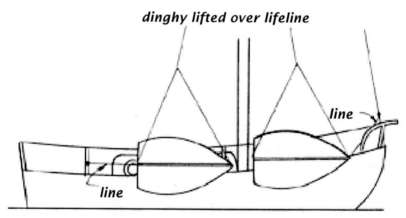

Figure 114. Dinghy over lifelines

You may find this same bow or stern line can be used to stop the bottom side of the dinghy from dipping into the water when it is lowered. If not, one has to be made in advance. I clip one end of this line to the oarlock socket on the bottom side of the dinghy and the other to the lifeline. When the dinghy is lowered, this line becomes taut. The dinghy rolls over, right side up into the water, as shown in Figure 115.

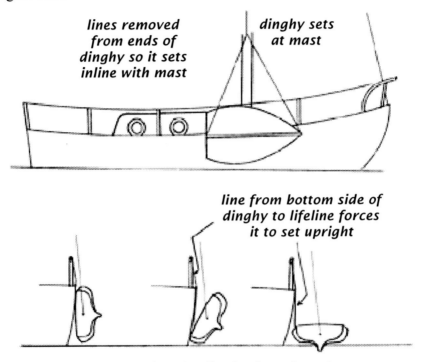

Figure 115. Setting the dinghy down into the water

The exact same procedure is used to raise the dinghy, except that the latter line between the oarlock socket and the lifeline is not needed. To raise the dinghy, the painter or lifting bridle is clipped to the transom eye, and the lifting halyard clipped to the center lifting ring. When the halyard begins to winch the dinghy up, the dinghy will automatically roll on to its side. It may be necessary to move the painter so that it is not caught on the down side of the stem and keel.

Continue to raise the dinghy until its lower side is just ready to pass over the lifeline, and then cleat the halyard. If the dinghy will set forward of the mast, attach the line that goes between the dinghy's stem fitting and the inner shroud. This line will prevent the dinghy from swinging aft alongside the mast when it passes over the lifeline.

If the dinghy will set aft of the mast, do the same with the dinghy's stern line.

Push the dinghy forward or aft until the bottom side of the dinghy passes over the lifeline, and it falls back until the bow or stern line is taut, then lower the dinghy to the deck. If this line between the stem fitting and the inner shroud is the right length, the dinghy will be in perfect position to be manually lowered over the hatch.

If the dinghy goes on the cabin, behind the mast, the rotation can be simple if the lifting line is at the horizontal pivot point on the dinghy. If the bridle is attached to the inside of the dinghy, it will be set right side up. If the existing painter is attached to the outside of the dinghy, it will set upside down. If it is difficult to keep the dinghy horizontal while moving it into position, a short line from the transom's corners to the bridle may be necessary.

One final comment: when raising the dinghy on its side, the bottom side of the dinghy will be rubbing against the side of the mother boat. Slip fenders or a sheet of carpet between the two to prevent any scratches or hang-ups.

Carrying the dinghy alone

When going ashore for the day, the dinghy has to be taken up the beach, so it isn't carried away at high tide. In some locations, the height difference between tides can be considerable. Dinghy wheels on the transom will make the chore easier. It seems like all too often, however, I go ashore and forget to attach the wheels on my dinghy. Depending on the size and type of dinghy, it may be easier to carry it than to drag it up the beach.

This method only works on smaller dinghies with a seat in the center. I mention it because I found it very useful. Stand the dinghy on its transom with the bow raised to nearly vertical. Step under the dinghy, and let the seat rest against your back or butt. Then support the dinghy with your arms, and bend over lifting the transom off the beach. It is easy to carry the dinghy a considerable distance using this method, shown in Figure 116.

**bend legs to get
under dinghy**

**stand upright to
lift dinghy**

Figure 116. Carrying dinghy alone

Medical issues

I am not really qualified to discuss medical issues. All I can do is to mention items that I have found useful during my cruising years and consider the minimum a person should carry. However, don't get sucked into buying too many prescription drugs that will expire before you need them or that can be purchased at a much lower cost in other countries.

The list of medical supplies one should have aboard a cruising boat is almost limitless. A lot will depend on the size of the boat, number and age of the crew, budget, and the type of cruise—gunk-holing along the coast or crossing oceans. The important thing is to have some basic first-aid knowledge and the minimum amount of medical supplies.

When I mention a particular brand name, it is simply because it is the brand that I am familiar with, not because I think it is the best product. Because of the fast turnover of goods, items may also be mentioned here that are no longer available today. What I am trying to say is do your own research to discover the best products for your purposes.

Check with each person aboard to see if they are allergic to any foods or medications. Make a written list of these items. If the allergy is severe, be sure to carry the proper medications to counter the allergy.

Because I am not qualified to give any medical advice, I strongly advise you to speak to your physician about the medications I mention and any other concerns for the particular needs of all aboard your own boat.

Tropical sores

I was surprised to discover that infectious bacteria and micro parasites live in tropical seawater. I was always under the impression that salt water was great for sterilizing cuts and open sores. I remember how quickly cuts healed when I swam or dove in salt water back home. This does not apply in the tropics.

I first learned about these sores when we arrived in the Marquesas. My girlfriend and I went for a walk through the jungle. When we returned to *Xiphias*, we discovered she had a few scratches on one ankle and a few mosquito bites. We both agreed that it would be a good idea to go swimming and let the salt water sterilize the scratches and bites. In less than a week, her ankle swelled to at least three times its normal size; she felt ill and had a fever. Fortunately, there was a medical clinic in town that treated her.

Tropical sores were a constant concern the entire time I was in the tropics. If they were not immediately treated, they quickly developed into a large sore. The sore did not have any pain, but developed into a volcano-looking open wound with a white core in the center. This core must be removed before the healing begins. If the sore heals over this core, applying topical ointments will be ineffective. The core will continue to grow beneath the skin and could develop into a severe problem, even staphylococcus.

External antibiotic ointment

We soon learned that the sore had to be kept wet with a good antibiotic ointment and covered to protect it and to prevent it from drying. We also discovered that the bacterial infection would not react to some types of antibacterial ointments, so we carried different kinds.

Staphylococcus infection

These tropical sores, if not properly treated, can quickly progress into a staphylococcus infection. The staphylococcus bacteria enters the blood and circulates through the body. Even the smallest mosquito bite can turn into a major sore that will not improve with topical treatment. Staphylococcus can be difficult to cure, and it requires oral antibiotics or even injections.

Oral antibiotics

Like with the external antibiotics, bacteria can quickly adjust to oral ones as well. There should be several different types of antibiotics aboard, and they should be clearly marked as to what they are and their intended purpose. Oral antibiotics do not last long in the tropics if they are not refrigerated. It may be better to buy them when you are in a local town that has a pharmacist. (In many countries, they are not called pharmacists but chemists instead.)

Sterilized solutions

Because these tropical sores are so serious and common, I got in the habit of washing my feet and legs from the knee down when I returned to the boat. The moment I saw an insect bite or any break in the skin, I washed it with a sterile solution. Overseas, I found a product called Milton Solution that could be used directly on the sore or mixed with water. There are many similar products that do the same thing. Carry plenty of it, and use it liberally if there is any doubt.

Coconut water

I was told that the liquid inside the coconut is sterile and can be used as a sterile wash if there is nothing else available.

Pain

I have a real low tolerance for pain. Perhaps it is psychological, but I still do not like to have to suffer with any pain of any sort. My problem has always been that no matter how bad the pain, I still had to perform because I was a single-handed sailor. I carried three levels of oral pain medications that still allowed me to function and sail my boat. The weakest was Tylenol and the strongest was Vicodin. This was many years ago; there may be better choices today.

Injections for pain

I was in the middle of a week passage, when I dropped and broke a glass jar. In the process of cleaning it up, I unknowingly knelt on a piece of broken glass. Blood was everywhere. It took some time to get the bleeding to stop, and I did not detect any glass in the wound. The next day, my knee began to swell. Two days later, it was so large that I thought it would burst. I knew I had to do something.

Fortunately, I had some Lidocane aboard and some syringes and needles. I filled the syringe with Lidocane and tried to stick the needle into my knee. Being the baby that I am, I couldn't do it. So I pricked the skin and squirted a little Lidocane on the pricked spot. As soon as it was numb, I did it again and again until I had the needle inside my knee. When it was fully numb, I used a scalpel to cut a half-inch incision where the glass had cut me. As I was cutting a little deeper, I felt the scalpel hit something hard. I was afraid it was a tendon or something I should not cut. I squeezed it and out came the piece of glass that was no more than a quarter-inch long. I dressed it normally, and by the next day, the swelling was gone.

I use this story to illustrate the importance of carrying some type of injection that will permit minor surgery. There are other local anesthetics available; ask your physician which is best.

Syringes, needles, scalpels and sutures

I think it should be apparent that all of these items must be aboard. They may not be that easy to purchase, so ask your physician for assistance. They are expensive, so depending on where you will be cruising, it may be easier and cheaper to buy them over the counter in the first country you visit.

Rash

Rashes are another common problem while cruising. Perhaps it is because cruisers do not bathe as often as they do at home, or because they are exposed to new and unfamiliar plant life.

I like to carry those disposable wash clothes that are sterile and will wipe off surface bacteria and spores. 'No Rinse Body Soap' and shampoo are also good to have aboard. These are available in most good drug stores where they carry adult diapers and other items for in-home adult care. There are excellent solutions available for rashes; carry plenty aboard.

Anti-diarrhea medications

When I left to go on my most recent cruise, I asked my physician for a prescription for something to stop diarrhea. He refused, stating that diarrhea was nature's way of flushing out bacteria or parasites, and stopping the diarrhea could cause major problems. He is probably right, and I will go along with this—for a while. But if I get it, there comes a time when I'll want it to stop. (Not to mention the possibility of dehydration). I think it is a good idea to have some over the counter anti-diarrhea medication aboard, as well as some prescription ones. Talk to your physician to find out when the prescription should be used.

Malaria prophylaxis

If you are heading into a region known for malaria, be sure you understand the symptoms. *It is important that malaria be treated immediately before it causes permanent damage.* The problem we encounter in the States is that there is little known about malaria, because it is not a concern in our country. If you go to your physician and ask for medication to prevent the disease, they may give you the wrong drug for the type of malaria you will encounter, or they will give you the medication used to cure malaria.

Malaria is a parasite carried by the females of a particular species of mosquitoes, the Anopheles mosquito. This parasite has proven to quickly adapt to the common prophylaxis issued today, making it ineffective. Years ago, the military and physicians prescribed

Chloroquine as a preventive treatment. Now, most countries of the world have Chloroquine-resistant malaria. The list of medications that are no longer effective against malaria is getting longer every day. When physicians continue to prescribe the cure for malaria as a prophylaxis, it is only a matter of time until there will be no cure at all for malaria. It is my understanding that we have almost reached such a condition.

I have had malaria three times; all three were while I was in Papua New Guinea. I had been taking Maloprim as a prophylaxis for several years. When I got malaria, I did not know that I had it. I was feeling rotten all the time and had daily periods of chills, normally at night. I went to the hospital numerous times, and although my white blood count was way up, they could not find the parasite in my blood. They did not want to treat me for malaria if they were not certain it was the disease, because the cure is radical and dangerous. One tablet too many could kill the infected person.

While I unknowingly had malaria, I had to return to California to testify at a federal trial. When I arrived in a different, colder climate, my symptoms became more severe. I don't even remember being questioned on the witness stand. I took an extra week to spend some time with my parents and brother. I was so ill that I was hallucinating at times. I went to a clinic, but they said they couldn't find anything wrong with me other than a high white blood count.

When I returned to Papua New Guinea, my symptoms were not as severe, but I still felt terrible most of the time. I was having lunch with a friend who had had malaria several years ago. While we were eating, I got a chill attack. My friend said that I must go to the hospital immediately. I was able to drive myself because I had been living like this for about eight months. When I walked through door, the physician met me with a syringe in his hand and took blood in the lobby. He said that my friend had called from the restaurant telling him I was on my way. Sure enough, they found the malaria parasites in my blood. I began taking the cure immediately. It was nearly as bad as the malaria.

My physician tried to explain in layman's terms how the malaria parasite works. The prophylaxis may not prevent malaria, but will subdue the symptoms. Sometimes, if the prophylaxis is new, strong, and is continued, it may kill the parasite in time, but this is not always the case. If the parasite has already been exposed to the prophylaxis, the malaria may continue to get worse. The problem is that the normal medication to cure the malaria cannot be administered if it has already been used as the prophylaxis, because the dosage would be too high.

What happened to me was that the malaria parasite had adjusted to Maloprim. The parasite continued to live and multiply, but at a much slower rate because of the Maloprim prophylaxis. The malaria parasite lives in the liver and comes out into the blood stream occasionally. While the parasite is in the blood stream, the white blood cells attack the parasite, causing a great deal of activity; this is the reason for the fever and chills. That is why they could not find the parasite in my blood until I got the chills.

There are different types of malaria. Obviously your local physician will not know which type you may encounter, so he might prescribe the wrong medication. If you insist on carrying the medication that is used to cure malaria, I strongly suggest it not be taken until you are sure you have the disease. When you get to a country that has the malaria-carrying mosquito, go to the local chemist (pharmacist) and buy the cure for the particular strain in that area. They sell the cure over the counter because the locals also get malaria, but not as severely as we do. I would carry at least one dose for each person aboard. I will say it again: *make sure you do not administer it until you are certain it is malaria.*

I also suggest you carry some glass slides that are used to test blood under a microscope. After I had malaria the second time, I carried these with me everywhere I went. If I got the chills, I pricked my finger and put a drop of blood on the slide, covered it with another slide, and took it to the hospital. This is how I discovered I had malaria the third time.

Ear infections

Another common problem that often occurs on cruising boats is ear infections. Carry the proper medications that treat both external and internal infections. If you do a lot of diving and swimming, it may be a good idea to flush the ear out with an ear syringe using white vinegar and water or hydrogen peroxide. Speak to your physician before doing this.

Wound dressings

Needless to say, many different kinds and sizes of dressings should be carried. This would include the normal Band-Aids, sterile dressing pads, gauze, sterile bandage rolls, and much more. I like the non-stick dressings rather than the absorbent kind, but there is a use for both.

I recently discovered a stick-on dressing that does not require any washing of the wound. It has its own anti-bacteria fighter in the dressing. They are a little more expensive than the regular dressing. I don't necessarily agree with this, but I suggest you speak to your physician about them. I know it as a Membrane Dot Dressing made by PolyMem.

Medical aloe vera

While I was in Malaysia, I rented a motorcycle to do some touring. A car that fortunately was not going too fast hit me. The motorcycle fell over my right foot, trapping it between the bike and the paved road. As I slid along the road, I tore off much of the skin on the right side of my foot. The skin was completely gone in about a three-inch circle near the bottom of my foot. I was taken to the hospital, where they lifted the remaining skin around this hole and cleaned the area under the skin. They said I needed a skin graft to seal this open wound. I figured that was all I needed: two wounds to heal. I asked what would happen if I did not get the skin graft. They said it would probably heal, but that it would take a long time, and there was always a chance of infection. I decided to have them stitch as much of it together as they could, then bandage it. After the stitching, the open wound was about two-inches in diameter.

I changed and cleaned the dressing twice a day. Betty Pearce, on a boat named *Crazy Lady*, suggested I use Aloe Vera on the wound to speed the healing. I tried this and found that it gave the wound a fresh, less painful feel, and I could see that it was healing much faster. It took about four months, and it was completely healed. Today, I can't find the scar.

Catheters

Fortunately, I do not have any personal experience with using one, yet. I do feel that there should be one aboard for any senior male or female. In fact, there should be one aboard for any adults. They come in various sizes and purposes. I suggest you speak to your physician on the size and type to carry. I know they have some catheters that they claim truck drivers use, which are easy to insert and reduce the other problems that occur by leaving a catheter in place.

Medical books

I suggest you carry several first-aid books aboard. The reason I say several is that I have yet to find the comprehensive first-aid book. I am not saying it doesn't exist, just that I have not found it. I also carry **Merick's Medical Manual** aboard; this is a little too technical for me, but it certainly is better than not having it aboard. There are other medical manuals that are written in more layman's terms; check them out as well.

To conclude this medical section, if you intend only to coastal cruise, the list of medical items will be far less. However, if you intend to make an ocean passage and sail through the South Pacific, there are considerable distances between medical facilities. Each person aboard may have special personal medical needs that should be considered. Again, I suggest you spend some time discussing your cruising intentions with your physician before stocking your first-aid kit.

Firearms

Most cruisers who consider carrying weapons aboard are apprehensive about pirates. I am not about to say that this is not a legitimate worry, because it is; however, it is not nearly as serious of a concern as most imagine.

§

Before sailing through Indonesian waters and the South China Sea, I was warned to be aware of pirates. My first encounter with what I considered were pirates was when I was making a passage through the Flores Sea between the Celebes (Sulawesi) and Java in Indonesia.

There was a 50-foot local fishing boat that stayed a few miles away from us for the full day. That evening, we found a small, uninhabited island that had a moderately protected anchorage on the lee side. Soon after we set anchor, the local fishing boat approached our stern. There was a man standing on the wide rub rail at the bow, holding on to the stem post. I was certain we were going to be boarded.

I had an Australian female crew aboard at the time. I told her to go below because she was wearing a skimpy bathing suit. I did not have any weapons aboard, but I did have my flare gun. I loaded it and set it in the bottom of the footwell. At least, this would stop one of them. Then I began to think, "What if they just want water, food, or money and do not intend to harm us?" I waited.

They sailed right up to my stern just a bit off to one side, so they could grab my backstay. The guy kept his foot on my boomkin to keep their boat from hitting mine. He held on for about a minute and made no attempt to come aboard. The other men on deck were yelling something and placed their hands in a circle like they were holding an imaginary plate by the edges. Then they would make a fist out of one hand and move it up and down like they were working a hand bilge pump. No one attempted to come aboard.

The Australian crewmember, who only had her head sticking out of the companionway, suggested that maybe they were taking on water and wanted a bucket. So I grabbed my bucket out of the side cockpit locker. As soon as they saw it, they nodded their heads in confirmation. I passed the bucket to the man standing on the bow who passed it back to the other 'pirates'. I continued to search for another bucket.

When I brought my head out of the locker with a collapsible canvas bucket, they handed my bucket back, filled over the brim with king prawns. They saw the astonished look in my eyes, smiled, and pushed off before I could even offer something in return.

§

I had many similar occurrences as I sailed up and down the Malacca Straits. Local fishing boats would come at me at high speed, then suddenly turn broadside so they were only a few feet away and toss me a large fresh fish. Sometimes they would ask for cigarettes or candy for their kids, but usually they just sped off, leaving a wake behind them.

I often wonder if I had kept a gun, what I would have done in these situations. At what point would I show the weapon or begin to shoot? This is a question I think everyone should seriously consider, before it occurs. Also, keep in mind that if they are real pirates, they probably have far more firearms and ammunition than you do.

When I left to go cruising, I carried a 300 Savage rifle with a scope and a 32-mm semi-automatic pistol. I am not sure why I carried the rifle; I guess I felt I could shoot a pirate out of the crow's nest at a distance. The pistol was for close range, but more importantly, it quickly killed big fish that I caught before attempting to bring them aboard.

The pistol I managed to hide, but the rifle had to be declared in each country. In those days, some countries permitted the rifle to remain aboard, but locked in bond. If the seal were broken, they would confiscate the weapon and possibly impose a fine.

Regulations are continually getting more severe. If a firearm is aboard, it must be declared. The customs officials will take the weapon with them and hold it until you depart the country. The problem is that the place where the firearm is removed from the boat is rarely the same place that the vessel departs the country. So, you either sail back to where the weapon was taken off the boat and continue from there, or let them keep it.

Many countries will confiscate any ammunition, even if the firearm is declared. They rationalize this by stating that ammunition has a safe life-expectancy. Since they don't know how old the ammunition is, it must be destroyed. It is difficult to impossible to buy ammunition in most countries other than the United States; consequently, this makes the firearm useless.

Because of the problems encountered declaring a firearm, many cruisers choose not to declare. This is extremely dangerous. *If the authorities discover the firearm, they can confiscate the vessel and put the skipper in jail.* I know of a yacht that sailed into New Caledonia that had four undeclared firearms aboard. At the time, the local French authorities were experiencing civil riots by the locals. The owner and the two crewmembers of the vessel were thrown in jail, and the boat became the property of the government. To this day, I do not know the final outcome.

After September 11, I expect that the search of cruising vessels is far more diligent than it was when I was cruising. I personally think it would be foolish for a cruiser to carry firearms and not declare them. There is too much at stake.

Bang Sticks or Shark Sticks were accepted in some countries. It wasn't considered a weapon, and the shells used in the Bang Stick were permitted. That has also changed. *No ammunition of any kind is permitted aboard a vessel.* This eliminates Shark Bang Sticks and converting a flare gun to shoot a 10-gauge shotgun shell.

If you are considering carrying a firearm aboard, try to imagine the situation when you would use it. Remember that many countries do not have officially marked government vessels when they come out to board. If they do, the markings may not be clearly visible or even legible. You may find yourself pulling out a firearm on a government official.

For some, this is a hard decision to make. We Americans are so "gun" oriented, we feel less vulnerable if we are armed. This is an individual issue; however, if you do carry firearms, I suggest do not mention this to anyone except the proper authorities.

This concludes this chapter. I know there are other or alternative methods and techniques that I have missed, but I hope you got some useful information from it. Every cruiser has his or her own ideas and suggestions that give them pleasure, comfort, or make their life a little easier. Share your ideas with others. The cruising life is difficult. With these suggestions, maybe you can make it just a little bit better.

Chapter Seven

INTERACTING WITH THE PEOPLE

It is the purpose of this chapter to provide information that, hopefully, will reveal the enjoyments and pleasures that can be anticipated while cruising. The general information presented will be seasoned with anecdotes that will help to illustrate my views. It is my wish that you will learn from these pages; at least, I hope you find them interesting.

Go with an open mind

One of the biggest problems I have witnessed while cruising is the number of cruisers who have a very negative attitude. Perhaps they don't agree with the check-in procedures or the cost to pay for a particular repair. There are those who can always find a reason to argue with the authorities and remind them that this would never happen in "Our Country". This does not only apply to Americans, but to cruisers from all over the world. The success of the cruise will directly depend on the attitude of all aboard, but most importantly, on the attitude of the skipper.

Avoid being the "Ugly American". Just because you are a citizen of what you may consider the world's best nation, it doesn't mean your values and customs are right for people of other countries. Don't brag about what you have and they don't, or how we do it differently or better.

Give yourself time to listen to what locals are saying and to experience how they live. You may discover that their way is actually better than you imagined, perhaps even better than back home. You will witness living examples of the extended family and how successfully it works, especially when raising children. This is one of the reasons most of the islands in the South Pacific are crime free. The children get their values from their great grandparents. I have never seen happier old people than in these extended families. There, the elderly are not only cared for, but revered. In the United States, we simply put old people in a nursing home to die and go on with our lives.

Try to learn as much as possible about the customs of a country before you rush around the village making social blunders. Try to show sincere interest in the people and the way they live. Learning a few words of their language will go a long way. When I enter a foreign country, I make it a point to let the immigration and customs officials know how honored I am to be in their country, and that I want to learn all that I can. I want to eat their foods, dress like they do, and most importantly, I don't want to offend anyone. I ask the officials to please take a little time to explain some of the things I should or should not do, so that I am more readily accepted and don't inadvertently do or say something rude or offensive. Often, I am invited home to meet the official's family and have my first locally made dinner.

The value of knowing local customs

I previously mentioned the importance of learning as much as you can about the customs and values of the locals you are visiting. To illustrate an example of the harm that can be done, let me refer you to Thor Heyerdahl's book *Fatu Hiva*.

Before I arrived in the Marquesas, I read his book about one of the islands named Fatu Hiva. Thor, who was an anthropologist, and his wife wanted to leave Norway to live someplace where they could live off the land and be politically independent. Thor spent a great amount of time doing his research for the perfect place to live. He concluded that Fatu Hiva was going to be their home.

I read his book with great interest. It was full of fascinating stories and interesting people. There were great photos of him holding up ancient bones and even sitting inside a sacred hollow tree. Towards the end of the book, he was suddenly hiding from the locals and actually in fear for his life. However, the book never clearly explained what had happened that changed the situation so dramatically. I was left wondering why.

While I was at Fatu Hiva, I met an old man named Daniel. I was amazed to learn that Daniel was the same Daniel mentioned in Thor's book. He had been Thor's guide and friend during the years they lived on the island. He and I sat and talked for hours. Through him, I learned that the people were upset with Thor for blatantly desecrating their holy grounds and taking the bones of their dead relatives. I guess Thor could not resist the anthropologist within him.

The point I am trying to make is that every village has certain taboos that must be respected. It is of utmost importance that you learn as much as you can about the customs and values of the country or village you plan to visit before arrival. One *faux pas* can quickly ruin your stay.

Some villages have strict religious beliefs. These beliefs are often reflected in the clothing they wear. For example, if a visiting female were to wear her normal bikini in public in a Muslim country, it would be considered a major offense. In many places, the missionaries were there long before, and some of the villagers take what they were taught to the extreme. *So before you offer perfume, jewelry, cigarettes, or magazines as gifts, be sure you know the local religious doctrine.*

I know of one incident in the Solomon Islands where a cruiser gave a local young woman one of her female magazines. She had forgotten that it had a nude male fold-out. Within an hour, the village Chief came out to their boat and insisted that they leave immediately.

When you set anchor near a village, children and young adults in dugout canoes will surround your boat. They will come alongside, and their number may be overwhelming. These canoes can do considerable damage to the yacht if they remain banging against the hull, so they must be kept away. Instead of using the deck washdown hose, sign language, or yelling, it is much better if it can be handled diplomatically.

Ask if any of them speaks English. If not, ask which one is the number one boy among them. Use polite sign language if necessary. If none of this works, select the eldest or biggest one of the group and invite only him to come aboard to be your representative.

Have him keep the rest of the canoes away from the yacht while you talk. Explain to your representative that the boat is your home, and it deserves the same respect as his home. Children are not to look into the portlights or windows, or come aboard without permission. After you are sure he understands, have him relate this to the others. This gives your representative some authority, and he will be your friend and helper as long as you are in the area. Then tell your representative to invite a few children aboard at a time, and to keep the canoes away from the boat, tied off the stern.

As soon as he is aboard, ask this young adult if it is okay to anchor where you are. This is because many of the villages have sacred ground in the water, and to anchor there would surely offend all of the villagers.

Strive to learn as much as you can about the village customs. Trying to communicate usually ends up being a lot of fun. You will have no idea what happened to cause all the children in the canoes to crack up suddenly at your expense, but this is what cruising is all about: learning and interacting. They have no idea what they do differently than you, so you will have to ask questions.

It is not necessary to give the children candy or cookies, but it is usually really appreciated. Often, they are excited just to be aboard and to see the interior of your floating home.

Do not spend too much time with the children, because the village Chief may become offended. When it is time for your representative to leave, give him a small gift for the village Chief. Ask him to extend an invitation to the Chief to visit your boat and to request his permission for you to come ashore to see their village.

When you go ashore, move slowly and be careful not to offend anyone, or to step where you shouldn't. While I was visiting an outer island in the Solomon's, I was invited ashore by the Chief and was permitted to go anywhere I wanted and to take photos. I walked freely and took pictures of all that interested me. No matter where I went, there was a crowd of children a few feet behind me. As I crossed a little bridge to go on to another small island, all the children began laughing. The children made all kinds of gestures that kept them in hysterics. I had a heck of a time learning that I was approaching Peck Peck Island. This is where all the locals go to defecate.

It is customary in many South Pacific islands for the local villagers to give you a small gift, and it is normally expected that you will return the custom. It does not have to be something special, unless you want it to be. A Polaroid snapshot of their family on your boat will be kept for a lifetime. *However, be sure to get permission before taking any pictures.* Many villagers are superstitious about seeing themselves in a photo because they fear that their spirit may also be in the picture.

Be careful when you select the proper gift to give. Magazines are excellent gifts, but be selective with your choice. They have no interest in sailing, sports, or technical magazines. They like newsmagazines, because they are isolated from the rest of the world and only hear about other places through their local radio. The women like women's magazines, but *make sure there are no nude photos of males. The same applies to men's magazines that have photos of nude females.* People and movie magazines are also a big success. Some magazines are considered pornographic, such as Playboy, Penthouse, or any that reveal more of the body than is accepted by their customs. Most locals won't or can't read magazines; they just look at the pictures. Eventually, the pages of the magazine will end up pasted to the inside of the house's walls for insulation.

The Chief may come out to your boat, but there are those who feel that you should visit them first. The Chief may want you to wear some kind of headdress, or sit in a special house for a period of time to rid you of evil spirits. Treat the Chief with the same respect you would show to the President, and in return, he will give you more privileges.

Consider it an honor if you are invited to a wedding, or a funeral, to go for a hunt, dive, or any other local activity. It would be foolish not to accept the adventure and the learning experience that may result. Spend evenings with the villagers sitting around the fire, and ask about their customs. Listen to their explanations and bring to their attention what you like about their methods. *Don't try to explain why you think your way is better.*

I found nearly all villagers on any island, in any country, love to sing. They have beautiful voices and the harmony they carry is amazing. There are no words to describe the way the sound of the deep, rich baritones harmonize at just the right moment with the high-pitched soprano voices. There were several anchorages I visited where the young local girls came down to the beach and sang to us on our boat for hours.

Many of the South Sea islands have special customs that involve drinking, eating, or smoking something special. Many of the islands drink Kava, or Yangona, as it is called in Fiji. The custom began as a ceremonial drink and still remains so today; however, its use has increased to the point that it is now consumed regularly, like we drink coffee or tea. Kava is a root that is mashed to a pulp, then mixed with water to make a mud-colored liquid. In past years, they used the saliva of young girls for the liquid; today, it isn't often done that way. (You might want to ask before you accept the offer to drink kava.) The effects appear to be cumulative, so the islanders seem to be affected by the drink more than we are. I am not sure what others feel after imbibing, but if I drink enough of it, I only get sleepy.

§

When I was cruising in the Tonga Islands, I had a friend named Jim sailing with me. He and I had tried drinking kava in every village we visited, and it never had any effect on us. So, when we saw a sign that said "Kava Haus", we decided to see how much we could drink.

We stuck our heads inside. We were greeted by long wooden tables, benches, and locals who called for us to join them. It was similar to a public bar, except that it was operated by the local Catholic Church. The Kava Haus only sold kava, nothing else. For about fifty cents, Tongan money, you could have all the kava you could drink, with the money going to the Church.

Jim and I looked at each other. We always said there must be something to this kava for everyone to drink it. "Let's do it!"

We each laid out fifty cents and started drinking—fast. In between bowls, we chatted with the other customers who were astonished at the amount we could drink in such a short time. After we downed several bowls of kava, I began feeling guilty for consuming so much for a measly fifty cents, so I donated a dollar. Jim did the same.

We lost track of how many bowls we'd finished when a guy across the table said, "You must be Americans. We had an American and his wife in here a couple years ago. They drank lots of kava like you two. Finally, they took some kava powder, rolled it like a cigarette, and smoked it. It was funny. They could hardly walk when they left. We had to show them the exit."

A smile creased Jim's face, and he said, "I'd like to buy some of that powder." He gave the man serving the muddy liquid a dollar. When I rose to leave, I felt a little lightheaded and my legs were weak, but otherwise I was fine.

Without incident, we made it to *Xiphias* and rolled our cigarettes. Jim inhaled first and then coughed uncontrollably. The smoke that he exhaled was enough to prompt my own hacking fit.

"What the hell are you coughing for?" he sputtered, and through my watering eyes, I saw his watering eyes. Then he continued, "I'm the idiot inhaling this wretched stuff, not you!"

"I just got some of your smoke," I responded, "that stuff must be solidified sulfuric acid."

Although Jim attempted one more drag, he couldn't suck it down his throat.

"That guy at the Kava Haus was putting us on," I said, wiping away fresh tears. "No one could smoke this stuff unless they had iron lungs, which they'd need after they smoked it."

This ended our attempts to get high smoking kava.

§

I had another experience drinking kava while I was in Fiji. I also learned a lot about their customs and their strong belief in witchcraft. At the time, I had my girlfriend and her two children aboard for our sail to New Zealand via New Caledonia.

We had met a local named Prasad. He had a lovely daughter about the same age as my girlfriend's daughter. They became great friends, as did my girlfriend and I with Prasad's family. We took turns making dinner for each other. One evening, we would go to Prasad's and eat East Indian food. Then, in a few days, they would come out to our boat. We would cook something American, or at least something different.

At one of our dinners at Prasad's, our host and I settled down for our after dinner kava drinking. We were joined by two Fijians we had drunk with previously, but this time Prasad asked my girlfriend to join us. Usually this wasn't permitted. While women weren't invited to partake in kava drinking, they were often expected to prepare the drink. My girlfriend was honored and really wanted to join in, talking and drinking with the men. However, she knew that Prasad's wife had not been invited, and she was keenly aware that this would violate their customs. She politely refused his offer, but he was insistent. To show her gratitude, she drank one cup and slipped back to the kitchen to be with Prasad's wife and the children. The Fijian men felt they had made a generous gesture to their guest and did not urge her to linger. Now, things could get back to normal.

I felt comfortable with these men I had come to know so well, so I asked, "Could I ask a few questions about some of your customs?"

They nodded, and in addition to answering, volunteered information I'd not considered.

I asked my first question, "Why are there three doors in most Fijian houses?"

It was Prasad who answered, "The front or center one is the public door for friends and visitors. The door to its left on the side wall, when looking from the outside of the house, is for family use exclusively. Unless you are invited to use the family door, use the public one. That door to the right of the public door, on the other side of the house, is for the Chief. Only the village Chief is allowed to use it; not even the family living in the house can enter or exit through that door."

The thin, tall Fijian next to Prasad took the next step by saying, "After a guest enters, he should sit on the floor immediately and should never stand taller than the host. If the guest is important, like the chief, then the host will sit or permit the honored guest to stand taller. This also applies to the depth in the house. A guest is to stay near the entry door. If the host invites his guest deep inside, that shows his respect for the guest or the guest's position."

I remembered that when we were in the Yasawa Islands, we all walked through the same door as our host and wandered around the room like it was a public house. I wasn't tall, but I towered over most of our hosts. I thought, "Good Lord, what they must have thought of me!"

I asked, "Is that what happened in Suva when the Queen of England visited? Everyone left the bleachers to sit on the ground."

Prasad laughed and explained, "With someone as important as the Queen, no one should sit higher than She. So, when She came out on the stage, below the public bleachers, a few Fijians left their seats to sit on the grass and the rest followed."

"What is the woman's role in the Fijian family?" I asked. The big, heavy Fijian sat up taller, squared his shoulders, and said, "They are to have our children, obey our orders, cook our meals, or we bash their heads in."

Everyone laughed except the speaker, but he grinned widely. The younger thin fellow explained, "Fijian women take care of their men. The men work hard in sugar cane or in gathering food. At home, she cooks and looks after the children. If the husband has guests, she stays away to give them privacy to talk and drink kava. She wouldn't dare eat or socialize with the men, because she has chores to do in the kitchen. Some men beat their wives, but that custom is looked down on, so it's not so common anymore."

We took a break for another hand-clapping drink of kava. I learned that hand clapping after drinking a cup or bowl of kava was a way of saying "Thank you" to the host, an old custom carried over to today, similar to our tradition of shaking hands on meeting.

When talk resumed, I heard several examples of why a wife would be beaten. Prasad told the story of a woman who clubbed her husband, bashed in his head, and then served him his kava.

Laughter began to die down when I asked, "What about witchcraft? I've heard Fiji has some strong witchcraft."

Instantly, total silence ensued. I could even make out words and phrases from the kitchen. To break the uneasy quiet, Prasad poured more kava and asked, "Do you mean magic?"

"Yes, I understand that the Fijians are one of the few peoples who still actively practice witchcraft or magic."

Prasad regarded both Fijians, but they sat stonily. When he spoke, his voice was cold, "We have special people who are born with a gift. It's passed on from generation to generation in the same family. We have a Fijian name for the gift, but we will call it magic. In the old days, the person of magic could do anything he wanted to someone else, using his powers. Nowadays, the few who practice it, use it mostly for good purposes—healing, finding lost children, or informing on a criminal. Many times, the police use a man of magic to learn who stole something, or where a criminal is hiding."

The stillness informed me that this was a sensitive subject. Prasad had been very careful in selecting his words. The kerosene lamp needed to be pumped up with pressure, for the room was slowly darkening. The women and children were quiet. It seemed silence ruled.

Prasad tried to change the subject. He poured more kava and after our round of clapping, said, "You must try the fine taste of the fruit bat, also called the Flying Fox…"

"But what about bad magic?" I nearly interrupted.

Impenetrable silence. Now, I felt uneasy. What had begun as a friendly party had become a reserved gathering. Rain spattered against the tin roof, but instead of alleviating the stillness, it merely heightened the tension.

The smaller Fijian stared at his empty kava bowl. Prasad looked into the wooden bowl half full of liquid, while the larger Fijian leaned against the wall, his gaze directed at Prasad.

I couldn't believe the enmity within this room. I longed to leap up, grab my girlfriend and the children, and run like hell for *Xiphias*, but it was miles away, and I didn't want to show any fear.

I felt it was necessary to say something, so I remarked, "Well, it's obvious you don't want to tell me about your magic. It's your culture, your custom, your magic, yours to keep to yourselves. Back home, we don't have magic, or at least I'm not aware of it. So, for me, it's new and exciting to hear of your magic and of the special gift someone possesses. Just ask your magic man to send us safely to New Zealand."

That eased the tension a bit, and the big man studied me. He straightened, sat erectly, and in a commanding voice I had not heard before, said, "I am a man with the gift. The other two are afraid to say anything because they know I inherited the gift from my father, and he inherited it from his father. I am now a Christian, so I don't practice magic anymore."

All of us stared at him, for he appeared bigger than before, exuding confidence and authority.

I felt more comfortable now. He was even smiling. I took my shot to continue the conversation and asked, "Would you mind explaining this power or gift, and how others with the gift are using it today? Please understand, this is something I know nothing about, and I really respect that this power still exists today. I just wonder if and how it is used by others."

The rain hissed. The darkness inside was broken by the mere flicker of a yellow flame from the lamp and by a line of light beneath the door to the kitchen. It must have been midnight, or later, but time had no meaning.

The big magic man began to speak, "First, if you want a man with the gift to perform a service for you through his magic, it would cost you a gift, money, or something. Secondly, all men with the gift drink kava to make their power stronger. As Prasad said, magic today is used mostly for good. Few people with the gift are known publicly, because the white society and Christianity frown upon this power and disclaim its existence."

After a short pause, I asked, "Does the person with the gift exercise voodoo, like making use of something from the person? Do they drink a potion other than kava, or is it all mind power?"

He glanced at me and at the other two, "It's helpful to have something belonging to the person who will be affected by the magic, but it's not mandatory. Some use dolls, but few do. Most just use kava; it seems to make the power stronger. The strength of the power of a person with the gift varies. For me, I see everything in my mind. I see an event or a situation, and sometimes I can change the event. I can recognize a thief amongst the people and in my mind see the theft. In my grandfather's day, he used to make bad people die. He would see them sick, and they would grow worse until they died. We don't do that anymore, because we have found God and know it's wrong to use our gift to harm or to kill."

I jumped in and asked, "But there must be others with the gift who haven't found God, and who still practice bad magic."

The big man leaned forward with his empty coconut bowl and motioned to Prasad. It was apparent that he now controlled the group, for customarily, a Fijian would not ask his host for additional kava.

As we drank and clapped our hands, he continued, "I suppose that's possible, but if people heard of it, they would try and stop the practitioner."

"I'd think people would be afraid to stop him because of his magic," I responded.

The big fellow was irritated. His smile became a tight slit. His eyes narrowed, and I felt their penetration deep within me. My backbone went rigid, and a cold chill coursed through my body. Damn, I'd pushed this too far. "Shut up, you fool," I told myself.

"You've always had too big a mouth that gets you into trouble. You've done it again, dumbhead."

Slowly, carefully, the speaker said, "People would tell others, and eventually, the police would jail him. As I said, there aren't any left who do bad. They only do good. They, like myself, never use their powers because we have found God."

Forcing a grin, I said, "Well, I've truly benefited from this discussion. I feel honored to be drinking kava with all of you, and especially with the one who has the gift, and who gave it away for Christianity. This night I will remember forever, but it's late, and we should get the children to bed."

Prasad borrowed a neighbor's old car to drive us back to the harbor. As we left, I said to the big Fijian, "All I ask for is a safe passage to New Zealand, be it through the gift or through God." In answer, he smiled, waved good-bye, and said, "I will pray for you all."

"Why did you say that?" my girlfriend asked from the back seat of the car.

"I want to leave no stone unturned."

§

Another example of the power of magic or witchcraft occurred while I was in Papua New Guinea. There, they call it Pori-Pori.

Papua New Guinea has over 200 dialects; each tribe speaks their own language. Because there are too many dialects for everyone to learn, they use Pidgin English as the National Language. If a person spoke the same dialect as others in the village, he was given the Pidgin term of "Wontok", meaning "One Talk". So, all people who speak only English are classed together as Wontoks.

While I was employed there, I had mostly local Papuan natives working for me. I was amazed at the variations in customs between each village. On weekends, I took a few of the locals day sailing. This made for a relaxed atmosphere and gave me an opportunity to gain some knowledge about their culture. The first thing I found out was that I would never learn anything if I had locals aboard from different Wontoks or villages. Tribal warfare is still strong there. They felt that if a rival tribe were to learn about some of their private customs, it would make them weaker. When I took only men from the same village or all Wontoks, they freely volunteered information about their customs. Without revealing the particular tribe, I would like to share some of their stories.

All the tribes have a Pori-Pori man or magic man. In one particular village, I was told that if a person dies from an unknown cause, they suspect that someone has put a Pori-Pori curse on him. To find out, they lay a piece of bamboo, pronounced "baboo", alongside the deceased overnight. This piece of bamboo is about 10 feet long and 4 inches in diameter. It is carved to an extremely sharp point at one end.

The next morning, the local Pori-Pori man and some other village men enter the deceased's grass house. If the bamboo has moved so that it is pointing toward the entrance to the house, it means that he died as a result of a Pori-Pori curse. If the bamboo remains as it was placed, the person died of natural causes.

If the bamboo points toward the door, they all lift it so that it rests in the outstretched palms of their hands. I am told that they cannot grasp it. When the bamboo begins to move, they move with it. Eventually, the bamboo is facing the door of another Pori-Pori man. When he opens his door, the village men tell him that the bamboo has revealed that he put a curse on the deceased villager. The bamboo thrusts forward, penetrating the man's chest and killing him. I am told that the bamboo does this on its own, while being supported by the carriers.

I asked them if the victim ever claims that he didn't do it. They responded, "Yes, every time, but the bamboo knows the truth."

I never felt comfortable opening my front door after I heard of this custom.

§

I heard many similar stories about the strong Pori-Pori of the various tribes. Most stories told of positive things like healing, but some conveyed bad circumstances in which a person was cursed with a slow deterioration of the vital organs.

I played squash with an Australian physician who was also a missionary. He devoted his life to assisting people who live in poverty around the world. I really admired this man for his convictions, his efforts, and sincerity in his beliefs. He never once tried to convert any of us. In fact, to this day, I do not even know his religious affiliation. He only wanted to do what was good for those who needed it.

He asked me if I would take him and a few medical staff out to the Mortlock Islands, about 150 nautical miles from Bougainville Island. I felt it an honor. It was truly an enlightening experience.

While we were sailing over to the Mortlock Islands, we talked about medical care and Pori-Pori. I was taken aback when this very religious man said that he couldn't ignore the power of Pori-Pori. He told me stories in which a family would bring a person who was slowly dying into the hospital. All the vital organs would be gradually shutting down, refusing to function, similar to how an older person might die. He explained that he and his staff would try everything they could to cure this person but with no success—they could not find the cause.

As a last resort, he permitted the family to bring in their own Pori-Pori man. Within two days after the Pori-Pori man performed his magic, the patient would begin to improve quickly. The doctor remarked that this situation occurred more than once, and he could never find a medical explanation for it.

When we arrived on the islands, we were immediately taken into a special Tamberan haus (house) that would rid us of any evil spirits. We also had to wear a special headdress that kept these evil spirits away while we were there. It must have worked, because as the doctor tended to his patients, I strolled around the island and was never bothered by any negative energy.

Wear the same type of clothing as the locals

The locals know what works best in their climate. It is also nice to show that you respect their customs. Not only will this make you more readily accepted, but you won't feel like you stand out, even if you are pink, 6 feet tall, and have red hair and blue eyes. Dressing like the locals may take a little getting used to, but it is well worth it. Of course, this would depend on the type of clothing, and whether it has any religious connotations.

However, I do not encourage going barefoot like the locals. In most places in the world, people wear western clothing, but without shoes. They have had many years of walking barefoot and have developed thick callused skin on the bottom of their feet. There is no way a cruiser will ever achieve the same protection.

Many tropical islanders wear no more than a colorful flower-patterned wrap. The men only cover from the waist down, while the women wear one that is full-length. Each country has a different name for this square piece of cloth, but they are all about the same. Cruising women seem to adjust to this different attire, but western men have a little more difficulty wearing a "skirt". The local men do not put on anything under the waist wrap. Since they have been using this type of garment all of their lives, they know how to hide their private parts. *Consequently, as a novice, be careful. Wear some undergarments, because the wrap may come off when you least expect it.* Also, we western men do not know how to sit properly without exposing ourselves; this may be more of a problem for some than others.

In some villages, the women will go topless. Before the bra goes over the side, talk to the village Chief or elder to see if this custom is also accepted for visitors. Today, most of the young women in the village cover themselves when there are strangers visiting. Just because the village women are topless, it does not necessarily mean that it is required. Use good judgement.

Most importantly, I want to discourage forcing your dress code on the locals. As I mentioned earlier, a bikini may be offensive in many cultures.

§

When I was visiting a tropical country, I had a female crewmember aboard. She invited her sister to join us for a week. When the sister arrived, she was insistent about going ashore wearing only her bikini bottom and no top. I told her that it would be inappropriate, and that she would not be going ashore if she dressed liked that.

An argument ensued, and she said, "They can dress any way they want when they are in my country, so why can't I wear what I want in theirs?" I tried to explain that this was a village that had a strict dress code for their own people, which applied to any visitors. If we were going to visit them, we had to respect their customs. I used as an example that a woman would not enter a Catholic Church without a head cover in her country. The same principle applied here.

My crewmember dressed appropriately, but her sister would not. I refused to take her ashore as she was attired. We did not go ashore at all that day. The rest of the time she was aboard was tense for all of us, and I was very relieved when she left to go home.

Eat local foods

When cruising, try to get away from your customary habits. Experiment with local foods, recipes, and eating methods; you may be pleasantly surprised. My first experience in eating local foods happened while I was in the Tuamotus atolls of French Polynesia. I was sailing with my girlfriend Cindy.

Soon after we set our anchor inside the lagoon at this particular atoll, we met André, a local native that was half-French and half-Polynesian. He brought his Polynesian wife out to the boat to visit. It didn't take long for us to feel comfortable with them. They spoke excellent English and appeared to be educated. We invited him and his wife to have dinner and some California red wine. We had an excellent evening with lots of nonstop talking, laughing, and great story telling.

The next day, André invited us ashore to see his village and to show us the way he caught fish. André had two fish catching methods that were next to his grass house. One technique was a corral-type fence in protected shallow water. He used chicken wire tied to bamboo poles driven into the shallow bottom. The chicken wire and poles made a funnel shape that was 30 to 50 feet long on both sides. It was wide at one end and narrowed at the other. At the narrow end, it opened up into a large corral or pond. This area had a considerable number of fish trapped inside. Fish would enter the funnel and swim through the small opening into the larger pond. Then they couldn't find the way back out through the small opening.

His second method called for the erection of a short chicken wire fence on similar bamboo poles that stretched across another shallow pond. At high tide, the fence was far below the surface, permitting fish to swim over it and into the pond. When the tide went out, exposing the fence, the fish were penned within the large pond. He also used one section of the pond to keep octopus and any fish he intended to eat soon. To get the fish into this littler pond, he had another smaller funnel-type fence. He would wade into the pond and herd the fish into the funnel and into this inner pond.

I was really impressed with the simplicity of this fish catching technique. There was enough fish in the inner ponds to feed the village for weeks.

"You must eat with us tonight," André insisted. "I have a large octopus I'll cook."

Cindy looked at me with a down-turned mouth. I agreed and said, "André, we'd love to stay, but…"

"Bullshit," André interrupted. "You will stay! And you will love my octopus, I promise."

It seemed we were stuck, so I accompanied André to the small, inner pond. Holding a stick with a large fishing hook lashed to its end, he reached down and hooked the octopus from its hole. Immediately, flailing tentacles wrapped around his arm. André shook the octopus until he could grab its head with the other hand. He slipped his thumb under a small slit in the back of the octopus's head, pressed down on top of the head with his fingers, and the head turned inside out. The octopus died instantly. Next, clutching it by the head, he beat the octopus against the coral rocks, working it back and forth. He explained, "This removes the slimy membrane that usually gives the strong taste that some don't like. When it becomes squeaky clean, it's ready to pound to tenderize it."

Repeatedly, he dipped the octopus into salt water and ran his hand down its skin to feel if the membrane was completely gone. After he was satisfied that the external membrane was removed, he pounded the octopus with a stick. "This will tenderize the meat," he explained. "You don't beat it so hard that you break the skin, but hard enough to soften the meat."

When he'd completed that step, he cooked it in a pressure cooker for 20 minutes. In the meantime, Cindy and André's wife cut up onions, potatoes, and made coconut milk. To make the coconut milk, André's wife removed the husk with a pointed stick, then sharply tapped around the nut's side with the back of a heavy knife. When a crack developed, she broke the nut into equal halves. She discarded the oily water and scraped the insides with a multiple-toothed grater. When grated meat filled the bowl, she selected a handful at a time and squeezed it through a cloth, extracting all the white milk. She set it aside to be cooked with the octopus.

André withdrew the cooked, shriveled octopus from the pot and cut it into thin pieces, which he tossed into a large frying pan full of previously cooked potatoes and onions. About ten minutes later, he added the coconut milk. After another few minutes of simmering, it began to thicken and was ready to eat.

It was fantastic! I never imagined octopus could taste so good. André kept our glasses full of a nice French white wine. As Cindy and I ate and ate, we felt we were feasting like royalty for the first time since we left the States. If this experience was any indication of what lay ahead, we were definitely going to enjoy cruising.

§

It is easy to meet local native Polynesians in French Polynesia. They are so friendly and outgoing that one would have to make an effort *not* to interact with them. My girlfriend had returned to the States and to her children. I was alone in Papeete, Tahiti. This particular day, I decided to get off the boat to do some shopping. As I tied my dinghy to *Xiphias's* stern lines running ashore, I saw an obese Tahitian standing close to the beach. As I walked by, I said my usual, "Bonjour," which was almost the limit of my French. He replied in rapid French, so I apologized in English for not speaking his language. He tried German, and I understood enough to realize he was asking if I could communicate in that language. Again I said, "No." Then he reverted to Spanish. I felt more comfortable with that, because I knew a smattering of Mexican Spanish.

For a very short while, we conversed in Spanish, but my Spanish was rusty and my vocabulary limited. At last, he chattered away in error-free English. "I'm Joe. Learning languages is a hobby of mine. Languages come easy for me. I can speak fluent Tahitian, French, German, Spanish, and English. Now, I'm working on mastering Portuguese. I often come to the harbor hoping to find yachts from foreign ports, so I can practice languages."

He fell into step beside me. We discussed world affairs, bomb tests in the Tuamotus, local French control, and then he said, "Why don't you have dinner with me and my wife? We live in Faaa, a small town near the airport."

Joe, his wife Opeta, and all their dogs and cats shared an open house that consisted of two one-room buildings. In one, they cooked and stored food. In the other, they slept and ate. They lived almost exclusively off the small piece of land they owned, growing fruits and vegetables, which they sold in the open market.

When I asked Joe if he worked, he answered, "Sure, on my land and studying languages."

Opeta volunteered that she had a salaried job, cleaning office buildings in Papeete. Their life was basic, but quite common for the Tahitian lifestyle. Opeta served a small reef fish, "Orare," which she'd deep-fried. Although she set a plate and utensils before me, I used my hands to eat, as did my hosts. Next, she brought in a plate of breadfruit, "Rare," which had been pounded to make a thick dough. We each took a handful, kneaded it in our hands, and dipped it into coconut milk before eating. We also ate wedges of fresh "Papaw" (papaya) and stacks of mangoes. Opeta kept our glasses full of sweet water from the green 'Ono' coconut.

After dinner, Joe and I relaxed and began talking. Shortly, he snored from his chair. I crossed over to the kitchen building where Opeta was cleaning up and thanked her for the meal. I said, "Maruru roa," and struck out for the *Xiphias*.

This was the beginning of an enduring friendship. Over the weeks and months that followed, I spent a lot of time with this couple, learning about Tahitian language and culture. Some of Joe's friends were surprised at my mastery of Tahitian—Joe was a good teacher. He never let me rest, insisting that we use Tahitian instead of English.

His teaching also included how to spear fish on the reef at night using only a kerosene lamp for light. Joe would wait until it was the right tide; then he would take a large aluminum pot, a kerosene lamp, and a spear and head for the reef. The water was only waist deep. He stuck the multiple pronged spearhead under water so he could see its deflection. He held the lamp out in front of him with his other hand. The huge pot was tethered to him with a short rope. When he saw a fish, he speared it and put it into the pot. This continued for hours, until the pot was nearly full. He often got lobster as well.

The next day, we went down to the reef again. This time he wanted to show me how to identify the fish that have poisonous ciguatera. The fish that have ciguatera are fish that feed off the reef, as well as predator fish that eat the reef-eating fish. This poison is cumulative in the body; therefore, a younger fish will have less ciguatera than an older one. The problem is that a particular type of fish on one side of the island may have ciguatera, while the same fish is safe to eat on the other side. As far as I know, there is still no definite explanation for this, but there must be a way of knowing if the fish is poisonous or not.

I know of other cruisers who would feed a bit of the fish to their cat before they ate it. If the cat got sick, they didn't eat it. Unfortunately, sometimes the cat died. I was not willing to take that chance with *Pintle*. Another way I was taught to detect contaminated fish was to eat a small chunk raw, then wait for an hour. If the mouth began to tingle or get numb, it was poisonous.

Joe taught me how the locals determine if the fish has ciguatera. They hang the freshly caught fish from a tree limb or from some other object. Then they watch the flies. If the flies land on the fish and stay there, the fish is safe to eat. If the flies buzz around the fish without landing or land only for a moment, the fish is unsafe to eat.

I really developed a taste for breadfruit There are many ways to prepare it, but my favorite was the way Joe did it. In an open fire, he placed the fresh breadfruit in the coals. When it burned to a black charcoal, the breadfruit was ready to eat. He determined if it was fully cooked by tapping it to see if it had a hollow sound. The outer, burnt skin was peeled away. After the skin was removed, the breadfruit was left to cool a little. When it was just cool enough to handle, it went into a bowl and was mashed with a stick. When it turned into a thick dough, like children's play clay, a piece was scooped out with the hands and rolled into an elongated ball. This ball was then dipped into fresh coconut milk and eaten.

I already mentioned earlier a bit about how to open a coconut in order to access the meat to make coconut milk. In case it was not clear, I will explain it again here in a little more detail. To make coconut milk, the old brown coconut lying on the ground is used. Joe husked the coconut by thrusting its side down on a strong, sharp stick stuck into the ground. Then he pried away a piece of the husk by rolling the coconut down the stick. This exposed a portion of the nut inside. He repeated this procedure until the husk was removed, which took about 30 seconds. Next, using the blunt edge of the blade of a large knife, he tapped the nut in a straight line around its circumference until the nut cracked, and he separated it into equal halves. Each half was grated on a sharp, round, multiple-tooth grater. The grated coconut was then put into a piece of cheesecloth and squeezed until the liquid coconut milk drained out of the meat. While coconut is an ingredient in nearly every Tahitian dish, it also goes very well with rum.

One of my favorite foods was roasted coconut. The same type of coconut that is used to get the coconut milk is used for this treat. After the husk is removed, one of the natural plugs on the end is punctured to remove the liquid inside. Then the nut is thrown into a fire. It burns for about 10 to 20 minutes; it is then removed and opened. The meat inside is sweet and tastes like popcorn.

Several times Joe mentioned his desire to go to Moorea and visit relatives. "Tahitians are great sailors," he kept reminding me, so we set a date to sail over on *Xiphias*. The morning we'd picked dawned rainy and stormy. I started raising the anchors as soon as the sky began to lighten.

It took me over an hour to raise and clean both anchors before motoring to where Joe was waiting.

"How about another day, Joe? " I asked. "The weather is bad and it will be rough out there".

"No, I'm a great sailor. All Tahitians are great sailors."

Previously, I had constructed a cover that extended from my boom gallows to my dodger. This completely enclosed the cockpit for special situations like today, when it was raining. However, although it provided protection from weather, it didn't leave any room to stand.

As we exited the pass from Papeete, the winds struck our beam, the seas turned rough, and Joe promptly vomited. "You want to go back?" I asked.

"No," he insisted, "I will be all right."

We made the 18-mile voyage to Moorea with Joe lying across the cockpit. His head hung over the stern, where he chucked up his morning breadfruit. To steer the boat was impossible, because Joe was bigger than the height of my tiller. Therefore, I removed the tiller and steered entirely by moving the wind vane's trim tab manually. I decided that sailing with Joe was like sailing with a dead horse in the cockpit—he consumed the whole area. To move from rudder to companionway, I had to crawl over him.

When we finally arrived, we found the wind blowing directly into the bay where we intended to anchor. I wanted to move elsewhere, but I glanced at Joe. He looked awful and I was tired. When we were inside the reef, I set the anchor in 20 feet of soft mud. He managed to move his bulk down to the pilot berth, which wasn't big enough for him. The passage had been abnormally tiring because of choppy seas and the obstruction in the cockpit. I was also exhausted, so I went below for some needed rest.

The screams of children roused me from sleep. Their voices were so close, that for one wild instant, I thought they were on board. I attempted to rush outside, but Joe got to the ladder before I did. There was no way to get around him. In slow motion, he took one lumbering step, then another. It seemed like ages crept by as he crawled out under the dodger. I pushed past him toward the stern to see Tahitian youngsters, about 10 feet away, standing in waist-high water. There was no doubt as to what they were saying: our anchor was dragging, and we were already into soft mud. I ordered Joe, "Get below." I realized I'd hurt his feelings, but I didn't have time to explain why I needed him out of the way.

I started the engine and put it in forward, then ran to the bow to bring in the anchor—to no avail. We were really stuck. The anchor continued to come to *Xiphias,* instead of *Xiphias* going to the anchor. Joe came forward to try to help. His weight on the bow lifted the stern enough so that we broke loose of our hold and began moving forward. Joe stayed forward as I motored us out of the bay to the inside of the reef, where I set the anchor in 20 feet of hard sand. Now safe, I prepared some food, and we both promptly fell asleep.

The following day, the weather improved. We returned to the muddy anchorage, so Joe could see his relatives. He spent the day with them, while I finished some needed varnishing on *Xiphias.* Joe invited me to go with him, but I explained that I would not leave the boat when I knew the bottom was not good holding for my anchor.

Mercifully, our sail back was uneventful, and Joe didn't get seasick. By the time we neared port, he began bragging anew about what great sailors all Tahitians were.

§

Another delicacy I love to eat is coconut crab. These large land crabs eat only fruit and coconuts. They have huge, strong pincers that cut though the tough husk of the coconut. My first experience eating the coconut crab was at Souverau Island in the Cook group of islands.

This is the island where Tom Neal, a New Zealander, used to live. Tom wrote a book titled *An Island to Myself*. He had been placed on the island to be a Japanese airplane spotter during World War II. He liked it there so much that the Tonga authorities agreed to give him permission to live on the island as long as he wanted. When we arrived, he had already passed away, but his house and the surrounding area was exactly how he left it. It was maintained entirely by passing cruising yachts. Tom had left a note to please look after his place until he returned. He also left a book for all visitors to sign. We found the place clean and probably exactly how he left it; apparently, the cruisers were doing a good job for Tom's spirit.

After a couple of days anchored at Anchorage Island, the main island where Tom Neal lived, we decided to sail across the lagoon to explore some atolls.

We arrived at one of the atolls and went ashore in the dinghy. We were about five miles upwind of a Taiwanese fishing boat that had wrecked on the reef some years ago. More than likely, the survivors had stayed on this island, because it was littered with pots, pans, bottles, lean-tos, etc. We rummaged through the debris and amassed a batch of glass balls they'd used on their fishing nets.

I climbed a coconut tree and cut down a few drinking nuts. With his machete, tool of the jungle, Jim hacked away the end of the husks. Then with a swift tap to the exposed nut, the tops were off. We drank a couple of coconuts each. As we sat there relaxed, a large coconut crab walked out of the bush and attacked the empty coconut at my side.

"His body must be at least eight inches across," I said. "Hell, the pincers are as long as my fist." Before I could comment further, Jim had a stick. I salvaged an old burlap bag the fishermen must have left, and we began catching coconut crabs. In less than an hour, we had six large crabs.

We debated about staying the night, for it was growing late, but we were on the downwind side of the lagoon, exposed to the southeast tradewinds. If we had to leave in darkness, we could never cross the lagoon because of the numerous coral heads right below the surface. When we arrived back at Anchorage Island, darkness was falling.

We'd just secured the boat, when the people from Wotan brought over a fish and large lobster they had caught on the reef. In exchange, we gave them two of our crabs. Jim started water boiling in the only two large pots we had. Meanwhile, I cleaned the fish. When the water was boiling, I submerged the lobster in one pot for only a couple of minutes. Then I cleaned and split it open. I smeared butter and garlic all over the lobster meat and fish before putting them into the hot oven. While we were cooking some brown rice in one pot, I cooked a crab in the other. The crabs were so big I had to cook them one at a time. Jim grabbed our last bottle of Riesling and put it into a wet sock to cool, as the lagoon water was too warm.

After I had cleaned the fish, I baited a large hook with its head, attached a stainless steel leader and 3/8-inch line, and hung it below the surface. It did its work, for just when our meal was nearly ready to serve, our fishing alarm went off: our tin can full of nuts and bolts rattled wildly. We had caught something big—a five-foot long gray reef shark.

It required all our energy to wrestle the beast alongside *Xiphias*. Jim held the line taut; I grasped the club and tried to smash its head. Because the shark thrashed furiously, I kept missing it and beat up *Xiphias*'s woodwork instead. With its teeth flashing, the shark leapt for me. He just missed my arm, but I felt its touch. My head spun. "Shit! It nearly got me. I wish it would spit out that damn hook and go away."

I handed the club to Jim, "You kill him. I've got to look after the rice."

Jim laughed, "You bastard. You can't leave me here alone; I can't kill this damn thing by myself. Come back here."

Chuckling, I went below to stir the rice. Every time the shark lurched, I could hear cursing. With renewed courage, I went topside and took the line from Jim. "Okay, I'll pull him up as far as I can. You club him good, but don't wipe out the boat."

With both hands wrapped tightly around the line, I started hauling up the shark. "Okay, get him!"

Jim surveyed the squirming fish, the 18-inch long club, and finally me. "I have to go check the rice," he said. He disappeared down the companionway, but reappeared shortly with a glass of wine.

"I would have poured you a glass, but you've got your hands full."

We finally managed to kill the shark without being bitten. It was heavier than we expected when we brought it on to the side deck to fillet. We decided we would fillet and salt it before we ate dinner.

Pintle went berserk from this windfall. He had had a taste of fresh fish, crab, and lobster. Now he wanted his share of the shark. He darted into it as if it were his kill. I let him attempt to penetrate the tough skin. After a few minutes, he realized that it wasn't possible and sat back to watch me begin cutting a fillet. The sight and smell of the shark meat sent him into a frenzy, running around the deck as fast as he could. He finally settled half on my shoulder and half on the top of my head. From this perch, he watched every movement I made. I cut a few pieces for him and set them aside. He knew they were his. In an instant, he was off my head and had consumed the lot. By then, he had chewed down so much seafood his stomach swelled hard.

When I finally finished filleting the shark, I salted it and set it aside until the next day.

At last, Jim and I sat down to a marvelous meal. Because its diet consists of coconut and fruit, the coconut crab tasted like king crab with a hint of roasted coconut. For an additional coconut flavor, we dipped the fine white meat into the mustard-colored sack at the base of its tail, which contains almost pure coconut oil.

The lobster, too, was superior, but very rich. We finished off the wine, stored the other two crabs for breakfast, and settled back to listen to the quietness of the night and enjoy the stars moving leisurely across the heavens.

The next morning, we went ashore and took the shark fillets with us. There, we ran into the folks of Wotan, who were cooking a late breakfast over an open fire. Earlier, we had found a recipe Tom Neal had left for smoking the gray reef shark. There was a large box made from corrugated metal just for smoking fish. Holes were already punched through the sides, which held rods used to support the fish fillets. The recipe calls for using a special bush that grows along the edge of the lagoon. A fire is started and reduced to coals, then the leaves from this bush are set atop the coals. The corrugated box is covered and left for a couple of hours.

The shark was the best smoked fish I had ever tasted. This was reinforced by all who tried it. An added bonus to smoked fish is that it will last a long time without refrigeration.

§

Anyone who goes cruising in the South Pacific will surely experience a custom banquet in the Tonga Islands. When we arrived, we met Issaa, the local feast maker. We took him around the chain of islands to his island, where he has these special meals. Here, we anchored for days to help Issaa build a small house and prepare for the feast.

Early one morning we took some of Issaa's village women out to the reef, so they could catch octopus for the feast. By hand, one woman jerked the octopus from its hole and then threw a woven basket into its tentacles. While the octopus fought the basket, the woman turned its head inside out and handed it to her son for cleaning. When the women got hungry, they picked up small sea cucumbers, bit off one end, spat that out, and squeezed the contents into their mouths. They said it was strong, but good. I took their word for it.

The men killed a pig for roasting on top of the "ume", the underground oven. Jim and I watched them open numerous coconuts and fill bowls with coconut milk. They arranged handfuls of chopped fish and crabs, onions, and coconut milk on banana leaves. Wrapped tight, the leaves were tied with bark strings. The same procedure was used with the octopus, but it was mixed with the coconut milk and put inside hollowed out green papaya. The papaya made the meat very tender. There were stuffed fruits, taro (a sweet potato-like root), onions, and much more, all placed in coconut milk and wrapped in another leaf.

After the pig's skin was charred to seal in the fat, the men put out the fire. The villagers shoveled hot rocks and some dirt into the bottom of a large hole, covered that with green banana leaves, and layered in the food. They set a damp burlap cloth on top, added more rocks, and the remaining coals. Finally, dirt concealed everything, making it appear like a mound of hot earth.

Issaa told us that it would cook for about three hours before it could be opened. Just about three hours later, one of the local charter boats pulled in and anchored. We hadn't been aware these guests were coming, but they'd obviously been invited.

The oven was opened, and we ate everything off banana leaves, using only our fingers. The food was superb. For entertainment, some of the villagers danced for us. One attractive young woman insisted Jim join her for a dance. He got a bit suggestive, as did she. Later we learned they'd participated in a marriage dance, and that Jim might have himself a wife. Luckily, the girl realized it was only in fun.

At the conclusion of the feast, we rowed each villager out to *Xiphias*. We must have had 30 people on board when we motored to the other end of the bay, where the path led to their settlement. The waterline was so low that there was water near the top of the sink. I motored in as close as I dared and kept the engine running while Jim rowed them ashore three at a time. Some couldn't wait and swam in.

§

While on the Mortlock Islands with the Australian doctor and his staff, I wandered around the village trying to find the family of one of my employees. He had given me a package for them. I found them gathered around a smoky fire with some long, skinny, snake-like things hanging from a stick placed across the fire.

I introduced myself in Pidgin English and was received as if I were a member of the family. We talked and drank fermented coconut sap. They actually drain the sap out of a coconut tree, mix it with coconut water, add some sugar, and let it age. I can't say that I enjoyed the taste, but it certainly did give quite a wallop.

Then, I was served the long, thin, snake-like things that had been smoking over the fire. They called them sea snakes, but when they described them, I learned that they were actually a type of sea worm. These live in the sand in shallow water and can be identified by a small mound with a hole in the top, like a small volcano. When the sun is nearly overhead, they stretch out like a long worm and absorb the microscopic animals in the water. They are difficult to catch, because they instantly draw back into their mounds. The taste was similar to lobster. There was little meat, mostly a chewy membrane. I was surprised to find that I really enjoyed it. I was also served smoked octopus and taro.

I love to eat food from the street vendors or anywhere the locals eat. If you visit India or any country inhabited by Indians, you will encounter some of the best tasting foods imaginable. One of my favorites was Lintel Dal with roti or nan. If you are real hungry, try a masala on rice. These common foods are very inexpensive. In the local cafes or street stands, they are served on banana leaves and eaten by hand.

In Thailand, they have corner stands that cook all varieties of shellfish, fish, meats, and vegetables in a boiling broth. This goes on all day long, and the flavor of the many items being cooked permeates the broth. By the end of the evening, this broth is strong. It can be diluted and eaten as soup.

Needless to say, the list of local foods could go on and on. I feel your cruise will be more enjoyable if you avoid the tourist restaurants, and eat where the locals eat. Try to eat using the same methods and utensils they use, even if you feel uncomfortable doing so. Not only will this broaden your tastes, it will introduce you to new customs and perhaps to new friends.

Humorous stories

In Papua New Guinea, the Central Price Index is based on the cost of the beetle nut, a mild narcotic. It is chewed along with a leaf from a local plant and lime made from burnt seashells. This all goes into the mouth at one time. As it is masticated, it turns a crimson, blood-red color. Like chewing tobacco, it should be spit out occasionally. It should not be swallowed, or it flows out the other end of the body. The locals get mouth cancer, their teeth fall out, and their eyes glaze over, but they still manage to function. I think it is addictive, because they continue to eat it, no matter how stoned they get.

Stan, a close friend of mine, visited me in Papua New Guinea, when I was working in the copper mine. One of my local native friends came over for a visit with a bag full of beetle nuts. My native friend insisted that Stan and I try it. We placed a big empty pot in the center of the table to take the red spit. We each started with our own beetle nut. First, the husk had to be removed to access the nut inside. Then we took a large bite, about half the nut. It had little if any taste, but was very bitter. (It is this bitterness that causes saliva to flow.) Then immediately, a leaf was dipped into the white lime and added to the mouth. This concoction turned hot and began to taste a bit like anise seed or liquorice. Stan and I managed to chew until it all turned red. We continued to chew for another few minutes, then spit it out.

I looked at Stan, Stan looked at me. He grabbed the bottle of scotch, and we both began to rinse out our mouths. The taste and the burning remained, so we took another swig, but this time we swallowed. Our mouths felt a little better, so we continued the cleansing process. An hour later, we weren't sure if the way we felt was from the beetle nut or the scotch.

If you have been to Britain, you probably noticed many colloquial terms that have different meanings than the same words we use in the States. Many of these British terms have been carried over to Commonwealth countries like Australia and New Zealand.

To illustrate what I am trying to say, the British and Australians call luggage 'port'. The hood of the car is the 'bonnet'. The trunk of the car is the 'boot'. An American is a 'Yank' or 'Septic' or 'God Damn'. (I guess it is apparent where they got those names.) Anyway, a common joke many 'Yanks' tell goes as follows: "When I arrived at the airport in Sydney, a porter asked me if he could put my port in my boot. I told him if he did, I would piss in his pocket."

§

I would like to tell a story that taught me to be careful of what I say. I had recently arrived in Queensland, Australia from New Zealand. I was alone. While in New Zealand, there had been a terrible tragedy aboard my boat, which left me very depressed. The story of the tragic accident circulated among the cruisers and many of the local Australians. A young Australian couple I had met invited me to go to a party. They said I needed some cheering up, and this would be the answer.

Jinni said, "Roger, you will enjoy the party, we all have so much fun. However, it is fancy dress, so you must be dressed."

Thinking that she meant black and white formal attire, I responded, "Gee, Jinni, I don't have anything like that aboard."

Laughing, Jinni continued, "Oh, you Americans, not that kind of fancy dress. I think you call it a costume party. You must come as your favorite movie title."

Then I understood. I got the date, time, and directions to her place. Then I began to wonder if Australia gets the same movies as we do. I know they make some excellent movies of their own, and I was afraid I might choose a title that would be too easy to identify, thus defeating the purpose of my costume. My other concern was that, in the States, many arrive at costume parties in normal everyday dress. I certainly did not want to make a fool of myself and be the only one there dressed in something silly.

After careful consideration, I decided everyone had heard of Superman. I could put on a Superman shirt and wear a normal shirt over it. I could wear my horn-rimmed glasses, and I would have all possibilities covered. I found a Superman T-shirt in the first store I entered.

The day came for the party. I dressed in my Superman shirt and put my dress shirt over it. I stuck my horn-rimmed glasses in my shirt pocket. Knowing I was going to spend some time in Australia, I had bought a used Australian made Holden automobile. I hopped in my car and left for the party. On the way, I stopped at a local bottle shop, or liquor store as we would call it, and bought a bottle of good scotch.

I didn't have any trouble finding her house and suddenly found myself knocking on the door. Jinni answered. She stood there in a lovely old wedding gown that had a bustle in the rear. She had a beer stein hanging around her neck with a hot dog inside.

She grinned at me and said, "Oh Roger, I am so glad you made it. Who am I? Who do you think I am?"

I stared at her lovely gown, the beer stein with the hot dog inside and said, "Sorry Jinni, I don't have a clue, but you look lovely."

"Oh you, I am the Bride of Frank-in-Stein."

"Jinni, that is really clever."

Then she lost her grin as she stared at me and said, "Roger, I am so sorry, I thought I explained, in Australia you must come to a fancy dress party in costume. The others will not be impressed if you don't make some effort. I should have made that clearer."

I unbuttoned my dress shirt, exposing my Superman T-shirt and put on my horn-rimmed glasses.

Jinni's smile returned. As she grabbed my hand and began pulling me inside, she said, "Oh, you are Superman, that's nice."

As she took me through the party, introducing me to her guests, I saw some of the cleverest costumes imaginable. As I passed from one guest to another, I heard the Red Baron tell Dracula, "Wouldn't you know the Yank would come as Superman."

Immediately, I felt out of place. Oh, how I wish I had put more effort into a proper costume. It was apparent that I had made a minor *faux pas*. I poured myself a stiff straight scotch and found a soft chair to sit it out.

No one made any effort to speak to me except Jinni. People were talking in groups, dancing, and having a really good time. I was ready to run out the door, but I felt that it was too early to leave. Then, the scotch kicked in. I didn't feel so bad. I thought that I should get up and mingle, when Jinni walked pass me. I couldn't resist the opportunity to break the ice. Trying to find a more familiar word than bustle, I said, "Jinni, I love your dress, especially the fanny."

Suddenly, it seemed the music stopped. Everyone stared at me. Jinni flushed. I felt like I was in a still scene in a movie. I had done something wrong.

A tall Australian with a huge beer gut looked over at me from across the room and said, "Hey Yank, do you know what you just told Jinni?"

"I… I am not sure what I said, but I think it wasn't what I meant," I responded in a quivering voice.

The Australian blurted in a loud voice that could be heard throughout the house. "Yank, you just told Jinni that you love her cunt."

Everyone cracked up laughing. At least the ice was broken. They began to explain that they couldn't believe that we Americans have Fanny Packs and even name someone Fanny.

The rest of the night was a real success; I had a lot of fun and made new friends.

While I am talking about Australia and some of their terms and customs, I would like to share another story. I was working at an engineering shop for a great guy named Grey. One day at the end of a hot, hard day's work, Grey said, "Hey, Roger, let me shout you a beer after work."

I had no idea what he was talking about, but I was ready for a cold beer. We entered the pub and Grey bought us both a beer. Then he asked, "Are you familiar with a *Shout*?"

I responded, "Only in the form of yelling."

Grey smiled and explained, "A shout is used when mates buy each other beers. I buy you a beer, you buy me a beer, and so it goes."

"We do the same thing, but we don't have a name for it," I said.

Grey responded, "It really isn't the same, because you Yanks do not feel you have to buy a person a drink back, nor is it really necessary; you do so only as a courtesy."

Soon we had finished our beers, and I ordered up another two. Then another guy came in and sat down next to Grey and asked, "Grey, is this your Yank friend you were telling me about?" Grey responded with an affirmative and introductions were made.

This new guy said, "Let me shout you guys a beer." Suddenly, there was another beer sitting in front of me.

Grey bought a round, and then I did the same. By now, I had consumed 5 beers. Another of Grey's friends or 'mates' came in. The routine was the same: an introduction, and then he shouted us all a beer.

This continued around the table, until I lost count of the number of beers I had consumed. I still had three full mugs sitting in front of me. It was apparent that there was no way I would be able to stay up with these guys. I leaned towards Grey and said, "Grey, I am getting drunk. How do I tactfully get myself out of this?"

Grey quietly responded, "Roger, are you pissed?" "No!" I jumped back, "I'm not mad, I'm drunk. How do I get out of this 'shout'?"

Grey carefully explained that I could not leave the beers the others had already paid for; it would be an insult to them. Also, it was my shout next, so I could buy a round but pass myself. I could drink what I had in front of me, then I could leave and still save face.

So, that was what I did. After everyone had a new beer, I chugged down the beers in front of me and excused myself.

When I stood, I realized just how drunk I really was, and my head began to spin. The pub had floor to ceiling windows, and I could not find the door out. I kept pushing on windows. I heard a voice behind me say, "Hey Grey, your Yank friend can't find his way out of the pub."

I made it outside and found my car, but I knew I couldn't drive. I threw up a few beers, crawled into the backseat, and went to sleep.

Since then, I learned that a shout can be avoided by simply saying that you don't have time for a shout, but would have one beer that you buy for yourself. If someone buys you a beer, you are committed. Another way to avoid the shout is to drink spirits. They cost more than beer, and no one wants to pay more for someone else's drinks. Therefore, you simply make it known that you are not getting into a shout, because you are drinking whiskey or something else more expensive than beer.

§

I was in Pago Pago, American Samoa, when an incident occurred that could happen to anyone. There were several boats in the harbor: Charles and Nita on *Mintaka*, Don and Muriel on *Aries*, Chuck and Lin on *Chucklin*, Steve and Sharon on *Blown Away*, Sid on *Doreen Beatrice*, and myself on *Xiphias*.

There was a little café at the end of the harbor, where we all regularly met for breakfast. One morning, Don and Muriel from *Aries* came in and told us a frightening experience they had the previous night.

Don told this story. "It was an extremely hot night, so I slept in the port settee berth and let Muriel have the forward 'V' berth. At about 0200, I woke from a deep sleep when Muriel screamed, 'There's a man in the boat!' I looked forward and, by God, there was a large, dark figure between the 'V' berth and me. I leaped out of my bunk, spread my legs far apart for stability, and threw both hands forward and high. In my deepest voice I ordered, 'Stop!' Unfortunately, the 'stop' didn't come out as I intended. It was pretty high-pitched and quivered.

Well, the dark figure stopped and Muriel turned on the light, which silhouetted this huge man. 'Don, he kissed me while I was sleeping.' With the light on, I could see how big this guy really was. I knew there was no way I was capable of doing anything.

But Muriel kept saying, 'He kissed me, honest he did, he kissed me.' This fellow looked at her and said, 'I never kissed you, lady, you were dreaming.'

Muriel insisted that he did and said, 'Don, do something.'

So, I asked him, 'what are you doing on our boat?' He didn't answer, but picked up a pairing knife from the galley bench top and palmed it so the handle was in his hand with the blade alongside his wrist so Muriel couldn't see it. I felt vulnerable as hell. I was stark naked, spread-legged, blocking the passageway.

'Must have the wrong boat,' the huge Samoan said. 'Earlier I had some drinks with a lady from a yacht, and she invited me to join her later.'

I felt in no position to restrain a knife-carrying guy who outweighed me by at least 90 pounds of pure muscle, so I stepped aside. In my most threatening voice that cracked with fright, I said, 'okay, get off now and don't ever come back, or I'll tear your head off next time.'

As the Samoan passed me, I crossed my legs feeling a bit embarrassed about being nude. He just smiled, handed me the knife, and then shook my hand. With a smile he said, 'I bet you would, wouldn't you?' Then as he dove over the side of the boat, he shouted, 'Thanks for the kiss, lady!' and was gone."

After hearing this story, everyone was aware that there was a really bold Samoan boarding boats at night and that we should all take care. A few mornings later, in the same café, Steve from *Blown Away* came in and immediately said, "I had the Samoan on my boat last night, but I took care of him. Sharon had gone to bed. I was reading when I felt the yacht heel slightly, only for an instant, the kind of movement a boat makes when someone is climbing aboard. I sneaked forward, but I couldn't see too well because my eyes had not adjusted to the dark."

Steve continued to tell his story. "I could just make out a figure holding on to the shrouds, trying to climb aboard. Just as the intruder was passing his leg over the lifeline, I kicked him in the chest. I think I knocked the breath out of him, because I could hear him gasping. He was in the water, but still holding on to the shroud and chain plate. So I put my foot on his head and pushed him under water. He immediately let go and swam away still gasping."

"I don't think this guy will be bothering any boats for awhile," Steve concluded.

As we ate our breakfast and drank our coffee, the elderly single-hander, Sid, from *Doreen Beatrice* came in and sat next to Steve. Steve began to recount the tale when Sid stopped him and told his own story, "Someone stole my dinghy last night, so I had to swim out to my boat. I am old and not a strong swimmer so I stopped at your boat Steve, to see if I could borrow your dinghy. You kicked me in the chest, knocked my breath out, and then tried to drown me. I barely had the strength to get back to my boat, and almost could not get aboard. Thanks, Steve!"

§

I entered Papua New Guinea at Bougainville Island, where there was a huge open pit copper mine. There was a very unofficial local yacht club where I was anchored. While they were working in the mine, I worked at building their jetty, so that they could bring their own boats alongside to board without using a dinghy.

One of the Australian yacht club members who owned a construction company was impressed with my skills and offered me a job. I explained that I couldn't legally work, but would like to find a job for a few months. He told me that if I performed as he expected, he would get me a working visa. I went to work the next day. We agreed that no money would exchange hands until I got my visa or was ready to depart.

It really wasn't labor-type work: I was the supervisor, overseeing the locally trained tradesmen who maintained and constructed the homes where the mine employees lived. It was not only easy, but also fun. I got to interact with the local men, and this gave me a chance to learn about their culture.

On one occasion, I found the truck driver who delivered the men to and from their job sites, drunk. I sent him home and drove the men around myself. I left my company car at one work site until the day ended. I told my superior what had happened. He called the driver in and gave him a severe warning that he was not to drink on the job.

A week later, I found the same driver drunk again. I did the same thing and reported him to my superior. He was immediately 'sacked', or fired as we say.

The next day when I dropped off some of the men at one of the sites, a workman showed me the head of a bird with other feathers tied around it. It was hanging from an overhead light fitting. He explained that one of the driver's Wontoks (from the same village who spoke the same dialect) had put a curse on our work site, and the men did not want to work there. I took them to another site and wondered how I could handle this problem.

The next day, I showed up with black charcoal streaks drawn down my cheeks and an eye on my forehead. I said nothing to the men, but they all stared at me.

I drove the men to the cursed work site and explained that I had my own magic, passed down to me from my Apache grandfather. The magic acted like a mirror: it reflected the curse back to the person who made it. I explained that it never failed, and that we would all be back to work at this site the next day, because the person who hung the bird's head would be very sick. Within 20 minutes, the bird's head and feathers were gone. I left the markings on my face for the day. My superior got a real kick out of the idea and the results.

After a few months working for the contractor, I was offered a position with the Bougainville Copper Mine. I became the Superintendent of Contract Services. This meant that I had about two dozen highly qualified tradesmen in each trade that would oversee the contractor's work. I often would go on site to reassure myself that my supervisors were doing a proper job. During some of these visits, I encountered the following situations.

In one home that needed to have the interior rebuilt because of severe dry rot, I asked a local contract tradesman to install a new door to the bathroom. I returned several hours later and found the door installed, but it was cut too short, resulting in a two-inch gap at the bottom. Rather than ask the tradesman to make a new door, I asked him to just add the piece he cut off to the bottom of the door and properly patch the join. When I returned, I found the door no longer had a gap at the bottom of the door—now it was on the top. I decided to let it go.

Then, I asked him to install a barrel-bolt lock on the door. I returned later and found the barrel bolt was installed, but on the outside of the door. I asked the tradesman why he installed the lock on the outside of the bathroom door, instead of on the inside. His response was that it was to keep intruders, who might come in through the bathroom window, out.

In another house, the kitchen sink and cupboards had to be replaced. In these particular homes, the double sink and double drains were all in one piece, formed in pre-molded stainless steel. The sink had a 2-inch apron around the front and both ends, so that it would fit over the cupboards. The problem was that it had to be installed against a blind wall that was just an inch wider than the formed sink.

This required the cupboard to be made a little shorter, to fit into the space and to have the stainless steel sink fit over it. First, the cupboard had to be centered between the two walls. Then, the stainless steel sink combination was set over the cupboards. After everything was properly installed, wood trim was added to hide the gap between the cupboard ends and walls.

In this particular house, the cupboard was set against the back wall, but it was hard against one of the side walls. I explained to the local tradesman that the cupboard must not be installed against a side wall, because the double sink would not fit over it. With a big smile, he agreed.

I returned later to find that it was all installed, with some of the wood trim fitted and ready to paint. All the cupboard doors were open, so it took me a minute to realize that the cupboard was installed hard against one wall, and there was a 2-inch gap between the cupboard and the other wall. The sink sat on top of the cupboard on one side, but over it at the other, so it was at a considerable slant.

When I asked the tradesman why he did this, he explained that it was easier to install against one wall, and he didn't feel it mattered that the sink and draining board were at a slant.

These few examples are common occurrences in Papua New Guinea. I found that most of the local natives were smart and capable. I had one man that worked for me who could tell me the name of every person who lived in any one of the over two thousand company homes. By memory, he could tell me the last time the house was maintained, and what was done at the time. He never failed to be right.

Not all cultures, however, think like we do. To us, the above anecdotes may seem funny, but to them, they are perfectly logical. Once shown how I wanted a project done, the locals were very quick to learn how to handle the new job. They needed to be shown only one time, and they would remember it and repeat the procedure exactly.

Hopefully, the stories and anecdotes related in this chapter will help to convince you of the wonderful learning experiences that await you when you go cruising. Not only will you have an opportunity to learn firsthand how other cultures live, but you will also forge friendships that will last a lifetime.

CONCLUSION

In this final section of the book, I would like to briefly summarize the most important points that need to be considered in order to make your cruise successful. Each individual will interpret this information based on his or her own personal experiences; so, take what is relevant for you and your level of cruising ability and skill.

Probably the most difficult step is making the decision to go cruising. Whether crossing oceans or sailing along the coast, many obstacles will have to be resolved before a definite decision can be reached. This must be the desire and dream of all who will be aboard. If it is not, one person can make everyone else aboard miserable by emphasizing the negative and ignoring the positive.

Once everyone is committed to the same goal, an interesting sort of tunnel vision will set in. Everything you do will be relevant to your future plans. Everyday life will take on a new and different focus: what you read, everything you buy, all of the commitments you make will be considered in relation to your ultimate plan to go cruising.

Another difficult decision to be made is deciding if your existing vessel is the one to achieve the objective. The vessel's soundness and seaworthiness removes worry, doubt, and fear when the weather gets rough. The size of the vessel must be carefully considered so that it is not too big or too small for the number of persons aboard. How the vessel sails in all wind directions will determine the amount of motoring that needs to be done. Too much motoring can create a feeling of despair that the passage is taking far too long and using too much fuel.

If the existing vessel seems to satisfy your needs, then there may have to be some modifications made to ensure that it is capable of serving its intended purpose. If the existing vessel is not the right one, then it must be sold and the proper boat found and prepared.

The most enjoyable part of pre-cruising is the preparation. Everything that is on the boat must have a purpose. The most important items will be the essentials. This will vary by the individual and the size of the boat. Everything else is for enjoyment, comfort, or simply to make life easier. As the boat is being prepared and provisioned, it is inevitable that you will mentally experience the various possible scenarios of your dream cruise. This is the fun part. The mind can take you to the best anchorages, to the friendliest cultures, and to the most exotic foods you have ever known.

Your mind can also portend possible fears and dangers. That's why the next phase must be to practice every imaginable situation that could occur. The more physical practice and experience gained, the higher the level of confidence that will result. Confidence is crucial in ensuring that the cruise will be enjoyable and not formidable.

I feel the final and most important key to a successful cruise it to have the right attitude. There are many factors involved or required that will influence this. The first is to reduce tension and fear. This comes from experience.

The right attitude, however, can also come from accepting that you are different from the rest of the world. You have decided to pursue a dream that many others do not have the courage to attempt.

There are cruisers who will have the right attitude before they ever leave port, others will develop it after years of building confidence, while some will never achieve it at all. If you can just accept that this is what you are going to do and that you will make the best of it, regardless of what others say or what happens, then you will have the right attitude.

The proper attitude can only be achieved if you accept that your life is going to change. For some, it will be a temporary change; for others, it will be for the rest of their lives. Regardless, your life will be totally different than it is now; accept this and look forward to the change. We have a tendency to become complacent in our everyday lives. To me, and many of you, this is boring. Change is good. Change in life is necessary to keep the mind open.

I know of cruisers who are still cruising after many years because they have made and adjusted to this change in lifestyle. However, some never adjust to certain aspects of cruising, like making ocean passages. They dread the passage and can only concentrate on the negative part of the trip.

I had a woman crewmember who was also my girlfriend sail with me when I left Papua New Guinea, on my way to Northern Australia and on to Thailand. She was an experienced sailor, and I felt confident leaving her on watch. Even with her ability and skill, she did not have the right attitude about the passages. She constantly complained about the boat's movement, the coldness and dampness, the lack of sleep, and fear for her life. She made my life miserable. Most of our passage was with clear skies and moonlit, starry nights. The wind was off our quarter at about 18 knots. Although these were perfect sailing conditions, she could never see it.

During each and every overnight passage, she swore she would catch a flight out at the next anchorage with an airport. When we arrived at our destination, she would begin to enjoy interacting with the locals and swimming and snorkeling. Even if there was an airport, she no longer wanted to leave. However, on the next passage with me, she would begin to complain again. When she finally left the boat, I was sad to see her go, but I was very happy to get rid of the negative attitude. She failed to realize that passage making is only a very small part of cruising. Much more time is spent in anchorages, visiting foreign countries, and experiencing other people and cultures. If she could have just committed to the cruising lifestyle and accepted the bad times along with the good, I am convinced that her experience would have been transformed.

On the other hand, some will develop the change and adopt the right attitude to make cruising enjoyable. I would like to use Lin and Larry Pardey as an example. Here is a couple that has made several circumnavigations on a boat without an engine or any electronics. They decided to do it simple and do it now. In their books, they state that they will continue to cruise as long as it is fun. This is a perfect example of the right attitude.

I was impressed with an article Lin Pardey wrote regarding her attitude towards making an ocean passage. Unfortunately, I don't remember the magazine or issue. (We call this a senior moment.) In this article, she eloquently explained the contentment and pleasure she felt while making a long ocean passage—the thing many cruisers dread the most. Only a seasoned sailor could really understand the meaning of what she wrote. I felt the same as she in my heart and wish I could recall the words she used that moved me so.

The point I am trying to make is that if you look at the cruise as being uncomfortable, cold, wet and formidable, that is exactly what you will get. Try to accept that the cruise is a new phase in your life—an adventure that few undertake. You will make new friends from all over the world. Only you can decide that your cruise will be successful and that you will enjoy every moment. This attitude will have a positive influence on everything you do and everything that happens. This type of attitude is contagious; those around you will begin to feel the same way.

§

It's time to end this book but before I do, I don't want to leave the reader with the impression that it is all fun and enjoyable. Unfortunately, there will be problems and bad times, just like there are at home. During my 13 years of cruising, I encountered several hurricanes or cyclones. I was carried, uncontrolled, down a river during a flash flood. Probably, the worst was the loss of the life of a small child who I loved as my own.

This may sound like I had many problems, probably more than most cruisers have over the same number of years. I was younger and more courageous then. I took chances and sailed during the cyclone season when I knew, deep inside, that I shouldn't. Some of my problems were a result of poor judgment; however, there were incidents that could not be controlled or prevented.

Personally, I feel there are more dangers at home or driving the freeway to and from work. A car accident can happen in a split second without giving you time to even consider a reaction. It is over that quickly. At least on a boat, there is always some advanced warning of a possible problem, and there is usually time to respond. This is one aspect of cruising that I like. I am left to my own skills, strengths, and judgments.

I feel I should emphasize once again that safety for all aboard, including pets, comes before anything else. The boat can be replaced or repaired, but a life is lost forever. Most prudent sailors can predetermine a course or route that will greatly reduce any chance of bad or severe weather. Add a sound vessel and a confident skipper and crew, and the chances are that the cruise will be enjoyable, pleasurable, and will leave memories that will last the rest of your life.

I mentioned earlier that one of my worst experiences cruising was the loss of the life of a small child who was on my boat while we were in New Zealand. I loved this child as if he were my own. Prior to this tragic accident, his mother had wanted me to give up cruising, and I refused. We took the child's remains back to the States, and I returned to New Zealand alone. A few days after I returned, there was a flash flood that tore my boat from its mooring and took me, out of control, roaring down the Keri-Keri River.

After this was over, the combination of the tragic accident, the loss of the woman I loved, and the shock of the flash flood sent me into a severe depression. I had to leave New Zealand and try to start my life over. I expressed these feelings to a friend named Bob Cleary. He is not only an excellent writer, but a poet as well. I would like to end this book with a poem that Bob wrote for me.

Our first day out, the morning greets my mourning with its first greyed light; my head feels it is trapped in a vise, the weather is wonderful but all the colours have been robbed from my sight. Pintle springs into action and gives me a love bite upon the chin before dashing out of the cabin. Am I to die alone out to sea with only this damned cat to mourn my death by slowly sharing my carcass with the sea gulls?

I don't know. I only know to stop now would be similar to Hamlet chucking everything this ghost is telling him, and simply walking off the stage of life. But my ghost is the voice of renewable futures. Then again, after all these miles and years at sea, why am I so adamant I continue? Could it be I suffer the same malaise the rest of humanity suffers in this world; a malaise I swear singularly voids the future... avarice?

No... I stand alone in my old age, I shall become my own master; I'll show them all there is a perfectly wonderful way to live... that voids no future. For the moment, I need to get my head out of this vise it seems stuck in, or I void my own future. The Indian Ocean in the longitudes west of New Zealand... is nothing to fool with and it calls.

B.C.

GLOSSARY

A

Abaft.	Further aft.
Abeam.	On the side of a vessel, or amidships, or at a 90 angle to the vessel.
Ablative paint.	A type of bottom paint used to protect the vessel's undersides from growth. These paints are partially soluble, with lower levels of toxicity than hard paints.
About.	When a sailing vessel is about to change tacks. The helmsman's command is "ready about!"
Abreast.	In line with, alongside or abeam.
Adrift.	Floating without mooring or direction at the mercy of wind and current.
Afore.	Further forward.
Aft.	Near the stern or at the rear of the vessel.
Aground.	A vessel whose keel is touching or resting on the bottom and is stuck there.
Ahead.	In front of the bow. Opposite of astern.
Ahoy.	Hello, in nautical terms. A call used to hail another vessel.
Ahull.	A vessel beam to the waves under bare poles.
Airfoil.	A part or surface, such as a wing, propeller blade, sail, or rudder, whose shape and orientation control stability, direction, lift, thrust, or propulsion.
Alee.	On the side of the ship away from the wind. Opposite of windward. When the crew is ready to come about, the helmsman's command as he changes tacks is "Hard-alee!"
Almanac.	An official annual publication for mariners, astronomers, farmers, etc. that gives in advance

the positions of the heavenly bodies and other calculations.

Aloft.................................High up in the rigging or up the mast; above the deck of a boat.

Anchor..............................A hook that holds on to the bottom to keep a vessel from drifting.

Anchorage.........................A place that is appropriate for dropping anchor.

Anchor light......................A light used at night on an anchored vessel to alert other vessels of its presence.

Anchor roller.....................A device usually on the foredeck that aids in leading the anchor rode up and down.

Anemometer......................An instrument designed to measure wind force and velocity.

Anopheles.........................A species of mosquito whose females carry and transmit the Malaria parasite.

Antifouling paint................A specially formulated paint designed to retard barnacle growth under the waterline of a hull.

Apparent wind...................The force and direction of the wind felt by a person aboard a moving vessel, which is affected by the speed and direction of movement of the vessel. Not the same as true wind.

Astern...............................In the direction of the stern, or behind.

Athwartship......................Perpendicular to the keel, across the vessel from side to side.

Atoll.................................A coral island or coral reef with a lagoon inside.

Autopilot...........................An electro-mechanical device attached to the tiller or wheel, used to steer the vessel on a given course.

Aweigh..............................Clearing the bottom. Used for an anchor that has broken loose from the bottom when raised.

Aye..................................Yes, in nautical terms.

B

Backing the jib.................Leaving the windward jib sheet cleated when coming about, until the boat crosses the eye of the wind during the tack.

Backstay..........................A wire that is attached from the aft portion of the masthead to the stern of the sailboat. Part of the standing rigging, it prevents the mast from falling forward.

Backwind.........................To put the sails in a position so the wind pushes against their forward surfaces, in order to stop the vessel.

Baffle. ....An obstructing wall to hold back or separate the flow of liquids in a tank.

Bail. ....A hoop-shaped fitting at the end of the boom.

Balanced.........................A sailboat with its center of effort and its center of lateral resistance on the same vertical axis, i.e., with neither weather helm nor lee helm.

Ballast. ....Heavy material located low in the hull or externally attached to the keel to ensure the vessel's stability and ability to right itself when knocked down.

Balsa. ....A very lightweight strong wood obtained from the balsa tree.

Bare poles.......................When the wind is too strong and all sails have been taken down, the vessel is sailing under bare poles.

Barometer.......................An instrument used for measuring the atmospheric pressure and thus for forecasting the weather. A falling barometer foretells bad weather; a rising barometer indicates better weather on its way.

Barometric pressure...........Atmospheric pressure shown on a device to help forecast changes in the weather.

Batten down the hatches......To secure loose objects aboard and close all the hatches of the boat in preparation for bad weather.

Battens...........................Thin flexible strips (usually made of wood or fiberglass) placed in pockets along the leach of the mainsail, to help the sail keep its shape.

BBB. ....The shorter type of chain links makes it compatible with most windlasses; usually made of low carbon steel.

Beam reach.....................Point of sail with the wind coming over the beam, at a 90 angle to the keel.

Beam. ....The widest part of a vessel.

Bear down.......................To approach another vessel on a collision course.

Bearing. ....The direction of an object in relation to the compass course of the vessel.

Beat................................To sail to weather, or to windward, alternating tacks.

Beaufort Scale.................Wind force scale that measures the strength of the wind, from force 0 to force 12. Force 12 is cyclone strength; gales start at around force 8.

Becalmed.........................A sailing vessel unable to move due to lack of wind.

Belay. ....To fasten a line to a cleat or pin.

Belaying pin.....................Any of various wooden or metal pegs or bolts used in fastening the rigging or stowing lines on a vessel.

Bells. ....On a striking clock aboard a vessel, the bells strike every half hour. The end of each watch is marked by eight bells.

Below. ....The part of the vessel underneath the deck.

Bend................................A type of knot used to fasten one rope to another.

Berth...............................(a) The place where a crewmember sleeps aboard. (b) The place where a vessel is normally docked.

Bight...............................A bend or coil in a rope.

Bilge pump......................Pump used to draw water collected in the bilge.

Bilge...............................The lowest part of the vessel's hull.

Binnacle.	The case in which the compass and a light are kept on a ship. On a yacht, a stand that holds the vessel's compass, usually just forward of the steering wheel.
Bitter end	The end of a line, chain or rode.
Bitts.	Deck posts used to fasten mooring lines.
Blade	Flat part of a propeller or an oar.
Blanket.	When or a vessel is passing to windward of another vessel and her sails steal the wind from the sails of the leeward vessel; also used when a vessel passes a landmass to windward.
Bleed	To let air out of a fuel line.
Block	A casing that holds a pulley or sheave in place. Two or more blocks and tackle are used to increase the force of the pull, in applications such as a boom vang.
Blow	A strong wind.
Boat hook	A pole with a hook on its end to fend off another vessel or to pick up a mooring buoy or your favorite wind-blown hat.
Bobstay.	A wire or chain from the stem of the boat above the waterline to the cranse iron, used to secure the bowsprit against the pull of the headstay.
Bollard.	Vertical post on a dock to fasten lines.
Boltrope	A line sewn to a sail's edge to make the cloth stronger along that edge.
Boom gallows	A support for the boom near the stern of the boat, used to support the boom when the mainsail is furled.
Boom vang.	A block and tackle attached between the boom and the deck, to help hold the boom down against the lift of the wind.
Boom.	A long pole or spar that holds the foot of the sail outstretched.
Boomkin	A spar or spars attached to the stern and extending aft of it, used to attach the backstay.

Boot stripe.....................A lengthwise strip of paint, usually just below the sheer, of a different color than the topsides.

Boot top.......................A strip of paint at the waterline, of a different color than the topsides.

Bosun's chair. ....A seat sling made of canvas and wood to hoist a crewmember aloft in order to inspect or work on the mast.

Bourd ....Military ordnance cargo parachute that can be used as a sea anchor.

Bow............................Stem. Front part of a boat.

Bow line......................Docking line led forward through bow hawsehole or chock.

Bowline. ....The most useful knot. It makes a loop or an eye at the end. It will not slip, yet it's easy to untie.

Bowsprit. ....A large tapered pole extending forward from the bow of a sailing vessel to attach the foremost stays.

Brackish water................A briny mixture of fresh and salt water.

Breaking wave.................A wave that spills its top water over itself.

Brightwork....................Varnished woodwork or polished metal aboard a vessel.

Broach. ....When a boat running downwind before a following sea swerves broadside to the wind, heeling dangerously.

Broad reach...................Point of sail with the wind off a vessel's quarter.

Bruce.........................A claw-type anchor.

Bulkhead......................Structural wall built athwartship in a hull.

Bulwarks......................High deck rails that prevent crewmembers and gear from washing overboard.

Bungee cord...................Shock cord. An elastic line with hooks at its ends used to hold objects secured in place.

Bunk..........................A berth to sleep in.

Buoy..........................A navigational aid floating on the water.

Buoyancy......................The quality of floating on the surface of water.

C

Cabin......................................A compartment for passengers or crew.

Cabintop............................The roof of the cabin.

Calm. ....No wind or very light wind (under one knot).

Cam Cleat.........................A fitting made of metal which has teethlike jaws to secure ropes or lines fastened to it. The line has to be released by pulling up or down to detach from the grabbing mechanism of these teeth.

Canoe stern.......................A pointed stern, like a canoe's. Also called double-ender.

Canopy..............................The billowy fabric dome of a parachute.

Capsize.............................To turn over accidentally (a boat).

Capstan............................A cylindrical mechanism set vertically on deck used to hoist heavy weights like an anchor. In a horizontal windlass, the rotating part that is used to haul rope or cable, opposite to the gypsy. In a vertical windlass, the tapered rotating part that is used to haul rope or cable above the gypsy.

Carbon fiber......................Strong, lightweight synthetic used to reinforce materials like epoxy resins in the fabrication of hulls and masts for modern boats.

Careen..............................To lie a vessel on her side.

Carvel..............................A smooth planked hull, flush at the seams.

Cast off............................To release mooring lines anticipating departure.

Catamaran........................A boat with twin hulls.

Catenary...........................The curve formed by a perfectly flexible cord or chain hanging freely between two points at the same level.

Celestial navigation...........The art and science of guiding a vessel by observing the positions of celestial bodies such as the sun, moon and stars.

Center of effort..................The point on the sail area where the force of the wind is concentrated.

Center of lateral resistance..The point on the keel where the force of lateral resistance from the water is concentrated.

Centerboard.......................A hinged board that can be dropped down from inside the hull to provide more lateral resistance. Daggerboard

Chafe................................Damage to sails and lines caused by friction when rubbing against other objects.

Chafing gear.....................Leather, plastic tubing, hoses, cloth or anything used to protect lines and sails against rubbing through.

Chain locker.....................Compartment in the forward part of the hull to stow the anchor chain.

Chainplates. ....Metal fittings attached to the sides of the hull or to the deck, to provide support for the shrouds.

Chandlery. ....A store that sells marine supplies and gear.

Channel buoys..................Buoys used to mark the navigable (dredged) part of a channel.

Charlie Noble. ....Smokestack on a vessel.

Chart...............................A map, in nautical terms.

Charted. ....Recorded on a chart.

Chartplotter,,,. ....Hardware that interfaces with the GPS, into which actual charts of an area can be loaded. The chartplotter will show on a screen your position on the chart. Depending on the degree of sophistication, some give depth, current, tidal info and more.

Cheeks.............................(a) Sides of a block. (b) Sides of a roller. (c) Wooden plates on the sides of an externally hung rudder, through which the tiller is inserted.

Chine...............................Sharp edge of a hull.

Chock..............................Metal fitting on a sailing vessel to lead docklines.

Chronometer. ....Accurate watch or clock for navigation.

Ciguatera. ....Food poisoning contracted from eating tropical fish and seafood containing ciguatoxin, a toxin derived from coral in reefs.

Claw off.	To beat to weather, away from a lee shore.
Clear.	(a) To steer out of shallow water. (b) To sail away from land. (c) To leave port after customs inspection. (d) To untangle a fouled line.
Clearing papers.	Documents needing approval by port authorities to authorize departure.
Cleat...............................	Wood or metal fitting used on decks and docks to secure lines.
Clew...............................	The aft lower corner of a sail, where the sheets are attached.
Clinometer........................	A device that indicates the angle of heel in degrees.
Closehauled.	Point of sail with the wind coming at a 45 to a 60 angle from the bow of the vessel. The highest point of sail a sailboat can sail to weather.
Close reach.......................	Point of sail with the wind coming at a 60 to a 90 angle from the bow of a vessel.
Closing.	A vessel approaching and overtaking another vessel.
Clove hitch......................	A knot made with two half hitches to temporarily fasten a line around a spar or line.
Clubbed jib.	A self-tending jib. A jib that has a boom.
Clutch.............................	The mechanism that controls the friction and rotational speed of the gypsy in a windlass, when pulling in or letting out the anchor chain.
Coamings.........................	Lateral splashguards surrounding a hatch or cockpit to prevent water from coming in.
Cockpit............................	A sunken area aft or in the center of a sailboat for the crew to sail the vessel.
Coil.	To stow away a rope in circular or figure 8 fashion.
Come about......................	To turn a sailing vessel from one tack to the other, with her bow crossing the eye of the wind.

Companionway.................Steps leading down below from the deck of a boat to the cabin.

Compass. ....A device with a magnetic needle on a pivot that always points to the Earth's magnetic north.

Compass point.................One of the subdivisions of the compass rose. Following clockwise from the North, they are: N, NNE, NE, ENE, E, ESE, SE, SSE, S, SSW, SW, WSW, W, WNW, NW, and NNW.

Compass rose...................A graduated circle on a compass or a chart, showing the compass points.

Compression post. ....On a boat whose mast is stepped on deck, a spar or steel strut that rests on the keel and supports and reinforces the part of the deck where the heel of the mast is stepped.

Corrosion.........................The effect of chemicals or moisture on metals.

Course. ....(a) Compass heading. (b) Direction in which a boat is steered.

Courtesy Flag..................The flag of the country a foreign yacht is visiting, raised on the flag halyard for the duration of the visit.

Cowl vent........................A hooded device set on deck or on a dorade box, used to scoop fresh air down inside a boat for ventilation.

CQR. ....A plow-type anchor with limited swiveling capability.

Cradle.............................A frame to hold a vessel on the hard when hauled out.

Cranse iron......................A metal ring fitting at the end of a bowsprit to attach the bobstay, whisker stays and headstay.

Crest...............................The crown or top ridge of a wave.

Crew...............................All the persons aboard a vessel able to sail it, except for the captain.

Cringle...........................Small metal ring or loop of rope on the edge of a sail, through which a rope can be run.

Crown............................(a) The lowest part of an anchor, where the arms are joined to the shank. (b) Convex curved surface of cabin top or deck, to facilitate water and spray to drain overboard.

Customs..............................Government authority in charge of admittance and departure of foreign vessels into a country.

Cutter.................................Single masted sail boat with a headstay and an inner stay, able to deploy two headsails.

Cyclone..............................Term used for a hurricane in some parts of the world. A violent circular storm with heavy rainfall, huge seas and winds of force 12 or greater rotating about a calm center of low atmospheric pressure (the eye).

D

Daggerboard.......................See centerboard.

Dan buoy...........................A pole with a float, used to mark a location.

Danforth.............................A fluke-type anchor.

Davits................................Metal cranes placed usually at the stern, to hoist a dinghy or tender.

Dead ahead.........................Directly ahead or in front of a vessel.

Dead calm...........................No wind, or very little wind (under one knot).

Dead reckoning...................Calculation of a vessel's position at sea, based on compass readings and data recorded into the vessel's log, such as speed, course and distance traveled.

Deck beams........................In a wooden boat, athwartship supports for the deck.

Deck...................................The horizontal floor of a vessel above the hull.

Degree................................A unit of measure of angles or arcs, the 360th part of a circumference.

Depth sounder.....................A device that measures the depth of the water under a vessel.

Diesel.................................A type of fuel commonly used in marine engines.

Dinghy...............................Tender. A small open boat, hard or inflatable, used to ferry cargo and crew.

Dismasted. ....A boat that has lost its mast or masts in a storm, or in a collision.

Displacement.....................The weight of the volume of water displaced by a vessel. The weight of the vessel when she is on the hard.

Dock...............................A pier or structure where a boat can tie up.

Dock lines.......................The ropes that tie the boat to the dock.

Dodger...........................A structure built over the companionway to provide protection from the weather.

Doldrums. ....(a) The dead calms and light fluctuating winds found on the oceans near the equator. (b) Equatorial ocean regions noted for dead calms and light fluctuating winds.

Dorade box......................A waterproof box installed on deck, on which a cowl vent can be mounted to provide ventilation below.

Double block....................A block encasing two sheaves.

Double sheet bend. ....A knot used to join two medium sized lines.

Double-ender....................A vessel with a pointed bow and a pointed stern, such as a canoe.

Douse. ....To bring down a sail quickly.

Downhaul. ....Line used to pull down a sail.

Draft.............................Depth of water needed to keep the vessel afloat. The deepest part of the keel, measured from the waterline.

Drag. ....The movement of an anchor that has lost its hold on the bottom.

Drift.............................Leeway. The deviation from its course suffered by a vessel, due to currents or winds. To drift: to move with the tidal current.

Drifter..........................A large headsail —larger than a genoa— used in very light winds. Also called a gennaker, it is a cross between a genoa and a spinnaker.

Drogue...........................(a) Anything that can be towed behind the stern of a boat to slow it down. (b) Sea anchor. A surface anchor, usually shaped like a funnel, to help hold the bow to the wind in a blow.

Drop board........................One of two or three boards that slide down into side grooves at the cabin's entry to prevent water from coming in the companionway.

Dropforge. ....To pound or stamp between dies with the force of a falling weight like a drop hammer.

Ductility. ....Ability to be stretched or hammered thin without breaking.

E

Ease. ....To slacken a sheet.

Ebb tide..........................Tidal change from high tide to low tide, when the tidal current flows out to sea.

Echo Sounder...................A depth sounder that measures the time it takes for a sound pulse to bounce off the bottom and return to the vessel's transducer. It converts the time into a depth reading and sometimes shows the contour of the bottom.

Eddy...............................A circular movement of water or air.

Electrolysis.....................The decomposition into ions of a chemical compound in solution by the action of an electric current passing through the solution.

E-meter...........................A device that monitors the condition of the battery: the number of amps being charged or drawn, the number of amps consumed since the batteries had a full charge, and the amount of time left before the batteries will be dead at the present rate of consumption.

End for end......................To completely pay out a line or rode and then reverse its ends.

Ensign. ....A flag that denotes a vessel's country of origin.

Entry. ....A vessel's bow that cuts the water above the waterline.

EPIRB............................Emergency Position Indicating Radio Beacon. A safety device that emits a homing radio signal to help locate the position of someone in trouble.

Equator. ....An imaginary line bisecting the Earth's sphere in two halves, the Northern Hemisphere and the Southern Hemisphere.

Even keel. ....A vessel that floats straight on her lines.

External Ballast..................A heavy mass that is cast separately from the hull in lead, steel, or iron. It is then bolted through the underside of the hull on the bottom of the keel to give the vessel stability.

Eye of the wind. ....The direction the wind is blowing from.

Eye splice...........................Spliced loop at the end of a rope. It can contain a thimble, for applications such as lazy jacks.

Eyebolt. ....A bolt with a built-in eye at one end.

Eyelets...............................Grommet holes used for attachment points. In a sail they are used for attaching halyards, downhauls and outhauls, as well as for reef points.

F

Fair wind............................A following, favorable wind.

Fairlead..............................A fitting with a hole or a block that acts as a guide for the running rigging or a rope, to prevent friction and its being cut or chafed.

Fall off...............................To steer downwind, away from the eye of the wind.

Fathom...............................A depth measurement of 6 feet. Charts' datums can have depth in fathoms, feet or meters.

Fender................................Inflatable cushion to prevent a hull from rubbing against a dock, or against another hull when rafting up.

Fenderboard. ....Rafting board. A wooden board with two or more fenders to prevent hulls from rubbing when tying next to each other or to a pier.

Ferro cement......................A material made of concrete and wire mesh used in boat construction.

Fiberglass...........................A material produced with filaments of glass made into yarn that is woven into textiles or used as insulation or hull building material mixed with resin.

Fid...................................A tapered tool made of wood or metal used to splice ropes.

Fiddle.............................A frame or railing on a vessel's table or shelf to keep objects from falling off.

Figure eight knot...............A knot shaped like an 8 used to stop a line from going through a small opening such as a fairlead or cleat.

Fin keel..........................A type of keel used in racing boats, bolted to the underside of the hull.

Finger............................A walkway perpendicular to the dock in a marina, where a boat can be tied.

Fish finder depth sounder...A depth sounder used by fishing boats to find schools of fish. Some read very deep waters and have the ability to show the contour of the bottom, indicating rocks, coral heads, and even wrecks, or whether the bottom is soft or hard.

Fisherman's reef................A method of spilling wind quickly to reduce heel by letting the sail out so the end will carry some wind while the rest flogs.

Fix................................To find a vessel's position by land observations in coastal navigation, or by celestial observations when sailing offshore.

Flake.............................To fold a sail.

Flange...........................A raised or projecting edge, rib or rim for strength.

Flare.............................A signal light for emergency use to help locate a distressed vessel's position.

Fleet.............................A group of vessels sailing together. A group of vessels of the same kind and make.

Flemish coil.....................A coil of rope running concentrically, with the bitter end at the center.

Flood tide.......................Opposite of ebb tide. Tidal change from low tide to high tide, when the tidal current flows in from the sea.

Flotation tanks....................Buoyancy tanks. Airtight tanks used to keep a holed vessel afloat.

Flotsam............................Floating objects at sea.

Flukes..............................The triangular, pointed blades on the arms of an anchor that hold on to the bottom.

Foghorn. ....A horn blown to give warning to other vessels in a fog.

Following sea....................An overtaking sea that is coming from astern.

Foot................................The bottom edge of a sail.

Force. ....A measurement of the wind's velocity described in the Beaufort Scale.

Fore................................Forward.

Fore-and-aft. ....Lengthwise, parallel to the keel. Opposite of athwartship.

Foredeck..........................The forward part of the deck.

Forward. ....Closer to the bow, or ahead of the bow.

Fouled.............................Dirty, clogged, choked, tangled, stuck.

Frame. ....Skeleton of a wooden boat.

Freak wave......................An unusually large and unexpected wave. See rogue wave.

Freeboard.........................The side of a vessel between the rail or gunwale and the waterline.

Furl................................To flake or to roll up a sail.

G

Gaff................................A spar or pole extending diagonally upward from the aft side of a mast used to support a fore-and-aft sail.

Gaff sail..........................A sail with a gaff spar at its head.

Gale................................Wind of force 8 or higher. See Beaufort Scale.

Galley.............................Kitchen area, in nautical terms.

Galvanic Scale..................A list of metals according to their ability to maintain their electrical charge. The list is descending from the most noble to least noble metal. The most noble metal is the one with the least chance of losing its electrons to other metals (more noble metals are affected less by electrolysis). The nobler the metal makes it a stronger cathode. The less noble makes it an anode.

Galvanize .... To hot-dip and plate metal with zinc in order to protect against rust and corrosion.

Gasket. .... (a) Sail tie. (b) A protective seal, often made of rubber or cork, used in engines.

Gel coat .... The first layer or coat applied to a mold in the production of a fiberglass hull, it is the outermost surface of the finished hull.

Generator .... A device used for transforming mechanical energy into electrical energy.

Genoa .... A jib sail larger than a 100% working jib that extends aft of the mast.

Geostrophic winds .... Winds 1,000 meters (3,300 feet) above ground, driven by pressure and temperature differences, and not influenced by the surface of the Earth.

Ghosting .... A sailboat making little headway in a very light breeze.

Gimbals .... Devices consisting of a pair of rings pivoted on axes at right angles, used to hold lamps, stoves, compasses and other gear in a horizontal position regardless of the vessel's motion or angle of heel.

Gland. .... A movable part that compresses the packing in a stuffing box. See packing gland.

Gooseneck .... Metal fitting used to attach the boom to the mast.

GPS .... Global Positioning System, a network of earth orbiting satellites that a vessel equipped with a GPS receiver can use to establish her position on the Earth's surface.

Grapnel .... Small anchor with four or five flukes or claws.

Grating. .... Open latticework frame used to cover hatches and cockpit floors.

Green sea.........................A large, foamless wave or quantity of water that breaks aboard.

Grommet.........................A ring of metal used to fasten the edge of a sail to its stay. A metal eyelet in cloth or leather used for attaching lines, bungees, etc.

Ground tackle.................Gear used for anchoring, including anchor, swivels, shackles, chain and rode.

Grounding.......................When a vessel touches bottom.

Gudgeon. ....Metal fitting with an eye, attached to a boat's transom, to accept an externally hung rudder's pintle.

Gunkholing. ....Cruising in shallow waters, sailing from anchorage to anchorage.

Gunwale.........................Gunnel. Upper railing of a dinghy, usually its rub rail. Uppermost edge of a ship's side, bulwark.

Gust...............................A sudden draft. A puff of wind.

Guy. ....A line used to steady a pole. When flying a headsail, the fore guy is attached from the bow to the end of the whisker pole, and the after guy is attached from the stern to the end of the whisker pole.

Gybe..............................British term for jibe. When a sailboat changes tacks with her stern crossing the eye of the wind.

Gypsy. ....In a horizontal windlass, the notched rotating part that is used to haul chain, opposite to the capstan. In a vertical windlass, the notched rotating part that is used to haul chain, just above the windlass base and below the capstan if there is one.

H

Hail. ....To call someone, or to call another vessel.

Halyards.........................Lines used to hoist sails.

Ham radio.......................A type of radio utilized exclusively by amateur radio operators. It uses different frequencies than the SSB, which permit the radio to transmit and receive short to long distance, even on the other side of the earth. A license and some knowledge of Morse code is required. No commercial use is permitted.

Hand. .... A crewmember.

Handrail .... Wooden rails attached on sides of the cabintop to provide support for crewmembers going forward.

Hanks. .... Small clips or rings used to attach headsails to their stays.

Harbor. .... A port or haven for vessels, offering shelter or safety.

Harbor master. .... An official in charge of a harbor.

Hard. .... A vessel is on the hard when it is stored on cradles on land.

Hard-alee. .... Command yelled by the helmsman when putting the helm to leeward in order to come about.

Harness. .... A set of straps with a buckle to which a tether can be attached, worn by a crewmember to stay connected to a jackline. Used for safely going forward in heavy weather. Also known as safety harness.

Hawseholes. .... Metal pipes set into the bulwarks through which the dock lines are led.

Head. .... (a) Bathroom, in nautical terms. (b) In a sail, the upper corner where the halyard is attached.

Headboard .... A hard board at the head of a sail.

Headsail .... Sail flown forward of the mast. Drifter, Genoa, Jib, Spinnaker, Reacher and Staysail are all headsails.

Headstay. .... The most forward stay, keeps the mast from falling aft.

Headway .... Forward movement of a vessel. Opposite of sternway.

Headwind. .... Wind coming from dead ahead.

Heave-to. ....To set the sails of a vessel and her helm so that the boat makes little or no headway. This maneuver can be used in a storm, or when a vessel needs to remain stationary.

Heavy weather..................Stormy weather with strong winds and high seas.

Heel................................Inclination. To lean to one side.

Helm...............................The tiller, wheel or steering mechanism.

Helmsman........................The person at the helm in charge of steering the boat.

High. ....In weather terms, high atmospheric pressure.

High and dry....................A vessel that is aground above the high water mark, therefore unable to float off with high tide.

Hike...............................To move crew or ballast to windward in order to reduce heel.

Hitch..............................A knot attaching a line to a cleat, or a spar, or a ring.

Hobbyhorse......................The movement of a boat fore and aft, depending on hull design and placement of the weight along its keel.

Hoist...............................To raise a sail or an anchor.

Hold. ....(a) To grip. An anchor holds when it has gripped the bottom and does not drag. (b) A storage compartment in a ship's hull.

Holding tank.....................A tank to store wastewater from the head in a vessel.

Horseshoe buoy................A Personal Flotation Device used for man overboard situations. It is shaped like a horseshoe and attached with a bracket to the stern rail or pushpit.

Hove-to...........................A vessel making no headway. Past participle of heave-to.

Hull. ....Body of a vessel, not including deck, house, masts or rigging.

Hull speed.......................The theoretical maximum speed of a vessel due to her hull's design.

Hurricane	A cyclone in the Atlantic and Caribbean, a tropical revolving storm with winds of force 12 or greater and huge seas.
Hurricane hole	A port of refuge offering protection from strong winds and heavy seas.

I

In irons	A sailboat pointing directly into the eye of the wind with her sails luffing and unable to make headway on either tack.
Inboard	(a) Toward the center of the vessel. Opposite of outboard. (b) An engine set inside the hull of a vessel.
Inner stay	Staysail stay. In a cutter or ketch, a stay from the bow to about 3/4 height of the mast, used to fly a staysail and storm jib.
Internal Ballast	The heavy weight placed inside the cavity of a hull to give the vessel stability. The internal ballast can be encapsulated inside the hull. The hull mold is made with the shape of the keel as part of the design. This provides a cavity to accept the lead ballast so the ballast material never makes contact with water.
Intracoastal Waterways	ICW. Rivers, canals and bays interconnected along the East Coast and the Gulf of Mexico, permitting vessels to travel along the coast in protected waters.
Inverter	A device for transforming direct current (DC) into alternating current (AC)
Isobars	Lines connecting points of equal atmospheric pressure on a weather map. The closer the isobars, the stronger the wind.

J

Jacklines	Strong webbing that extends from the bow to the stern, to which the tether of a crewmember's harness is attached, permitting free movement fore and aft.

Jerry Jugs.............................Containers for liquids, usually fuel and water.

Jetsam...............................Objects thrown overboard to lighten a vessel.

Jettison.............................To throw something overboard.

Jetty................................A kind of wall built out into the water to restrain waves and currents, in order to protect a harbor or the end of a pier.

Jib. ....A triangular sail set forward of the mast. Jibs can vary in size, measured in percentages. A working jib is a 100% jib. A genoa is a jib greater than 100% (usually from 110% to 150%).

Jib boom. ....A spar used as a boom on club-footed jibs.

Jibe or gybe......................When a sailboat changes tacks with her stern crossing the eye of the wind.

Jiffy reefing.....................One of the most common methods of reducing the sail area of modern sailboats. See slab reefing.

Jigger or mizzen..................A small sail used on the aft mast of a ketch or a yawl.

Junk................................A flat-bottomed ship with battened sails used in China and Japan.

Jury rig...........................A temporary replacement of a damaged part improvising with whatever material is available.

K

Kedge. ....(a) A light anchor used especially in pulling a vessel or freeing it when aground. (b) To warp or pull a vessel along by means of a rope fastened to an anchor dropped at some distance.

Keel................................Main structural member or backbone, extending from stem to stern, laid at the bottom of a vessel. Its primary function is to provide steering ability and lateral resistance to leeway.

Ketch...............................A two masted vessel, with her aft or mizzen mast shorter than the forward mast, and the steering station forward of the mizzenmast.

Kevlar ....Lightweight synthetic material known for its strength, used on hulls and sails of modern boats.

Killet................................A weight that, added to a rode's swivel, helps keep the rode submerged under the keel.

Kink.................................A twist in a rope.

Knees. ....Structural members of a hull connecting and reinforcing two parts that meet, for example the sternpost and the keel, or the ribs and the deckbeams.

Knockdown. ....A yacht turned on its side by a wave, with the mast touching the water.

Knot................................(a) A fastening made with a rope. (b) A unit of speed: one knot equals one nautical mile per hour.

L

Landfall............................Sighting of land from a vessel at sea after an ocean passage.

Landmark. ....A distinctive object on land that is charted.

Lanyard............................(a) A short rope or line used on board to hold or fasten an object. (b) A cord used to hang a knife around a sailor's neck.

Lapstrake..........................In boatbuilding, a type of planking where each plank overlaps the edge of another.

Lash. ....To bind, to make fast a line or rope.

Latitude............................Horizontal distance of a point on the Earth's surface from the Equator expressed in degrees, can be north or south.

Latitude lines. ....Imaginary circles parallel to the Equator.

Launch. ....To put a vessel in the water.

Lay..................................The direction a rope is twisted, usually to the right.

Lazarette..........................Storage compartment at the stern of a boat.

Lazy guy	Preventer. A line attached from the bow to the end of the boom, used to prevent an accidental gybe.
Lazy jacks	Lines attached from both sides of the mast to the aft sides of the boom to facilitate lowering the mainsail on any point of sail.
Leach or leech	The trailing edge of a sail, opposite to the luff.
Leach line	A line sewed into the leach to tighten it.
Lead	(a) The weight attached to the end of a leadline. (b) A metal used for ballast on some sailboats.
Leading edge	The forward edge of a sail, also known as the luff.
Leadline	A marked line with a lead weight attached at its end, used to measure the depth of the water.
Lee	The direction in which the wind is blowing.
Leeboard	A piece of wood affixed to the side of a bunk, to prevent the occupant from falling out.
Lee board	A board attached to the lee side of a sailing dinghy, to provide lateral resistance.
Lee helm	The tendency of a sailboat to sail off the wind.
Lee shore	A shore that is to the lee of a vessel.
Leech	See leach.
Leecloth	A piece of fabric (usually canvas) affixed to the side of a bunk, to prevent the occupant from falling out.
Leeward	In the direction the wind is blowing. Toward the lee.
Leeway	Sideways drift of a sailboat caused by the push of the wind or current.
Length	The distance from bow to stern on a vessel. Length Over All (LOA) is the maximum length of a vessel, including her bowsprit and boomkin. Length on deck (LOD) is the actual distance on deck from bow to stern. Length of the waterline (LWL) is the length of the vessel measured along her waterline or line of flotation.

Life preserver...................A personal flotation device, such as life ring, a vest or a cushion.

Lifelines. ....Lines made of rope or vinyl covered wire attached to stanchions along the sides of the boat to prevent crewmembers from falling overboard.

Lifesling...........................A brand name device that facilitates lifting a stunned or unconscious person from the water. Most come with their own quick deploy storage cases

Lift...................................The force that pushes upward on a wing's airfoil and pulls forward on a sail.

Line..................................Any rope used aboard a sailing vessel.

LOA.................................Length Over All. See length.

Locker..............................Closet, storage bin or space.

LOD.................................Length on Deck. See length.

Log..................................(a) A device used to measure a vessel's speed though the water. (b) A daily record of a vessel's speed and progress, as well as the weather encountered, radio transmissions and receptions, navigational and maintenance details, notable events, etc., usually entered in a book called a log book.

Longitude. ....Angular distance in degrees measured east or west of the Greenwich meridian.

Longitudinal. ....Lengthwise.

Lubber line.......................A fixed line inside the case of compass indicating the bow of the vessel, therefore its heading.

Luff..................................(a) The forward edge of a sail, opposite to the leach. (b) To cause a sail to flutter by turning too close to the wind.

Lunch hook.......................Small anchor used for a brief stop.

Lurch...............................Sudden roll.

LWL. ....Length of the Waterline. See length.

M

Main mast. ....The tallest mast on a schooner, ketch or yawl.

Mainsail. ....The sail set on the mast of a sloop or cutter, or the sail set on the main mast of a schooner, ketch or yawl.

Malaria. ....An infectious disease, generally intermittent and recurrent, caused by parasitic protozoa in the red blood cells, and transmitted to man by the bite of an infected anopheles mosquito in swampy, tropical areas.

Man overboard. ....(a) Shouted command used to attract the crew's attention when someone has fallen into the water. (b) A maneuver used to bring a vessel about and close to a crewmember gone overboard, in order to rescue the crewmember from the water.

Marlinspike. ....Tool for opening the strands of rope while splicing.

Mast. ....A vertical spar to support sails and running rigging. It is supported by the standing rigging.

Mast collar. ....A raised frame on deck in which the mast is aligned and installed.

Masthead. ....The top part of the mast.

Masthead light. ....A light set on the masthead. On small sailing vessels, it is usually a tricolor light.

Mast step. ....The place on the keel or deck where the mast is mounted.

Mast steps. ....Steps attached to the sides of a mast to facilitate climbing aloft.

Mayday. ....A radio distress call, to be used only if the vessel or crew is in imminent danger. It comes from the French "m'aidez!" (help me!) In Morse code, the distress call is SOS (...---...)

Meridian. ....An imaginary circle running from the North Pole to the South Pole. On a chart, meridians are lines of longitude, measured east or west from the Greenwich meridian.

Mildew................................A fungus among us that usually grows due to moisture in poorly ventilated areas.

Mile. ....A unit of distance. A nautical mile is equal to 6076.12 feet. A statute mile (land mile) is 5280 feet. A geographical mile is the length of one minute of latitude at the Equator, or 6087.2 feet.

Millibar ....A unit of measure of atmospheric pressure, equal to one thousand dynes per square centimeter.

Mizzen. ....The aftermost sail in a ketch or a yawl.

Mizzen mast......................The aft mast in a ketch or yawl.

Mizzen staysail.................A staysail flown between the mainmast and the mizzenmast in a ketch or yawl.

Mold ....A pattern, hollow form, or matrix for giving a certain shape or form to something in a plastic or molten state.

Monel..............................An alloy of nickel, copper, iron, manganese, silicon and carbon, very resistant to corrosion. Monel wire is used for seizing anchor swivels and shackles for ocean use.

Monohull..........................A sailing vessel with a single hull.

Mooring............................A permanent ground tackle, where a vessel can be made fixed or secured, usually consisting of a very heavy object such as a mushroom anchor or cement block with a chain and rode, and a buoy or float attached to the rode for easy retrieval.

Morse code........................A communication language invented by Samuel Morse, used in the early days of the telegraph. It consisted of long and short taps of the transmission key. Modified for radio transmission, it is now described in dots and dashes. Every letter, number and special sign of the alphabet has its unique signature in dots and dashes. The international distress signal in Morse code is S O S (...---...)

Mould...A growth produced by any fungi, especially in the presence of dampness or decay. Also spelled mold.

Multihull....................................A sailing vessel with more than one hull, such as a catamaran (two hulls) or a trimaran (three hulls).

Mushroom..................................A heavy anchor shaped like an inverted mushroom used for a permanent mooring.

N

Nautical mile.............................A unit of distance. A nautical mile is equal or 6076.12 feet. See mile.

Naval architect..........................A person schooled in naval design. A boat designer.

Navigation. ....The art and science of guiding a vessel from one place to another.

Navigation lights.......................Lights on a vessel displayed at night to give other vessels information such as movement, size, and purpose or activity of vessel. Basic lights used are white stern light, red port light and green starboard light.

Neap tides.................................Tides that occur just after the first and third quarters of the lunar month. At these times, the difference between high and low tides is the smallest. Opposite of spring tides.

Neptune. ....In Roman mythology, the ruler of the sea, who is appeased by offering libations. Known as Poseidon in Greek mythology.

Nip. ....A short turn in a rope, often the anchor rode, passing through a chock or hawsehole, in danger of being chafed.

Nylon..A very strong, elastic polymer that can be produced as a monofilament, used for fishing lines, or to make three-strand rope used for anchor rodes.

O

Oarlock............................Pivoting device in which an oar is set for rowing.

Offshore. ....Out at sea, away from the shore.

Osmosis...........................The diffusion of fluids through a membrane or porous partition.

Outboard..........................(a) A portable engine that hangs from the transom of a boat. (b) Outside, or away from, a vessel's centerline. Opposite to inboard.

Outhaul............................A line attached to the clew of a mainsail, used to tighten the foot of the sail to the boom.

P

Packing gland...................A movable part that compresses the packing in a stuffing box.

Pad or pad eye..................A metal eye bolted to a deck, bulwark or cabin top.

Painter.............................A line used to tow a dinghy or to tie it up.

Palm................................(a) The broad part of an anchor's fluke. (b) A leather device like a thimble used to push a needle for sewing sails or whipping lines.

Parachute anchor...............A surface anchor shaped like a parachute, deployed off the bow for offshore use in heavy weather.

Passage............................(a) An ocean crossing. (b) A journey by water. (c) One leg of a voyage.

Pay out............................To release a line, rode or chain in a controlled fashion.

Pea coat...........................Heavy wool coat originally used by the US Navy.

Pedestal...........................A base or support for the steering wheel of a boat.

Pennant...........................(a) A short line or cable attached to the tack or to the head of a sail. (b) A small flag, usually a signal flag. (c) A tackle for hoisting goods aboard a vessel (also known as pendant).

PFD...................................Personal Flotation Device. An object used to keep a person afloat. PFD's include vests, cushions, horseshoes and life preserver rings.

Pier...................................A structure built out over the water, supported by pilings, used as a landing place or loading platform.

Piling...............................A wooden or metal beam with its lower end driven into the ground sometimes under water, used for moorings, or to support floating docks, piers and floats.

Pilot................................A person licensed to steer vessels in and out of a harbor or through difficult waters.

Pilot Charts......................Charts used for coastwise piloting and navigation.

Pin..................................Any of various wooden or metal pegs or bolts used in fastening the rigging or stowing lines on a vessel.

Pinch..............................To steer pointing higher than closehauled, with sails beginning to luff.

Pin rail...........................A rack or board used to stow belaying pins.

Pintle.............................(a) Metal fitting attached to the rudder, with a pin that slides down into the eye of a gudgeon. (b) Roger Olson's cat.

Pitch..............................(a) The rise and fall of the bow and stern of a vessel in a seaway. (b) The distance a propeller moves forward with one revolution. (c) Mixture of tar and resin used for caulking wooden boats.

Pitch poling.....................A vessel turning end over end, when the bow sinks deep into the water acting as a pivot point and the stern does a somersault.

Plow...............................A type of anchor that looks and behaves like a farmer's plow.

Plug...............................A tapered pin, usually made of wood, that can be used to stop a leak in a through-hull.

Polypropylene...................Lightweight synthetic material used to make ropes that float.

Poop..............................A vessel is pooped when a wave breaks over her stern or quarter.

Port.	(a) The left side of a vessel looking forward. Opposite of starboard. Larboard in old-fashioned terms. (b) A harbor or haven for vessels. (c) An opening for light and or ventilation on the side of a vessel, also called porthole or portlight.
Porthole	See portlight.
Portlight	An opening in a vessel's side to admit light and air; also known as porthole.
Port of entry	The first port of a country with customs officials entered by a vessel.
Port tack.	When a sailboat is sailing with the wind coming over her port side. A sailing vessel on a port tack must stand down (give right-of-way) to a vessel sailing on a starboard tack.
Pram	A dinghy with a transom bow and stern.
Preventer.	A line attached from the bow of a sailing vessel to the end of her boom, used to avert an accidental gybe.
Privileged vessel	A vessel that has right-of-way over another vessel and must maintain her present course.
Proof coil	The longer type links of chain, less compatible with windlasses, usually made of low carbon steel.
Prop.	Propeller.
Propeller.	A series of blades mounted at an angle in a revolving hub used to propel a craft forward as it rotates like a screw through the water.
Pulpit	Forward railing and support for the lifelines at the bow of a boat, used to prevent crewmembers from falling overboard.
Purchase.	A block and tackle, a mechanical device used for pulling or lifting. A two-part purchase gives twice the pulling power; a four-part purchase gives four times the pulling power.
Pushpit.	Opposite of pulpit. Stern railing and support for the lifelines at the stern of a boat, used to prevent crewmembers from falling overboard.

Q

Quarantine. ....A period (originally of forty days) when a vessel is restricted from disembarking passengers or crew until cleared by health, customs and immigration officials.

Quarantine Flag.................A yellow flag raised when a cruising vessel arrives in a new country, used to hail health, customs and immigration officials for clearing purposes.

Quarter............................The side of a vessel from her beam to her stern.

Quartering sea...................When the wind and waves are coming from a vessel's quarter.

Quinine............................A bitter, crystalline alkaloid ($C_{20}H_{24}N_2O_2$), or any compound of it, such as quinine sulfate, commonly used in medicine for the treatment of Malaria.

R

Radar...............................An electronic system or device that uses transmitted and reflected radio waves for detecting a reflecting object and determining its direction, distance, height and speed.

Radar reflector..................A device used to return radar waves along the same path they arrived so your boat can be seen by the vessel sending out the radar signal.

Rafting up........................A mooring technique where two or more boats are tied together side by side, at anchor, at a dock, a float or a mooring.

Rake. ....The slant of a mast fore or aft from the perpendicular.

Reach..............................All points of sail between running and closehauled. They include broad reach, beam reach and close reach.

Ready about......................Command yelled by the helmsman to alert the crew to prepare to change tacks.

Reef................................(a) A ridge of sand, rock or coral lying at or near the surface of the water. (b) The act of reducing sail area in preparation for stronger winds. (c) The part of a sail which can be folded together and tied down in order to reduce the sail area exposed to the wind.

Reef knot............................A knot used to tie in a reef point. Also known as a square knot.

Reef points.......................Short lines tied around the boom and through grommets in the sail to secure the shortened sail to the boom.

Rhumb line.......................The course of a vessel that maintains a constant compass course, drawn as a straight line on a chart.

Rib...................................On a wooden boat, one of the structural hull support members perpendicular to the keel.

Rig...................................(a) The type of sailing equipment and setup of a sailing vessel. Rigs appropriate for cruising include the sloop, the cutter, the ketch, the yawl and the schooner. (b) To fit a vessel with sails, shrouds, stays, braces, etc.

Rigging............................All lines and wires necessary to set up a sailing vessel. The standing rigging consists of the permanent stays, such as headstays, innerstays, bobstays, whisker stays, backstays, and shrouds that support the mast or masts of a sailing vessel. The running rigging consists of the adjustable lines used to control spars and sails, such as halyards, downhauls, outhauls, topping lifts, guys, preventers, running backstays, and sheets.

Right-of-way.....................In the rules of the road, the privileged vessel has right-of-way over the stand-down vessel. The privileged vessel must maintain present course and speed, while the stand-down vessel must alter course and speed to give way to the privileged vessel. Under most conditions, sailing vessels under sail without a motor running have right-of-way over motor vessels. A sailing vessel on a starboard tack has right-of-way over a sailing vessel on a port tack.

Roach. ....The outer curved edge of a battened sail that extends beyond the leach. It can be positive or negative.

Rode. ....The anchor line, generally nylon, chain or a combination of both.

Rogue wave ....An unusually large and unexpected wave. See freak wave.

Roll. ....The sideways motion of a boat.

Roller furling ....A device that allows a sail to be wound around its stay. Most commonly used on headsails, it is also available for mainsails, housed inside the boom or the mast.

Roller reefing. ....A way to reef a mainsail by winding it around a rotating boom.

Rolling hitch ....A knot in which one or more turns are made between two hitches, used to attach a line to another line, chain or spar.

Rope. ....A strong cord made of inter-twisted strands of fiber. On a sailing vessel, all ropes put to use are usually called lines, except the rope used for anchoring, which is called rode. A coiled line aboard reverts back to being a rope.

Rub rail. ....A hard wood or metal strip outboard of the topsides, to protect a hull from damage by pounding or rubbing of the hull against other hulls or docks.

Rudder. ....A broad flat movable piece of wood, fiberglass or metal at the stern used to steer a vessel through the water by rotating it left or right. The rudder can be governed by a tiller or by a steering wheel. The most common types of rudders on cruising boats are spade rudders, skeg rudders and externally hung rudders.

Rudderpost. ....A post that holds a spade rudder or a skeg rudder.

Rules of the Road. ....The set of rules and regulations governing the movement of vessels on coastal waters in order to avoid collisions.

Running.............................Point of sail with the eye of the wind directly aft of the vessel.

Running backstays.............Removable stays that facilitate control of the upper portion of the mast, and to adjust the shape of the upper portion of the sail.

Running lights...................Also known as Navigation Lights, they are required for operation of a vessel at night or during periods of reduced visibility in order to show her course, position and activity (such as fishing or towing).

Running rigging. ....The lines used to control spars (booms, whisker poles) and sails on a sailing vessel. See rigging.

S

Safety harness...................See harness.

Sail trim..........................The correct set of the sails according to the point of sail.

Sails. ....In modern sailboats, triangular pieces of cloth with an aerodynamic shape, used to drive a sailing vessel using the force of the wind. A sail has three edges: the luff or fore edge, the foot or bottom edge, and the leach or leech, its aft or trailing edge. A sail has also three corners: the tack, or fore bottom corner, the clew, or aft bottom corner, and the head, or top corner.

Satellite navigation............The art and science of navigating a vessel using data obtained from Global Positioning System satellites. See GPS.

Schooner..........................A two or more masted sailing vessel whose foremast is shorter than her mainmast.

Scope. ....Length of rode paid out for an anchor to hold. It is usually a multiple of the vessel's depth. When anchoring with an all chain rode, the scope is usually 5 to 1. When anchoring with chain and rope rode, a 7 to 1 scope is recommended. If a vessel is anchored at a depth of 20 feet of water, a 5 to 1 scope means the length of the rode should be 100 feet, whereas a 7 to 1 scope means the length of the rode should be 140 feet. In general, the greater the scope used, the better the holding power of the ground tackle.

SCUBA .... Self-Contained Breathing Apparatus. The tanks, regulator and other gear needed to dive under water for extended periods of time.

Scull. .... (a) An oar twisted from side to side over the stern to propel a small sailboat. (b) The act of propelling a small sailboat by twisting an oar from side to side over her stern.

Scuppers. .... Drain holes on the sides of a vessel.

Scuttle hatch. .... A small opening in the deck to admit light and air, usually with a lid or cover.

Sea anchor. .... A surface anchor generally shaped like a floating canvas cone with a hole at its vertex, and a bridle at its widest part connecting to the rode, for offshore use.

Seacock. .... A through-hull valve with a flange used for shut-off on plumbing or drainpipes under the waterline.

Sea room. .... Enough space and depth to maneuver a vessel without danger of grounding or collision.

Seaway. .... (a) A way or route by sea. (b) The movement of a vessel through the water. (c) A rough sea.

Seaworthy. .... A sturdy, properly designed and built vessel fit to travel on the open sea.

Seizing. .... (a) To fasten together by lashing. (b) To bind using a light waxed line called seizing line; (c) to bind anchor swivels and shackles using Monel wire.

Set. .... The distance and direction of a vessel due to the current flow.

Sextant. .... A navigational instrument used to determine the altitude of celestial bodies and their angles over the horizon, thereby determining the latitude of the observer at sea.

Shackle. .... A U-shaped or D-shaped fitting with a movable pin or bolt across the open end.

Shakedown cruise.............The first cruise; the purpose is to test the performance of a vessel and her crew.

Shake out.........................To let out a reef and set more sail area when the winds lighten.

Shank. ....The straight or stemlike part of an anchor.

Shear pin........................A pin used to attach a propeller to the shaft, designed to break if the propeller hits a solid object, in order to avoid damage to the prop.

Sheave............................A grooved wheel in a pulley, masthead or block.

Sheer. ....The curvature of a vessel's deck seen from the side.

Sheet. ....A line attached to the clew of a sail, shortened or slackened to adjust the trim of the sail. Every sail has two sheets, or a single sheet with two parts, the windward sheet and the leeward sheet.

Sheet bend......................A knot used in fastening a rope to the bight of another line or to an eye.

Shipshape. ....In order, snug, trim, properly stowed.

Shipwright.......................One whose occupation is to build and repair boats or ships.

Shoal. ....A shallow place in a body of water.

Shore up.........................To prevent a sailing vessel hard aground from heeling excessively due to the action of the waves, using lines and kedge anchors.

Shorten sail.....................To reduce area by reefing, dropping sail or furling.

Short-handed....................A vessel with not enough crew.

Shrouds. ....Standing rigging wires providing lateral support for the mast.

Single-handed ....Unassisted, by oneself. As in single-handed sailor, who is one that sails alone.

Skeg. ....A support for the rudder, usually the aft part of the keel or an extension of it on which the rudderpost is mounted.

Slab reefing.....................Most common way to reduce sail. The sail is loosened and lowered to a set of grommets higher up the sail. The new foot that is created is tied off at the boom. The tack and clew are adjusted to the new, higher position. The smaller sail is then hoisted. See jiffy reefing.

Slack water.....................The period between flood tide and ebb tide, when the tide runs slowly or the water is at rest.

Slick.....................A track of confused water left behind by the hull of a hove-to vessel, that protects the boat from breaking waves.

Slip knot.....................A knot that is easy to untie quickly.

Sloop.....................A single masted sailboat with only one headstay.

Snubber.....................A line with some elasticity, attached between the anchor rode and a bitt or Samson post.

Sole.....................The floor of a cabin or cockpit.

SOS.....................Emergency call spelled out in Morse Code as 3 short blasts, followed by 3 long blasts and ending with 3 short blasts. (...---...)

Sound.....................(a) To determine water depth, generally using a lead line. (b) Seaworthy.

Soundings.....................Measured depths found on a chart. Soundings on charts' datums can be measured in feet, fathoms or meters. Soundings on charts usually also indicate the type of bottom.

Spade rudder.....................A type of rudder that hangs by the rudderpost.

Spars.....................Any pole used for supporting or extending the sails of a sailing vessel, such as masts, booms, yards, gaffs and sprits.

Spinnaker.....................A large, light, triangular sail usually made of nylon that is used when running downwind. Spinnakers can be asymmetrical, used in racing sailboats, or cruising spinnakers, which are easier to deploy.

Splice.....................(a) To join lines or make eyes by unraveling and interweaving the strands. (b) A join of two lines.

Spreaders................................	Structural members attached to the mast athwartship, to help spread out the shrouds.
Spring lines............................	Docking lines used to control the fore and aft motion of a vessel.
Spring tides............................	Tides that occur at or soon after a full moon or a new moon. Spring tides have the highest range between high tide and low tide. Opposite of neap tides.
Squall.....................................	A sudden, violent windstorm usually accompanied by heavy rains, occuring frequently in the tropics.
Square knot.............................	A knot generally used to tie in a reef point or to tie two similar lines together. See reef knot.
SSB.......................................	Single Side Band radio. The SSB can transmit and receive voice communications for short as well as long distances. It can also receive weather fax, and send and receive emails.
Stability.................................	The ability of a sailboat to right herself. A tender boat has little stability, while a stiff boat has excessive stability.
Stanchion...............................	Upright metal post attached to the deck and bulwarks, to support the lifelines.
Stand down............................	To alter course and speed in order to allow a privileged vessel to pass.
Stand down vessel..................	A vessel that does not have the right-of-way.
Standing rigging.....................	The permanent stays and shrouds used to support the mast(s) and counteract the force of the sails.
Starboard...............................	The right side of a vessel when looking forward. Opposite of port or larboard.
Starboard tack........................	A vessel sailing with the wind coming over her starboard side. A sailing vessel on a starboard tack has right-of-way over a vessel sailing on a port tack.
Statute mile............................	A land mile, equal to 5280 feet. See mile.
Stays.....................................	Wires that form part of the standing rigging, providing fore and aft support for the mast(s).

The headstay provides support to fly the headsails.

Staysail..............................A smaller headsail used on a cutter or ketch, hanked on to the inner stay.

Staysail stay.......................Inner stay. In a cutter or ketch, a stay from the bow to about 3/4 height of the mast, used to fly a staysail or storm jib.

Steaming lights.................Navigation lights on a mast used when motoring.

Steerage............................The effect of the helm on a vessel.

Steerageway.......................Minimum forward movement of a vessel which allows her to be governed by the helm.

Steering wheel...................A wheel usually with spokes, mounted on a pedestal and connected to the rudder, used to steer a vessel.

Stem ....Bow. Forward part of the hull.

Step..................................The area on the keel or deck where the heel of the mast is set.

Stern................................The aft part of the hull.

Stern line..........................A docking line used at the stern.

Sternway...........................The backward movement of a vessel. Opposite of headway.

Stiff..................................The property of a sailing vessel that does not heel easily. Opposite of tender.

Stock ....The crossbar at the end of the shank of the anchor, opposite to the crown.

Storm anchor.....................A heavy weight anchor used in strong winds.

Storm jib...........................A small triangular jib of very strong material and construction.

Storm trysail......................A small triangular sail of very strong material and construction, usually set on a separate track on the mast.

Strip planking....................A boat building technique. In a wooden hull, narrow strips of wood are applied over the frame; then, they are butted, screwed and glued together.

Stuffing box......................A watertight through-hull chamber that holds packing material tightly around a moving part such as the engine shaft or rudderpost.

Surveyor...........................A person who specializes in inspecting all aspects of a boat for insurance assessment or before a purchase.

Swamp. ....To be overcome by a large amount of water from a wave that breaks over the side of a vessel.

Swell...............................A train of large waves that do not crest and are caused by the winds of a faraway storm.

Swing the compass...........To take an onboard compass through all the compass points, in order to establish the deviation of the compass caused by metallic objects nearby.

Swivel.............................A device with two parts that can turn independently of each other, commonly used in ground tackle.

T

Tabernacle......................An elevated socket stepped on deck, to which a vessel's mast may be hinged to facilitate the raising or lowering of the mast.

Tack..............................(a) The forward bottom corner of a triangular sail. (b) The course of a vessel in regard to the position of the sails. If the wind is coming over the starboard side, the vessel is sailing on a starboard tack. If the wind is coming over the port side, the vessel is sailing on a port tack. (c) A change in direction of a sailing vessel made when her bow crosses the eye of the wind.

Tack cloth.......................A sticky cloth used to wipe off saw dust after sanding, before varnish can be applied to brightwork.

Tackle. ....A system of ropes and pulleys used to lower, raise or move weights. A tackle with two or more blocks increases the pulling power of the purchase.

Taffrail..........................A rail around the stern of a vessel, usually made of wood.

Tangs...........................Metal fittings attached to the mast, where stays and shrouds are affixed.

Telltales......................Indicators of wind direction attached to the shrouds, sails and masthead.

Tender........................(a) A small boat to transport the crew and supplies. See dinghy. (b) An unstable sailing vessel. Opposite of stiff.

Teredo.........................Sea worm that lives in salt water and eats all kinds of wood except teak.

Thimble.......................A grooved metal ring used as reinforcement in an eye splice, to protect the eye from chafing.

Tidal current.................The current produced by the rise and fall of the tides.

Tide............................The rise and/or fall of the ocean due to the gravitational pull of the sun and the moon.

Tide tables...................Annual publications that give the time for high and low tides in a particular area.

Tiller..........................A spar attached to the rudder, to steer a sailing vessel.

Topping lift..................A part of the running rigging that is usually attached between the masthead and the end of a boom or a whisker pole and is used to control the height of the spar.

Topsides......................(a) The sides of a hull above the waterline. (b) On deck, opposite of below.

Tow...........................To pull another vessel through the water.

Track..........................A metal fitting attached to the mast and/or to the deck, to control sails and spars and blocks used in the running rigging.

Tradewinds..................Winds that blow toward the equator from the same quarter throughout the year, in an area from about 30 N to 30 S. North of the equator, tradewinds blow in the general direction from NE to SW, while south of the equator tradewinds blow in the general direction from SE to NW.

Transducer.........................The device on a depth sounder that is mounted on the hull that sends and receives underwater signals to determine the depth of the water under it.

Transom. ....A flat crosspiece usually at the stern of a vessel.

Traveler.........................A transversal track used to adjust the sheets of the mainsail.

Trim tab.........................A small rudder attached to the trailing edge of a sailboat's externally hung rudder that is governed by a windvane or autopilot.

Trim. ....The set and adjustment of the sails.

Trimaran.........................A vessel with three hulls. The center hull is for living and the other two for flotation.

Trip line.........................A strong nylon line attached to the crown of the anchor with a buoy attached at the other end, used to free the anchor easily if it is fouled or buried too deeply. Also used to collapse a sea anchor so it can be brought aboard.

Trough...........................The depression in the sea between the crests of two waves.

True course......................A course that has been corrected taking into account the magnetic variation and the compass deviation.

True wind........................The actual direction and force of the wind felt by a stationary observer.

Trysail.........................Small strong triangular storm sail set on a separate track on the main mast.

Tumble home.....................The part of a boat that inclines inward above the extreme breadth.

Tune............................To adjust rigging and sails for utmost effectiveness.

Turnbuckle......................A threaded fitting used to adjust stays and shrouds.

Typhoons........................Cyclones that occur in the China Sea and adjacent regions, comparable to the hurricanes that blow in the North Atlantic and Caribbean Sea.

U

Undertow..........................The undercurrent flowing seaward beneath the breaking surf.

Upstream. ....Moving against a river stream or tidal current.

Upwind..............................To windward.

V

Vane..................................A wind direction indicator set on the masthead.

Variation...........................The divergence of a compass needle from true north and south.

Venturi Effect....................An increase in velocity as a fluid (air or liquid) passes from a wide to a narrow area.

VHF radio..........................A radio communications device that operates at Very High Frequency.

W

Wake,, ...The track left in the water by a moving vessel.

Warp..................................To move a vessel by hauling on lines or hawsers fastened to or wrapped around piles, cleats on a dock or anchors.

Watch. ....One of the periods of duty into which the day and night are divided aboard a vessel to split the labor of sailing the vessel or being on the lookout.

Waterline. ....The line around a vessel's hull where the surface of the water meets the hull. The line of flotation of a hull, separating the topsides from the wetted surface.

Waterway...........................A navigable river or channel.

Weather. ....(a) The area to windward. (b) The state of the air or atmosphere at a given time or place, with respect to the temperature, pressure, humidity, cloudiness, wind velocity or any other meteorological phenomena.

Weathercock......................To point more into the wind.

Weather helm......................A sailboat's tendency to round up into the wind. Opposite of lee helm. Most sailboats are designed with a small amount of weather helm as a safety factor.

Weather shore..................A shore to windward of a vessel. Opposite of lee shore.

Weigh.............................To hoist anchor.

Well. ....(a) A pit, such as the cockpit well. (b) A watertight trunk, such as the place where the centerboard or daggerboard is stowed.

Well found......................A properly equipped and adequately supplied vessel.

Wetted surface.................The propeller, rudder and all the surface areas of the hull under water that affect the speed of a vessel.

Whipping.........................To wind or bind a twine around the end of a line or at an eye splice, to strengthen it and avoid unraveling.

Whisker Pole...................A pole used as a boom for the jib or spinnaker when reaching or running downwind.

Widowmaker ....Term used for a bowsprit, implying its dangerous nature. (Many women lost their husbands, who risked their lives going out on the bowsprit to change sails.)

Winch.............................A mechanical device mounted on deck, on the cabintop, on the mast, and/or on the boom, used to increase the pulling power of sheets, halyards and slab reefing lines.

Winch handle...................A handle that fits inside a winch and provides more leverage when rotating it.

Windage. ....Resistance to the wind due to a vessel's surface area exposed to it.

Wind Generator.................A device with blades that uses the wind to generate electrical power.

Windlass.............................A specially designed winch that can be mounted horizontally or vertically, used to haul in chain and anchor rode. The part of the windlass that hauls chain is called the gypsy. The tapered part of the windlass that hauls rode is called the capstan.

Windrose ....A diagram that shows the frequency and intensity of wind from different directions for a particular place.

Windvane...........................A device that is driven by the wind and is attached to a trim tab, allowing a sailing vessel to be steered by the wind without a helmsman.

Windward. ....The direction from which the wind is blowing. Opposite of leeward.

Wing and wing.................Running downwind with the jib set on the opposite side of the main.

Wontok.............................Pidgin English for One Talk. One who speaks the same language or comes from the same village.

Working sails...................The set of sails used under normal wind conditions.

Y

Yacht................................Pleasure craft.

Yachtie. ....Owner operator or crew of a yacht.

Yaw..................................To turn or deviate unintentionally off course, generally due to a quartering sea.

Yawl.................................A type of sailing rig with the mizzenmast aft of the rudderpost.

Z

Zig zag..............................(a) A type of reinforced stitching used in sails. (b) A course followed by a sailboat beating to windward and changing tacks.

INDEX

ablative paint, 508
ahull, 278, 339
air conditioning, 57, 475, 479
airblock, 324, 325, 326
airfoil, 31, 65, 66, 311, 315, 316
almanac, 449, 463
alternator, 433
aluminum, 78, 100, 102, 103, 104, 105, 107, 132, 133, 134, 141, 142, 162, 194, 404, 405, 406, 436, 453, 456, 470, 482, 495, 498, 499, 501, 516, 559
anchor buoy, 222, 242, 259
anchor light, 214, 432
Anchor Mooring, 243
anchor roller, 193
anode, 104, 123, 135
Anopheles, 533
anti-siphon, 391, 418, 419
atoll, 190, 233, 504, 556
autopilot, 51, 124, 321, 430, 440, 474, 475
awning, 368, 399, 465, 466, 467, 468, 469, 470, 471, 472, 473, 506
baffles, 378, 380, 392, 487
bail, 341, 409, 410
balance, 56, 59, 62, 66, 69, 70, 71, 72, 286, 287, 307, 331, 343, 396, 398, 459
ballast, 77, 79, 80, 81, 83, 85, 86, 88, 89, 91, 93, 94, 95, 96, 97, 98, 106, 107, 109, 111, 133, 134, 142, 455, 459, 499
balsa, 119, 128, 129, 453
Barbecue, 483
barometer, 150, 302, 303, 307, 345, 347, 353
barometric pressure, 301, 303
battens, 285, 327, 398, 400
batteries, 202, 292, 308, 383, 422, 426, 427, 429, 433, 438, 439, 441, 458, 478, 479
battery charger, 438, 479
BBB, 183, 184, 185, 188, 189, 204
beanbags, 473, 474, 514
Beaufort Scale, 276, 278, 297
beetle nuts, 569
bilge, 27, 89, 93, 95, 119, 131, 133, 143, 160, 191, 192, 193, 196, 203, 206, 288, 294, 375, 377, 379, 385, 391, 394, 424, 445, 446, 497, 503, 509, 538
bilge pump, 27, 206, 288, 294, 391, 497, 509, 538
bleed, 414, 415, 416
boltrope, 398, 401

Inverters, 438
isobars, 301, 303, 304, 306
Isotemp, 383
J measurement, 70
jacklines, 293, 307, 327, 399, 400, 452
Kava, 545, 546, 547, 549, 550, 551, 552
keel bolts, 93, 96, 97, 98
kerosene, 17, 214, 375, 376, 377, 388, 389, 432, 460, 509, 549, 559
ketch, 72, 73, 152, 175, 290, 343, 344, 345, 470
Kevlar, 99, 112, 114, 133
killet, 244
knife, 458
knockdown, 56, 282, 285, 289, 291, 292, 293, 339, 343, 352, 353, 360, 368
knot-log, 446
lanolin, 423
lapstrake, 105
Laundry, 501
LaVac, 390, 391, 392
lazarette, 82
Lazy jacks, 328, 396, 398, 408
lee helm, 59, 62, 65, 73, 124, 126
lee shore, 283
Leeboards, 371, 372
leecloths, 371, 373
life raft, 287, 294, 339, 453, 454, 511, 512, 513
lifelines, 33, 36, 250, 281, 313, 319, 338, 368, 451, 452, 469, 470, 472, 506, 524
Lifesling, 455
lightning, 98, 134, 171, 172, 173, 175, 177, 359, 449, 450, 498, 499, 501
lightning protection, 134, 307, 498, 501
linear polyurethane, 133
liner, 109, 110, 118, 119, 133, 144, 362, 369, 379, 385, 386
magic, 4, 549, 550, 551, 552, 553, 554, 576
Malaria, 533
Maloprim, 534, 535
Mast steps, 405, 406
masthead light, 214, 432
matt, 112, 113, 114, 116, 143
Mayday, 289
Mediterranean method, 148, 258
Merick's Medical Manual, 537
Mid-Link Connector, 185
mildew, 385
millibars, 301, 302, 303, 304
Milton Solution, 531

radar, 134, 280, 447, 448, 449, 456, 457, 458, 489

radar detector, 457

radar reflector, 456, 457

rats, 386, 484, 485, 486

reef, 31, 32, 58, 91, 92, 96, 152, 164, 190, 215, 233, 246, 278, 285, 287, 291, 293, 309, 312, 313, 314, 318, 319, 321, 322, 323, 326, 327, 328, 330, 333, 341, 342, 343, 344, 347, 396, 400, 453, 497, 504, 506, 559, 560, 562, 563, 564, 566

reef lines, 285, 293, 319, 322, 323, 326, 327, 401, 506

reef points, 284, 287, 313, 317, 318, 321, 322, 341, 400, 401

reefing, 52, 56, 285, 293, 294, 309, 312, 314, 315, 316, 317, 318, 321, 322, 323, 324, 326, 327, 328, 342, 524

refrigeration, 21, 476, 477, 478, 479, 480, 566

regulator, 433

ribs, 101, 102, 105, 107, 109, 349

right-of-way, 458

ring buoy, 455

roach, 285, 398, 400

rogue waves, 276, 342

roller furling, 68, 248, 250, 264, 273, 286, 292, 307, 309, 315, 316, 347, 401

roller reefing, 30, 70, 309, 315, 316

rolling hitch, 211, 227, 257, 337, 339, 398, 471, 472, 506, 523

rope clutch, 319, 321, 322, 324, 327

roving, 112, 113, 143

rubrail, 366

rudderpost, 70, 71, 72, 89, 121, 122, 123, 125, 126, 364

rules of the road, 458

running lights, 343, 431, 432

Sail tracks, 404

Sailing Directions, 14

sailmaker, 310, 312, 314, 400, 401

Sam L. Morse, 142

Sanipotties, 390

satellite phone, 443

schooner, 73, 74, 75

scope, 58, 157, 190, 192, 201, 202, 203, 207, 211, 221, 226, 227, 228, 229, 232, 236, 240, 247, 248, 252, 260, 266, 539

Scotsman, 328

SCUBA, 3, 57, 191, 198, 219, 507

scuttle hatch, 350, 384, 524

sea anchor, 35, 37, 351

seacock, 373, 374, 375, 381, 461

Seraffyn, 28, 142, 474

shackle, 179, 183, 187, 188, 189, 192, 195, 213, 238, 240, 241, 244, 268, 271, 313, 338, 341, 350, 353, 401, 402, 409, 410, 518

For your notes

ABOUT THE AUTHOR

Roger Olson, M. Ed., taught for fifteen years in Southern California, spending his summer vacations cruising in the Sea of Cortez. He eventually sailed a 20-foot trailersailer around Baja California. This adventure, published in Yachting Magazine in 1976, created an intense desire to experience other foreign lands. After owning many boats, he found the perfect sailing vessel. He named her *Xiphias* and set sail to cruise around the world.

After thirteen years of blue water cruising, he returned to the United States and bought the Sam L. Morse Company, a boatyard that produces fine offshore sailing yachts. He worked there for ten years. Today, he is back at sea aboard his new yacht *Nereus*, doing what he loves best – cruising.

Printed in the United States
58624LVS00003B/2

9 781418 405762